Advanced Database Query Systems:

Techniques, Applications and Technologies

Li Yan
Northeastern University, China

Zongmin Ma
Northeastern University, China

A volume in the Advances in Data Mining and Database Management (ADMDM) Book Series

Senior Editorial Director:	Kristin Klinger
Director of book publications:	Julia Mosemann
Editorial Director:	Lindsay Johnston
Acquisitions editor:	Erika Carter
Development editor:	Michael Killian
Production coordinator:	Jamie Snavely
Typesetters:	Michael Brehm, and Milan Vracarich Jr.
Cover design:	Nick Newcomer

Published in the United States of America by
Information Science Reference (an imprint of IGI Global)
701 E. Chocolate Avenue
Hershey PA 17033
Tel: 717-533-8845
Fax: 717-533-8661
E-mail: cust@igi-global.com
Web site: http://www.igi-global.com

Library of Congress Cataloging-in-Publication Data

Advanced database query systems : techniques, applications and technologies / Li Yan and Zongmin Ma, editors.
    p. cm.
  Includes bibliographical references and index.
  Summary: "This book focuses on technologies and methodologies of database queries, XML and metadata queries, and applications of database query systems, aiming at providing a single account of technologies and practices in advanced database query systems"--Provided by publisher.
  ISBN 978-1-60960-475-2 (hardcover) -- ISBN 978-1-60960-476-9 (ebook) 1. Databases. 2. Query languages (Computer science) 3. Querying (Computer science) I. Yan, Li, 1964- II. Ma, Zongmin, 1965-
  QA76.9.D32A39 2011
  005.74--dc22
                                   2010054423

This book is published in the IGI Global book series Advances in Data Mining and Database Management (ADMDM) (ISSN: 2327-1981; eISSN: 2327-199X).

British Cataloguing in Publication Data
A Cataloguing in Publication record for this book is available from the British Library.

Advances in Data Mining and Database Management (ADMDM) Book Series

David Taniar
Monash University, Australia

ISSN: 2327-1981
EISSN: 2327-199X

MISSION

With the large amounts of information available to businesses in today's digital world, there is a need for methods and research on managing and analyzing the information that is collected and stored. IT professionals, software engineers, and business administrators, along with many other researchers and academics, have made the fields of data mining and database management into ones of increasing importance as the digital world expands. The **Advances in Data Mining & Database Management (ADMDM) Book Series** aims to bring together research in both fields in order to become a resource for those involved in either field.

COVERAGE

- Cluster Analysis
- Customer Analytics
- Data Mining
- Data Quality
- Data Warehousing
- Database Security
- Database Testing
- Decision Support Systems
- Enterprise Systems
- Text Mining

IGI Global is currently accepting manuscripts for publication within this series. To submit a proposal for a volume in this series, please contact our Acquisition Editors at Acquisitions@igi-global.com or visit: http://www.igi-global.com/publish/.

Titles in this Series

For a list of additional titles in this series, please visit: www.igi-global.com

Data Mining in Dynamic Social Networks and Fuzzy Systems
Vishal Bhatnagar (Ambedkar Institute of Advanced Communication Technologies and Research, India)
Information Science Reference • copyright 2013 • 412pp • H/C (ISBN: 9781466642133) • US $195.00 (our price)

Ethical Data Mining Applications for Socio-Economic Development
Hakikur Rahman (University of Minho, Portugal) and Isabel Ramos (University of Minho, Portugal)
Information Science Reference • copyright 2013 • 359pp • H/C (ISBN: 9781466640788) • US $195.00 (our price)

Design, Performance, and Analysis of Innovative Information Retrieval
Zhongyu (Joan) Lu (University of Huddersfield, UK)
Information Science Reference • copyright 2013 • 508pp • H/C (ISBN: 9781466619753) • US $195.00 (our price)

XML Data Mining Models, Methods, and Applications
Andrea Tagarelli (University of Calabria, Italy)
Information Science Reference • copyright 2012 • 538pp • H/C (ISBN: 9781613503560) • US $195.00 (our price)

Graph Data Management Techniques and Applications
Sherif Sakr (University of New South Wales, Australia) and Eric Pardede (LaTrobe University, Australia)
Information Science Reference • copyright 2012 • 502pp • H/C (ISBN: 9781613500538) • US $195.00 (our price)

Advanced Database Query Systems Techniques, Applications and Technologies
Li Yan (Northeastern University, China) and Zongmin Ma (Northeastern University, China)
Information Science Reference • copyright 2011 • 410pp • H/C (ISBN: 9781609604752) • US $180.00 (our price)

Knowledge Discovery Practices and Emerging Applications of Data Mining Trends and New Domains
A.V. Senthil Kumar (CMS College of Science and Commerce, India)
Information Science Reference • copyright 2011 • 414pp • H/C (ISBN: 9781609600679) • US $180.00 (our price)

Data Mining in Public and Private Sectors Organizational and Government Applications
Antti Syvajarvi (University of Lapland, Finland) and Jari Stenvall (Tampere University, Finland)
Information Science Reference • copyright 2010 • 448pp • H/C (ISBN: 9781605669069) • US $180.00 (our price)

Text Mining Techniques for Healthcare Provider Quality Determination Methods for Rank Comparisons
Patricia Cerrito (University of Louisville, USA)
Medical Information Science Reference • copyright 2010 • 410pp • H/C (ISBN: 9781605667522) • US $245.00 (our price)

www.igi-global.com

701 E. Chocolate Ave., Hershey, PA 17033
Order online at www.igi-global.com or call 717-533-8845 x100
To place a standing order for titles released in this series, contact: cust@igi-global.com
Mon-Fri 8:00 am - 5:00 pm (est) or fax 24 hours a day 717-533-8661

Editorial Advisory Board

Table of Contents

Preface xiv

Acknowledgment.. xix

Section 1

Chapter 1

Automatic Categorization of Web Database Query Results 1

Xiangfu Meng, Liaoning Technical University, China

Li Yan, Northeastern University, China

Z. M. Ma, Northeastern University, China

Chapter 2

Practical Approaches to the Many-Answer Problem 28

Mounir Bechchi, LINA-University of Nantes, France

Guillaume Raschia, LINA-University of Nantes, France

Noureddine Mouaddib, LINA-University of Nantes, Morocco

Chapter 3

Concept-Oriented Query Language for Data Modeling and Analysis.............................. 85

Alexandr Savinov, SAP Research Center Dresden, Germany

Chapter 4

Evaluating Top-k Skyline Queries Efficiently 102

Marlene Goncalves, Universidad Simón Bolívar, Venezuela

María Esther Vidal, Universidad Simón Bolívar, Venezuela

Chapter 5

Remarks on a Fuzzy Approach to Flexible Database Querying, its Extension and Relation
to Data Mining and Summarization.. 118

Janusz Kacprzyk, Polish Academy of Sciences, Poland

Guy De Tré, Ghent University, Belgium

Sławomir Zadrożny, Polish Academy of Sciences, Poland

Chapter 6
Flexible Querying of Imperfect Temporal Metadata in Spatial Data Infrastructures 140
    Gloria Bordogna, CNR-IDPA, Italy
    Francesco Bucci, CNR-IREA, Italy
    Paola Carrara, CNR-IREA, Italy
    Monica Pepe, CNR-IREA, Italy
    Anna Rampini, CNR-IREA, Italy

Chapter 7
Fuzzy Querying Capability at Core of a RDBMS 160
    Ana Aguilera, Universidad de Carabobo, Venezuela
    José Tomás Cadenas, Universidad Simón Bolívar, Venezuela
    Leonid Tineo, Universidad Simón Bolívar, Venezuela

Chapter 8
An Extended Relational Model & SQL for Fuzzy Multidatabases 185
    Awadhesh Kumar Sharma, M.M.M. Engg College, India
    A. Goswami, IIT Kharagpur, India
    D. K. Gupta, IIT Kharagpur, India

Section 2

Chapter 9
Pattern-Based Schema Mapping and Query Answering in Peer-to-Peer XML
Data Integration System 221
    Tadeusz Pankowski, Poznan University of Technology, Poland

Chapter 10
Deciding Query Entailment in Fuzzy OWL Lite Ontologies 247
    Jingwei Cheng, Northeastern University, China
    Z. M. Ma, Northeastern University, China
    Li Yan, Northeastern University, China

Chapter 11
Relational Techniques for Storing and Querying RDF Data: An Overview 269
    Sherif Sakr, University of New South Wales, Australia
    Ghazi Al-Naymat, University of New South Wales, Australia

Section 3

Chapter 12
Making Query Coding in SQL Easier by Implementing the SQL Divide Keyword:
An Experimental Query Rewriter in Java 287
  Eric Draken, University of Calgary, Canada
  Shang Gao, University of Calgary, Canada
  Reda Alhajj, University of Calgary, Canada & Global University, Lebanon

Chapter 13
Querying Graph Databases: An Overview 304
  Sherif Sakr, University of New South Wales, Australia
  Ghazi Al-Naymat, University of New South Wales, Australia

Chapter 14
Querying Multimedia Data by Similarity in Relational DBMS 323
  Maria Camila Nardini Barioni, Federal University of ABC, Brazil
  Daniel dos Santos Kaster, University of Londrina, Brazil
  Humberto Luiz Razente, Federal University of ABC, Brazil
  Agma Juci Machado Traina, University of São Paulo at São Carlos, Brazil
  Caetano Traina Júnior, University of São Paulo at São Carlos, Brazil

Compilation of References 360

About the Contributors 378

Index 386

Detailed Table of Contents

Preface xiv

Acknowledgment... xix

Section 1

Chapter 1

Automatic Categorization of Web Database Query Results 1
Xiangfu Meng, Liaoning Technical University, China
Li Yan, Northeastern University, China
Z. M. Ma, Northeastern University, China

This chapter proposes a novel categorization approach which consists of two steps. The first step analyzes query history of all users in the system offline and generates a set of clusters over the tuples, where each cluster represents one type of user preference. When a user issues a query, the second step presents to the user a category tree over the clusters generated in the first step such that the user can easily select the subset of query results matching his needs. The chapter develops heuristic algorithms to compute the min-cost categorization. The efficiency and effectiveness of the proposed approach are demonstrated by experimental results.

Chapter 2

Practical Approaches to the Many-Answer Problem 28
Mounir Bechchi, LINA-University of Nantes, France
Guillaume Raschia, LINA-University of Nantes, France
Noureddine Mouaddib, LINA-University of Nantes, Morocco

This chapter reviews and discusses several research efforts that have attempted to provide users with effective and efficient ways to access databases. The focus is on a simple but useful strategy for retrieving relevant answers accurately and quickly without being distracted by irrelevant ones. The chapter presents a very recent but promising approach to quickly provide users with structured and approximate representations of users' query results, a must have for decision support systems. The underlying algorithm operates on pre-computed knowledge-based summaries of the queried data, instead of raw data themselves.

Chapter 3

Concept-Oriented Query Language for Data Modeling and Analysis...85
Alexandr Savinov, SAP Research Center Dresden, Germany

This chapter describes a novel query language, called the concept-oriented query language, and demonstrates how it can be used for data modeling and analysis. The query language is based on a novel construct, called concept, and two relations between concepts, inclusion and partial order. Concepts generalize conventional classes and are used for describing domain-specific identities. Inclusion relation generalized inheritance and is used for describing hierarchical address spaces. Partial order among concepts is used to define two main operations: projection and de-projection. The chapter demonstrates how these constructs are used to solve typical tasks in data modeling and analysis such as logical navigation, multidimensional analysis and inference.

Chapter 4

Evaluating Top-k Skyline Queries Efficiently 102
Marlene Goncalves, Universidad Simón Bolívar, Venezuela
María Esther Vidal, Universidad Simón Bolívar, Venezuela

This chapter describes existing solutions and proposes to use the TKSI algorithm for the Top-k Skyline problem. TKSI reduces the search space by computing only a subset of the Skyline that is required to produce the top-k objects. In addition, the Skyline Frequency Metric is implemented to discriminate among the Skyline objects those that best meet the multidimensional criteria. The chapter empirically studies the quality of TKSI, and the experimental results show the TKSI may be able to speed up the computation of the Top-k Skyline in at least 50% percent with regards to the state-of-the-art solutions.

Chapter 5

Remarks on a Fuzzy Approach to Flexible Database Querying, its Extension and Relation
to Data Mining and Summarization... 118
Janusz Kacprzyk, Polish Academy of Sciences, Poland
Guy De Tré, Ghent University, Belgium
Sławomir Zadrożny, Polish Academy of Sciences, Poland

This chapter is meant to revive the line of research in flexible querying languages based on the use of fuzzy logic. Details of a basic technique of flexible fuzzy querying are recalled and some newest developments in this area are discussed. Moreover, it is shown how other relevant tasks may be implemented in the framework of such queries interface. In particular, the chapter considers fuzzy queries with linguistic quantifiers and shows their intrinsic relation with linguistic data summarization. Moreover, so called bipolar queries are mentioned and advocated as a next relevant breakthrough in flexible querying based on fuzzy logic and possibility theory.

Chapter 6
Flexible Querying of Imperfect Temporal Metadata in Spatial Data Infrastructures 140

Gloria Bordogna, CNR-IDPA, Italy
Francesco Bucci, CNR-IREA, Italy
Paola Carrara, CNR-IREA, Italy
Monica Pepe, CNR-IREA, Italy
Anna Rampini, CNR-IREA, Italy

This chapter discusses the limitations of current temporal metadata in discovery services of spatial data infrastructures (SDIs) and proposes some solutions. The proposal of a formal and operational method is presented to represent imperfect temporal metadata values and allow users to express flexible search conditions, i.e. tolerant to under-satisfaction. In doing so, discovery services can apply partial matching mechanisms between the "desired" metadata, expressed by the user, and the archived metadata: this would allow retrieving geodata in decreasing order of relevance to the user needs, as it usually occurs on the Web when using search engines. Finally, the chapter illustrates the proposal with an example.

Chapter 7
Fuzzy Querying Capability at Core of a RDBMS 160

Ana Aguilera, Universidad de Carabobo, Venezuela
José Tomás Cadenas, Universidad Simón Bolívar, Venezuela
Leonid Tineo, Universidad Simón Bolívar, Venezuela

This chapter concentrates on incorporating the fuzzy capabilities to a relational database management system (RDBMS) of open source. The fuzzy capabilities include connectors, modifiers, comparators, quantifiers and queries. The extensions consider a more flexible DDL and DML languages. The aim is to show the design and implementation details in the RDBMS PostgreSQL. For this, a fuzzy query processor and fuzzy access mechanism are designed and implemented. The physical fuzzy relational operators are also defined and implemented. The flow of a fuzzy query through the different modules (parser, planner, optimizer and executor) is shown. The chapter includes some experimental results to demonstrate the performance of the proposal solution. These results show that the extensions do not decrease the performance of the RDBMS.

Chapter 8
An Extended Relational Model & SQL for Fuzzy Multidatabases 185

Awadhesh Kumar Sharma, M.M.M. Engg College, India
A. Goswami, IIT Kharagpur, India
D. K. Gupta, IIT Kharagpur, India

This chapter investigates the problems in integration of fuzzy relational databases and extends the relational data model to support fuzzy multidatabases of type-2 that contain integrated fuzzy relational databases. The extended model named fuzzy tuple source (FTS) relational data model is provided with a set of FTS relational operations to manipulate the global relations called FTS relations from such fuzzy multidatabases. The chapter proposes and implements a full set of FTS relational algebraic operations capable of manipulating an extensive set of fuzzy relational multidatabases of type-2 that include fuzzy data values in their instances. To facilitate formulation of global fuzzy query over FTS relations in such fuzzy multidatabases, an appropriate extension to SQL is done so as to get fuzzy tuple source structured query language (FTS-SQL).

Section 2

Chapter 9
Pattern-Based Schema Mapping and Query Answering in Peer-to-Peer XML
Data Integration System.. 221
Tadeusz Pankowski, Poznan University of Technology, Poland

This chapter discusses a method for schema mapping and query reformulation in a P2P XML data integration system. The discussed formal approach enables us to specify schemas, schema constraints, schema mappings, and queries in a uniform and precise way. Based on this approach, the chapter defines some basic operations used for query reformulation and data merging, and proposes algorithms for automatic generation of XQuery programs performing these operations in real. Some issues concerning query propagation strategies and merging modes are discussed, when missing data is to be discovered in the P2P integration processes. The approach is implemented in 6P2P system. Its general architecture is presented and the way how queries and answers are sent across the P2P environment is sketched.

Chapter 10
Deciding Query Entailment in Fuzzy OWL Lite Ontologies 247
Jingwei Cheng, Northeastern University, China
Z. M. Ma, Northeastern University, China
Li Yan, Northeastern University, China

This chapter focuses on fuzzy (threshold) conjunctive queries over knowledge bases encoding in fuzzy DL SHIF(D), the logic counterpart of fuzzy OWL Lite language. The decidability of fuzzy query entailment in this setting is shown by providing a corresponding tableau-based algorithm. It is also shown that the data complexity for answering fuzzy conjunctive queries in fuzzy SHIF(D) is in coNP, as long as only simple roles occur in the query. Regarding combined complexity, the chapter proves a co3NExpTime upper bound in the size of the knowledge base and the query.

Chapter 11
Relational Techniques for Storing and Querying RDF Data: An Overview....................... 269
Sherif Sakr, University of New South Wales, Australia
Ghazi Al-Naymat, University of New South Wales, Australia

This chapter concentrates on using relational query processors to store and query RDF data. An overview of the different approaches is given and these approaches are classified according to the storage and query evaluation strategies.

Section 3

Chapter 12
Making Query Coding in SQL Easier by Implementing the SQL Divide Keyword:
An Experimental Query Rewriter in Java..287

Eric Draken, University of Calgary, Canada
Shang Gao, University of Calgary, Canada
Reda Alhajj, University of Calgary, Canada & Global University, Lebanon

This chapter intends to provide SQL expression equivalent to explicit relational algebra division (with static divisor). The goal is to implement a SQL query rewriter in Java which takes as input a divide grammar and rewrites it to an efficient query using current SQL keywords.

Chapter 13
Querying Graph Databases: An Overview...304

Sherif Sakr, University of New South Wales, Australia
Ghazi Al-Naymat, University of New South Wales, Australia

This chapter provides an overview of different techniques for indexing and querying graph databases. An overview of several proposals of graph query language is also given and a set of guidelines for future research directions is provided.

Chapter 14
Querying Multimedia Data by Similarity in Relational DBMS 323

Maria Camila Nardini Barioni, Federal University of ABC, Brazil
Daniel dos Santos Kaster, University of Londrina, Brazil
Humberto Luiz Razente, Federal University of ABC, Brazil
Agma Juci Machado Traina, University of São Paulo at São Carlos, Brazil
Caetano Traina Júnior, University of São Paulo at São Carlos, Brazil

This chapter presents an already validated strategy that adds similarity queries to SQL, supporting a powerful set of similarity operators. The chapter also describes techniques to store and retrieve multimedia objects in an efficient way and show existing DBMS alternatives to execute similarity queries over multimedia data.

Compilation of References 360

About the Contributors 378

Index...386

Preface

Databases are designed to support the data storage, processing, and retrieval activities related to data management. The wide usage of databases in various applications has resulted in an enormous wealth of data, which populate various types of databases around the worlds. Ones can find many types of database systems, for example, relational databases, object-oriented databases, object-relational databases, deductive databases, parallel databases, distributed databases, multidatabase systems, Web databases, XML databases, multimedia databases, temporal/spatial databases, spatiotemporal databases, and uncertain databases. As a result, databases have become the repositories of large volumes of data.

Database query is closely related to data management. Database query processing is such a procedure that database management systems (DBMSs) obtain the information needed by the users from the databases according to users' requirements, and then provides them to the users after this useful information is organized. It is very critical to deal with the enormity and retrieve the worthwhile information for effective problem solving and decision making. It is especially true when a variety of database types, data types, and users' requirements, as well as large volumes of data, are available. The techniques of database queries are challenging today's database systems and promoting their evolvement. There is no doubt that database query systems play an important role in data management, and data management requires database query support.

The research and development of information queries over a variety of databases are receiving increasing attention. By means of query technology, large volumes of information in databases can be retrieved, and Information Systems are hereby built based on databases to support various problem solving and decision making. So database queries are the fields which must be investigated by academic researchers together with developers and users both from database and industry areas.

This book focuses on the following issues of advanced database query systems: the technologies and methodologies of database queries, XML and metadata queries, and applications of database query systems, aiming at providing a single account of technologies and practices in advanced database query systems. The objective of the book is to provide the state of the art information to academics, researchers and industry practitioners who are involved or interested in the study, use, design, and development of advanced and emerging database queries with ultimate aim to empower individuals and organizations in building competencies for exploiting the opportunities of the data and knowledge society. This book presents the latest research and application results in advanced database query systems. The different chapters in the book have been contributed by different authors and provide possible solutions for the different types of technological problems concerning database queries.

This book, which consists of fourteen chapters, is organized into three major sections. The first section discusses the technologies and methodologies of database queries, over the first eight chapters. The next three chapters covering XML and metadata queries comprise the second section. The third section, containing the final three chapters, focuses on the design and applications of database query systems.

First of all, we take a look at the issues of the technologies and methodologies of database queries.

Web database queries are often exploratory. The users often find that their queries return too many answers and many of them may be irrelevant. Based on different kinds of user preferences, Xiangfu Meng, Li Yan and Z. M. Ma propose a novel categorization approach which consists of two steps. The first step analyzes query history of all users in the system offline and generates a set of clusters over the tuples, where each cluster represents one type of user preference. When a user issues a query, the second step presents to the user a category tree over the clusters generated in the first step such that the user can easily select the subset of query results matching his needs. The problem of constructing a category tree is a cost optimization problem and the authors develop heuristic algorithms to compute the min-cost categorization. The efficiency and effectiveness of their approach are demonstrated by experimental results.

Database systems are increasingly used for interactive and exploratory data retrieval. In such retrievals, user queries often result in too many answers, so users waste significant time and efforts sifting and sorting through these answers to find the relevant ones. Mounir Bechchi, Guillaume Raschia and Noureddine Mouaddib first review and discuss several research efforts that have attempted to provide users with effective and efficient ways to access databases. Then, they focus on a simple but useful strategy for retrieving relevant answers accurately and quickly without being distracted by irrelevant ones. They present a very recent but promising approach to quickly provide users with structured and approximate representations of users' query results, a must have for decision support systems. The underlying algorithm operates on pre-computed knowledge-based summaries of the queried data, instead of raw data themselves. Thus, this first-citizen data structure is also presented.

Alexandr Savinov describes a novel query language, called the concept-oriented query language (COQL), and demonstrates how it can be used for data modeling and analysis. The query language is based on a novel construct, called concept, and two relations between concepts, inclusion and partial order. Concepts generalize conventional classes and are used for describing domain-specific identities. This includes relation generalized inheritance and is used for describing hierarchical address spaces. Partial order among concepts is used to define two main operations: projection and de-projection. Savinov demonstrates how these constructs are used to solve typical tasks in data modeling and analysis such as logical navigation, multidimensional analysis, and inference.

Criteria that induce a Skyline naturally represent user's preference conditions useful to discard irrelevant data in large datasets. However, in the presence of high-dimensional Skyline spaces, the size of the Skyline can still be very large. To identify the best k points among the Skyline, the Top-k Skyline approach has been proposed. Marlene Goncalves and María-Esther Vidal describe existing solutions and propose to use the TKSI algorithm for the Top-k Skyline problem. TKSI reduces the search space by computing only a subset of the Skyline that is required to produce the top-k objects. In addition, the Skyline Frequency Metric is implemented to discriminate among the Skyline objects those that best meet the multidimensional criteria. They empirically study the quality of TKSI, and their experimental results show the TKSI may be able to speed up the computation of the Top-k Skyline in at least 50% percent with regards to the state-of-the-art solutions.

Janusz Kacprzyk, Guy De Tré, and Sławomir Zadrożny briefly present the concept of, a rationale for and various approaches to the use of fuzzy logic in flexible querying. They discuss first some historical developments, and then the main issues related to fuzzy querying. Next, they concentrate on fuzzy queries with linguistic quantifiers, and discuss in more detail their FQUERY for Access fuzzy querying system. They indicate not only the straightforward power of that fuzzy querying system but its great potential as a tool to implement linguistic data summaries that may provide an ultimately human consistent way of data mining and data summarization. Also, they briefly mention the concept of bipolar queries that may reflect positive and negative preferences of the user, and may be a breakthrough in fuzzy querying. In the context of fuzzy querying and linguistic summarization they mention a considerable potential of their new recent proposals to explicitly use in linguistic data summarization some elements of natural language generation (NLG), and some natural language generation related elements of Halliday's systemic functional linguistics (SFL). They argue that this may be a promising direction for future research.

Gloria Bordogna *et al*. discuss the limitations of current temporal metadata in discovery services of Spatial Data Infrastructures (SDIs) and propose some solutions. They present their proposal of a formal and operational method to represent imperfect temporal metadata values and allow users to express flexible search conditions, i.e. tolerant to under-satisfaction. In doing so, discovery services can apply partial matching mechanisms between the "desired" metadata, expressed by the user, and the archived metadata: this would allow retrieving geodata in decreasing order of relevance to the user needs, as it usually occurs on the Web when using search engines. The proposal is finally illustrated with an example.

Ana Aguilera, José Tomás Cadenas and Leonid Tineo concentrate on incorporating the fuzzy capabilities to a relational database management system (RDBMS) of open source. The fuzzy capabilities include connectors, modifiers, comparators, quantifiers, and queries. The extensions consider a more flexible DDL and DML languages. The aim is to show the design and implementation details in the RDBMS PostgreSQL. For this, they design and implement a fuzzy query processor and fuzzy access mechanism. Also, they define and implement the physical fuzzy relational operators. They show the flow of a fuzzy query through the different modules (parser, planner, optimizer, and executor). They include some experimental results to demonstrate the performance of the proposal solution. These results show that the extensions do not decrease the performance of the RDBMS.

Awadhesh Kumar Sharma, A. Goswami, and D.K. Gupta investigate the problems in integration of fuzzy relational databases and extend the relational data model to support fuzzy multidatabases of type-2 that contain integrated fuzzy relational databases. The extended model is given the name fuzzy tuple source (FTS) relational data model which is provided with a set of FTS relational operations to manipulate the global relations called FTS relations from such fuzzy multidatabases. They propose and implement a full set of FTS relational algebraic operations capable of manipulating an extensive set of fuzzy relational multidatabases of type-2 that include fuzzy data values in their instances. To facilitate formulation of global fuzzy query over FTS relations in such fuzzy multidatabases, an appropriate extension to SQL can be done so as to get fuzzy tuple source structured query language (FTS-SQL).

The second section deals with the issues of XML and metadata queries.

Tadeusz Pankowski addresses the problem of data integration in a P2P environment, where each peer stores schema of its local data, mappings between the schemas, and some schema constraints. The goal of the integration is to answer queries formulated against a chosen peer. The answer must consist of data stored in the queried peer as well as data of its direct and indirect partners. Pankowski focuses on defining and using mappings, schema constraints, query propagation across the P2P system, and query answering in such scenario. Schemas, mappings, constraints (functional dependencies) and queries are all expressed using a unified approach based on tree-pattern formulas. He discusses how functional dependencies can be exploited to increase information content of answers (by discovering missing values) and to control merging operations and propagation strategies. He proposes algorithms for translating high-level specifications of mappings and queries into XQuery programs, and shows how the discussed method has been implemented in SixP2P (or 6P2P) system.

Significant research efforts in the Semantic Web community have recently been directed toward the representation and reasoning with fuzzy ontologies. Description logics (DLs) are the logical foundations of standard Web ontology languages. Conjunctive queries are deemed as an expressive reasoning service for DLs. Jingwei Cheng, Z. M. Ma, and Li Yan focus on fuzzy (threshold) conjunctive queries over knowledge bases encoding in fuzzy DL SHIF(D), the logic counterpart of fuzzy OWL Lite language. They show decidability of fuzzy query entailment in this setting by providing a corresponding tableau-based algorithm. Also they show data complexity for answering fuzzy conjunctive queries in fuzzy SHIF(D) is in coNP, as long as only simple roles occur in the query. Regarding combined complexity, they prove a co3NExpTime upper bound in the size of the knowledge base and the query.

The Resource Description Framework (RDF) is a flexible model for representing information about resources in the Web. With the increasing amount of RDF data which is becoming available, efficient and scalable management of RDF data has become a fundamental challenge to achieve the Semantic Web vision. The RDF model has attracted attentions in the database community, and many researchers have proposed different solutions to store and query RDF data efficiently. Sherif Sakr and Ghazi Al-Naymat concentrate on using relational query processors to store and query RDF data. They give an overview of the different approaches and classify these approaches according to the storage and query evaluation strategies.

In the third section, we see the design and application aspects of database query systems.

Relational Algebra (RA) and structured query language (SQL) are supposed to have a bijective relationship by having the same expressive power. That is, each operation in SQL can be mapped to one RA equivalent and vice versa. RA has an explicit relational division symbol ($\div$) whereas SQL does not have a corresponding explicit division keyword. Division is implemented using a combination of four core operations, namely cross product, difference, selection, and projection. The work described by Eric Draken, Shang Gao, and Reda Alhajj is intended to provide SQL expression equivalent to explicit relational algebra division (with static divisor). The goal is to implement a SQL query rewriter in Java which takes as input a divide grammar and rewrites it to an efficient query using current SQL keywords. The developed approach could be adapted as front-end or as a wrapper to existing SQL query system.

Recently, there has been a lot of interest in the application of graphs in different domains. Graphs have been widely used for data modeling in different application domains such as: chemical compounds, protein networks, social networks, and Semantic Web. Given a query graph, the task of retrieving related graphs as a result of the query from a large graph database is a key issue in any graph-based application. This has raised a crucial need for efficient graph indexing and querying techniques. Sherif Sakr and Ghazi Al-Naymat provide an overview of different techniques for indexing and querying graph databases. They also give an overview of several proposals of graph query language. Finally, they provide a set of guidelines for future research directions.

Multimedia objects–such as images, audio, and video–do not present the total ordering relationship, so the relational operators are not suitable to compare them. Therefore, similarity queries are the most useful, and often the only types of queries adequate to search multimedia objects stored in a database. Unfortunately, the ubiquitous query language SQL–the most widely employed language in Database Management Systems (DBMS)–does not provide effective support for similarity queries. Maria Camila

Nardini Barioni *et al.* present an already validated strategy that adds similarity queries to SQL, supporting a powerful set of similarity operators. They also describe techniques to store and retrieve multimedia objects in an efficient way and show existing DBMS alternatives to executing similarity queries over multimedia data.

Li Yan
Northeastern University, China

Zongmin Ma
Northeastern University, China

Acknowledgment

The editors wish to thank all of the authors for their insights and excellent contributions to this book and would like to acknowledge the help of all involved in the collation and review process of the book, without whose support, the project could not have been satisfactorily completed. Most of the authors of chapters included in this book also served as referees for chapters written by other authors. Thanks go to all those who provided constructive and comprehensive reviews.

A further special note of thanks goes to all the staff at IGI Global, whose contributions throughout the whole process from inception of the initial idea to final publication have been invaluable. Special thanks also go to the publishing team at IGI Global. This book would not have been possible without the ongoing professional support from IGI Global.

The idea of editing this volume stems from the initial research work that the editors did in past several years. The research work of the editors was supported by the *National Natural Science Foundation of China* (60873010 and 61073139), the *Fundamental Research Funds for the Central Universities* (N090504005, N100604017 and N090604012), and the *Program for New Century Excellent Talents in University* (NCET- 05-0288).

Li Yan
Northeastern University, China

Zongmin Ma
Northeastern University, China

June 2010

Section 1

Chapter 1
Automatic Categorization of Web Database Query Results

Xiangfu Meng
Liaoning Technical University, China

Li Yan
Northeastern University, China

Z. M. Ma
Northeastern University, China

ABSTRACT

Web database queries are often exploratory. The users often find that their queries return too many answers and many of them may be irrelevant. Based on different kinds of user preferences, this chapter proposes a novel categorization approach which consists of two steps. The first step analyzes query history of all users in the system offline and generates a set of clusters over the tuples, where each cluster represents one type of user preference. When a user issues a query, the second step presents to the user a category tree over the clusters generated in the first step such that the user can easily select the subset of query results matching his needs. The problem of constructing a category tree is a cost optimization problem and heuristic algorithms were developed to compute the min-cost categorization. The efficiency and effectiveness of our approach are demonstrated by experimental results.

INTRODUCTION

As internet becomes ubiquitous, many people are searching their favorite cars, houses, stocks, etc. over the Web databases. However, Web database queries are often exploratory. The users often find that their queries return too many answers, which are commonly referred to as "information overload". For

DOI: 10.4018/978-1-60960-475-2.ch001

Figure 1. Tree generated by the Greedy method

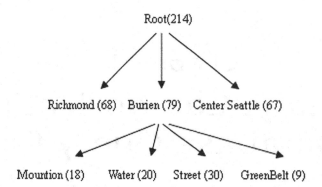

example, when a user submits a query to MSN House&Home Web site to search for a house located in Seattle with a price between $200,000 and $300,000, 1,256 tuples are returned. Information overload makes it hard for the user to separate the interesting items from the uninteresting ones, and thereby lead to a huge wastage of user's time and effort. In such a situation, the user would pose a broad query in the beginning to avoid exclusion of potentially interesting results, and then iteratively refine their queries until a few answers matching their preferences are returned. However, this iterative procedure is time-consuming and many users will give up before they reach the final stage.

In order to resolve the problem of "information overload", two types of solutions have been proposed. The first type categorizes the query results into a category tree (Chakrabarti, Chaudhuri & Hwang, 2004; Chen & Li, 2007), and second type ranks the results (Agrawal, Chaudhuri, Das & Gionis, 2003; Agrawal, Rantzau &Terzi, 2006; Bruno, Gravano & Marian, 2002; Chaudhuri, Das, Hristidis & Weikum, 2004; Das, Hristidis, Kapoor & Sudarshan, 2006). The success of both approaches depends on the utilization of user preferences. But these approaches always assume that all users have the same user preferences, but in real life different users often have different preferences. Let us look at the following example.

Example 1. Consider a real estate searching Web site. Figure 1 and Figure 2 respectively show a fraction of category trees generated by using the methods of *Greedy* (Chakrabarti, Chaudhuri & Hwang, 2004) and *C4.5-Categorization* (Chen & Li, 2007) over 214 houses returned by a query with the condition "Price between 250000 and 350000 ∧ City = Seattle". Each of tree nodes specifies the range or equality conditions on an attribute, and the number in the parentless is the number of tuples satisfying all conditions from the root to the current node. Users can use this tree to select the houses they are interested in.

Consider three users U_1, U_2, and U_3. Assume that U_1 prefers houses with large square, U_2 prefers houses with water views, and U_3 prefers both water views and Burien living area. The *Greedy* method assumed that all users have the same preferences. As a result, attributes "Livingarea" and "Schooldistrict" are placed at the first two levels of the tree because more users are concerned with "Livingarea" and "Schooldistrict" than other attributes. However, there may be some users (such as U_2 and U_3) who want to first visit the large square and water view houses. Then they have to visit many nodes if they go along with the tree built in Figure 1. Considering the diversity of user preferences and the cost of both visiting intermediate nodes and leaf nodes, the *C4.5-Categorization* method took advantage of C4.5 algorithm

Figure 2. Tree generated by the C4.5-Categorization method

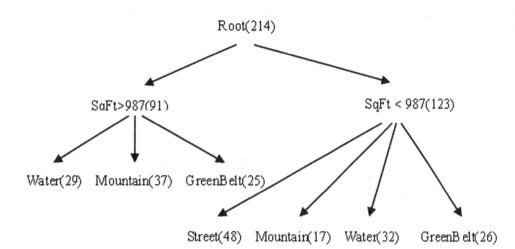

to create the navigational tree. But the created category tree (Figure 2) has two drawbacks: (i) the tuples under the intermediate nodes cannot be explored by the users, i.e., users can only access the tuples under the leaf nodes but cannot examine the tuples in the intermediate nodes; (ii) the cost of visiting the tuples of intermediate node is not considered if the user choose to explore the tuples of intermediate node.

User preferences are often difficult to obtain because users do not want to spend extra efforts to specify their preferences, thus there are two major challenges to address the diversity issue of user preferences: (i) how to summarize different kinds of user preferences from the behavior of all users already in the system, and (ii) how to categorize or rank the query results according to the specific user preferences. Query history has been widely applied to infer the preferences of all users in the system (Agrawal, Chaudhuri, Das & Gionis, 2003; Chaudhuri, Das, Hristidis & Weikum, 2004; Chakrabarti, Chaudhuri & Hwang, 2004; Das, Hristidis, Kapoor & Sudarshan, 2006).

In this chapter, we present techniques to automatically categorize the results of user queries on Web databases in order to reduce information overload. We propose a two-step approach to address both challenges for the categorization case. The first step analyzes query history of all users already in the system offline and then generates a set of clusters over the data. Each cluster corresponds to one type of user preferences and is associated with a probability that users may be interested in the cluster. Assume that an individual user's preference can be represented as a subset of these clusters. When a specific user submits a query, the second step first compute the similarity between the query and the representative queries in the query clusters, and then the data clusters the user may be interested in can be inferred by the query. Next, the set of data clusters generated in the first step is intersected with the query answers and then a labeled hierarchical category structure is generated automatically based on the contents of the tuples in the answer set. Consequently, a category tree is automatically constructed over these intersected clusters on the fly. This tree is finally presented to the user.

This chapter presents a domain-independent approach to addressing the information overload problem. The contributions are summarized as follows:

- We propose a clustering approach to cluster queries and summarize preferences of all users in the system using the query history. This approach uses query pruning, pre-computation and query clustering to deal with large query histories and large data sets.
- We propose a cost-based algorithm to construct a category tree over these clusters pre-formulated in the offline processing phrase. Unlike the existing categorization and decision tree construction approaches, our approach shows tuples for intermediate nodes and considers the cost for users to visit both intermediate nodes and leaves.

The rest of this chapter is organized as follows. Section 2 reviews some related work. Section 3 formally defines some notions. Section 4 describes the queries and tuples clustering method. Section 5 proposes the algorithm for the category tree construction. Section 6 shows the experimental results. The chapter is concluded in Section 7.

RELATED WORK

Two kinds of automatic categorization approaches have been proposed by *Chakrabarti et. al.* (Chakrabarti, Chaudhuri & Hwang, 2004) and *Chen et. al.* (Chen & Li, 2007), respectively. *Chakrabarti et.al.* proposed a greedy algorithm to construct a category tree. This algorithm uses query history of all users in the system to infer an overall user preference as the probabilities that users are interested in each attribute. Taking advantage of C4.5 decision tree constructing algorithm, *Chen* (Chen & Li, 2007) proposed a two-step solution which first clusters user query history and then constructs the navigated tree for resolving the user's personalized query. We make use of some of these ideas, but enhance the category tree with the feature of showing tuples in the intermediate nodes and focus on how the clusters of query history and the cost of visiting both intermediate nodes and leaves have impact on the categorization.

For providing query personalization, several approaches have been proposed to define a user profile for each user and use the profile to decide his preferences (Koutrika &Ioannidis, 2004; Kießling, 2002). As *Chen* (Chen & Li, 2007) pointed out that, however, in real life, user profiles may not be available because users do not want to or cannot specify their preferences (if they can, they can form the appropriate query and there is no need for either ranking or categorizing). The profile may be derived from the query history of a certain user, but this method does not work if the user is new to the system, which is exactly true when the user needs help.

There has been a rich body of work on categorizing text documents (Dhillon, Mallela, & Kumar, 2002; Joachims, 1998; Koller,& Sahami, 1997) and Web search results (Liu, Yu & Meng, 2002; Zeng, He, Chen, Ma & Ma, 2004). But categorizing relational data presents unique challenges and opportunities. First, relational data contains numerical values while text categorization methods treat documents as bags of words. This chapter tries to minimize the overhead for users to navigate the generated tree (it will be defined in Section 3), which is not considered in the existing text categorization methods. Also there has been a rich body of work on information visualization techniques (Card, MacKinlay & Shneiderman, 1999). Two popular techniques are dynamic query slider (Ahlberg & Shneiderman, 1994) and brushing histogram (Tweedie, Spence, Williams & Bhogal, 1994). The former allows users to visualize dynamic query results by using sliders to represent range search conditions, and the latter employs interactive histograms to represent each attribute and helps users exploring correlations between attributes. Note that they do not take query history into account. Furthermore, information visualization techniques require users to specify what information to visualize (e.g., by setting the slider or selecting histogram buckets). Since our approach generates the information to visualize, i.e., the category tree, our approach is a complementary to visualization techniques. If the leaf of the tree still contains many tuples, for example, a query slider or brushing histogram can be used to further narrow down the scope.

Concerning the ranked retrieval from databases, user relevance feedback (Rui, Huang & Merhotra, 1997; Wu, Faloutsos, Sycara & Payne, 2000) is employed to learn the similarity between a result tuple and the query, which is used to rank the query results in relational multimedia databases. The SQL query language is extended to allow the user to specify the ranking function according to their preference for the attributes (Kießling, 2002; Roussos, Stavrakas & Pavlaki, 2005). Also, the importance scores of result tuples (Agrawal, Chaudhuri, Das & Gionis, 2003; Chaudhuri, Das, Hristidis & Weikum, 2004; Geerts, Mannila & Terzim, 2004) are extracted automatically by analyzing the past workloads, which can reveal what users are looking for and what they consider as important. According to the scores, the tuples can be ranked. Ranking is a complementary to categorization. We can use ranking in addition to our techniques (e.g., we rank tuples stored in the intermediate nodes and leaves). However, most existing work does not consider the diversity issue of user preferences. In contrast, we focus on addressing the diversity issue of user preferences for the categorization approach.

Also there has been a lot of work on information retrieval (Card, MacKinlay & Shneiderman, 1999; Shen, Tan & Zhai, 2005; Finkelstein &Gabrilovich, 2001; Joachims, 2006; Sugiyama & Hatano, 2004) using query history or other implicit feedbacks. However, these work focuses on searching text documents, while this chapter focuses on searching relational data. In addition, these studies typically rank query results, while this chapter categorizes the results. Of course, ones could use the existing hierarchical clustering techniques (Mitchell, 1997) to create the category tree. But the generated trees are not easy for users to navigate. For example, how do we describe the tuples contained in a node? We can use a representative tuple, but such a tuple may contain many attributes. It is difficult for users to read. On the contrary, the category tree used in this chapter is easy to understand because each node just uses one attribute.

BASICS OF CATEGORIZATION

This section introduces the query history firstly, and then defines the category tree and the category cost. The categorical space and exploration model are finally described.

Query History

Consider a database relation D with n tuples $D = \{t_1,..., t_n\}$ with schema R $\{A_1,...,A_m\}$. Let $\text{Dom}(A_i)$ represent the active domain of attribute A_i.

Let H be a query history $\{(Q_1, U_1, F_1),..., (Q_k, U_k, F_k)\}$ in chronological order, where Q_i is a query, U_i is a session ID (a session starts when a user connects to the database and ends when the user disconnects), and F_i is the importance weight of the query, which is evaluated by the frequency of the query in H. Assume that the queries in the same session are asked by the same user, which will be used later to prune queries. The query history can be collected using the query log of commercial database systems.

We assume that all queries only contain point or range conditions, and the query is of the form: $Q = \wedge_{i \in m}(A_i \theta a_i)$, where $a_i \in \text{Dom}(A_i)$, $\theta \in \{>, <, =, \geq, \leq, \text{between, in}\}$. Note that if θ is the operator *between*, $A_i \theta a_i$ has the format of "A_i between a_{i1} and a_{i2}"or "$a_{i1} \leq A_i \leq a_{i2}$", where $a_{i1}, a_{i2} \in \text{Dom}(A_i)$.

D can be partitioned into a set of disjoint preference-based clusters $C = \{C_1,..., C_q\}$, where each cluster C_j corresponds to one type of user preferences. Each C_j is associated with a probability P_j that users are interested in C_j. This set of clusters over D is inferred from the query history. We assume that the dataset D is fixed. But, in practice D may get modified from time to time. For the purpose of this chapter, we will assume that the clusters are generated periodically (e.g., once a month) as the set of queries evolve and database is updated.

Category Tree

Category Tree

Definition 1 (Category tree). A category tree $T(V, E, L)$ consists of a node set V, an edge set E, and a label set L. Each node $v \in V$ has a label $\text{lab}(v) \in L$ which specifies the condition on an attribute such that the following should be satisfied: (i) such conditions are point or range conditions, and the bounds in the range conditions are called partition points; (ii) v contains a set of tuples $N(v)$ that satisfy all conditions on its ancestors including itself, in other words, $N(v)$ is the subset of tuples in D that satisfies the conjunction of catalog labels of all nodes on the path from the root to v; (iii) conditions associated with subcategory of an intermediate node v are on the same attribute (called partition attribute), and define a partition of the tuples in v.

The label of a category (or a node), therefore, solely and unambiguously describes to the user which tuples, among those in the tuple set of the parent of v, appear under v. Hence, user can determine whether v contains any item that is relevant to her or not by looking just at the label and hence decide whether to explore or ignore v. The $\text{lab}(v)$ has the following structure:

If the categorizing attribute A is a categorical attribute: $\text{lab}(v)$ is of the form '$A \in S$' where $S \subset \text{Dom}(A)$ ($\text{Dom}(A)$ denotes the domain of values of attribute A in D). A tuple t satisfied the predicate $\text{lab}(v)$ if $t.A \in S$, otherwise it is false ($t.A$ denotes the value of tuple t on attribute A).

If the categorizing attribute A is a numeric attribute: $\text{lab}(v)$ is of the form '$a_1 \leq A < a_2$' where $a_1, a_2 \in \text{Dom}(A)$. A tuple t satisfies the predicate $\text{lab}(v)$ is true if $a_1 \leq t.A < a_2$, otherwise it is false.

Exploration Model

Given a category tree T over the query results, the user starts the exploration by exploring the root node. Suppose that she has decided to explore the node v, if v is an intermediate node, she non-deterministically (i.e., not known in advance) chooses one of the two options:

Option 'ShowTuples': Browse through the tuples in $N(v)$. Note that the user needs to examine all tuples in $N(v)$ to make sure that she finds every tuple relevant to her.

Option 'ShowCat': Examine the labels of all the n subcategories of v, exploring the ones relevant to her and ignoring the rest. More specifically, she examines the label of each subcategory v_i of v staring form the first subcategory and no-deterministically chooses to either explore it or ignore it. If she chooses to ignore v_i, she simply proceeds and examines the next label (of v_{i+1}). If she chooses to explore

v_i, she does so recursively based on the same exploration model, i.e., by choosing either 'ShowTuples' or 'ShowCat' if it is an intermediate node or by choosing 'ShowTuples' if it is a leaf node. After she finishes the exploration of v_i, she goes ahead and examines the label of the next subcategory of v (of v_{i+1}). When the user reaches the end of the subcategory list, she is done. Note that we assume that the user examines the subcategories in the order it appears under v; it can be from top to bottom or from left to right depending on how the tree is rendered by the user interface.

Category Cost

We assume that a user visits T in a top-bottom fashion, and stops at a node (intermediate node or leaf node) that contains the tuples that she is interested in.

Let v be a node (intermediate node or leaf node) of T with $N(v)$ tuples and C_j be a cluster in C. $C_j \cap v \neq \phi$ denotes that v contains tuples in C_j. $Anc(v)$ denotes the set of ancestors of v including v itself, but excluding the root. $Sib(v)$ denotes the set of nodes at the same level as the node v including itself. Let K_1 and K_2 represent the weights of visiting a tuples in the node and visiting an intermediate tree node, respectively. Let P_j be the probability that users will be interested in cluster C_j, and let P_{st} be the probability that user goes for option 'ShowTuples' for an intermediate node v given that she explores v. The category cost is defined as follows.

Definition 2 (category cost). The category cost

$$\text{Cost}\,(T, C) =$$
$$\sum_{v \in Node(T)} \sum_{C_j \cap v \neq \phi} P_j (K_1 \mid N(v) \mid + K_2 \sum_{v_i \in Anc(v)} (\mid Sib(v_i) \mid + \sum_{j=1}^{\mid Sib(v_i) \mid} P_{st_j} (N(v_j)))) \tag{1}$$

The category cost of a leaf node v consists of three terms: the cost of visiting tuples in leaf node v, the cost of visiting intermediate nodes, and the cost of visiting tuples in intermediate nodes if the user chooses to explore it. Users need to examine the labels of all sibling nodes to select a node on the path from the root to v, thus users have to visit $\sum_{v_i \in Anc(v)} \mid Sib(v_i) \mid$ intermediate tree nodes. Users may also like to examine the tuples of some sibling nodes on the path from the root to v, thus users have to visit $\sum_{v_i \in Anc(v)} \sum_{j=1}^{\mid Sib(v_i) \mid} P_{st_j}(N(v_j))$ tuples of intermediate tree nodes. When users reach the node v which they would like to explore it, they have to look at $N(v)$ tuples in v. P_{st} is the probability that the user exploring v using 'ShowTuples', $P_{st} = N(A_v)/N$, where $N(A_v)$ denotes the number of queries in the query history that contain selection condition on attribute A of node v and N is the total number of queries in the query history. Definition 2 computes the expected cost over all clusters and nodes.

Query Results Categorization

For resolve the problem of query results categorization, we propose a solution which consists of two steps, the offline data clustering step and the online category tree construction step. In this Section, we first describe data clustering and then present the category tree construction approach.

Data Clustering

We generate preference-based clusters as follows. We first define a binary relationship R over tuples such that $(r_i, r_j) \in R$ if and only if two tuples r_i and r_j appear in the results of the exactly same set of queries in H. If $(r_i, r_j) \in R$, according to the query history, r_i and r_j are not distinguishable because each user that requests r_i also requests r_j and vice versa. Clearly, R is reflexive, symmetric, and transitive. Thus R is an equivalence relation and it partitions D into equivalence classes $\{C_1, ..., C_q\}$, where tuples equivalent to each other are put into the same class. Those tuples not selected by any query will also form a cluster associated with zero probability (since no users are interested in them). Thus, we can define the data clustering problem as follows.

Problem 1. Given database D, query history H, find a set of disjoint clusters $C = \{C_1, ..., C_q\}$ such that for any tuples r_i and $r_j \in C_l$, $1 \leq l \leq q$, $(r_i, r_j) \in R$, and for any tuples r_i and r_j not in the same cluster, $(r_i, r_j) \notin R$.

Since the query history H may contain many queries, thus we need to cluster the queries in H, and then to cluster the tuples depending on the clusters of query history. We will propose the algorithm for query history and data clustering in the next section.

Category Tree Construction

We next define the problem of category tree construction.

Problem 2. Given D, C, Q, find a tree $T(V, E, L)$ such that (i) it contains all tuples in the results of Q, and (ii) there does not exist another tree T' satisfying (i) and with Cost $(T', C) <$ Cost (T, C).

The above problem can be proved to be NP-hard in a way similar to proving that the problem of finding an optimal decision tree with a certain average length is NP-hard. Section 5 will present an approximate solution. The category tree construction algorithm is shown in Algorithm 1.

CLUSTERING FOR QUERY HISTORY AND DATA TUPLES

This section describes the algorithm to cluster tuples using query history. We propose the preprocessing steps to refine the query history, which include prune unimportant queries and cluster the queries. Based on different kinds of user preferences, we propose the method of generating tuples clusters.

Algorithm 1. The category tree construction algorithm

```
Input: query history H, database D, query Q
Output: a category tree T
1. (Offline step) Cluster tuples in query results D using H. The results are a set
of clusters C₁,..., C_q, and each cluster C_j, 1 ≤ j ≤ q, is assigned a probability P_j.
2. (Online step) For the query Q, create a category tree T with minimal
LCost(T, C) over tuples in results of Q, using C₁,..., C_q as class labels.
```

Query Refinement and Clustering

Query Prune

The query pruning algorithm is based on the following heuristics: (i) queries with empty answers are not useful, (ii) in the same session, a user often starts with a query with general conditions and return many answers, and then continuously refines the previous query until the query returns a few interesting answers. Therefore, only the last query in such a refinement sequence is important. The queries prune algorithm is shown in Algorithm 2.

We identify the relationship "$\subseteq$" between queries by using the following method. Let Q_i's condition on attribute A_i ($i = 1,\ldots,m$) is $a_{i1} \leq A_i \leq a_{i2}$, and Q_j's condition on attribute A_i is $a'_{i1} \leq A_i \leq a'_{i2}$. $Q_i \subseteq Q_j$ if for every condition in Q_i, Q_j either does not contain any condition on A_i or has a condition $a'_{i1} \leq A_i \leq a'_{i2}$, such that $a'_{i1} \leq a_{i1} \leq A_i \leq a_{i2} \leq a'_{i2}$. For simplicity, we use H to denote the pruned query history H' in the following sections.

Query Clustering

Since there are too many queries in the query history, we should cluster the similar queries into the same cluster and find the representative queries.

The Problem of Queries Clustering

In order to quantify the similarity between the query Q_1 and Q_2, we adopt a typical definition of similarity, the cosine similarity. For this to be defined we first need to form the vector representations of query Q_1 and Q_2. Consider the set Δ of all distinct <attribute, attribute-value> pairs appearing in the D, that is, $\Delta = \{<A_i, a_i> \mid \forall i \in \{1,\ldots, d\}$ and $\forall a \in \text{Dom}(A_i)\}$. Since $\text{Dom}(A_i)$ is the active domain of attribute A_i the cardinality of this set is finite. Let it be $N = |\Delta|$ and let O_D be an arbitrary but fixed order on the pairs appearing in Δ. We refer to the i-th element of Δ based on the ordering O_D by $\Delta[i]$. A vector representation of query $Q_1 = \wedge_{j \in m}(A_j \theta a_j)$ is a binary vector V_{Q1} of size N. The i-th element of the vector corresponds to pair $\Delta[i]$. If $\Delta[i]$ is contained in the conjunctions of Q_1 then $V_{Q1}[i] = 1$. Otherwise it is 0. Analogously, the vector representation of a query Q_2 is a binary vector V_{Q2} of size N. The i-th element of the vector corresponds to pair $\Delta[i]$. If $\Delta[i]$ is contained in the conjuncts of Q_2, then $V_{Q2}[i] = 1$; otherwise it is 0.

Algorithm 2. The queries pruning algorithm

```
Input: query history H, database D
Output: pruned query history H'
1. Eliminate queries with empty answers by executing the query over D.
2. Order the remaining queries by session ID in chronological order.
3. For each sequence (Q_i, U_i, F_i), ..., (Q_j, U_j, F_j) in H such that U_i = U_{i+1} = ... =U_j
and Q_i ⊆Q_{i+1}...⊆Q_j and (Q_j ⊄ Q_{j+1} or U_j ≠ U_{j+1}).
4. Eliminate all queries Q_i, ..., Q_{j-1}.
```

Now, we can define the similarity between Q_1 and Q_2 using their vector representations V_{Q1} and V_{Q2} as follows:

$$\text{Sim}(Q_1, Q_2) = \cos(V_{Q1}, V_{Q2}) = \frac{V_{Q1} \cdot V_{Q2}}{|V_{Q1}| |V_{Q2}|} \tag{2}$$

In order to quantify how well a query Q_1 is represented by another query Q_2, we need to define a distance measure between two queries. Based on the similarity mentioned above, the distance between Q_1 and Q_2 can be defined as

$$d(Q_1, Q_2) = 1 - \text{Sim}(Q_1, Q_2) \tag{3}$$

Based on the definitions above, the queries clustering problem can be defined. Let H be the set of m queries in query history: $H = \{Q_1, ..., Q_m\}$. The we need to find a set of k queries $H_k = \{\overline{Q}_1, ..., \overline{Q}_k\}$ ($k < m$) such that:

$$\cos t(H_k) = \sum_{Q \in H} d(Q, QC_k) \tag{4}$$

is minimized. The distance of a query Q_i from a set of queries H is defined as

$$d(Q_i, H) = \min_{Q_j \in H} d(Q_i, Q_j) \tag{5}$$

We call the queries in set H_k representative queries and associate with each representative query $\overline{Q}_i$ a set of queries $QC_j = \{Q_i \mid \overline{Q}_j = \arg\min_{j'} d(Q_i, \overline{Q}_{j'})\}$.

Complexity of the Queries Clustering Problem

The problem of queries clustering is the same as the k-median problem. The k-median problem is well known to be NP-hard. An instance of the metric k-median problem consists of a metric space $\chi = (X, c)$, where X is a set of points and c is a distance function (also called the cost) that specifies the distance $c_{xy} \geq 0$ between any pair of nodes $x, y \in X$. The distance function is reflexive, symmetric, and satisfies the triangle inequality. Given a set of points $F \subseteq X$, the cost of F is defined by $\text{cost}(F) = \sum_{x \in X} c_{xF}$, where $c_{xF} = \min_{f \in F} c_{xF}$ for $x \in X$. The objective is to find a k-element set $F \subseteq X$ that minimizes $\text{cost}(F)$ (Chrobak, Keynon & Young, 2005). Obviously, the queries clustering problem can be treated as the k-median problem and it is also NP-hard. Thus, we have to think of approximation algorithms for solving it.

Algorithm 3. The Greedy-Refine algorithm of queries clustering

```
Input: A pruned query history H with m queries: H = {Q₁,..., Qₘ}, a set of all
Stars: U = {⟨Qᵢ, QCᵢ⟩ | Qᵢ ∈ H, QCᵢ ⊆ H}, k
Output: A set of k query clusters Hₖ = {⟨Q̄₁,QC₁⟩...⟨Q̄ₖ, QCₖ⟩}
1. Let B = {} be a buffer that can hold m ⟨Qᵢ, QCᵢ⟩
2. While H ≠ ∅ and k > 0 Do
3.    B ← ∅
4.    For each Qᵢ ∈ H Do
5.       Pick sᵢ = ⟨Qᵢ, QCᵢ⟩ with minimum rₛᵢ from Uᵢ = {⟨Qᵢ, QCᵢ⟩ | QCᵢ ⊆ H, | QCᵢ |
= [2, |H| - k + 1]}
6.       B ←B +{sᵢ}
7.    End For
8.    Pick s = ⟨Qᵢ, QCᵢ⟩ with minimum rₛ from B
9.    H←H -QCᵢ - {Qᵢ}, Hₖ ←Hₖ + s, k← k - 1
10. End While
11. Return Hₖ
```

Algorithmic Solution

For clustering queries, we propose a novel approach, which can discover the near-globally optimal solution and has the low time complexity of the algorithm as well. The approach is described as follows.

Observing the solution of the queries clustering, we can find that every representative query connects with some other queries of H and these connections are like star structures. Here, we call a connection as a *Star*. Then we can re-define the queries clustering problem as follows: Let U be the set of all Stars, i.e., $U = \{\langle Q_i, QC_i \rangle \mid Q_i \in H, QC_i \subseteq H\}$. The cost of each *Star* $s = \langle Q_i, QC_i \rangle \in U$ can be denoted as: $c_s = \sum_{Q_j \in QC_i} d(Q_i, Q_j)$. Let $r_s = c_s/|QC_i|$ be the performance-price ratio. Our objective is to find a set of *Star S*, such that $S \subseteq U$, which minimizes the cost and enables that there are k representative queries in S and any original query $Q_j \in H$ appears at least once at *Star* $s \in S$.

For solving this problem, we propose an approach which consists of two parts: a pre-processing part and a processing part. In the processing part, we build a sequential permutation $k_i = \{Q_{i1}, Q_{i2},..., Q_{im}\}$ over H for each query $Q_i \in H$, where $\{Q_{i1}, Q_{i2},..., Q_{im}\} \in H$ and the queries in k_i are arranged non-decreasing according to their cost corresponding to Q_i, that is, $d(Q_i, Q_{i1}) \leq d(Q_i, Q_{i2}) \leq ... \leq d(Q_i, Q_{im})$. Such permutations can help us only consider the first l queries in k_i other than all queries in k_i when we build the *Star* for Q_i. Note that, the number l should be chosen appropriately. It can be seen that the complexity of pre-processing part is $O(|H|^2 \log|H|)$, where $|H|$ denotes the number of queries of H.

The task of processing part is to cluster queries by using the Greedy-Refine algorithm (Algorithm 3) based on the Stars formed in pre-processing part. The input is a set of all Stars formed in preprocessing part. For each $Q_i \in H$, the algorithm picks up the Star s_i with the minimal r_s in U_i (the set of all Stars in U corresponding to Q_i, $U_i \subseteq U$) and put it in the set B. From the set B, the algorithm chooses the *Star* s with the minimal r_s and adds it to the objective set H_k. And then, the algorithm removes Q_i and QC_i from H. The algorithm stops when the set H_k has k elements. The output is a set of k pairs of the form $\langle \overline{Q}_i,$

QC_i), where $\overline{Q}_i$ is a representative query (i.e., it is the center of clustering QC_i), and $\overline{Q}_i$ corresponds to the query cluster QC_i. The time complexity in the processing part is $O(|H|k)$, and thus the algorithm is polynomial solvable (Meng & Ma, 2008).

Generation of Data Clusters

After queries pruning and clustering, we get a set of query clusters $QC_1, ..., QC_k$. For each tuple t_i, we generate a set S_i consisting of query clusters such that one of the queries in that cluster returns t_i. That is, $S_i = \{QC_p \mid \exists Q_i \in QC_p \text{ such that } t_i \text{ is returned by } Q_j\}$. We then group tuples according to their S_i, and each group forms a cluster. Each cluster is assigned a class label. The probability of users being interested in cluster C_i is computed as the sum of probabilities that a user asks a query in S_i. This equals the sum of frequencies of queries in S_i divided by the sum of frequencies of all queries in the pruned query history H.

Example 2. Suppose that there are four queries Q_1, Q_2, Q_3, and Q_4 and 15 tuples $r_1, r_2, ..., r_{15}$. Q_1 returns first 10 tuples $r_1, r_2, ..., r_{10}$, Q_2 returns the first 9 tuples $r_1, r_2, ..., r_9$, and r_{14}, Q_3 returns r_{11}, r_{12} and r_{14}, and Q_4 returns r_{15}. Obviously, the first 9 tuples $r_1, r_2, ..., r_9$ are equivalent to each other since they are returned by both Q_1 and Q_2. The data can be divided into five clusters $\{r_1, r_2, ..., r_9\}$ (returned by Q_1, Q_2), $\{r_{10}\}$ (returned by Q_1 only), $\{r_{11}, r_{12}, r_{14}\}$ (returned by Q_3), $\{r_{15}\}$ (returned by Q_4), and $\{r_{13}\}$ (not returned by any query).

In example 2, after clustering we get two clusters $\{Q_1, Q_2\}$, $\{Q_3\}$ and $\{Q_4\}$. Four clusters $C_1, C_2, C3$, and C_4 will be generated. The cluster C_1 corresponds to Q_1 and Q_2 and contains the first 10 tuples, with probability $P_1 = 2/4 = 0.5$. The cluster C_2 corresponds to Q_3 and contains r_{11}, r_{12}, r_{14}, with probability $P_2 = 1/4 = 0.25$. The cluster C_3 corresponds to Q_4 and contains r_{15}, with probability $P_3 = 1/4 = 0.25$. The cluster C_4 contains r_{13}, with probability 0, because r_{13} is not returned by any query. The data clusters generating algorithm is shown in Algorithm 4.

Algorithm 4. The algorithm for generating the preference-based data clusters

```
Input: pruned query history H, query results R
Output: data clusters of query results C₁,…, C_q
1. QueryCluster (H, U) → {QC₁, …, QC_k}.
2. For each tuple r_i ∈ R, identify S_i = {QC_p | ∃ Q_j∈QC_p such that r_i is returned
by Q_j}.
Group tuples in R by S_i.
3. Output each group as a cluster C_j, assign a class label for each cluster,
and compute
```

$$\text{probability } P_j = \frac{\sum_{Q_i \in S_j} F_i}{\sum_{Q_p \in H} F_i}.$$

CATEGORY TREE CONSTRUCTION

This section proposes the category tree construction algorithm. Section 5.1 gives an overview of our algorithm. Section 5.2 presents a novel partitioning criterion that considers the cost of visiting both intermediate and leaves nodes.

Algorithm Overview

A category tree is very similar to a decision tree. There are many well-known decision construction algorithms such as ID3 (Quinlan, 1986), C4.5 (Quinlan, 1993), and CART (Breiman, Friedman & Stone, 1984). However, the existing decision tree construction algorithm aims at minimizing the impurity of data (Quinlan, 1993) (represented by information gain, etc.). Our goal is to minimize the category cost, which includes both the cost of visiting intermediate tree nodes (and the cost of visiting tuples in the intermediate nodes if the user explores it) and the cost of visiting tuples stored in leaf nodes.

For building the category tree, we make use some ideas of solution presented by *Chen* (Chen & Li, 2007) and propose the improved algorithms for solving it. The problems of our algorithm have to resolve including (i) eliminating a subset of relatively unattractive attributes without considering any of their partitions, and (ii) for every attribute selected above, obtaining a good partition efficiently instead of enumerating all the possible partitions. Finally, we construct the category tree by choosing the attribute and its partition that has the least cost.

Reducing the Choices of Categorizing Attribute

Since the presence of a selection condition on an attribute in query history reflects the user's interest in that attribute, attributes that occur infrequently in the query history can be omitted while constructing the category tree. Let $N(A)$ be the number of queries in the query history that contain selection condition on attribute A and N be the total number in the query history. We eliminate the uninteresting attributes using the following solution: if an attribute A occurs in less than a fraction x of the queries in the query history, i.e., $N(A)/N < x$, we eliminate A. The threshold x will need to be specified by the system domain expert. For example, for the real estate searching application, if we use $x = 0.4$, only 7 attributes, namely Price, SqFt, Livinarea, View, Neighborhood, Schooldistrict, and Bedrooms, are retained from among 25 attributes in the MSN House&Home dataset. The algorithm for eliminating the uninterested attributes is shown in Algorithm 5.

Algorithm 5. Eliminate uninterested attribute algorithm

```
Input: pruned query history H, threshold x
Output: A_R = {A_1, ..., A_k} which are the attribute set retained after eliminating
the uninterested attributes in H
1. For each attribute A_i of the attribute set A_H appeared in H, Compute its
N(A_i)/N, eliminate A_i if its N(A_i)/N < x.
2. Output A_R = {A_1, ..., A_k}.
```

Partitioning for Categorical Attribute

For a categorical attribute, a new subcategory will be created with one branch for each value of the attribute, and the information gain (we will discuss how to compute the information gain in Section 5.2) will be computed over that subcategory. If a categorical attribute have too many values and thus generate too many branches, we can add intermediate levels to that attribute. The categorical attribute can only generate one possible partition, and it will be removed from A_R if it is selected as the partition attribute.

Partitioning for Numeric Attribute

For a numeric attribute A_i, we use binary partition, i.e., $A_i \leq v$ or $A_i > v$. For a numerical value attribute, the algorithm will generate one subcategory for every possible partition point, and compute the information gain for that partition point. The best partition point will be selected and the gain of the best partition

Algorithm 6. The category tree building algorithm

Function: BuildTree (A_R, D_Q, C, λ)
Input: A_R is the set of attributes retained after eliminating, D_Q is the query results, C is the class labels assigned in the clustering step for each tuple in D_Q, λ and is a user defined stopping threshold.
Output: a category tree T.
1. Create a root r.
2. If all tuples in D_Q have the same class label stop.
3. For each attribute $A_i \in A_R$.
4.   If A_i is a categorical attribute then
5.   For each value v of A_i, create a branch under the current root. Add those tuples with "$A_i = v$" to that branch.
6.   Compute the attribute A_i's gain g(A_i, T_i) where T_i is the subcategory created.
7.   Else
8.   For each value v of A_i, create a tree T_i^v with r as the root and two branches, one for those tuples with $A_i \leq v$ or A_i, one for those tuples with $A_i > v$ or A_i.
9.   Compute the gain g(A_i, T_i^v) for each partition point v and choose the maximal one as g(A_i, T_i).
10.   End If
11. End For
12. Choose the attribute A_j with the maximal g(A_j, T_j), remove A_j from A_H if A_j is categorical.
13. If g(A_j, T_j) > λ then
14.   Replace r with the subcategory T_j, for each leaf n_k in T_j with tuples in D_{Qk},
BuildTree (A_H, D_{Qk}, C, λ).
15. End If

is the gain of the attribute. If the gain-ratio of the attribute with the maximal gain-ratio exceeds a predefined threshold λ, the tree will be expanded by adding the selected subcategory to the current root.

Algorithm Solution

Based on the solutions mentioned above, we can now describe how we construct a category tree. Since the problem of finding a tree with minimal category cost is NP-hard, we propose an approximate algorithm (see Algorithm 6).

After building the category tree, the user can go along with the branches of tree to find the interesting answers. As mentioned above, the user can explore category tree using two models, i.e., showing tuples (option 'ShowTuples') and showing category (option 'ShowCat'). When the user chosen the option 'ShowTuples' on a node (an intermediate node or a leaf node), the system will provide the items satisfying all conditions from the root to the current node. The category tree accessing algorithm is shown in Algorithm 7.

Partition Criteria and Cost Estimation

We first describe how to compute the information gain which acts as the partition criteria, and then we give the cost estimation of visiting the intermediate nodes and the leaves.

Partition Criteria

Existing decision tree construction algorithms such as C4.5 compute an information gain to measure how good an attribute classifies data. Given a decision tree T with N tuples and n classes, where each class C_i in T has N_i tuples. The entropy can be defined as follows,

$$E(T) = -\sum_{i=1}^{n} \frac{N_i}{N} \log \frac{N_i}{N} \qquad (6)$$

Algorithm 7. The algorithm of accessing category tree

```
1. For each intermediate node
2.   If option = 'ShowTuples'
3.     List the tuples satisfying all conditions from the root to the current
node
4.   Else
5.     List the subcategory of the current node
6. End For
7. For each leaf node
8.   The explore model is only the option 'ShowTuples'
9.   List the tuples satisfying all conditions from the root to the current node
10. End For
```

In real applications, there may be several distinct values in the domain of an attribute A. For each attribute value v of A, let N_{Ti} be the number of tuples with the attribute value v of A in class C_i, and thus the conditional entropy can be defined as

$$E_A(v) = \sum_{i=1}^{n} \left[\frac{N_{Ti}}{N} \times E(T_i) \right] \tag{7}$$

And then, the information gain of attribute A can be computed by

$$g(A) = E(T) - E_A(v) \tag{8}$$

For example, consider a fraction results (showed in Table 1) returned by MSN house&home Web database for a query with the condition "Price between 250000 and 350000 and City = Seattle". We then use it to describe how to obtain a best partition attribute by using the formulas defined above.

Here, we assume the decision attributes are View, Schooldistrict, Livingarea, and SqFt. We first compute the entropy of tree T,

$$E(T) = E(C_1, C_2, C_3) = -\left[\frac{5}{15} \log \frac{5}{15} + \frac{6}{15} \log \frac{6}{15} + \frac{4}{15} \log \frac{4}{15} \right] = 0.471293.$$

And then, we compute the entropy of each decision attributes. For attribute "View", it contains four distinct values which are 'Water', 'Mountain', 'GreenBelt', and 'Street', the entropy of each value are

Table 1. The fraction of query results

ID	Price	Bedrooms	Livingarea	Schooldistrict	View	SqFt	Cluster
01	329000	2	Burien	Highline	Water	712	C1
02	335000	2	Burien	Tukwila	Water	712	C1
03	325000	1	Richmond	Shoreline	Water	530	C1
04	325000	3	Richmond	Shoreline	Water	620	C1
05	328000	3	Richmond	Shoreline	Water	987	C1
06	264950	1	Burien	Seattle	Mountain	530	C2
07	264950	1	C-seattle	Seattle	Mountain	530	C2
08	328000	3	Burien	Seattle	GreenBelt	987	C2
09	349000	2	Burien	Seattle	Water	955	C2
10	339950	2	C-seattle	Seattle	GreenBelt	665	C2
11	339950	3	Burien	Seattle	Street	852	C2
12	264950	4	Richmond	Highline	Street	1394	C3
13	264950	5	C-seattle	Seattle	Mountain	1400	C3
14	338000	5	Burien	Tukwila	Street	1254	C3
15	340000	3	Burien	Tukwila	GreenBelt	1014	C3

$$E_{\text{View}}(\text{Water}) = -\left[\frac{5}{6}\log\frac{5}{6} - \frac{1}{6}\log\frac{1}{6}\right] = 0.195676,$$

$$E_{\text{View}}(\text{Mountain})\left[\frac{0}{3}\log\frac{0}{3} - \frac{2}{3}\log\frac{2}{3} - \frac{1}{3}\log\frac{1}{3}\right] = 0.276434,$$

$$E_{\text{View}}(\text{GreenBelt}) = -\left[\frac{0}{3}\log\frac{0}{3} - \frac{2}{3}\log\frac{2}{3} - \frac{1}{3}\log\frac{1}{3}\right] = 0.276434,$$

$$E_{\text{View}}(\text{Street})\left[\frac{0}{3}\log\frac{0}{3} - \frac{2}{3}\log\frac{2}{3} - \frac{1}{3}\log\frac{1}{3}\right] = 0.276434.$$

Next,

$E(\text{View}) = 6/15 * 0.195676 + 3/15 * 0.276434 + 3/15 * 0.276434 + 3/15 * 0.276434 = 0.2441308.$

Thus, the gain

$g(\text{View}) = E(T) - E(\text{View}) = 0.2271622.$

Analogously,

$g(\text{Schooldistrict}) = 0.2927512, g(\text{Livingarea}) = 0.1100572, g(\text{SqFt}) = 0.251855,$

where, we choose the value '987' as the partition value.

Finally, the attribute "Schooldistrict" will be selected as the first level partition attribute of decision tree T by using the C4.5 algorithm.

However, the main difference between our algorithm and the existing decision tree construction algorithm is how to compute the gain of a partition. Our approach wants to reduce the category cost of visiting intermediate nodes (includes the tuples in them if user choose to explore them) and the cost of visiting tuples in the leaves. Our following analysis will show that information gain ignores the cost of visiting tupes, and the existing category tree construction algorithm proposed by *Chakrabarti et. al.* (Chakrabarti, Chaudhuri & Hwang, 2004) ignores the cost of visiting intermediate nodes generated by future partitions while the category tree construction algorithm proposed by *Chen et. al.* (Chen & Li, 2007) ignores the cost of visiting tuples in the intermediate nodes.

Cost Estimation

Cost of Visiting Leave

Let v be the node to be partitioned and $N(v)$ be the number of tuples in v. Let v_1 and v_2 be children generated by a partition. Let P_i be the probability that users are interested in cluster C_i. The gain equals the reduction of category cost when v is partitioned into v_1 and v_2. Thus based on the category cost defined in Definition 2, the reduction of the cost of visiting tuples due to partition v into v_1 and v_2 equals

$$N(t) \sum_{C_l \cap t \neq \phi} P_l - \sum_{j=1,2} N(t_j)(\sum_{C_i \cap t_j} P_i) \tag{9}$$

The decision tree construction algorithms do not consider the cost of visiting leaf tuples. For example, consider a partition that generates two nodes that contain tuples with labels (C_1, C_2, C_1) and (C_2), and a partition that generates two nodes that contain tuples with labels (C_2, C_1, C_2) and (C_1). According to the discussion in Section 5.4.1, these two partitions have the same information gain. However, if $P_1 = 0.5$ and $P_2 = 0$, then the category cost for the first partition is smaller because the cost is 1.5 for the first partition and is 2 for the second partition.

Cost of Visiting Intermediate Nodes

For estimate the cost of visiting intermediate nodes, we adopted the method proposed by *Chen et. al.* (Chen & Li, 2007). According to the definition in (Chen & Li, 2007), the *perfect* tree is that their leaves only contain tuples of on class and can not be partitioned further. In fact, the perfect tree is a decision tree. Given a perfect tree T with N tuples and k classes, where each class C_i in T has N_i tuples. The entropy $E(T) = -\sum_{i=1}^{k} \frac{N_i}{N} \log \frac{N_i}{N}$ approximates the average length of root-to-leaf paths for all tuples in T. Since T is a perfect tree, its leaves contain only one class per node. For each such leaf L_i that contains N_i tuples of class C_i, it can be further expanded into a smaller subtree T_i which is rooted at L_i, and its leaf contains exactly one record in C_i. Each such small subtree T_i contains N_i leaves. All these subtrees and T compose a big tree T_b that contains $\sum_{1 \leq i \leq k} N_i = N$ leaves. We further assume that each T_i and the big tree T_b are balanced, thus the height for T_i is $\log N_i$ and the height for T_b is $\log N$. Note that for the i-th leaf L_i in T, the length of the path from root to L_i equals the height of big tree T_b minus the height of small tree T_i. There are N_i tuples in L_i, all with the same path from the root. Thus the average length of root-to-leaf paths for tuples is defined as follows,

$$\sum_{1 \leq i \leq k} \frac{N_i}{N}(\log N - \log N_i) = -\sum_{i=1}^{k} \frac{N_i}{N} \log \frac{N_i}{N} \tag{10}$$

This is exactly the entropy $E(t)$. Note that most existing decision tree algorithms choose the partition that maximizes information gain. Information gain is the reduction of entropy due to a partition and is represented in the following formula,

$$IGain(t, t_1, t_2) \;=\; E(t) - \frac{N_1}{N} E(t_1) - \frac{N_2}{N} E(t_2) \tag{11}$$

Thus a partition with a high information gain will generate a tree with a low entropy. And, this tree will have short root-to-leaf paths as well. Since the cost of visiting intermediate nodes equals the product of path lengths and fan-out in Definition 2, if we assume the average fan-out is about the same for all trees, then the cost of visiting intermediate nodes is proportional to the length of root-to-leaf paths. Therefore, the cost reduction of visiting intermediate nodes can be used information gain to estimate.

Cost of Visiting Tuples in Intermediate Nodes

Since user may choose to examine the tuples in an intermediate node, thus we need to consider the cost of visiting these tuples. Let P_{st} be the probability that user goes for option 'ShowTuples' for an intermediate node v given that she explores v, and $N(t)$ be the number of tuples in the intermediate node t. Next, the cost of visiting tuples in an intermediate node equals $P_{st} \cdot N(t)$.

Combining Costs

The remaining problem is how to combine the three types of costs. Here we take a normalization approach, which uses the following formula to estimate the gain of partitioning t into t_1 and t_2,

$$\frac{IGain(t, t_1, t_2) / E(t)}{((\sum_{j=1,2} N(t_j)(\sum_{C_i \cap t_j \neq \phi} P_i)) / (N(t) \sum_{C_l \cap t \neq \phi} P_l)) * P_{st} N(t)} \tag{12}$$

The denominator is the product of the cost of visiting leaf tuples after partition normalized by the cost before partition multiplying the cost of visiting the tuples in t. A partition always reduces the cost of visiting tuples (the proof is straightforward). Thus the denominator ranges from (0, 1]. The nominator is the information gain normalized by the entropy of t. We compute a ratio between these two terms rather than sum of the nominator and (1-denominator) because in practice the nominator (information gain) is often quite small. Thus the ratio is more sensitive to the nominator when the denominator is similar.

Complexity Analysis

Let n be the number of tuples in query results, m be the number of attributes, and k be the number of classes. The gain in Formula 5 can be computed in $O(k)$ time. C4.5 also uses several optimizations such as computing the gains for all partition points of an attribute in one pass, sorting all tuples on different attribute values beforehand, and reusing the sort order. The cost of sorting tuples on different attribute values is $O(mn\log n)$, and the cost of computing gains for all possible partitions at one node is $O(mnk)$ because there are at most m partition attributes and n possible partition points, and each gain can be computed in $O(k)$ time. If we assume the generated tree has $O(\log n)$ levels, the total time is $O(mnk\log n)$.

EXPERIMENTAL EVALUATION

In this section, we describe our experiments, report the experimental results and compare our approach with several existing approaches.

Experimental Setup

We used Microsoft SQL Server 2005 RDBMS on a P4 3.2-GHz PC with 1 GB of RAM for our experiments.

Dataset: For our evaluation, we setup a real estate database HouseDB (Price, SqFt, Bedrooms, Bathrooms, Livingarea, Schooldistrict, View, Neighborhood, Boat, Garage, Buildyear...) containing 1,700,000 tuples extracted from MSN House&Home Web site. There are 27 attributes, 10 numerical and 17 categorical. The total data size is 20 MB.

Table 2. Test queries used in user study

Queries	Result size
Q_1: Price between 250000 and 300000 and SqFt > 1000	323
Q_2: Schooldistrict = Tukwila and View = GreenBelt	894
Q_3: Price < 250000 and Neighborhood in { Winslow, Shoreline}	452
Q_4: Schooldistrict = Seattle and View in {Water, GreenBelt}	558
Q_5: SqFt between 600 and 1000	16213

Query history: In our experiments, we requested 40 subjects to behave as different kinds of house buyers, such as rich people, clerks, workers, women, young couples, etc. and post queries against the database. We collected 2000 queries for the database and these queries are used as the query history. Each subject was asked to submit 15 queries for HouseDB, each query had 2~6 conditions and had 4.2 specified attributes on average. We assume each query has equal weight. We did observe that users started with a general query which returned many answers, and then gradually refined the query until it returned a small number of answers.

Algorithm: We implemented all algorithms in C# and connected to the RDBMS through ADO. The clusters are stored by adding a column to the data table to store the class labels of each tuple. The stopping threshold λ in build tree algorithm is set to 0.002. We have developed an interface that allows users to classify query results using generated trees.

Comparison: We compare our create tree algorithm (henceforth referred to as *Cost-based* algorithm) with the algorithm proposed by *Chakrabarti et. al.* (Chakrabarti, Chaudhuri & Hwang, 2004) (henceforth referred to as *Greedy* algorithm). It differs from our algorithm on two aspects: (i) it does not consider different user preferences, and (ii) it does not consider the cost of intermediate nodes generated by future partitions. We also compare the algorithm proposed by *Chen et. al.* (Chen & Li, 2007) (henceforth referred to as *C4.5-Categorization* algorithm), it first uses the merging queries step to generate data clusters and corresponding labels, then uses modified C4.5 to create the navigational tree. It differs from our algorithm on two aspects: (i) it needs to execute queries on the dataset to evaluate the queries similarity and then to merging the similar queries, and (ii) it can not expand the intermediate nodes to show tuples and it thus does not consider the cost of visiting tuples of intermediate nodes.

Setup of user study: We conduced an empirical study by asking 5 subjects (with no overlap with the 40 users submitting the query history) to use this interface. The subjects were randomly selected colleagues, students, etc. Each subject was given a tutorial about how to use this interface. Next, each subject was given the results of 5 queries listed in Table 2, which do not appear in the query history. For each such query, the subject was asked to go along with the trees generated by the three algorithms mentioned above, and to select 5-10 houses that he would like to buy.

Categorization Cost Experiment

The experiment aims at comparing the cost of three categorization algorithms and showing the efficiency of our categorization approach. The actual category cost is defined as follows:

Figure 3. Total actual cost

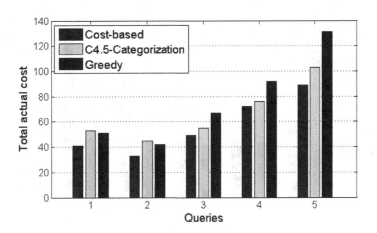

Figure 4. Average number of selected houses per subject

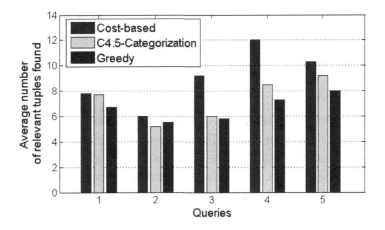

$$\text{ActCost} = \sum_{\forall leaf\ v\ visited\ by\ a\ subject} (K_1 N(v) + K_2 \sum_{v_i \in Anc(v)} (\mid Sib(v_i) \mid + \sum_{j=1}^{|Sib(v_i)|} P_{st_j}(N(v_j)))) \tag{13}$$

Unlike the category cost in Definition 2, this cost is the real count of intermediate (including siblings) and tuples visited by a subject. We assume the weight for visiting intermediate nodes and visiting tuples are equal, i.e. $K_1 = K_2 = 1$. In general the lower the total category cost, the better the categorization method.

Figure 3 shows the total actual cost, averaged over all the subjects, for *Cost-based, C4.5-Categorization,* and *Greedy* algorithm. Figure 4 reports the average number of houses selected by each subject. Figure 5 reports the average category cost of per selected house for these algorithms.

The results show that the category trees generated by *Cost-based* algorithm have the lowest actual cost and the lowest average cost per selected house (the number of query clusters *k* was set to 30). Users

Figure 5. Average category cost of per selected house

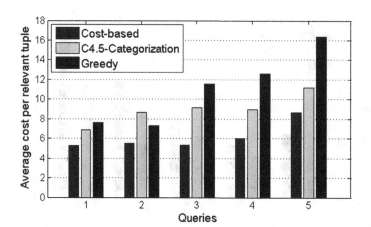

Table 3. Results of survey

Categorization algorithm	#subjects that called it best
Cost-based	16
C4.5-categorization	4
Greedy	2

have also found more houses worth considering to buy using our algorithm than the other two algorithms, suggesting our method makes it easier for users to find interesting houses. The tree generated by *Greedy* algorithm has the worst results. This expected because the *Greedy* algorithm ignores different user preferences, and dose not consider future partitions when generating category trees. The *C4.5-Categorization* algorithm also has higher cost than our method. The reason is that our algorithm uses a partitioning criterion that considers the cost of visiting the tuples in intermediate nodes, while *C4.5-Categorization* algorithm does not. Moreover, our algorithm can use a few clusters to representative a large scale tuples without lose accuracy (it will be tested in the next experiment).

The results show that using our approach, on average a subject only needs to visit no more than 8 tuples or intermediate nodes for queries Q_1, Q_2, Q_3, and Q_4 to find the first relevant tuple, and needs to visit about 18 tuples or intermediate nodes for Q_5. The total navigational cost for our algorithm is less than 45 for the former four queries, and is less than 80 for Q_5. At the end of the study, we asked subjects which categorization algorithm worked the best for them among all the queries they tried. The result of that survey is reported in Table 3 and shows that a majority of subjects considered our algorithm the best.

Queries Clustering Experiment

This experiment aims at testing the quality of the algorithm for the queries clustering, whose accuracy has a great impaction on the accuracy of the clusters of the tuples. We first translated each query in the query history into its corresponding vector representation, and then we adopt the following strategies to generate synthetic datasets. Every dataset is characterized by 4 parameters: *n, m, l, noise*. Here the *n*

Figure 6. Algorithms' performance for the queries clustering

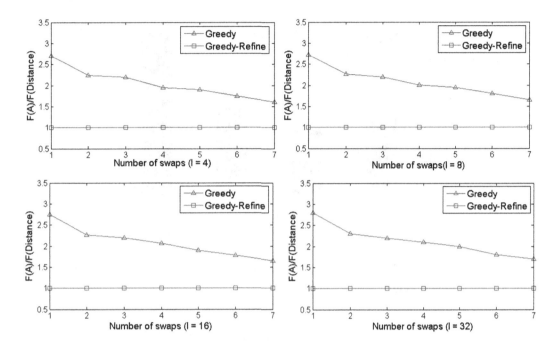

is the number of vector elements in <attribute, value> pairs set of Δ (note that, each query in the query history is translated into vector representations), m is the number of input queries, and l is the number of true underlying clusters. We set '0' and '1' at random on the n elements and we then generate l random queries by sampling at random the space of all possible permutations of n elements. These initial queries form the centers around which we build each one of the clusters. The task of the algorithms is to rediscover the clustering model used for the data generation. Given a cluster center, each query from the same cluster is generated by adding to the center a specified amount of *noise* of a specific type. We consider two types of noise: *swaps* and *shifts*. The *swap* means that '0' and '1' elements from the initial order are picked and their positions in the order are exchanged. For the shifts we pick a random element and we move it to a new position, either earlier (or later) in the order. All elements that are between the new and the old positions of the element are shifted on position down (or up). The amount of noise is the number of swaps or shifts we make.

We experiment with datasets generated for the following parameters: $n = 300$, $m = 600$, $l = \{4, 8, 16, 32\}$, *noise* $= \{2, 4, 8,\dots, 128\}$ for swaps. Figure 6 shows the performance of the algorithms as a function of the amount of noise. The y axis is the ratio: $F(A)/F(INP)$, for $A = \{\text{Greedy, Greedy-Refine}\}$, where the Greedy- Refine algorithm is proposed in this chapter (Algorithm 3), while the Greedy algorithm is proposed in [2]. We compare them here since they all aim at solving the same problem (clustering problem). The $F(A)$ is the total cost of the solution provided by algorithm A when the distance showed in Equation (3) is used as a distance measure between queries. The $F(INP)$ corresponds to the cost of the clustering structure (Equation 4) used in the data generation process.

From Figure 6 we can see that: Greedy- Refine algorithm performs greatly better than Greedy algorithm. The reason is that: the Greedy- Refine is executed on the queries which were arranged according

Figure 7. Execution time for Q_1 to Q_4

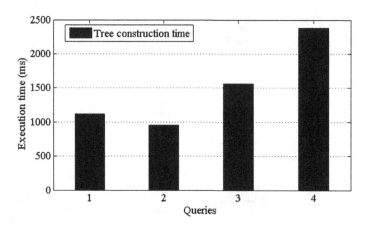

to their cost in pre-processing phrase and makes twice greedy selection in processing phrase, so that it can obtain the near-globally optimization solution.

Performance Report

Figure 7 report the tree construction time of our algorithm for the 5 test queries (since the execution time of Q_5 is much longer than the first 4 queries, we do not show its histogram in the figure). Our algorithm took no more than 2.4 second for the first 4 queries queries that returned several hundred results. It took about 4 seconds for the 5th query that returned 16,213 tuples. Thus our algorithm can be used in an interactive environment.

CONCLUSION

This chapter proposed a categorization approach to address diverse user preferences, which can help users navigate many query results. This approach first summarized preferences of all users in the system by clustering the query history, and then divided tuples into clusters using the different kinds of user preferences. When a specific user issues a query, our approach create a category tree over the clusters appearing in the results of the query to help users navigate these results. Our approach differs from the several existing approaches in two aspects: (i) our approach does not require a user profile or a meaning-ful query when deciding the user preferences for a specific user, and (ii) the category tree construction algorithm proposed in this chapter considers both the cost of visiting intermediate nodes (including the cost of visiting the tuples in intermediate nodes) and the cost of visiting the tuples in leaf nodes. In the future, we will investigate how to accommodate the dynamic nature of user preferences and how to integrate the ranking approach into our approach.

REFERENCES

Agrawal, R., Rantzau, R., & Terzi, E. (2006). Context-sensitive ranking. *Proceedings of the ACM SIG-MOD International Conference on Management of Data*, (pp. 383-394).

Agrawal, S., Chaudhuri, S., Das, G., & Gionis, A. (2003). Automated ranking of database query results. *ACM Transactions on Database Systems*, *28*(2), 140–174.

Ahlberg, C., & Shneiderman, B. (1994). *Visual information seeking: tight coupling of dynamic query filters with starfield displays* (pp. 313–317). Proceedings on Human Factors in Computing Systems.

Breiman, L., Friedman, J., Stone, C. J., & Olshen, R. (1984). *Classification and regression trees*. Boca Raton, FL: CRC Press.

Bruno, N., Gravano, L., & Marian, A. (2002). Evaluating top-k queries over Web-accessible databases. *Proceedings of the 18th International Conference on Data Engineering*, (pp. 369-380).

Card, S., MacKinlay, J., & Shneiderman, B. (1999). *Readings in information visualization: using vision to think*. Morgan Kaufmann.

Chakrabarti, K., Chaudhuri, S., & Hwang, S. (2004). Automatic categorization of query results. *Proceedings of the ACM SIGMOD International Conference on Management of Data*, (pp. 755–766).

Chaudhuri, S., Das, G., Hristidis, V., & Weikum, G. (2004). Probabilistic ranking of database query results. *Proceedings of the 30th International Conference on Very Large Data Base*, (pp. 888–899).

Chen, Z. Y., & Li, T. (2007). Addressing diverse user preferences in SQL-Query-Result navigation. *Proceedings of the ACM SIGMOD International Conference on Management of Data*, (pp. 641-652).

Chrobak, M., Keynon, C., & Young, N. (2005). The reverse greedy algorithm for the metric k-median problem. *Information Processing Letters*, *97*, 68–72. doi:10.1016/j.ipl.2005.09.009

Das, G., Hristidis, V., Kapoor, N., & Sudarshan, S. (2006). Ordering the attributes of query results. *Proceedings of the ACM SIGMOD International Conference on Management of Data*, (pp. 395-406).

Dhillon, I. S., Mallela, S., & Kumar, R. (2002). Enhanced word clustering for hierarchical text classification. *Proceedings of the 8th ACM SIGKDD International Conference*, (pp. 191–200).

Finkelstein, L., Gabrilovich, E., Matias, Y., Rivlin, E., Solan, Z., Wolfman, G., et al. (2001). Placing search in context: The concept revisited. *Proceedings of the 9th International World Wide Web Conference,* (pp. 406–414).

Geerts, F., Mannila, H., & Terzim, E. (2004). Relational link-based ranking. *Proceedings of the 30th International Conference on Very Large Data Base*, (pp. 552-563).

Joachims, T. (1998). Text categorization with support vector machines: Learning with many relevant features. *Proceedings of the European Conference on Machine Learning*, (pp. 137–142).

Joachims, T. (2002). Optimizing search engines using clickthrough data. *Proceedings of the ACM Conference on Knowledge Discovery and Data Mining*, (pp. 133–142).

Kießling, W. (2002). Foundations of preferences in database systems. *Proceedings of the 28th International Conference on Very Large Data Bases*, (pp. 311-322).

Koller, D., & Sahami, M. (1997). Hierarchically classifying documents using very few words. *Proceedings of the 14th International Conference on Machine Learning*, (pp. 170–178).

Koutrika, G., & Ioannidis, Y. (2004). Personalization of queries in database systems. *Proceedings of the 20th International Conference on Database Engineering*, (pp. 597-608).

Liu, F., Yu, C., & Meng, W. (2002). Personalized Web search by mapping user queries to categories. *Proceedings of the ACM International Conference on Information and Knowledge Management*, (pp. 558-565).

Meng, X. F., & Ma, Z. M. (2008). A context-sensitive approach for Web database query results ranking. *Proceedings of IEEE/WIC/ACM International Conference on Web Intelligence and Intelligent Agent Technology*, (pp. 836-839).

Mitchell, T. (1997). *Machine learning*. McGraw Hill.

Quinlan, J. R. (1986). Induction of decision trees. *Machine Learning*, *1*(1), 81–106. doi:10.1007/BF00116251

Quinlan, J. R. (1993). *C4.5: Programs for machine learning*. San Francisco: Morgan Kaufmann Publishers Inc.

Roussos, Y., Stavrakas, Y., & Pavlaki, V. (2005). Towards a context-aware relational model. *Proceedings of the International Workshop on Context Representation and Reasoning, Paris*, (pp. 101-106).

Rui, Y., Huang, T. S., & Merhotra, S. (1997). Content-based image retrieval with relevance feedback in MARS. *Proceedings of the IEEE International Conference on Image Processing*, (pp. 815-818).

Shen, X., Tan, B., & Zhai, C. (2005). Context-sensitive information retrieval using implicit feedback. *Proceedings of the 28th Annual International ACM SIGIR Conference on Research and Development in Information Retrieval*, (pp. 43–50).

Sugiyama, K., Hatano, K., & Yoshikawa, M. (2004). Adaptive Web search based on user profile constructed without any effort from users. *Proceedings of the 13th International World Wide Web Conference*, (pp. 975-990).

Tweedie, L., Spence, R., Williams, D., & Bhogal, R. S. (1994). The attribute explorer. *Proceedings of the International Conference on Human Factors in Computing Systems*, (pp. 435–436).

Wu, L., Faloutsos, C., Sycara, K., & Payne, T. (2000). FALCON: Feedback adaptive loop for content-based retrieval. *Proceedings of the 26th International Conference on Very Large Data Bases*, (pp. 297-306).

Zeng, H. J., He, Q. C., Chen, Z., Ma, W. Y., & Ma, J. (2004). Learning to cluster Web search results. *Proceedings of the 19th Annual International ACM SIGIR Conference on Research and Development in Information Retrieval*, (pp. 210–217).

KEY TERMS AND DEFINITIONS

Categorizing Attribute: an attribute that is used for partitioning the set of tuple into an ordered list of mutually disjoint subcategories.

Category Cost: an estimated cost of finding all relevant tuples by exploring the category tree, it consists of the cost of visiting tuples in a leaf node, the cost of visiting intermediate nodes, and the cost of visiting tuples in intermediate nodes if the user chooses to explore it.

Category Tree: a labeled hierarchical category structure that is generated automatically based on data clusters.

Data Cluster: a closely-packed group of data tuples, the tuples in the same cluster are similar to each other in semantic.

Query History: the log of past user queries on the database, it can reflect the user preferences.

User Preferences: an implicit need of a specific user for liking one thing.

Web Database: a non-local autonomous database that is accessible only via a Web from-based interface.

Chapter 2
Practical Approaches to the Many-Answer Problem

Mounir Bechchi
LINA-University of Nantes, France

Guillaume Raschia
LINA-University of Nantes, France

Noureddine Mouaddib
LINA-University of Nantes, Morocco

ABSTRACT

Database systems are increasingly used for interactive and exploratory data retrieval. In such retrievals, users' queries often result in too many answers, so users waste significant time and efforts sifting and sorting through these answers to find the relevant ones. This chapter first reviews and discusses several research efforts that have attempted to provide users with effective and efficient ways to access databases. Then, it focuses on a simple but useful strategy for retrieving relevant answers accurately and quickly without being distracted by irrelevant ones. Generally speaking, the chapter presents a very recent but promising approach to quickly provide users with structured and approximate representations of their query results, a must have for decision support systems. The underlying algorithm operates on pre-computed knowledge-based summaries of the queried data, instead of raw data themselves. Thus, this first-citizen data structure is also presented in this chapter.

1. INTRODUCTION

With the rapid development of the World Wide Web, more and more accessible databases are available online; A July 2000 study (Bergman, 2001) estimated 96000 relational databases were online and the number increased by seven times in 2004 (Chang, He, Li, Patel & Zhang, 2004). The increased visibility of these structured data repositories made them accessible to a large number of lay users, typically lacking a clear view of their content, moreover, not even having a particular item in mind. Rather,

DOI: 10.4018/978-1-60960-475-2.ch002

they are attempting to discover potentially useful items. In such a situation, user queries are often very broad, resulting in too many answers. Not all the retrieved items are relevant to the user. Unfortunately, she/he often needs to examine all or most of them to find the interesting ones. This too-many-answers phenomenon is commonly referred to as information overload - "a state in which the amount of information that merits attention exceeds an individual's ability to process it" (Schultz & Vandenbosch, 1998).

Information overload often happens when the user is not certain of what she/he is looking for, i.e., she/he has a vague and poorly defined information need or retrieval goal. Thus, she/he generally poses a broad query in the beginning to avoid exclusion of potentially interesting results and next, she/he starts browsing the answer looking for something interesting. Information overload makes it hard for the user to separate the interesting items from the uninteresting ones, thereby leading to potential decision paralysis and wastage of time and effort. The dangers of information overload are not to be underestimated and are well illustrated by buzzwords such as *Infoglut* (Allen, 1992), *Information Fatigue Syndrome* (Lewis, 1996), *TechnoStress* (Weil & Rosen, 1997), *Data Smog* (Shenk, 1997), *Data Asphyxiation* (Winkle, 1998) and *Information Pollution* (Nielsen, 2003).

In the context of relational databases, *automated ranking* and *clustering of query results* are used to reduce information overload. Automated ranking-based techniques first seek to clarify or approximate the user's retrieval goal. Then, they assign a score to each answer, representing the extent to which it is relevant to the approximated retrieval goal. Finally, the user is provided with a ranked list, in descending order of relevance, of either all query results or only a top-k subset. In contrast, clustering-based techniques assist the user to clarify or refine the retrieval goal instead of trying to learn it. They consist in dividing the query result set into dissimilar groups (or clusters) of similar items, allowing users to select and explore groups that are of interest to them while ignoring the rest. However, both of these techniques present two major problems:

- the first is related to *relevance*. With regard to automated ranking-based techniques, the relevance of the results highly depends on their ability to accurately capture the user's retrieval goal, which is not an obvious task. Furthermore, such techniques also bring the disadvantage of match homogeneity, i.e., the user is often required to go through a large number of similar results before finding the next different result. With regard to clustering-based techniques, there is no guarantee that the resulting clusters will match the meaningful groups that a user may expect. In fact, most clustering techniques seek to only maximize some statistical properties of the clusters (such as the size and compactness of each cluster and the separation of clusters relative to each other) ;
- the second is related to *scalability*. Both ranking and clustering are performed on query results and consequently occur at query time. Thus, the overhead time cost is an open critical issue for such a posteriori tasks.

To go one step beyond an overview of these well-established techniques, we investigate a simple but useful strategy to alleviate the two above problems. Specifically, we present an efficient and effective algorithm coined Explore-Select-Rearrange Algorithm (*ESRA*) that provides users with hierarchical clustering schemas of their query results. *ESRA* operates on pre-computed knowledge-based summaries of the data, instead of raw data themselves. The underlying summarization technique used in this work is the SAINTETIQ model (Raschia & Mouaddib, 2002; Saint-Paul, Raschia, & Mouaddib, 2005), which is a domain knowledge-based approach that enables summarization and classification of structured data stored into a database. Each node (or summary) of the hierarchy provided by *ESRA* describes a subset of the result set in a user-friendly form based on domain knowledge. The user then navigates through this hierarchy structure in a top-down fashion, exploring the summaries of interest while ignoring the rest.

The remaining of this chapter is organized as follows. In the first part of the chapter, we first survey techniques that have been proposed in the literature to provide users with effective and efficient ways to access relational databases, and then propose a categorization of these techniques based on the problem that they are supposed to address. In the second part of the chapter, we present the *ESRA* algorithm and the query answering system that supports *ESRA*-based summary hierarchies.

2. ADVANCED QUERY PROCESSING IN DATABASES

As internet becomes ubiquitous, many people are searching their favorite houses, cars, movies, cameras, restaurants, and so on over the Web. Most Web sites use databases to store their data and provide SQL-based query interfaces for users to interact with databases (Bergman, 2001; Chang, He, Li, Patel & Zhang, 2004). Database systems provide well-maintained and high-quality structured data. However, unlike Web search engines that take a few keywords, look up the index and provide a listing of best-matching Web pages, they expect users to know the name of the relation to query, the field to look in, and at times even the field type (Nambiar, 2005). Moreover, database query processing models have always assumed that the user knows what she/he wants and is able to formulate a query that accurately expresses her/his needs. Therefore, most database systems have always used a boolean model of query processing where there is a set of answer tuples that exactly satisfy all the constraints of the query and thus are equally relevant to the query.

While extremely useful for third-party applications and expert users, the above retrieval model is inadequate for lay users who cannot articulate the perfect query for their needs - either their queries are very specific, resulting in no (or too few) answers, or are very broad, resulting in too many answers. Hence, to obtain a satisfactory answer from a database, users must reformulate their queries a number of times before they can obtain a satisfactory answer. However, this process is frustrating, tedious and time-consuming.

In following subsections, we review and discuss several research efforts that have attempted to handle the dual issues of empty and many answers. Although the list of approaches described below is not exhaustive, it provides a representative list of some commonly used approaches. In Section 2.1, we review a number of approaches for handling the *empty-answer* problem, that is, the problem of not being able to provide the user with any data fitting her/his query. Section 2.2 presents some works addressing the *many-answers* problem, i.e., the situation where the user query results in overabundant answers. Then, in Section 2.3 we give an overview of flexible and user-friendly querying techniques, the main objective of which is to provide intelligent interfaces to access databases in a more human-oriented fashion and hence diminish the risk of both empty and many answers. A discussion is presented in Section 2.4.

2.1 Handling the Empty-Answer Problem

Most probably, one has encountered answers like 'no houses, hotels, vehicles, flights, etc. could be found that matched your criteria; please try again with different choices'. The case of repeatedly receiving empty query result turns out to be extremely disappointing to the user, and it is even more harmful for the e-merchant.

This problem, which is known as *empty-answer* problem, happens when the user submits a very restrictive query. A simple way to remedy this problem is to retry a particular query repeatedly with alternative values of certain conditions until obtaining satisfactory answers from a database. This solution, however, can be applied only if the user is aware of the close alternatives, otherwise it is infeasible (especially for users who lack knowledge about the contents of the database they wish to access). Many techniques are proposed to overcome this problem, namely query relaxation (Section 2.1.1) and similarity based search (Section 2.1.2).

2.1.1 Query Relaxation

Query relaxation aims to modify the failed query to provide the user with some alternative answers or at least to identify the cause of the failure, rather than just to report the empty result. A database system with such capability is also known as a cooperative information system (Gaasterland, Godfrey & Minker, 1994).

Consider a database EmpDB with information on employees, including their Name, Age, Gender, Salary, Job and Department, and a query '*get all employees who make less than 15K€ and work in the R&D department*'. Note that this query may fail for two different reasons (Motro, 1986): either no employee in R&D department makes less than 15K€ or the company does not have an R&D department. The former is a genuine null answer (i.e., the null answer is appropriate since query fails to match any data), while the latter is a fake null answer (i.e., it is due to the erroneous presupposition that the company has an R&D department).

The first system (CO-OP[i]) with such human behavior was developed by Kaplan (Kaplan, 1983) and was designed for natural language interaction. The main idea of CO-OP is to follow up a query that failed with several more general queries (i.e., the query with some of its conditions relaxed). If even these general queries fail, then the conclusion is that some of the presuppositions of the user who composed the original query are erroneous. If all these general queries succeed, a query that fails produces a genuine null. Furthermore, assume q' and q'' are both relaxations of the failed query q, but q'' is more general than q'. If both succeed, then the partial answer returned by q' is better (i.e., the best the system could do to satisfy the initial query q). If both fail, then the erroneous presupposition indicated by q'' is stronger. This leads to the conclusion that only Minimal Generalizations that Succeed (MGSs) and maXimal Generalizations that Fail (XGFs) are significant. Indeed, XGFs provide explanation for the failure and some assistance for relaxing the query into a non-failing query, whereas MGSs produce alternative answers to the failing query.

Since then, several systems that adapt CO-OP's techniques to relational databases have been proposed, including SEAVE (Motro, 1986), CoBase (Chu, Yang, Chiang, Minock, Chow & Larson, 1996) and Godfrey's system (Godfrey, 1997). These systems differ only in the way they perform generalizations. SEAVE considers all possible generalizations of the query. CoBase uses prior knowledge of the domain to guide the generalization process. Godfrey's system generalizes the query by only removing some of its conditions.

SEAVE

Given a query that fails, SEAVE[ii] (Motro, 1986) constructs a lattice of its generalized queries and uses it to find all MGSs/XGFs. The query generalizations are obtained by relaxing to a degree some of the

Figure 1. Lattice of generalized queries of q (cf. Motro, 1986)

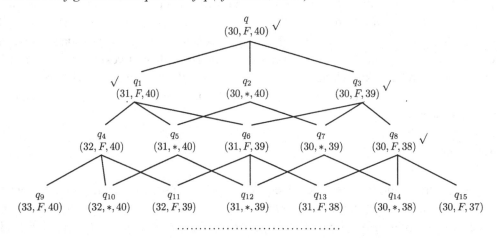

conditions in the query. As an example (cf. Motro, 1986), consider the following query q over the Employees' relation EmpDB:

SELECT *
FROM EmpDB
$Q \equiv$ WHERE Age ≤ 30
AND Gender = F
AND Salary $\geq 40K€$.

Figure 1 shows a portion of the lattice of relaxations of q generated by SEAVE, where nodes indicate generalizations (or presuppositions) and arcs indicate generalization relationships. (x, y, z) denotes a query which returns the employees whose age is under x, whose sex is y, and whose yearly salary is at least z. The symbol * indicates any value; once it appears in a query, this query cannot be generalized any further. Assume in this example that q fails and all its relaxed queries are successful queries except those that are marked √ in Figure 1 (i.e., q_1, q_3 and q_8). Thus, the failed relaxed queries q_1 and q_3 are XGFs, whereas the successful relaxed queries q_2, q_4, q_6 and q_{15} are MGSs. The queries q_2, q_4, q_6 and q_{15} produce alternative answers to the original query q: (q_2) all employees under 30 who earn at least 40K€; (q_4) all female employees under 32 who earn at least 40K€; (q_6) all female employees under 31 who earn at least 39K€; and (q_{15}) all female employees under 30 who earn at least 37K€. These answers can be delivered by SEAVE to the user as 'the best it could do' to satisfy the query q.

The main drawback of SEAVE is its high computational cost, which comes from computing and testing a large number of generalizations (i.e., various combinations of the values of attributes) to identify MGSs/XGFs.

CoBase

The CoBase[iii] (Chu, Yang, Chiang, Minock, Chow & Larson, 1996) system augments the database with Type Abstraction Hierarchies (TAHs) to control the query generalization process. A TAH represents attribute values at different levels of granularity. The higher levels of the hierarchy provide a more abstract data representation than the lower levels (or attribute values). Figure 2 shows an example of TAH for

Figure 2. TAH defined on the attribute Salary

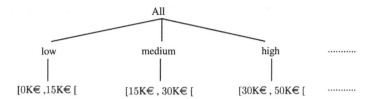

attribute Salary in which unique salary values are replaced by qualitative ranges of high, medium, or low. To relax a failing query, CoBase uses some types of TAH-based operators such as generalization (moving up the TAH) and specialization (moving down the TAH). For example, based on the type abstraction hierarchy given in Figure 2, the condition 'Salary = 20K€' could be generalized (i.e., move-up operator) to 'Salary = medium'.

CoBase considerably reduces the number of generalizations to be tested. Note that how close the results are to the user's initial expectations depends on the TAHs used.

Godfrey's System

In (Godfrey, 1997), Godfrey proposed to generalize the user failed query by just removing some of its conditions. Thus, instead of searching all MGSs/XGFs, the proposed system looks for all maXimal Succeeding and Minimal Failing Sub-queries (XSSs and MFSs, respectively) of the failed query. The author also proves that this problem is NP-hard. Indeed, the size of the search space grows exponentially with the number of attributes used in the failed query, i.e., if a query involves m attributes, there exist $(2^m - 2)$ sub-queries that have to be examined, disregarding the query itself and the empty query ϕ. For instance, the lattice of the possible sub-queries of q is illustrated in Figure 3, using the same notation as in Figure 1.

Hence, recently some heuristics (Muslea, 2004; Muslea & Lee, 2005; Nambiar & Kambhampati, 2004) have been proposed to prune the search space. In (Muslea, 2004) and (Muslea & Lee, 2005), Muslea et al. respectively used decision tree and Bayesian network learning techniques on a randomly-chosen subset of the target database to identify potential relaxations (or sub-queries) of the failing query to be tested. Then, they use nearest-neighbor techniques to find the relaxed query that is the most similar to the failing query. Nambiar et al. (Nambiar & Kambhampati, 2004) employed approximate

Figure 3. Lattice of possible sub-queries of q

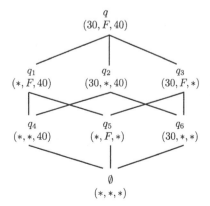

functional dependency to get the importance degree of the schema attributes in a database, according to which the order of the relaxed attributes is specified. The data samples used to compute the importance degree are also chosen randomly. Note that both Muslea et al's and Nambiar et al's approaches reduce the search space considerably, but the output relaxed queries, while succeed, are not necessary XSSs.

2.1.2 Similarity Search

A similarity-based search uses a notion of non-exact matching. In other words, when available data stored in the database do not exactly match a user's query, database records which best fit (i.e., which are the most similar to) the query are retrieved and ranked according to their similarity to the query.

Consider a tourist looking for a hotel, with a rent price at 100€ a day, and located in the city center. She/he will unfortunately fail to find such a hotel by means of the traditional database systems if the city center does not have any hotel rented at that price. However, a similarity-based search system would return the most similar hotels (i.e., hotels having attributes values very close to those specified in the query) instead of the empty result set. In fact, the user might accept a hotel near the city center and the rent price can also be a little lower or higher 100€ per day.

In the literature, several approaches have been proposed to enhance conventional databases with similarity search capabilities, such as ARES (Ichikawa & Hirakawa, 1986), VAGUE (Motro, 1988), IQE (Nambiar & Kambhampati, 2003) and Nearest-Neighbors (Roussopoulos, Kelley, & Vincent, 2003). The former three approaches (ARES, VAGUE and IQE) make use of an explicit operator 'similar-to', which extends the usual equality. The latter (Roussopoulos, Kelley, & Vincent, 2003) views the records in the database as points in a multidimensional space and the queries about these records are transformed into the queries over this set of points.

ARES

ARES[iv] (Ichikawa & Hirakawa, 1986) is the first system that has addressed the basic issue of similarity matching. It introduces a new operator named 'similar-to' and denoted $\approx$, meaning 'approximately equal to'. $\approx$ can be used as a comparison operator inside queries instead of the usual equality operator (=) in order to express vague conditions, e.g., $A \approx v$ will select values of an attribute A that are similar to a constant v. The interpretation of $\approx$ is based on dissimilarity relations tied to each domain. A dissimilarity relation, $DR_A(A_1, A_2, Distance)$, on the domain D_A of attribute A contains triples of the form $(v_1, v_2, dist)$, where $v_1 D_A$, $v_2 D_A$ and $dist$ represents the distance (dissimilarity) value between v_1 and v_2 (a smaller value means v_1 and v_2 are more similar). Table 1 illustrates an example dissimilarity relation for the attribute Job of a relation EmpDB.

In a given query, which contains vague conditions (i.e., conditions involving the similarity operator $\approx$), the following process takes place. First of all, for each vague condition, the user gives a maximum

Table 1. Dissimilarity relation defined on the attribute Job

Job$_1$	Job$_2$	Distance
Student	PhD. Student	1
Student	Supervisor	3
Supervisor	PhD. Student	2
…	…	…

accepted distance value. ARES then accesses dissimilarity relations to produce a boolean query which will be processed by a conventional database system. For example, the vague condition $A \approx v$ is transformed to the boolean one $A\{x\ D_A \mid (v, x, dist)\ DR_A \wedge dist \leq \tau\}$, where τ is the maximum allowed distance given by the user on D_A. In other words, x and v are considered somewhat close as far as $dist \leq \tau$. The produced query will then select acceptable tuples for which a global distance is calculated, by summing up the elementary distances tied to each vague condition in the query. Finally, the tuples are sorted in ascending order according to their global distance (dissimilarity) values and the system will output as many tuples as possible within the limit that has been specified by the user.

The main drawback of ARES is its high storage and maintenance costs of dissimilarity relations: each dissimilarity relation needs m^2 entries with respect to m different attribute values in the corresponding conventional relation; and when a new attribute value is added, $2m + 1$ additional entries are necessary for the corresponding dissimilarity relation. Moreover, ARES does not allow defining dissimilarity between attribute values for infinite domains because the dissimilarities can only be defined by means of tables.

VAGUE

VAGUE[v] (Motro, 1988) is a system that resembles ARES in its overall goals. It is an extension to the relational data model with data metrics and the SQL language with a comparator $\approx$. Indeed, each attribute domain D is endowed with a metric M_D to define distance (dissimilarity) between its values. M_D is a mapping from the cartesian product $D \times D$ to the set of non-negative reals which is:

- *reflexive*, i.e., $M_D(x, x) = 0$, for every value x in D;
- *symmetric*, i.e., $M_D(x, y) = M_D(y, x)$, for all values x and y in D; and
- *transitive*, i.e., $M_D(x, y) \leq M_D(x, z) + M_D(z, y)$, for all values x, y and z in D.

Furthermore, M_D is provided with a radius r. This notion is very similar to the maximum dissimilarity allowed in ARES. Thus, two values v_1 and v_2 in D are considered to be similar if $M_D(v_1, v_2) \leq r$. During query processing, each vague condition expressed in the query is translated (in a similar way to ARES) into a boolean one using the appropriate metric and the resulting query is used to select tuples. Then, an ordering process takes place, relying on the calculation of distances (by means of associated metrics) for the elementary vague conditions. The global distance attached to a selected tuple in case of a disjunctive query is the smallest of distances related to each vague condition. For conjunctive queries, the global distance is obtained as the root of the sum of the squares (i.e., the Euclidean distance) of distances tied to each vague condition.

Note that in VAGUE, the users cannot provide their own similarity thresholds for each vague condition but when a vague query does not match any data, VAGUE doubles all searching radii simultaneously. Thus the search performance can be considerably deteriorated.

IQE

Another system that supports similarity-based search over relational databases is the IQE[vi] system (Nambiar & Kambhampati, 2003). IQE converts the imprecise query (i.e., conditions involving the similarity operator $\approx$) into equivalent precise queries that appear in an existing query workload. Such queries are then used to answer the user given imprecise query. More precisely, given the workload, the main idea of IQE is to map the user's imprecise query q_i to a precise query q_p by tightening the operator in the query condition. For example, tightening the operator 'similar-to' ($\approx$) to 'equal-to' ($=$) in the imprecise query 'Salary $\approx$ 40K€' gives us the precise query 'Salary = 40K€'. Then IQE computes the similarity of q_p to all queries in the workload. To estimate the similarity between two queries, IQE uses the document Jaccard similarity metric over the answer sets of the two queries. A minimal similarity threshold τ is used to prune the number of queries similar to q_p. Finally, the answer to q_i is the union of the answers of the precise queries similar to q_p, with each tuple in the union inheriting the similarity of its generating precise query. Although IQE is a useful system, a workload containing past user queries is required, which is unavailable for new online databases.

Nearest Neighbors

In the approach known as nearest neighbors (Roussopoulos, Kelley, & Vincent, 2003), database records and queries are viewed as points (i.e., feature vectors) in a multidimensional space S with a metric M_S (e.g., the Euclidean distance). Here a typical query is given by an example (Moshé, 1975) and its result set corresponds to the set of database records which are close to it according to M_S. For instance, in image databases, the user may pose a query asking for the images most similar to a given image. This type of query is known as nearest neighbor query and it has been extensively studied in the past (Kevin, Jonathan, Raghu & Uri, 1999).

The two most important types of nearest neighbor queries (NNQ) in databases are:

- **ε-Range Query.** The user specifies a query object q S and a query radius ε. The system retrieves all objects from the database DB S that have a distance from q not exceeding ε (Figure 4-(a)). More formally, the result set RQ_ε^q is defined as follows: $RQ_\varepsilon^q = \{t \in DB \mid M_S(q,t) \leq \varepsilon\}$

- **k-Nearest Neighbor Query.** The user specifies a query object q and the cardinality k of the result set. The system retrieves the k objects from the database DB S that have the least distance from q (Figure 4-(b)). More formally, the result set NN_k^q is defined as follows: $\forall t \in NN_k^q, \forall t' \in DB - NN_k^q, M_S(q,t) \quad M_S(q,t')$

A naive solution for answering a given NNQ query is to scan the entire database and test for each object if it is currently among the results. Obviously, this solution is very expensive and not feasible for a very large set of objects. Several multidimensional index structures, that enable to prune large parts of the search space, were proposed. The most popular are R-Tree and its variants R*-tree, X-Tree, SS-

Figure 4. Nearest neighbor query types

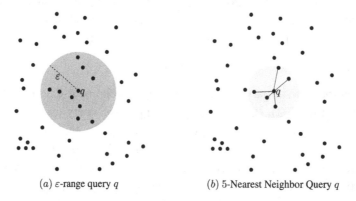

(a) ε-range query q (b) 5-Nearest Neighbor Query q

Tree, etc. For a more detailed elaboration on multidimensional access methods and on the corresponding query processing techniques, we refer the interested reader to (Volker & Oliver, 1998) and (Christian, Stefan & Daniel, 2001).

While the approaches described in both previous subsections differ in their implementation details, their overall goal is the same - allowing the database system to return answers, related to the failed query, which is more convenient than returning nothing. In the following section, we review some works addressing the *many-answers* problem, i.e., the situation where the original query results in overabundant answers.

2.2 Handling the Many-Answers Problem

Due to the ever increasing amount of information stored each day into databases, user's queries often result in too many answers - many of them irrelevant to the user. This phenomenon is also commonly referred to as 'information overload', as the user expends a huge amount of effort sifting through the result set looking for interesting results.

The many-answers problem often stems from the specificity of the user query that is too general. A solution to reduce the number of answers consists in narrowing the query by adding new conditions. However, it is quite impossible to find conditions that can effectively restrict the retrieved data without any knowledge of the database content. To circumvent this initial issue, several techniques have been proposed, including automated ranking (Section 2.2.1) and clustering (Section 2.2.2) of query results.

2.2.1 Automated Ranking of Query Results

Automated ranking of query results is a popular aspect of the query model in Information Retrieval. It consists in providing a user with a list ranked in descending order of relevance (though the user may not have explicitly specified how) of either all query results or only the top-k subset, rather than thousands of answers ordered in a completely uninformative way. In contrast, the Boolean query model used in traditional database systems does not allow for any form of relevance ranking of the retrieved tuple set. Indeed, all tuples that satisfy the query conditions are returned without any relevance distinction between them. Thus, the result of any query is simply a partition of the database into a set of retrieved tuples, and a set of not-retrieved tuples. It is only recently that top-k queries have been introduced (see (Ilyas, Beskales & Soliman, 2008) for a survey). Top-k queries provide the user with the k most relevant results of a given query ranked according to some scoring function. Consider a realtor database HouseDB with information on houses for sale, including their Price, Size, Age, City, Zip, Location, SchoolDistrict, View, #Bedrooms, #Bathrooms, Garage and BoatDock. The following query is an example of a top-k query:

SELECT Price AS *p*, Size AS *s*, Age AS *a*
FROM HouseDB
WHERE Zip = 75000
ORDER BY $f(d_{Price}(p), d_{Size}(s), d_{Age}(a))$
LIMIT 5

where LIMIT limits the number of results reported to the user, $d_A(x)$ measures the extent (score) to which the value *x* of attribute *A* is relevant to the user and *f* determines how to combine the ranking according to each feature in an overall ranking. As one can observe, a fundamental requirement of top-k based approaches is that they require a scoring function that specifies which result from a large set of potential answers to a query is most relevant to the user. Achieving this requirement is generally not a straightforward endeavor, especially when users do not really know what might be useful or relevant for them.

Automatic methods of ranking answers of database (DB) queries have been recently investigated to overcome this problem, most of them being an adaptation of those employed in Information Retrieval (IR). Before discussing these methods in detail, we first review existing Information Retrieval ranking techniques. Then, we discuss related work on top-k query processing techniques in relational database systems.

2.2.1.1 IR Ranking Techniques

Automated ranking of query results has been extensively investigated in Information Retrieval (Salton & McGill, 1986; Robertson, 1997; Brin & Page, 1998; Bharat & Henzinger, 1998; Kleinberg, 1999; Borodin, Roberts, Rosenthal & Tsaparas, 2001; Ng, Zheng & Jordan, 2001). Indeed, the Web pages that are returned as a result to a query expressed by a set of keywords are automatically ranked so that the more 'relevant' the page is to the query, the higher it is ranked. Furthermore, among the Web pages that are equally relevant, those that are more 'important' should precede the less 'important' ones. Models that have been used for this purpose include vector space and probabilistic information retrieval models which are eventually combined with link-based ranking methods to offer the user not only relevant documents but also high quality Web pages.

Vector Space Model

Vector space model (Salton, & McGill, 1986) represents documents as term vectors in an N-dimensional space where N corresponds to the number of terms in the collection. Each element in a vector captures a term and its weight, defined as $w = tf * idf$, where *tf* is the term frequency in the document and *idf* is the inverse document frequency reflecting the general importance of the term in the entire document collection. Specifically, *idf* decreases the weight of terms that occur in numerous documents and, therefore, have low discriminating value. Queries are also represented as vectors of keywords. Hence, given a keyword query, the retrieved documents are ranked based on their similarity to the query. A range of measures exists to calculate this similarity; the most common one is the cosine similarity measure defined as the Cosine of the angle between the query and the document vector representations.

Probabilistic Model

In the probabilistic model (Robertson, 1997), documents and queries are also viewed as vectors, whereas the vector space similarity measure is replaced by a probabilistic matching function. More precisely, given a document collection D and a query q, probabilistic-based approaches formally rank documents by decreasing order of their odds of relevance to non-relevance using a score function defined as follows:

$$score(d) = \frac{P(\mathrm{Re}\,l \mid d)}{P(\overline{\mathrm{Re}\,l} \mid d)} = \frac{\dfrac{P(d \mid \mathrm{Re}\,l)P(\mathrm{Re}\,l)}{P(d)}}{\dfrac{P(d \mid \overline{\mathrm{Re}\,l})P(\overline{\mathrm{Re}\,l})}{P(d)}} \approx \frac{P(d \mid \mathrm{Re}\,l)}{P(d \mid \overline{\mathrm{Re}\,l})}$$

where Rel denotes the set of relevant documents, $\overline{\mathrm{Re}l} = (D - \mathrm{Re}l)$ the set of irrelevant ones and $P(\mathrm{Re}l \mid d)$ (resp., $P(\overline{\mathrm{Re}l} \mid d)$) the probability of relevance (resp., non-relevance) of document d w.r.t. the query q. The higher the ratio of the probability of relevance to non-relevance is w.r.t. a document d, then the more likely document d is to be relevant to a user query q.

In the above formula, the second equality is obtained using the Bayes formula, whereas the final simplification follows from the fact that $P(\mathrm{Re}l)$ and $P(\overline{\mathrm{Re}l})$ are the same for every document d and thus are mere constant values that do not influence the ranking of documents.

Note that $\mathrm{Re}l$ and $\overline{\mathrm{Re}l}$ are unknown at query time and consequently are estimated as accurately as possible, on the basis of whatever data has been made available to the system for this purpose. The usual techniques in Information Retrieval make some simplifying assumptions, such as estimating $\mathrm{Re}l$ through user feedback, approximating $\overline{\mathrm{Re}l}$ as D (since $\mathrm{Re}l$ is usually small compared to D) and assuming some form of independence between query terms (e.g., the Binary Independence Model, the Linked Dependence Model, or the Tree Dependence Model. INQUERY (Callan, Croft & Harding, 1992) is an example of this model.

Link-Based Ranking Methods

The link-based ranking methods are based on how the pages on the Internet link to each other (Brin & Page, 1998; Bharat & Henzinger, 1998; Kleinberg, 1999; Borodin, Roberts, Rosenthal & Tsaparas, 2001; Ng, Zheng & Jordan, 2001). Indeed, the relevance of a page is not only decided by the page content, but is also based on the linkage among pages. An example of a ranking algorithm based on link analysis is the PageRank algorithm (Brin & Page, 1998) introduced by Google[vii]. PageRank computesWeb page scores by exploiting the graph inferred from the link structure of the Web. Its underlying motivation is that pages with many backlinks are more important than pages with only a few backlinks. So basically, a page's rank in Google's search results is higher if many, preferably important, pages link to that page. The higher the PageRank is, the more relevant the page is (according to Google). Another example of a ranking algorithm using link analysis is the HITS[viii] algorithm (Kleinberg, 1999). The HITS algorithm suggests that each page should have a separate 'authority' rating (based on the links going to the page) and a 'hub' rating (based on the links going from the page). The intuition behind the algorithm is that important hubs have links to important authorities and important authorities are linked by important hubs.

For more details and more general sources about Information Retrieval ranking methods, please refer to (Manning, Raghavan & Schtze, 2008).

2.2.1.2 DB Ranking Techniques

Automated ranking of database query results has been extensively investigated in recent years. Examples include (Chaudhuri & Das, 2003; Chaudhuri, Das, Hristidis & Weikum, 2004; Su, Wang, Huang & Lochovsky, 2006; Wu, Faloutsos, Sycara & Payne, 2000; MacArthur, Brodley, Ka & Broderick, 2002). These approaches take a user's query - which typically specify simple selection conditions on a small set of attributes - and use diverse knowledge sources to automatically estimate the ranking of its results. For instance, the systems proposed in (Chaudhuri & Das, 2003; Chaudhuri, Das, Hristidis & Weikum, 2004; Su, Wang, Huang & Lochovsky, 2006) use workload and/or database statistics while (Wu, Faloutsos, Sycara & Payne, 2000) and (MacArthur, Brodley, Ka & Broderick, 2002) use relevance feedback from the user.

Chaudhuri et al's System

In (Chaudhuri & Das, 2003), the authors proposed a ranking function (QF_W) that leverages workload information to rank the answers to a database query. It is based on the frequency of occurrence of the values of unspecified[ix] attributes. For example, consider a home-buyer searching for houses in HouseDB. A query with a not very selective condition such as 'City = Paris AND #Bedrooms = 2' may result in too many tuples in the answer, since there are many houses with two bedrooms in Paris. The proposed system uses workload information and examines attributes other than City and #Bedrooms (i.e., attributes that are not specified in the query) to rank the result set. Thus, if the workload contains many more queries for houses in Paris's 15th arrondissement (precinct) than for houses in Paris's 18th arrondissement, the system ranks two bedroom houses in the 15th arrondissement higher than two bedroom houses in the 18th arrondissement. The intuition is that if the 15th arrondissement is a wonderful location, the workload will contain many more queries for houses in the 15th than for houses in the 18th.

More formally, consider one relation R. Each tuple in R has N attributes $A_1, ..., A_N$. Further, let q be a user's query with some number of attributes specified (e.g., $A_1, A_2, ..., A_i$ and $i < N$) and the rest of them unspecified (e.g., $A_{i+1}, ..., A_N$). The relevance score of an answer t is defined as follows:

$$QF_W(t) = \sum_{k=i+1}^{N} \frac{F(t.A_k)}{F_{max}}$$

where $F(t.A_k)$ is the frequency of occurrence of value $t.A_k$ of attribute A_k in the workload W and F_{max} the frequency of the most frequently occurring value in W.

PIR

In the PIR[x] system (Chaudhuri, Das, Hristidis & Weikum, 2004), the authors adapted and applied principles of probabilistic models from Information Retrieval to structured data. Given a query, the proposed ranking function depends on two factors: (a) a global score that captures the global importance of unspecified attribute values, and (b) a conditional score that captures the strengths of dependencies (or correlations) between specified and unspecified attribute values. For example, for the query 'City = Marseille AND View = Waterfront', a house with 'SchoolDistrict = Excellent' gets a high rank because good school districts are globally desirable. A house with also 'BoatDock = Yes' gets a high rank because people desiring a waterfront are likely to want a boat dock. These scores are estimated using past workloads as well as data analysis, e.g., past workload may reveal that a large fraction of users seeking houses with a waterfront view have also requested boat docks. More precisely, under the same notations and hypotheses that we have used for the previous approach, the relevance score of a tuple t is computed as follows:

$$PIR(t) = \frac{P(\mathrm{Rel} \mid t)}{P(\overline{\mathrm{Rel}} \mid t)} \approx \prod_{k=i+1}^{N} \frac{P(t.A_k \mid W)}{P(t.A_k \mid R)} * \prod_{k=i+1}^{N} \prod_{l=1}^{i} \frac{P(t.A_l \mid t.A_k, W)}{P(t.A_l \mid t.A_k, R)}$$

where the quantities $P(t.A_k \mid W)$ and $P(t.A_k \mid R)$ are simply the relative frequencies of each distinct value $t.Ak$ respectively in the workload W and in the relation R, while the quantities $P(t.A_l \mid t.A_k, W)$

and $P(t.A_l \mid t.A_k, R)$ are estimated by computing the confidences of pair-wise association rules (Agrawal, Mannila, Srikant, Toivonen & Verkamo, 1996) in W and R, respectively. Note that the score in the above formula is composed of two large factors. The first factor is the global part of the score, while the second one is the conditional part of the score. This approach is implemented in STAR (Kapoor, Das, Hristidis, Sudarshan & Weikum, 2007).

Note that in both Chaudhuri's system (Chaudhuri & Das, 2003) and the PIR system (Chaudhuri, Das, Hristidis & Weikum, 2004), the atomic quantities $F(x)$, $P(x|W)$, $P(x|R)$, $P(y|x,W)$ and $P(y|x,R)$ are pre-computed and stored in special auxiliary tables for all distinct values x and y in the workload and the database. Then at query time, both approaches first select the tuples that satisfy the query condition, then scan and compute the score for each such tuple using the information in the auxiliary tables, and finally returns the top-k tuples. The main drawback of both (Chaudhuri & Das, 2003) and (Chaudhuri, Das, Hristidis & Weikum, 2004) is their high storage and maintenance costs of auxiliary tables. Moreover, they require a workload containing past user queries as input, which is not always available (e.g., new online databases).

QRRE

In the QRRE[xi] system (Su, Wang, Huang & Lochovsky, 2006), the authors proposed an automatic ranking method, which can rank the query results from an E-commerce Web database R using only data analysis techniques. Consider a tuple $t = \langle t.A_1, ..., t.A_N \rangle$ in the result set T_q of a query q that is submitted by a buyer. QRRE assigns a weight w_i to each attribute A_i that reflects its importance to the user. w_i is evaluated by the difference (e.g., The Kullback-Leibler divergence (Duda, Hart & Stork, 2000)) between the distribution (histogram) of A_i's values over the result set T_q and their distribution (histogram) over the whole database R. The bigger the divergence, the more A_i is important for a buyer. For instance, suppose the database HouseDB contains houses for sale in France and consider the query q with the condition 'View = Waterfront'. Intuitively, the Price values of the tuples in the result set T_q distribute in a small and dense range with a relatively high average, while the Price values of tuples in HouseDB distribute in a large range with a relatively low average. The distribution difference shows a close correlation between the unspecified attribute, namely, Price, and the query 'View = Waterfront'. In contrast, attribute Size is less important for the user since its distribution in houses with a waterfront view may be similar to its distribution in the entire database HouseDB. Besides the attribute weight, QRRE also assigns a preference score p_i to each attribute value $t.A_i$. p_i is computed based on the following two assumptions:

- a product with a lower price is always more desired by buyers than a product with a higher price if the other attributes of the two products have the same values. For example, between two houses that differ only in their price, the cheapest one is preferred. Hence, QRRE assigns a small preference score to a high Price value and a large preference score to a low Price value;
- a non-Price attribute value with higher 'desirableness' for the user corresponds to a higher price. For example, a large house, which most buyers prefer, is usually more expensive than a small one. Thus, in the case of a non-Price attribute A_i, QRRE first converts its value $t.A_i$ to a Price value pv which is the average price of the products for $A_i = t.A_i$ in the database R. Then, QRRE assigns a large preference score to $t.A_i$ if pv is large.

Finally, the attribute weight and the value preference score are combined to calculate the ranking score for each tuple $t \in T_q$, as follows:

$$QRRE(t) = \sum_{i=1}^{N} w_i * p_i$$

The tuples' ranking scores are sorted and the top-K tuples with the largest ranking scores are presented to the user first. QRRE is a useful automated ranking approach for the *many-answers* problem. It does not depend on domains nor require workloads. However, this approach may imply high response times, especially in the case of low selectivity queries, since different histograms need to be constructed over the result set (i.e., at query time).

Feedback-Based Systems

Another approach to rank query's results, which is different from those discussed above, is to prompt the user for feedback on retrieval results and then use this feedback on subsequent retrievals to effectively infer which tuples in the database are of interest to the user. Relevance Feedback techniques were studied extensively in the context of image retrieval (Wu, Faloutsos, Sycara & Payne, 2000; MacArthur, Brodley, Ka & Broderick, 2002) and were usually paired with the query-by-example approach (Moshé, 1975). The basic procedure of these approaches is as follows:

1.   the user issues a query;
2.   the system returns an initial set of results;
3.   the user marks some returned tuples as relevant or non-relevant;
4.   the system constructs a new query that is supposed to be close to the relevant results and far from those which are non-relevant; and
5.   the system displays the results that are most similar to the new query.

This procedure can be conducted iteratively until the user is satisfied with the query results. Relevance feedback-based approaches provide an effective method for reducing the number of query results. However, they are not necessarily popular with users. Indeed, users are often reluctant to provide explicit feedback, or simply do not wish to prolong the search interaction. Furthermore, it is often harder to understand why a particular tuple is retrieved after the relevance feedback algorithm has been applied.

Once the scoring function is defined, the DB ranking techniques discussed in this subsection adapt and use available top-k query processing algorithms (Ilyas, Beskales & Soliman, 2008) in order to quickly provide the user with the k most relevant results of a given query. In the following subsection, we briefly review top-k query processing methods in relational database systems.

2.2.1.3 Efficient Top-k Query Processing

Assume a relation R with attributes $A_1,...,A_N$ and a query q over R. Further, one supposes that each tuple $t = \langle t.A_1,...,t.A_N \rangle$, in the result set T_q of q, has N attribute-oriented scores $s_1,...,s_N$. Each s_i measures the extent (score) to which the value $t.A_i$ of tuple t on attribute A_i is relevant to the user. For the top-k problem, T_q could alternatively be seen as a set of N sorted lists L_i of $\left|T_q\right|$ (the number of tuples in T_q) pairs $(t, s_i), t \in T_q$. Hence, for each attribute A_i, there is a sorted list L_i in which all $\left|T_q\right|$ results are ranked in descendant order. Entries in the lists could be accessed randomly from the tuple identifier or sequentially from the sorted score. The main issue for top-k query processing is then to obtain the k tuples with the highest overall scores computed according to a given aggregation function $agg(s_1, ..., s_N)$ of the attribute scores s_i. The aggregation function *agg* used to combine ranking criteria has to be monotone; that is, *agg* must satisfy the following property:

$$agg(s_1, ..., s_N) \leq agg(s'_1, ..., s'_N) \text{ if } s_i \leq s'_i \text{ for every i}$$

The naive algorithm consists in looking at every entry t, s_i in each of the sorted lists L_i, computing the overall grade of every object t, and returning the top k answers. Obviously, this approach is unnecessarily expensive as it does not take advantage of the fact that only the k best answers are part of the query answer and the remaining answers do not need to be processed. Several query answering algorithms have been proposed in the literature to efficiently process top-k queries. The most popular is the Threshold Algorithm (TA) independently proposed by several groups (Fagin, Lotem & Naor, 2001; Nepal & Ramakrishna, 1999; Güntzer, Balke & Kießling, 2000).

The TA algorithm works as follows:

1. do sorted access in parallel to each of the N sorted lists. As a tuple t is seen under sorted access in some list, do random access to the other lists to find the score of t in every list and compute the overall score of t. Maintain in a set TOP the k seen tuples whose overall scores are the highest among all tuples seen so far;
2. for each list L_i, let s_i be the last score seen under sorted access in L_i. Define the threshold to be $\ddot{A} = agg(s_1, ..., s_N)$. If TOP involves k tuples whose overall scores are higher than or equal to τ, then stop doing sorted access to the lists. Otherwise, go to step 1;
3. return TOP.

Table 2 shows an example with three Lists L_1, L_2 and L_3. Assume that the top-k query requests the top-2 tuples and the aggregation function *agg* is the summation function SUM. TA first scans the first tuples in all lists which are t_5, t_4, and t_3. Hence the threshold value at this time is $\tau = 21+34+30 = 85$. Then TA calculates the aggregated score for each tuple seen so far by random accesses to the three lists. We get the aggregated score for t_5 SUM(t_5) = 21+9+7 = 37, for t_4 SUM(t_4) = 11+34+14 = 59 and for t_3 SUM(t_3) = 11+26+30 = 67. TA maintains the top-2 tuples seen so far which are t_3 and t_4. As neither of them has an aggregated score greater than the current threshold value $\tau = 85$, TA continues to scan the tuples at the second positions of all lists. At this time, the threshold value is recomputed as $\tau = 17 + 29 + 14 = 60$. The new tuples seen are t_1 and t_2. Their aggregated scores are retrieved and calculated as SUM(t_1) = 0 + 29 + 0 = 29 and SUM(t_2) = 17 + 0 + 1 = 18. TA still keeps tuples t_3 and t_4 since their aggregated scores are higher than those of both t_1 and t_2. Since only t_3 has an aggregated score greater than the current threshold value $\tau = 60$, TA algorithm continues to scan the tuples in the third positions. Now the threshold value is $\tau = 11 + 29 + 9 = 49$ and the new tuple seen is t_0. TA computes the aggregated score for t_0 which is 38. t_3 and t_4 still maintain the two highest aggregated scores which are now greater

Table 2. The Threshold Algorithm - an example with 3 lists

Position	L_1	L_2	L_3
1	*(t_5, 21)*	*(t_4, 34)*	*(t_3, 30)*
2	*(t_2, 17)*	*(t_1, 29)*	*(t_4, 14)*
3	*(t_4, 11)*	*(t_6, 29)*	*(t_6, 9)*
4	*(t_3, 11)*	*(t_3, 26)*	*(t_5, 7)*
5	*(t_6, 10)*	*(t_5, 9)*	*(t_2, 1)*
6	*(t_7, 10)*	*(t_9, 7)*	*(t_8, 1)*

than the current threshold value $\tau = 49$. Thereby, TA terminates at this point and returns t_3 and t_4 as the top-2 tuples. Note that, in this example, TA avoids accessing the tuples t_6, t_7, t_8 and t_9.

For more details about top-k processing techniques in relational databases, we refer the interested reader to (Ilyas, Beskales & Soliman, 2008).

2.2.2 Clustering of Query Results

Clustering of query results is the operation of grouping the set of answers into meaningful clusters (or groups). This allows the user to select and browse clusters that most closely match what she/he is looking for while ignoring the irrelevant ones. This idea has been traditionally used for organizing the results of Web search engines (Jardine & Van Rijsbergen, 1971; Van Rijsbergen & Croft, 1975; Croft, 1980; Voorhees, 1985; Hearst & Pedersen, 1996; Jain, Murty & Flynn, 1999; Zamir & Etzioni, 1999; Zeng, He, Chen, Ma & Ma, 2004; Cheng, Kannan, Vempala & Wang, 2006; Ferragina & Gulli, 2005) but has only recently been adapted in the context of relational database (Chakrabarti, Chaudhuri & Hwang, 2004; Bamba, Roy & Mohania, 2005; Li, Wang, Lim, Wang & Chang, 2007). In the following, we review existing search results clustering techniques in both information retrieval (IR) and relational database (DB) systems.

2.2.2.1 IR Clustering Techniques

Document clustering has been used in information retrieval for many years. Originally, it aimed at improving search efficiency by reducing the number of documents that needed to be compared to the query. The rationale was that by partitioning the document collection in clusters, an information retrieval system could restrict the search to only some of them. It was only with the work of Jardine and Van Rijsbergen that clustering became associated with search effectiveness (Jardine & Van Rijsbergen, 1971).

The motivation for the use of clustering as a way to improve retrieval effectiveness lies in the cluster hypothesis. The cluster hypothesis, as proposed by Jardine and van Rijsbergen, states that the association between documents conveys information about the "relevance of documents to the request" (Jardine & Van Rijsbergen, 1971). In other words, if a document is relevant to an information need expressed in a query[xii], then similar documents are also likely to be relevant to the same information need. So, if similar documents are grouped into clusters, then one of these clusters contains the relevant documents (or most of them). Therefore, finding this cluster could improve search effectiveness.

There are various ways in which the cluster hypothesis could be exploited. One way is to implement cluster-based retrieval. In cluster-based retrieval, the strategy is to build a clustering of the entire collection in advance and then retrieve clusters based on how well their representations (e.g., a set of keywords) match the upcoming query. A hierarchical clustering technique is typically used in these approaches, and different strategies for matching the query against the document hierarchy have been proposed, most notably a top-down or a bottom-up search and their variants (Jardine & Van Rijsbergen, 1971; Van Rijsbergen & Croft, 1975; Croft, 1980; Voorhees, 1985). Similarly, search engines (e.g., Yahoo) and product catalog search (e.g., eBay) use a category structure created in advance and then group search results into separate categories. In all these approaches, if a query does not match any cluster representation of one of the pre-defined clusters or categories, then it fails to match any documents even if the document collection contains relevant results. It is worth noticing that this problem is not intrinsic to clustering, but is due to the fact that keyword representation of clusters is often insufficient to apprehend the meaning of documents in a cluster.

An alternative way of using the cluster hypothesis is in the presentation of retrieval results, that is by presenting, in a clustered form, only documents that have been retrieved in response to the query. This idea was first introduced in the Scatter/Gather system (Hearst & Pedersen, 1996) which is based on a variant of the classical k-means algorithm (Hartigan & Wong, 1979). Since then, several classes of algorithms have been proposed such as STC (Zamir & Etzioni, 1999), SHOC (Zeng, He, Chen, Ma & Ma, 2004), EigenCluster (Cheng, Kannan, Vempala & Wang, 2006), SnakeT (Ferragina & Gulli, 2005). Note that such algorithms introduce a noticeable time overhead to the query processing, due to the large number of results returned by the search engine. The reader is referred to (Manning, Raghavan & Schtze, 2008) for more details on IR clustering techniques.

All the above approaches testify that there is a significant potential benefit in providing additional structure in large answer sets.

2.2.2.2 DB Clustering Techniques

The SQL group-by operator allows grouping query results. It classifies the results of a query into groups based on a user-selected subset of fields. However, it partitions the space only by identical values. For instance, if there are 1000 different zip-codes, 'group-by Zip' returns 1000 groups. In the last few years, traditional clustering techniques have been employed by the database research community to overcome this shortcoming (Chakrabarti, Chaudhuri & Hwang, 2004; Bamba, Roy & Mohania, 2005; Li, Wang, Lim, Wang & Chang, 2007).

Chakrabarti et al's System

In (Chakrabarti, Chaudhuri & Hwang, 2004), the authors proposed an automatic method for categorizing query results. This method dynamically creates a navigation tree (i.e., a hierarchical category structure) for each query q based on the contents of the tuples in the answer set T_q. A hierarchical categorization of T_q is a recursive partitioning of the tuples in T_q based on the data attributes and their values, i.e., the query results are grouped into nested categories. Figure 5 shows an example of a hierarchical categorization of the results of the query 'City = Paris AND Price [150, 300] K€'. At each level, the partitioning is done based on a single attribute in the result set T_q, and this attribute is the same for all nodes at that level. Furthermore, once an attribute is used as a categorizing attribute at any level, it is not repeated at a later level. For example, Price is the categorizing attribute of all nodes at Level 2. The partitions are assigned descriptive labels and form a categorization of the result set based on that attribute. For example, the first child of the root in Figure 5 has label 'Location = 18th arrondissement' while its own first child has label 'Price [200, 225] K€'.

Figure 5. Example of hierarchical categorization of query results

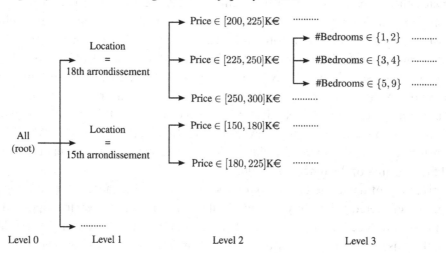

The order in which the attributes appear in the tree, and the values used to split the domain of any attribute are inferred by analyzing the aggregate knowledge of previous user behaviors - using the workload. Indeed, the attributes that appear most frequently in the workload are presented to the user earlier (i.e., at the highest levels of the tree). The intuition behind this approach is that the presence of a selection condition on an attribute in a workload reflects the user's interest in that attribute. Furthermore, for each attribute A_i, one of the following two methods is used to partition the set of tuples $tset(C)$ contained in a category C depending on whether A_i is categorical or numeric:

- If A_i is a categorical attribute with discrete values $\{v_1, ..., v_k\}$, the proposed algorithm simply partitions $tset(C)$ into k categories, one category C_j corresponding to a value v_j. Then, it presents them in the decreasing order of $occ(A_i = v_j)$, i.e., the number of queries in the workload whose selection condition on A_i overlaps with $A_i = v_j$;
- Otherwise, assume the domain of attribute A_i is the interval $[v_{min}, v_{max}]$. If a significant number of query ranges (corresponding to the selection condition on A_i) in the workload begins or ends at $v[v_{min}, v_{max}]$, then v is considered as a good point to split $[v_{min}, v_{max}]$. The intuition here is that most users would be interested in just one bucket, i.e., either in the bucket $A_i \leq v$ or in the bucket $A_i > v$ but not both.

This approach provides the user with navigational facilities to browse query results. However, it requires a workload containing past user queries as input, which is not always available. Furthermore, the hierarchical category structure is built at query time, and hence the user has to wait a long time before the results can be displayed.

OSQR

In Bamba, Roy & Mohania (2005), the authors proposed OSQR[xiii], an approach for clustering database query results based on the agglomerative single-link approach (Jain, Murty & Flynn, 1999). Given an SQL query as input, OSQR explores its result set, and identifies a set of terms (called the query's context) that are the most relevant to the query; each term in this set is also associated with a score quantifying its relevance. Next, OSQR exploits the term scores and the association of the rows in the query result with the respective terms to define a similarity measure between the terms. This similarity measure is then used to group multiple terms together; this grouping, in turn, induces a clustering of the query result rows. More precisely, consider a query q on a table R, and let T_q denote the result of the query q. OSQR works as follows:

1. scan T_q and assign a score s_x to each attribute value x (or term) in T_q. The terms' scores (similar to *tf * idf* scores used in information retrieval) are defined in such a way that higher scores indicate attributes values that are popular in the query result T_q and are rare in $R\text{-}T_q$;
2. compute the context of q as the set of terms $q_{context}$ with scores exceeding a certain threshold (a system parameter);
3. associate to each term x in $q_{context}$ the cluster C_x, i.e., the set of tuples of T_q in which the attribute value x appears. The tuples in T_q that are not associated with any term $xq_{context}$ are termed 'outliers'.

These rows are not processed any further; iteratively merge the two most similar clusters until a stopping condition is met. The similarity $sim(C_x, C_y)$ between each pair of clusters C_x and C_y ($x, y\ q_{context}$) is defined as follows:

$$sim\ C_x, C_y = \frac{s_y\ |C_x - C_y| + s_x\ |C_y - C_x|}{s_y\ |C_x| + s_x\ |C_y|}$$

where |.| denotes the cardinality of a set.

OSQR's output is a dendrogram that can be browsed from its root node to its leaves, where each leaf represents a single term x in $q_{context}$ and its associated tuple set C_x.

The above approach has many desirable features: it generates overlapping clusters, associates a descriptive 'context' with each generated cluster, and does not require the query workload. However, note that some query results (tuples that are not associated with any term in $q_{context}$) are ignored and therefore not included in the output result. Moreover, this approach may imply high response times, especially in the case of low selectivity queries, since both scoring and clustering of terms are done on the fly.

Li et al's System

In a recent work (Li, Wang, Lim, Wang & Chang, 2007), the authors generalized the SQL group-by operator to enable grouping (based on the proximity of attribute values) of database query results. Consider a relation R with attributes $A_1, ..., A_N$ and a user's query q over R with a group-by clause on a subset X of R's numeric attributes. The proposed algorithm first divides the domain of each attribute A_iX into p_i disjoint intervals (or bins) to form a grid of $\prod p_i$ buckets (or cells). Next, this approach identifies the set of buckets $C = \{b_1, ..., b_m\}$ that holds the results of q, and associates to each bucket b_i a virtual point v_i, located at the center of that bucket. Finally, a k-means algorithm is performed on these virtual points (i.e., $\{v_1, ..., v_m\}$) to obtain exactly k clusters of q's results. The k parameter is given by the end-user. For example, consider a user's query that returns 10 tuples $t_1, ..., t_{10}$ and the user needs to partition these tuples into 2 clusters, using two attributes A_1 and A_2. Figure 6 shows an example of a grid over $t_1, ..., t_{10}$ by partitioning attributes A_1 and A_2. The bins on A_1 and A_2 are {[0, 3), [3, 6), [6, 9)} and {[0, 10), [10, 20), [20, 30)}, respectively. The two clusters C_1 (i.e. A_1 [0, 3] A_2 [10, 30]) and C_2 (i.e., A_1 [6,

Figure 6. Example of a grid in two dimensions

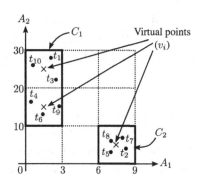

9] A_2 [0, 10]) are returned to that user. C_1 contains 6 tuples t_1, t_3, t_4, t_6, t_9 and t_{10}, whereas C_2 contains 4 tuples t_2, t_5, t_7 and t_8.

This approach is efficient. Indeed, it relies on a bucket-level clustering, which is much more efficient than the tuple-level one, since the number of buckets is much smaller than the number of tuples. However, the proposed algorithm requires the user to specify the number of clusters k, which is difficult to know in advance, but has a crucial impact on the clustering result. Further, this approach generates flat clustering of query results and some clusters may contain a very large number of results, although, this is exactly the kind of outcome this technique should avoid.

2.3 Flexible/User-Friendly Database Querying

A typical problem with traditional database query languages like SQL is a lack of flexibility. Indeed, they are plagued by a fundamental problem of specificity (as we have seen in Sections 2.1 and 2.2): if the query is too specific (with respect to the dataset), the response is empty; if the query is too general, the response is an avalanche. Hence, it is difficult to cast a query, balanced on this scale of specificity, that returns a reasonable number of results. Furthermore, they expect users to know the schema of the database they wish to access.

Recently, many flexible/user-friendly querying techniques have been proposed to overcome this problem. The main objective of these techniques is to provide human-oriented interfaces which allow for a more intelligent and human-consistent information retrieval and hence, diminish the risk of both empty and many answers. Examples include preference queries (Section 2.3.1), fuzzy queries (Section 2.3.2) and keyword search (Section 2.3.3).

2.3.1 Preference Queries

The first way of introducing flexibility within the query processing is to cope with user preferences. More precisely, the idea is to select database records with Boolean conditions ('hard' constraints) and then to use preferences ('soft' constraints) to order the previously selected records.

Lacroix and Lavency (Lacroix & Lavency, 1987) were the first to introduce the notion of a preference query to the database field. They proposed an extension of the relational calculus in which preferences for tuples satisfying given logical conditions can be expressed. For instance, one could say: pick the

Figure 7. An example of a personalization graph (cf. (Koutrika & Ioannidis, 2005))

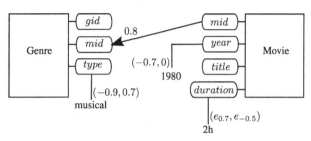

tuples of R satisfying QP_1P_2; if the result is empty, pick the tuples satisfying $Q_{\zeta}^{\neg\zeta} P_1P_2$; if the result is empty, pick the tuples satisfying $Q^{\neg} P_1P_2$. In other words, Q is a 'hard' constraint, whereas P_1 and P_2 are preferences or 'soft' constraints. Since then extensive investigation has been conducted, and two main types of approaches have been distinguished in the literature to deal with the user's preferences, namely, quantitative and qualitative (Chomicki, 2003).

2.3.1.1 Quantitative Preferences

The quantitative approach expresses preferences using scoring functions, which associate a numeric score with every tuple of the query, e.g. 'I like tuple t with score 0.5'. Then tuple t_1 is preferred over tuple t_2 if and only if the score of t_1 is higher than the score of t_2. Agrawal et al. (Agrawal & Wimmers, 2000) provided a framework for expressing and combining such kinds of preference functions.

Recently, Koutrika et al. (Koutrika & Ioannidis, 2005) presented a richer preference model which can associate degrees of interest (like scores) with preferences over a database schema. Thus, from this aspect, it seems to follow a quantitative approach. These preferences are all kept in a user profile. A user profile is viewed as a directed graph $\zeta\langle \vartheta, E\rangle$ (called Personalization Graph), where ϑ is the set of nodes and E the set of edges. Nodes in ϑ are (a) relation nodes, one for each relation in the schema, (b) attribute nodes, one for each attribute of each relation in the schema, and (c) value nodes, one for each value that is of any interest to a particular user. Edges in E are (a) selection edges, representing a possible selection condition from an attribute to a value node, and (b) join edges, representing a join between attribute nodes. An example of a user profile is given in Figure 7. It indicates among others a preference for movies of duration around 2h and a big concern about the genre of a movie. The first value between brackets indicates the preference for the presence of the associated value, the second indicates the preference for the absence of the associated value. The function e stands for an elastic preference. Furthermore, the authors proposed a query personalization algorithm which exploits the user profile to dynamically enrich (personalize) user queries prior to their execution. For example, the personalization of a user query can add selection conditions to a query, meaning that the user obtains a subset of the answer to the initial query. In general, it is expected that this subset contains the most interesting tuples (with respect to the user preferences) of the global answer.

Koutrika et al's approach (Koutrika & Ioannidis, 2005) provides one of the first solutions towards modelling of user preferences in Database systems in the form of a structured profile. In (Kostadinov, Bouzeghoub & Lopes, 2007), the authors elaborated a taxonomy of the most important knowledge composing a user profile and proposed a generic model that can be instantiated and adapted to each specific application.

2.3.1.2 Qualitative Preferences

The qualitative approach intends to directly specify preferences between the tuples in the query answer, typically using binary preference relations, e.g., 'I prefer tuple t_1 to tuple t_2'. These kinds of preference relations can be embedded into relational query languages through relational operators or special preference constructors, which select from their input the set of the most preferred tuples. This approach is, among others, taken by Chomicki (Chomicki, 2002; Chomicki, 2003) using the winnow operator and Kießling (Kießling, 2002) in his PreferenceSQL best match only model.

To get an idea of the representation for this approach, consider the following preference from (Chomicki, 2003), which specifies a preference of white wine over red when fish is served, and red wine over white, when meat is served, over a relation MealDB with attributes Dish (d), DishType (dt), Wine (w), WineType (wt):

$$\left(d, dt, w, wt\right) (d', \ dt', w', wt') = (d = d' \ dt = fish \ wt = w$$
$$dt' = fish \ wt' = red)$$
$$(d = d' \ dt = meat \ wt$$
$$dt' = meat \ wt' = whii$$

Another example representation of a qualitative preference, over a relation CarDB with attributes Make, Year, Price and Miles, is the following preference for cheap cars manufactured by Benz, and prior to 2005 but not before 2003, using PreferenceSQL from (Kießling, 2002):

```
SELECT *
FROM CarDB
WHERE Make = Benz
PREFERRING (LOWEST(Price) AND Year BETWEEN 2003, 2005)
```

Note that the qualitative approach is more general than the quantitative one, since one can define preference relations in terms of scoring functions, whereas not every preference relation can be captured by scoring functions. For example, consider the relation BookDB(ISBN, Vendor, Price) and its instance shown in Table 3. The preference 'if the same ISBN, prefer lower price to higher price' gives the preferences 'b_2 to b_1' and 'b_1 to b_3'. There is no preference between the first three books (i.e., b_1, b_2 and b_3) and the fourth one (i.e., b_4). Thus, the score of the fourth tuple should be equal to all of the scores of the first three tuples. But this implies that the scores of the first three tuples are the same, which is not possible since the second tuple is preferred to the first one which in turn is preferred to the third one.

2.3.2 Fuzzy Queries

The second and most popular approach of flexible query processing advocates the use of the fuzzy sets theory. More precisely, the idea is to allow end-users to formulate database queries using fuzzy terms that best capture their perception of the domain and then to use them to filter and rank relevant data.

Table 3. Excerpt of the BookDB relation

ID	ISBN	Vendor	Price
b_1	0679726691	BooksForLess	14.75
b_2	0679726691	LowestPrices	13.50
b_3	0679726691	QualityBooks	18.80
b_4	0062059041	BooksForLess	7.30

2.3.2.1 Fuzzy Sets Theory

Fuzzy set theory, introduced by Zadeh (Zadeh, 1956; Zadeh, 1975, Zadeh, 1999), is a mathematical tool for translating user's perception of the domain (often formulated in a natural language) into computable entities. Such entities are called fuzzy terms (linguistic labels). Fuzzy terms are represented as fuzzy sets and may be fuzzy values (e.g., *young*), fuzzy comparison operators (e.g., *much greater than*), fuzzy modifiers (e.g., *very, really*) or fuzzy quantifiers (e.g., *most*).

Mathematically, a fuzzy set F of a universe of discourse[xiv] U is characterized by a membership function μ_F given by:

$$\mu_F: \quad U \quad \rightarrow \quad \left[0,1\right]$$
$$u \quad \rightarrow \quad \mu_F(u)$$

where $\mu_F(u)$, for each uU, denotes the degree of membership of u in the fuzzy set F. An element u U is said to be in the fuzzy set F if and only if $\mu_F(u)\mu 0$ and to be a full member if and only if $\mu_F(u) = 1$. We call support and kernel of the fuzzy set F respectively the sets:

$$\text{support}(F) = \left\{u \in U \mid \mu_F(u)\; 0\right\} \text{ and } \text{kernel}(F) = \left\{u \in U \mid \mu_F(u) = 1\right\}.$$

Furthermore, if m fuzzy sets $F_1, F_2, \ldots$ and F_m are defined over U such that $\forall i = \left[1,m\right], F_i \neq \varphi, F_i \neq U$ and $\forall u \in U, \sum \mu_{F_i}(u)$, the set $\{F_1, \ldots, F_m\}$ is called a fuzzy partition (Ruspini, 1969) of U.

For example, consider the attribute Salary with domain $D_{\text{Salary}} = [0, 110]$ K€. A typical fuzzy partition of the universe of discourse D_{Salary} (i.e., the employees' salaries) is shown in Figure 8, where the fuzzy sets (values) *none, miserable, modest, reasonable, comfortable, enormous* and *outrageous* are defined. Here, the crisp value 60K€ has a grade of membership of 0.5 for both the *reasonable* and the *comfortable* fuzzy sets, i.e., $\mu_{reasonable}(60\text{K€}) = \mu_{comfortable}(60\text{K€}) = 0.5$.

2.3.2.2 Practical Extensions of SQL

In the literature, several extensions of SQL have been proposed to allow the use of fuzzy terms in database queries. Examples include the work of Tahani (Tahani, 1977), FQUERY (Zadrozny & Kacprzyk, 1996) and SQLf (Bosc & Pivert, 1995).

Figure 8. An example of fuzzy partition defined for the attribute Salary

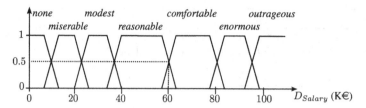

Tahani's Approach

Tahani (Tahani, 1977) was the first to propose a formal approach and architecture to deal with simple fuzzy queries for crisp relational databases. More specifically, the author proposed to use in the query condition fuzzy values instead of crisp ones. An example of a fuzzy query would be 'get employees who are *young* and have a *reasonable* salary". This query contains two fuzzy predicates 'Age = *young*' and 'Salary = *reasonable*', where *young* and *reasonable* are words in natural language that express or identify a fuzzy set (Figure 9).

Tahani's approach takes a relation R and a fuzzy query q over R as inputs and produces a fuzzy relation R_q, that is an ordinary relation in which each tuple t is associated with a matching degree γ_q within [0, 1] interval. The value γ_q indicates the extent to which tuple t satisfies the fuzzy predicates involved in the query q. The matching degree, γ_q, for each particular tuple t is calculated as follows. For a tuple t and a fuzzy query q with a simple fuzzy predicate $A = l$, where A is an attribute and l is a fuzzy set defined on the attribute domain of A, $\gamma_{A=l}$ is defined as follows:

$$\gamma_{A=l}(t) = \mu_l(t.A)$$

where $t.A$ is the value of tuple t on attribute A and μ_l is the membership function of the fuzzy set l.

For instance, consider the relation EmpDB in Table 4. The fuzzy relation corresponding to the fuzzy predicate 'Age = *young*' (resp., 'Salary = *reasonable*') is shown in Table 5-(a) (resp., Table 5-(b)). Note that when $\gamma_q(t) = 0$, the tuple t does not belong to the fuzzy relation R_q any longer (for instance, tuple #1 in Table 5-(a)).

The matching function γ for a complex fuzzy query with multiple fuzzy predicates is obtained by applying the semantics of the fuzzy logical connectives, that are:

$$\gamma_{p_1 \wedge p_2}(t) = \min(\gamma_{p_1}(t), \gamma_{p_2}(t))$$
$$\gamma_{p_1 \vee p_2}\, t = \max\, \gamma_{p_1}\, t\,, \gamma_{p_2}\, t$$
$$\gamma_{\neg p_1}\, t = 1 - \gamma_{p_1}\, t$$

Figure 9. The fuzzy sets (values) young and reasonable

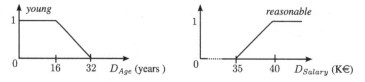

Table 4. Excerpt of the EmpDB relation

Id	Salary	Age	...
1	45000	62	
2	38750	24	
3	37500	28	

where p_1, p_2 are fuzzy predicates.

Table 6 shows the fuzzy relation corresponding to the query 'Age = *young* AND Salary= *reasonable*'. Note that the *min* and *max* operators may be replaced by any *t-norm* and *t-conorm* operators (Klement, Mesiar & Pap, 2000) to model the conjunction and disjunction connectives, respectively.

FQUERY

In (Zadrozny & Kacprzyk, 1996), the authors proposed FQUERY, an extension of the Microsoft Access SQL language with capability to manipulate fuzzy terms. More specifically, they proposed to take into account the following types of fuzzy terms: fuzzy values, fuzzy comparison operators, and fuzzy quantifiers. Given a query involving fuzzy terms, the matching degree of relevant answers is calculated according to the semantics of fuzzy terms (Zadeh, 1999). In addition to the syntax and semantics of the extended SQL, the authors have also proposed a scheme for the elicitation and manipulation of fuzzy terms to be used in queries. FQUERY has been one of the first implementations demonstrating the usefulness of fuzzy querying features for a traditional database.

SQLf

In contrast to both Tahani's approach and FQUERY which concentrated on the fuzzification of conditions appearing in the 'WHERE' clause of the SQL's SELECT statement, the query language SQLf (Bosc & Pivert, 1992; Bosc & Pivert, 1995; Bosc & Pivert, 1997) allows the introduction of fuzzy terms into SQL wherever they make sense. Indeed, all the operations of the relational algebra (implicitly or explicitly used in SQL's SELECT instruction) are redefined in such a way that the equivalences that occur in the crisp SQL are preserved. Thus, the projection, selection, join, union, intersection, Cartesian product and

Table 5. Fuzzy relations

(a) EmpDB$_{Age=young}$				
Id	Salary	Age	...	$\gamma_{Age=young}$
1	45000	62		0.0
2	38750	24		0.5
3	37500	28		0.25
(b) EmpDB$_{Salary=reasonable}$				
Id	Salary	Age	...	$\gamma_{Salary=reasonable}$
1	45000	62		1
2	38750	24		0.75
3	37500	28		0.25

*Table 6. The fuzzy relation EmpDB*_(Age=young Salary=reasonable)

Id	Salary	Age	...	$\gamma_{Age=young\,Salary=reasonable}$
1	45000	62		0
2	38750	24		0.5
3	37500	28		0.25

set difference operations are considered. Special attention is also paid to the division operation which may be interpreted in a different way due to many possible versions of the implication available in fuzzy logic (Bosc, Pivert & Rocacher, 2007). Other operations typical for SQL are also redefined, including the 'GROUP BY' clause, the 'HAVING' clause and the operators 'IN' and 'NOT IN' used along with sub-queries. A query in SQLf language has the following syntax:

SELECT $[n|t|n,t]$ set of attributes
FROM set of relations
WHERE set of fuzzy predicates

where the parameters n and t of the select block limit the number of the answers by using a quantitative condition (the best n answers) or a qualitative condition (ones which satisfy the fuzzy predicates according to a degree higher than t).

For more details and more general sources about fuzzy querying, please refer to (Galindo, 2008).

2.3.3 Keyword Search

Keyword-searchable database systems offer a simple keyword-based search interface where users need to neither understand the underlying database schemas and structures in advance nor know complex query languages like SQL. Instead, users are only required to submit a list of keywords, and the system will return ranked answers based on their relevance to query keywords.

Consider the example of Figure 10, which illustrates a small subset of the DBLP database. If a user wants to get the papers co-authored by '*Hristidis Vagelis*' and '*Papakonstantinou Yannis*', she/he should learn the schema of the DBLP database first, and then she/he must write intricate SQL queries like this:

(
SELECT title
FROM Paper, Writes, Author
WHERE Paper.pid = Writes.pid
AND Writes.aid = Author.aid
AND Author.name = '*Hristidis Vagelis*'
) (
SELECT title
FROM Paper, Writes, Author
WHERE Paper.pid = Writes.pid
AND Writes.aid = Author.aid

Figure 10. The DBLP database

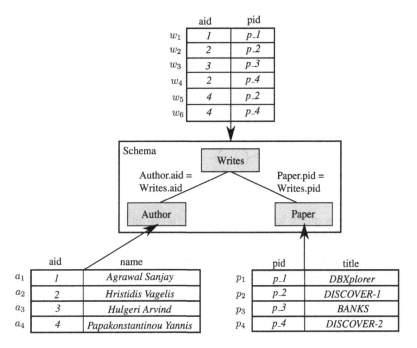

AND Author.name = '*Papakonstantinou Yannis*'
)

Obviously, this model of search is too complicated for ordinary users. Several methods aim at decreasing this complexity by providing keyword search functionality over relational databases. With such functionality, a user can avoid writing an SQL query; and she/he can just submit a simple keyword query '*Hristidis Vagelis* and *Papakonstantinou Yannis*' to the DBLP database. Examples include BANKS (Bhalotia, Hulgeri, Nakhe, Chakrabarti & Sudarshan, 2002), DBXplore (Agrawal, Chaudhuri & Das, 2002) and DISCOVER (Hristidis & Papakonstantinou, 2002). The former system (BANKS) models the database as a graph and retrieves results by means of traversal, whereas the latter ones (DBXplore and DISCOVER) exploit the database schema to compute the results.

BANKS

BANKS[xv] (Bhalotia, Hulgeri, Nakhe, Chakrabarti & Sudarshan, 2002) views the database as a directed weighted graph, where each node represents a tuple, and edges connect tuples that can be joined (e.g., according to primary-foreign key relationships). Node weight is inspired by prestige ranking such as PageRank; node that has large degree[xvi] get a higher prestige. Edge weight reflects the importance of the relationship between two tuples or nodes[xvii]; lower edge weights correspond to greater proximity or stronger relationship between the involved tuples. At query time, BANKS employs a *backward* search strategy to search for results containing all keywords. A result is a tree of tuples (called tuple tree), that is, sets of tuples which are associated on their primary-foreign key relationships and contain all the keywords of the query. Figure 11 shows two tuple trees for query q = '*Hristidis Vagelis* and *Papakonstantinou Yannis*' on the example database of Figure 10. More precisely, BANKS constructs paths starting from

Figure 11. Tuple trees for query q = 'Hristidis Vagelis and Papakonstantinou Yannis'

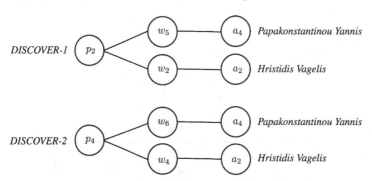

each node (tuple) containing a query keyword (e.g., a_2 and a_4 in Figure 11) and executes a Dijkstra's single source shortest path algorithm for each one of them. The idea is to find a common vertex (e.g., p_2 and p_4 in Figure 11) from which a forward path exists to at least one tuple corresponding to a different keyword in the query. Such paths will define a rooted directed tree with the common vertex as the root containing the keyword nodes as leaves, which will be one possible answer (tuple tree) for a given query. The answer trees are then ranked and displayed to the user. The ranking strategy of BANKS is to combine nodes and edges weights in a tuple tree to compute a score for ranking.

DBXplorer

DBXplorer (Agrawal, Chaudhuri & Das, 2002) models the relational schema as a graph, in which nodes map to database relations and edges represent relationships, such as primary-foreign key dependencies. Given a query consisting of a set of keywords, DBXplorer first searches the symbol table to find the relations of the database that contain the query keywords. The symbol table serves as an inverted list and it is built by preprocessing the whole database contents before the search. Then, DBXplorer uses the schema graph to find join trees that interconnect these relations. A join tree is a subtree of schema graph that satisfies two conditions: one is that the relation corresponding to a leaf node contains at least one query keyword; another is that every query keyword is contained by a relation corresponding to a leaf node. Thus, if all relations in a join tree are joined, the results might contain rows having all keywords. For each join tree a relevant SQL query is then created and executed. Finally, results are ranked and displayed to the user. The score function that DBXplorer uses to rank results is very simple. The score of a result is the number of joins involved. The rationale behind this simple relevance-ranking scheme is that the more joins are needed to create a row with the query keywords, the less clear it becomes whether the result might be meaningful or helpful.

DISCOVER

DISCOVER (Hristidis & Papakonstantinou, 2002) also exploits the relational schema graph. It uses the concept of a candidate network to refer to the schema of a possible answer, which is a tree interconnecting the set of tuples that contain all the keywords, as in DBXplorer. The candidate network generation algorithm is also similar. However, DISCOVER can be regarded as an improvement of DBXplorer. In fact, it stores some temporary data to avoid re-executing joins that are common among candidate networks. DISCOVER, like DBXplorer, ranks results based on the number of joins of the corresponding candidate network.

Figure 12. Basic database searching process

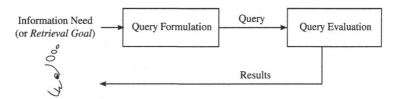

Note that all afore-mentioned approaches (BANKS, DBXplore and DISCOVER) are useful to users who do not know SQL or are unfamiliar with the database schema. However, they present a semantic challenge because the metadata of attributes and relations that are in an SQL statement are lacking in keyword search. Furthermore, because a keyword may appear in any attributes and in any relations, the result set may be large and include many answers users do not need.

2.4 Discussion

Database search processes basically involve two steps, namely query formulation and query evaluation (Figure 12). In the query formulation step, the user formulates her/his information need (or *retrieval goal*) in terms of an SQL query. The query evaluation step runs this query against the database and returns data that match it exactly.

Thus, formulating a query that accurately captures the user's retrieval goal is crucial for obtaining satisfactory results (i.e., results that are both useful and of manageable size for human analysis) from a database. However, it is challenging to achieve for several reasons:

- users may have *ill-defined* retrieval goals, i.e., they do not really know what might be useful for them, merely an expectation that interesting data may be encountered if they use the database system (e.g., *'I can't say what I want, but I will recognize it when I see it'*) ;
- even if users have *well-defined* retrieval goals, they may not know how to turn them into regular SQL queries (e.g., *'I know what I want, but I don't know how to get it'*). This may be either because they are not familiar with the SQL language or with the database schema. It may also be due to an expressiveness limit of SQL. In fact, an information need is a mental image of a user regarding the information she/he wants to retrieve and it is difficult to capture it using an unnatural exact language such as SQL.

Note that even if users have *well-defined* retrieval goals and know how to formulate them in terms of SQL queries (e.g., *'I know what I want and I know how to get it'*), they may not obtain what they need (e.g., *'I am not satisfied'*). This occurs if the database they wish to access contains no data that satisfy their retrieval goals.

One can clearly notice that the *Many-Answers* and the *Empty-Answer* problems are immediate consequences of the above problems. In fact, if the user has an *ill-defined* retrieval goal, her/his queries are often very broad, resulting in too many answers; otherwise, they are very specific and often return no answers.

In Figure 13, we propose a classification of the techniques presented and discussed in this chapter. This classification is based on the situation or problem, from those mentioned above, that they are supposed to address.

The first category (**Group A** in Figure 13) contains query relaxation (Section 2.1.1) and similarity-based search (Section 2.1.2) techniques. These techniques address situations in which a user approaches the database with a query that exactly captures her/his retrieval goal but she/he is delivered an empty result set. These techniques allow the database system to retrieve results that closely (though not completely) match the user's retrieval goal.

The second (**Group B** in Figure 13) contains preference-based (Section 2.3.1), fuzzy-based (Section 2.3.2) and keyword-based search (Section 2.3.3) techniques. These techniques provide human-oriented interfaces which allow users to formulate their retrieval goals in a more natural or intuitive manner. Note, however, that these techniques, while useful, do not help users to clarify or refine their retrieval goals; therefore they are not designed for the problem of ill-defined retrieval goal.

Finally, the third category (**Group C** in Figure 13) contains automated ranking and clustering-based techniques. These techniques address situations in which a database user has an ill-defined retrieval goal. Automated ranking-based techniques (Section 2.2.1) first seek to clarify or approximate the retrieval goal. For this purpose, they use either past behavior of the user (derived from available workloads) or relevance feedback from the user. Then, they compute a score, by means of a similarity measure, of each answer that represents the extent to which it is relevant to the approximated user's retrieval goal. Finally, the user is provided with a ranked list, in descending order of relevance, of either all query results or only a top-k subset. The effectiveness of these approaches highly depends on their ability to accurately capture the user's retrieval goal, which is a tedious and time consuming task. Note that such approaches also bring the disadvantage of match homogeneity, i.e., the user is often required to go through

Figure 13. A classification of advanced database query processing techniques

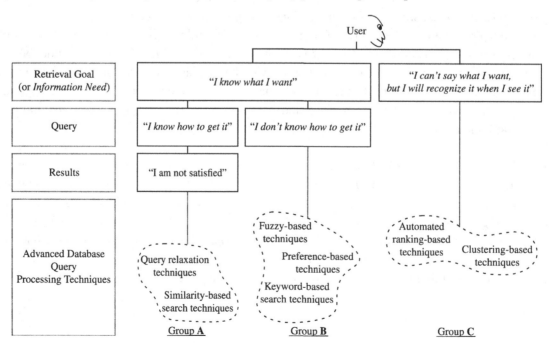

a large number of similar results before finding the next different result. In contrast, clustering-based techniques(Section 2.2.2) assist the user to clarify or refine the retrieval goal instead of trying to learn it. They consist in dividing the query result set into homogeneous groups, allowing the user to select and explore groups that are of interest to her/him. However, such techniques seek to only maximize some statistical property of the resulting clusters (such as the size and compactness of each cluster and the separation of clusters relative to each other), and therefore there is no guarantee that the resulting clusters will match the meaningful groups that a user may expect. Furthermore, these approaches are performed on query results and consequently occur at query time. Thus, the overhead time cost is an open critical issue for such a posteriori tasks.

In the second part of this chapter, we focus on the *Many-Answers* problem that is critical for very large database and decision support systems. Thus, we investigate a simple but useful strategy to handle this problem.

3. KNOWLEDGE-BASED CLUSTERING OF RESULT SET

Database systems are being increasingly used for interactive and exploratory data retrieval. In such retrieval, user's queries often result in too many answers. Not all the retrieved items are relevant to the user; typically, only a tiny fraction of the result set is relevant to her/him. Unfortunately, she/he often needs to examine all or most of the retrieved items to find the interesting ones. As discussed in Section 2, this phenomenon (commonly referred to as 'information overload') often happens when the user submits a 'broad' query, i.e., she/he has an *ill-defined* retrieval goal.

For example, consider a realtor database HouseDB with information on houses for sale in Paris, including their Price, Size, #Bedrooms, Age, Location, etc. A user who approaches that database with a broad query such as 'Price [150k€, 300k€]' may be overloaded with a huge list of results, since there are many houses within this price range in Paris. A well-established theory in cognitive psychology (Miller, 1962; Mandler, 1967) contends that humans organize items into logical groups as a way of dealing with large amounts of information. For instance, a child classifies his toys according to his favorite colors; a direct marketer classifies his target according to a variety of geographic, demographic, and behavioral attributes; and a real estate agent classifies his houses according to the location, the price, the size, etc. Furthermore, the *Cluster Hypothesis* (Jardine & Van Rijsbergen, 1971) states that "closely associated items tend to be relevant to the same request". Therefore, clustering analysis (Berkhin, 2006) which refers to partitioning data into dissimilar groups (or clusters) of similar items is an effective technique to overcome the problem of information overload. However, applying traditional clustering methods directly to the results of a user's query presents two major problems:

1. the first is related to *relevance*. Most clustering algorithms seek to only maximize some statistical property of the clusters (e.g., the size and compactness of each cluster and the separation of clusters relative to each other), and therefore there is no guarantee that the resulting clusters will match the meaningful groups that a user may expect;
2. the second is related to *scalability*. Clustering analysis is a time-consuming process, and doing it on the fly (i.e., at query time) may compromise seriously the response time of the system.

Now suppose that the user poses her/his query to a real estate agent. The estate agent often provides that user with better results than the ones obtained using traditional database systems, as she/he has a large amount of knowledge in the field of house buying. Let us briefly discuss two important features of the estate agent that contribute to her/his ability to fit the user's information requirements:

1. the first is her/his ability to organize, abstract, store and index her/his knowledge for future use. In fact, besides organizing her/his knowledge into groups (Miller, 1962; Mandler, 1967), the estate agent stores (in her/his memory) these groups as a knowledge representation and such groups often become an automatic response of her/him. This interesting statement comes from the central tenet of semantic network theory (Quillian, 1968; Collins & Quillian, 1969), which argues that information is stored in human memory as a network of linked concepts (e.g., the concept 'house' is related by the word 'is' to the concept 'home'). Moreover, psychological experiments (Miller, 1956; Simon, 1974; Halford, Baker, McCredden & Bain, 2005) show that humans can deal with a large amount of information, exceeding their memory limitations, when such information are supplemented with additional features such as a relationship to a larger group (or concept). Hence, cognitive theories assume that humans arrange their knowledge in a hierarchical structure that describes groups at varying levels of specificity. Furthermore, Ashcraft (Ashcraft, 1994) found that humans assign meaningful words from natural language to groups and retrieve information by those words (i.e., group representatives) rather than blindly traversing all information;

2. the second feature is her/his ability to assist the user to refine and clarify her/his information need as well as to make a decision. In fact, the estate agent establishes a dialog with the user during which she/he asks pertinent questions. Then, for each user's response (i.e., a new information need), the estate agent uses her/his knowledge to provide the user with concise and comprehensive information. Such information is retrieved by matching user query words with group representatives (Ashcraft, 1994) stored in her/his memory.

From these cognitive and technical observations, we propose a simple but useful strategy, that emulates the interaction a user might have with a real estate agent to some extent, to alleviate the two previously mentioned problems (i.e., *relevance* and *scalability*). It can be summarized as follows (see Figure 14):

Figure 14. Our proposal

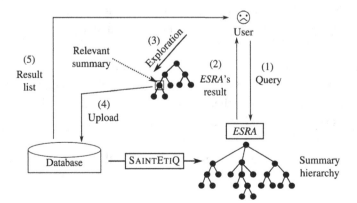

- In a pre-processing step, we compute knowledge-based summaries of the queried data. The underlying summarization technique used in this paper is the SAINTETIQ model (Raschia & Mouaddib, 2002; Saint-Paul, Raschia, & Mouaddib, 2005), which is a domain knowledge-based approach that enables summarization and classification of structured data stored into a database. SAINTETIQ first transforms raw data into high-level representations (summaries) that fit the user's perception of the domain, by means of linguistic labels (e.g., *cheap, reasonable, expensive, very expensive*) defined over the data attribute domains and provided by a domain expert or even an end-user. Then it applies a hierarchical clustering algorithm on these summaries to provide multi-resolution summaries (i.e., summary hierarchy) that represent the database content at different abstraction levels. The summary hierarchy can be seen as an analogy for knowledge representation estate agent.

- At query time, we use the summary hierarchy of the data, instead of the data itself, to quickly provide the user with concise, useful and structured answers as a starting point for an online analysis. This goal is achieved thanks to the Explore-Select algorithm (*ESA*) that extracts query-relevant entries from the summary hierarchy. Each answer item describes a subset of the result set in a human-readable form using linguistic labels. Moreover, answers of a given query are nodes of the summary hierarchy and every subtree rooted by an answer offers a 'guided tour' of a data subset to the user. The user then navigates this tree, in a top-down fashion, exploring the summaries of interest while ignoring the rest. Note that the database is accessed only when the user requests to download (*Upload*) the original data that a potentially relevant summary describes. Hence, this framework is intended to help the user iteratively refine her/his information need in the same way as done by the estate agent.

However, since such the summary hierarchy is independent of the query, the set of starting point answers could be large and consequently dissimilarity between items is susceptible to skew. It occurs when the summary hierarchy is not perfectly adapted to the user query. To tackle this problem, we first propose a straightforward approach (*ESA-SEQ*) using the clustering algorithm of SAINTETIQ to optimize the high-level answers. The optimization requires post-processing and therefore, it incurs overhead time cost. Thus, we finally develop an efficient and effective algorithm (*ESRA*, i.e., ES-Rearrange Algorithm) that rearranges answers based on the hierarchical structure of the pre-computed summary hierarchy, such that no post-processing task (but the query evaluation itself) have to be performed at query time.

The rest of this section is organized as follows. First, we present the SAINTETIQ model and its properties and we illustrate the process with a toy example. Then, in Section 3.2 we detail the use of SAINTETIQ outputs in a query processing and we describe the formulation of queries and the retrieval of clusters. Thereafter, we discuss in Section 3.3 how such results help facing the many-answers problem. The algorithm that addresses the problem of dissimilarity (discrimination) between the starting point answers by rearranging them is presented in Section 3.4. Section 3.5 discusses an extension of the above process that allows every user to use her/his own vocabulary when querying the database. An experimental study using real data is presented in Section 3.6.

3.1 Overview of the SAINTETIQ System

In this subsection, we first introduce the main ideas of SAINTETIQ (Raschia & Mouaddib, 2002; Saint-Paul, Raschia, & Mouaddib, 2005). Then, we briefly discuss some other data clustering techniques, and argue that SAINTETIQ is more suitable for interactive and exploratory data retrieval.

Figure 15. Fuzzy linguistic partition defined on the attribute Price

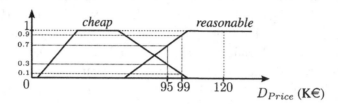

3.1.1 A Two-Step Process

SAINTETIQ takes tabular data as input and produces multi-resolution summaries of records through an online mapping process and a summarization process.*3.1.1.1 Mapping Service*SAINTETIQ system relies on Zadeh's fuzzy set theory (Zadeh, 1956), and more specifically on linguistic variables (Zadeh, 1975) and fuzzy partitions (Ruspini, 1969), to represent data in a concise form. The fuzzy set theory is used to translate records in accordance with a Knowledge Base (*KB*) provided by a domain expert or even an end-user. Basically, the operation replaces the original values of each record in the table by a set of linguistic labels defined in the *KB*. For instance, with a linguistic variable on the attribute Price (Figure 15), a value *t*.Price = 95000€ is mapped to {0.3/*cheap*, 0.7/*reasonable*} where 0.7 is a membership grade that tells how well the label *reasonable* describes the value 95000. Extending this mapping to all the attributes of a relation could be seen as mapping the records to a grid-based multidimensional space. The grid is provided by the *KB* and corresponds to the user's perception of the domain.

Thus, tuples of Table 7 are mapped into two distinct grid-cells denoted by c_1 and c_2 in Table 8. *old* is a fuzzy label a priori provided by the *KB* on attribute Age and it perfectly matches (with degree 1) range [19, 24] of raw values. Besides, 0.3/*cheap* says that *cheap* fits the data only with a small degree (0.3). The degree is computed as the maximum of membership grades of tuple values to cheap in c_1.

Flexibility in the vocabulary definition of *KB* permits to express any single value with more than one fuzzy descriptor and avoid threshold effect due to a smooth transition between two descriptors. Besides, *KB* leads to the point where tuples become indistinguishable and then are grouped into grid-cells such that there are finally many more records than cells. Every new (coarser) tuple stores a record count and attribute-dependant measures (min, max, mean, standard deviation, etc.). It is then called a summary.

3.1.1.2 Summarization Service

The summarization service (*SEQ*) is the second and the most sophisticated step of the SAINTETIQ system. It takes grid-cells as input and outputs a collection of summaries hierarchically arranged from the most generalized one (the root) to the most specialized ones (the leaves). Summaries are clusters of grid-cells, defining hyperrectangles in the multidimensional space. In the basic process, leaves are grid-cells themselves and the clustering task is performed on L cells rather than n tuples ($L \ll n$).

From the mapping step, cells are introduced continuously in the hierarchy with a top-down approach inspired of D.H. Fisher's CobWeb, a conceptual clustering algorithm (Fisher, 1987). Then, they are incorporated into best fitting nodes descending the tree. Three more operators could be apply, depending on partition's score, that are *create*, *merge* and *split* nodes. They allow developing the tree and updating its current state. Figure 16 represents the summary hierarchy built from the cells c1 and c2 of Table 8.

Table 7. Raw data (R)

Id	Age	Price
$t_1 t_2 t_3$	221924	9500099000120000

Table 8. Grid-cells mapping

Cell	Age	Price	Id
c_1	old	0.3/cheap	t_1
c_2	old	reasonable	t_1, t_2, t_3

For the sake of simplicity, we have only reported the linguistic labels (*intent*) and the row Ids (*extent*) that point to tuples described by those linguistic labels.

3.1.2 Discussion about SAINTETIQ

Cluster analysis is one of the most useful tasks in data mining (Maimon & Rokach, 2005) process for discovering groups and identifying interesting distributions and patterns in the underlying data. The clustering problem is about partitioning a given data set into groups (clusters) such that the data points in a cluster are more similar to each other than to points in different clusters.

Up to now, many clustering methods (Berkhin, 2006) have been proposed and, among them, grid-based clustering methods (e.g., STING (Wang, Yang & Muntz, 1997), BANG (Schikuta & Erhart, 1998), WaveCluster (Sheikholeslami, Chatterjee & Zhang, 2000), etc.). Grid-based clustering methods first partition the data by applying a multidimensional grid structure on the feature space. Second, statistical information (e.g., min, max, mean, standard deviation, distribution) is collected for all the database records located in each individual grid cell and clustering is performed on populated cells to form clusters. These methods have been proved as valuable tools for analyzing the structural information of very large databases. One of the most appealing factors is the excellent runtime behavior. In fact, their processing time only depends on the number of populated cells L which is usually much less than the number of database records n ($L << n$) (Berkhin, 2006). More specifically, the time complexity T_{SEQ} of the SAINTETIQ process and especially, its summarization service (*SEQ*) - the mapping service will not be further discussed as it is a straightforward rewriting process, can be expressed as:

$$T_{SEQ} = k_{SEQ} L \log(L) \in O(L \log(L))$$

Figure 16. Example of SAINTETIQ hierarchy

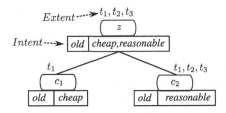

where L is the number of cells of the output hierarchy and d its average width. In the above formula, the coefficient k_{SEQ} corresponds to the set of operations performed to find the best learning operator (*create*, *merge* or *split*) to apply at each level of the hierarchy, whereas $L \log L$ is an estimation of the average depth of this hierarchy.

The SAINTETIQ model, besides being a grid-based clustering method, has many other advantages that are relevant for achieving the targeted objective of this chapter. First, SAINTETIQ uses prior domain knowledge (the Knowledge Base) to guide the clustering process, and to provide clusters that fit the user's perception of the domain. This distinctive feature differentiates it from other grid-based clustering techniques which attempt to only maximize some statistical property of the clusters, and therefore there is no guarantee that the resulting clusters will match the meaningful groups that a user may expect. Second, the flexibility in the vocabulary definition of *KB* leads to clustering schemas that have two useful properties: (1) the clusters have 'soft' boundaries, in the sense that each record belongs to each cluster to some degree, and thus undesirable threshold effects that are usually produced by crisp (non-fuzzy) boundaries are avoided; (2) the clusters are presented in a user-friendly language (i.e., linguistic labels) and hence the user can determine at a glance whether a cluster's content is of interest. Finally, SAINTETIQ applies a conceptual clustering algorithm for partitioning the incoming data in an incremental and dynamic way. Thus, changes in the database are reflected through such an incremental maintenance of the complete hierarchy (Saint-Paul, Raschia, & Mouaddib, 2005).

Of course, for new application, the end-user or the expert has to be consulted to create linguistic labels as well as the fuzzy membership functions. However, it is worth noticing that, once such knowledge base is defined, the system does not require any more setting. Furthermore, the issue of estimating fuzzy membership functions has been intensively studied in the fuzzy set literature (Galindo, 2008), and various methods based on data distribution and statistics exist to assist the user designing trapezoidal fuzzy membership functions.

3.2 Querying the SAINTETIQ Summaries

In an exploratory analysis of a massive data set, users usually have only a vague idea of what they could find in the data. They are then unable to formulate precise criteria to locate the desired information. The querying mechanism presented here allows such users to access a database (previously summarized) using vague requirements (e.g., *cheap*) instead of crisp ones (e.g., [100k€, 200k€]). In fact, users only need to select the right criteria from an existing set of linguistic labels defined on each attribute domain in the *KB*, to filter a set of clusters (summaries) that can then be browsed to find potentially interesting pieces of information. However, choosing the linguistic labels from a controlled vocabulary compels the user to adopt a predefined categorization materialized by the grid-cells. In section 3.5, we deal with user-specific linguistic labels to overcome this pitfall. In this subsection, we first introduce a toy example that will be used throughout that chapter. Then, we present all aspects of the querying mechanism from the expression and meaning of a query to its matching against summaries.

3.2.1 Running Example

To illustrate the querying mechanism, we introduce here a sample data set R with 30 records (t_1-t_{30}) represented on three attributes: Price, Size and Location. We suppose that {*cheap* (ch.), *reasonable* (re.), *expensive* (ex.), *very expensive* (vex.)}, {*small* (sm.), *medium* (me.), *large* (la.)} and {*downtown* (dw.), *suburb* (su.)} are sets of linguistic labels defined respectively on attributes Price, Size and Location. Figure 17 shows the summary hierarchy H_R provided by SAINTETIQ performed on R.

3.2.2 Expression and Evaluation of Queries

The querying mechanism proposed here intends to evaluate queries such as Q_1:

Example 3.1 (Q_1)

SELECT *
FROM R
WHERE Location IN {*suburb*}
AND Size IN {*medium* OR *large*}

In the following, we denote by X the set of attributes specified in the user's input query Q and by Y the set of missing attributes which is the complement of X relatively to R: $XY=R$ and $XY=\varphi$. Further, for each attribute AX, Q_A denotes the set of required features defined on attribute A. For instance, given Q_1, we have $X=\{Location, Size\}$, $Y=\{Price\}$, $Q_{Location}=\{suburb\}$, $Q_{Size}=\{medium, large\}$.

Let $z.A$ be the set of descriptors that appear in a summary z on attribute A. When matching z with a query Q to decide whether it corresponds to that query and can then be considered as a result, three cases might occur:

a: no correspondence (i.e., $\exists A\in X, z.A\cap Q_A=\varphi$). For one attribute or more, z has no required feature, i.e., it shows none of the linguistic labels mentioned in query Q.

b: exact correspondence (i.e., $\forall A\in X, z.A\subseteq Q_A$). The summary z matches the query Q semantics. It is considered as a result.

Figure 17. Summary hierarchy H_R of the data set R

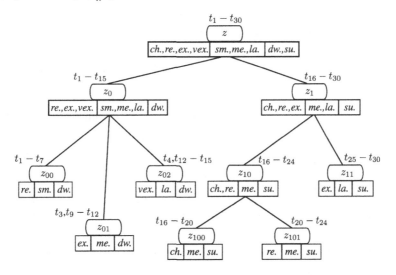

c: no decision can be made (i.e., $\exists A \in X, z.A - Q_A \neq \varphi$). There is one attribute A for which z exhibits one or many linguistic labels besides those strictly required (i.e., those in Q_A). The presence of required features in each attribute of z suggests, but does not guarantee, that results may be found in the subtree rooted by z. Exploration of the subtree is necessary to retrieve possible results: for each branch, it will end up in situations categorized by case **a** or case **b**. Thus, at worst at leaf level, an exploration leads to accepting or rejecting summaries; the indecision is always solved.

The situations stated above reflect a global view of the matching of a summary z with a query Q.

3.2.3 Search Algorithm

The Explore-Select Algorithm (*ESA*) applies the matching procedure from the previous section over the whole set of summaries, organized in a hierarchy, to select relevant summaries. Since the selection should take into account all summaries that correspond to the query, the exploration of the hierarchy is complete. Algorithm 1 (shown on the next page) describes *ESA* with the following assumptions:

- the function returns a list of summaries;
- function Corr symbolizes the matching test reported in Section 3.2.2;
- operator '+' performs a list concatenation of its arguments;
- function Add is the classical constructor for lists, it adds an element to a list of the suitable type;
- Lres is a local variable.

The *ESA* algorithm (see Algorithm 1) is based on a depth-first search and relies on a property of the hierarchy: the generalization step in the SAINTETIQ model guarantees that any label that exists in a node of the tree also exists in each parent node. Inversely, a label is absent from a summary's intent if and only if it is absent from all subnodes of this summary. This property of the hierarchy permits branch cutting as soon as it is known that no result will be found. Depending on the query, only a part of the hierarchy is explored.

Thus, results of Q_1 (Example 3.1), when querying the hierarchy shown in Figure 17, look like Table 9.

In this case, the *ESA* algorithm first confronts z (root) with Q_1. Since no decision can be made, Q_1 is respectively confronted to z_0 and z_1, the children of z. The subtree rooted by z_0 is then ignored because there is no correspondence between Q_1 and z_0. Finally z_1 is returned because it exactly matches Q_1. Thus, the process tests only 30% of the whole hierarchy.

Note that, the set of records R_z summarized by z_1 can be returned if the user requests it (SHOW-TUPLES option). This is done by simply transforming the *intent* of z_1 into a query q_{z_1} and sending it as a usual query to the database system. The WHERE clause of q_{z_1} is generated by transforming the linguistic labels (fuzzy sets) contained in the intent of z_1 into crisp ones. In other words, each linguistic label l on an attribute A is replaced by its support, i.e., the set of all values in the domain of A (D_A) that belong to l with non-zero membership. Then, the obtained crisp criteria on each summary's attribute are connected with OR operator and summary's attributes are connected with AND operator to generate the WHERE clause. Thus, performing a SHOWTUPLES operation takes advantage of the optimization mechanisms that exist in the database system. Furthermore, tuples covered by z_1 can also be sorted, thanks to their satisfaction degrees to the user's query, using an overall satisfaction degree. We assign

Algorithm 1.

```
Function Explore-Select(z,Q)
L   ← ⟨ ⟩
 res
if Corr(z,Q) = indecisive then
        for all child node z     of z do
                             child
                L   ← L   + Explore-Select(z     ,Q)
                 res    res                   child
        end for
else
        if Corr(z,Q) = exact then
                Add(z, L   )
                        res
        end if
end if
return L
        res
```

to each tuple the degree to which it satisfies the fuzzy criteria of the query. Usually, the minimum and maximum functions stand for the conjunctive and disjunctive connectives. There are many propositions in the literature for defining aggregation connectives (Klement, Mesiar & Pap, 2000).

The *ESA* algorithm is particularly efficient. In the worst case (exploration of the hierarchy is complete), its time complexity is given by:

$$T_{ESA} = \varepsilon \frac{L-1}{d-1} \in O\ L$$

where L is the number of leaves (cells) of the queried summary hierarchy, d its average width and coefficient ε corresponds to the time required for matching one summary in the hierarchy against the query. In the above formula, $\frac{L-1}{d-1}$ gives an estimation of the number of nodes in the summary hierarchy.

In the following subsection, we discuss how *ESA*'s answers help facing the *many-answers* problem.

3.3 Multi-Scale Summarized Answers

Given a query Q, the *ESA* algorithm produces a set of clusters (summaries) from a SAINTETIQ hierarchy instead of a list of tuples *tset(Q)*. Each answer item z describes a subset of the query result set *tset(Q)*. Hence, the user can unambiguously determine whether R_z contains relevant tuples only by looking at the intentional description of z and particularly on unspecified attributes (Y) because all answer tuples satisfy the specified conditions related to attributes in X. Three cases might occur:

1:   summary z doesn't fit the user's need. It means that for at least one unspecified attribute AY, all linguistic labels (the set $z.A$) are irrelevant to the user. For instance, consider the Q_1 results (Table 9). z_1 doesn't contain any relevant tuple if the user is actually looking for *very cheap* houses because *very cheap* z_1.Price. In other words, none of the records in R_{z_1} is mapped to very cheap on attribute

Table 9. Q_1 results

Id_Sum	Price	Size	Location
z_1	*cheapreasonableexpensive*	*mediumlarge*	*suburb*

Price and consequently a new broad query with less selective conditions may be submitted or the task may be abandoned (we denote this with the IGNORE option).

2: summary z exactly fits the user's need. It means that for each AY, all linguistic labels in $z.A$ are relevant to the user. Assume that the user is interested in *cheap, reasonable* as well as *expensive* houses. Thus, all tuples contained in R_{z_1} are relevant to her/him. In such cases, she/he uses SHOW-TUPLES option to access tuples stored in R_{z_1}.

3: summary z partially fits the user's need. In this case, there is at least one attribute AY for which $z.A$ exhibits too many linguistic labels w.r.t. the user's requirement. For instance, the set R_{z_1} partially matches the needs of a user who is looking for *cheap* as well as *reasonable* houses because R_{z_1} contains also tuples that are mapped to *expensive* on attribute Price. In this case, a new query with more selective conditions (e.g., Price IN {*cheap* OR *reasonable*}) may be submitted or a new clustering schema of the set R_z, i.e., which allows to examine more precisely the dataset, is required. Since z is a subtree of the summary hierarchy, we present to the user the children of z (SHOWCAT option). Each child of z represents only a portion of tuples in R_z and gives a more precise representation of the tuples it contains. For example, $\{z_{10}, z_{11}\}$ is a partitioning of R_{z_1} into two subsets $R_{z_{10}}$ and $R_{z_{11}}$; z_{10} exactly fits user needs. Since the entire tree is pre-computed, no clustering at all would have to be performed at feedback time.

More generally, a set of summaries or clusters $S = \{z_1 \ldots z_m\}$ is presented to the user as a clustering schema of the query result *tset(Q)*. The three options IGNORE (case **1**), SHOWTUPLES (case **2**) and SHOWCAT (case **3**) give the user the ability to browse through the S structure (generally a set of rooted subtrees), exploring different datasets in the query results and looking for potentially interesting pieces of information. Indeed, the user may navigate through S using the basic exploration model given below:

i. start the exploration by examining the intensional description of z_iS (initially $i = 0$);
ii. if case 1, ignore z_i and examine the next cluster in S, i.e., z_{i+1};
iii. if case 2, navigate through tuples of R_{z_1} to extract every relevant tuple and thereafter, go ahead and examine z_{i+1};
iv. if case 3, navigate through children of z_i, i.e., repeat from step (i) with S, the set of children of z_i. More precisely, examine the intensional description of each child of z_i starting from the first one and recursively decide to ignore it or examine it (SHOWTUPLES to extract relevant tuples or

Figure 18. Summary z_1

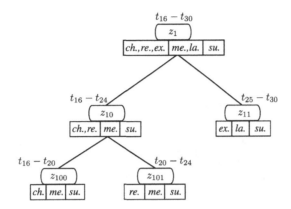

SHOWCAT option for further expansion). At the end of the exploration of the children of z_i, go ahead and examine z_{i+1}.

For instance, suppose a user is looking for *medium, large* as well as *expensive* houses in the *suburb* but issues the broad query Q_1 (Example 3.1): 'find *medium* or *large* houses in the *suburb*'. The set of summaries S presented to that user is $\{z_1\}$, where z_1 is a subtree (Figure 18) in the pre-computed summary hierarchy shown in Figure 17. In this situation, the user can explore the subtree rooted by z_1 as follows to reach relevant tuples: analyze the intent of z_1 and explore it using SHOWCAT option, analyze the intent of z_{10} and ignore it, analyze the intent of z_{11} and use SHOWTUPLES option to navigate through the tuples in $R_{z_{11}}$ (i.e., t_{25}-t_{30}) to identify each relevant tuple.

Note that when the set $S = \{z\}$ is a singleton, i.e., z is a node of the pre-computed clustering tree, its exploration is straightforward. Indeed, given a summary of the tree rooted by z that the user wishes to examine more closely (SHOWCAT option), its children are well separated since SAINTETIQ is designed to discover summaries (clusters) that locally optimize the objective function U. Furthermore, the number of clusters presented to the user, at each time, is small; the highest value is equal to the maximum width of the pre-computed tree. However, since the summary hierarchy is independent of the query, the set of starting point answers S could be large and consequently dissimilarity between summaries is susceptible to skew. It occurs when the summary hierarchy is not perfectly adapted to the user query. In this situation, it is hard for the user to separate the interesting summaries from the uninteresting ones, thereby leading to potential decision paralysis and wastage of time and effort.

In the next subsection, we propose an original rearranging query results algorithm to tackle this problem.

3.4 Rearranging the Result Set

The problem of discrimination (dissimilarity) between *ESA*'s results occurs when these results are scattered over the queried summary hierarchy. This situation is illustrated in Figure 19 (Left), where the set of summaries $S = \{z_{00}, z_{01}, z_{1000}, z_{101}, z_{11}\}$ is returned by *ESA* as the result of a query Q over the summary hierarchy H.

A straightforward way to address this problem would be to, first, execute the SAINTETIQ summarization service (*SEQ*) on the cells populated by records of *tset(Q)*, i.e., the cells covered by summaries

Figure 19. (Left) A pre-computed hierarchy H (Right) Rearranging Q summary results

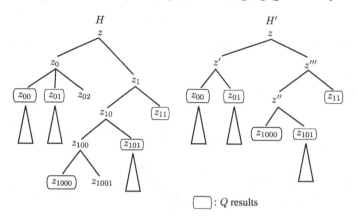

$\square$: Q results

of S. Then, we present to the user the top-level partition of the result tree. We will refer to this approach as *ESA+SEQ* (i.e., search step followed by summarization step) for the remainder of this chapter.

Size reduction and discrimination between items in S are clearly achieved at the expense of an overhead computational cost. Indeed, the search step time complexity T_{ESA} is in $O(L)$ where L is the number of leaves of the queried summary hierarchy (see Section 3.2.3). Furthermore, the summarization step time complexity T_{SEQ} is in $O(L' \cdot log \, L')$ with L' the number of cells populated by answer records (see Section 3.1.2). Therefore, the global time complexity $T_{ESA+SEQ}$ of the *ESA+SEQ* approach is in $O(L \cdot log \, L)$: LL' since the query is expected to be broad. Thus, *ESA+SEQ* doesn't fit the querying process requirement (see experimental results in Section 3.6), that is to quickly provide the user with concise and structured answers.

To tackle this problem, we propose an algorithm coined Explore-Select-Rearrange Algorithm (*ESRA*) that rearranges answers, based on the hierarchical structure of the queried summary hierarchy, before returning them to the user. The main idea of this approach is rather simple. It starts from the summary partition S (a clustering schema of the query results) and produces a sequence of clustering schemas with a decreasing number of clusters at each step. Each clustering schema produced at each step results from the previous one by merging the '*closest*' clusters into a single one. Similar clusters are identified thanks to the hierarchical structure of the pre-computed summary hierarchy. Intuitively, summaries which are closely related have a common ancestor lower in the hierarchy, whereas the common ancestor of unrelated summaries is near the root. This process stops when it reaches a single hyperrectangle (the root $z*$). Then, we present to the user the top-level partition (i.e., children of $z*$) in the obtained tree instead of S.

For instance, when this process is performed on the set of summaries $S = \{z_{00}, z_{01}, z_{1000}, z_{101}, z_{11}\}$ shown in Figure 19, the sequence of clustering schemas in Table 10 is produced.

The hierarchy H' obtained from the set of query results S is shown in Figure 19 (Right). Thus, the partition $\{z', z'''\}$ is presented to the user instead of S. This partition has a small size and defines well separated clusters. Indeed, all agglomerative methods, including the above rearranging process, have a monotonicity property (Hastie, Tibshirani & Friedman, 2001): the dissimilarity between the merged clusters is monotonically increasing with the level. In the above example, it means that the dissimilarity value of the partition $\{z', z'''\}$ is greater than the dissimilarity value of the partition $\{z_{00}, z_{01}, z_{1000}, z_{101}, z_{11}\}$.

Table 10.

1	z_{00}	z_{01}	z_{1000}	z_{101}	z_{11}
2	$z_{00}+z_{01}$	$z_{1000}+z_{101}$	z_{11}		
3	$z_{00}+z_{01}$	$z_{1000}+z_{101}+z_{11}$			
4	$z_{00}+z_{01}+z_{1000}+z_{101}+z_{11}$				

Algorithm 2 describes *ESRA*. It is a modified version of *ESA* (Algorithm 1) with the following new assumptions:

- it returns a summary ($z*$) rather than a list of summaries;
- function AddChild appends a node to caller's children;
- function NumberofChildren returns the number of caller's children;
- function uniqueChild returns the unique child of the caller;
- function BuildIntent builds caller's intent (hyperrectangles) from intents of its children;
- Z_{res} and Z' are local variables of type summary.

The *ESRA* cost is only a small constant factor γ larger than that of *ESA*. In fact, the rearranging process is done at the same time the queried summary hierarchy is being scanned. It means that no post-processing task (but the query evaluation itself) have to be performed at query time. More precisely, the time complexity of the *ESRA* Algorithm is in the same order of magnitude (i.e., $O(L)$) than the *ESA* Algorithm:

$$T_{ESRA} = \gamma + \varepsilon \cdot \frac{L-1}{d-1} \in O\ L$$

where the coefficient γ is the time cost for the additional operations (addChild, uniqueChild and BuildIntent). L is the number of leaves (cells) of the queried summary hierarchy and d its average width.

3.5 Discussion about Extension to any Fuzzy Predicate

A limitation of our proposal relies in the fact that *ESRA* restrains the user to queries using a controlled vocabulary (i.e., the summary vocabulary). Indeed, consider a user looking for *cheap* houses. What is meant by *cheap* can vary from one user to another one, or from one kind of users to another one (e.g., *cheap* does not have the same meaning for house buyers and for apartment tenants). Regarding the query cost and accuracy, the ideal solution consists in building a summary hierarchy for every user such that queries and summaries share the same vocabulary. Thus, *ESRA* can be used in its current state. But maintaining user-specific summaries is hardly conceivable in a system with multiple users. Two alternatives are then envisaged.

The first one is to consider group profiles in order to reduce the number of managed summaries (e.g., one for buyers and the other for tenants). In this case, *ESRA* can also be used directly since users formulate queries within the vocabulary of their groups. In this approach, users would subscribe to

Algorithm 2.

```
Function Explore-Select-Rearrange(z, Q)
Z_res ← Null
Z' ← Null
if Corr(z,Q) = indecisive then
        for all child node z_child of z do
                Z' ← Explore-Select-Rearrange(z_child,Q)
                if Z' Null then
                        Z_res.addChild (Z')
                end if
        end forif Z_res.NumberofChildren() > 1 then
                Z_res.BuildIntent()
        Else
                Z_res ←Zres.uniqueChild()
        end if
else
        if Corr(z,Q) = exact then
                Z_res ← z
        end if
end ifreturn Z_res
```

groups that share the same (or similar) vocabulary as theirs. In addition, they have to be familiar with their group's linguistic labels before using them accurately. As a result, this option is not much more convenient than using ad-hoc linguistic labels predetermined by a domain expert. Moreover, it only transposes the problem of user-specific summaries maintenance to group-specific ones.

The second alternative, investigated in the following, consists in building only one SAINTETIQ summary hierarchy using an ad-hoc vocabulary, and querying it with user-specific linguistic labels. Since the vocabulary of the user's query Q is different from the one in the summaries, we first use a fuzzy set-based mapping operation to translate predicates of Q from the user-specific vocabulary to the summary language. It consists in defining an accepting similarity threshold τ to decide whether the mapping of two fuzzy labels is valid. In other words, the user's label l_u is rewritten with a summary label l_s if and only if the similarity of l_u to ls ($\sigma(l_u, l_s)$) is greater than or equal to τ. There are many propositions in the literature for defining $\sigma(l_u, l_s)$ (e.g., degree of satisfiability (Bouchon-Meunier, Rifqi & Bothorel, 1996)). Then, the *ESRA* Algorithm is performed using the rewritten version of Q. Finally, results are sorted and flirted thanks to their similarity degrees to the initial user's query Q.

3.6 Experimental Results

Evaluating and comparing the effectiveness of different approaches that address the *Many-Answers* problem in databases is challenging. Unlike Information Retrieval where there exist extensive user studies and available benchmarks (e.g., the TREC[xviii] collection), such infrastructures are not available today in the context of Relational Databases. Nonetheless, in this subsection, we discuss the efficiency and the effectiveness of *ESA*, *ESA+SEQ* and *ESRA* algorithms based on a real database.

3.6.1 Data Set

Through an agreement, the CIC Banking Group provided us with an excerpt of statistical data used for behavioral studies of customers. The dataset is a collection of 33735 customers defined on 10 attributes (e.g., age, income, occupation, etc.). On each attribute, marketing experts defined between 3 and 8 linguistic labels leading to a total of 1036800 possible label combinations (i.e., 1036800 possible cells). Note that all the experiments were done on a 1.7GHz P4-based computer with 768MB memory.

3.6.2 Results

All experiments reported in this section were conducted on a workload composed of 150 queries with a random number of selection predicates from all attributes (i.e., each query has between 1 and 3 required features on 1, 2, 3 or 4 attributes).

Quantitative Analysis
The CIC dataset is summarized by the SAINTETIQ system as described in Section 3.1. The dataset, consisting of 33735 records, yields a summary tree with 13263 nodes, 6701 leaves or cells, maximum depth of 16, average depth of 10.177, maximum width of 14 and an average width of 2.921. The data distribution in the summary tree reveals a 0.6% ($\frac{6701}{1036800}$) occupation rate.

From the analysis of theoretical complexities, we claim that *ESA* and *ESRA* are much faster than the post-clustering approach *ESA+SEQ*. That is the main result of Figure 20 that shows the performance evolution according to the number of cells populated by query answer records. Furthermore, we plot the number of summary nodes visited (#*VisitedNodes*) per query (right scale) and finally, the normalized *ESRA* time cost ($t_{N.\ ESRA}$) to evaluate the performance of *ESRA* regardless of how the query fits the pre-clustering summary hierarchy. $t_{N.\ ESRA}$ is computed as follows:

$$t_{N.ESRA} = \frac{t_{ESRA} TreeNodes}{VisitedNodes}$$

As one can observe, Figure 20 verifies experimentally that *ESA+SEQ* is quasi-linear ($O(L \cdot log\ L)$) in the number of cells L whereas *ESA*, *ESRA* and *N.ESRA* are linear ($O(L)$). Besides, the time cost incurred by rearranging query results (i.e., t_{ESRA}-t_{ESA}) is insignificant compared to the search cost (i.e., t_{ESA}). For instance, for $L = 1006$, t_{ESA} and t_{ESRA} are 0.235*sec* and 0.287*sec*, respectively. Thus, the *ESRA* algorithm is able to drastically reduce the time cost of clustering query results.

Qualitative Analysis
Due to the difficulty of conducting a large-scale[xix] real-life user study, we discuss the effectiveness of the *ESRA* algorithm based on structural properties of results provided to the end-user. It is worth notic-

Figure 20. Time cost comparison

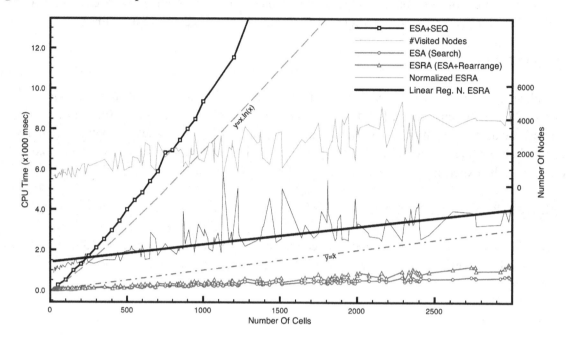

ing that the end-user benefit is proportional to the number of items (clusters or tuples) the user needs to examine at any time as well as to the dissimilarity between these items.

We define the 'Compression Rate' (*CR*) as the ratio of the number of clusters (summaries) returned as a starting point for an online exploration over the total number of cells covered by such summaries. Note that *CR* = 1 means no compression at all, whereas smaller values represent higher compression. As expected, Figure 21 shows that *CR* values of *ESRA* and *ESA+SEQ* are quite similar and much smaller than that of *ESA*. Thus, size reduction is clearly achieved by the *ESRA* algorithm.

We could also see that the dissimilarity (Figure 22) of the first partitioning that *ESRA* presents to the end-user is greater than that of *ESA* and is in the same order of magnitude than that provided by *ESA+SEQ*. It means that *ESRA* significantly improves discrimination between items when compared against *ESA* and is as effective as the post-clustering approach *ESA+SEQ*. Furthermore, the dissimilarity of the *ESA* result is quite similar to that of the most specialized partitioning, i.e., the set of cells. Thus the rearranging process is highly required to provide the end-user with well-founded clusters.

Now assume that the user decides to explore a summary z returned by *ESRA*. We want to examine the number of hops *NoH* (i.e., the number of SHOWTUPLES/SHOWCAT operations) the user might employ to reach a relevant tuple. *NoH* ranges from 1 up to $d_z + 1$, where d_z is the height of the tree rooted by z (i.e., subtree H_z). The best case (*NoH* = 1) occurs when z exactly fits the user's need, whereas the worst case (*NoH* = d_z + 1) occurs when the relevant information is reached by following a path of maximal length in H_z. Note that these two scenarios are on opposite extremes of the spectrum of possible situations: the generalized case ($0 \leq NoH \leq d_z + 1$) is that the user's need is successfully served by a node at height h such that $0 \leq h \leq d_z$.

In the following experiment (Figure 23), one considers a user query q with selectivity of η, i.e., the number of tuples returned by q divided by the total number of tuples in the database (33735). We look for all the possible summaries (subtrees) in the pre-computed summary hierarchy that can be returned

Figure 21. Compression rate comparison

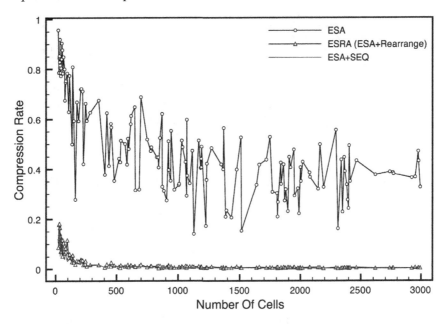

Figure 22. Dissimilarity comparison

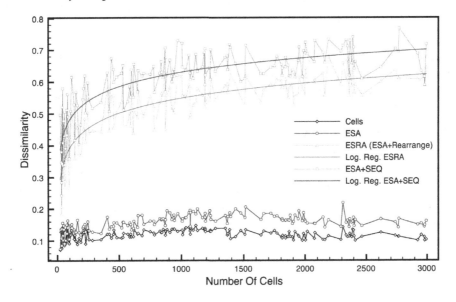

as the result of q and, for each one, we compute its maximum depth, its average depth and the average length of all paths emanating from that node (summary). Then, we pick out the highest (maximum) value observed for each of these measures. The three values obtained, for each value of η (η {0.2%, 0.4% … 2%}), evaluate respectively:

1. the worst number of hops required to reach the deepest leaf node (*Worst NoH2C*) containing relevant data;

Figure 23. The number of SHOWTUPLES/SHOWCAT operations

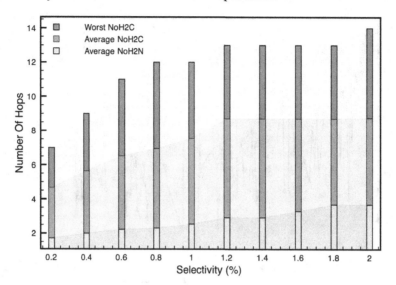

2. the average number of hops needed to reach any leaf node (*Average NoH2C*) containing relevant data (i.e., not necessarily the deepest one);

3. the average number of hops required to reach any node (*Average NoH2N*) containing relevant data (i.e., not necessarily a leaf node).

Figure 23shows that the *Worst NoH2C* and the *Average NoH2C* are relatively high, but bounded respectively by the maximum (16) and the average (10.177) depth of the pre-computed tree. It is worth noticing that, in real life situation, the user finds out that her/his need has been successfully served by an inner node of the tree rooted by *z*. Thus, the *Average NoH2N* is more adapted to evaluating the effectiveness of our approach (*ESRA*). As one can observe, the *Average NoH2N* is quite small given the number of tuples in the *q* result set. For instance, *NoH2N* = 3.68 is the number of hops the user takes to reach relevant information within a set of 674 tuples (η = 2).Those experimental results validate the claim of this work, that is to say the *ESRA* algorithm is very efficient (Figure 20) and provides useful clusters of query results (Figure 21 and Figure 22) and consequently, makes the exploration process more effective (Figure 23).

4. CONCLUSION

Interactive and exploratory data retrieval are more and more suitable to database systems. Indeed, regular 'blind' queries often retrieve too many answers. Users then need to spend time sifting and sorting through this information to find relevant data.

In this chapter, we proposed an efficient and effective algorithm coined Explore-Select-Rearrange Algorithm (*ESRA*) that uses database SAINTETIQ summaries to quickly provide users with concise, useful and structured representations of their query results. Given a user query, *ESRA* (i) explores the summary hierarchy (computed offline using SAINTETIQ) of the whole data stored in the database;

(ii) selects the most relevant summaries to that query; (iii) rearranges them in a hierarchical structure based on the structure of the pre-computed summary hierarchy and (iv) returns the resulting hierarchy to the user. Each node (or summary) of the resulting hierarchy describes a subset of the result set in a user-friendly form using linguistic labels. The user then navigates through this hierarchy structure in a top-down fashion, exploring the summaries of interest while ignoring the rest.

Experimental results showed that the *ESRA* algorithm is efficient and provides well-formed (tight and clearly separated) and well-organized clusters of query results. Thus, it is very helpful to users who have vague and poorly defined retrieval goals or are interested in browsing through a set of items to explore what choices are available.

REFERENCES

Agrawal, R., Mannila, H., Srikant, R., Toivonen, H. & Verkamo, A.I. (1996). Fast discovery of association rules. *Advances in Knowledge Discovery and Data Mining*, 307-328.Allen, D. (1992). Managing infoglut. *BYTE magazine, 17*(6), 16.

Agrawal, R. & Wimmers, E.L. (2000). *A framework for expressing and combining preferences.*

Agrawal, S., Chaudhuri, S., & Das, G. (2002). Dbxplorer: enabling keyword search over relational databases. *Proceedings of the ACM SIGMOD international conference on Management of data*, (pp. 627-627).

Ashcraft, M. (1994). *Human memory and cognition*. Addison-Wesley Pub Co.

Bamba, B., Roy, P., & Mohania, M. (2005). OSQR: Overlapping clustering of query results. *Proceedings of the 14th ACM international conference on Information and knowledge management*, (pp. 239-240).

Bergman, M. K. (2001). The deep Web: Surfacing hidden value. *Journal of Electronic Publishing, 7*(1). doi:10.3998/3336451.0007.104

Berkhin, P. (2006). A survey of clustering data mining techniques. In Kogan, J., Nicholas, C., & Teboulle, M. (Eds.), *Grouping multidimensional data: Recent advances in clustering* (pp. 25–71). doi:10.1007/3-540-28349-8_2

Bhalotia, G., Hulgeri, A., Nakhe, C., Chakrabarti, S., & Sudarshan, S. (2002). Keyword searching and browsing in databases using banks. *Proceedings of the International Conference on Data Engineering*, (pp. 431-440).

Bharat, K., & Henzinger, M. R. (1998). Improved algorithms for topic distillation in a hyperlinked environment. *Proceedings of the International Conference on Research and development in information retrieval*, (pp. 104–111).

Borodin, A., Roberts, G. O., Rosenthal, J. S., & Tsaparas, P. (2001). Finding authorities and hubs from link structures on the World Wide Web. *Proceedings of the International Conference on World Wide Web*, (pp. 415-429).

Bosc, P., & Pivert, O. (1992). Fuzzy querying in conventional databases. In *Fuzzy logic for the management of uncertainty*. (pp. 645-671).

Bosc, P., & Pivert, O. (1995). Sqlf: A relational database language for fuzzy querying. *IEEE Transactions on Fuzzy Systems, 3*, 1–17. doi:10.1109/91.366566

Bosc, P., & Pivert, O. (1997). Fuzzy queries against regular and fuzzy databases. In *Flexible query answering systems*. (pp. 187-208).

Bosc, P., Pivert, O. & Rocacher, D. (2007). *About quotient and division of crisp and fuzzy relations.*

Bouchon-Meunier, B., Rifqi, M., & Bothorel, S. (1996). Towards general measures of comparison of objects. *Fuzzy Sets and Systems, 84*(2), 143–153. doi:10.1016/0165-0114(96)00067-X

Brin, S. & Page, L. (1998). The anatomy of a large-scale hypertextual Web search engine. *Computer Networks and ISDN Systems, 30*(1-7), 107-117.

Callan, J. P., Croft, W. B., & Harding, S. M. (1992). The inquery retrieval system. *Proceedings of the Third International Conference on Database and Expert Systems Applications*, (pp. 78–83).

Chakrabarti, K., Chaudhuri, S., & Hwang, S. W. (2004). Automatic categorization of query results. *Proceedings of the ACM SIGMOD International Conference on Management of Data*, (pp. 755-766).

Chang, K. C. C., He, B., Li, C., Patel, M., & Zhang, Z. (2004). Structured databases on the Web: Observations and implications. *Proceedings of the ACM SIGMOD International Conference on Management of Data, 33*(3), 61-70.Chaudhuri, S. & Das, G. (2003). *Automated ranking of database query results.* In CIDR, (pp. 888-899).

Chaudhuri, S., Das, G., Hristidis, V., & Weikum, G. (2004). Probabilistic ranking of database query results. *Proceedings of the Thirtieth international conference on Very Large Data Bases*, (pp. 888-899).

Cheng, D., Kannan, R., Vempala, S., & Wang, G. (2006). A divide-and-merge methodology for clustering. *ACM Transactions on Database Systems, 31*(4), 1499–1525. doi:10.1145/1189769.1189779

Chomicki, J. (2002). Querying with intrinsic preferences. *Proceedings of the 8th International Conference on Extending Database Technology*, (pp. 34-51).

Chomicki, J. (2003). Preference formulas in relational queries. *ACM Transactions on Database Systems, 28*(4), 427–466. doi:10.1145/958942.958946

Christian, B., Stefan, B., & Daniel, A. K. (2001). Searching in high-dimensional spaces: Index structures for improving the performance of multimedia databases. *ACM Computing Surveys, 33*(3), 322–373. doi:10.1145/502807.502809

Chu, W. W., Yang, H., Chiang, K., Minock, M., Chow, G., & Larson, L. (1996). Cobase: A scalable and extensible cooperative information system. *Journal of Intelligent Information Systems, 6*(2-3), 223–259. doi:10.1007/BF00122129

Collins, A., & Quillian, M. (1969). Retrieval time from semantic memory. *Journal of Verbal Learning and Verbal Behavior, 8*(2), 240-247.Croft, W.B. (1980). A model of cluster searching based on classification. *Information Systems, 5*, 189–195.

Duda, R. O., Hart, P. E., & Stork, D. G. (2000). *Pattern classification* (2nd ed.). Wiley-Interscience.

Fagin, R., Lotem, A., & Naor, M. (2001). Optimal aggregation algorithms for middleware. *Proceedings of the Twentieth ACM SIGMOD-SIGACT-SIGART Symposium on Principles of Database Systems*, (pp. 102-113).

Ferragina, P., & Gulli, A. (2005). A *personalized search engine based on Web-snippet hierarchical clustering.* Special interest tracks and posters of the 14th International Conference on World Wide Web, (pp. 801-810).

Fisher, D. H. (1987). Knowledge acquisition via incremental conceptual clustering. *Machine Learning, 2*(2), 139–172. doi:10.1007/BF00114265

Gaasterland, T., Godfrey, P., & Minker, J. (1994). An overview of cooperative answering. In *Nonstandard queries and nonstandard answers: studies in logic and computation* (pp. 1–40). Oxford: Oxford University Press.

Galindo, J. (2008). *Handbook of research on fuzzy information processing in databases.* Hershey, PA: Information Science Reference.

Godfrey, P. (1997). Minimization in cooperative response to failing database queries. *IJCIS, 6*(2), 95–149.

Güntzer, U., Balke, W. T., & Kießling, W. (2000). Optimizing multi-feature queries for image databases. *Proceedings of the 26th International Conference on Very Large Data Bases*, (pp. 419-428).

Halford, G. S., Baker, R., McCredden, J. E., & Bain, J. D. (2005). How many variables can humans process? *Psychological Science, 15*, 70–76. doi:10.1111/j.0956-7976.2005.00782.x

Hartigan, J. A., & Wong, M. A. (1979). A K-means clustering algorithm. *Applied Statistics, 28*, 100–108. doi:10.2307/2346830

Hastie, T., Tibshirani, R., & Friedman, J. H. (2001). *The elements of statistical learning.* Springer.

Hearst, M. A., & Pedersen, J. O. (1996). Reexamining the cluster-hypothesis: Scatter/gather on retrieval results. *Proceedings of the 19th annual international ACM SIGIR conference on Research and development in information retrieval*, (pp. 76-84).

Hristidis, V., & Papakonstantinou, Y. (2002). Discover: Keyword search in relational databases. *Proceedings of the International Conference on Very Large Data Bases*, (pp. 670-681).

Ichikawa, T., & Hirakawa, M. (1986). Ares: A relational database with the capability of performing flexible interpretation of queries. *IEEE Transactions on Software Engineering, 12*(5), 624–634.

Ilyas, I. F., Beskales, G., & Soliman, M. A. (2008). A survey of top-k query processing techniques in relational database systems. *ACM Computing Surveys, 40*(4), 1–58. doi:10.1145/1391729.1391730

Jain, A. K., Murty, M. N., & Flynn, P. J. (1999). Data clustering: A review. *ACM Computing Surveys, 31*(3), 264–323. doi:10.1145/331499.331504

Jardine, N. & Van Rijsbergen, C.J. (1971). *The use of hierarchical clustering in information retrieval.*

Kaplan, S. J. (1983). Cooperative responses from a portable natural language database query system. In Brady, M., & Berwick, R. C. (Eds.), *Computational models of discourse* (pp. 167–208). Cambridge, MA: MIT Press.

Kapoor, N., Das, G., Hristidis, V., Sudarshan, S., & Weikum, G. (2007). Star: A system for tuple and attribute ranking of query answers. *Proceedings of the International Conference on Data Engineering*, (pp. 1483-1484).

Kevin, S. B., Jonathan, G., Raghu, R., & Uri, S. (1999). Nearest neighbor queries When is nearest neighbor meaningful? *Proceedings of the International Conference on Database Theory*, (pp. 217-235).

Kießling, W. (2002). Foundations of preferences in database systems. *Proceedings of the 28th International Conference on Very Large Data Bases*, (pp. 311-322).

Kleinberg, J. M. (1999). Authoritative sources in a hyperlinked environment. *Journal of the ACM, 46*(5), 604–632. doi:10.1145/324133.324140

Klement, E. P., Mesiar, R., & Pap, E. (2000). *Triangular norms*. Kluwer Academic Publishers.

Kostadinov, D., Bouzeghoub, M., & Lopes, S. (2007). *Query rewriting based on user's profile knowledge. Bases de Données Avancées*. BDA.

Koutrika, G., & Ioannidis, Y. (2005). A unified user profile framework for query disambiguation and personalization. *Proceedings of Workshop on New Technologies for Personalized Information Access*, (pp. 44-53).

Lacroix, M., & Lavency, P. (1987). Preferences: Putting more knowledge into queries. *Proceedings of the 13th International Conference on Very Large Data Bases*, (pp. 217-225).

Lewis, D. (1996). Dying for information: An investigation into the effects of information overload in the usa and worldwide. *Reuters Limited*. Li, C., Wang, M., Lim, L., Wang, H. & Chang, K.C.C. (2007). Supporting ranking and clustering as generalized order-by and group-by. *Proceedings of the ACM SIGMOD International Conference on Management of data*, (pp. 127-138).

MacArthur, S. D., Brodley, C. E., Ka, A. C., & Broderick, L. S. (2002). Interactive content-based image retrieval using relevance feedback. *Computer Vision and Image Understanding, 88*(2), 55–75. doi:10.1006/cviu.2002.0977

Maimon, O. & Rokach, L. (2005). *The data mining and knowledge discovery handbook*.

Mandler, G. (1967). Organization in memory. In Spense, K. W., & Spense, J. T. (Eds.), *The psychology of learning and motivation* (pp. 327–372). Academic Press.

Manning, C. D., Raghavan, P., & Schtze, H. (2008). *Introduction to information retrieval*. USA: Cambridge University Press.

Miller, G. A. (1956). The magical number seven, plus or minus two: Some limits on our capacity for processing information. *Psychological Review, 63*, 81–97. doi:10.1037/h0043158

Miller, G. A. (1962). Information input overload. In M.C. Yovits, G.T. Jacobi, and G.D. Goldstein, (Eds.), *Conference on Self-Organizing Systems*. Spartan Books.

Moshé, M. Z. (1975). Query-by-example: The invocation and definition of tables and forms. *Proceedings of the ACM SIGMOD international conference on Very Large Data Bases,* (pp. 1-24).

Motro, A. (1986). Seave: A mechanism for verifying user presuppositions in query systems. *ACM Transactions on Information Systems, 4*(4), 312–330. doi:10.1145/9760.9762

Motro, A. (1988). Vague: A user interface to relational databases that permits vague queries. *ACM Transactions on Information Systems, 6*(3), 187–214. doi:10.1145/45945.48027

Muslea, I. (2004). Machine learning for online query relaxation. *Proceedings of the International Conference on Knowledge discovery and data mining,* (pp. 246-255).

Muslea, I., & Lee, T. (2005). Online query relaxation via Bayesian causal structures discovery. *Proceedings of the National Conference on Artificial Intelligence,* (pp. 831-836).

Nambiar, U. (2005). *Answering imprecise queries over autonomous databases.* Unpublished doctoral dissertation, University of Arizona, USA.

Nambiar, U., & Kambhampati, S. (2003). Answering imprecise database queries: a novel approach. *Proceedings of the International Workshop on Web Information and Data Management,* (pp. 126-133).

Nambiar, U., & Kambhampati, S. (2004). Mining approximate functional dependencies and concept similarities to answer imprecise queries. *Proceedings of the International Workshop on the Web and Databases,* (pp. 73-78).

Nepal, S., & Ramakrishna, M. V. (1999). Query processing issues in image (multimedia) databases. *Proceedings of the 15th International Conference on Data Engineering,* (pp. 23-26).

Ng, A. Y., Zheng, A. X., & Jordan, M. I. (2001). Stable algorithms for link analysis. *Proceedings of the International ACM SIGIR Conference on Research and Development in Information Retrieval,* (pp. 258-266).

Nielsen, J. (2003). Curmudgeon: IM, not IP (information pollution). *ACM Queue; Tomorrow's Computing Today, 1*(8), 76–75. doi:10.1145/966712.966731

Quillian, M. R. (1968). Semantic memory. In Minsky, M. (Ed.), *Semantic information processing* (pp. 227–270). The MIT Press.

Raschia, G., & Mouaddib, N. (2002). SAINTETIQ: A fuzzy set-based approach to database summarization. *Fuzzy Sets and Systems, 129*(2), 137–162. doi:10.1016/S0165-0114(01)00197-X

Robertson, S. E. (1997). The probability ranking principle in IR. *Readings in Information Retrieval,* 281–286.Roussopoulos, N., Kelley, S. & Vincent, F. (2003). Nearest neighbor queries. *Proceedings of the ACM SIGMOD International Conference on Management of Data,* (pp. 71-79).

Ruspini, E. (1969). A new approach to clustering. *Information and Control, 15,* 22–32. doi:10.1016/S0019-9958(69)90591-9

Saint-Paul, R., Raschia, G., & Mouaddib, N. (2005). General purpose database summarization. *Proceedings of the International Conference on Very Large Data Bases,* (pp. 733-744).

Salton, G., & McGill, M. J. (1986). *Introduction to modern information retrieval.* USA: McGraw-Hill, Inc.

Schikuta, E., & Erhart, M. (1998). Bang-clustering: A novel grid-clustering algorithm for huge data sets. *Proceedings of the Joint IAPR International Workshops on Advances in Pattern Recognition,* (pp. 867-874).

Schultz, U., & Vandenbosch, B. (1998). Information overload in a groupware environment: Now you see it, now you don't. *Journal of Organizational Computing and Electronic Commerce, 8*(2), 127–148. doi:10.1207/s15327744joce0802_3

Sheikholeslami, G., Chatterjee, S., & Zhang, A. (2000). Wavecluster: A wavelet-based clustering approach for spatial data in very large databases. *The VLDB Journal, 8*(3-4), 289–304. doi:10.1007/s007780050009

Shenk, D. (1997). *Data smog: Surviving the information glut.* HarperCollins Publishers.

Simon, H. A. (1974). How big is a chunk? *Science, 183,* 482–488. doi:10.1126/science.183.4124.482

Su, W., Wang, J., Huang, Q., & Lochovsky, F. (2006). Query result ranking over e-commerce Web databases. *Proceedings of the International Conference on Information and Knowledge Management,* (pp. 575-584).

Tahani, V. (1977). A conceptual framework for fuzzy query processing: A step toward very intelligent database systems. *Information Processing & Management, 13,* 289–303. doi:10.1016/0306-4573(77)90018-8

Van Rijsbergen, C. J., & Croft, W. B. (1975). Document clustering: An evaluation of some experiments with the Cranfield 1400 collection. *Information Processing & Management, 11*(5-7), 171–182. doi:10.1016/0306-4573(75)90006-0

Volker, G., & Oliver, G. (1998). Multidimensional access methods. *ACM Computing Surveys, 30*(2), 170–231. doi:10.1145/280277.280279

Voorhees, E. M. (1985). The cluster hypothesis revisited. *Proceedings of the 8th Annual International ACM SIGIR Conference on Research and Development in Information Retrieval,* (pp. 188-196).

Wang, W., Yang, J., & Muntz, R. R. (1997). STING: A statistical information grid approach to spatial data mining. *Proceedings of the International Conference on Very Large Data Bases,* (pp. 186-195).

Weil, M. M., & Rosen, L. D. (1997). *TechnoStress: Coping with technology work home play.* John Wiley and Sons.

Winkle, W.V. (1998). Information overload: Fighting data asphyxiation is difficult but possible. *Computer Bits magazine, 8*(2).

Wu, L., Faloutsos, C., Sycara, K. P., & Payne, T. R. (2000). Falcon: Feedback adaptive loop for content-based retrieval. *Proceedings of the International Conference on Very Large Data Bases,* (pp. 297-306).

Zadeh, L. A. (1956). Fuzzy sets. *Information and Control, 8*, 338–353. doi:10.1016/S0019-9958(65)90241-X

Zadeh, L. A. (1975). Concept of a linguistic variable and its application to approximate reasoning. *Information Systems, 1*, 119–249.

Zadeh, L. A. (1999). Fuzzy sets as a basis for a theory of possibility. *Fuzzy Sets and Systems, 100*, 9–34. doi:10.1016/S0165-0114(99)80004-9

Zadrozny, S., & Kacprzyk, J. (1996). Fquery for access: Towards human consistent querying user interface. *Proceedings of the ACM Symposium on Applied Computing*, (pp. 532-536).

Zamir, O., & Etzioni, O. (1999). Grouper: A dynamic clustering interface to Web search results. *Proceedings of the Eighth International Conference on World Wide Web*, (pp. 1361-1374).

Zeng, H. J., He, Q. C., Chen, Z., Ma, W. Y., & Ma, J. (2004). Learning to cluster Web search results. *Proceedings of the 27th Annual International ACM SIGIR Conference on Research and Development in Information Retrieval*, (pp. 210-217).

ENDNOTES

[i] A COOPerative Query System.

[ii] Supposition Extraction And VErification.

[iii] A Cooperative DataBase System.

[iv] Associative Information REtrieval System.

[v] A User Interface to Relational Databases that Permits VAGUE Queries.

[vi] Imprecise Query Engine.

[vii] http://www.google.com

[viii] Hyperlink-Induced Topic Search.

[ix] In the case of information retrieval, ranking functions are often based on the frequency of occurrence of query values in documents (term frequency, or *tf*). However, in the database context, *tf* is irrelevant as tuples either contain or do not contain a query value. Hence ranking functions need to consider values of unspecified attributes.

[x] Probabilistic Information Retrieval.

[xi] Query Result Ranking for E-commerce.

[xii] In information retrieval systems, the information need is what the user desires to know from the stored data, to satisfy some intended objective (e.g., data analysis, decision making). However, the query is what the user submits to the system in an attempt to fulfill that information need.

[xiii] Overlapping cluStering of Query Results.

[xiv] Fuzzy sets can be defined in either discrete or continuous universes.

[xv] Browsing ANd Keyword Searching.

[xvi] A degree of a node is the number of edges incident to this node.

[xvii] The intuition is that a node that has many links with others has relative small possibility of having a close relationship to any of them, and thus edges incident on it have large weights.

^{xviii} http://trec.nist.gov

^{xix} A potential problem with real-user evaluation techniques is that users' opinions are very subjective. Hence, even if we obtain positive feedback from a small set of test users, we cannot be more convinced and affirmative about the effectiveness of our approach.

Chapter 3
Concept–Oriented Query Language for Data Modeling and Analysis

Alexandr Savinov
SAP Research Center Dresden, Germany

ABSTRACT

This chapter describes a novel query language, called the concept-oriented query language (COQL), and demonstrates how it can be used for data modeling and analysis. The query language is based on a novel construct, called concept, and two relations between concepts, inclusion and partial order. Concepts generalize conventional classes and are used for describing domain-specific identities. Inclusion relation generalizes inheritance and is used for describing hierarchical address spaces. Partial order among concepts is used to define two main operations: projection and de-projection. This chapter demonstrates how these constructs are used to solve typical tasks in data modeling and analysis such as logical navigation, multidimensional analysis, and inference.

INTRODUCTION

A model is a mathematical description of a world aspect and a data model provides means for data organization in the form of some structural principles. These structural principles are used to break all elements into smaller groups making access to and manipulation of data more efficient for end-users and applications. The concept-oriented model (COM) is a novel general-purpose approach to data model-

DOI: 10.4018/978-1-60960-475-2.ch003

ing (Savinov, 2009a) which is intended to solve a wide spectrum of problems by reducing them to the following three structural principles distinguishing it from other data models:

- **Duality principle** answers the question *how* elements exist by assuming that any element is a *couple* of one identity and one entity (called also reference and object, respectively)
- **Inclusion principle** answers the question *where* elements exist by postulating that any element is *included* in some domain (called also scope or context)
- **Order principle** answers the question what an element *is*, that is, how it is defined and what is its meaning by assuming that all elements are partially ordered so that any element has a number of greater and lesser elements

Formally, the concept-oriented model is described using a formalism of nested partially ordered sets. The syntactic embodiment of this model is the concept-oriented query language (COQL). This language reflects the principles of COM by introducing a novel data modeling construct, called *concept* (hence the name of the approach), and two relations among concepts, *inclusion* and *partial order*. Concepts are intended to generalize conventional classes and inclusion generalizes inheritance. Concepts and inclusion are used also in a novel approach to programming, called concept-oriented programming (COP) (Savinov, 2008, 2009b). Partial order relation among concepts is intended to represent data semantics and is used for complex analytical tasks and reasoning about data.

The concept-oriented model and query language are aimed at solving several general problems which are difficult to solve using traditional approaches. In particular, the following factors motivated this work:

- **Domain-specific identities.** In most existing data models elements are represented either by *plat-form-specific* references like oids or by weak identities based on entity properties like primary keys. These approaches do not provide a mechanism for defining strong *domain-specific* identities with arbitrary structure. Concepts solve this problem by making it possible to describe *both* identities and entities using only one common construct. This produces nice symmetry between two branches: identity modeling and entity modeling.
- **Hierarchical address spaces.** Elements cannot exist outside of any space, domain or context but existing data models do not support this abstraction as a core notion of the model. A typical solution consists in modeling spaces and containment like any other domain-specific relationship. The principled solution proposed in COM is that all elements are supposed to exist within a hierarchy where a parent is a space, context, scope or domain for its child elements. Thus inclusion relation between concepts turns an element into a set of its child elements. Since identities of internal elements are defined relative to the space they are in, we simultaneously get a hierarchical address space for the elements. Each element within this hierarchy is identified by a domain-specific hierarchical address like a conventional postal address.
- **Multidimensionality.** Dimension is one of the fundamental constructs which is used to represent information in various areas of human knowledge. There exist numerous approaches to multidimensional modeling which are intended for analytical processing. The problem is that there exist different models for analytical and transactional processing which rely on different assumptions and techniques. The goal of COM in this context is to rethink dimensions as a first-class construct of the data model which plays a primary role for describing both transactional and analytical aspects. Data should be represented as originally existing in a multidimensional space and dimension should be used in most operations with data.

- **Semantics.** The lack of semantic description in traditional approaches to data modeling is a strong limiting factor for the effective use of data and this significantly decreases its value including possibility of information exchange, integration, consistency, interoperability and many other functions. Semantics in databases "should enable it to respond to queries and other transactions in a more intelligent manner" (Codd, 1979). Currently, semantics is supposed to exist at conceptual level while logical data models have rather limited possibilities for representing semantic relationships. In this context, the goal of COM is to make semantics integral part of the logical data model so that the database can be directly used for reasoning about data. To reach this goal, COM makes a principled assumption that database is a *partially ordered set* (as opposed to a set without any structure). Partial order is supposed to be represented by references which are used as an elementary semantic construct in COM.

CONCEPT-ORIENTED MODEL

The smallest unit of data in COM is a *primitive value* like integer or text string. They are normally provided by DBMS and therefore their structure is not part of the model. More complex elements are produced by means of *tuples* which are treated in their common mathematical sense as a combination of primitive values or other tuples. Each member of a tuple has its unique position which is referred to as a *dimension*. If $e=(x=a,y=b,z=c,\dots)$ is a tuple then x, y and z are dimensions while a, b and c are members of this tuple. According to the duality principle, an element in COM is defined as a couple of two tuples: identity tuple and entity tuple. Identity tuples are values which are passed by-copy while entity tuples are passed by-reference. Identity tuples are used as locations or addresses for entity tuples. If tuple a is a member within tuple b then only identity part of a is included by-value in b. It is assumed that it is always possible to access entity tuple if its identity tuple is available. In terms of conventional computer memory, identity tuple has the structure of memory addresses and entity tuple has the structure of memory cells.

Inclusion principle in COM is implemented via *extension operator* denoted by semicolon. If a and b are two elements then $e=a{:}b$ is a new element where a is a base and b is an extension (so b is said to extend a). It is analogous to object-oriented extension with the difference that this operation is applied to couples of identity-entity tuples rather than to individual tuples. If entity tuple is empty then this operation can be used to extend values and model value domains. If identity tuple is empty then it is used to extend objects or records. With the help of extension any element can be represented as a sequence of couples starting from some common root element and ending with the last extension. Extension operator induces *strict inclusion relation* $\subset$ among elements by assuming that extended element is included in its base element, that is, if $e=a{:}b$ then $a{\subset}e$. All elements from set R in this case are represented as a nested set $(R,\subset)$ where parents are referred to as *super-elements* and children (extended elements) are referred to as *sub-elements*. Inclusion relation among elements is analogous to the nested structure of elements in XML.

According to the order principle, elements in COM are (strictly) partially ordered by assuming that a tuple is less than any of its members, that is, if $e=(\dots,a,\dots)$ is a tuple then $e<a$. All elements of set R in this case are represented as a partially ordered set $(R,<)$. If $a<b$ then a is said to be a *lesser* element and b is referred to as a *greater* element. In particular, this assumption means that a tuple cannot have itself as a member directly or indirectly, that is, cycles are prohibited. According to the duality principles,

tuple members are represented by storing identities which correspond to conventional object references. Hence this principle means that object references represent greater elements.

Inclusion and partial order relations are connected using *type constraint*:

$e \subset b \vdash ex \subseteq bx$

In terms of the extension operator it can be equivalently written as follows:

$b:e \vdash (bx):(ex)$

This condition means that if an element sets some value for its dimension then its extensions are permitted to extend this value using this same dimension but they cannot set arbitrary value for it.

A concept-oriented database is formally defined as a *nested partially ordered set* $(R, \subset, <)$ where elements are identity-entity couples and strict inclusion and strict partial order relations satisfy type constraint. This structure can be produced from a partially ordered set if we assume that an element can itself be a partially ordered set. Alternatively, it can be produced from a nested set if we assume that its elements are partially ordered. An example of a nested partially set is shown in Figure 1. Nested structure spreads horizontally while partially ordered structure spreads vertically. For example, element *a* consists of elements *b* and *c* which are its extensions. Simultaneously, element *a* has two greater elements *f* and *d*.

MODELING IDENTITIES

Object identity is an essential part of any programming and data model. Although the role of identities has never been underestimated (Khoshafian et al, 1986; Wieringa et al, 1995; Abiteboul et al, 1998; Kent, 1991; Eliassen et al, 1991), there exists a very strong bias towards modeling entities. There is a

Figure 1. Nested partially ordered set

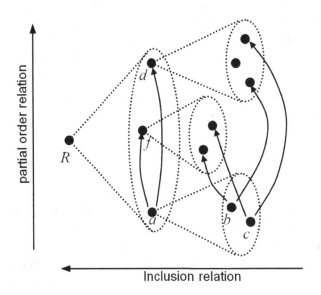

very old and very strong belief that it is entity that should be in the focus of a programming and data model while identities simply serve entities. As a consequence, there is a strong asymmetry between entities and identities in traditional approaches to data modeling: entities have *domain-specific* structure while identities have *platform-specific* structure. Accordingly, classes are used to model domain-specific structure and behavior of entities while identities are provided by the underlying environment with some built-in platform-specific structure.

The concept-oriented model treats entities and identities symmetrically so that *both* of them may have arbitrary domain-specific structure and behavior. More specifically, it is assumed that *any element is a couple consisting of one identity and one entity*. To model such identity-entity couples, a new construct is introduced, called *concept*. Concept is defined as a *couple* of two classes: one identity class and one entity class. Concept fields are referred to as *dimensions* in COM. This produces a nice yin-yang style of balance and symmetry between two orthogonal branches – identity modeling and entity modeling. If traditional approaches use classes to model entities then COQL uses concepts to model identity-entity couples. The shift of paradigm is that things (data elements) are *couples* and identities are made explicit part of the model. Informally, elements in COM can be thought of as complex numbers in mathematics which also have two constituents manipulated as one whole.

Identity is an observable part which is manipulated directly in its original form. It is passed by-value (by-copy) and does not have its own separate representative. Entity can be viewed as a thing-in-itself or reality which is radically unknowable and not observable in its original form. The only way to do something with an entity consists in using its identity as an intermediate. This means that there is no other way to access an entity rather than using its reference.

Entities are persistent *objects* while identities are transient *values* which are used to represent and access objects. In most cases identities are immutable and cannot be changed over the whole lifetime of the represented entity while entities are supposed to be mutable so that their properties reflect the current state of the problem domain. The entity itself is then considered a kind of a point in space while its reference is thought of as a coordinate. It is important to note that references in COM are abstract addresses from a virtual address space. Therefore the represented object can actually reside anywhere in the world (not even necessarily in a computer system). References in COM (just as values) are *domain-specific* because they are designed taking into account properties and requirements of the application being created. In contrast, references in most existing models are *platform-specific* because they are provided by the compiler taking into account the available run-time environment.

If identity class of a concept is empty then this concept is equivalent to conventional class which is used for describing objects. In this case entities are supposed to be represented by some platform-specific reference. If entity class is empty then this concept describes a type of values (value domain). Values are very important notion in data modeling because they are considered terminal elements for any model. Essentially, values are what any model or computation is about. Values are characterized by the following properties: they are immutable, passed by-copy, do not have their own reference. Values are used in modeling because they have some meaning which can be passed to other elements, stored, retrieved or computed. An example of a primitive value is an integer number which could represent city population or a double number which could represent the quantity of some resource. A complex system requires complex value types which are made of simpler types and it is precisely where concepts (with empty entity class) are intended to be used. For example, the following concept describes amount in some currency (like USD or EUR) as a value:

```
CONCEPT Amount
  IDENTITY
    DOUBLE amount
    CHAR(3) currency
  ENTITY // Empty
```

If both constituents of a concept are non-empty then identity class describes references for representing its objects. For example, let us assume that we need to model bank accounts. In this problem domain any bank account is identified by an account number and characterized by its current balance and owner. The existence of domain-specific identity and entity is easily described by means of the following concept:

```
CONCEPT Account
  IDENTITY
    CHAR(10) accNo
  ENTITY
    Amount balance
    Person owner
```

Each instance of this concept will be a pair of account reference identifying this element and account object consisting of two fields. Variables of this concept will store account numbers which identify the corresponding account objects. Account owners can be modeled using the following concept:

```
CONCEPT Person
  IDENTITY
    CHAR(11) ssn
  ENTITY
    CHAR(11) name
    Date dob
```

The difference from the relational model (Codd, 1970) is that concept dimensions contain the whole identity of the referenced element treated as one value. The difference from object data models (Dittrich, 1986; Bancilhon, 1996) is that identities may have arbitrary domain-specific structure. And the general specific feature of this approach is that both identities and entities are modeled together within one data modeling construct.

MODELING HIERARCHIES

Any element must have some identity which manifests the fact of its existence. But if something exists then there has to be some space to which it belongs, that is, elements are not able to exist outside of any space. In COM, existence within space means that the element is identified relative to this space. Space is a normal element of the model and all elements exist within a hierarchy where a child is said to be *included* in its parent interpreted as a space, scope, context or domain. Parents in the inclusion hierarchy are said to be super-elements while their children are called sub-elements. Parent element is also referred to as a domain, scope or context for its children.

To model a hierarchy of elements, COQL introduces a special relation among concepts, called *inclusion*. For example, assume that concept Savings describing savings accounts is included in concept Account:

```
CONCEPT Savings IN Account
  IDENTITY
    CHAR(2) savAccNo
  ENTITY
    Amount balance
```

This declaration means that instances of the Savings concept will be identified by two digits within an instance of the Account concept. Any reference to a savings account consists of two segments: main account number and relative savings account number. An account in this case is a set of savings accounts which are all distinguished within this main context by means of their relative identifier. The most important difference from inheritance is that one parent may have many children. In contrast, if Savings were a class inheriting from class Account then any new instance of Savings would get its own account. Thus the advantage of concepts is that they allow us to describe a hierarchy where one account may contain many sub-accounts which in turn may have their own child objects. This hierarchy is analogous to conventional postal addresses where one country has many cities and one city has many streets so that any destination has a unique hierarchical address. Inclusion is also analogous to element nesting in XML where any element may have many child elements.

An important property of inclusion is that it is equivalent to inheritance under certain simplifying conditions and this is why we say that inclusion generalizes inheritance. Namely, inclusion relation is reduced to conventional inheritance if identity class of the child concept is empty. In this case only one child can be created and this child shares identity with its parent. For example, if concept Special describing accounts with special privileges has no identity and is included in concept Savings then effectively it extends the parent concept and behaves like a normal class:

```
CONCEPT Special IN Savings
  IDENTITY // Empty
  ENTITY
    INT privileges
```

This compatibility allows us to make smooth transition from classical inheritance to more powerful inclusion which is a novel, more general, treatment of what inheritance is. In concept-oriented terms, to inherit something means to be included into it and to have it as a domain, scope or context.

Inheritance is one of the corner stones of object data models but it has one problem: classes exist as a hierarchy while their instances exist in flat space. Indeed, parent classes are shared parts of the child classes while parent objects are allocated for each new child and all objects have the same type of identity. Concepts and inclusion eliminate this asymmetry so that both concepts and their instances exist within a hierarchy.

Having object hierarchy is very important in data modeling because it is a way how one large set of objects can be broken into smaller groups. Probably, it is the solid support of set-oriented operations that is the main reason why the relational model (Codd, 1970) has been dominating among other data models. And insufficient support of the set-oriented view on data is why object-orientated paradigm is much less popular in data modeling than in programming. Concepts and inclusion allow us to turn object data models into a set-based approach where any element is inherently a set and the notion of set is supported at the very basic level. Also, the use of inclusion relation makes COM similar to the hierarchical model (Tsichritzis et al, 1976).

Inclusion in the case of empty entity class can be used to extend values by adding additional fields and describing a hierarchy of value types. For example, if we need to mark an amount with the date of transaction then it can be described as follows:

```
CONCEPT DatedAmount IN Amount
  IDENTITY
    Date date
  ENTITY // Empty
```

Of course, the same can be done using conventional classes but then we would need to have two kinds of classes for values and for objects while concepts and inclusion describe *both* values and objects types. In relational terms, this allows us to model *two* hierarchies of domains and relations using only one construct (concept) and one relation (inclusion). In this sense, it is a step in the direction of unifying object-oriented and relational models by uniting two orthogonal branches: domain modeling and relational modeling.

PARTIAL ORDER

Logical Navigation

Concepts in COQL are partially ordered using the principle that dimension types are greater concepts. For example, let us consider the following concept:

```
CONCEPT Account
  IDENTITY
    CHAR(10) accNo
  ENTITY
    Person owner
```

Here concept Account has a dimension which represents its owner the type of which is Person. Accordingly, concept Person is a greater concept and concept Account is a lesser concept. The number of greater concepts is equal to the number of dimensions (concept fields). And the number of lesser concepts is equal to the number of uses of this concept as a dimension type. In diagrams, greater concepts are positioned over lesser concepts.

Concept instances are also partially ordered using the following principle: *a referenced element is greater than the referencing element*. Thus a reference always points to a greater element in the database. For example, a bank account element (instance of concept Account) is less than the referenced account

Figure 2. Projection and de-projection operations

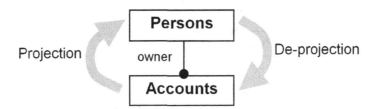

owner (instance of concept Person). Thus references are not simply a navigational tool but rather allow us to represent partial order which is a formal basis for representing data semantics.

Two operations of *projection* and *de-projection* are defined in COM by using partially ordered structure of elements. Projection is applied to a set of elements and returns all their greater elements along the specified dimension. Since greater elements are represented by references, this definition can be formulated as follows: projection of a set is a set of all elements referenced by some dimension. For example (Figure 2, left), in order to find all owners of the bank accounts we can project these accounts up to the collection of owners:

```
(Accounts)
  -> owner -> (Persons)
```

The set of accounts and owners can be restricted so that the selected accounts are projected to the selected persons:

```
(Accounts | balance > 1000)
  -> owner
  -> (Persons | age < 30)
```

This query returns all young owners of the accounts with large balance.

De-projection is applied to a set of elements and returns all their lesser elements along the specified dimension. In terms of references, de-projection is defined as follows: de-projection of a set is a set of all elements referencing them by some dimension. For example (Fig. 2, right), in order to find all accounts of the persons we can de-project these persons down to the collection of accounts:

```
(Persons)
  <- owner <- (Accounts)
```

The owners and accounts can be restricted and then this query returns all accounts with large balance belonging to young owners:

```
(Persons | age < 30)
  <- owner
  <- (Accounts | balance > 1000)
```

Figure 3. Inference by automatic constraint propagation

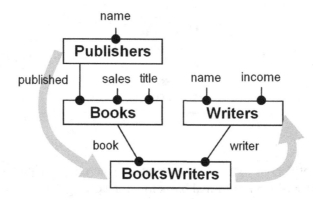

In the general case, operations of projection and de-projection can be combined so that it has a zig-zag form and consists of upward (projection) and downward (de-projection) segments in the partially ordered structure of collections (Savinov, 2005a, 2005b).

Inference

Logical navigation using projection and de-projection can be used for constraint propagation along explicitly specified dimension paths. In this section we describe an inference procedure which can *automatically* propagate source constraints through the model to the target without complete specification of the propagation path (Savinov, 2006b). This inference procedure is able to choose a natural propagation path itself. This means that if something is said about one set of elements then the system can infer something specific about other elements in the model. The main problem is *how* concretely the source constraints are propagated through the model.

In COM, the inference procedure consists of two steps:

1. De-projecting source constraints down to the chosen fact collection
2. Projecting the obtained fact elements up to the target collection

Let us consider a concept-oriented database schema shown in Figure 3 where it is assumed that each book is published by one publisher and there is a many-to-many relationship between writers and books. If we want to find all writers of one publisher then this can be done by specifying concrete access path for propagating publishers to writers:

```
(Publishers | name = "XYZ")
  <- published <- (Books)
  <- book <- (BooksWriters)
  -> writer -> (Writers)
```

Here we select a publisher, de-project it down to the Books collection, then again de-project the result further down to the BooksWriters collections with fact elements, and finally project the facts up to the Writers collection.

If we apply the inference procedure then the same query can be written in a more compact form:

```
(Publishers | name = "XYZ")
  <-* (BooksWriters)
  *-> (Writers)
```

This query consists of two parts which correspond to the two-step inference procedure. On the first step we de-project the source collection down to the BooksWriters fact collection using '<-*' operator. On the second step we project the facts up to the target Writers collection using '*->' operator. Note that we use stars in projection and de-projection operators to denote arbitrary dimension path. We can write this query in even more concise form if de-projection and projection steps are united in one inference operator denoted <-*->:

```
(Publishers | name = "XYZ")
  <-*-> (Writers)
```

The system will de-project the source collection down to the most specific collection and then project it up to the target collection. Note how simple and natural this query is. We essentially specify what we have and what we need. The system then is able to propagate these constraints to the target and return the result.

Multidimensional Analysis

Projection and de-projection allow us to navigate through the partially ordered structure of the database following only one dimension path. For multidimensional analysis it is necessary to have an operation which could take several collections and produce a multidimensional cube from them (Savinov, 2006a). In COQL, this operation is prefixed with the CUBE keyword followed by a sequence of source collections in round brackets. For example (Figure 4), given two source collections with countries and product categories we can produce a 2-dimensional cube where one element is a combination of one country and one produce category:

```
ResultCube =
  CUBE (Countries, Categories)
```

By default, all input dimensions will be included in the result collection, that is, a cube in our example will have two dimensions: a country and a product category. An arbitrary structure of the result collection is specified my means of the RETURN keyword. For example, we might want to return only country and category names:

```
ResultCube =
  CUBE(Countries co, Categories ca)
    RETURN co.name, ca.name
```

Figure 4. Multidimensional analysis

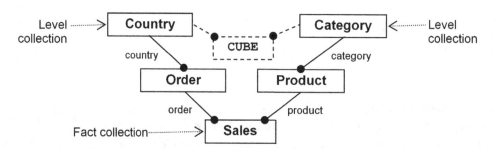

The main application of the CUBE operator is multidimensional analysis where data is represented in aggregated form over a multidimensional space with user-defined structure. The analyzed parameter, measure, is normally computed by aggregating data for each cell of the cube. Measure can be computed within query body denoted by the BODY keyword. For example, if we need to show sales over countries and categories then it can be done as follows:

```
ResultCube =
  CUBE(Countries co, Categories ca)
  BODY {
    cell = co <-* Sales AND
           ca <-* Sales
    measure = SUM(cell.price)
  }
  RETURN co.name, ca.name, measure
```

In this query it is assumed that the Sales collection is a common lesser collection for Countries and Categories. The result is a combination of country and category names along with the total sales for them. To compute the total sales figure we first find all facts belonging to one cell (to a combination of the current country and category). It is done by de-projecting the country and category down to the Sales fact collection and then finding their intersection (denoted by AND). Then we sum up all sales within one cell of the cube using only one numeric dimension for aggregation and store this result in the measure variable. Finally, the value computed for this country and this category is then returned in the result.

RELATED WORK

Although the concept-oriented model is based on only three principles, it is able to simulate many widespread mechanisms and data modeling patterns provided in other model. For example, the existence of hierarchies in COM makes it very similar to the classical hierarchical data model (HDM) (Tsichritzis et al, 1976). In both models data exist within a hierarchy where any element has a unique position. Therefore, this can be viewed as a reincarnation of the hierarchical model on a new cycle of the development spiral. The main distinguishing feature of COM is that it proposes to use domain-specific identities by providing means for modeling hierarchical address space for each problem domain. Another novelty is that inclusion relation simultaneously generalizes inheritance and can be used for type modeling like it is done in object data models.

Both the relational model and COM are tuple-based and set-based. The main difference of COM is that it introduces two types of tuples: identity tuples and entity tuples. Another difference is that instead of using conventional sets, COM considered partially ordered sets. In other words, COM assumes that in data modeling it is important to consider the structure of the set and partial order is assumed to be an intrinsic and primary property of data while other properties are derived from it. One of the main achievements of the relational model was independence from physical representation which was reached by removing physical (platform-specific) identities from the model. In this sense COM reverses the situation by recognizing the importance of identity modeling. COM makes a clear statement that identities are at least as important as entities and introduces special means for modeling them using concepts. If we assume that surrogates are used for identifying rows in the relational model and then these surrogates may have arbitrary structure then we get the mechanism of identity modeling similar to that used in COM.

The idea that partial order can be laid at the foundation of data management was also developed by Raymond (1996) where "a partial order database is simply a partial order". However, this approach assumes that partial order underlies type hierarchies while COM proposes to use a separate inclusion relation for modeling types. It also focuses on manipulating different partial orders and relies more on formal logic while COM focuses on manipulating elements within one nested poset with strong focus on dimensional modeling, constraint propagation and inference.

The notion of direct acyclic graph (DAG) has frequently been used in data modeling as a constraint imposed on a graph structure. When used informally, DAGs and partial orders can be easily confused although they are two different mathematical constructs created for different purposes. DAGs are more appropriate for graph-based models to impose additional constraints on its relationships (edges of the graph). COM is not a graph-based model and its main accent is made on dimensional modeling and analytical functions where order theoretic formalism is much more appropriate. For example, in graphs (including DAGs) we still rely on navigational approach for data access while in COM we rely on projection and de-projection operations along dimensions which change the level of details.

Hierarchies in the concept-oriented model are as important as they are in object data models (Dittrich, 1986, Bancilhon, 1996). However, object hierarchies are interpreted as inheritance and one of its main purposes consists in re-use of parent data and behavior. COM inclusion relation generalizes inheritance which means that inclusion can be used as inheritance. However, inclusion hierarchy is simultaneously a means for identity modeling so that elements get their unique addresses within one hierarchical container. Essentially, establishing the fact that inheritance is actually a particular case of inclusion is one of the major contributions of the concept-oriented approach. From this point of view, hierarchy in the hierarchical model and inheritance in object models are particular cases of inclusion hierarchy in COM. The treatment of inclusion in COM is very similar to how inheritance is implemented in prototype-based programming (Lieberman, 1986; Stein, 1987; Chambers et al, 1991) because in both approaches parent elements are shared parts of children.

The use of partial order in COM makes it similar to multidimensional models (Pedersen et al, 2001) widely used in OLAP and data warehousing. In most multidimensional models (Li et al, 1996; Agrawal et al, 1997; Gyssens et al, 1997), each dimension type is defined as a partially ordered set of category types (levels) and two special categories T (top) and L (bottom). The main difference is that COM proposes to partially order the whole model without assigning special roles to dimensions, cube, fact table and measures as it is done in multidimensional models. Thus instead of defining dimensions as several partially ordered sets of levels, COM unites all levels into one model. The assignment of such roles as dimension, cube, fact table and level is done later during each concrete analysis which is defined in terms of set-based projection and de-projection operations. This extension of partial order on the whole model (rather than considering it within the scope of each individual dimension) allows us to treat it as a model of data rather than a model of analysis (OLAP model).

One of the main characteristics of any semantic data model is its ability to represent complex relationships among elements and then using them for automating complex tasks like reasoning about data. There has been a large body of research on semantic data models (Hull et al, 1987; Peckham et al, 1988) but most of them propose a conceptual model which needs to be mapped to some logical model. COM proposes a new approach to representing and manipulating data semantics where different abstractions of conventional semantic models such as aggregation, generalization and classification are expressed in terms of a partially ordered set. From the point of view of aggregation, greater elements are constituents of this aggregate. From the point of view of generalization, greater elements are more general elements. One important feature of COM is that references change their role from navigational tool to an elementary semantic construct. Another unique property of COM is that it uses two orthogonal structures: inclusion and partial order. A similar approach is used in (Smith et al, 1977) where data belongs to two structures simultaneously: aggregation and generalization.

The functional data model (FDM) is based upon sets and functions (Sibley et al, 1977; Shipman, 1981). COM is similar to this model because dimensions can be expressed as functions which return a super-element. However, COM restricts them by only single-valued functions while set-valued functions are represented by inverted dimensions which are expressed via de-projection operator. In addition, COM imposes a strong constraint on the structure of functions by its order principle which means that a sequence of functions cannot return a previous element.

CONCLUSION

In this paper we described the concept-oriented model and query language which propose to treat elements as identity-entity couples structured using two relations: inclusion and partial order. The main distinguishing features of this novel approach are as follows:

- **Concepts instead of classes.** COQL introduces a novel construct, called concept, which generalizes classes. If classes have only one constituent then concepts are made up of two constituents: identity class and entity class. Data modeling is then broken into two orthogonal branches: identity modeling and entity modeling. This creates a nice ying-yang style of symmetry between two sides of one model. Informally speaking, it can be compared to manipulating complex numbers in mathematics which also have two constituents: real and imaginary parts. In practice, this generalization allows us to model domain-specific identities instead of having only platform-specific ones.

- **Inclusion instead of inheritance.** Classical inheritance is not very effective in data modeling because class instances exist in flat space although classes exist in hierarchy. Inclusion relation introduced in COM permits objects to exist in a hierarchy where they are identified by hierarchical addresses. Data modeling is then reduced to describing such hierarchical address space where data elements are supposed to exist. Importantly, inclusion retains all properties of classical inheritance. This use of inclusion turns objects into sets (of their sub-objects) and makes the whole approach intrinsically set-based rather than instance-based.

- **Partial order instead of graph.** COM proposes to partially order all data elements by assuming that references represent greater elements and dimension types of concepts represent greater concepts. Data modeling is then reduced to ordering elements so that other properties and mechanisms are derived from this relation. Note that partial order also allows us to treat elements as sets of their lesser elements.

These principles are rather general and support many mechanisms and patterns of thought currently being used in data modeling. In particular, we demonstrated how this approach can be used for logical navigation using operations of projection and de-projection, inference where constraint propagation path is chosen automatically, and multidimensional analysis where cube and measures are easily constructed using the partially ordered structure of the model. Taking into account its simplicity and generality, COM and COQL seem rather perspective direction for further research and development activities in the area of data modeling.

REFERENCES

Abiteboul, S., & Kanellakis, P. C. (1998). Object identity as a query language primitive. [JACM]. *Journal of the ACM, 45*(5), 798–842. doi:10.1145/290179.290182

Agrawal, R., Gupta, A., & Sarawagi, S. (1997). *Modeling multidimensional databases*. In 13th International Conference on Data Engineering (ICDE'97), (pp. 232–243).

Bancilhon, F. (1996). Object databases. [CSUR]. *ACM Computing Surveys, 28*(1), 137–140. doi:10.1145/234313.234373

Chambers, C., Ungar, D., Chang, B., & Hölzle, U. (1991). Parents are shared parts of objects: Inheritance and encapsulation in self. *Lisp and Symbolic Computation, 4*(3), 207–222. doi:10.1007/BF01806106

Codd, E. (1970). A relational model for large shared data banks. *Communications of the ACM, 13*(6), 377–387. doi:10.1145/362384.362685

Codd, E. F. (1979). Extending the database relational model to capture more meaning. [TODS]. *ACM Transactions on Database Systems, 4*(4), 397–434. doi:10.1145/320107.320109

Dittrich, K. R. (1986). Object-oriented database systems: The notions and the issues. In *Proceedings of the International Workshop on Object-Oriented Database Systems*, (pp. 2–4).

Eliassen, F., & Karlsen, R. (1991). Interoperability and object identity. *SIGMOD Record, 20*(4), 25–29. doi:10.1145/141356.141362

Gyssens, M., & Lakshmanan, L. V. S. (1997). A foundation for multi-dimensional databases. In *Proceedings of the 23rd International Conference on Very Large Data Bases (VLDB'97)*, (pp. 106–115).

Hull, R., & King, R. (1987). Semantic database modeling: Survey, applications, and research issues. [CSUR]. *ACM Computing Surveys, 19*(3), 201–260. doi:10.1145/45072.45073

Kent, W. (1991). A rigorous model of object references, identity and existence. *Journal of Object-Oriented Programming, 4*(3), 28–38.

Khoshafian, S. N., & Copeland, G. P. (1986). Object identity. *Proceedings of OOPSLA'86, ACM SIG-PLAN Notices, 21*(11), 406–416.

Li, C., & Wang, X. S. (1996). A data model for supporting on-line analytical processing. In *Proceedings of the Conference on Information and Knowledge Management*, Baltimore, MD, (pp. 81–88).

Lieberman, H. (1986). Using prototypical objects to implement shared behavior in object-oriented systems. In *Proceedings of OOPSLA'86, ACM SIGPLAN Notices, 21*(11), 214–223.

Peckham, J., & Maryanski, F. (1988). Semantic data models. [CSUR]. *ACM Computing Surveys, 20*(3), 153–189. doi:10.1145/62061.62062

Pedersen, T. B., & Jensen, C. S. (2001). Multidimensional database technology. *IEEE Computers, 34*(12), 40–46.

Raymond, D. (1996). *Partial order databases.* Unpublished doctoral thesis, University of Waterloo, Canada

Savinov, A. (2005a). Hierarchical multidimensional modeling in the concept-oriented data model. *3rd International Conference on Concept Lattices and Their Applications (CLA'05)* Olomouc, Czech Republic, (pp. 123–134)

Savinov, A. (2005b). Logical navigation in the concept-oriented data model. *Journal of Conceptual Modeling, 36.*

Savinov, A. (2006a). Grouping and aggregation in the concept-oriented data model. In *Proceedings of the 21st Annual ACM Symposium on Applied Computing (SAC'06)*, Dijon, France, (pp. 482–486).

Savinov, A. (2006b). Query by constraint propagation in the concept-oriented data model. *Computer Science Journal of Moldova, 14*(2), 219–238.

Savinov, A. (2008). Concepts and concept-oriented programming. *Journal of Object Technology, 7*(3), 91–106. doi:10.5381/jot.2008.7.3.a2

Savinov, A. (2009a). Concept-oriented model. In Ferraggine, V. E., Doorn, J. H., & Rivero, L. C. (Eds.), *Handbook of research on innovations in database technologies and applications: Current and future trends* (pp. 171–180). Hershey, PA: IGI Global.

Savinov, A. (2009b). Concept-oriented programming. In Khosrow-Pour, M. (Ed.), *Encyclopedia of Information Science and Technology* (2nd ed., pp. 672–680). Hershey, PA: IGI Global.

Shipman, D. W. (1981). The functional data model and the data language DAPLEX. [TODS]. *ACM Transactions on Database Systems, 6*(1), 140–173. doi:10.1145/319540.319561

Sibley, E. H., & Kerschberg, L. (1977). Data architecture and data model considerations. In *Proceedings of the AFIPS Joint Computer Conferences,* (pp. 85-96).

Smith, J. M., & Smith, D. C. P. (1977). Database abstractions: Aggregation and generalization. [TODS]. *ACM Transactions on Database Systems, 2*(2), 105–133. doi:10.1145/320544.320546

Stein, L. A. (1987). Delegation is inheritance. In *Proceedings of OOPSLA'87, ACM SIGPLAN Notices, 22*(12), 138–146.

Tsichritzis, D. C., & Lochovsky, F. H. (1976). Hierarchical data-base management: A survey. [CSUR]. *ACM Computing Surveys, 8*(1), 105–123. doi:10.1145/356662.356667

Wieringa, R., & de Jonge, W. (1995). Object identifiers, keys, and surrogates-object identifiers revisited. *Theory and Practice of Object Systems, 1*(2), 101–114.

KEY TERMS AND DEFINITIONS

Access Path: is a sequence of projection and de-projection operations applied to a set of elements possibly with intermediate constraints. Access path is used for logical navigation and retrieval of related data elements.

Concept: is a data modeling and programming construct which is defined as a couple of one identity class and one entity class. Concept instances are identity-entity couples. Concepts generalize conventional classes and are used instead of them for declaring type of elements.

Concept-Oriented Model: is a model of data which is based on three structural principles: duality principle postulates that an element is an identity-entity entity couple, inclusion principle postulates that all elements exist in an inclusion hierarchy, and order principle assumes that all elements are partially ordered.

Concept-Oriented Query Language: is a syntactic embodiment of the concept-oriented model. It is based on a novel data modeling construct, concept, which participates in two relations, inclusion and partial order. Main operations of this query language are projection, de-projection and product (cube).

De-Projection: is an operation applied to a set of elements and returning all their lesser elements which reference the source elements along the specified dimension.

Entity Class: is one of two constituents of a concept. Its instances are objects which are passed by-reference using identities. Entity classes are analogous to conventional classes.

Identity Class: is one of two constituents of a concept. Its instances are values which are passed by-copy and represent entities. It is assumed that by storing an identity we can always access the represented entity. Identity classes are used to describe domain-specific address spaces however they can exist only as part of a concept.

Inclusion Relation: is used to specify a super-concept this concept is included in. Inclusion relation among concepts generalizes inheritance relation among classes.

Projection: is an operation applied to a set of elements and returning all their greater elements which are those referenced by the source elements along the specified dimension.

Chapter 4
Evaluating Top–k Skyline Queries Efficiently

Marlene Goncalves
Universidad Simón Bolívar, Venezuela

María Esther Vidal
Universidad Simón Bolívar, Venezuela

ABSTRACT

Criteria that induce a Skyline naturally represent user's preference conditions useful to discard irrelevant data in large datasets. However, in the presence of high-dimensional Skyline spaces, the size of the Skyline can still be very large. To identify the best k points among the Skyline, the Top-k Skyline approach has been proposed. This chapter describes existing solutions and proposes to use the TKSI algorithm for the Top-k Skyline problem. TKSI reduces the search space by computing only a subset of the Skyline that is required to produce the top-k objects. In addition, the Skyline Frequency Metric is implemented to discriminate among the Skyline objects those that best meet the multidimensional criteria. This chapter's authors have empirically studied the quality of TKSI, and their experimental results show the TKSI may be able to speed up the computation of the Top-k Skyline in at least 50% percent with regard to the state-of-the-art solutions.

INTRODUCTION

Emerging technologies such as Semantic Web, Grid, Semantic Search, Linked Data and Cloud and Peer-to-Peer computing have become available very large datasets. For example, by the time this paper has been written at least 21.59 billion pages are indexed by the Web (De Kunder, 2010) and the Cloud of Linked Data has at least 13,112,409,691 triples (W3C, 2010). The enormous growth in the size of data has a direct impact on the performance of tasks that are required to process on very large datasets and

DOI: 10.4018/978-1-60960-475-2.ch004

Table 1. Estimated Skyline Cardinality

#Dimensions	Cardinality
2	191
3	2,637
4	36,431
5	503,309
6	6,953,471
7	96,065,749
8	1,327,197,371
9	18,335,909,288
10	253,319,948,365

whose complexity depends on the size of the database. Particularly, the task of evaluating queries based on user preferences may be considerably affected by this situation.

Skyline (Börzsönyi et al., 2001) approaches have been successfully used to naturally express user preference conditions useful to characterize relevant data in large datasets. Even though, Skyline may be a good choice for huge data sets its cardinality may become very large as the number of criteria or dimensions increases. The estimated cardinality of the Skyline is $O(\ln^{d-1}n)$ when the dimensions are independent where n is the size of the input data and d the number of dimensions (Bentley et al., 1978).

Consider Table 1 that shows estimates of the skyline cardinality when the number of dimensions ranges from 2 to 10 in a database comprised of 1,000,000 tuples. We may observe in Table 1 that Skyline cardinality rapidly increases making unfeasible for users to process the whole skyline set. In consequence, users may have to discard useless data manually and consider just a small subset or a subset of the Skyline that best meet the multidimensional criteria. To identify these points, the Top-k Skyline has been proposed (Goncalves and Vidal, 2009; Chan et al., 2006b; Lin et al., 2007). Top-k Skyline uses a score function to induce a total order of the Skyline points, and recognizes the top-k objects based on these criteria.

Several algorithms have been defined to compute the Top-k Skyline, but they may be very costly (Goncalves and Vidal, 2009; Chan et al., 2006b; Lin et al., 2007; Vlachou and Vazirgiannis, 2007). First, they require the computation of the whole Skyline; second, they execute probes of the multidimensional function over the whole Skyline points. Thus, if k is much smaller than the cardinality of the Skyline, these solutions may be very inefficient because a large number of non-necessary probes may be evaluated, i.e., at least Skyline size minus k performed probes will be non-necessaries.

Top-k Skyline has become necessary in many real-world situations (Vlachou and Vazirgiannis, 2007), and a wide range of ranking metrics to measure the interestingness of each Skyline tuple has been proposed. Examples of these ranking metrics are skyline frequency (Chan et al., 2006b), k-dominant skyline (Chan et al., 2006a), and k representative skyline (Lin et al., 2007). Skyline frequency ranks Skyline in terms of the number of times in which a Skyline tuple belongs to a non-empty subset or subspace of the multi-dimensional criteria. k-dominant skyline metric identifies Skyline points in k ≤ d dimensions of multi-dimensional criteria. Finally, k representative skyline metric produces the k Skyline points that have the maximal number of dominated object.

Skyline frequency is one of the most significant metrics that measures interestingness of each Skyline point in the answer. Intuitively, a high Skyline frequency value indicates that the point is dominated only in few subsets of multidimensional criteria and therefore, it is considered a very interesting point because it may dominate in many of the subsets.

In (Chan et al., 2006b), the authors proposed an efficient approximated algorithm to estimate the skyline frequency values. (Yuan et al., 2005) define two algorithms to efficiently calculate the Skycube or the union of the Skylines of the non-empty subsets of multidimensional criteria. Both algorithms make uses of the Skyline point properties to speed the Skycube computation. But, they compute the Skycube completely.

To overcome these limitations, we propose an algorithm that takes advantages of the properties of the skyline frequency metric, and identifies the subset of the Skyline points that are needed to compute the top-k ones in the answer. In this chapter, we will address the problem of computing Top-k Skyline queries efficiently (Goncalves and Vidal, 2009; Chan et al., 2006b) in a way that number of probes of the multidimensional function or score function is minimized.

This chapter comprises five sections in addition to section 1 that motivates the problem. Section 2 presents the background required to understand the Top-k Skyline problem. Section 3 will present our Top-k Skyline approach. We will describe an algorithm that is able to compute only the subset of the Skyline that will be required to produce the top-k objects. In Section 4, the quality and performance of the proposed technique will be empirically evaluated against the state-of-the-art solutions. Finally, the conclusions of our work will be pointed out in Section 5.

BACKGROUND

In this section, we present a motivating example and preliminary definitions, and we summarize existing approaches to compute the Skyline and Top-k points. Then, we will outline the advantages and limitations of each approach, and we will consider existing solutions defined to calculate Top-k Skyline. Finally, we will present some metrics proposed to rank the Skyline which allows to score the importance of the Skyline without necessity of defining a score function.

Motivating Example

To motivate the problem of computing Top-k Skyline queries efficiently, consider the DBLP Computer Science Bibliography database (Ley, 2010) and a research institute which offers a travel fellowship to the best three researchers based on their number of publications on the main four database conferences: EDBT, ICDE, VLDB and SIGMOD. The DBLP database provides information on researcher's performance, which include number of papers in each conference. The summarized information is organized in the Researcher relational table, where the candidates are described by an identifier, author name, total number journals in SIGMODR, VLDBJ, TODS, TKDE, and DKE, and number of papers in EDBT, ICDE, VLDB SIGMOD.

According to the research institute policy, all criteria are equally important and relevant; hence, either a weight or a score function cannot be assigned. A candidate can be chosen for granting an award, if and only if, there is no other candidate with more papers in EDBT, ICDE, VLDB and SIGMOD. To nominate a candidate, the research institute must identify the set of all the candidates that are non-dominated by any

Table 2. Nominees for three awards

Id	Author	Journals	EDBT	ICDE	VLDB	SIGMOD	SFM
5932	Divesh Srivastava	19	6	37	24	32	7
8846	H. V. Jagadish	27	10	23	35	28	12
19660	Philip S. Yu	62	9	49	21	18	8
20259	Raghu Ramakrishnan	18	2	16	30	30	4
23870	Surajit Chaudhuri	19	3	27	26	39	10

other candidate in terms of these criteria. Thus, tuples in table Researcher must be selected in terms of the values of EDBT, ICDE, VLDB and SIGMOD. Following these criteria, the nominees are computed, and presented in Table 2; also the Skyline frequency metric (SFM) for each researcher is reported. In total, DBLP database contains information at least 1.4 million publications (Ley, 2010).

Since the research institute only can grant three awards, it has to select the top-3 researchers among the five nominees. Thus, criteria to discriminate the top-3 researchers among nominees are needed. The number of journals may be used as a score function; therefore, three candidates are the new nominees: 19660, 8846 and 5932 (or 23870).

On the other hand, in the literature, several metrics have been proposed to distinguish the top-k elements in a set of incomparable researchers. For example, consider the skyline frequency metric (SFM) that measures the number of times a researcher belongs to a skyline set when different sub-sets of the conditions in the multi-dimensional criteria are considered. To compute SFM the algorithms presented in (Yuan et al., 2005) may be applied. Both algorithms build non-empty subsets of multidimensional criteria as shown in Table 3. However, the Skyline may be huge, and it will be completely built by these algorithms (Goncalves and Vidal, 2009). Therefore, to calculate the skyline frequency values, a large number of non-necessary points in all subsets of multidimensional criteria may be computed.

Based on the values of the SFM, three of the researchers 8846, 23870 and 19660 are the winners of the research institute request. Intuitively, to select the awarded researchers, queries based on user preferences have been posted against the table Researcher. Skyline (Börzsönyi et al., 2001) and Top-k (Carey and Kossmann, 1997) are two user preference languages that could be used to identify some of he granted researchers. However, none of them will provide the complete set, and post-processing will be needed to identify the top-3 researchers (Goncalves and Vidal, 2009). To overcome limitations of existing approaches, we propose a query evaluation algorithm that minimizes the number of non-necessary probes, i.e., this algorithm is able to identify the top-k objects in the Skyline, for which there are not k better Skyline objects in terms of the SFM.

Preliminaries

Given a set $DO = \{o_1, ..., o_n\}$ of database objects, where each object o_i is characterized by p attributes $(A_1, ..., A_p)$; r different score functions $s_1, ..., s_q, ..., s_r$ defined over some of the p attributes, where each $s_i: O \rightarrow [0, 1]$, $1 \leq i \leq r$; a score function f defined on some scores s_i, which induces a total order of the objects in DO; and a multicriteria function m defined over a subspace S of the score functions s_1, ..., s_q, which induces a partial order of the objects in DO. For simplicity, we suppose that scores related to the multicriteria function need to be maximized, and the score functions $s_1, ..., s_q, ..., s_r$ respect a

Table 3. Skyline for each subset of multidimensional criteria

Subset	Skyline
{EDBT, ICDE, VLDB, SIGMOD}	{5932; 8846; 19660; 20259; 23870}
{ICDE, VLDB, SIGMOD}	{5932; 8846; 19660; 20259; 23870}
{EDBT, VLDB, SIGMOD}	{5932; 8846; 20259; 23870}
{EDBT, ICDE, SIGMOD}	{5932; 8846; 19660; 23870}
{EDBT, ICDE, VLDB}	{5932; 8846; 19660; 23870}
{VLDB, SIGMOD}	{8846; 20259; 23870}
{ICDE, SIGMOD}	{5932; 19660; 23870}
{ICDE, VLDB}	{5932; 8846; 19660; 23870}
{EDBT, SIGMOD}	{5932; 8846; 23870}
{EDBT, VLDB}	{8846}
{EDBT, ICDE,}	{8846; 19660}
{EDBT}	{8846}
{ICDE}	{19660}
{VLDB}	{8846}
{SIGMOD}	{23870}

natural ordering over p attributes. We define the Skyline SKY_S on a space S according to a multicriteria function m as follows:

$$SKY_S = \{o_i | \; o_i \in DO: (\neg \exists \; o_j | \; o_j \in DO: s_1(o_j) \geq s_1(o_i) \wedge \ldots \wedge s_q(o_j) \geq s_q(o_i) \wedge (\exists x \; | \; 1 \leq x \leq q: s_x(o_j) \succ s_x(o_i)))\}$$

The conditions to be satisfied by the answers of a Top-k Skyline query with respect to the functions m and f, are described as follows:

$$\xi_{<f,m,k>} = \{ \; o_i | \; o_i \in SKY_S \wedge (\neg \exists^{k \cdot |SKYs|} \; o_j | \; o_j \in SKY_S: f(o_j) \geq f(o_i))\}$$

Where, $\exists^t$ means that exists at most t elements in the set. Additionally, the Skyline Frequency may be used as a score function to rank the Skyline:

$$\xi_{<sf,m,k>} = \{ \; o_i | \; o_i \in SKY_S \wedge (\neg \exists^{k \cdot |SKYs|} \; o_j | \; o_j \in SKY_S: sf(o_j) \geq sf(o_i))\}$$

Where the Skyline Frequency of a object $o \in SKY_S$, denoted by *sf(o)*, is the number of subspaces S' of S in which o is a Skyline object, this is:

$$sf(o) = (\sum S' \; | \; S' \in S \wedge o \in SKY_{S'}: 1)$$

The Skycube or lattice is the set of the all Skylines for any subspace S' of S defined as:

$$SkyCube = \{\cup SKY_{S'} \; | \; S' \subseteq S\}$$

Finally, the probes of the functions m and sf required to identify the top-k objects in the Skyline correspond to necessary probes, i.e., a probe p of the functions m or f is necessary if and only if p is performed on an object $o \in \xi_{<sf,m,k>}$. In this work, we define an algorithm that minimizes the number of non-necessary probes, while computing the Top-k Skyline objects with respect to the functions m and sf.

Related Work

Skyline (Börzsönyi et al., 2001) and Top-k (Carey and Kossmann, 1997) approaches have been defined in the context of databases to distinguish the best points that satisfy a given ranking condition. A Skyline-based technique identifies a partially ordered set of points whose order is induced by criteria comprised of conditions on equally important parameters. Top-k approaches select the top-k elements based on a score function or discriminatory criteria that induce a totally ordered of the input set.

(Bentley et al., 1978) proposed the first Skyline algorithm, referred to as the maximum vector problem and it is based on the divide & conquer principle. Progress has been made as of recent on how to compute efficiently such queries in a relational system and over large datasets. Block-Nested-Loops (BNL) (Börzsönyi et al., 2001), Sort-Filter-Skyline (SFS) (Godfrey et al., 2005) and LESS (Linear Elimination Sort for Skyline) (Godfrey et al., 2005) are three algorithms that identify the Skyline by scanning the whole dataset.

On the other hand, progressive (or online) algorithms for computing Skyline have been introduced: the Tan et al.'s algorithm, NN (Nearest Neighbor) and BBS (Branch-and-Bound Skyline) (Kossmann et al., 2002; Papadias et al., 2003; Tan et al., 2001). A progressive algorithm returns the first results without having to read the entire input and produces more results during execution time. Although these strategies could be used to implement our approach, they may be inefficient because they may perform a number of non-necessary probes or require index structures which are not accessible in Web data sources.

In order to process Skyline queries against Web data sources, efficient algorithms have been designed considering sequential and random accesses. Each data source contains object identifiers and their scores. A sequential access retrieves an object from a sorted data source while a random access returns the score from a given object identifier. The Basic Distributed Skyline (BDS) defined by (Balke et al., 2004) is one of the algorithms to solve this kind of Skyline queries. BDS is a twofold solution which builds a Skyline superset in a first phase and then, it discards the dominated points in a second phase. A second algorithm known as Basic Multi-Objective Retrieval (BMOR) is presented by (Balke and Güntzer, 2004); in contrast to BDS, BMOR compares all the seen objects until a seen object that dominates the virtual object is found. The virtual object is constantly updated and is comprised of all the highest values seen so far. Both algorithms avoid to scan the whole dataset, and minimize the number of probes.

A new hybrid approach that combines the benefits of Skyline and Top-k has been proposed and it is known as Top-k Skyline (Goncalves and Vidal, 2009). Top-k Skyline identifies the top-k objects using discriminatory criteria that induces a total order of the objects that compose the skyline of points that satisfy a given multi-dimensional criteria. Top-k Skyline has become necessary in many real-world situations (Vlachou and Vazirgiannis, 2007), and a variety of ranking metrics have been proposed to discriminate among the points in the Skyline, e.g., Skyline Frequency (Chan et al., 2006b), k-dominant sky-line (Chan et al., 2006a), and k representative skyline (Lin et al., 2007). The Skyline Frequency Metric is one of the most significant metrics that ranks skyline points in terms of how many times a skyline point belongs to the skyline induced by the subsets of the multidimensional criteria; it measures how much a skyline point satisfies the different parameters in the multidimensional criteria. Intuitively, a high Skyline Frequency value indicates that a point may be dominated on smaller subsets of the multidimensional criteria, and it can be considered a very good point because it may dominate in many of the other subsets; in contrast, a skyline point with a low Skyline Frequency value shows that other skyline points dominate it in subsets of the multidimensional criteria. Approaches in (Pei et al., 2006; Yuan et al., 2005) propose two algorithms to compute Skyline Frequency values by building the Skycube or the union of the skylines of the non-empty subsets of the multidimensional criteria. The Bottom-Up Skycube algorithm (BUS) (Yuan et al., 2005) identifies the Skycube of d dimensions in a bottom-up fashion. BUS sorts dataset on each dimension of the multidimensional criteria in a list and it calculates the skyline points from one to d dimensions. BUS makes use of the skyline point properties to speed the Skycube computation. On the other hand, the Top-Down Skycube algorithm (TDS) (Pei et al., 2006) computes the Skycube in a top-down manner based on a Divide and Conquer (DC) Skyline algorithm (Börzsönyi et al., 2001). TDS computes a minimal set of paths in the lattice structure of the Skycube and then, it identifies skylines in these paths. Thus, multiple related skylines are built simultaneously. BUS and TDS can be used to compute the Top-k Skyline. However, some overhead may have to be paid, because both algorithms compute the Skycube completely. (Goncalves and Vidal, 2009) propose an index-based technique called TKSI, to compute the Top-k Sky-line points by just probing the minimal subset of incomparable points and using a given score function to distinguish the best points.

TOP-K SKYLINE

The Top-k Skyline approach identifies the objects that best meet the multi-dimensional criteria based on the Skyline Frequency Metric (SFM). The problem of efficient implementation of Top-k Skyline (EITKS) is defined as the problem of building the set $\xi_{<sf,m,k>}$ minimizing the number of non-necessary probes; a probe p on the multidimensional criteria function m and the Skyline Frequency metric sf is necessary if and only if p is perfomed on an object $o \in \xi_{<sf,m,k>}$.

Skyline frequency of an object o returns the number of times in which o belongs to a non-empty subset the multidimensional criteria. There are $2^q - 1$ non-empty subspaces for multidimensional criteria m with q dimensions. In Figure 1, we illustrate that the structure of lattice of for our example contains $2^4 - 1$ subspaces. Moreover, there exists a containment relationship property between the skylines of subspaces when data are non-duplicated: Given two subspaces U, V where $U \subset V$, then $SKY_U \subseteq SKY_V$. Since $o \in SKY_U$, none object may be better than o in all criteria of V (Chan et al., 2006b). For example, the object $8846 \in SKY_{\{VLDB\}}$ also belongs to $SKY_{\{VLDB,SIGMOD\}}$ because of Skyline definition formula, i.e., any object o in $SKY_{\{VLDB,SIGMOD\}}$ may dominate 8846 in {SIGMOD} but not in {VLDB, SIGMOD}.

BUS is based on the containment relationship property in order to save probes among subspaces. Instead of constructing Skylines of each subspace individually, BUS builds the lattice in a bottom-up fashion sharing results of the skylines in order to minimize probes of the multidimensional criteria. To illustrate the behavior of the BUS with an example, consider the following query: the top-1 candidates with maximum number of papers in EDBT, ICDE, VLDB, and SIGMOD. To answer this query, BUS calculates the Skyline for each subspace of 1-dimension EDBT, ICDE, VLDB, SIGMOD; then shares results for the skyline of subspaces of 2-dimensions {EDBT,ICDE}, {EDBT,VLDB}, {EDBT,SIGMOD}, {ICDE,VLDB}, {ICDE,SIGMOD}, {VLDB, SIGMOD} using the containment relationship property; so and so until $2^4 - 1$ all Skylines for subspaces of multidimensional criteria are built. The Skylines of each subspace are in Table 3.

Figure 1. Lattice for the multidimensional criteria

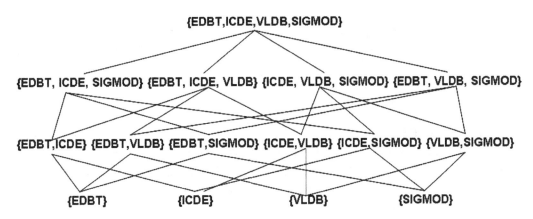

BUS may be adapted to build the Top-k Skyline. First, BUS computes the lattice including the whole Skyline; second, it calculates the SFM values for each Skyline object; and finally, it sorts the Skyline by the SFM and returns the top-k objects. However, time complexity for Skyline queries is high and it depends on the size of the input data set and the number of probes performed. In general, the problem of identifying the Skyline is $O(n^2)$ (Godfrey et al., 2005); this is because all the input objects need to be compared against themselves to probe the multidimensional criteria. Our goal is to minimize non-necessary probes building the Skyline partially until the top-k objects are produced.

BUS requires the computation of the entire Skyline and executes probes of the multidimensional function over the whole Skyline objects. Thus, we propose the use of Top-k Skyline Index (TKSI) to efficiently solve this problem based on the Skyline Frequency Metric (SFM).

Consider Table 4 that shows a set of sorted indices $I_1, ..., I_5$ on each attribute of multidimensional criteria and SFM values, and the first object *8846* characterized by the highest SFM value. $I_1, ..., I_5$ contain the objects sorted descendantly. We may observe that not exists an object above *8846* in all indices $I_1, ..., I_4$, and therefore *8846* is not dominated by any object and it is a Skyline object. Since *8846* is a Skyline and has the highest SFM value, *8846* is the Top-1 Skyline. Thus, it is not necessary to completely build the Skyline whose size is five in order to produce the answer for our Top-1 Skyline query. Next, we introduce the following property:

Table 4. Indices

I_1			I_2			I_3			I_4			I_5	
Id	**EDBT**		**Id**	**ICDE**		**Id**	**VLDB**		**Id**	**SIGMOD**		**Id**	**SFM**
8846	10		19660	49		8846	35		23870	39		8846	12
19660	9		5932	37		20259	30		5932	32		23870	10
5932	6		23870	27		23870	26		20259	30		19660	8
23870	3		8846	23		5932	24		8846	28		5932	7
20259	2		20259	16		19660	21		19660	18		20259	4

Table 5. The TKSI Algorithm Execution

Id	Publication/GPA/Experience	Index
8846	12	I_5
8846	10	I_1
19660	9	I_1

Property 1. Given a set of sorted indices $I_1, ..., I_q$ on each attribute of multidimensional criteria m; an index I_{q+1} defined on values of SFM sf; the Skyline SKY_S; an integer k such as $0 < k \leq |SKY_S|$; and object o indexed by I_{q+1}. Then, o is an Top-k Skyline object if not exists an object above o in all indices $I_1, ..., I_q$ and not exists Top $k - 1$ Skyline objects with higher SFM value than it.

TKSI focuses on performing sorted accesses on the SFM index I_{q+1} firstly and then, verifying if each accessed object is a Top-k Skyline using the indices on multidimensional criteria $I_1, ..., I_q$. Basically, TKSI receives a set of indices on each attribute of multidimensional criteria m and the Skyline Frequency metric sf, and an integer k; and it builds the Top-k Skyline using the indices (Table 4). Since the indices on multidimensional criteria are sorted, TKSI has not to scan the entire index and builds the whole skyline while k is smaller than the Skyline size.

Following with our example, TKSI accesses the objects from I_5 sequentially until the top-1 object is produced. For each accessed object o from I_5, TKSI verifies that o is a Top-k Skyline object. Because objects are sorted, it is very likely that any object with the higher values in each index of function m dominates the next objects in the indices. For this reason, TKSI must select one of the indices I_1, I_2, I_3, or I_4 in order to minimize the necessary probes over the multicriteria function m. The objects could be accessed in a round robin fashion. However, in order to speed up the computation, TKSI determines what is the index whose distance with respect to o is the lowest, i.e., the index that will avoid the access of more non-necessary objects. To do this, TKSI computes the distance D_1 as the difference between the last seen value from I_1 and the value for EDBT of o $(min_1 - s_1(o))$, D_2 as the difference between the last seen value from I_2 and the value for ICDE of o $(min_2 - s_2(o))$, D_3 as the difference between the last seen value from I_3 and the value for VLDB of o $(min_3 - s_3(o))$, and D_4 as the difference between the last seen value from I_4 and the value for SIGMOD of o $(min_4 - s_4(o))$. Next, TKSI selects the minimum value between D_1, D_2, D_3, and D_4.

Initially, TKSI accesses the first object *8846* from I_5, and their values for EDBT, ICDE, VLDB and SIGMOD randomly. Because of the objects from I_1, I_2, I_3, and I_4 have not been seen yet; TKSI assumes the last seen value is the maximum value possible for the attribute. Therefore, the best distance between $D_1 = 10 - 10$, $D_2 = 49 - 23$, $D_3 = 35 - 35$, and $D_4 = 39 - 28$ is calculated. In this case, I_1 and I_3 have the minimum distance. Note that *8846* is placed in the indices I_1 and I_3 in a lower position than the same object in I_2 and I_4. The objects of I_1 are accessed until the object *19660* with a value lower in EDBT is found. All these objects are compared against *8846* to verify if some of them dominate it. Since, none of the objects dominates *8846*, the object *8846* is a Top-k Skyline object. If some object indexed by I_1 dominates *8846*, a new object from I_5 is accessed. However, the algorithm decides to stop here because the objects behind *19660* have worse values in Publication than *8846*, and they may not dominate *8846*. The detailed TKSI execution is showed in Table 5.

Figure 2. The TKSI Algorithm

INPUT:

- m: Multicriteria Function;

- *SFM*: Precomputed Skyline Frequence Metric;

- k: Integer;

- $I = \{I_1, \ldots, I_q, \ldots, I_r\}$: Set of indexes on attributes in m;

OUTPUT:

- ξ: Top-k Skyline objects

1) Initialize $\xi \leftarrow \emptyset$; $cont \leftarrow 0$;

2) **WHILE** ($cont < k$ and exists values in *SFM*) **DO**

    a) Select the following best object o_t for SFM;

    b) Perform all random accesses to retrieve scores of o_t using indexes I;

    c) $I_i \leftarrow SelectBestIndex(o_t.I)$;

    d) **IF** exists an object o in I_i, o is between the first object and the object o_t in I_i, and o dominates to o_t, **THEN** discard dominated object o_t

    e) **IF** o_t is incomparable, **THEN** Add o_t to ξ; $cont \leftarrow cont + 1$;

3) return ξ

The TKSI algorithm is presented in Figure 2. In the first step, TKSI initializes the set of Top-k Skyline objects ξ and the variable *cont* registers the number of top objects produced by the algorithm. In step 2, TKSI identifies the Top-k objects in terms of SFM. In the step 2a-b), the next best object o_t from the SFM metric is completely accessed. This object is a Top-k Skyline candidate because it has the following best skyline frequency value. However, TKSI must verify if o_t is incomparable. TKSI may select sorted indices in a round-robin way in order to check if an object is incomparable. Nevertheless, based on the properties of SFM, we have implemented a heuristic that guides TKSI in the space of possibly good objects, and avoids excessive accesses of non-necessary objects. For simplicity, we suppose that attributes of the multidimensional criteria are maximized. Since $2^q - 1$ subspaces are calculated to compute the skyline frequency metric, TKSI computes a monotonic function $\sum_{\forall a \in m} s(a) / (2^q - 1)$ with respect to the last object seen in each source, in order to select the best one. Intuitively, while this function is close to 1.0, it indicates that the object belongs to a large number of skylines. We are interested in this kind of objects because they may discard quickly dominated objects. Because objects are sorted, it is very likely that any object with the higher values in each index dominates the next objects in the other indices. Thus, sources with the maximum value of the monotonic function will be selected, and scanned for minimizing the number of accesses. Finally, if o_t is dominated by some seen intermediate object in the selected index, then in step 2d) the object o_t is discarded. In case of o_t is non-dominated with respect to the seen objects; then, in step 2e) the object o_t is a Top-k Skyline Frequency object and it is inserted into ξ. Thus, the algorithm continues until k objects are found.

Finally, the Theorem 1 shows lower bound for TKSI algorithm.

Table 6. DBLP features

Name	#nodes	#edges	Size (MB)
DBLP	876,110	4,166,626	3,950

Theorem 1. Given a set of sorted indices I_1, ..., I_q on each attribute of multidimensional criteria m; an index I_{q+1} defined on values of SFM sf; the Skyline SKY_s; and an integer k such as $0 < k \leq |SKY_s|$. Then, a lower bound of the number of probes performed by TKSI is 2k.

The best case for the TKSI algorithm is each object o accessed by the index I_{q+1} is compared against a only object o' of some index I_1, ..., I_q and each object o is in the answer. Thus, 2k probes are necessary because k objects are compared and TKSI verifies by each object in I_{q+1} if each object o dominates o', and o' dominates o.

EXPERIMENTAL STUDY

Dataset and Query Benchmark: We shredded the downloaded DBLP file (Ley, 2010) into the relational database; DBLP features are shows in Table 6. We randomly generated 25 queries by restricting the numbers of papers by each author in the DBLP dataset; the queries are characterized by the following properties: (a) only one table in the FROM clause; (b) the attributes in the multicriteria function were selected following a uniform distribution; (c) directives for each attribute of the multicriteria function were selected considering only maximizing; (d) the number of attributes of the multicriteria function is five, six and seven; and (e) k is 3.

- **Evaluation Metrics:** we report on the Number of Probes (NP), the ratio of the skyline size and the Normalized Skyline Frequency value (NSF). NP is the number of the probes of the multidimensional criteria and Skyline Frequency Metric evaluations performed by the algorithm. NSF is a quality metric that represents a percent of non-empty subspaces of the multidimensional criteria; it indicates how good a Skyline object is. NSF is computed as follows: SFM / $(2^q - 1)$.
- **Implementations:** TKSI and BUS algorithms were developed in Java (64-bit JDK version 1.5.0 12) on top of Oracle 9i. A set of sorted queries are executed for each criterion of the multicriteria and the score functions, and the resultsets are stored on indices. The resultsets are sorted descendantly according to the MAX criteria of the multicriteria function. Each resultset is accessed on-demand.

Furthermore, a set of hash maps are built, one for each index. These hash maps are comprised of objects accessed by each index. Also, a variable for each index is updated with the last value seen in that index. Initially, these variables are set with the best values. Lately, they are updated according to the last object accessed by each index.

Thus, TKSI accesses the first object o from the index over the score function. It selects which is the index I_i that has the lowest gap with respect to o. The resultset of the selected index I_i is scanned until

Figure 3. Skyline size

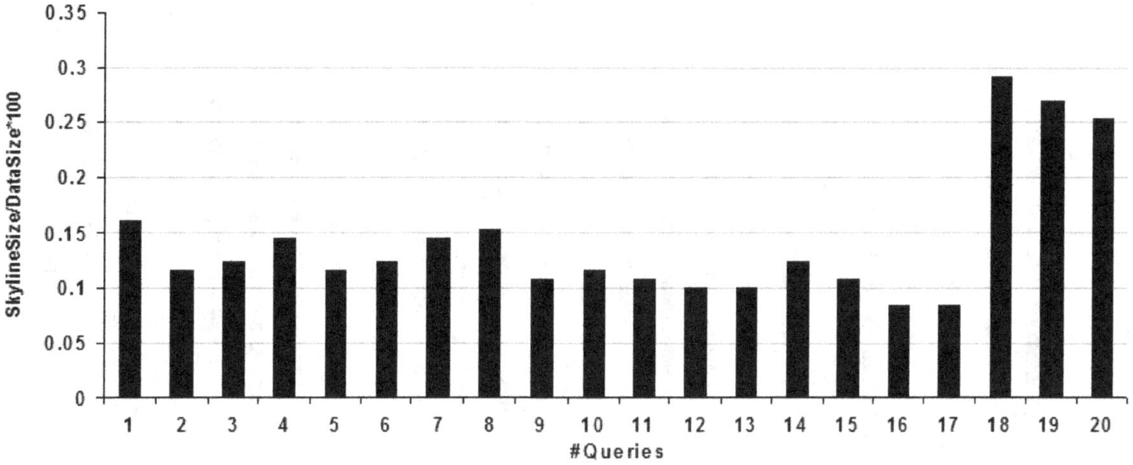

some object from I_i dominates o or none of the objects better than o in the attribute i dominates to o. If o is incomparable, then o is a Top-k Skyline object and it is added in the set of answers. This process continues until computing the top k objects.

DBLP data were stored in relational tables on Oracle 9i, and sorted based on each dimension. The experiments were evaluated on a SunFire V440 machine equipped with 2 processors Sparcv9 of 1.281 MHZ, 16 GB of memory and 4 disks Ultra320 SCSI of 73 GB running on SunOS 5.10 (Solaris 10).

Quality and Performance of the Top-Skyline Technique

We studied the quality of the TKSI, and we compare its performance with respect to the BUS algorithm. We ran 25 queries on subset of 13,029 objects.

In Figure 3, we report the ratio of the skyline size based on the multidimensional criteria. In general, we observe that the skyline size is larger for high dimensional queries. In the studied queries, the skyline size ranges from 6% to 43% of the total number of objects that satisfy the multidimensional criteria.

Figure 4 reports on the number of probes performed by TKSI and BUS (logarithmic scale). We can observe that TKSI reduces the number of probes by at least three and half orders of magnitude with respect to the bottom-up solution implemented by the BUS algorithm. This is because TKSI does not build the skyline completely.

Additionally, the quality of the Top-k Skyline objects identified by the ranking engine is shown in Figure 5. NSF values are between 0.37 and 0.75, i.e., the retrieved objects dominate in at most 75% of the subspaces of the multidimensional criteria and they may be of good quality. For Top-k Skyline queries for six and seven dimensions, NSF is near to 0.5; this indicates that selected objects dominate in almost 50% of the subspaces of the multidimensional criteria. For Top-k Skyline queries with five dimensions, NSF is between 0.6 and 0.75; thus, selected objects are more dominators.

Figure 4. Number of probes (logarithmic scale)

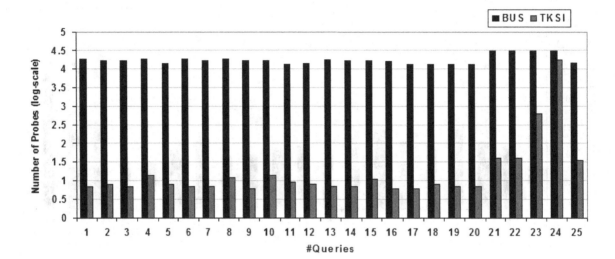

Figure 5. Quality of the Top-k Skyline

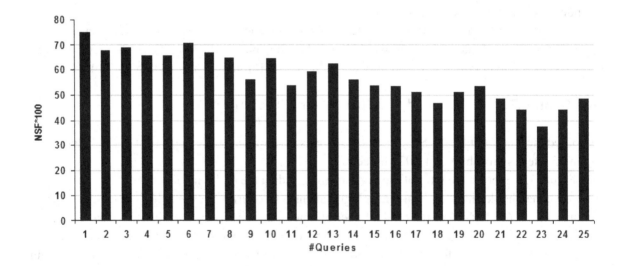

CONCLUSION

Skyline size can be very large in the presence of high-dimensional Skyline spaces, making unfeasible for users to process this set of points. Top-k Skyline has been proposed in order to identify the top k points among the Skyline. Top-k Skyline uses discriminatory criteria to induce a total order of the points that comprise the Skyline, and recognizes the best k objects based on these criteria.

Different algorithms have been defined to compute the top-k objects among the Skyline; while existing solutions are able to produce the Top-k Skyline, they may be very costly. First, state-of-the-art Top-k Skyline solutions require the computation of the whole Skyline; second, they execute probes of the multicriteria function over the whole Skyline points. Thus, if k is much smaller than the cardinality of the Skyline, these solutions may be very inefficient because a large number of non-necessary probes may be evaluated.

In this chapter, we showed the problem of identifying the Top-k that best meet multidimensional criteria and adapt the TKSI, an efficient solution for the Top-k Skyline that overcomes existing solutions drawbacks. The TKSI is an index-based algorithm that is able to compute only the subset of the Skyline that will be required to produce the top-k objects; thus, the TKSI is able to minimize the number of non-necessary probes. TKSI was empirically compared to extensions of the state-of-the-art algorithms: BUS. BUS relies on the computation of the whole set of Skyline to identify the Top-k Skyline while TKSI builds the Skyline until it has computed the k objects. Initial experimental results show that TKSI computes the Top-k Skyline performing less number of probes, and have shown that our approach is able to identify good quality objects and outperform state-of-the-art solutions.

REFERENCES

W3C Semantic Web discussion list. (2010). *Kit releases 14 billion triples to the linked open data cloud.* Retrieved from http://permalink.gmane.org/gmane.org.w3c.semantic-web/12889

Balke, W., & Güntzer, U. (2004). Multi-objective query processing for database systems. In *Proceedings of the International Conference on Very Large Databases* (VLDB), (pp. 936-947).

Balke, W., Güntzer, U., & Zheng, J. (2004). Efficient distributed skylining for Web Information Systems. In *Proceedings of International Conference on Extending Database Technology* (EDBT), (pp. 256-273).

Bentley, J., Kung, H.T., Schkolnick, M. & Thompson, C.D. (1978). On the average number of maxima in a set of vectors and applications. *Journal of ACM* (JACM).

Börzsönyi, S., Kossmann, D., & Stocker, K. (2001). The skyline operator. In *Proceedings of the 17th International Conference on Data Engineering*, (pp. 421- 430). Washington, DC, USA. IEEE Computer Society.

Carey, M. J., & Kossmann, D. (1997). On saying \Enough already! in SQL. *SIGMOD Record, 26*(2), 219–230. doi:10.1145/253262.253302

Chan, C.-Y., Jagadish, H. V., Tan, K.-L., Tung, A. K. H., & Zhang, Z. (2006a). Finding k-dominant skylines in high dimensional space. In SIGMOD '06: *Proceedings of the 2006 ACM SIGMOD International Conference on Management of Data*, (pp. 503-514). New York: ACM.

Chan, C. Y., Jagadish, H. V., Tan, K.-L., Tung, A. K. H., & Zhang, Z. (2006b). On high dimensional Skylines. In *Proceedings of International Conference on Extending Database Technology* (EDBT), (pp. 478-495).

De Kunder, M. (2010). *The size of the World Wide Web.* Retrieved from http://www.worldwidewebsize.com

Godfrey, P., Shipley, R., & Gryz, J. (2005). Maximal vector computation in large data sets. In VLDB '05: *Proceedings of the 31st International Conference on Very Large Data Bases* (VLDB), (pp. 229-240).

Goncalves, M., & Vidal, M.-E. (2009). Reaching the top of the Skyline: An efficient indexed algorithm for Top-k Skyline queries. In *Proceedings of International Conference on Database and Expert Systems Applications* (DEXA), (pp. 471-485).

Kossmann, D., Ramsak, F., & Rost, S. (2002). Shooting stars in the sky: An online algorithm for skyline queries. In *Proceedings of the 28th International Conference on Very Large Data Bases* (VLDB), (pp. 275-286).

Ley, M. (2010). *The dblp computer science bibliography*. Retrieved from http://www.informatik.uni-trier.de/~ley/db

Lin, X., Yuan, Y., Zhang, Q., & Zhang, Y. (2007). Selecting Stars: The k Most Represen-tative Skyline Operator. In Proceedings of International Conference on Database Theory (ICDE), pp. 86-95.

Papadias, D., Tao, Y., Fu, G., & Seeger, B. (2003). An optimal and progressive algorithm for skyline queries. In SIGMOD '03: *Proceedings of the 2003 ACM SIGMOD International Conference on Management of Data*, (pp. 467-478). New York: ACM Press.

Pei, J., Yuan, Y., Lin, X., Jin, W., Ester, M., & Wang, Q. L. W. (2006). Towards multidimensional subspace skyline analysis. *ACM Transactions on Database Systems, 31*(4), 1335–1381. doi:10.1145/1189769.1189774

Tan, K., Eng, P., & Ooi, B. (2001). Efficicient progressive skyline computation. In *Proceedings of the 28th International Conference on Very Large Data Bases* (VLDB), (pp. 301-310).

Vlachou, A., & Vazirgiannis, M. (2007). Link-based ranking of skyline result sets. In *Proceedings of the 3rd Multidisciplinary Workshop on Advances in Preference Handling* (M-Pref).

Yuan, Y., Lin, X., Liu, Q., Wang, W., Yu, J. X., & Zhang, Q. (2005). Efficient computation of the skyline cube. In VLDB '05: *Proceedings of the 31st International Conference on Very Large Data Bases* (VLDB), (pp. 241-252). VLDB Endowment.

KEY TERMS AND DEFINITIONS

Dominance: An object *a* dominates another object *b* if and only if of *a* is better than or equal to *b* on all dimensions of a multidimensional function and *a* is better than *b* on at least one dimension.

K-Dominant Skyline: A metric to identify Skyline objects in k ≤ d dimensions of multidimensional criteria.

K Representative Skyline: A metric that produces the *k* Skyline objects that have the maximal number of dominated objects.

Multidimensional Function: Criteria comprised of conditions on equally important dimensions or attributes.

Score Function: A function that scores an object of the input dataset.

Skyline: Set of non-dominated objects based on a multidimensional function. Skyline uses a multidimensional function to induce a partial order of the input dataset.

Skyline Frequency: A metric to rank the Skyline in terms of the number of times in which a Skyline object belongs to a subset of the multidimensional criteria.

Top-k: Set of the best k objects based on a score function. Top-k uses a score function to induce a total order of the input dataset.

Top-k Skyline: The top-k objects among the Skyline. Top-k Skyline uses a score function to induce a total order of the Skyline points, and recognizes the top-k objects based on these criteria.

Skycube: The Skylines of the subsets of multidimensional criteria.

Chapter 5
Remarks on a Fuzzy Approach to Flexible Database Querying, Its Extension and Relation to Data Mining and Summarization

Janusz Kacprzyk
Polish Academy of Sciences, Poland

Guy De Tré
Ghent University, Belgium

Sławomir Zadrożny
Polish Academy of Sciences, Poland

ABSTRACT

For an effective and efficient information search of databases, various issues should be solved. A very important one, though still usually neglected by traditional database management systems, is related to a proper representation of user preferences and intentions, and then their representation in querying languages. In many scenarios, they are not clear-cut, and often have their original form deeply rooted in natural language implying a need of flexible querying. Although the research on introducing elements of natural language into the database querying languages dates back to the late 1970s, the practical commercial solutions are still not widely available. This chapter is meant to revive the line of research in flexible querying languages based on the use of fuzzy logic. This chapter recalls details of a basic technique of flexible fuzzy querying, discusses some newest developments in this area and, moreover, shows how other relevant tasks may be implemented in the framework of such queries interface. In particular, it considers fuzzy queries with linguistic quantifiers and shows their intrinsic relation with linguistic data summarization. Moreover, the chapter mentions so called "bipolar queries" and advocates them as a next relevant breakthrough in flexible querying based on fuzzy logic and possibility theory.

DOI: 10.4018/978-1-60960-475-2.ch005

INTRODUCTION

Databases are a crucial element of all kinds of information systems that are in turn the "backbone" of virtually all kinds of nontrivial human activities. The growing power, and falling prices of computer hardware and software, including those that have a direct impact on database technology, have implied an avalanche growth of data volume stored all over the world. That huge volume makes an effective and efficient use of information resources in databases difficult. On the other hand, the use of databases is not longer an area where database professionals are only active and, in fact, nowadays most of the users are novice. This implies a need for a proper human-computer (database) interaction which would adapt to the specifics of the human being, mainly – in our context – to the fact that for the human user the only fully natural means of articulation and communication is natural language with its inherent imprecision.

The aspects mentioned above, the importance of which has been growing over the lasts decades or years, have triggered many research efforts, notably related to what is generally termed *flexible* querying, and some human consistent approaches to data mining and knowledge discovery, including the use of natural langue, for instance in linguistic data summarization.

Basically, the construction of a database query consists in spelling out conditions that should be met by the data sought. Very often, the meaning of these conditions is deeply rooted in natural language, i.e., their original formulation is available in the form of natural language utterances. It is then, often with difficulty, translated into mathematical formulas requested by the traditional query languages. For example, looking for a suitable house in a real estate agency database one may prefer a *cheap* one. In order to pose a query, the concept of "cheap" has to be expressed by an interval of prices. The bounds of such an interval will usually be rather difficult to assess. Thus, a tool to somehow define the notion of "being cheap" may essentially ease the construction of a query. The same definition may be then used, in other queries referring to this concept, also in the context of other words, as, e.g., *very*. The words of this kind, interpreted as so-called *modifiers*, modify the meaning of the original concept in a way that may be assumed context-independent and expressed by a strict mathematical formula.

It seems obvious that a condition referring to such terms as "cheap", "large" etc. should be considered, in general, to be satisfied to *a degree* rather than as satisfied or not satisfied – as it is assumed in the classical approach to database querying. Thus, the notion of the *matching degree* is one of the characteristic features of flexible fuzzy queries.

Moreover, usually, a query comprises more than just one condition. In such a case, the user may require various combinations of conditions to be met. Classically, directly only the satisfaction of *all* conditions may be required or the satisfaction of *any one* condition may be required. However, these are in fact only some extreme cases of conceivable *aggregation* requirements. For instance, a user may be completely satisfied with the data satisfying *most* of the his or her conditions.

The study of modeling of such natural language terms as "cheap", "very" or "most" for the purposes of database querying is the most important part of the agenda of the flexible fuzzy querying research.

In this paper we will present a focused overview of the main research results on the development of flexible querying techniques that are based on fuzzy set theory (Zadeh, 1965). The scope of the chapter is further limited to an overview of those techniques that aim to enhance database querying by introducing various forms of user specified fuzzy preferences (Bosc, Kraft & Petry, 2005). We will not consider other techniques that are relevant in this area, exemplified by self-correcting, navigational, cooperative, etc. querying systems.

For our purposes, we will view a *fuzzy query* as a combination of a number of imprecisely specified (fuzzy) *conditions* on attribute values to be met. The fuzzy preferences in queries are introduced *inside* query conditions and *between* query conditions. For the former, fuzzy preferences introduced *inside* query conditions via flexible search criteria which make possible to indicate a graded desirability of particular values. For the latter, fuzzy preferences *between* query conditions are given via grades of importance of particular query conditions.

The research on fuzzy querying has already a long history, starting with the seminal works of Zadeh during his stay at the IBM Almaden Research Center in the late 1970s, and the first attempt to use fuzzy logic in database querying by Zadeh's doctoral student Tahani (1977). The area has soon enjoyed a great popularity, with many articles in the early period, related both to database querying per se and a relevant area of textual information retrieval [cf. (Bookstein, 1980; Bosc & Pivert,1992a; Kacprzyk & Ziółkowski, 1986; Kacprzyk, Zadrożny & Ziółkowski, 1989), etc.], and books, cf. (Zemankova & Kandel, 1984). Later, the field has become an area of huge research efforts. For an early account of main issues and perspectives, we can refer the reader to Zemankova & Kacprzyk (1993), while for recent, comprehensive state of the art type presentation – Rosado, Ribeiro, Zadrożny & Kacprzyk (2006), Zadrożny, De Tré & De Caluwe (2008), etc.

Some novel and practically relevant developments in broadly perceived data mining and data warehousing have greatly increased interest in fuzzy querying. A notable examples are here works on the combination of fuzzy querying and data mining interfaces for an effective and efficient linguistic summarization of data [cf. (Kacprzyk & Zadrożny, 2000a; Kacprzyk & Zadrożny, 2000b)] or fuzzy logic and the OLAP (Online Analytical Processing) technology (Laurent, 2003).

The purpose of this paper is to present those developments of, and related to fuzzy querying in a focused way to show their essence and applicability. We will start with a general introduction to fuzzy querying in (numeric) relational databases, adding some remarks on the use of object oriented paradigm. Then, we will mention some attempts to add an additional information of user specified preference via so called *bipolar queries* which, in their particular form, make possible to include mandatory and optional requirements. Then, we will show the usefulness of fuzzy queries as a vehicle for an effective and efficient generation of linguistic summaries.

BACKGROUND

A *relational database* is meant as a collection of relations, characterized by sets of *attributes* and populated with *tuples*, which are represented by tables comprising *rows* and *columns*. In what follows we will freely use interchangeably both notions of relations and tables what should not lead to any misunderstandings. Each relation R is defined via the *relation schema*:

$$R\left(A_1 : Dom\left(A_1\right), A_2 : Dom\left(A_2\right),...,A_n : Dom\left(A_n\right)\right) \tag{1}$$

where A_i's are the names of *attributes* (*columns*) and $Dom(A_i)$'s are their associated *domains*.

To retrieve data, a user forms a *query* specifying some conditions (criteria). The retrieval process may be meant, in our context of fuzzy querying, as the calculation of a *matching degree* for each tuple of relevant relation(s), usually from [0,1], as opposed to {0,1} as in the traditional querying.

Basically, one can follow the two general formal approaches to the querying: the *relational algebra* and the *relational calculus*. However, for our purposes the exact form of queries is not that important as we focus on the condition part of queries.

A *fuzzy set F* in the universe *U* is characterized by a membership function

$$\mu_F : U \rightarrow \left[0,1\right] \tag{2}$$

where for each element $x \in U$, $\mu F(x)$ denotes the membership grade or extent to which *x* belongs to *F*.

Fuzzy sets make it possible to represent vague concepts, like "*tall* man" by reflecting the graduality of such a concept.

Fundamentals of Flexible Fuzzy Querying of Databases

The basic idea behind the concept of flexible fuzzy queries is the use of natural language (fuzzy) terms in their conditions. The main approaches include: modelling linguistic terms in queries using fuzzy logic (Tahani, 1977); enhancements of the fuzzy query formalism with flexible aggregation operators (Kacprzyk & Ziółkowski, 1986; Kacprzyk, Zadrożny & Ziółkowski, 1989; Bosc & Pivert, 1993; Dubois & Prade, 1997), and embedding fuzzy constructs in the syntax of the standard SQL (Bosc & Pivert, 1992a; Bosc & Pivert, 1992b; Umano & Fukami, 1994; Bosc & Pivert, 1995; Kacprzyk & Zadrożny, 1995; Galindo et al., 1998; Bosc, 1999; Galindo, Urrutia & Piattini, 2006; De Tré et al., 2006).

Fuzzy Preferences Inside Query Conditions

The first proposal to use fuzzy logic to improve the flexibility of crisp database queries is due to Tahani (1977) who proposed, within SQL to use vague linguistic terms as, e.g., "high" and "young" in "WHERE salary = *HIGH* AND age = *YOUNG*", represented by fuzzy sets. Then, for a tuple *t* and a simple (elementary) condition *q* of type *A = l*, where *A* is an attribute (e.g., "age") and *l* is a linguistic (fuzzy) term (e.g., "YOUNG"), the value of the *matching degree,* γ, is:

$$\gamma\left(q,t\right) = \mu_l\left(x\right) \tag{3}$$

where *x* is *t*[*A*], i.e. the value of tuple *t* for attribute *A* and μ_l is the membership function of the fuzzy set representing the linguistic term *l*. The γ for complex conditions, as, e.g., "age = *YOUNG* AND (salary = *HIGH* OR empyear = *RECENT*)" is obtained using the fuzzy logical connectives, i.e.,

$$\gamma\left(p \wedge q,t\right) = \min\left(\gamma\left(p,t\right),\gamma\left(q,t\right)\right) \tag{4}$$

$$\gamma\left(p \vee q,t\right) = \max\left(\gamma\left(p,t\right),\gamma\left(q,t\right)\right) \tag{5}$$

$$\gamma\left(\neg q,t\right) = 1 - \gamma\left(q,t\right) \tag{6}$$

where p, q are conditions. The minimum and maximum may be replaced by, e.g., t-norm and t-conorm (Klement, Mesiar & Pap, 2000) to model the conjunction and disjunction connectives, respectively.

Among earlier contributions, using the *relational calculus* instead of the relational algebra, is Takahashi (1995) where he proposes the FQL (Fuzzy Query Language), meant as a fuzzy extension of the *domain relational calculus* (DRC). A more complete approach has been proposed Buckles, Petry & Sachar (1989) in a more general context of *fuzzy databases*, which is however also applicable for the crisp relational databases considered here. Zadrożny & Kacprzyk (2002) proposed to interpret elements of DRC in terms of a variant of fuzzy logic. This approach makes it also possible to account for preferences between query conditions in an uniform way.

Fuzzy Preferences Between Query Conditions

A query usually comprises several conditions and they may differ in their importance. For instance, a user may look for a cheap car with a low mileage but the price may be much more important to him or her. Thus, it may be wortwhile to offer him or her the possibility to assign different *importance weights* to various parts of a query condition. A weight w_i is usually assumed to be represented by a real number, $w_i \in [0,1]$, and $w_i=0$ models 'not important at all' and $w_i=1$ represents 'fully important'. A weight w_i is associated with each part of a (fuzzy) condition p_i. The matching degree of a condition p_i with an importance weight w_i is denoted by $\gamma\left(p_i^*, t\right)$.

In order to be meaningful, weights should satisfy some natural conditions [cf. (Dubois & Prade, 1997; Dubois, Fargier & Prade, 1997)]. An interesting disctinction is between static and dynamic weights. Basically, for the static weights which are used in most approaches, Dubois and Prade (1997) propose the following framework. Assume that a query condition p is a conjunction (or disjunction) of weighted elementary query conditions p_i, and denote by $\gamma\left(p_i, t\right)$ the matching degree for a tuple t of p_i without any importance weight assigned. Then, the matching degree, $\gamma\left(p_i^*, t\right)$, of an elementary condition p_i with an importance weight $w_i \in [0,1]$ assigned is:

$$\gamma\left(p_i^*, t\right) = \left(w_i \Rightarrow \gamma\left(p_i, t\right)\right) \tag{7}$$

where $\Rightarrow$ is fuzzy implication connective. The overall matching degree of the whole query composed of the conjunction of conditions p_i is calculated using the standard min-operator.

Depending on the type of the fuzzy implication operator used we get various interpretations of importance weights. For example, using the Dienes implication we obtain from (7):

$$\gamma\left(p_i^*, t\right) = \max\left(\gamma\left(p_i, t\right), 1 - w_i\right) \tag{8}$$

for the Gödel implication:

$$\gamma\left(p_i^*, t\right) = \begin{cases} 1 & \text{if} \quad \gamma\left(p_i, t\right) \geq w_i \\ \gamma\left(p_i, t\right) & \text{otherwise} \end{cases} \tag{9}$$

and for the Goguen implication:

$$\gamma\left(p_i^*, t\right) = \begin{cases} 1 & \text{if} \quad \gamma\left(p_i, t\right) \geq w_i \\ \gamma\left(p_i, t\right)\big/ w_i & \text{otherwise} \end{cases} \qquad (10)$$

In the case of dynamic weights, Dubois & Prade (1997) deal with a variable importance $w_i \in [0,1]$ depending on the matching degree of the associated elementary condition. Basically, while using dynamic weights and dynamic weight assignments, neither the weights nor the associations between weights and criteria are known in advance. Both the weights and their assignments then depend on the attribute values of the record(s) on which the query criteria act as, for example, if the condition "*high salary*" is not important, unless the salary value is extremely high.

Other Flexible Aggregation Schemes

The use of other flexible aggregation schemes is also a subject of intensive research in flexible, fuzzy logic based querying. In (Kacprzyk & Ziółkowski, 1986) and (Kacprzyk, Zadrożny & Ziółkowski, 1989) the aggregation of partial queries (conditions) driven by a *linguistic quantifier* has been firstly described by considering conditions:

$$p = Q \text{ out of } \left\{ p_1, \ldots, p_k \right\} \qquad (11)$$

where Q is a linguistic (fuzzy) quantifier and p_i are elementary conditions to be aggregated. For example, in the context of a US based company, one may classify an order as troublesome if it meets *most* of the following conditions: "comes from outside of USA", "its total value is *low*", "its shipping costs are *high*", "employee responsible for it is known to be not completely reliable", "the amount of order goods on stock is *not much greater* than the amount ordered", etc.

The overall matching degree may be computed using any of the approaches used to model the linguistic quantifier driven aggregation. In (Kacprzyk & Ziółkowski, 1986; Kacprzyk, Zadrożny & Ziółkowski, 1989) first the linguistic quantifiers in the sense of Zadeh (Zadeh, 1983) and later the OWA operators (Yager, 1994) are used (cf. Kacprzyk & Zadrożny, 1997; Zadrożny & Kacprzyk, 2009b).

In Zadeh's approach (1983), a linguistically quantified proposition, exemplified by

"*Most* conditions are *satisfied*", $\qquad (12)$

is written as:

Qy's are F $\qquad (13)$

where Q is a linguistic quantifier (e.g., most), $Y=\{y\}$ is a set of objects (e.g., conditions), and F is a property (e.g., satisfied). Importance B may be added yielding:

QBy's are F $\qquad (14)$

e.g.,

"Most (Q) of the important (B) conditions (y's) are satisfied (F)". (15)

The problem is to find truth(Qy's are F) or truth(QBy's are F) respectively, knowing truth(y is F), $\forall y \in Y$. To this end property F and importance B are represented by fuzzy sets in Y, and a (proportional, nondecreasing) linguistic quantifier Q is assumed to be a fuzzy set in $[0,1]$ as, e.g.

$$\mu_Q(x) = \begin{cases} 1 & \text{for } x \geq 0.8 \\ 2x - 0.6 & \text{for } 0.3 < x < 0.8 \\ 0 & \text{for } x \leq 0.3 \end{cases}$$ (16)

Then, due to Zadeh (1983)

$$\text{truth}(Qy's \text{ are } F) = \mu_Q[\tfrac{1}{n}\sum_{i=1}^{n}\mu_F(y_i)]$$ (17)

$$\text{truth}(QBy's \text{ are } F) = \mu_Q[\sum_{i=1}^{n}(\mu_B(y_i) \wedge \mu_F(y_i)) / \sum_{i=1}^{n}\mu_B(y_i)]$$ (18)

There is a lot of works on this topic studying various possible interpretations of linguistic quantifiers for the flexible querying purposes; cf., e.g., (Bosc, Pivert & Lietrad, 2001; Bosc, Lietrad & Pivert, 2003; Galindo, Urrutia & Piattini, 2006; Vila, Cubero, Medina & Pons, 1997).

The linguistic quantifier guided aggregation is also relevant for our further considerations concerning data mining related extensions of flexible fuzzy querying discussed in what follows.

Towards Implementable Fuzzy Querying Systems

Among the best known approaches to an implementable fuzzy querying systems, one can mention: SQLf (SQLfuzzy) (Bosc & Pivert, 1995), an extension of the SQL introducing linguistic (fuzzy) terms wherever it makes sense, Galindo et al.'s (1998) FSQL (FuzzySQL), a more comprehensive approach, along the lines of SQLf and beyond, and FQUERY (FuzzyQUERY) for Access (Kacprzyk & Zadrożny, 1995), an implementation of a specific "fuzzy extension" of SQL for Microsoft Access®.

We will only present in more detail FQUERY for Access proposed in a series of papers by Kacprzyk & Zadrożny starting with (Kacprzyk & Zadrożny, 1995). It is relevant for our discussion.

FQUERY for Access package is a result of a practical approach to flexible fuzzy querying. We first identified the classes of linguistic terms most useful for the purposes of database querying. These resulted in the following classification:

1. terms representing inherent imprecision of some queries' conditions, including:
    a. numeric fuzzy values (e.g., "cheap"),
    b. modifiers (e.g. "very" in "very cheap"),
    c. fuzzy relations (e.g., "much greater than"),
    d. fuzzy sets of scalar values (e.g., "well-developed countries")

2. terms corresponding to the non-standard aggregation operators, including:
   a. fuzzy (linguistic) quantifiers (e.g., "most"),
   b. importance coefficients (e.g., "important to a degree 0.8" or "very important" etc.)

The query languages of the classic DBMSs do not provide any means for representing such linguistic terms, and some extensions of a classic query language, the SQL are needed. These extensions concern both the syntax of the language and a proper interpretation of particular new linguistic constructs accompanied with some scheme for their representation, elicitation and manipulation. Here we discuss these issues on the example of FQUERY for Access.

The Syntax

We will focus our attention on the well-known SELECT...FROM...WHERE command of the SQL, and will deal only with its WHERE clause. Starting with its simplified version, e.g., excluding subqueries, we propose the following additions to the usual syntax of this clause providing for the direct use of linguistic terms:

```
<WHERE-clause>::= WHERE <condition>
<condition>::= <linguistic quantifier> <sequence of subconditions> ;
    <sequence of subconditions>::= <subcondition> | <subcondition> OR
                <sequence of subconditions>
    <subcondition>::= <importance coefficient> <linguistic quantifier>
                <sequence of atomic conditions>
<sequence of atomic conditions>::=    <atomic condition> |
                <atomic condition> AND
                <sequence of atomic conditions>
<atomic condition>::=    <attribute> = <modifier> <fuzzy value> |
                <attribute> <fuzzy relation> <attribute> |
                <attribute> <fuzzy relation> <number> |
                <single-valued-attribute> IN <fuzzy-set constant> |
<multi-valued-attribute> <compatibility operator> <fuzzy-set constant>
                |
<attribute>::= <numeric field>
<linguistic quantifier>::= <OWA-tag> <quantifier name>
<OWA-tag>::= OWA |
<modifier>::= VERY | MORE OR LESS | RATHER | NOT |
    <compatibility operator>::= possible matching | necessary matching |
                Jackard compatibility
```

Now, let us discuss particular categories of linguistic terms listed above. In what follows, we mainly use examples referring to a hypothetical database of a real estate agency. Particular houses are characterized by: price, land area, location (region), number of bedrooms and bathrooms and other life quality indicators as, e.g., an overall assessment of the environment, transportation infrastructure or shopping facilities.

Atomic condition. The basic building block of a query condition is the *atomic condition*. Basically, it contains a name of an attribute and a constraint imposed on the value of this attribute. Such a constraint may be a traditional, crisp one as, e.g., in

Price <= 200,000

It may also employ one of linguistic terms as, e.g.:

1. *Price =**low*** (numeric fuzzy value)
2. *Land area =**very large*** (numeric fuzzy value + modifier)
3. *Price**is not much greater than**250,000* (fuzzy relation)
4. *Location belongs to**favorite regions*** (fuzzy set constant)
5. **Life quality indicators** are **compatible**
    *with **high quality of life pattern*** (multi-valued-attribute + fuzzy set constant)

Numeric fuzzy values are to be used in connection with numeric fields as, e.g., with the field *Price*. Meaning of such a linguistic term is intuitively obvious, although rather subjective. Thus, it should be possible for each user to define his or her meaning of the linguistic term *low*. On the other hand, it would be advantageous to make it possible to use an already once defined term, like *low*, in various fields. Numeric fuzzy values may be accompanied by *modifiers* as, e.g., *very*, that directly correspond to the similar structures of the natural language.

Fuzzy relations make it possible to soften rigidness of crisp relations. In the third example given above, the atomic condition employs the *much greater than* fuzzy relation accompanied with the negation operator treated as a modifier. Thus, such a condition will accept the price of, e.g., 255,000, which seems to be much more practical than treating 250,000 as a sharp limit.

The examples discussed so far employed linguistic terms to be used along with the numeric data. The fourth example introduces a *fuzzy set constant* which is similar to numeric fuzzy values but meant to be used with scalar data. In this example, the *favorite regions* constant represents the user's preferences as to the location of the house sought. The concept of favorite regions will quite often turn out to be fuzzy, i.e., some regions will be perceived by the user as the best location, some will be completely rejected, and the rest will be acceptable to a degree. Obviously, such a concept is highly subjective.

Finally, the fifth example presents the concept of a *multi-valued attribute* but we will not discuss this case here, for simplicity, referring the reader to (Zadrożny & Kacprzyk, 1996).

The *sequence of atomic conditions* is just a conjunction of atomic conditions. Due to the fact that particular atomic conditions may be satisfied to a degree, we need to employ some generalization of the classical AND logical connective, notably using a *t*-norm, in particular the min operator. In order to achieve a flexibility of the aggregation postulated earlier, linguistic quantifiers are implemented in FQUERY for Access.

Each sequence of atomic conditions may be additionally assigned an importance coefficient. That way, the user may vary the degree to which given sequence contributes to the overall satisfaction degree of the whole query.

Finally, the sequence of atomic conditions, possibly accompanied by a linguistic quantifier and an importance coefficient, is called a *subcondition*.

The *sequence of subconditions* is the disjunction of subconditions. This structuring of various elements of the condition adheres to the scheme assumed in Microsoft Access. As in case of the AND connective, the OR connective is replaced by the corresponding *max* operator of fuzzy logic. Again, it may be further replaced by a linguistic quantifier and importance coefficients may be assigned to subconditions.

Representation and Definitions of Linguistic Terms

Basically, all linguistic terms are represented as fuzzy sets. Obviously, the universe used to define particular fuzzy set depends on the type of their corresponding linguistic term. Namely, in order to represent terms used along with the *numeric* fields (attributes) we use trapezoidal fuzzy numbers. It seems obvious, that these fuzzy numbers are defined over the domains of corresponding fields. Namely, if the *price* of the house ranges from, say, 10,000 up to 100,000 USD, then the fuzzy value *low*, to be used in the atomic condition "price is low", should be defined as a fuzzy number over the interval [10,000, 100,000]. However, then if we strictly stick to this scheme, we have to define *low* separately for each field which we are going to use together with this linguistic term. In order to avoid this apparent inconvenience, we propose to use, in parallel, "context-free" definitions of numeric linguistic terms. Namely, the corresponding fuzzy numbers are defined over the universal interval, e.g., [-10, 10]. Additionally, for each relevant field, its range of variability, the [LowerLimit, UpperLimit] interval, has to be provided before a given linguistic term may be used along with this field in an atomic condition. Then, during the calculation of a matching degree the definitions of relevant fuzzy numbers are translated into the domains of corresponding fields.

The same approach is adopted for dealing with *fuzzy relations*. Basically, a fuzzy relation is a fuzzy set defined in the universe of the Cartesian product of two domains. In the context considered here, these are the domains of one or two *numeric* attributes involved. Obviously, it would be rather tedious to define a fuzzy relation directly on this Cartesian product. Thus, in our approach as the universe for the definition of a fuzzy relation we use the set of possible values of the difference of values of the two attributes involved. More precisely, the same universal interval [-10,10] is used for the definition which is then translated into the real interval of possible differences during the matching degree calculation. The definitions again take the form of trapezoidal fuzzy numbers.

The idea of a *universal* domain is also applied for the definition of a linguistic quantifier. In fact, such a universal domain in the form of the [0,1] interval is present in the original Zadeh's (1983) approach to modeling a special class of so-called *proportional linguistic quantifiers*, which is most relevant for our purposes. Particular numbers from the interval [0,1] are interpreted as expressing proportion of elements possessing a property – in our case, this is a proportion of satisfied conditions.

In FQUERY for Access, a linguistic quantifier has to be first defined in the sense of Zadeh (1983). Then, for the matching degree calculation two options exist. First, the quantifier's original form may be employed directly. Second, an original definition may be automatically translated in order to obtain a corresponding Yager's *OWA operator* (cf. Yager, 1988; Yager & Kacprzyk, 1997).

The linguistic terms meant for the use along with scalar attributes, i.e., *fuzzy set constants*, have to be defined directly in the appropriate universe of discourse corresponding to the domain of a given scalar attribute. More precisely, the set of given attribute values is taken as the universe of discourse. Thus, these constants are, by definition, context dependent. Their discrete membership functions are defined as arrays of numbers. Fuzzy set constants may be defined for any field of character (text) type. Fuzzy set constants may also be defined for - and used together with - *multi-valued attributes*. Obviously, these attributes have to be separately defined, according to the explanation given in the previous section. The definition consists in indicating the list of fields which may then be treated jointly as a virtual attribute.

Computation of a Matching Degree

Flexible fuzzy queries contain ambiguously and imprecisely specified conditions and thus they are assumed to match data to a *degree*. The matching degree is computed for particular linguistic terms as shown in Table 1. We omit some details in Table 1 – for a comprehensive discussion see, e.g., (Kacprzyk & Zadrożny, 2001b).

The partial matching degrees calculated for atomic conditions (subconditions) are aggregated in linguistic quantifier guided way, in accordance with Zadehs' approach (Zadeh, 1983), i.e., using the following formula:

$$md = \mu_Q \left(\frac{\sum_{i=1}^{n} md_i}{n} \right) \tag{19}$$

where *md* stands for the overall matching degree and md_i's denote partial matching degrees computed for *n* component conditions.

BIPOLAR QUERIES AS A NEXT STEP IN FUZZY QUERYING

In the previous sections we have presented the use of fuzzy logic in database querying in a rather traditional setting by essentially extending the standard SQL querying language in a straightforward way. Now, we will briefly outline some new direction in flexible querying which makes possible to even better represent complex user's preferences.

Another aspect of dealing with user preferences which is becoming more and more a topic of intensive research is related to so called *bipolar queries* that are basically meant as involving both positive and negative evaluation of data sought. The name "bipolar queries" was introduced by Dubois & Prade (2002). However, the roots of this concept should be traced back to a much earlier work of Lacroix &

Table 1. Matching degree calculation of a tuple t and atomic conditions containing various linguistic terms where: AT_1, AT_2, AT denote attributes; AT[t] denotes the value of attribute AT at a tuple t; FV and μ_{FV} denote numeric fuzzy values and their membership function; μ_{FV}; MOD and η denote modifiers and their associated functions; FR, μ_{FR} denote fuzzy relations and their membership functions; FS, μ_{FS} denote fuzzy set constants and their membership functions.

Linguistic term type	Atomic condition form	Formula for the calculation of matching degree
Numeric fuzzy value	$AT = FV$	$\mu F_{V}(AT[t])$
Numeric fuzzy value with a modifier	$AT = MOD\ FV$	$\eta(\mu F_{V}(AT[t]))$
Fuzzy relation	$AT_1\ FR\ AT_2$	$\mu F_{R}(AT1[t]-AT2[t])$
Fuzzy set constant	$AT\ in\ FS$	$\mu F_{S}(AT[t])$

Lavency (1987). Their approach was quickly followed by Bosc & Pivert (1992c, 1993), and then extended and discussed in detail by Dubois & Prade (2002, 2008) and in our papers (Matthé & De Tré, 2009; Zadrożny, 2005; Zadrożny & Kacprzyk, 2006, 2007, 2009a; De Tré et al., 2009).

In the most general setting relevant for our considerations, bipolarity is understood as follows. The user expressing his or her preferences concerning the data sought is assumed to consider both *positive* and *negative* aspects. Both may be considered more or less independently and may be aggregated (or not) by the user in many different ways. Thus, our aim should be to provide the user with means making expression of such bipolar preferences as convenient as possible.

Bipolarity may be modeled by using the two basic models (Grabisch, Greco & Pirlot, 2008): *bipolar univariate* and *unipolar bivariate.* The former assumes one scale with three main levels of, respectively, negative, neutral and positive evaluation, gradually changing from one end of the scale to another, giving rise to some intermediate levels. The latter model of bipolarity assumes two independent scales which separately account for positive and negative evaluation. In the first case the negative and positive assessments are somehow combined by the user and only an aggregated overall assessment is expressed as one number, usually from the [-1, 1] interval. Intuitively, the negative numbers express an overall negative assessment, 0 expresses the neutral assessment and the positive numbers express an overall positive assessment. In the case of the unipolar bivariate scale, the positive and negative assessments are expressed separately on two unipolar scales, usually by two numbers from the [0,1].

Now, we will briefly discuss various aspects of the concept of bipolarity in the context of flexible fuzzy queries because we think it is important to distinguish various interpretations of this term used in the literature.

First, in the classic fuzzy approach a unipolar univariate scale is tacitly assumed as we have a degree to which given attribute value is compatible with the meaning of a given linguistic term *l* and, thus, the degree to which this value satisfies a query condition. There is no way to distinguish between "negative" ("rejected", "bad") and "positive" ("accepted", "good") values.

The bipolarity may manifest itself *at the level of each attribute domain* or *at the level of the comprehensive evaluation* of the whole tuple. In the former case, the user may see particular elements of the domain as "negative", "positive" or "neutral", to a degree. This classification should, of course, influence the matching degree of a tuple having particular element of the domain as the value of the attribute under consideration. In the latter case the user is expected to express some conditions, involving possibly many attributes, which – when satisfied by a tuple – make it "negative" or "positive".

In case of the unipolar bivariate model we can distinguish a special interpretation which is further discussed in this paper. Namely, the negative and positive assessments are treated as corresponding to the conditions which are *required* and *preferred* to be satisfied, respectively. Thus, the former condition has to be satisfied necessarily and the latter only *if possible*. The negative assessment in this interpretation is identified with the degree to which the required condition is *not* satisfied. For example, if a person sought has to be young (the required condition), then its negative assessment corresponds to the degree to which he or she is not young, i.e., to which it satisfies the negation of the required condition. The preferred condition, on the other hand, characterizes those tuples (persons) which are really desired, with an understanding that the violation of such a condition by a tuple does not necessarily cause its rejection.

The above special interpretation of bipolarity is in fact predominant in the literature. Lacroix and Lavency (1987) first introduced a query comprising two categories of conditions: one which is mandatory (*C*) and another which expresses just mere preferences (desires) (*P*). The bipolarity of these conditions becomes evident when one adopts the following interpretation. The former condition *C* expresses a *negative* preference: the tuples which do not satisfy it are definitely not matching the whole query while the latter condition *P*, on the other hand, expresses a *positive* preference. These conditions will be referred to as a positive and negative condition, for short, and the whole query will be denoted as (*C*,*P*).

We will identify the negative and positive condition of a bipolar query with the predicates that represent them and denote them as *C* and *P*, respectively. Let us denote the set of all tuples under consideration with *T*. For a tuple $t \in T$, $C(t)$ and $P(t)$ will denote that the tuple *t* satisfies the respective condition. The bipolar query in this approach may be expressed in natural language as follows:

Find tuples t satisfying C and possibly satisfying P

exemplified by: "Find a house cheaper than USD 250,000 *and possibly* located not more than two blocks from a railway station", and such a query may be formally written as

C and possibly P (20)

The key problem, which we consider here, is a proper modeling of the aggregation of both types of conditions which is expressed here with the use of the "and possibly" operator. Thus, we are mainly concerned with how to combine both negative and positive evaluations (assessments) in order to come up with a "standard" evaluation on a unipolar univariate scale which provides for an obvious ordering of the tuples in an answer to the query. An alternative way is to not aggregate and order the tuples with respect to their matching of required and preferred conditions taken separately – this way is adopted, e.g., by Dubois and Prade (2002). However, it seems that the interpretation of the "and possibly" operator is quite intuitive and possesses some interesting properties [cf. also (Bordogna & Pasi, 1995)].

According to the original (crisp) approach by Lacroix & Lavency (1987) such an operator has an important property: the aggregation result depends not only on the explicit arguments, i.e., $C(t)$ and $P(t)$, but also on the content of the database. If there are no tuples meeting both conditions then the result of the aggregation is determined by the negative condition *C* alone. Otherwise the aggregation becomes a regular conjunction of both conditions. This dependence is best expressed by the following logical formula (Lacroix & Lavency, 1987):

$$C(t) \text{ and possibly } P(t) \Leftrightarrow C(t) \wedge \exists s \, (C(s) \wedge P(s)) \Rightarrow P(t) \quad (21)$$

If conditions *C* and *P* are crisp, then this characteristic property is preserved if the "first select using *C* and then order using *P*" interpretation of (20) is adopted, i.e., when first tuples satisfying *C* are selected and then ordered according to *P*. However if both conditions *C* and *P* are fuzzy then it is no longer clear what it should mean that a tuple satisfies the condition *C* as the satisfaction of this condition is now a matter of the degree.

In our approach we start with the formula (24) and, using standard fuzzy counterparts of the classical logical connectives, interpret it in terms of fuzzy logic obtaining the membership function of the fuzzy answer set to a bipolar query (*C*, *P*), with respect to a set of tuples *T*, ans(*C*,*P*,*T*), as:

$$\mu_{ans(C,P,T)}(t) = \min \left(C(t), \max \left(1 - \max_{s \in T} \min(C(s), P(s)), P(t) \right) \right) \quad (22)$$

The matching degree of a tuple against a bipolar query (C, P) is thus meant here as the truth value of (21), computed in the framework of fuzzy (multivalued) logic using the right-hand side of (22). Thus, the evaluation of a bipolar query in this approach produces a fuzzy set of tuples, where the membership function value for a tuple t corresponds to the matching degree of this tuple against the query. The answer to a bipolar query is then a list of the tuples, non-increasingly ordered according to their membership degree.

In (22), the min, max and $1-x$ operators are used to model the connectives of conjunction, disjunction and negation, respectively. Moreover, the implication connective $\Rightarrow$ is modeled by the Kleene-Dienes implication operator and the existential quantifier $\exists$ is modeled via the maximum operator. As there are many other alternatives the issue arises how to appropriately model the logical connectives in (22). For more information on this issue, as well as on other issues related to bipolar queries, we refer the reader to our works (Zadrożny & Kacprzyk, 2007, 2009a; Matthé & De Tré, 2009; De Tré et al., 2009).

Concluding this section, it has to be stressed that the research on bipolarity in the framework of database querying is still at its infancy. Despite some very advanced theoretical treatments [cf. (Dubois & Prade, 2008)] still a vast area of possible interpretations is not covered yet and further research is definitely needed.

FUZZY QUERIES AND LINGUISTIC DATA SUMMARIES

Though the power of FQUERY for Access, or maybe more appropriately its underlying idea of using a linguistic quantifier in the query, is quite obvious for retrieving information of interest to a human user from a database, it has been proven even more effective and efficient as a tool for the implementation of linguistic data summarization. This is one of basic capabilities needed by any "intelligent" system that is meant to operate in real life situations, and – since for the human being the only fully natural means of communication is natural language - then a linguistic (say, by a sentence or a small number of sentences in a natural language) summarization of a set of data would be very desirable and human consistent.

Unfortunately, data summarization is still in general unsolved a problem in spite of vast research efforts. In this paper we will use a simple yet effective and efficient approach to the linguistic summarization of data sets (databases) proposed by Yager (1982), and then presented in a more advanced, and implementable form by Kacprzyk & Yager (2001), and Kacprzyk, Yager & Zadrożny (2000). This will provide a point of departure for our further analysis of more complicated and realistic summaries.

Let us assume the following notation and terminology:

- V is a quality (attribute) of interest, e.g. salary in a database of workers,
- $Y=\{y_1,\ldots,y_n\}$ is a set of objects (records) that manifest quality V, e.g. the set of workers; hence $V(y_i)$ are values of quality V for object $y_i \in Y$;
- $D = \{V(y_1),\ldots,V(y_n)\}$ is a set of data (the "database" in question)

A *linguistic summary* of a data set D consists of:

- a *summarizer* S (e.g. young),
- a *qualifier* R (e.g. recently hired),
- a *quantity in agreement* Q (e.g. most),
- truth T - e.g. 0.7,

as, e.g.,

"Most of recently hired employees are young"   (23)

with "T(*most* of *recently hired* employees are *young*)=0.7". The truth T may be meant in a more general sense, e.g. as validity or, even more generally, as some quality or goodness of a linguistic summary.

The quantity in agreement, Q, is an indication of the extent to which the data satisfy the summary, and two types of a linguistic quantity in agreement can be used:

- absolute as, e.g., "about 5", "more or less 100", "several", and
- relative as, e.g., "a few", "more or less a half", "most", "almost all"etc.

Notice that the above linguistic expressions are again the fuzzy linguistic quantifiers use of which we advocate in the framework of fuzzy flexible querying. Thus, they may be modeled and processed using Zadeh's (1983) approach and this way we obtain the truth T of a linguistic summary.

The basic validity criterion, i.e. the truth of a linguistically quantified statement given by (13) and (14), is certainly the most natural and important but it does not grasp all aspects of a linguistic summary, and hence some other criteria have been proposed, notably by Kacprzyk & Yager (2001), and Kacprzyk, Yager & Zadrożny (2000). These include the degrees of imprecision, covering, appropriateness, the length of a summary, etc. (cf. Kacprzyk & Zadrożny, 2010).

The problem is to find a best summary, i.e. with the highest value of some weighted average of the satisfactions of the criteria assumed. One can clearly notice that a fully automatic determination of a best linguistic summary may be infeasible in practice due to a high number of possible summaries obtained via a combination of all possible linguistic quantifiers, summarizers and qualifiers. In (Kacprzyk & Zadrożny, 2001a) an *interactive approach* was proposed with a *user assistance* in the selection of summarizers, qualifiers and linguistic quantifiers. Basically, given a set of data D, we can hypothetize any appropriate summarizer S, qualifier R and any quantity in agreement Q, and the assumed measure of truth will indicate the quality of the summary.

In our interactive approach it is assumed that such hypothetic summaries are proposed by the user via a flexible fuzzy querying interface, such as provided by FQUERY for Access. It may be easily noticed that components of linguistic summaries are also components of fuzzy queries, as implemented in FQUERY for Access. In particular, atomic conditions with fuzzy values are perfect simple summarizers and qualifiers which may be further combined to obtain more sophisticated summaries. Linguistic quantifiers are used in fuzzy queries to aggregate partial matching degrees but exactly the same computations are required in order to obtain the truth of a linguistic summary. Therefore, the derivation of a linguistic summary may proceed in an interactive (user assisted) way as follows:

- the user formulates a set of linguistic summaries of interest (relevance) using the fuzzy querying add interface,
- the system retrieves records from the database and calculates the validity of each summary adopted, and
- a best (most appropriate) linguistic summary is chosen.

Table 2. Classification of linguistic summaries ($S^{structure}$ denotes that attributes and their connection in a summary are known, while S^{value} denotes a non-instantiated part of a protoform (a summarizer sought)).

Type	Given	Sought	Remarks
1	S	Q	Simple summaries through ad-hoc queries
2	$S\ B$	Q	Conditional summaries through ad-hoc queries
3	$Q\ S^{structure}$	S^{value}	Simple value oriented summaries
4	$Q\ S^{structure}\ B$	S^{value}	Conditional value oriented summaries
5	Nothing	$S\ B\ Q$	General fuzzy rules

Kacprzyk & Zadrożny (2005, 2009) proposed to use the concept of a *protoform* in the sense of Zadeh (2006) as a template underlying both the internal representation of linguistic summaries and their formation in a dialogue with the user. A protoform is defined as an abstract prototype of a linguistically quantified proposition, and its most abstract form is given by (14). Less abstract protoforms are obtained by instantiating particular elments of (14), i.e., for example by replacing F with a condition/property "price is cheap". A more subtle instantiation is also possible where, e.g., only an attribute "price" is specified and its (fuzzy) value is left over. Thus, the user is constructing a more or less abstract protoform and the role of the system is to complete it with all missing elements (e.g., referring to our previous example of the protoform, all possible fuzzy values representing the price) and check the truth value (or other quality indicator) of each thus obtained lingustic summary. Of course, this is fairly easy for a fully instantiated protoform, such as (23) but much more difficult, if possible at all, for fully abstract protoform (14).

In Table 1 we show a classification of linguistic summaries into 5 basic types corresponding to protoforms of an increasingly abstract form.

Type 1 and 2 summaries may be easily produced by a simple extension of a fuzzy querying interface as provided by FQUERY for Access. Basically, the user has to construct a query – a candidate summary, and it has to be determined what is the fraction of rows matching this query and what linguistic quantifier best denotes this fraction. Type 3 summaries require much more effort. Their primary goal is to determine typical (exceptional) values of an attribute. So, query S consists of only one simple condition built of the attribute whose typical (exceptional) value is sought, the "=" relational operator and a placeholder for the value sought. The latter corresponds to the non-instantiated part of an underlying protform. For example, using the following summary in the context of personnel database: $Q = $ *"most"* and $S = $ "age=?" (here "?" denotes a placeholder mentioned above) we look for a typical value of age. A Type 4 summary may produce typical (exceptional) values for some, possibly fuzzy, subset of rows. From the computational point of view Type 5 summaries, corresponding to the most abstract protoform (14), represent the fuzzy rules describing dependencies between specific values of particular attributes. The summaries of Type 1 and 3 have been actually implemented in the framework of FQUERY for Access.

As for possible future directions, we can mention the new proposals to explicitly base linguistic data summarization in the sense considered here, i.e. founded on the concept of Zadeh's *computing with words*, on some developments in computational linguistics. First, Kacprzyk & Zadrożny (2010a) have proposed to consider linguistic summarization in the context of natural language generation (NLG). Second, Kacprzyk & Zadrozny (2010b) suggested the use of some natural language generation (NLG) related elements of Halliday's *systemic functional linguistics* (SFL). We think that these new directions of research will play a considerable role to find better tools and techniques for linguistic data summarization that will better take into account an intrinsic imprecision of natural language.

SOME FUTURE RESEARCH DIRECTIONS AND CONCLUSION

We briefly presented the concept of, a rationale for and various approaches to the use of fuzzy logic in flexible querying. We discussed first some historical developments, then the main issues related to fuzzy querying. Next, we concentrated on fuzzy queries with linguistic quantifiers, and discussed in more detail our FQUERY for Access fuzzy querying system. We indicated not only the straightforward power of that fuzzy querying system but its great potential as a tool to implement linguistic data summaries that may provide an ultimately human consistent way of data mining and data summarization. We briefly mentioned also the concept of bipolar queries that may reflect positive and negative preferences of the user, and may be a breakthrough in fuzzy querying. In the context of fuzzy querying and linguistic summarization we mentioned a considerable potential of our new recent proposals to explicitly use in linguistic data summarization some elements of natural language generation (NLG), and some natural language generation related elements of Halliday's systemic functional linguistics (SFL). We argue that this may be a promising direction for future research.

There may still be many other promising research directions in this area. First, an interesting future line of research may be the incorporation of bipolar queries as an element of flexible (fuzzy) querying to be used in the linguistic summarization context. Second, the inclusion of (fuzzy) ontologies, and maybe even their combination with protoforms of linguistic summaries, may also be a useful paradigm for the human-computer interaction (HCI) in the context of fuzzy logic based data mining and knowledge discovery.

REFERENCES

Bookstein, A. (1980). Fuzzy requests: An approach to weighted Boolean searches. *Journal of the American Society for Information Science American Society for Information Science, 31*, 240–247. doi:10.1002/asi.4630310403

Bordogna, G., & Pasi, G. (1995). Linguistic aggregation operators of selection criteria in fuzzy information retrieval. *International Journal of Intelligent Systems, 10*(2), 233–248. doi:10.1002/int.4550100205

Bosc, P. (1999). Fuzzy databases. In Bezdek, J. (Ed.), *Fuzzy sets in approximate reasoning and Information Systems* (pp. 403–468). Boston: Kluwer Academic Publishers.

Bosc, P., Kraft, D., & Petry, F. E. (2005). Fuzzy sets in database and Information Systems: Status and opportunities. *Fuzzy Sets and Systems, 153*(3), 418–426. doi:10.1016/j.fss.2005.05.039

Bosc, P., Lietard, L., & Pivert, O. (2003). Sugeno fuzzy integral as a basis for the interpretation of flexible queries involving monotonic aggregates. *Information Processing & Management, 39*(2), 287–306. doi:10.1016/S0306-4573(02)00053-5

Bosc, P., & Pivert, O. (1992a). Some approaches for relational databases flexible querying. *International Journal on Intelligent Information Systems, 1*, 323–354. doi:10.1007/BF00962923

Bosc, P., & Pivert, O. (1992b). Fuzzy querying in conventional databases. In Zadeh, L. A., & Kacprzyk, J. (Eds.), *Fuzzy logic for the management of uncertainty* (pp. 645–671). New York: Wiley.

Bosc, P., & Pivert, O. (1992c). Discriminated answers and databases: Fuzzy sets as a unifying expression means. In *Proceedings of the IEEE International Conference on Fuzzy Systems (FUZZ-IEEE)*, (pp. 745-752). San Diego, USA.

Bosc, P., & Pivert, O. (1993). An approach for a hierarchical aggregation of fuzzy predicates. In *Proceedings of the 2nd IEEE International Conference on Fuzzy Systems (FUZZ-IEEE'93)*, (pp. 1231—1236). San Francisco, USA.

Bosc, P., & Pivert, O. (1995). SQLf: A relational database language for fuzzy querying. *IEEE Transactions on Fuzzy Systems, 3*, 1–17. doi:10.1109/91.366566

Bosc, P., Pivert, O., & Lietard, L. (2001). Aggregate operators in database flexible querying. In *Proceedings of the IEEE International Conference on Fuzzy Systems (FUZZ-IEEE 2001)*, (pp. 1231-1234), Melbourne, Australia.

Buckles, B. P., Petry, F. E., & Sachar, H. S. (1989). A domain calculus for fuzzy relational databases. *Fuzzy Sets and Systems, 29*, 327–340. doi:10.1016/0165-0114(89)90044-4

De Tré, G., De Caluwe, R., Tourné, K., & Matthé, T. (2003). Theoretical considerations ensuing from experiments with flexible querying. In T. Bilgiç, B. De Baets & O. Kaynak (Eds.), *Proceedings of the IFSA 2003 World Congress*, (pp. 388—391). (LNCS 2715). Springer.

De Tré, G., Verstraete, J., Hallez, A., Matthé, T., & De Caluwe, R. (2006). The handling of select-project-join operations in a relational framework supported by possibilistic logic. In *Proceedings of the 11th International Conference on Information Processing and Management of Uncertainty in Knowledge-based Systems (IPMU)*, (pp. 2181—2188). Paris, France.

De Tré, G., Zadrożny, S., Matthe, T., Kacprzyk, J., & Bronselaer, A. (2009). *Dealing with positive and negative query criteria in fuzzy database querying*. (LNCS 5822), (pp. 593-604).

Dubois, D., & Prade, H. (1997). Using fuzzy sets in flexible querying: Why and how? In Andreasen, T., Christiansen, H., & Larsen, H. L. (Eds.), *Flexible query answering systems*. Dordrecht: Kluwer Academic Publishers.

Dubois, D., & Prade, H. (2002). *Bipolarity in flexible querying*. (LNAI 2522), (pp. 174-182).

Dubois, D., & Prade, P. (2008). Handling bipolar queries in fuzzy information processing. In Galindo, J. (Ed.), *Handbook of research on fuzzy information processing in databases* (pp. 97–114). New York: Information Science Reference.

Galindo, J., Medina, J. M., Pons, O., & Cubero, J. C. (1998). A server for Fuzzy SQL queries. In T. Andreasen, H. Christiansen & H.L. Larsen (Eds.), *Proceedings of the Third International Conference on Flexible Query Answering Systems*, (pp. 164-174). (LNAI 1495). London: Springer-Verlag.

Galindo, J., Urrutia, A., & Piattini, M. (2006). *Fuzzy databases: Modeling, design and implementation.* Hershey, PA: Idea Group Publishing.

Grabisch, M., Greco, S., & Pirlot, M. (2008). Bipolar and bivariate models in multicriteria decision analysis: Descriptive and constructive approaches. *International Journal of Intelligent Systems, 23,* 930–969. doi:10.1002/int.20301

Kacprzyk, J., & Yager, R. R. (2001). Linguistic summaries of data using fuzzy logic. *International Journal of General Systems, 30,* 133–154. doi:10.1080/03081070108960702

Kacprzyk, J., Yager, R. R., & Zadrożny, S. (2000). A fuzzy logic based approach to linguistic summaries of databases. *International Journal of Applied Mathematics and Computer Science, 10,* 813–834.

Kacprzyk, J., & Zadrożny, S. (1995). FQUERY for Access: Fuzzy querying for windows-based DBMS. In Bosc, P., & Kacprzyk, J. (Eds.), *Fuzziness in database management systems* (pp. 415–433). Heidelberg, Germany: Physica-Verlag.

Kacprzyk, J., & Zadrożny, S. (1997). Implementation of OWA operators in fuzzy querying for Microsoft Access. In Yager, R. R., & Kacprzyk, J. (Eds.), *The ordered weighted averaging operators: Theory and applications* (pp. 293–306). Boston: Kluwer Academic Publishers.

Kacprzyk, J., & Zadrożny, S. (2000a). On a fuzzy querying and data mining interface. *Kybernetika, 36,* 657–670.

Kacprzyk, J., & Zadrożny, S. (2000b). On combining intelligent querying and data mining using fuzzy logic concepts. In Bordogna, G., & Pasi, G. (Eds.), *Recent research issues on fuzzy databases* (pp. 67–81). Heidelberg: Physica-Verlag.

Kacprzyk, J., & Zadrożny, S. (2001a). Data mining via linguistic summaries of databases: An interactive approach. In Ding, L. (Ed.), *A new paradigm of knowledge engineering by soft computing* (pp. 325–345). Singapore: World Scientific. doi:10.1142/9789812794604_0015

Kacprzyk, J., & Zadrożny, S. (2001b). Computing with words in intelligent database querying: Standalone and Internet-based applications. *Information Sciences, 134,* 71–109. doi:10.1016/S0020-0255(01)00093-7

Kacprzyk, J., & Zadrożny, S. (2005). Linguistic database summaries and their protoforms: Towards natural language based knowledge discovery tools. *Information Sciences, 173,* 281–304. doi:10.1016/j.ins.2005.03.002

Kacprzyk, J., & Zadrożny, S. (2009). Protoforms of linguistic database summaries as a human consistent tool for using natural language in data mining. *International Journal of Software Science and Computational Intelligence, 1*(1), 100–111.

Kacprzyk, J., & Zadrozny, S. (2010). Computing with words and systemic functional linguistics: Linguistic data summaries and natural language generation. In Huynh, V.-N., Nakamori, Y., Lawry, J., & Inuiguchi, M. (Eds.), *Integrated uncertainty management and applications* (pp. 23–36). Heidelberg: Springer-Verlag. doi:10.1007/978-3-642-11960-6_3

Kacprzyk, J., & Zadrożny, S. (in press). Computing with words is an implementable paradigm: Fuzzy queries, linguistic data summaries and natural language generation. *IEEE Transactions on Fuzzy Systems.*

Kacprzyk, J., Zadrożny, S., & Ziółkowski, A. (1989). FQUERY III+: A human-consistent database querying system based on fuzzy logic with linguistic quantifiers. *Information Systems*, *14*, 443–453. doi:10.1016/0306-4379(89)90012-4

Kacprzyk, J., & Ziółkowski, A. (1986). Database queries with fuzzy linguistic quantifiers. *IEEE Transactions on Systems, Man, and Cybernetics*, *16*, 474–479. doi:10.1109/TSMC.1986.4308982

Klement, E. P., Mesiar, R., & Pap, E. (Eds.). (2000). *Triangular norms*. Dordrecht, Boston, London: Kluwer Academic Publishers.

Lacroix, M., & Lavency, P. (1987). Preferences: Putting more knowledge into queries. In *Proceedings of the 13 International Conference on Very Large Databases*, (pp. 217-225). Brighton, UK.

Laurent, A. (2003). Querying fuzzy multidimensional databases: Unary operators and their properties. *International Journal of Uncertainty. Fuzziness and Knowledge-Based Systems*, *11*, 31–46. doi:10.1142/S0218488503002259

Matthé, T., & De Tré, G. (2009). Bipolar query satisfaction using satisfaction and dissatisfaction degrees: Bipolar satisfaction degrees. In S.Y. Shin & S. Ossowski (Eds.), *Proceedings of the SAC Conference*, (pp. 1699-1703). ACM.

Rosado, A., Ribeiro, R., Zadrożny, S., & Kacprzyk, J. (2006). Flexible query languages for relational databases: An overview. In Bordogna, G., & Psaila, G. (Eds.), *Flexible databases supporting imprecision and uncertainty* (pp. 3–53). Berlin, Heidelberg: Springer Verlag. doi:10.1007/3-540-33289-8_1

Tahani, V. (1977). A conceptual framework for fuzzy query processing: A step toward very intelligent database systems. *Information Processing & Management*, *13*, 289–303. doi:10.1016/0306-4573(77)90018-8

Takahashi, Y. (1995). A fuzzy query language for relational databases. In Bosc, P., & Kacprzyk, J. (Eds.), *Fuzziness in database management systems* (pp. 365–384). Heidelberg, Germany: Physica-Verlag.

Umano, M., & Fukami, S. (1994). Fuzzy relational algebra for possibility-distribution-fuzzy relational model of fuzzy data. *Journal of Intelligent Information Systems*, *3*, 7–27. doi:10.1007/BF01014018

Vila, M. A., Cubero, J.-C., Medina, J.-M., & Pons, O. (1997). Using OWA operator in flexible query processing. In Yager, R. R., & Kacprzyk, J. (Eds.), *The ordered weighted averaging operators: Theory and applications* (pp. 258–274). Boston: Kluwer Academic Publishers.

Yager, R. R. (1982). A new approach to the summarization of data. *Information Sciences*, *28*, 69–86. doi:10.1016/0020-0255(82)90033-0

Yager, R. R. (1988). On ordered weighted averaging aggregation operators in multi-criteria decision making. *IEEE Transactions on Systems, Man, and Cybernetics*, *18*, 183–190. doi:10.1109/21.87068

Yager, R. R., & Kacprzyk, J. (1997). *The ordered weighted averaging operators: Theory and applications*. Boston: Kluwer.

Zadeh, L. A. (1965). Fuzzy sets. *Information and Control*, *8*(3), 338–353. doi:10.1016/S0019-9958(65)90241-X

Zadeh, L. A. (1983). A computational approach to fuzzy quantifiers in natural languages. *Computers & Mathematics with Applications (Oxford, England)*, *9*, 149–184. doi:10.1016/0898-1221(83)90013-5

Zadeh, L. A. (2006). From search engines to question answering systems-the problems of world knowledge relevance deduction and precisiation. In Sanchez, E. (Ed.), *Fuzzy logic and the Semantic Web* (pp. 163–210). Amsterdam: Elsevier.

Zadrożny, S. (2005). Bipolar queries revisited. In V. Torra, Y. Narukawa & S. Miyamoto (Eds.), *Modelling decisions for artificial intelligence (MDAI 2005)*, (pp. 387-398). (LNAI 3558). Berlin, Heidelberg: Springer-Verlag.

Zadrożny, S., De Tré, G., De Caluwe, R., & Kacprzyk, J. (2008). An overview of fuzzy approaches to flexible database querying. In Galindo, J. (Ed.), *Handbook of research on fuzzy information processing in databases* (pp. 34–54). Hershey, PA/ New York: Idea Group, Inc.

Zadrożny, S., & Kacprzyk, J. (1996) Multi-valued fields and values in fuzzy querying via FQUERY for Access. In *Proceedings of FUZZ-IEEE.96 - Fifth International Conference on Fuzzy Systems New Orleans, USA,* (pp. 1351-1357).

Zadrożny, S., & Kacprzyk, J. (2002). Fuzzy querying of relational databases: A fuzzy logic view. In *Proceedings of the EUROFUSE Workshop on Information Systems,* (pp. 153-158). Varenna, Italy.

Zadrożny, S., & Kacprzyk, J. (2006). Bipolar queries and queries with preferences. In *Proceedings of the 17th International Conference on Database and Expert Systems Applications (DEXA'06)*, Krakow, Poland, (pp. 415-419). IEEE Computer Society.

Zadrożny, S., & Kacprzyk, J. (2007). *Bipolar queries using various interpretations of logical connectives* (pp. 181–190).

Zadrożny, S., & Kacprzyk, J. (2009a). Bipolar queries: An approach and its various interpretations. In J.P. Carvalho, D. Dubois, U. Kaymak, & J.M. da Costa Sousa (Eds.), *Proceedings of the IFSA/EUSFLAT Conference*, (pp. 1288-1293).

Zadrożny, S., & Kacprzyk, J. (2009b). Issues in the practical use of the OWA operators in fuzzy querying. *Journal of Intelligent Information Systems*, *33*(3), 307–325. doi:10.1007/s10844-008-0068-1

Zemankova, M., & Kacprzyk, J. (1993). The roles of fuzzy logic and management of uncertainty in building intelligent Information Systems. *Journal of Intelligent Information Systems*, *2*, 311–317. doi:10.1007/BF00961658

Zemankova-Leech, M., & Kandel, A. (1984). *Fuzzy relational databases-a key to expert systems*. Cologne, Germany: Verlag TÜV Rheinland.

KEY TERMS AND DEFINITIONS

Bipolar Query: A database query which separately specifies the positive and negative conditions. The former should be satisfied by the data sought while the latter should not.

Database: A collection of persistent data. In a database, data are modeled in accordance with a database model. This model defines the structure of the data, the constraints for integrity and security, and the behavior of the data.

Fuzzy Query: A database query which involves imprecisely specified search conditions. These conditions are often expressed using terms of a natural language which are modeled using fuzzy logic.

Linguistic Quantifier: a natural language expression such as ¨most¨, around 5¨ which expresses an imprecise proportion or quantity.

Linguistic Summary of Data: a linguistic (by a sentence or a small number of sentences in a natural language) summarization of a set of data.

Protoform: an abstract prototype of a linguistically quantified proposition, i.e. of an expression such as ¨Most employees are young¨.

Relational Database: A relational database is a database that is modeled in accordance with the relational database model. In the relational database model, the data are structured in relations that are represented by tables. The behavior of the data is defined in terms of the relational algebra, which originally consists of eight operators (union, intersection, division, cross product, join, selection, projection and division), or in terms of the relational calculus, which is of a declarative nature.

Chapter 6
Flexible Querying of Imperfect Temporal Metadata in Spatial Data Infrastructures

Gloria Bordogna
CNR-IDPA, Italy

Francesco Bucci
CNR-IREA, Italy

Paola Carrara
CNR-IREA, Italy

Monica Pepe
CNR-IREA, Italy

Anna Rampini
CNR-IREA, Italy

ABSTRACT

Spatial Data Infrastructures (SDI) allow users connected to the Internet to share and access remote and distributed heterogeneous geodata that are managed by their providers at their own Web sites. In SDIs, available geodata can be found via standard discovery geo-services that makes available query facilities of a metadata catalog. By expressing precise selection conditions on the values of the metadata collected in the catalog, the user can discover interesting and relevant geodata and then access them by means of the services of the SDI. An important dimension of geodata that often concerns such users' requests is the temporal information that can have multiple semantics. Current practice to perform geodata discovery in SDIs is inadequate for several reasons. First of all, with respect to the temporal character- ization, available recommendations for metadata specification, for example, the INSPIRE Directive of the European community do not consider the multiple semantics of the temporal metadata. To this aim,

DOI: 10.4018/978-1-60960-475-2.ch006

this chapter proposes to enrich the current temporal metadata with the possibility to indicate temporal metadata related to both the observations, i.e., the geodata, the observed event, i.e., the objects in the geodata, and the temporal resolution of observations, i.e., their timestamps. The chapter introduces also a proposal to manage temporal series of geodata observed at different dates. Moreover, in order to represent the uncertain and incomplete knowledge of the time information on the available geodata, the chapter proposes a representation for imperfect temporal metadata within the fuzzy set framework. Another issue that is faced in this chapter is the inadequacy of current discovery service query facilities: in order to obtain a list of geodata results, corresponding values of metadata must exactly match the query conditions. To allow more flexibility, the chapter proposes to adopt the framework of fuzzy databases to allow expressing soft selection conditions, i.e., tolerant to under-satisfaction, so as to retrieve geodata in decreasing order of relevance to the user needs. The chapter illustrates this proposal by an example.

INTRODUCTION

Infrastructures are complex systems in which a network of interconnected but autonomous components is used for the exchange and mobility of goods, persons, information. Their successful exploitation requires technologies, policies, investments in money and personnel, common standards and harmonized rules. Typical examples of infrastructures which are critical for society are transportation and water supply. In Information Technology, the term infrastructure could be related to communication channels through which information can be located, exchanged, accessed, and possibly elaborated.

The importance of Spatial Data Infrastructures (SDIs) has been recognized since the United Nations Conference on Environment and Development in Rio de Janeiro in 1992.

Geographic information is vital to making sound decisions at the local, regional, and global levels. Crime management, business development, flood mitigation, environmental restoration, community land use assessments and disaster recovery are just a few examples of areas in which decision-makers can benefit from geographic information, together with the associated Spatial Data Infrastructure (SDI) that support information discovery, access, and use of this information in the decision-making process.

In time, the role of discovery services of data with a geographic reference (geodata) has become a main issue of governments and institutions, and central to many activities in our society. In order to take political and socio-economics decisions, administrators must analyze data with geographic reference; for example, the governments define funding strategies on the basis of CO_2 pollution distribution. Even in everyday life, people need considering data regarding the area in which they live, move, work and act; for example, consider a family wishing to reach mountains for a skiing holiday, and looking for meteorological data. In order to be useful, the data they are looking for should fit the area and period of time of their interest; they should trust in the quality of the data; if possible, they should obtain what they need with simple searching operations, and in a way that allows evaluating the fitness of the data with respect to their needs and purposes.

In 2007, the INSPIRE Directive of the European Parliament and of the Council entered into force (INSPIRE Directive, 2007) to trigger the creation of a European Spatial Data Infrastructure (ESDI) that delivers to the users integrated spatial information services. These services should allow users to discover and possibly access spatial or geographical information from a wide range of sources, from the local to the global level, in an inter-operable way for a variety of uses. Discovery is performed through services that should follow INSPIRE standards and can be implemented through some products (either proprietary or not) that declare their compliance.

Nevertheless, current technologies adopted in SDIs, and consequently the actual practice for searching geographic information, do not comply with the way users express their needs and search for information and hamper the ability and practices of geodata providers.

One main problem is due to the characteristics of the information on the available geodata, i.e., metadata. Metadata is an essential requirement for locating and evaluating available geodata, and metadata standards can increase and facilitate geodata sharing through time and space. For this reason considerable efforts have been spent to define "standard" and minimum core metadata for geodata to be used in SDIs. INSPIRE is nowadays a directive of the European community that comprehends metadata specifications (European Commission, 2009).

Nevertheless, such specifications are still incomplete and inadequate for they do not allow specifying all the necessary information on geodata as far as the temporal dimension, and force providers to generate precise metadata values, which are missing in many real cases (Dekkers, 2008; Bordogna et al., 2009).

This chapter, analyses the utility of temporal metadata on geodata and proposes a framework to represent its imprecise and uncertain values as well as to express its possible multiple semantics..

Another problem with the current information search practice in SDIs is that the user is forced to express precise conditions on the metadata values that must be perfectly satisfied in order to obtain a result. Further, the results are unordered, with no indication of relevance to the user who must access the remote geodata to become aware of its actual adequacy to his/her needs. Even when a web service is invoked, this may case useless network overloading.

A framework that this chapter proposes for optimizing this search practice is to allow users to express flexible queries, with tolerant (soft) conditions on the metadata values, so as to retrieve results ranked in decreasing order of their satisfaction to the query.

To this aim the fuzzy database framework can provide an effective way to model the discovery service of SDIs, since it allows both representing and flexibly querying imperfect metadata (Bosc and Pivert, 2000).

In the next paragraph, this chapter will discuss the limitations of current temporal metadata in discovery services of SDIs and propose some solutions. Then, the proposal of a formal and operational method to represent imperfect temporal metadata values and allowing users to express soft search conditions, i.e., tolerant to under-satisfaction, is presented. In doing so, discovery services can apply partial matching mechanisms between the "desired" metadata, expressed by the user, and the archived metadata: this would allow retrieving geodata in decreasing order of relevance to the user needs, as it usually occurs on the Web when using search engines. In the last paragraph, the proposal is illustrated with an example, while the concluding paragraph describes the context of this research work.

ARCHITECTURE OF A SPATIAL DATA INFRASTRUCTURE

An overview of the current understanding of the technical architecture of INSPIRE is depicted in figure 1; it has been adopted by the European SDI (for a through description of this figure, see INSPIRE Cross Drafting Teams, 2007). It is a layered structure that makes available several facilities executed by the functional components (depicted by the rounded boxes).

Figure 1. INSPIRE technical architecture overview

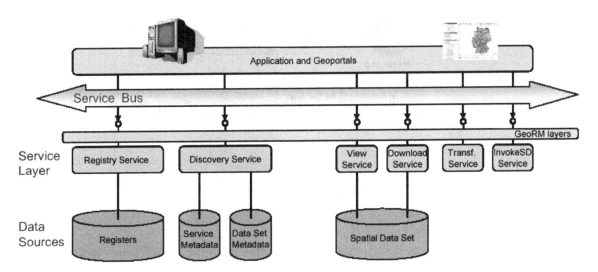

The object of our attention is the data discovery service that is in charge of both providing the discovery services and the management of the metadata. Such metadata are defined to support distinct purposes, namely:

Geodata Discovery- What geodata holds the characteristics I am interested in? This enables users to know what geodata the organizations have and make available.

Exploration activity - Do the identified geodata contain sufficient information for my purposes? This is documentation on the geodata that must be provided to ensure that others can use the geodata correctly.

Exploitation activity – What is the process of obtaining and using the required geodata? This helps end users and provider organisations to effectively store, reuse, maintain and archive their data holdings.

Two kinds of metadata sets are managed by the discovery service:

- the metadata data set that describes the summary information and characteristics of the available geodata (these include human-generated textual description of geodata and machine-generated data),
- and the service metadata, that are descriptions of the service characteristics made available by the SDI, for example services to discover geodata.

The discovery service works by comparing the users' requests for information, coming from the Application and Geoportal Layer, with the metadata that describe available resources, following a well know and widely developed retrieval model.

Figure 2 illustrates the three main components of a retrieval model, i.e. data representation, query representation, and matching mechanism. In order to improve effectiveness of the discovery, representations must be comparable and matching adequate to them (Cater and Kraft, 1989; Salton, 1989; Bordogna, Carrara, Pasi, 1991). The matching mechanism is deputed at identifying all metadata whose content satisfies (at least partially) users' selection conditions. In order to allow automatic matching,

Figure 2. Components of a generic retrieval model

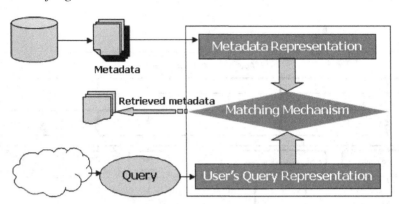

selection conditions and resource descriptions must be expressed in the same formal representation at some stage of the matching process.

In particular, in the discovery of geodata sets, the query selection conditions expressed by a user should clearly specify "what" is of interest through content keywords (e.g., landslides), "where" the interesting features should be located (e.g., in a bounding box surrounding the Alps), "when" these features should have been observed (e.g., the date/s of the observation), and "why" they are searched (e.g., to detect recurrence of landslides).

On the provider side, metadata should describe georesources following the same four aspects.

TEMPORAL METADATA IN THE EUROPEAN SDI

Within the context of a SDI discovery service, temporal aspects play a major role at multiple levels, especially when considering some outstanding applications of geodata that involve dynamic phenomena. This is the case of research on climate change, meteorological forecast, monitoring the impact of natural and anthropic events on the environment, etc.

In the perspective of the hugely populated European SDI envisioned by INSPIRE, it is necessary to filter out geographic resources that not only refer to a given spatial location, but also match both the temporal coverage of interest and the temporal resolution suitable to the application purposes. This implies an adequate temporal description by the metadata providers, who should be guided in characterizing their resources as far as their temporal aspects, also when temporal descriptions cannot be precisely assessed (such as for resources regarding the past).

Recommended temporal specifications in the Implementing Rules of metadata in INSPIRE (European Commission, 2007) are listed in Table 1.

They are inadequate to satisfy the multiple semantics of the temporal conditions. In fact, they are mainly devoted to time stamping resource lifecycle, while only the element "Temporal extent" contains dates related to the resource content whose meaning is ambiguous and does not help in characterizing both temporal coverage and resolution.

To improve temporal metadata definition, some proposals have been formulated and a set of six new recommendations is now available (Dekkers, 2008). Their main role is to specify the type and format

Table 1. Temporal metadata elements in INSPIRE Implementing Rules

Metadata element	Metadata sub-element	Definition
Temporal reference	-	It addresses the Directive's requirement to have information on the temporal dimension of the data (Article 8-2 (d)). At least one of the following metadata sub-elements shall be provided
Temporal reference	Temporal extent	It defines the time period covered by the content of the resource. This time period can be expressed as: • an individual date, • an interval of dates expressed through the starting date and end date of the interval; or • a mix of individual dates and intervals of dates. The default reference system shall be the Gregorian calendar, with dates expressed in accordance with ISO 8601
Temporal reference	Date of publication	This is the date of publication of the resource when available, or the date of entry into force
Temporal reference	Date of last revision	This is the date of last revision of the resource, if the resource has been revised
Temporal reference	Date of creation	This is the date of creation of the resource, if it has not been revised

of time values to be adopted either in expressing dates or time periods and to suggest how to preserve precision in exchange or conversion processes.

However, these recommendations are still limited, with respect to both the requirements of time stamping by metadata providers, and the representation of the temporal search conditions necessary to geodata users.

EXTENDING TEMPORAL METADATA AND MANAGING TIME SERIES

Based on actual experience gained in the European Projects IDE-Univers (http://www.ideunivers.eu) and AWARE (http://www.aware-eu.info), we verified the usefulness of series of temporal datasets and realized that some extensions should be adopted to improve temporal characterization of datasets and dataset series in the metadata of an SDI. In fact, as discussed in the previous paragraph, the current specification of INSPIRE (European Commission, 2009) does not allow specifying the time relative to the occurrence of the event that is observed in one, several or a series of spatial data, nor their temporal granularity. As experienced in our practice, these aspects could not be considered irrelevant for INSPIRE applications as argued also in (Dekkers, 2008). Therefore, in the following subparagraphs we first introduce a proposal for managing temporal series of data sets, and then discuss the need for metadata extensions in the temporal domain.

Temporal Data Set Series

In many real applications it is worth pointing out that a set of geographic resources is a collection of data that share common spatial properties (e.g., they cover the same area, they are the products of the same application) but are distinct with respect to their temporal attribute. An example could be the set of snow cover maps of the Alpine region, resulting from the processing of satellite images taken in different days along one melting season.

Current metadata specification allows to create a unique metadata item for the whole set of maps, assigning the value "series" to the metadata element "ResourceType" (see section 2.2.3, European Commission, 2009). This unique metadata item is used to describe the whole set, since all satellite products share all their attributes (e.g., geographic bounding-box, lineage, provider, etc.) but time.

In particular, the "temporal extent" element of the metadata describing the series should address the whole temporal range targeted by the maps: this goal can be achieved specifying a time period either starting with the first image date and ending with the date of the last image, or declaring a sequence of time instants, each of them corresponding to an image date (see Table 2). A combination of the two specifications could be adopted too.

From the metadata provider point of view, managing the map collection like a time series avoids a long and error-prone metadata creation activity for each map; from the user point of view, the discovery service presents to her/him a unique resource, instead of a huge amount of similar results. However, in terms of discovery, it is not possible to filter a single image in the set, on the basis of its own timestamp.

However, the problem of temporal filtering can be solved by filling the resource locator metadata element "Resource locator" (see section 2.2.4, European Commission, 2009), which could be used to link the metadata of the series to a Web service providing the maps. In this way, a proper client application could allow users to search dates or periods that are automatically combined with the service URL, and submit a correctly formatted request to the service that provides related maps.

Further Metadata Elements for Temporal Resolution and Events

The spatial characterization of a dataset presents two complementary aspects, i.e., spatial coverage and spatial resolution; in the same way its temporal characterization cannot be considered complete without specifying temporal coverage together with temporal resolution, which is also mentioned in the literature as granularity. An example: a data set contains the daily (time resolution) mean precipitation in a year (time coverage) as measured by a rain-gauge. Another example is represented by a collection of satellite products such as 16-day (time resolution) biomass maps from the beginning to the end of operation (time coverage) of a sensor. The temporal resolution of repeated observations is a key element of such data set attributes as well as it is crucial to assess their appropriateness for specific purposes, e.g., as related to environmental modelling or monitoring.

Though the current Implementing Rules for INSPIRE metadata (European Commission, 2009) account for describing both the spatial characterization aspects (see sect. 2.7.2 for Spatial Resolution), the dual temporal description is missing since there is no element to specify the temporal resolution.

Time resolution can be expressed by the use of ISO 8601:2004 (ISO 8601, 2004), in the form of Recurring time interval that is specified by adding "R[n]/" to the beginning of a time interval expression, where "R" is used as the letter itself and [n] is replaced by the number of repetitions, whose unit is specified in the following part of the same expression (for example R8760/2008-01-01T0:00/P0Y0M-0DT1H00M, means hourly for the year 2008).

However, it is preferable to provide a separate metadata element, in order to allow for an easier compilation and discovery of metadata. This solution makes it possible to use a linguistic label for expressing the temporal resolution (such as hourly, daily, monthly, yearly, etc.) instead of a numeric value - the number of repetitions -, which should be computed on a case-base, and that is not easily interpretable (as in the example reported). For the use of linguistic temporal specifications in metadata elements see the following paragraph 3.

Table 2. Specification of the temporal extent of a time series of maps

```
...
<gmd:extent>
<gmd:EX_Extent>
<!-- temporal Extent as unique range covering the whole melting season period -->
<gmd:temporalElement>
<gmd:EX_TemporalExtent>
<gmd:extent>
<gml:TimePeriod gml:id="IDd2febb...">
<gml:beginPosition>2003-04-01T11:45:30</gml:beginPosition>
<gml:endPosition>2003-08-31-T11:56:30</gml:beginPosition>
</gml:TimePeriod>
</gmd:extent>
</gmd:EX_TemporalExtent>
</gmd:temporalElement>

<!-- temporal Extent as a series of dates, each one corresponding to an image in the series -->
<gmd:temporalElement>
<gmd:EX_TemporalExtent>
<gmd:extent>
<gml:TimeInstant>
<gml:timePosition>2003-04-01</gml:timePosition>
</gml:TimeInstant>
</gmd:extent>
</gmd:EX_TemporalExtent>
</gmd:temporalElement>
<gmd:temporalElement>
<gmd:EX_TemporalExtent>
<gmd:extent>
<gml:TimeInstant>
<gml:timePosition>2003-04-15</gml:timePosition>
</gml:TimeInstant>
</gmd:extent>
</gmd:EX_TemporalExtent>
</gmd:temporalElement>
<!-- date corresponding to other images in the series -->
</gmd:EX_Extent>
</gmd:extent>

...
```

As regards events and observations, Dekkers, (2008) has reported that "*looking at the use of temporal information for discovery, users may be interested in [...] a particular date or time period during which an event took place which is described in the resource*". The supporting example regards the statistics of rainfall in a particular time period. However, though in the example there is a semantic agreement between the event and its observations - that constitutes the content of the resource -, in many other cases this is not applicable.

For example, if a provider has to describe the metadata of remote sensing products acquired and processed in order to monitor a landslide that occurred in 1986, the current specification of temporal extent just allows indicating the time of the observations (acquisitions of the satellite image) and not the time of the event, i.e., of the landslide occurrence. Nevertheless, this can be very important information for the user of a discovery service, because she/he can be interested in comparing the status of the landslide in different periods of time, as they appear in distinct products. She/he must be sure that the compared images refer to the same event, and not to distinct ones.

While the description of the event associated to the different resources can be included in the resource abstract, there is no way to specify the temporal characterization of the event.

In summary, this chapter proposes to introduce the possibility to include in metadata one or more events/processes/phenomena of reference for the geodata: a satellite image can be an observation of fires in a region; a set of meteo records are measures of a rainfall; some thematic maps can be subsequent representations of urban growth, etc. A temporal extent element should be defined also for the reference event(s), of course. Notwithstanding further extensions are possible, this chapter proposes to include the following temporal metadata:

- Instant in which the observation/event occurred:
    ◦ Date, time (e.g. the landslide occurred 11-07-2008 at 8:00:00)
- Period of validity, or duration of an observation/event:
    ◦ period (interval of dates, times) (e.g. the duration of a fire was from 11-07-2008 to 13-07-2008)
- Sequence of instances of occurrences/events:
    ◦ multiple instants of time or dates, periodic or aperiodic (e.g. the dates of the distinct fires were 11-07-2008, and 12-07-2008)
- Sequence of periods of validity or duration of occurrences/events:
    ◦ multiple periods or durations, periodic or aperiodic (e.g. the times of the distinct fires were from 11-07-2008 to 13-07-2008 and from 20-08-2008 to 23-08-2008)

Moreover, the following paragraph introduces a framework to allow the definition of imperfect temporal values in the temporal extent metadata elements regarding both geodata and related event(s).

A FRAMEWORK FOR IMPERFECT TEMPORAL METADATA VALUES

The formats specified in the guidelines based on ISO 19115 and ISO 19119 which regard metadata (European Commission, 2009) do not allow specifying imperfect values for metadata, both temporal, spatial, and thematic, which, sometimes, are the only values that metadata producers can provide, given that they often do not have enough information to define precise values. In real situations, it often happens that the date or time of occurrence of an event is ill-known. This is due to several reasons: either because the event was not observed during its occurrence, and thus the date can only be estimated by experts, or because it occurred long time ago so that its date can be deduced only imprecisely by the dating methods available (e.g., this is the case of archaeological, geological and paleontological data).

To allow the definition in metadata of imprecise temporal values on the temporal elements of both geodata and related event(s), fuzzy values should be admitted in the expression of single time points (e.g., the landslide occurred in the night of 15th December, 2005), of time intervals (e.g., snow precipitation of three days starting from 14th December 2008), and of subsequent either periodic or aperiodic dates/intervals (e.g., fires occurring each summer), i.e., to allow the specification of ill-known instants, intervals and time series by means of fuzzy instant, fuzzy intervals and fuzzy time series.

First of all a formal framework is described in which all these fuzzy temporal indications are modelled, adopting the proposal of De Caluwe et al. (1999). In order to express such fuzzy temporal indications into an XML-type language, TimeML specification language (http://www.timeml.org/site/publications/specs.html) is adopted.

The use of TimeML is motivated by the fact that it is a textual meta-language - thus easy to read and to index by common Information Retrieval techniques - and can be employed in a discovery service context in order to represent the metadata contents for a successive search and discovery. It is enough flexible to allow the annotation (description) of the kind of event and observations, and their temporal information, possibly imprecise and approximate.

In the following, let us first describe the representation within fuzzy set theory and possibility theory of time expressions, then, introduce TimeML and, specifically, the adopted tags, and finally, the proposed partial matching mechanism.

Definition of Imperfect Time Indications

The representation of temporal information requires the choice of a numeric scale to describe the order of events and phenomena; this scale is defined by an origin (time t=0) and a time unit, so that events occurred before t=0 have negative time values and those occurred after have positive values.

The choice of the time unit depends on the cycles of an observed periodic phenomenon, such as the movement of the sun.

Nevertheless, almost every time scale shares the basic unit *second*, and other units with lower granularity such as *minute*, *hour* and *day*. Besides these units of time, there are other natural language time indications such as *week, month, season, year, century,* that are artificial notions, defined within a calendar such as the Julian and Gregorian ones. Other notions of time, related to human experience such as *now, soon, recent, often, end of the year*, are approximate time indications.

Several time models have been proposed (Tsotras and Kumar, 1996), their common limitation is that they deal with crisp time indications.

A flexible framework has been defined within fuzzy set and possibility theory (Zadeh, 1978) to express approximate hierarchical time indications close to natural language at distinct level of granularity (De Caluwe et al., 1999; De Caluwe et al., 2000). It takes inspiration from the time hierarchy proposed in (Maiocchi et al., 1992) and by the time granularity defined as a mapping from the set of positive integers to the absolute time proposed in (Wang et al., 1997): it builds up a multi-granular hierarchical time structure in which also approximate and imprecise time granules can be defined. s

The proposal in this chapter is based on this approach. This way it is possible to express temporal indications in several time units with distinct granularities, the less refined ones obtained by grouping units of the higher level granularity.

A *basic domain* G_0, consists of granules of time points below which the elements are not discernable. For example, if G_0 is *hour* we cannot discern the *minutes* within an hour. Notice that, a granule of a domain G' (e.g. G'=*week*) that is not the basic domain G_0 (e.g. G_0=*hour*) can be defined by recursively grouping granules (G=*day* and G_0) of its parent domains in the hierarchy. For example, G'=7*G=7*24*G_0=168*hours*.

The adopted temporal specifications are listed here following:

- A *time point* indication is defined as a pair [t, G] in which t is an ordinal indicating the position with respect to the time origin on a domain G of granules. An example is: [t=2, *day*] that indicates the second day from the time origin. Also approximate time points can be specified and represented by fuzzy sets on the basic temporal domain. A fuzzy time point is [t={0.8/3, 1./4, 0.7/5}, *day*] that means around the fourth day after the time origin. Specifically, a fuzzy or imprecise time point defined on a basic temporal domain assigns a membership degree in [0,1] to each element of the domain: in the previous example, the time point 4 has the maximum membership degree 1, whose meaning is that 4 is fully possible as value of the defined approximate time point, while 3 and 5 have membership degrees 0.8 and 0.5 respectively, indicating that they are also possible values of the approximate time point, but to a lower extent than 4.

- A duration in time, i.e. a *time span*, is a pair $[\Delta t, G]$ and can be denoted by either a set or a range of time points. A fuzzy time span example is $[\Delta t = \{0.8/3, 1./4, 0.7/5\}, year]$ that means a duration of about 4 years.

- A temporal distance from the origin, i.e. a *time distance*, is defined as a pair $[d, G]$ in which d is a positive or negative value, indicating the distance in time granules on G from the origin. In this case $[d=2, day]$ means two days after the origin. As t, also d can be a fuzzy set indicating a fuzzy time distance.

- A *time interval* is a triple $[t, \Delta d, G]$; in a crisp case $[t=1991, \Delta d=3, year]$ means a range of 3 years from 1991.

- A *composite span* is a union of spans $\cup[\Delta t_i, G_i]$, not necessarily adjacent and on the same basic domain G.

- An *aperiodic time element* is a union of time intervals $\cup[t_i, \Delta d_i, G_i]$. The crisp example $[t=1\text{-}11\text{-}2008, \Delta d=28, day] \cup [t=30\text{-}11\text{-}2008, \Delta d=31, day]$ means 28 days from 1-11-2008 and 31 days from 30-11-2008.

- Finally, a *periodic time element* is a union of time intervals separated by time distances: $\cup[t_i, \Delta d_i, G_i], [d_k, G_k]$. For example $\cup[t=1\text{-}8\text{-}2000, \Delta d=31, day], [d=1, year]$ means every August from year 2000. An example of approximate periodic time element is $\cup [t=1\text{-}2000, \Delta d=\{0.2/1, 0.8/2, 1./3, 0,8/4\}, week], [d=1, year]$ that means around the third week of every January from year 2000.

Since in the context of metadata compilation we may have time series that are related to finite repetitions of observations or events, a *finite periodic time element* is defined as composed of a periodic time element and a time point:

$$\cup[t_i, \Delta d_i, G_i], [d_k, G_k][t, G]$$

in which the time point t specifies the end of the repetition.

An example of finite periodic time element is "*every autumn from 2000 to 2005*" that is formally expressed as:

$$\cup[21\text{-}09\text{-}2000, 91, day], [1, year][21\text{-}12\text{-}2005, day].$$

TimeML for Expressing Imperfect Time Indications in Temporal Metadata

TimeML is a markup language of the XML family for describing events, signals and temporal expressions into a text written in natural language. It is designed to address four situations:

1. Time stamping of events (identifying an event in time, instant or interval of validity).
2. Ordering events with respect to one another (relative ordering).
3. Reasoning with contextually underspecified temporal expressions (temporal functions such as 'last week' and 'two weeks before').

Table 3. TimeML tags adopted in this proposal

EVENT
Tag used to annotate the semantics of the event described. Syntactically, EVENT can be a verb (such as "raining"), but also a nominal, such as "fire"
MAKEINSTANCE
It indicates different instances (observations) of a given event. Different instances can have different attribute values, and every EVENT introduces at least one corresponding MAKEINSTANCE
TIMEX3
This tag is central since it is primarily used to mark up explicit temporal expressions, such as times, dates, durations, etc. TIMEX3 allows marking up the following types of temporal indications specified by the attribute type: *Durations* such as "four weeks", "half a year"; *Calendar dates* (points in time equal or bigger than a day) both precise such as "13 August 2007" and imprecise or approximate such as "few days ago", "end of July", "at the beginning of summer"; *Times of day* (smaller than a day) both precise such as "at 9.50.00 a.m." and imprecise or approximate such as "before noon"; *Sets* (Recurring time expressions) such as "every month", "twice a week" The value attribute of this tag can assume XML datatypes based on the 2002 TIDES guideline, which extends the ISO 8601 standard for representing dates, times, and durations. E.g. "twelve weeks" becomes "P12W" and "21 February 2008 at 8.30.00 a.m." becomes "2008-2-21T8:30:00" The mod attribute allows specifying temporal modifiers that can be expressed neither within value attribute, nor via links or temporal functions, such as "before", "after", "equal or less", "end".
TLINK
one of the TimeML link tags which encodes the relations that exist between two temporal elements (e.g., BEGINS, HOLDS, IN-CLUDES, AFTER)

4.   Reasoning about the persistence of events (how long does an event or the outcome of an event last).

The tags of TimeML[1] adopted to extend the INSPIRE metadata, and modelled within the fuzzy framework previously described, are listed and illustrated in Table 3.

For example the expression *"every beginning of autumn from 2000 to 2005"* can be formulated in TimeML as in Table 4.

Finally, in TimeML it is possible to mark confidence values to be assigned to any tag and to any attribute of any tag. The confidence value associated with the value attribute of TIMEX3 expresses the uncertainty that the metadata provider has in assigning the temporal indication to an event or observation. For example, if we are unsure that the observation was performed on the first or second of January 2000 we could add the confidence annotation to TimeX3 as in Table 5.

MANAGING IMPERFECT TEMPORAL METADATA

The frameworks and assumptions of the previous paragraphs can be used to define the temporal fields associated with events and observations in the metadata of an SDI discovery service.

Table 4. TimeML expression for "every beginning of autumn from 2000 to 2005"

```
<TIMEX3 tid="t10" type="SET" value="R6/2000-09-21/P1Y0M0D">
Every beginning of autumn from 2000 to 2005
</TIMEX3>
```

Table 5. TimeML expression for "more likely 1 January 2000 than 2 January 2000"

```
<TIMEX3 tid="t1" type="DATE" value="2000-01-01">
On January 1st, 2000
</TIMEX3>
<CONFIDENCE tagType="TIMEX3" tagID="t1" confidenceValue="1."/>
<TIMEX3 tid="t2" type="DATE" value="2000-01-02">
On January 2nd, 2000
</TIMEX3>
<CONFIDENCE tagType="TIMEX3" tagID="t2" confidenceValue="0.80"/>
```

The metadata provider should define the time indications of events and observations by means of a metadata editor.

A running example of the metadata of two thematic maps representing subsequent observations of the same event, i.e., the melting of the "*Lys Glacier*" (a glacier of the Italian Alps), during Summer 2007, is discussed.

In this example, the temporal specification of the first occurrence of the observation is known precisely, while the second date of the observation is affected by some uncertainty. Following the proposed extension, in the metadata of the first map we have fields such as:

```
Metadata 1
...
Event="Lys Glacier melting"
Occurrence="observation of Lys Glacier melting"
        Time Position of Occurrence="1.7.2007"
...
```

In the metadata of the second map we have:

```
Metadata 2
...
Event="Lys Glacier melting"
Occurrence="observation of Lys Glacier melting"
Time Position of Occurrence="3.9.2007" with confidence 0.7 or ="4.9.2007" with
confidence 0.3
...
```

The Metadata items are translated into TimeML sentences as in Table 6.

To allow partial matching with respect to soft selection conditions specified by a user, a parser translates the external TimeML definitions of temporal metadata element into its internal fuzzy set representation.

In this phase we can obtain fuzzy sets defined on distinct domains (G) having different time granularity.

On the other side, the user specifies her/his temporal selection conditions Q within a discovery service client interface. The expression of temporal selection conditions could be performed by the support of

Table 6. TimeML expression for Metadata 1 and Metadata 2

```
Lys Glacier
<EVENT eid="e10" class="OCCURRENCE">
is melting
</EVENT>
<MAKEINSTANCE eiid="ei1" eventID="e10" pos="VERB" tense="PRESENT" aspect="PROGRESSIVE" />
<TIMEX3 tid="t1" type="DATE" value="2007-07-01">
On July 1st, 2007
</TIMEX3>
<TLINK eventInstanceID="ei1" relatedToTime="t1" relType="DURING"/>
<MAKEINSTANCE eiid="ei2" eventID="e10" pos="VERB" tense="PRESENT" aspect="PROGRESSIVE" />
<TIMEX3 tid="t2" type="DATE" value="2007-09-03">
On September 3rd, 2007
</TIMEX3>
<TLINK eventInstanceID="ei2" relatedToTime="t2" relType="DURING"/>
<CONFIDENCE tagType="TIMEX3" tagID="t2" confidenceValue="0.7"/>
<TIMEX3 tid="t3" type="DATE" value="2007-09-04">
On September 4th, 2007
</TIMEX3>
<TLINK eventInstanceID="ei2" relatedToTime="t3" relType="DURING"/>
<CONFIDENCE tagType="TIMEX3" tagID="t3" confidenceValue="0.3"/>
```

a graphic user interface that allows depicting the semantics of the (possibly) soft temporal conditions on the timeline such as in Figure 3.

The soft temporal conditions are defined as soft constraints, i.e., with a desired membership function μ_Q, defined on a time line with a given granularity, chosen among the available ones (Zadeh, 1978).

An example of user selection condition for the *Lys Glacier* melting example reported in table 6 could be:

Search for observations of glacier melting events, occurring close to late Summer 2007.

The soft constraint of this example can correspond to a fuzzy *time interval*, defined as follows: [t=1-8-2007, Δd={ 0, 15, 43, 17}, *day*], where Δd specifies the fuzzy time span in days from the date 1-8-2007. This definition corresponds to a membership function with a trapezoidal shape such as the obe depicted in Figure 4 [1-8-2007, 15-8-2007, 23-9-2007, 10-10-2007] (Bosc and Pivert, 2000).

The matching is performed by first filtering the observations that are related to the "Lys Glacier". This is done by matching the strings in the metadata "EVENT" and "MAKEINSTANCE" fields.

Then, if an instance is found, in order to obtain two homogeneous temporal representations, we have to convert either the temporal metadata values in TIME3X or the soft query condition to which it is matched into a temporal indication, defined on a common basic domain with the same granularity. This can be done as explained in the following paragraph.

Conversion of a Time Indication

In order to convert a temporal indication defined on a domain into a semantically equivalent one, defined on a domain with different granularity, we need a time hierarchy such as the one depicted in Figure 5.

This hierarchy defines the relationships between pairs of temporal granules with distinct granularity. It is a graph in which each node is a time granule, and an edge connecting two nodes *i* and *j* expresses the composition of the coarser time granule into the finer time granule: a mapping function $F_{i,j}$ allows

Figure 3. Examples of two soft temporal constraints defined on two timelines with distinct granularity (months and years, respectively). The constraint "every autumn from 2000 to 2005" is defined as a fuzzy periodic time element, while "after the second world war" as a fuzzy time interval

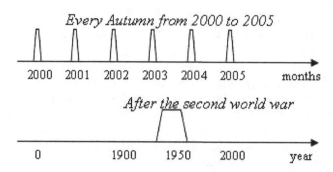

Figure 4. Trapezoidal membership function corresponding to a soft constraint representing a fuzzy time interval

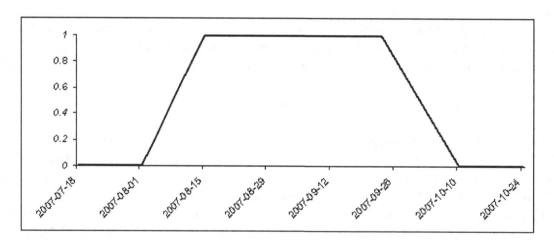

converting the current coarser granule of the *i*-th node in terms of aggregation of finer granules of the *j*-th node (Figure 5 is a simplification to illustrate how the concept works).

The function $F_{i,j}$:G'→G, where G⊂G', with *i*-th node defined on domain G' and *j*-th defined on G, defines the mapping of a granule g'∈G' into a fuzzy set $F_{i,j}$(g')∈G of granules defined on G.

Notice that a precise temporal expression can be converted into a fuzzy temporal expression: for example a *month* is defined in figure 5 by the following fuzzy set of *days:*

month={0.3/30 *days*; 0.08/28 *days*, 0.58/31 *days* }, meaning that it can consist of 30 days with confidence 0.3, 28 days with confidence 0.08, or 31 days with confidence 0.58.

A temporal indication *t*, defined on a coarser domain G' (e.g., year) can be converted on another finer domain G (e.g., day) at a distance greater than 1 on the graph, by repeatedly applying the mapping

Figure 5. Simplified example of the graph representing the relationships between time granules: on each edge the fuzzy set defines the conversion function F of granules

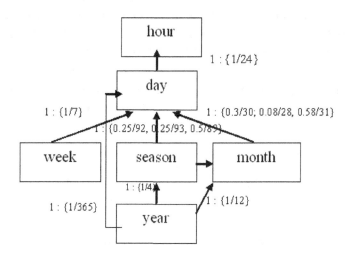

functions $F_{i,j}$ associated to the edges of the path from node *G'* to node *G* as proposed in (De Caluwe et al., 2000).

Nevertheless, since there can be more than a single path $P_1...P_k$ connecting two nodes in the hierarchy (e.g. in figure 5 we have two paths connecting *year* to *day*: P_1=*year, season, day* and P_2= *year, month, day*), by applying a transformation using the distinct paths, depending on the followed path, one can obtain multiple definitions $t_{P1},.. t_{Pk}$ of the same temporal indication *t*.

In order to reconcile these definitions we select the shortest path connecting the two nodes. If more paths with same length exist we generate the maximum bound of their definitions:

$$t_{P1 \oplus P2 \oplus Pk} (g)= \max(t_{P1}(g).. t_{Pk}(g))$$

The reason for this choice is that the maximum bound comprehends all possible definitions of the temporal indication on the domain G.

When matching a temporal metadata item with a temporal query condition, we transform the one defined on the coarser granularity domain into the finer domain so that we obtain two homogenous temporal indications expressed with same granularity.

At this point the users' temporal query specifications and the temporal metadata are converted into their internal fuzzy set representations μ_t and μ_Q respectively, and can be matched as described in the following paragraph.

Partial Matching of Homogenous Imperfect Temporal Indications

In order to match the fuzzy temporal metadata, represented by μ_t, and the soft temporal constraint, represented by μ_Q we rely on the fuzzy database framework by adopting the representation-based approach proposed in (Bosc and Pivert, 2000; Bordogna and Pasi, 2007).

We are aware that temporal reasoning methods on fuzzy temporal constraints could be a more adequate and specific framework to face this task (Vila, 1994; Vila and Godo, 1995; Deng et al., 2009), but we wanted to adopt a general framework that could be used also for other kinds of metadata elements, such as those for spatial descriptions.

In the representation-based approach, both the metadata values μ_t, possibly uncertain, and the soft query condition μ_Q are interpreted as soft constraints and one can match them to obtain a degree of satisfaction, the Retrieval Status Value, indicated by $RSV(t,Q) \in [0,1]$, by computing several measures between the two fuzzy sets μ_Q and μ_t, such as a measure of similarity or a fuzzy inclusion measure (see Figure 6).

When one is interested in selecting observations of an event taken in a date *close* to another date, or for matching events that took place *close* to a desired date a similarity matching function can be used, defined for example as follows:

$$RSV(t,Q) = Close(\mu_t, \mu_Q) = \frac{\sum_{i \in G} \min(\mu_t(i), \mu_Q(i))}{\sum_{i \in G} \max(\mu_t(i), \mu_Q(i))}$$

in which $\mu_t(i)$ and $\mu_Q(i)$ are the membership degrees of a date *i* of the temporal domain to a fuzzy temporal metadata value *t*, and in the query constraint Q, respectively. By this definition if the two fuzzy sets have at least a time point in common, i.e., have some overlapping, the metadata item is retrieved.

Another case is when one wants to select observations or events that occurred *within* a period: this corresponds to select a matching function defined as a fuzzy inclusion:

$$RSV(t,Q) = Within(\mu_t, \mu_Q) = \frac{\sum_{i \in G} \min(\mu_t(i), \mu_Q(i))}{\sum_{i \in G} (\mu_t(i))}$$

Further, other matching functions could be defined corresponding with other temporal relations such as "*close before*" "*close after*" "*recent*" defined based on the generalization of the Allen's temporal relations (Allen, 1983).

Figure 6. Schema of the partial matching mechanism between a soft query condition and an imperfect temporal metadata item

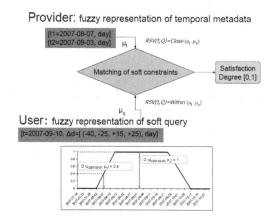

The retrieved metadata, based on *RSVs* evaluated by the chosen matching function can be ranked in decreasing order with respect to the user query, thus avoiding empty answers and suggesting an access order to the geodata.

In the example proposed, by using the *close* matching function, both metadata are retrieved: Metadata 2 has a membership degree "1" being situated in late Summer, while Metadata 1 is also retrieved since it partially satisfies the query condition *"close"*, thus meaning that it is associated to an observation of glacier melting that is in proximity of the required temporal range 'late Summer'.

CONCLUSION

The proposal in this chapter originated within the context of a recent experience in European projects where we had to cope with the actual job of both filling metadata of our georesources and training other colleagues to create their own ones in order to create a discovery service for a European SDI. In carrying out this activity we encountered several difficulties derived mainly by the constraints on metadata type and formats imposed by the current INSPIRE implementation rules.

In fact, it happens very often that information on the geodata is not well known or completely trusted, or it is even lacking. In some cases, the available geodata is produced manually by distinct experts in charge of performing land surveys. Only successively this information is transformed into electronic format, so that there can be a substantial temporal gap between the time of geodata creation and their metadating, time in which pieces of information can get lost. Such imperfect information on metadata call for new data models capable to represent and manage imprecision and uncertainty of the metadata values. This aspect is particularly evident as far as the temporal metadata used to describe geodata, and this is the aspect that has been analyzed in this chapter. We observed in particular that temporal resolution, time series and imperfect and/or linguistic temporal values are missing in the current INSPIRE Implementing Rules, so we proposed distinct metadata elements to represent them and proposed a fuzzy database framework to allow the representation of imperfect metadata and their flexible querying in catalog services.

ACKNOWLEDGMENT

Two out of five authors of this paper carried out this research under temporary contracts. We wish to acknowledge European Commission funding for this possibility, without which our work couldn't be performed.

REFERENCES

Allen, J. F. (1983). Maintaining knowledge about temporal intervals. *Communications of the ACM*, 832–843. doi:10.1145/182.358434

Bordogna, G., Carrara, P., Pagani, M., Pepe, M., & Rampini, A. (2009). Extending INSPIRE metadata to imperfect temporal descriptions, In the *Proceedings of the Global Spatial Data Infrastructures Conference (GSDI11), June 15-19 2009, Rotterdam (NL)*, CD Proceedings, Ref 235.

Bordogna, G., Carrara, P., & Pasi, G. (1991). Query term weights as constraints in fuzzy information retrieval. *Information Processing & Management, 27*(1), 15–26. doi:10.1016/0306-4573(91)90028-K

Bordogna, G., & Pasi, G. (2007). A flexible approach to evaluating soft conditions with unequal preferences in fuzzy databases. *International Journal of Intelligent Systems, 22*(7), 665–689. doi:10.1002/int.20223

Bosc, P., & Pivert, O. (2000). On the specification of representation-based conditions in a context of incomplete databases. In the *Proceedings of Database and Expert Systems Applications, 10th International Conference (DEXA '99), August 30 - September 3, 1999, Florence (It)*, (pp. 594-603).

Cater, S. C., & Kraft, D. H. (1989). A generalization and clarification of the Waller-Kraft wish-list. *Information Processing & Management, 25*, 15–25. doi:10.1016/0306-4573(89)90088-5

Cross Drafting Teams, I. N. S. P. I. R. E. (2007). *INSPIRE technical architecture overview, INSPIRE cross drafting teams report*. Retrieved on February 17, 2009, from http://inspire.jrc.ec.europa.eu/reports.cfm

De Caluwe, R., & De Tré, G. G., Van der Cruyssen, B., Devos, F. & Maesfranckx, P. (2000). Time management in fuzzy and uncertain object-oriented databases. In O. Pons, A. Vila & J. Kacprzyk (Eds.*), Knowledge management in fuzzy databases*. (pp. 67-88). Heidelberg: Physica-Verlag.

De Caluwe, R., Devis, F., Maesfranckx, P., De Trè, G., & Van der Cruyssen, B. (1999). Semantics and modelling of flexible time indication. In Zadeh, L. A., & Kacprzyk, J. (Eds.), *Computing with words in Information/Intelligent Systems* (pp. 229–256). Physica Verlag.

Dekkers, M. (2008). *Temporal metadata for discovery-a review of current practice*. M. Craglia (Ed.), (EUR 23209 EN, JRC Scientific and Technical Report).

Deng, L., Cai, Y., Wang, C., & Jiang, Y. (2009). Fuzzy temporal logic on fuzzy temporal constraint metworks. In the *Proceedings of the Sixth International Conference on Fuzzy Systems and Knowledge Discovery*, 6, (pp. 272-276).

Directive, I. N. S. P. I. R. E. 2007/2/EC of the European Parliament and of the Council of 14. (2007). *INSPIRE*. Retrieved on February 17, 2009, from www.ecgis.org/inspire/directive/l_10820070425en00010014.pdf

European Commission. (2007). *Draft implementing rules for metadata* (v. 3). INSPIRE Metadata Report. Retrieved on February 17, 2009, from http://inspire.jrc.ec.europa.eu/reports.cfm

European Commission. (2009). *INSPIRE metadata implementing rules: Technical guidelines based on EN ISO 19115 and EN ISO 19119*. INSPIRE Metadata Report. Retrieved on February 18, 2009, from http://inspire.jrc.ec.europa.eu/reports.cfm

ISO8601. (2004). *Data elements and interchange formats–information interchange- Representation of dates and times*. (Ref: ISO 8601).

Maiocchi, R., Pernici, B., & Barbic, F. (1992). Automatic deduction of temporal indications. *ACM Transactions on Database Systems, 17*(4), 647–668. doi:10.1145/146931.146934

Salton, G. (1989). *Automatic text processing: The transformation, analysis and retrieval of information by computer*. Addison Wesley.

Tsotras, V. J., & Kumar, A. (1996). Temporal database bibliography update. *SIGMOD Record, 25*(1), 41–51.

Vila, L. (1994). A survey on temporal reasoning in artificial intelligence. *AI Communications, 7*(1), 4–28.

Vila, L., & Godo, L. (1995). Query answering in fuzzy temporal constraint networks. In the *Proceedings of FUZZ-IEEE/IFES'95*, Yokohama, Japan. IEEE Press.

Wang, X. S., Bettini, C., Brodsky, A., & Jajodia, S. (1997). Logical design for temporal databases with multiple granularities. *ACM Transactions on Database Systems, 22*(2), 115–170. doi:10.1145/249978.249979

Zadeh, L. A. (1978). Fuzzy sets as a basis for a theory of possibility. *Fuzzy Sets and Systems, 1*, 3–28. doi:10.1016/0165-0114(78)90029-5

KEY TERMS AND DEFINITIONS

Discovery Geo-Services: a web portal that allows users to search into a catalogue of metadata describing geodata.

Geodata: Spatial or textual data containing information about a territory.

Imperfect Temporal Metadata: metadata describing temporal information with imprecise values, i.e. time values that are not a single element of the temporal domain, but a subset or a fuzzy subset. They are used in case of uncertain and incomplete knowledge

Metadata: data about data, i.e., a structured description of data aimed at depicting their main features. They are used for several purposes such as data searching, discovering, indexing.

Partial Matching: a function or algorithm that is used to compare two entities and that returns as a results a degree on an ordinal or numeric scale, expressing the degree of satisfaction of the matching.

Spatial Data Infrastructure: communication channels through which spatial data can be located, exchanged, accessed, and possibly elaborated. Its components are: metadata, spatial data themes, spatial data services; network services and technologies; agreements on data and service sharing, access and use; coordination and monitoring mechanisms, processes and procedures.

ENDNOTE

[1]   TimeML vers. 1.2.1 <http://www.timeml.org>

Chapter 7
Fuzzy Querying Capability at Core of a RDBMS

Ana Aguilera
Universidad de Carabobo, Venezuela

José Tomás Cadenas
Universidad Simón Bolívar, Venezuela

Leonid Tineo
Universidad Simón Bolívar, Venezuela

ABSTRACT

This chapter is focused in incorporating the fuzzy capabilities to a relational database management system (RDBMS) of open source. The fuzzy capabilities include connectors, modifiers, comparators, quantifiers, and queries. The extensions consider a more flexible DDL and DML languages. The aim is to show the design and implementation details in the RDBMS PostgreSQL. For this, a fuzzy query processor and fuzzy access mechanism has been designed and implemented. The physical fuzzy relational operators have been also defined and implemented. The flow of a fuzzy query through the different modules (parser, planner, optimizer, and executor) has been shown. Some experimental results have been included to demonstrate the performance of the proposal solution. These results show that the extensions have not decreased the performance of the RDBMS.

INTRODUCTION

The language used by human beings is imprecise, but for the computer the opposite stands true. Scientists are continually investigating how to create an intermediate point to enhance the communication between these different worlds. Moreover, the capacity to store large quantities of data is growing in an exponen-

DOI: 10.4018/978-1-60960-475-2.ch007

tially form, we now dispose of technology that is normally interconnected to support many terabytes or petabytes of data, consequently we need systems that are able to efficiently manipulate this data.

The problem resides in the fact that human reasoning is very different from the logic involved in software. In order to narrow this gap, there exists a branch in the scientific community which studies different techniques to model the human mind. This branch is known as soft computing (Zadeh, 1994). The aim of this work is to describe, in a general form, how to render the constraints of the queries on a database more flexible, therefore making a Database Management System (RDBMS) flexible without affecting in a considerable way its performance to manipulate large quantities of data.

Natural language is imprecise, vague and inexact; for example, when we say *Juan is a young person* or *Milton is very tall*, we are expressing imprecise terms like *young* and *very tall*; how does the computer interpret these terms? Normally, we have to employ precise terms: a person is young if she/he is 30 years old or less; but, what about the person who is 31 years old? One day I am young (I was 30 years old), and the day after my birthday, Am I no longer young?

Furthermore, Juan is 50 years old and he considers himself to be young. That is true for him but false for others. If Milton is 1.80 meters, do you think that he is very tall? A lot of persons will say no, but if Milton is being selected to ride horses as a jockey? Then he is very tall; truthfulness or falseness is relative, and depends on many factors. People have different points of view (preferences) and the role of context is also important.

In a computer system, objects are clearly divided into white and black, but in the real world there is an infinite grey area between the two and most things normally fall in the grey area. Morin (1999) states that "Reality is not easily legible. Ideas and theories are not a reflection of reality they are translations, and sometimes mistranslations. Our reality is nothing more than our idea of reality" (p. 44). Morin, a French philosopher and sociologist, recognizes ambiguity and uncertainty as the hallmark of science and of human experience.

Morin´s approach, complex thought, is in harmony with a culture of uncertainty. Morin (1999) asserts "But in life, unlike crossword puzzles, there are boxes without definitions, boxes with false definitions, and no neat framework to define the limits" (p. 45). How can we manipulate these boxes into the computers?

An example is the evaluation of young ladies for top models. There are many requirements to be fulfilled and nobody satisfies all of them. However, *Lolita* was disqualified because she is 1.79 meters tall and there exists a clear (*crisp*) condition stipulating a minimum height of 1.80 meters. But what about the other prerequisites met? What happen if *Lolita* was the best candidate based on the rest of them? This system may be very unfair, due to the rigidity of precise conditions.

We have proposed the enhancement of an RDBMS to support flexible queries and help users to define preferences depending on the context by using fuzzy conditions in their SQL queries.

The contribution of this chapter is to describe the design and implementation of flexible queries (using fuzzy logic) in a Relational Database Management System (RDBMS) without affecting its performance to manipulate large quantities of data in a considerable form. The approach is Tightly Coupling, with modification in the source code on the query processor engine in order to process fuzzy queries.

BACKGROUND

Traditional RDBMS suffer from rigidity: data are considered to be perfectly known and query languages do not allow natural expression of user preferences. In order to provide flexible queries over databases, several efforts have been made, such as: RankSQL (Li, Chen-chuan, Ihab, Ilyas & Song, 2005) retrieving the top-k ranked answers; SKYLINE (Börzsönyi, Kossmann, & Stocker, 2001) selection of best rows or all non-dominated based on a crisp multi criteria comparison; SQLf (Bosc & Pivert, 1995) allowing fuzzy conditions anywhere SQL expects Boolean ones; Soft-SQL (Bordogna & Psaila, 2008) allowing customizable fuzzy terms definitions for querying; FSQL (Galindo, 2005) using Fuzzy Sets for imperfect data representation; MayBMS (Koch, 2009), MystiQ (Boulos, Dalvi, Mandhani, Mathur, Re & Suciu, 2009) and Trio (Widom, 2009) are proposals to implement probabilistic uncertain databases; there are also proposals for fuzzy queries combination on multiple data sources (Fagin, 2002).

Fuzzy Set based is the more general approach to solve the problem of database rigidity (Bosc & Pivert, 2007; Goncalves & Tineo, 2008). Nevertheless, Fuzzy Set handling adds extra processing costs to database systems that must be controlled (Bosc & Pivert, 2000; Tineo, 2006). We need efficient evaluation mechanisms in order to make the use of fuzzy queries possible in real world applications (Lopez & Tineo, 2006). Moreover, it would be appreciated to enhance existing RDBMS with native fuzzy query capability in order to improve performance and scalability; this is the focus and contribution of present chapter.

Fuzzy Sets

Zadeh (1965) introduced Fuzzy Sets in order to model fuzzy classes in Control Systems, since then Fuzzy Set has been infiltrating into many branches of pure and applied mathematics that are set theory based. A Fuzzy Set is defined as a subset F of a domain X characterized by a membership function μ_F ranked on the real interval [0,1]. Some correspondence operators between a Fuzzy Set F and regular ones are defined: *support(F)* is the set of elements with $\mu_F(x)>0$; *core(F)* is the set of elements with $\mu_F(x)=1$; *border(F)* is the set of elements with $\mu_F(x)\notin\{0,1\}$; *α-cut(F)* is the set of elements with $\mu_F(x)\geq\alpha$.

In the numeric domain, trapezoidal shape functions are often used, they are described by $\mu_F =(x_1, x_2, x_3, x_4)$, where the range $[x_2, x_3]$ is the *core*, the interval $]x_1, x_4[$ is the *support*, the interval $]x_1, x_2[$ is the increasing part or the *border* where the membership function is given by the line segment from $(x_1, 0)$ to $(x_2, 1)$ and the interval $]x_3, x_4[$ is the decreasing side or the *border* characterized by the segment from $(x_3, 1)$ to $(x_4, 0)$. A trapezoidal shape Fuzzy Set is said to be *Monotonous* if it is has only an increasing or a decreasing side but not both $(x_1=x_2$ or $x_3=x_4)$. We say that is *unimodal* when it has both increasing and decreasing sides $(x_1\neq x_2$ and $x_3\neq x_4.)$

Fuzzy Sets give meaning to linguistic terms (predicates, modifiers, comparators, connectors and quantifiers), giving rise to a fuzzy logic where sentence S truth-value, $\mu(S)$ is in [0,1], being 0 completely false, and 1 completely true. Conjunction and disjunction are extended by means of operators t-norm and t-conorm (s-norm) respectively, satisfying the properties: boundary in [0,1], monotonicity, commutativity, associativity and neutral element (1 and 0 respectively). Most common used t-norm and t-conorm couple are *minimum* and *maximum* operators.

SQLf Fuzzy Querying Language

There are several different proposals of Fuzzy Set based flexible querying languages; SQLf is one that has been proposed by Bosc and Pivert (1995) from IRISA-ENSSAT. SQLf is a fuzzy extension of the standard SQL that allows the use of fuzzy conditions in any place where SQL allows a classical or boolean. Goncalves and Tineo (2001a; 2001b) have proposed extensions to SQLf.

SQLf was conceived for fuzzy querying relational databases. Its basic query structure is:

SELECT <attributes> FROM <relations>
WHERE <fuzzy condition> WITH CALIBRATION k|α|k,α.

The result of this query is a fuzzy relation with the attributes of the SELECT clause projected from the Cartesian product of the relations in the FROM clause that satisfy the fuzzy condition in the WHERE clause. The optional WITH CALIBRATION clause, proposed by Tineo (2006) to maintain the orthogonality of the original SQL, indicate the best rows choice in two senses: — Quantitative, retrieving the top k answers, according to satisfaction degree. — Qualitative, obtaining rows with membership greater or equal to a threshold α (*alpha cut*).

Goncalves and Tineo (2008) have previously worked towards a real implementation of a flexible querying system based in SQLf and its extensions. Result of such work is the flexible querying system named SQLfi. This system implements fuzzy querying capabilities on top of an existing RDBMS by means of a processing strategy known as the Derivation Principle that we briefly describe here after. At present time SQLfi is compatible with most popular RDBMS (Oracle, PostgreSQL, MySQL, IBM/ DB2, Firebird and SQL/Server). Nevertheless, SQLfi uses a Loose Coupling strategy (Timarán, 2001) that has scalability problems.

In this chapter we provide another way of implementing SQLf that surpasses such problems due to a Tightly Coupling implementation strategy at core of a RDBMS.

Derivation Principle

Fuzzy querying supposes extra cost of processing when compared to crisp ones. For SQLf processing, in order to minimize this added cost, the Derivation Principle has been conceived (Bosc & Pivert, 2000; Tineo, 2006). It takes advantage of support and α-cut concepts. Given an SQLf query φ it is possible to derive a crisp SQL query $DQ(\varphi)$ retrieving relevant rows for φ, ie *support(result(φ))⊆result(DQ(φ))*. Then φ is processed on *result(DQ(φ))*, membership degrees are computed and rows are filtered according to desired query calibration. When we find $DQ(\varphi)$ such that *support(result(φ))=result(DQ(φ))*, the derivation is said to be strong and the processing does not make unsuccessful computation. Otherwise, the derivation is said to be weak. Fuzzy queries with boolean connectors (AND, OR, NOT) allow strong derivation. With the Derivation Principle, SQLf processing is made on top of the RDBMS. This kind implementation strategy is known as Loose Coupling architecture (Timarán, 2001). Previous works (Bosc & Pivert 2000; Lopez & Tineo, 2006) have proved Derivation Principle based processing strategy to be the best in performance respects existing ones. Nevertheless, it has some overhead because rows in *result(DQ(φ))* are rescanned for the fuzzy query processing to compute the membership degree. This is one reason for the scalability problem of Loose Coupling. We would like to provide a fuzzy query processing mechanism with the advantage of Derivation Principle but without problems of Loose Coupling. For so doing we must extend functionality of RDBMS inner modules. In this chapter we propose needed extensions. Moreover, we present a real implementation into PostgreSQL source code. Experimental evidences of this strategy feasibility and benefice are also in this chapter.

Database Management Systems Architecture

Relational Database Management Systems are mainly built from these components (Connolly & Begg, 2005): *Storage Manager,* responsible for data blocks interchange between disc and main memory; *Transaction Manager,* responsible for maintaining the system data integrity ensuring concurrency and recovery from system failures; *Query Processor (or Query Engine),* responsible for gathering a data manipulation or querying statement, expressed in SQL, to transform it into a series of requests regarding the database, guarantying semantics and performance constraints.

The Query Engine is composed of inner modules that work in this way: The *Parser* takes the SQL statement, verifies the syntax and searches in the *Catalog* for objects definitions and tables and generates an abstract data structure called a *query tree*. The *Planner-Optimizer* takes the *query tree*, translates it into a *relational algebra tree*, applies a process to obtain a good *execution plan* that is a relational algebra tree in which each operator is annotated with the chosen physical mechanisms for evaluating it (Connolly & Begg, 2005), such as: sequential scan, index scan, bitmap heap scan, nested loop join, hash join and merge join. The *Executor* processes the execution plan building the result set.

In order to support fuzzy queries as native feature in an RDBMS, in this chapter, we propose the extension of a query engine. To the best of our knowledge, the present work constitutes the first proposal to extend a query engine for processing SQLf queries at the core of an RDBMS.

SCOPE DELIMITATION

SQLf is the most complete fuzzy extension to SQL due to the diversity of fuzzy queries that allows the extension of all SQL constructions with Fuzzy Sets. SQLf Data Definition Language (SQLf-DDL) allows inside its syntactic structure the following *fuzzy terms*:

- Atomic Predicates interpreted by Fuzzy Sets (we call *fuzzy predicates*).
- Modifiers build predicates by Fuzzy Set transformations.
- Comparators as fuzzy binary relations.
- Connectors as operation over membership values.
- Quantifiers represented as Fuzzy Sets over natural numbers.

Fuzzy terms allows building fuzzy conditions that can be used in SQLf anyplace where standard SQL allows a boolean logic condition. Thus, SQLf is a rather complex language.

Processing model that we propose in this chapter may be applied to all SQLf querying features. Nevertheless, due to complexity of this language, we delimit the scope of our actual implementation to the following characteristics.

Fuzzy Data Definition

Selected subset of SQLf allows the definition of fuzzy terms as shown in Box 1. We will call here SQLF-DDL this set of SQLf statements.

Box 1.

```
Atomic Predicates with the syntax:
     CREATE FUZZY PREDICATE <name> ON <dom> AS <fset>
where
     <name>        is a string of characters,
     <dom>         is the domain (possible values over the linguistic variable),
     <fset>        is the specification of a Fuzzy Set with one of the follow-
ing forms:
          A trapezoidal function with four parameters
               (<support₁>, <core₁>, <core₂>, <support₂>)
          A Fuzzy Set for extension, i.e.
               {<value₁>/<μ₁>,...,<valueₙ>/< μ ₙ>}
          An arithmetic expression with the variable <x> that indicates the
predicate´s argument.
Fuzzy modifiers with the syntax:
     CREATE MODIFIER <name> AS POWER <n>
or
     CREATE MODIFIER <name> AS <exp> POWER <n>
or
     CREATE MODIFIER <name> AS TRANSLATION <d>
where
     <name>        is a string of characters,
     <n>           is a power to the membership degree,
     <exp>         is an arithmetic expression with the variables <x> and <y>
indicating the first and second term respectively
     <d>           is a value for translation of the original predicate
Fuzzy comparison with the syntax:
     CREATE COMPARATOR <name> ON <dom> AS <exp>
where
     <name>        is a string of characters
     <dom>         is the domain (possible values over the linguistic variable)
     <exp>         is an expression to calculate the value of the comparator
through two elements. It may be a Fuzzy Set like:
          A trapezoidal function with four parameters (<exp₁>, <exp₂>, <exp₃>,
<exp₄>) that are arithmetic expressions with the variables <x> and <y> indicat-
ing the first and second term respectively,
               {<(value₁₁, value₁₂)>/<μ₁>,..., <(valueₙₙ, valueₙₘ)>/<μₙ>} and valueᵢⱼ (i
between 1 and n, j between 1 and m) are pairs of values in the domain with re-
spective membership degrees.
Fuzzy connectors with the syntax:
     CREATE CONNECTOR <name> AS <exp>
where
     <name>        is a string of characters
```

Box 1. Continued

```
     <exp>          is an expression that led to compute the value of the com-
pound predicate. The variables <x> and <y> indicate the first and second term
respectively
Fuzzy quantifiers with the syntax:
     CREATE [ABSOLUTE/RELATIVE] QUANTIFIER <name> AS <fset>
where
     <name>         is a string of characters
     <fset>         is the specification of a Fuzzy Set with one of the follow-
ing forms:
          A trapezoidal function with four parameters
               (<support₁>, <core₁>, <core₂>, <support₂>)
          An arithmetic expression with the variable <x> that indicates the
predicate´s argument.
Checks fuzzy conditions with the syntax:
     CHECK(<fuzzy condition>)
Views based in fuzzy subquery:
     CREATE VIEW <name> AS <fuzzy subquery>
```

Fuzzy Querying and Data Manipulation

Between all different SQLf querying structures and data manipulation sentences, we focus our attention in this chapter to provide the functionality shown in Box 2. In the rest of this chapter we will refer to this sub language as SQLf-DML.

DESIGN OF A FUZZY QUERY PROCESSOR

We propose a fuzzy query processor as the extension of an existing querying engine. For so doing, first we must to extend the RDBMS' catalog in order to record the fuzzy terms (predicates, comparators, modifiers and quantifiers). Thereafter, we extend the parser module in order to accept SQLf-DML and SQLf-DDL syntax. Then a general processing algorithm involving different modules may be applied according the kind of recognised sentence.

Statement Processing

The general algorithm for term definition is:

1. The parser accepts the creation of a *fuzzy term* (i.e. create fuzzy predicate…, create fuzzy modifier…, create fuzzy quantifier …)
2. If the *fuzzy term* does not exists then record it with parameters on the fuzzy catalog, else report to the user that the *fuzzy term is* already on the fuzzy catalog.

Box 2.

```
Fuzzy queries with the syntax:
    SELECT <attributes> FROM <tables> WHERE <fuzzy condition>
Queries with fuzzy conditions in partitioning:
    SELECT <attributes> FROM <tables> WHERE <condition>
    GROUP BY <attributes> HAVING <quantified fuzzy condition>
Updates with fuzzy condition:
    UPDATE <table>  SET <attribute>= <value> WHERE <fuzzy condition>
Queries with fuzzy subquery  at FROM clause:
    SELECT <attributes> FROM <fuzzy subquery> AS <alias>
    WHERE <fuzzy condition>
Fuzzy Set operations:
    (<Q1> INTERSECT/UNION/EXCEPT <Q2>)
where,
    At least one of the queries (Q1 or Q2) is a fuzzy subquery.
A <fuzzy condition> is a fuzzy logic expression of the form:
    <exp> = <pred>
or
    (<fuzzy condition>)
or
    NOT <fuzzy condition>
or
    <fuzzy condition> <conn> <fuzzy condition>
where
    <exp>        is a traditional SQL value expression
    <pred>       is a fuzzy predicate term that may be:
        an user defined fuzzy predicate identifier <name>
        a combination <mod><pred>, being <mod> the name of a user defined
modifier or a built-in modifier ANT/NOT
    <conn>       is a fuzzy logic connector that may be:
        a built in fuzzy logic operator AND/OR
        a <name> identifying an user defined fuzzy connector
A <quantified fuzzy condition> is a fuzzy logic expression of the form:
    <quant> ARE <fuzzy condition>
where
    <quant>      is a <name> identifying an user defined fuzzy quantifier
```

The main thing is that the fuzzy catalog is composed of system tables and we can maintain or view them trough sentences of the standard SQL, with the constraints of the RDBMS and system privileges.

The general algorithm to process a SQLf-DML with a fuzzy term would be:

1. The parser module, after having verified that a term is not standard, search on the fuzzy catalog.
2. If the term is on the fuzzy catalog then
    a. Create a new *fuzzy node* (memory structure) with the parameters of the *fuzzy term*, i.e. *A_ fuzzy_predicate* node.
    b. Insert into the parser tree the *fuzzy node*.
    c. Set on a boolean *fuzzy* variable in the parser state, i.e. set on *has_fuzzy_predicate* else report error to the user and finish.
3. The *fuzzy parser tree* is converted in a *Fuzzy Query Tree*, the query condition has the *fuzzy term* and the *fuzzy node* is hold on the query tree as a list of *fuzzy terms*. The boolean *fuzzy* variable is hold on the query state.
4. The analyzer module applies the Derivation Principle to transform the *fuzzy* query condition to a classical query condition, then this *Fuzzy Query Tree* has a classical SQL query but with the information about the fuzzy term.
5. The optimizer module applies the usual algorithm of query optimization to obtain a *fuzzy execution plan*. It has annotated the *fuzzy leaf* (base table with a linguistic label over a linguistic variable).
6. The executor module applies the extended *fuzzy access mechanism* (i.e. *fuzzy sequential scan*) to the *fuzzy leaf*, then the calculated membership degree is propagated bottom-up using the extended physical *fuzzy algebra relational operator* (i.e. *fuzzy hash join*).
7. Each row is showed with a membership degree (*fuzzy row*)

This algorithm is easily extended for more fuzzy terms. In special we implement a recursive algorithm to derive a fuzzy condition into a classical condition, furthermore put all the fuzzy nodes in a chained list; and finally, we extended the parser, query and plan tree with other parameters according with each particular fuzzy condition, quantifier, comparator, modifier or fuzzy partition.

Access Methods

The access methods (like sequential scan and index scan) used in classical relations were extended in order to process fuzzy conditions over classical relations and obtain fuzzy relations (rows with membership degree); furthermore, the physical relational operators (like nested loop join, hash join and merge join) were extended to propagated the membership degree until the fuzzy row is showed.

Main extension for these mechanisms was to compute membership degree (through Fuzzy Access Methods) recording it in the resulting temporal tables and propagating it (through Fuzzy Physical Relational Operators) until the result set is showed.

The innovation consists in the fact that we calculate the membership degree while the execution plan is running, then we avoid calculating it later after having obtained the result set, this job is undertaken by the preceding approach at top of the RDBMS.

Access methods are entrusted to calculate the membership degree in base tables and choose the resulting rows according to the support and core of the membership function, thus we extended the classical access mechanism (based in sequential and index scan). In the following sections, we specify the fuzzy access mechanisms when we apply the selection algebra operator (because these are tightly related to choose the rows of the tables) and we explain the implementation for execution like a fuzzy access mechanism.

Physical Operators

When applying fuzzy queries, the Fuzzy Query Tree is converted into a fuzzy relational tree, where the physical operators of Selection, Projection and Join must use the fuzzy relational algebra theory. We obtain a fuzzy relation as the result of applying a fuzzy physical operator to classical relations that is why we have to record the membership degree for each resulting row.

Fuzzy Selection

For the classical selection, there are various algorithms denominated file scans because we have to scan all the records and obtain only rows that accomplish the condition of the query. If the scan algorithm involves an index, we denominate it index scan. The most frequently used algorithms for implementing an ordinary condition are: lineal search (naïve), binary search (if file is sorted), using a primary index, using a cluster index or using a secondary index (B$^+$ tree) over an equal condition.

In this case we extended the file scan, index scan and bitmap heap scan to calculate the membership degree of each row when the base table is annotated with a fuzzy term (there is a linguistic label over a linguistic variable); furthermore these physical operators record the membership degree of each fuzzy row in order to propagate it bottom-up through the execution plan.

The membership is computed applying the theoretical frame of Fuzzy Sets, when we have a membership function (i.e. trapezoidal) we take the value of the linguistic variable and apply the corresponding membership function. When we have Boolean connectors in a fuzzy condition we use minimum (AND), maximum (OR) or complement (NOT) as $1 - \mu_x$.

Fuzzy Projection

This operator only has to delete the attributes that are not projected and record the membership degree of each fuzzy row. When duplicates need to be deleted (Distinct clause) we have to apply a partition access mechanism for the project attributes, and furthermore, calculate the maximum (t-conorm mostly used) membership degree when we have equal rows. The membership degree is propagated bottom up through the execution plan.

Fuzzy Join

We extended this operator when at least one involved relation is fuzzy, that is, it arises from the application of a fuzzy access mechanism or from another fuzzy relational operator. If any of the relations is classical we assumed that the membership degree is one (1), in accordance with the theory of Fuzzy Sets (each row pertains completely to the Fuzzy Set). With these conditions, we only have to compute the minimum (t-norm mostly used) for each pair of rows and record it to propagate bottom-up through the execution plan. So we extended the nested loop join, hash join and merge join.

Optimizer

The fuzzy querying engine optimizer module takes the Fuzzy Query Tree arising from the parser module and uses the same algorithm to optimize a classical query (i.e. query optimizer from System R). This is because, from fuzzy condition, we derive a classical condition and annotate the fuzzy terms (fuzzy algebra tree). The output of the optimizer is a fuzzy execution plan, that is, an algebra relational tree with the physical operators and the fuzzy conditions for each base table (linguistic labels over the linguistic variables), we annotate the fuzzy algebra operators, the fuzzy terms and a new projected attribute to record the membership degree when the executor calculate it.

Executor

The executor must apply the fuzzy access mechanism and Fuzzy Physical Relational Operators recording the membership degree in each resulting row using a bottom-up approach (from leaf to the top of tree), as we have to sort in descending order over the membership degree. Previous works compute the membership degree starting from the top down causing overhead due to the post-processing applied at the top for processing SQLf.

Processing Example

Let's illustrate fuzzy query processing by means of a simple example. We assume the following simple database schema (primary keys are underlined):

STUDENT(SID, SName, Age, RecordS) index on SName
COURSE(CNO, CName, Credits, AverageC) index on CName
ENROLL(SID,CNO,Period,Section, Grade)

Further, consider the following SQLf query:

SELECT SName, Period FROM STUDENT S, ENROLL E
WHERE Grade = *middle* AND Age = *old* AND S.SID = E.SID ;

In this query *middle* and *old* are fuzzy predicates defined by trapezoidal membership functions according user's preferences statements like:

CREATE FUZZY PREDICATE middle ON 0..100 AS (60,70,80,90);
CREATE FUZZY PREDICATE old ON 0..120 AS (65,100, INFINITE, INFINITE);

The syntax of this type of statements was defined in previous works and used in applications with SQLfi (Goncalves & Tineo, 2008). The first and last parameter represents the support, also the second and third the core of the membership function. The fuzzy predicate *old* is a monotonous increasing function, for this reason the two last parameters are *infinite* (unbounded). Also *middle* is a linguistic label that refers to the *linguistic variable* grade and *old is another* that refers to age.

We propose fuzzy algebra operators that might calculate the membership degree in any query tree's node or leaf, i.e. Figure 1 show a fuzzy algebra tree for the SQLf query given before.

This fuzzy relational algebra query tree can't be processed by classical query optimizer, we propose to apply the Derivation Principle and extend the classical query annotated by fuzzy conditions like is shown in Figure 2.

Figure 1. Fuzzy Relational Algebra Tree

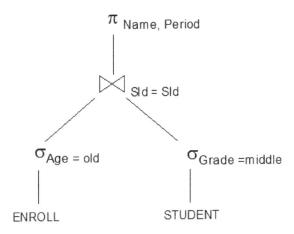

This derived Fuzzy Query Tree with boolean conditions can be processed by classical query optimizer, then we propose to extend access mechanisms (sequential scan, index scan) and physical algebra operators (projection, selection, join) such that the query evaluator might apply fuzzy sequential scan, fuzzy index scan, fuzzy projection, fuzzy selection or fuzzy join.

The fuzzy operators can compute the degree of membership and send to the next fuzzy algebra operator the membership degree, additionally if the query optimizer push the projection below, this operator must to project the linguistic variable (age and grade in this case) as is shown in Figure 3.

We consider for fuzzy mechanisms access and algebra operators that they may have a classical relation as input but a fuzzy relation (classical relation with a membership degree) as output. In case of join with two fuzzy relations as input the output fuzzy relation will have the minimum between the membership degrees.

Figure 2. Derived Fuzzy Query Tree

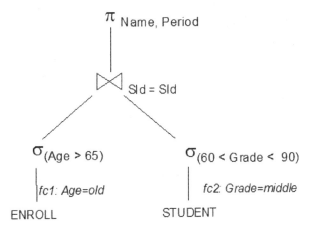

Figure 3. Fuzzy Query Tree Derived with push Projection

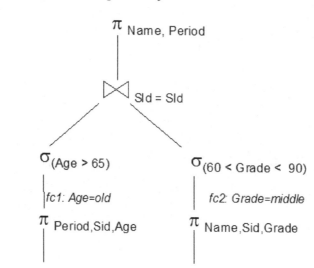

DATA STRUCTURES

This section presents main data structures that we must implement in order to give support of fuzzy query processing at core of a RDBMS. This data structures are given here according to actual PortgreSQL structures and code. We have extended PostgreSQL querying engine for processing fuzzy queries in SQLf. We name PosgreSQLf our extension.

Fuzzy Terms Catalog

The fuzzy predicates, comparators, connectors, modifiers and quantifiers are stored in the PostgreSQLf's catalog. We create a fuzzy catalog with various tables as a subset of the full catalog; this data is very important to process the fuzzy query.

The catalog structure named pg_fuzzpred will store the fuzzy predicates' name domain and parameters of the membership function (extension, expression or trapezoidal). It is defined in Box 3.

We store the name of the fuzzy modifier, the power, name of the expression, left term and right term and type of modifier. Such information is contained in the catalog structure p g_fuzzymod (see Box 4).

Fuzzy comparators will be stored in a catalog structure named pg_fuzzy comp. It will contain the name, the domain (discrete or real), support and core (if the membership function is trapezoidal), the extension membership function and type of comparator (see Box 5).

We define also a new catalog structure pg_fuzzyconn. It is intended to store the name of the fuzzy connector and the expression associated as shown in Box 6.

Finally, we will store fuzzy quantifiers' definitions in the catalog structure pg_fuzzyquan. Stored definition comprises the name, the type and the Fuzzy Set describing the fuzzy quantifier (see Box 7).

Box 3.

```
#define RelationFuzzyPredId  2859
CATALOG(pg_fuzzypred,2859) BKI_BOOTSTRAP BKI_WITHOUT_OIDS{
     NameData       predname;          // predicate name
     int2           predbegd;          // domain range begin
     int2           predendd;          // domain range end
     int2           predminfp;         // support's left bound
     int2           predcore1;         // core's left bound (included)
     int2           predcore2;         // core's right bound (included)
     int2           predmaxfp;         // support's right bound
     int2           predtypefp;        // shape 1(trapz.) 2(increases) 3(decreases)
     NameData       preddisd;          // discrete domain
     text           predcompfplist[1]; // fuzzy predicates compare list name
     NameData       predexprfp;        // expression
} FormData_pg_fuzzypred;
```

Box 4.

```
#define RelationFuzzyModId  2879
CATALOG(pg_fuzzymod,2879) BKI_BOOTSTRAP BKI_WITHOUT_OIDS {
     NameData       modname;           // modifier name
     int2           modtype;           // modifier type
     int2           modpower;          // modifier power
     NameData       modnorms;          // t-norms and t-conorms name
     NameData       modfirstarg;       // t-norms and t-conorms left arg
     NameData       modsecarg;         // t-norms and t-conorms rigth arg
} FormData_pg_fuzzymod;
```

Fuzzy Terms Nodes

If the parser module finds a fuzzy term then a new fuzzy node is created, i.e.: *A_FuzzyPred* (a fuzzy predicate), *A_FuzzyComp* (a fuzzy comparator) or *A_FuzzyQuan* (a fuzzy quantifier); we record in these memory structures the data retrieved from the fuzzy catalog tables.

Box 8 shows the node structure for holding in memory fuzzy predicate information.

In a similar way, the node structure for fuzzy query information in parsing structure is (see Box 9).

For the case of a fuzzy comparator, the representation as a node is in Box 10.

Fuzzy Parse Tree

The parser module has the mission of recognizing the statements in SQLf. In case of a well formed query, the parser generates a in memory abstract structure named the parse tree. When the query contains some

Box 5.

```
#define RelationFuzzyCompId  2857
CATALOG(pg_fuzzycomp,2857) BKI_BOOTSTRAP BKI_WITHOUT_OIDS {
     NameData      compname;           // comparator name
     int2          compbegd;           // domain range begin
     int2          compendd;           // domain range end
     NameData      compmin;            // support's left bound
     NameData      compcore1;          // core's left bound (included)
     NameData      compcore2;          // core's right bound (included)
     NameData      compmax;            // support's right bound
     int2          comptype;           // comparator type
     NameData      compdisd;           // discrete domain
     text          complist[1];        // compare list name
} FormData_pg_fuzzycomp;
```

Box 6.

```
#define RelationFuzzyConnId  2880
CATALOG(pg_fuzzyconn,2880) BKI_BOOTSTRAP BKI_WITHOUT_OIDS{
     NameData      connname;           // connector name
     NameData      connexpr;           // defining expresion
} FormData_pg_fuzzyconn;
```

Box 7.

```
#define RelationFuzzyQuanId  2878 CATALOG(pg_fuzzyquan,2878) BKI_BOOTSTRAP
BKI_WITHOUT_OIDS{  NameData  uanname;   // quantifier name
     NameData      quanminfp;          // support's left bound
     NameData      quancore1;          // core's left bound (included)
     NameData      quancore2;          // core's right bound (included)
     NameData      quanmaxfp;          // support's right bound
     int2          quantypefp;         // shape 1(trapz.) 2(increases) 3(decreases)
     int2          quantypefq;         // nature 1 (absolute) 2 (proportional)
} FormData_pg_fuzzyquan;
```

fuzzy condition, generated structure is a Fuzzy Parse Tree. It is characterized by the presence of fuzzy terms nodes as defined in previous section.

Let's illustrate this abstract structure by means of the the following query:

SELECT FirstName, LastName FROM STUDENT WHERE age = young

Box 8.

```
typedef struct A_FuzzyPred {
    NodeTag        type;
    char           *pred;              // predicate name
    int            minfp;              // support's left bound
    int            modminfp;
    int            core1;              // core's left bound (included)
    int            modcore1;
    int            core2;              // core's right bound (included)
    int            modcore2;
    int            maxfp;              // support's right bound
    int            modmaxfp;
    int            typefp;             // shape 1(trapz.) 2(increases) 3(decreases)
    int            modtypefp;
    unsigned int   vno;                // table number
    int            vattno;             // relative attribute number
    Oid            rorigtab;
    Oid            rorigcol;
    List           *compfplist;        // compare fuzzy predicate list
    List           *modcompfplist;
    char           *exprfp;            // fuzzy expression
    char           *disd;              // discrete domain
    bool           hasfm;              // has fuzzy modificator
    char           *fuzzymod;          // fuzzy modificator
    int            Mtype;              // modificator type
    int            Mpower;             // modificator power
    int            normType;
    int            vtype;
} A_FuzzyPred;
```

As we can see in Figure 4, the parser module generates a parser tree composed of: a root node *Select-Stm,* a *TargelList* (projected attributes) and for each attribute contained in the clause Select a *ResTarget node* that has a pointer to a node *Attr*, it contains the table name and a pointer to a *Value node* where is indicated the name of the attribute. The *SelectStmt node also* has a *fromClause* list with a *RangeVar node* for each input at the FROM clause, and a pointer to a node *RelExpr* with the table name, moreover the list *whereClause* has a *A_Expr node* with the name of the operation, this is a subtree with two leaves: *lexpr* (left term, in this case attribute "Age") and *rexpr* (right term, in this case, *A_FuzzyPred node* "young").

Fuzzy Query Tree

Next the parser module of PostgreSQLf transforms the fuzzy parser tree into a Fuzzy Query Tree. The fuzzy condition is stored at the *qualification structure*, moreover the list of tables (or subquerys) are stored at the *rtable field* as shown in Figure 5.

Box 9.

```
typedef struct A_FuzzyQuan {
     NodeTag        type;
     char           pred;        // quantifier name
     char           *minfp;      // support's left bound
     char           *core1;      // core's left bound (included)
     char           *core2;      // core's right bound (included)
     char           *maxfp;      // support's right bound
     int            typefp;      // shape 1(trapz.) 2(increases) 3(decreases)
     int            typefq;      // nature 1 (absolute) 2 (proportional)
     List           *args;       // the arguments (list of exprs)
     unsigned int   vno;         // table number
     int            vattno;      // relative attribute number
} A_FuzzyQuan;
```

Box 10.

```
typedef struct A_FuzzyComp {
     NodeTag        type;
     char           *pred;       // comparator name
     char           *minfp;      // support's left bound
     int            modminfp;
     char           *core1;      // core's left bound (included)
     int            modcore1;
     char           *core2;      // core's right bound (included)
     int            modcore2;
     char           *maxfp;      // support's right bound
     int            modmaxfp;
     int            typefp;      // shape 1(trapz.) 2(increases) 3(decreases)
     int            modtypefp;
     unsigned int   vno;         // table number
     int            vattno;      // relative attribute number
     Oid            rorigtab;
     Oid            rorigcol;
     List           *compfclist; // compare fuzzy predicate list.
     char           *disd;       // discrete domain.
     bool           hasfm;       // has fuzzy modifier
     char           *fuzzymod;   // modifier name
     int            Mtype;       // modifier type
     int            Mpower;      // modifier power
     int            normType;
     A_Const        *secarg;
     int            vtype;
} A_FuzzyComp;
```

Figure 4. Fuzzy Parse Tree

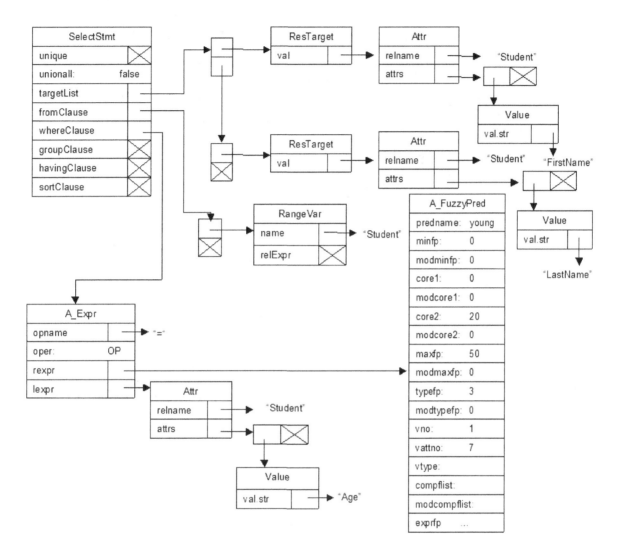

The *Planner Module* takes the *Fuzzy Query Tree* transforming the fuzzy condition into a Boolean condition after applying the Derivation Principle. We have indicators like a boolean variable named *hasFuzzPred*. It indicates if the query tree is fuzzy and we store a list name *fuzzypred* with the fuzzy terms as shown in Figure 6.

Fuzzy Plan Tree

After that, the *optimizer module* takes the enhanced Fuzzy Query Tree structure to produce a *Fuzzy Plan Tree*. The extension of the *optimizer* consists in pushing each fuzzy predicate to the corresponding leaf (Base table) of the *Fuzzy Plan Tree*. It also generates an attribute (*Gr_memb*) at top of the plan tree intended for the membership degree calculation (a new *Target Entry*). A similar structure is added in each node of the plan involving physical mechanisms for fuzzy relational operators as shown in Figure 7.

Figure 5. Fuzzy Query Tree

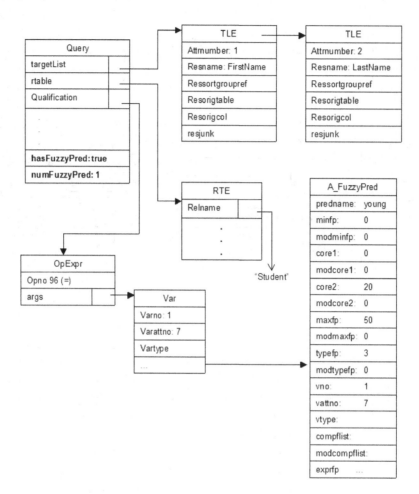

Executor module's physical access mechanisms: *sequential scan*, i*ndex scan* and *bitmap heap scan* were extended as follows: if the node has a fuzzy predicate then it computes the membership degree of each row taking into account the node's fuzzy predicate attached to the list *FuzzyPred*, and it is projected in the *Gr_memb* attribute attached to the *Target Entry List* (*tlist*), thus is generated *fuzzy rows*. Also *nested loop*, *hash* and *merge* physical join operators were extended, so once they receive a fuzzy row then propagate the membership degree bottom-up for the next operator through the attribute *Gr_memb*.

Additional tasks are carried out if we find a fuzzy subquery at FROM clause, we identify this in the *rtable* structure and process the fuzzy subquery. Furthermore, the Executor module computes the membership degree according to the fuzzy term (predicate, comparator, quantifier, connector, modifier or partition)

Finally if we find Fuzzy Set operations, we determined the type of these operations (INTERSECT, UNION or EXCEPT) in order to apply the Fuzzy Set operation (classical operation extended).

Figure 6. Derived Fuzzy Query Tree

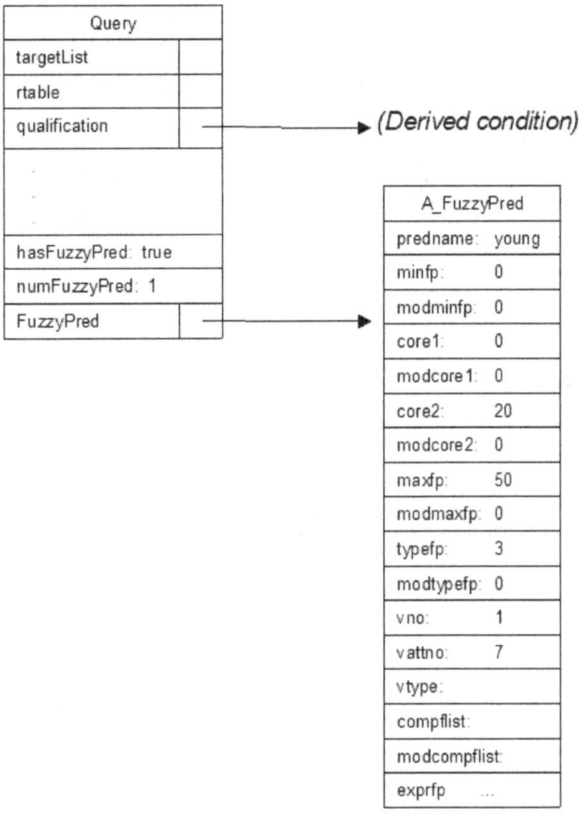

EXPERIMENTAL RESULTS

We have designed and tested a set of queries on PostgreSQLf in order to verify functionality and perfor-mance results. In general, the results obtained are good. The functionality tests and validation of results are done with a 100% level of effectiveness. The performance tests are very good because the time is not incremented much and in some instances the mean time is very similar than in the classical case.

We have designed and tested a set of queries on PostgreSQLf in order to verify functionality and performance results over the TPC Benchmark™H (TPC-H) available at http://www.tpc.org/tpch/.

For such tests several fuzzy terms were created. Some of them are shown in Box 11.

We have designed 28 fuzzy queries with different querying structures and fuzzy condition. One of such queries is in Box 12.

We compare the performance of processing fuzzy queries in PostgreSQLf regarding regular querying processing in PostgreSQL. For each designed fuzzy query we run a boolean version obtained as the corresponding derived query according the Derivation Principle. This comparisos allows showing the added extra cost for fuzzy query processing with mechanism that has been proposed and implemented in this work.

We generate two volumes of data (low 1 gigabyte and high 5 gigabytes) and we obtain execution time of fuzzy queries and their corresponding classical queries, of course, in the first case we addition-

Figure 7. Fuzzy Plan Tree

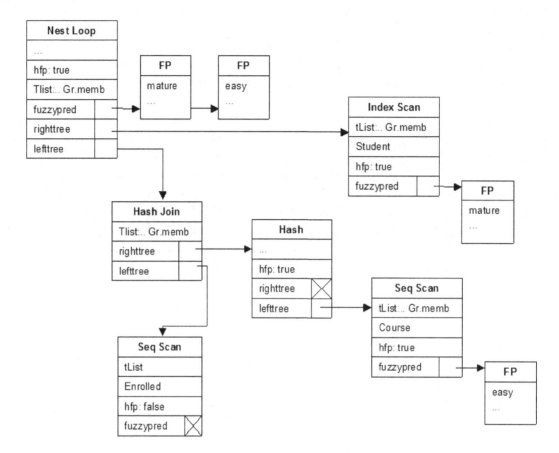

ally obtain the membership degree. We run 56 queries in total: 28 for each data volume and within each level of data volume 14 classical y 14 fuzzy queries.

With these data we make a statistical study using a multifactorial analysis (ANOVA), taking account the factors: type of query (boolean or fuzzy), volume of data (low or high). Statistically we obtain that observed processing times are completely explained by the volume of data (Pr(>F) 2.361e-05)and there is no significant difference between times for fuzzy and boolean queries (Pr(>F) 0.8554).

We can see in Figure 8 that observed times are similar for fuzzy or boolean queries. This behavior is due to fuzzy query processing mechanism proposed in this chapter.

CONCLUSION AND FUTURE WORK

We have designed a way to extend a RDBMS for native processing of SQLf fuzzy queries. This extension uses a Tightly Coupling integration strategy to modify the query engine on the core of RDBMS. We extend physical evaluation mechanisms of algebra operators to implement fuzzy relational algebra. We implemented it in the RDBMS PostgreSQL, as it allows modifications of query engine, and dem-

Box 11.

```
CREATE FUZZY PREDICATE LOWAVAIL ON 0 .. 10000 AS (
     INFINITE, INFINITE, 1000, 1500
);
CREATE RELATIVE QUANTIFIER most_of AS (
     0.5, 0.75, 1.0, 1.0
);
CREATE COMPARATOR '~' ON 1 .. 100 AS (
     'y-5','y','y','y+5'
);
CREATE COMPARATOR '<<' ON 1 .. 100 AS (
     INFINITE, INFINITE,'y/3','y'
);
CREATE COMPARATOR '>>' ON 1 .. 100 AS (
     'y','y*3', INFINITE, INFINITE
);
CREATE COMPARATOR 'cerca' on 'nation' AS (
     '(ALGERIA,ETHIOPIA)/0.1', '(ALGERIA,KENYA)/0.2',
     '(ALGERIA,MOROCCO)/0.3', '(ALGERIA,MOZAMBIQUE)/0.4',
     '(ARGENTINA,BRAZIL)/0.9', '(ARGENTINA,CANADA)/0.1',
     '(ARGENTINA,PERU)/0.5', '(FRANCE,GERMANY)/0.7',
     '(FRANCE,ROMANIA)/0.5', '(FRANCE,RUSSIA)/0.1'
);
```

Box 12.

```
SELECT p_name, s_name
FROM part, partsupp, supplier
WHERE (p_partkey=ps_partkey AND ps_suppkey=s_suppkey)
      AND ps_availqty '<<' LOWAVAIL
INTERSECT
SELECT p_name, s_name
FROM part, partsupp, supplier
WHERE (p_partkey=ps_partkey AND ps_suppkey=s_suppkey)
             AND ps_supplycost '~' affordable;
```

onstrate the feasibility of the proposed design. We used the principal characteristics of SQLf according to SQL2 and SQL3 standards.

Accordingly to benchmark test using TPC Benchmark™H, the proposed design was validated through functionality tests. With statistical analysis over 56 queries the implementation proved scalability and performance compared to classical queries. Main result is the fact that fuzzy querying with our proposed strategy has not a significant impact in query processing time. This behavior is due to fuzzy query pro-

Figure 8. Experimental Results

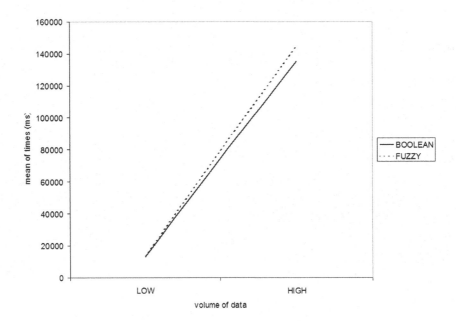

cessing mechanism proposed in this chapter. There are two keys of advantage in this mechanism. First key is the derivation of boolean conditions form fuzzy ones at optimizer level. It avoids superfluous computation of unnecessary satisfaction degrees for fuzzy conditions. Second key is the computation of satisfaction degrees into access methods and physical operator. It avoids the rescanning of result set for the computation of satisfaction degrees. It has been possible because we have proposed fuzzy query processing at core of the RDBMS engine. With this approach we avoid overhead due to the post-processing applied at the top for processing SQLf in previous works.

Proposed extension for fuzzy query processing with reported benefits would lead to wider acceptance and use of fuzzy querying systems for real applications.

The development of PostgreSQLf is still open. There are features of SQLf that has not been implemented yet at core of this RDBMS, it may be matter of future works. Up to present time we have assumed that cost model for the optimizer is not significantly affected and we have shown in practice that, nevertheless, it would be very interesting to do a formal study of cost model for this kind of queries. Also it is possible to think about more powerful fuzzy algebra specific physical operators to be implemented and considered bye the planner optimizer.

Additionally we are designing various benchmark tests to compare our approach with other implementations of flexible queries.

ACKNOWLEDGMENT

We acknowledge financial help of Venezuela's FONACIT Project G-2005000278 and France's IRISA/ENSSAT Project Pilgrim. "I will lift up mine eyes unto the hills, from whence cometh my help. My help cometh from the LORD, which made heaven and earth" (Psalms121:1-2).

REFERENCES

Bordogna, G., & Psaila, G. (2008). Customizable flexible querying classic relational databases . In Galindo, J. (Ed.), *Handbook of research on fuzzy information processing in databases* (pp. 191–217). Hershey, PA: Information Science Reference.

Börzsönyi, S., Kossmann, D., & Stocker, K. (2001). The Skyline operator. *In Proceedings of 17th International Conference on Data Engineering*, (pp. 421-430).

Bosc, P., & Pivert, O. (1995). SQLf: A relational database language for fuzzy querying. *IEEE Transactions on Fuzzy Systems, 3*(1). doi:10.1109/91.366566

Bosc, P., & Pivert, O. (2000). SQLf query functionality on top of a regular relational RDBMS. *Knowledge Management in Fuzzy Databases*, 171-190. Heidelberg: Physica-Verlag.

Boulos, J., Dalvi, N., & Mandhani, B. Mathur, S., Re, C. & Suciu, D. (2005). *MystiQ: A system for finding more answers by using probabilities.* System Demo in 2005 ACM SIGMOD International Conference on Management of Data. Retrieved October 18, 2009, from http://www.cs.washington.edu/homes/suciu/demo.pdf

Connolly, T., & Begg, C. (2005). *Database systems-a practical approach to design, implementation, and management.* United Kingdom: Pearson Education Limited.

Fagin, R. (2002). Combining fuzzy information: An overview . *SIGMOD Record, 31*(2), 109–118. doi:10.1145/565117.565143

Galindo, J. (2005). New characteristics in FSQL, a fuzzy SQL for fuzzy databases. *WSEAS Transactions on Information Science and Applications, 2*(2), 161–169.

Goncalves, M., & Tineo, L. (2001a). *SQLf: Flexible querying language extension by means of the norm SQL2.* The 10th IEEE International Conference on Fuzzy Systems, (pp. 473-476).

Goncalves, M., & Tineo, L. (2001b). *SQLf3: An extension of SQLf with SQL3 features.* The 10th IEEE International Conference on Fuzzy Systems, (pp. 477-480).

Goncalves, M., & Tineo, L. (2008). SQLfi y sus aplicaciones. [Medellín, Colombia]. *Avances en Sistemas e Informática, 5*(2), 33–40.

Koch, C. (2009). MayBMS: A database management system for uncertain and probabilistic data . In Aggarwal, C. (Ed.), *Managing and mining uncertain data* (pp. 149–184). Springer. doi:10.1007/978-0-387-09690-2_6

Li, C., Chen-chuan, K., Ihab, C., Ilyas, F., & Song, S. (2005). RankSQL: Query algebra and optimization for relational top-k queries. *In Proceedings of the 2005 ACM SIGMOD International Conference on Management of Data*, (pp. 131-142). ACM Press.

López, Y., & Tineo, L. (2006). About the performance of SQLf evaluation mechanisms. *CLEI Electronic Journal, 9*(2), 8. Retrieved October 10, 2009, from http://www.clei.cl/cleiej/papers/v9i2p8.pdf

Morin, E. (1999). *Seven complex lessons in education for the future*. United Nations Educational, Scientific and Cultural Organization. Retrieved October 18, 2009, from http://www.unesco.org/education/tlsf/TLSF/theme_a/mod03/img/sevenlessons.pdf

Timarán, R. (2001). Arquitecturas de integración del proceso de descubrimiento de conocimiento con sistemas de gestión de bases de datos: Un estado del arte. [Universidad del Valle, Colombia.]. *Ingeniería y Competitividad, 3*(2), 44–51.

Tineo, L. (2006) *A contribution to database flexible querying: Fuzzy quantified queries evaluation*. Unpublished doctoral dissertation, Universidad Simón Bolívar, Caracas, Venezuela.

Widom, J. (2009). Trio: A system for integrated management of data, uncertainty, and lineage . In Aggarwal, C. (Ed.), *Managing and mining uncertain data* (pp. 113–148). Springer. doi:10.1007/978-0-387-09690-2_5

Zadeh, L. (1994). Soft computing and fuzzy logic. *IEEE Software, 11*(6), 48–56. doi:10.1109/52.329401

Zadeh, L. A. (1965). Fuzzy sets. *Information and Control, 8*, 338–353. doi:10.1016/S0019-9958(65)90241-X

KEY TERMS AND DEFINITIONS

Derivation Principle: Given a (fuzzy) SQLf query, we can derive a (boolean) SQL query that retrieves same rows (strong derivation) or a set of row with some (few) extra rows (weak derivation).

Fuzzy Access Methods: Stored tables are scanned with different methods according physical organization and querying conditions, such methods are extended to compute satisfaction degree in case of fuzzy queries, these are the Fuzzy Access Methods.

Fuzzy Parse Tree: Memory structure that the query engine parse module will generate for representing and manipulating a fuzzy query.

Fuzzy Physical Relational Operators: Relational Algebra operators join, selection and projection have their different implementations, they are extended to compute satisfaction degree in case of fuzzy queries, these are the Fuzzy Physical Relational Operators.

Fuzzy Plan Tree: Planner/optimizer generated memory structure that holds a fuzzy relational algebra tree where each node is annotated with the Fuzzy Physical Relational Operators or Fuzzy Access Methods that executor module will use in order to compute the query answer.

Fuzzy Query Tree: Query engine internal memory structure that holds a fuzzy relational algebra tree corresponding to the fuzzy query that is been processed.

Fuzzy Set: Special kind of set where elements are characterized by a membership function in the real interval [0,1] where 1 indicates element completely included, o indicates element completely excluded, otherwise, element is gradually included.

Loose Coupling: Software architecture strategy for adding extra functionality to an existing system by means of a logic layer implemented in an external program.

SQLf: Extension of the relational database standard query language SQL allowing querying conditions in fuzzy logic based on linguistic terms that user defines according own preferences.

Tightly Coupling: Software architecture strategy for adding extra functionality to an existing system by means of source code extension preserving original system architecture.

Chapter 8

An Extended Relational Model & SQL for Fuzzy Multidatabases

Awadhesh Kumar Sharma
M.M.M. Engg College, India

A. Goswami
IIT Kharagpur, India

D.K. Gupta
IIT Kharagpur, India

ABSTRACT

This chapter investigates the problems in integration of fuzzy relational databases and extends the relational data model to support fuzzy multidatabases of type-2 that contain integrated fuzzy relational databases. The extended model is given the name fuzzy tuple source (FTS) relational data model which is provided with a set of FTS relational operations to manipulate the global relations, called FTS relations, from such fuzzy multidatabases. The chapter proposes and implements a full set of FTS relational algebraic operations capable of manipulating an extensive set of fuzzy relational multidatabases of type-2 that include fuzzy data values in their instances. To facilitate formulation of global fuzzy query over FTS relations in such fuzzy multidatabases, an appropriate extension to SQL can be done so as to get fuzzy tuple source structured query language (FTS-SQL).

Many real world problems involve imprecise and ambiguous information rather than crisp information. Recent trends in the database paradigm are to incorporate fuzzy sets to tackle imprecise and ambiguous information of real world problems. Fuzzy query processing in multidatabases have been extensively studied, however, the same has rarely been addressed for fuzzy multidatabases. This chapter attempts to extend the SQL to formulate a global fuzzy query on a fuzzy multidatabase under FTS relational model discussed earlier. The chapter provides architecture for distributed fuzzy query processing with a strategy for fuzzy query decomposition and optimization. Proofs of consistent global fuzzy operations and some of algebraic properties of FTS Relational Model are also supplemented.

DOI: 10.4018/978-1-60960-475-2.ch008

INTRODUCTION

Databases hold data that represent properties of real-world objects. Ideally, a set of real-world objects can be described by the constructs of a single data model and stored in one and only one database. Nevertheless, in reality, one can usually find two or more databases storing information about the same real-world objects. There are several reasons that result in the overlapping representations. These include:

- Different roles played by the same real-world objects in different applications. For example, a company can be the customer as well as the supplier for a firm. Hence, the company's information can be found in both the customers' database and supplier's database.
- For performance reasons, a piece of information may be fully or partially duplicated and stored in databases at different geographical locations. For example, the customers' information may be stored in both the branches and headquarter.
- Different ownership of information can also lead to information stored in different databases. For example, the information of a raw material item may be stored in different production databases because each production line wants to own a copy of the information and to exercise control over the information.

When two or more databases represent overlapping sets of real world objects, there is a strong need to integrate these databases in order to support applications of cross- functional information systems. It is therefore important to examine strategies for database integration. An important aspect of database integration is the definition of a global schema that captures the description of the combined (or integrated) database. Here, we define schema integration to be the process of merging schemas of databases, and instance integration to be the process of integrating the database instances. Schema integration is a problem well studied by database researchers (Batini, Lenzerini, and Navade, 1986; Hayne and Ram, 1990; Kaul, Drosten, and Neuhold, 1990; Larson, Navade and Elmasari, 1989; Spaccapietra, Parent and Dupont, 1992). The solution approaches identify the correspondences between schema constructs (e.g. entity types, attributes, etc.) from different databases and resolve their differences. The end result is a global schema which describes the integrated database. In contrast, instance integration focuses on merging the actual values found in instances from different databases. There are two major problems in instance integration:

a. entity identification; and
b. attribute value conflict resolution

The entity identification problem involves matching data instances that represent the same real-world objects. The attribute value conflict resolution problem involves merging the values of matching data instances. These two problems have been studied in (Chatterjee and Segev, 1991; Lim, Srivastava, Prabhakar and Richardson, 1993; Wang and Madnick, 1989) and (DeMichiel 1989; Lim, Srivastava, Prabhakar and Richardson, 1993; Lim, Srivastava and Shekhar, 1994; Tasi and Chen, 1993) respectively. It is not possible to have attribute value conflicts resolved without entity identification because attribute value conflict resolution can only be done for matching data instances. In defining the integrated database, one has to choose a global data model so that the global schema can be described by the constructs provided by the data model. The queries that can be formulated against the integrated database also depend on the global data model. The selection of global data model depends on a number of factors including the semantic richness of the local databases (Saltor, Castellanos and Garcia-Solaco, 1991; Seth and Larson, 1990) and the global application requirements. Nevertheless, the impact of instance integration on the global data model has not been well studied so far. In this chapter, we study this impact in the context of fuzzy relational data model.

In this research, we assume that the schema integration process has been carried out to the extent that a global schema has been obtained from a collection of existing (local) fuzzy relational databases. Hence, global users or applications will formulate their queries based on the global schema. Moreover, export schemas that are compatible with respect to the global schema have been defined upon the local fuzzy databases. We classify instance integration into three distinct levels according to the extent to which instance integration is carried out:

- Level-0: Neither entity identification nor attribute value conflict resolution is performed. Since no instance integration is involved, the integrated database is defined merely by collecting the instances from different local databases into relations specified by the global schema.
- Level-1: Entity identification is performed but not attributes value conflict resolution. Hence, local database instances which correspond to the same real-world objects are matched and combined in the global relations. However, the attributes of these matching database instances are not merged.
- Level-2: (complete integration). Both entity identification and attribute value conflicts are resolved. In this case, the local database instances are completely integrated.

Earlier research on database integration indicates that complete integration of instances is the only ideal solution for database integration. Nevertheless, we argue that there are some reasons advocating different levels of instance integration.

1. Firstly, it may not be possible to acquire sufficient knowledge to perform complete instance integration.
2. Secondly, data quality of local databases may be low and it is not worthwhile to perform complete instance integration.
3. Thirdly, performing instance integration may be costly, especially for the case of virtual database integration in which instance integration is being performed for every global query. For many organizations, the benefits of complete instance integration may not outweigh costs associated with the integration.
4. Lastly, in some cases, the global users or applications may not require complete instance integration.

Apart from level-2 instance integration which represents the complete integration, the levels 0 and 1 impose some constraints upon the global data model:

- Due to incomplete instance integration, the integrated database is expected to accommodate some remaining instance level heterogeneities. It is the responsibility of global applications to resolve remaining instance-level conflicts when the need arises.
- On the other hand, there exists the possibility that the levels 0 and 1 integrated databases may be needed to be fully integrated with human involvement combined with additional domain knowl-

edge. In order to achieve the complete integration requirement, a global data model must preserve source information for partially integrated databases.

- An extended global data model associated with source information requires new set of data manipulation operations. On one hand, these operations allow us to query the integrated database. On the other hand, one can make use of these operations to achieve complete database integration.

When complete instance integration has not been performed on multiple databases, it is necessary to augment source information to the global data model in order to identify where the instances in the integrated database come from. The source information allows us to:

i.   provide the context information to better interpret the non-fully integrated instances;
ii.   support meaningful and flexible query formulation on the partially integrated databases; and
iii. perform entity identification and attribute value conflict resolution within queries or applications if the need arises.

A number of different data models have been proposed for multidatabase systems (MDBSs). They can be broadly classified into three main categories according to the degrees of integration:

- Type-1: These MDBSs choose not to handle any semantic heterogeneity, e.g. MSQL (Litwin, Abdellatif, Zeroual and Nicolas, 1989; Lakshman, Saderi and Subramanian, 1996; Wang, Madnick, Wang and Madnick 1990). In other words, they do not provide global integrated schemas over the preexisting databases.
- Type-2: These MDBSs may support global integrated schemas but not integrated instances. In these MDBSs, the pre-existing database instances representing the same real world objects are not entirely integrated together (Agrawal, Keller, Wiederhold and Saraswat, 1995; Liu, Pu and Lee, 1996)
- Type-3: These are MDBSs that integrated both the pre-existing database schemas and instances (Clements, Ganesh, Hwang, Lim, Mediratta, Srivastava, Stenoein, Myriad, and Yang, 1994).

In (Agrawal, Keller, Wiederhold and Saraswat, 1995), a multidatabase is defined to be a set of flexible relations in which local instances that represent the same real-world entities are stored together as group of tuples. Hence, some implicit grouping of tuples in a flexible relation is required. Flexible relations also capture the source, consistency and selection information of their tuples. A corresponding set of flexible relational operations has been developed to manipulate the flexible relations. Nevertheless, flexible relational model is not a natural extension of the relational model. Furthermore, the join between flexible relations has not been defined. A universal relational approach to model and query multidatabases is proposed in (Zhao, Segev and Chatterjee, 1995). In this approach, a multidatabase is a universal relation instead of a set of relations. Queries on the universal relation are translated into multiple local queries against the local relations. The final query results are formed by unioning the local query results. Source information is attached to tuples in the final query results to indicate where the tuples come from. However, the source attribute is included in neither the universal relation nor its query specification. Joins and other operations that involve multiple component databases are not allowed in this model.

BACKGROUND

Database Integration Process

Database integration, involving both schemas and instances of databases, should be performed in database migration/ consolidation, data warehouse, and multidatabase systems. Regardless of the mode of integration, the basic database integration tasks are essentially the same. We view the entire database integration as a set of processes which derives the integrated schema and instances that can be implemented on either multidatabase or data warehouse systems.

Logical steps in which the integrated database is derived from the existing (local) databases does not dictate exactly how and when the steps should be performed. For example, for the actual consolidation of databases, schema integration and instance integration should be performed together. However, if only a virtual integration is required, schema integration will be performed once but the instance integration will be performed whenever queries are evaluated against the integrated database. The actual schema and instance integration techniques adopted will depend on a number of factors such as the global applications' requirements, types of conflicts found among local databases and data quality of local databases.

Schema Integration Process

Each local database consists of a schema and a set of data instances. The schema integration process requires knowledge about the local database schemas. The knowledge about database schema can be discovered from the database content. For example, database reverse engineering extracts applications' domain knowledge by analyzing not only the database schema but also database instances of an existing database (Chiang, Barron and Storey, 1994). However, we always require the database designers or administrators to supply additional knowledge manually. Schema integration produces the global schema as well as the mappings between the global schema elements and the local schema elements. Very often, a local schema can be vastly different from the global schema. This can be caused by different data models or database design decisions adopted by local databases and the integrated database. We may therefore have to introduce a view of the local schema, called export schema, such that the local database through the export schema can be seen compatible with the global schema. An export schema also defines the portion or subset of a local database to be integrated. The local database to export database conversion usually involves schema transformation. Efforts in this area are reported in (Fahrner and Vossen 1995; Meier A. et al, 1994; Zaniolo, 1979)

Instance Integration Process

During instance integration process the entity identification always precedes attribute value conflict resolution since only the conflicting attribute values of matching data instances should be resolved. Throughout the entire instance integration, any detected erroneous integration result (e.g. two data instances from the same existing databases is matched to one single data instance from another database) is forwarded to the schema integration process as a feedback if the error is possibly caused by incorrect schema integration. This can happen when the schema integration makes use of hypothesis obtained by sampling the local databases. However, this hypothesis may not hold for all local database instances.

While considering real world objects another very important consideration that needs to be taken into account is the inherent fuzziness in the data instances. Often the data we have to manage are far from being precise and certain. Indeed, the attribute value of an item may be completely unknown or partially known (a probability distribution is known on the possible values of attribute, for example). Besides an attribute may be irrelevant for some of the considered items; moreover, we may not know whether the values does not exist or is simply unknown. In such circumstances fuzzy relations are incorporated in the database. Integration of fuzziness in database provides means of representing, storing, and manipulating imprecise and uncertain information. Since our knowledge of the real world is often imperfect, one's ability to create databases of integrity poses a great challenge. To maintain the integrity of database in situations where knowledge of the real world is imperfect, one may either restrict the model of database to the portion about which only perfect information is available leading to the loss of valuable information, keeping relevant data unexplored, unanswered queries, unsatisfied user requests and resulting in degraded quality of information delivery. To overcome the aforesaid hazards, formalism has been suggested that allow the representation, storage, retrieval and manipulation of uncertain information. In this research work the term FUZZY is used as a generalized term implying imprecision, uncertainty, partial knowledge, vagueness and ambiguity.

Fuzzy relations have been treated by Kaufman (1975) and Zadeh (1965). A considerable work on solving the equality problem among fuzzy data values are in the literature. Buckles and Petry (1983), and Prede and Testamale (1984) introduced the concept of similarity measure to test the two domains for equality of fuzzy data values. Rundensteiner (1989) introduced a new equality measure termed as resemblance relation. The concept behind the resemblance relation and proximity relation are somewhat similar and has been exploited by Raju and Majumdar (1986). A fuzzy probabilistic relational data model is proposed by Zhang, Laun and Meng (1997) to integrate local fuzzy relational databases into a fuzzy multidatabase system by identifying and resolving new types of conflicts in local fuzzy database schemas. Another approach in (Ma, Zhang and Ma, 2000) addressed the fuzzy multidatabase systems for identifying and resolving the involved conflicts in their schema integration.

FUZZY TUPLE SOURCE RELATIONAL DATA MODEL

Definition: Let U be a universe of discourse. A set F is a fuzzy set of U if there is a membership function $\mu_F : U \to [0,1]$, which associates with each element $u \in U$ a membership value $\mu_F(u)$ in the interval $[0,1]$. The membership value $\mu_F(u)$ for each $u \in U$ represents the grade of membership of the element u in the fuzzy set F. F may be represented by $F = \{\mu_F(u) \, / \, u \mid u \in U\}$.

Definition: Let $U^* = U_1 \times U_2 \times \cdots \times U_n$ be the cartesian product of n universes and $A_1, A_2, \cdots, A_n$ be fuzzy set in $U_1, U_2, \cdots, U_n$ respectively. Then the cartesian product $A_1 \times A_2 \times \cdots \times A_n$ is defined to be a fuzzy subset (denoted by $\overset{f}{\subseteq}$) of $U_1 \times U_2 \times \cdots \times U_n$, with $\mu_{A_1 \times A_2 \times \cdots \times A_n}(u_1, u_2, \cdots, u_n) = \min\left(\mu_{A_1}(u_1), \mu_{A_2}(u_2), \cdots, \mu_{A_n}(u_n)\right)$, Where $u_i \in U_i, i = 1, 2, \cdots, n$. An n-ary fuzzy relation R in U^* is a relation that is characterized by a n-variate membership function ranging over U^*, that is, $\mu_R : U^* \to [0,1]$.

Table 1. Instances of two export fuzzy relations

Faculty: DB_1						
Name	**Age**	**Health**	**Dept**	**Exp**	**Pay**	**IT**
Datta	$y_3\big/old$	$y_1\big/poor$	CS	$y_3\big/high_E$	$y_3\big/high_P$	$y_2\big/\mathrm{mod}_T$
John	$u_2\big/mid$	$u_2\big/avrg$	CE	$u_2\big/\mathrm{mod}_E$	$u_2\big/\mathrm{mod}_P$	$u_2\big/\mathrm{mod}_T$
Soma	$y_2\big/mid$	$y_3\big/good$	MA	$y_1\big/low_E$	$y_2\big/\mathrm{mod}_P$	$y_3\big/high_T$
Emp: DB_2						
Datta	$y_{33}\big/old$	$y_{11}\big/poor$	CS	$y_{33}\big/high_E$	$v_{16}\big/high_P$	$v_{17}\big/high_T$
Dhar	$v_{22}\big/old$	$v_{23}\big/poor$	ME	$v_{25}\big/\mathrm{mod}_E$	$y_{32}\big/high_P$	$y_{24}\big/high_T$
John	$v_{32}\big/old$	$v_{33}\big/good$	CE	$y_{33}\big/high_E$	$v_{36}\big/\mathrm{mod}_P$	$y_{24}\big/high_T$
Mona	$v_{42}\big/mid$	$v_{43}\big/good$	EC	$y_{33}\big/high_E$	$y_{32}\big/high_P$	$v_{47}\big/low_T$
Ram	$v_{52}\big/old$	$v_{53}\big/avrg$	CS	$v_{55}\big/\mathrm{mod}_E$	$y_{32}\big/high_P$	$y_{24}\big/high_T$
Soma	$y_{22}\big/mid$	$y_{32}\big/good$	MA	$y_{13}\big/\mathrm{mod}_E$	$y_{22}\big/\mathrm{mod}_P$	$y_{31}\big/\mathrm{mod}_T$

At level-0 instance integration, export fuzzy database instances are not integrated at all although the mapping from export fuzzy schemas to global fuzzy schema has been identified. It is necessary to attach the source information to the export instances when they appear in the global fuzzy relations. For example, consider the two export fuzzy relations *Emp* and *Faculty* as given in Table 1.

It has already been shown in (Sharma, Goswami and Gupta, 2004) that the set $\sum^f$ of fuzzy inclusion dependencies between the two export fuzzy relations *Emp* and Faculty is not empty. This establishes the fact that the two export fuzzy relations *Emp* and Faculty are related and hence can be integrated. While integrating (at level-0) two databases, only the related relations are merged as illustrated in Table 2.

As shown in Table 2, we have assigned the (export fuzzy database identifier), DB_1, for instances that come from the *Emp* relation in FRDB1, and assigned DB_2 for instances that come from the *Faculty* in FRDB2. Since we only have one export database for each local database, the export database identifier can be treated as the local database identifier. In this way, we have extended the relational fuzzy data model with an additional source attribute, and we call the relational data model with such extension the Fuzzy Tuple Source (FTS) Relational data Model. Note that even when the fuzzy schemas of our two export fuzzy relational database examples are compatible with the global schema, there may still be global database attributes that cannot be found in all export databases. In that case, we assume *Null* values for the missing attributes in the export instances.

At first glance, one may want to treat the additional source attribute like just another normal attribute. While this may be correct at the data storage level, we advocate that the source attribute deserves special treatment at both the data modeling and the query processing perspectives. The source attribute, unlike other normal attributes, must be present in every FTS relation and has a special meaning which not only relates the instances to the local fuzzy databases they come from, but also identify the context of data instances. Furthermore, it should be manipulated differently from the other normal attributes in the query processing. For the FTS relational model, the values of source attributes are used purely for implementation purpose. They do not provide any semantics regarding local fuzzy relational databases. In order to maintain and provide source (context) semantics in a fuzzy relational multidatabase, we can establish a source table with at least two attributes. The first attribute stores the local fuzzy relational database identifiers, whereas the other attributes store information about the local fuzzy relational databases. Information could be the application domains, the names of geographical locations, the types of database management systems, persons in charge (e.g., DBA), and even the assessment of the data quality's level of each local fuzzy relational database. This source table is employed to retain the context semantics which can be inferred by users to interpret global fuzzy queries' results of fuzzy relational multidatabase with level-0 instance integration, or used by other data analysis tools. In addition, this table contains useful information for level-1 instance integration. For example, the context semantics of our example can be stored in the source table as given in Table 3.

Being an extension to the traditional fuzzy relational data model, FTS relational data model can represent relations which do not require source information by assigning * values to the source attributes. The standard fuzzy relational operations can still operate on the FTS relations by ignoring the source

Figure 1. Membership functions and mappings for databases in Table 1

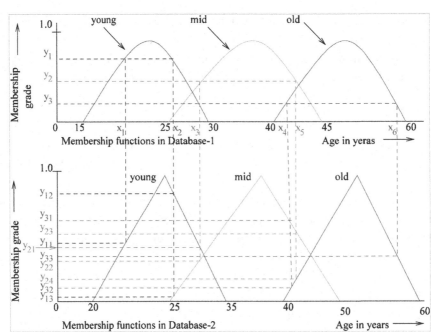

attributes. Note that the resultant fuzzy relations may no longer retain the values of the source attributes. With the special meaning attached to the source attribute, we design manipulation operations that involve the source attributes, which are called fuzzy tuple source (FTS) relational algebraic operators.

Data Types and Their Manipulation Methods

Data Types: FTS model considers all the eight different data types for fuzzy relational representations proposed by Rundensteiner et al (1989) as given below that correspond to the approach of Zemankova and Kandel (Kandel, 1986; Zemankova and Kandel, 1985).

i. A single scalar (e.g. Aptitude=good),

Table 3. Source relation to provide source(context) semantics

Source	Organization Unit	Location	DBMS	DBA
DB_1	Personnel Dept.	IIT Delhi	ORACLE7	Gupta
DB_2	Commercial Dept	IIT Kanpur	ORACLE9	Nanda

Table 2. Integration of two export fuzzy instances

Employee=merge(Faculty, Emp)							
Name	**Age**	**Health**	**Dept**	**Exp**	**Pay**	**IT**	**Source**
Datta	y_3/old	$y_1/poor$	CS	$y_3/high_E$	$y_3/high_P$	y_2/mod_T	DB_1
John	u_2/mid	$u_2/avrg$	CE	u_2/mod_E	u_2/mod_P	u_2/mod_T	DB_1
Soma	y_2/mid	$y_3/good$	MA	y_1/low_E	y_2/mod_P	$y_3/high_T$	DB_1
Datta	y_{33}/old	$y_{11}/poor$	CS	$y_{33}/high_E$	$v_{16}/high_P$	$v_{17}/high_T$	DB_2
Dhar	v_{22}/old	$v_{23}/poor$	ME	v_{25}/mod_E	$y_{32}/high_P$	$y_{24}/high_T$	DB_2
John	v_{32}/old	$v_{33}/good$	CE	$y_{33}/high_E$	v_{36}/mod_P	$y_{24}/high_T$	DB_2
Mona	v_{42}/mid	$v_{43}/good$	EC	$y_{33}/high_E$	$y_{32}/high_P$	v_{47}/low_T	DB_2
Ram	v_{52}/old	$v_{53}/avrg$	CS	v_{55}/mod_E	$y_{32}/high_P$	$y_{24}/high_T$	DB_2
Soma	y_{22}/mid	$y_{32}/good$	MA	y_{13}/mod_E	y_{22}/mod_P	y_{31}/mod_T	DB_2

ii.   A single number (e.g. Age=22),

iii.   Set of scalars (e.g. Aptitude={average, good}),

iv.   Set of numbers (e.g. {20, 21, 25}),

v.   A possibilistic distribution of scalar domain values (e.g. Age={0.4/average, 0.7/good}),

vi.   A possibilistic distribution of scalar domain values (e.g. Age={0.4/23, 1.0/24, 0.8/25}),

vii.   A real number from [0,1] (e.g. Heavy=0.9),

viii.   A designated null value (e.g. Age=unknown).

Arithmetic Operations

Arithmetic operations on different fuzzy data types are already discussed in Sharma, Goswami & Gupta, (2008).

Fuzzy Comparison Operators

FTS relational Model is designed to support the different data types as proposed by Rundensteiner et al (1989) for fuzzy relational representations that correspond to the approach of Zemankova and Kandel (1984, 1985). To supports queries that may contain qualifications involving imprecise and uncertain values, FTS relational model is equipped with fuzzy comparison operators. These operators (*EQ,NEQ*) and (*GT,GOE,LT,LOE*) are defined as follows:

Definition: A resemblance relation, EQ of *U* is a fuzzy binary relation on *U×U*, that fulfills the following properties $\forall x, y \in U$, where *U* is the universe of discourse.

i.   Reflexive: $\mu_{EQ}(x, x) = 1$,

ii.   Symmetric: $\mu_{EQ}(x, y) = \mu_{EQ}(y, x)$

Lemma: Let *EQ* be a resemblance relation on a set *U*. For all α with 0<α≤10, α-*level* sets EQ_{α} are tolerance relation on U.

The concept of an α-resemblance was introduced by Rundensteiner et al (1989).

Definition: Given a set *U* with a resemblance relation *EQ* as previously defined. Then, $\langle U, EQ \rangle$ is called a resemblance space. An α-level set EQ_{α} induced by E*Q* is termed as an α-resemblance set. Define the relationship of two values x,y∈U that resemble each other with a degree larger than or equal to α (i.e. $\mu_{EQ}(x, y) \geq \alpha$) as α-resemblant. The following notation is proposed for the notion of two values *x,y* being α-resemblant: $xEQ_{\alpha}y$. A set $P \subseteq U$ is called an α-preclass on $\langle U, EQ \rangle$, if $x, y \in P$, x and y are α-resemblant (i.e. $xEQ_{\alpha}y$ holds).

To define fuzzy relations GREATER THAN (*GT*) and LESS THAN (*LT*), let us consider a proximity relation *P* defined as given below:

Definition: A proximity relation *P* over a universe of discourse *U* is reflexive, symmetric and transitive fuzzy relation with $\mu_P(u_1, u_2) \in [1, 0]$, where $u_1, u_2 \in U$ (Kandel, 1986).

Definition: Let P_1 is a proximity relation defined over *U*. Fuzzy relational operator *GT* is defined to be a fuzzy subset of *U×U*, where μ_{GT} satisfies the following properties $\forall u_1, u_2 \in U$:

$$\mu_{GT}(u_1, u_2) = \begin{cases} 0 & if \quad u_1 \le u_2 \\ \mu_{P_1}(u_1, u_2) & otherwise. \end{cases}$$

Definition: Let P_2 is a proximity relation defined over a universe of discourse U. The fuzzy relational operator LT is defined to be a fuzzy subset of $U \times U$, where μ_{LT} satisfies the following properties $\forall u_1, u_2 \in U$:

$$\mu_{LT}(u_1, u_2) = \begin{cases} 0 & if \quad u_1 \ge u_2 \\ \mu_{P_1}(u_1, u_2) & otherwise. \end{cases}$$

Membership functions of fuzzy relations 'NOT EQUAL' (*NEQ*), 'GREATER THAN OR EQUAL' (*GOE*) and 'LESS THAN OR EQUAL' (*LOE*) can be defined based on that of *EQ*, *GT* and *LT* as follows:

$$\begin{aligned} \mu_{NEQ}(u_1, u_2) &= [1 - \mu_{EQ}(u_1, u_2)] \\ \mu_{GOE}(u_1, u_2) &= \max[\mu_{GT}(u_1, u_2), \mu_{EQ}(u_1, u_2)] \\ \mu_{LOE}(u_1, u_2) &= \min[\mu_{LT}(u_1, u_2), \mu_{EQ}(u_1, u_2)] \end{aligned}$$

Integration of Fuzzy Relational Databases

The merge operation defined in (Lim, Chiang and Cao, 1999) can be used to integrate local fuzzy relational databases into a fuzzy relational multidatabase of type-2 as given below.

In deriving level-0 global fuzzy relations from export fuzzy relations, we assume that each global fuzzy relation is formed by one or none export fuzzy relation from each export fuzzy relational database. This assumption is reasonable since the export fuzzy relational database should have a schema compatibility with that of integrated fuzzy relational database. To combine the export fuzzy relations of a global fuzzy relation, we need a merge operation.

Let $DB_1, \cdots, DB_n$ be n export fuzzy relational databases, and let L_{ij} be a fuzzy relation in DB_i. The fuzzy relation L_{ij} is a component of the global fuzzy relation G_j which is derived from $L_{1j}, \cdots, L_{nj}$ by $G_j = merge(L_{1j}, \cdots, L_{nj})$.

Definition: (merge operation) Let DB be the set of all export fuzzy relational databases, $DB_1, \cdots, DB_n$. Let $L_{1j}, \cdots, L_{nj}$ be export fuzzy relations from $DB_1, \cdots, DB_n$ respectively. They all correspond to the same global fuzzy relation G_j. L_{ij} is empty if no export fuzzy relation from DB_i correspond to G_j. Let $A = Attr(L_{1j}) \cup \cdots \cup Attr(L_{nj})$, then

$$merge(L_{1j}, \cdots, L_{nj}) = extends(L_{1j}, A, DB_1) \cup \cdots \cup extends(L_{nj}, A, DB_n),$$

where *extends*(L_{ij},*A*,*B$_i$*) augments records in L_{ij} with Null values for attributes in *A* that are not found in L_{ij}, and DB_i for the source attribute.

Table 4. Set of Export fuzzy relation from databases DB_1 & DB_2

[DB_1]: Emp_1				[DB_1]: $Dept_1$			
Name	Age	Hall	μ_r	Dname	HoD	Fund	μ_r
Jaya	.5/old	MT	.50	Chem.	Jaya	.63/low	.63
Apu	.5/mid	JCB	.50	Eco	Maya	.63/mod	.63

[DB_2]: Emp_2				[DB_2]: $Dept_2$			
Name	Age	μ_r	Dname	Staff	HoD	Fund	μ_r
Jaya	.5/mid	.50	Eco	10	Maya	.6/mod	.60
Maya	.5/mid	.50	Chem.	15	Jaya	.63/mod	.63

In some way the merge operation is similar to an outer-union except that an additional source attribute is added before they are outer-unioned. An integrated global fuzzy relation thus obtained by the use of merge operation is given the name FTS relations. A set of such FTS relations is called Fuzzy Multidatabase.

FTS Relational Operations

Let $\left(a_R, \mu_R(a_R), s_{a_R}\right)$ and $\left(a_s, \mu_S(a_s), s_{a_s}\right)$ be two fuzzy tuples in FTS relations R and S respectively where a_R and a_S denote fuzzy attributes values, $\mu_R(a_R), \mu_S(a_s)$ denote their membership grades to R and S respectively, and s_{a_R}, s_{a_s} denote their source export fuzzy database identifiers ($DB_{id}s$). Let T be the FTS relation obtained as a result of applying an FTS relational operation over R and/or S. FTS relational algebraic operators are mounted with a flag fs(viz. $\overset{fs}{\sigma}, \overset{fs}{\pi}, \overset{fs}{\bowtie}, \overset{fs}{\cup}, \overset{fs}{\cap}, \overset{fs}{-}$) and fuzzy relational algebraic operators are mounted with a flag f(viz. $\overset{fs}{\sigma}, \overset{fs}{\pi}, \overset{fs}{\bowtie}, \overset{fs}{\cup}, \overset{fs}{\cap}, \overset{fs}{-}$) to distinguish them from each other.

Now, we introduce the formal definition of FTS relational operators as follows:

$$\text{Definition: FTS} select(\sigma): T = \overset{fs}{\sigma}_{p,\alpha,\beta}(R) = \left\{\left(a_R, \mu_R(a_R), s_{a_R}\right) \mid p_\alpha(a_R, s_{a_R}) \wedge \mu_R(a_R) \geq \beta\right\}$$

where, $p_\alpha(a_R, s_{a_R})$ is a fuzzy predicate that uses fuzzy comparison operators. Value of α is used while deciding α-resemblance of two fuzzy values in the predicate. The predicate may involve both fuzzy and

Table 5. FTS Relations: Level-0 Integration of DB_1 & DB_2

Emp=merge(Emp_1, Emp_2)					$Dept$=merge($Dept_1$, $Dept_2$)					
Name	Age	Hall	μ_r	source	Dname	Staff	HoD	Fund	μ_r	source
Jaya	.5/old	MT	.50	DB_1	Chem.	Null	Jaya	.63/low	.63	DB_1
Apu	.5/mid	JCB	.50	DB_1	Eco	Null	Maya	.63/mod	.63	DB_1
Jaya	.5/old	Null	.50	DB_2	Eco	10	Maya	.6/mod	.60	DB_2
Maya	.5/mid	Null	.50	DB_2	Chem.	15	Jaya	.63/mod	.63	DB_2

Table 6. Result of FTS select operation on the FTS relation Dept from Table-5.

$$\sigma^{fs}_{\sigma} HoD = Maya, .5 Dept$$

Dname	Staff	HoD	Fund	μ_r	source
Eco	Null	Maya	.63/mod	.63	DB_1
Eco	10	Maya	.6/mod	.60	DB_2

source attributes $\left(s \in \left\{DB_{set}, *\right\}\right)$, and DB_{set} is set of $DB_{id}s$ for local fuzzy databases. The predicate is defined only on those tuples that qualify the threshold of tuple membership given by $\beta \in [0,1]$. It gives another level of precision while applying FTS relational operations (see Table 6).

Definition: FTS $project(\pi^{fs})$

$$T_1 = \pi^{fs\,sameDB}_{A,\alpha,\beta}(R) = \left\{(t.A, \mu_{T_1}, (t.A) \mid t \in R \wedge \mu_{T_1}(t.A) \geq \beta \wedge t.s \neq * \right\}$$

$$T_2 = \pi^{fs\,anyDB}_{A,\alpha,\beta}(R) = \left\{\left(t.A, \mu_{T_2}, smerge(\pi_s \sigma_{\mu_{EQ}(A,t.A)\geq\alpha} R)\right) \mid t \in R \wedge \mu_{T_2}(t.A) \geq \beta\right\}$$

where A is subset of fuzzy attributes in R, and

$$smerge(S) = \begin{cases} s & if \forall s_1, s_2 \in S, s_1 = s_2, where \quad S \quad is \\ & set \quad of \quad source \quad DB_{id}s, \\ * & otherwise. \end{cases}$$

Here equality of tuples has a special meaning. Two tuples from FTS relations are said to be equal iff each of its attribute values (both crisp and fuzzy) are α-resemblant (i.e for the case of projected relation T_1, if $t_1, t_2 \in R$ and $\mu_{EQ}(t_1.A, t_2.A) \geq \alpha$, then $\left(t_1.A, \mu_{T_1}(t_1.A), t_1.s\right) \in T_1$ if $\mu_{T_1}(t_1.A) \geq \mu_{T_1}(t_2.A)$, otherwise $\left(t_2.A, \mu_{T_1}(t_2.A), t_2.s\right) \in T_1$.

Table 7. Result of FTS project operation on FTS relation Dept from Table-5.

$\pi^{fs\,sameDB}_{Dname,Fund,.8,.6} Dept$

$\pi^{fs\,anyDB}_{Dname,Fund,.8,.6} Dept$

Dname	Fund	μ_r	source	Dname	Fund	μ_r	source
Chem	.63/low	.63	DB_1	Chem	.63/low	.63	DB_1
Eco	.63/mod	.63	DB_1	Eco	.63/mod	.63	*
Eco	.6/mod	.60	DB_2	Chem	.63/mod	.63	DB_2
Chem.	.63/mod	.63	DB_2				

Table 8. Result of FTS join operation to join the FTS relations Emp & Dept from Table-5.

$$\pi_{A,.5}^{fs\,sameDB}\left(Emp \underset{Name=HoD,.5}{\overset{fs\ sameDB}{\bowtie}} Dept\right) \qquad \pi_{A,.5}^{fs\,anyDB}\left(Emp \underset{Name=HoD,.5}{\overset{fs\ anyDB}{\bowtie}} Dept\right)$$

Dname	Staff	Fund	μ_r	source	Dname	Staff	Fund	μ_r	source
Chem	Null	.5/low	.50	DB_1	Chem	Null	.5/low	.50	DB_1
Chem	15	.5/mod	.50	DB_2	Chem	15	.5/mod	.50	*
Eco	10	.5/mod	.50	DB_2	Chem	Null	.5/low	.50	*
					Chem	15	.5/mod	.50	DB_2
	Where A={Dname, Staff, Fund}				Eco	Null	.5/mod	.50	*
					Eco	10	.5/mod	.50	DB_2

A flag (*sameDB* or *anyDB*) is attached to $\overset{fs}{\pi}$ to indicate if projected attributes from different export fuzzy databases sharing the same fuzzy attributes should be merged or not. *smerge*() produces $*$ for resultant tuples that have multiple sources. Original source values are not maintained because (1) the source attribute values should be atomic, (2) By maintaining set of values for source information, it is not possible to tell the exact source of each individual attribute for a given FTS relation. (see Table 7).

Definition: FTS *join* ($\overset{fs}{\bowtie}$)

$$T_1 = R \underset{\alpha,\beta}{\overset{fs\ sameDB}{\bowtie}} S = \left\{ \left(a_R, a_S, \mu_{T_1}(a_R, a_S)\right) \middle| \begin{array}{l} \mu_{T_1}(a_R, a_S) = \min\left(\mu_R(a_R), \mu_S(a_S)\right) \geq \beta \\ \wedge p_\alpha(a_R, a_S, s_{a_R}, s_{a_S}) \wedge (s = s_{a_R} = s_{a_S} \neq *) \end{array} \right\}$$

$$T_2 = R \underset{\alpha,\beta}{\overset{fs\ anyDB}{\bowtie}} S = \left\{ \begin{array}{l} \left(a_R, a_S, \mu_{T_2}(a_R, a_S),\right. \\ \left. smerge\left(\{s_{a_R}, s_{a_S}\}\right)\right) \end{array} \middle| \begin{array}{l} \mu_{T_2}(a_R, a_S) = \min\left(\mu_R(a_R), \mu_S(a_S)\right) \geq \beta \wedge \\ p_\alpha(a_R, a_S, s_{a_R}, s_{a_S}) \wedge (s = s_{a_R} = s_{a_S} \neq *) \end{array} \right\}$$

where p_α is a conjunction of fuzzy predicates which may include the source related predicates. It can be observed that the operator $\underset{\alpha,\beta}{\overset{fs\ anyDB}{\bowtie}}$ produces a $*$source value for its resultant fuzzy tuple whenever it joins two fuzzy tuples from different sources, whereas the operator $\underset{\alpha,\beta}{\overset{fs\ sameDB}{\bowtie}}$ retains the original non-$*$ source values.

Definition:FTS *union*($\overset{fs}{\cup}$)

$$T_1 = R \underset{\alpha,\beta}{\overset{fs\,sameDB}{\cup}} S = \left\{ \left(t.A, \mu_{T_1}(t.A), t.s\right) \middle| \begin{array}{l} \mu_{EQ}(t.A, t_R.A) \geq \alpha \wedge \mu_{T_1}(t.A) = \max\left(\mu_{T_1}(t.A), \mu_R(t_R.A)\right) \geq \\ \beta \wedge (t.s = t_R \neq *) \vee \mu_{EQ}(t.A, t_S.A) \geq \alpha \wedge \mu_{T_1}(t.A) = \max \\ \left(\mu_{T_1}(t.A), \mu_S(t_S.A)\right) \geq \beta \wedge (t.s = t_S \neq *) \end{array} \right\}$$

$$T_2 = R \underset{\alpha,\beta}{\overset{fs\,anyDB}{\cup}} S = \left\{ \left(t.A, \mu_{T_1}(t.A), smerge\left(\pi_{s,\beta}^{f}\left(\sigma_{\mu_{EQ}(A,t.A)}^{f}\left(R \underset{\beta}{\overset{f}{\cup}} S\right)\right)\right)\right) \middle| t.A \in \left((\pi_{A,\alpha,\beta}^{f} R) \underset{\alpha,\beta}{\overset{f}{\cup}} (\pi_{A,\alpha,\beta}^{f} S)\right) \right\}$$

Definition: FTS $intersection(\overset{fs}{\cap})$

$$T_1 = R \overset{fs\;sameDB}{\cap_{\alpha,\beta}} S = \left\{ \left(t.A, \mu_{T_1}(t.A), t.s\right) \middle| \begin{array}{l} \mu_{EQ}(t.A, t_R.A) \geq \alpha \wedge \mu_{T_1}(t.A) = \max\left(\mu_{T_1}(t.A), \mu_R(t_R.A)\right) \geq \\ \beta \wedge (t.s = t_R \neq *) \wedge \mu_{EQ}(t.A, t_S.A) \geq \alpha \wedge \mu_{T_1}(t.A) = \max \\ \left(\mu_{T_1}(t.A), \mu_S(t_S.A)\right) \geq \beta \wedge (t.s = t_S \neq *) \end{array} \right\}$$

$$T_2 = R \overset{fs\;anyDB}{\cap_{\alpha,\beta}} S = \left\{ \left(t.A, \mu_{T_1}(t.A), smerge(\pi_{s,\beta}(\sigma_{\mu_{EQ}(A,t.A)}(R \overset{f}{\cup_\beta} S)))) \middle| t.A \in ((\overset{f}{\pi}_{A,\alpha,\beta} R) \overset{f}{\cap_{\alpha,\beta}} (\overset{f}{\pi}_{A,\alpha,\beta} S)) \right\}$$

Definition: FTS $minus(\overset{fs}{-})$

$$T_1 = R \overset{fs\;sameDB}{\cap_{\alpha,\beta}} S = \left\{ \left(t.A, \mu_{T_1}(t.A), t.s\right) \middle| \begin{array}{l} \mu_{EQ}(t.A, t_R.A) \geq \alpha \wedge \mu_{T_1}(t.A) = \max\left(\mu_{T_1}(t.A), \mu_R(t_R.A)\right) \geq \\ \beta \wedge (t.s = t_R \neq *) \wedge \mu_{EQ}(t.A, t_S.A) < \alpha \wedge \mu_{T_1}(t.A) = \max \\ \left(\mu_{T_1}(t.A), \mu_S(t_S.A)\right) < \beta \wedge (t.s = t_S \neq *) \end{array} \right\}$$

$$T_2 = R \overset{fs\;anyDB}{\cap_{\alpha,\beta}} S = \left\{ \left(t.A, \mu_{T_1}(t.A), smerge(\pi_{s,\beta}(\sigma_{\mu_{EQ}(A,t.A)\geq\alpha} R))) \middle| t.A \in ((\overset{f}{\pi}_{A,\alpha,\beta} R) \overset{f}{-}_{\alpha,\beta} (\overset{f}{\pi}_{A,\alpha,\beta} S)) \right\}$$

Remark: In definition of *union, intersection, & minus*, A is set of fuzzy attributes that are common to R and S. Default value of α and β is 1.

FTS-SQL: AN EXTENSION OF SQL

Many users usually have their data in several databases and frequently need to jointly manipulate data from different databases. For example: a traveler looking for cheapest route may need to fuzzy query several airline, rail, and bus databases. The manager of a company may need to see the account balances that the company has at different bank branches. Therefore, he would like to fuzzy query all the relevant bank databases and his own databases.

Formulation of such a fuzzy query needs functions that do not exist in classical data manipulation languages such as SQL, which is designed to manipulate data in a single database. Classical SQL deals with single relation as an object of manipulation where as the current need is to allow sets of relations as the objects. A system for the manipulation of data in autonomous databases is called a multidatabase system (MDBS) and the corresponding language is called a multidatabase manipulation language (MML) (Litwin W. et al, 1982). Databases may be manipulated together without global integration is called interoperable (Litwin and Abdellatif, 1986). (Litwin, Abdellatif, Zeroual and Nicolas, 1989) present the multidatabase extension of SQL called MSQL that contains new functions designed for nonprocedural manipulation of data in different and nonintegrated SQL databases. A theoretical foundation for such languages has been proposed in (Grant, Litwin, Roussopoulos and Sellis, 1993) by presenting a multirelational algebra and calculus based on relational algebra and calculus. In (Lee, Jeong-Oog, Baik and Doo-Kwon, 1999) a semantic fuzzy query language, SemQL, has been provided to enable users to issue queries to a large number of autonomous databases without prior knowledge of their schema. (Juan Lavariega, Susan and Urban, 2002) presents an unique approach to fuzzy query decomposition in a multidatabase environment which is based on performing transformations over an object algebra that can be used as the basis for a global fuzzy query language.

Table 9. Result of FTS union, intersection & minus operations on FTS relations R and S

FTS relation R

Name	Subject	Grade	μ_r	source
Gupta	DBMS	.5/C	.50	DB_1
Raja	OOPS	B	1.0	DB_2
Datta	OOPS	.65/A	.65	DB_1

FTS relation S

Name	Subject	Grade	μ_r	source
Datta	OOPS	.63/A	.63	DB_2
Sonu	Graph	.73/A	.73	DB_2
gupta	DBMS	.5/C	.50	DB_1

$R \overset{fs_{sameDB}}{\underset{\cup_{.8,.5}}{}} S$

$R \overset{fs_{anyDB}}{\underset{\cup_{.8,.5}}{}} S$

Name	Subject	Grade	μ_r	source
Gupta	DBMS	.5/C	.55	DB_1
Raja	OOPS	B	1.0	DB_2
Datta	OOPS	.65/A	.65	DB_1
Datta	OOPS	.63/A	.63	DB_2

Name	Subject	Grade	μ_r	source
Gupta	DBMS	.5/C	.50	DB_1
Raja	OOPS	B	1.0	DB_2
Datta	OOPS	.65/A	.65	*

$R \overset{fs_{sameDB}}{\underset{\cap_{.8,.5}}{}} S$

$R \overset{fs_{anyDB}}{\underset{\cap_{.8,.5}}{}} S$

Gupta	DBMS	.5/C	.50	DB_1

Gupta	DBMS	.5/C	.50	DB_1
Datta	OOPS	.65/A	.65	*

$R \overset{fs_{sameDB}}{\underset{-_{.8,.5}}{}} S$

$R \overset{fs_{anyDB}}{\underset{-_{.8,.5}}{}} S$

Raja	OOPS	B	1.0	DB_2
Datta	OOPS	.65/A	.65	DB_1

Raja	OOPS	B	1.0	DB_2

Many real world problems involve imprecise and ambiguous information rather than crisp information. Recent trends in the database paradigm are to incorporate fuzzy sets to tackle imprecise and ambiguous information of real world problems. Fuzzy query processing in multidatabases have been extensively studied, however, the same has rarely been addressed for fuzzy multidatabases. In this chapter we have made an attempt to extend the SQL to formulate a global fuzzy query on a fuzzy multidatabase under FTS relational model discussed earlier. We have also provided architecture for distributed fuzzy query processing with a strategy for fuzzy query decomposition and optimization.

Assumptions

Our system configuration basically consists of one global site and a number of local sites. One of the local sites can be the global site, in which case we save a data communication cost for the site and the global site. Each local site maintains its own data management system that support FSQL (Galindo, Medina, Cubero and Garca, 2001; Galindo, Medina, Pons and Cubero, 1998) and is independent of other sites. A user communicates only with the global site. A global fuzzy query using FTS-SQL is entered at the global site, and results are received from the global site. The global site maintains information about each local fuzzy database structure, such as fuzzy schema definitions and which kind of fuzzy relations are stored in which local fuzzy database. This allows the global site to efficiently schedule a global fuzzy query processing plan. Each local fuzzy database can accommodate any number of fuzzy relations and optimally process each local fuzzy query given by the global site.

The Fuzzy Query Syntax

Well defined semantics of FTS-relational operations may not be directly suitable for fuzzy query formulation; hence we have designed FTS-SQL (the fuzzy version of TS-SQL (Lim, Chiang and Cao, 1999)). Demonstration of syntax of a simple FTS-SQL fuzzy query may be given as follows:

SELECT < target attributes >[anyDB]/[sameDB]
WITH Source Context {optional}
FROM < FTS relation >
WHERE < selection/join conditions > [anyDB]/[sameDB]
HAVING < value of α,β >

It may be noted that the keyword *anyDB* or *sameDB* are optional for SELECT clause and WHERE clause and at the same time, a simple FTS-SQL fuzzy query has an optional WITH clause and HAVING clause which makes it different from normal SQL. For both clauses, default keyword used is anyDB. If WITH clause is specified in a FTS-SQL fuzzy query, the fuzzy query result will also include the source context allowing the user to interpret the fuzzy query tuples using source context. The HAVING clause specifies the value of $\alpha,\beta \in [0,1]$ where α is used for α-resemblance (Rundensteiner, Hawkes and Bandler, 1989) of fuzzy attribute values and β is used as a threshold of the membership grade of fuzzy tuple to the fuzzy relation to satisfy the selection criteria. A FTS-SQL fuzzy query can be written as:

SELECT R.A, S.B [sameDB]
FROM R,S
WHERE R.X EQ S.X and R.U EQ `abc' and S.V EQ HIGH [anyDB]
HAVING 0.8, 0.6

This fuzzy query can be translated into an equivalent FTS-relational expression as shown below:

$$\pi^{fs\ sameDB}_{R.A,S.B,.8.6}\left(\left(\sigma^{fs}_{R.U\ EQ'abc'.8,.6}R\right)\bowtie^{fs\ anyDB}_{R.U\ EQ\ S.X,.8,.6}\left(\sigma^{fs}_{S.V\ EQ\ High,.8.6}S\right)\right)$$

This translation is allowed because both $\bowtie^{fs\ sameDB}_{\alpha,\beta}$ and $\bowtie^{fs\ anyDB}_{\alpha,\beta}$ are commutative and associative, however, source predicate must be evaluated before any FTS join is carried out, since attributes of operand relations are merged during the join. A FTS-SQL fuzzy query involving union, intersection or subtraction of two or more FTS-relation, can be written as given below:

SELECT < target attributes >[anyDB]/[sameDB]
WITH SOURCE CONTEXT {optional}

FROM < FTS ¡ relation >
HAVING < value of α,β >
WHERE < selection=join conditions >[anyDB]/[sameDB]
Union/Intersection/Minus [anyDB]/[sameDB]
SELECT <target attributes >[anyDB]/[sameDB]
WITH SOURCE CONTEXT {optional}
FROM < FTS relation >
WHERE < selection/join conditions >[anyDB]/[sameDB]
HAVING < value of α,β >

In summary, the main features offered by FTS-SQL include:

- FTS-SQL satisfies the closure property. Given FTS-relations, queries produce FTS-relations as result.
- FTS-SQL allows source options [anyDB]/[sameDB] to be specified on the SELECT and WHERE clauses, as well as on the *union, intersection & minus* FTS operations. Source option on SELECT clause determines if tuples from different local databases can be combined during projection. Source option on WHERE clause determines if tuples from different local databases can be combined during join.
- Defining source predicates to operand FTS-relations, can make formulation of queries to a specific local database. A source predicate is represented by <relation name>.source in <set of local DB_{id}>
- Queries can be on both crisp and fuzzy attributes. By specifying different values of α,β in the HAVING clause, the precision in fuzzy query formulation can be adjusted. $\alpha \in [0,1]$ is used for α-resemblance of fuzzy values in fuzzy predicates, where as $\beta \in [0,1]$ imposes a constraint while selecting a fuzzy tuple. Default value for both of them is 1 which corresponds to crisp values. It can be shown that some of the FTS-SQL queries involving the *anyDB* option can not be performed both directly and indirectly by the normal SQL. Even when some of the FTS-SQL queries can be computed by FSQL expressions, we believe that FTS-SQL will greatly reduce the effort of fuzzy query formulation on fuzzy relational multidatabase of type-2.
- Using the clause WITH SOURCE CONTEXT, tuples in the fuzzy query results can be joined with its source related information available in *source relation* table.

Figure 2.

Example Q_1: *Retrieve the Department name and the name of head of the department who has the departmental fund greater than .6/mod.*

SELECT	T.Dname. T.HoD,	T.Dname	T.HoD	T.Fund	μ_r	source
	T.Fund[sameDB]	Chem	Jaya	.63/low	.63	DB_1
FROM	Dept T	Eco	Maya	.63/mod	.63	DB_1
WHERE	T.Fund EQ_α .66/mod	Eco	Maya	.6/mod	.6	DB_2
HAVING	.8,.6	Chem	Jaya	.63/mod	.6	DB_2

In the following, we show a number of simple global fuzzy queries formulated using FTS-SQL over the FTS relations given in Table 5, and explain their semantics. In every example we have assumed $\alpha=0.8$ and $\beta=0.6$ to indicate the precision of the fuzzy query.

With the source option [*sameDB*] assigned to SELECT clause, $Q1$ requires the projection of *Dept* to include the source attribute (see Figure 2). Hence the fuzzy tuples with the identical projected attribute values not source values remain to be separate in the fuzzy query result, e.g. information about *Eco* department. The two fuzzy values.6/mod and.63/mod are α-resemblant but the tuples related with *Eco* department are not merged rather remain to be separate in the fuzzy query result. If the source option [*anyDB*] is not important during the projection, the source option can be assigned to the SELECT clause as shown in the next fuzzy query example.

As shown in result of the fuzzy query $Q2$, fuzzy tuples that are α-resemblant are merged using fuzzy *union* and the source value of the merged tuple is indicated by '*' if the parent tuples come from different source.

If it is required to view the result source context with the result tuples, the WITH clause is used as shown in the next example $Q3$.

It can be observed that the addition of WITH clause causes the source relation given in Table 3 to be joined with the FTS relation(s) in the WHERE clause using the source attribute. When the tuple has '*' as the source value, its source context will carry 'Null' values for the context attribute.

DISTRIBUTED FUZZY QUERY PROCESSING ARCHITECTURE

Fuzzy Query Mediator and Fuzzy Query Agents

The proposed distributed fuzzy query processor has a fuzzy query mediator and for each local database there is one fuzzy query agent. The responsibilities of a fuzzy query mediator are:

1. to take the global queries as input given by multi-database applications, and decompose it into multiple sub-queries to be evaluated by the fuzzy query agents of the respective local databases. For this decomposition process it has to refer to Global Fuzzy Schema to Export Fuzzy Schema Mapping information. This unique information is supposed to be stored in the FMDBS.
2. to forward the decomposed queries to respective local fuzzy query agents.

Figure 3.

Example Q_2: *Retrieve the Department name and the departmental fund regardless where the department records come from.*

```
SELECT   T.Dname, T.Fund[anyDB]
FROM     Dept T
HAVING   .8,.6
```

T.Dname	T.Fund	μ_r	source
Chem	.63/low	.63	DB_1
Eco	.63/mod	.63	*
Chem	.63/mod	.6	DB_2

Figure 4.

Example Q_3: *Retrieve the Department name and the departmental fund regardless where the department record come from and include the source context information.*

SELECT T.Dname, T.Fund[anyDB], WITH SOURCE CONTEXT, FROM Dept T,HAVING .8,.6

T.Dname	T.Fund	Org-Unit	Location	DBMS	DBA	μ_r	source
Chem	.63/low	Personnel	IITD	ORACLE7	Gupta	.63	DB_1
Eco	.63/mod	Null	Null	Null	Null	.63	*
Chem	.63/mod	Commercial	IITK	ORACLE9	Datta	.6	DB_2

3. to assemble the sub-fuzzy query results returned by fuzzy query agents and further process the assembled results in order to compute the final fuzzy query result.
4. to transform back the format of final fuzzy query result into a format that is acceptable to multi-database applications. Here again it refers to Global fuzzy Schema to Export Fuzzy Schema Mapping information.

The responsibilities of fuzzy query agents are:

1. to transform sub-queries into local queries that can be directly processed by the local database systems. This transformation process refers to Export Schema and Export to Local Schema Mapping information. This information is supposed to be stored in respective local databases.
2. to transform back (using Export Schema and Export to Local Schema Mapping information) the local fuzzy query results into a format that is acceptable to the fuzzy query mediator and forward the formatted results to the fuzzy query mediator.

Sub-queries are independent hence they may be processed in parallel at respective local databases. This reduces the fuzzy query response time. Fuzzy query agents hide heterogeneous fuzzy query interfaces of local database systems from the fuzzy query mediators. Distributed fuzzy query processing steps designed for global FTS-SQL queries can be described briefly as follows:

Global FTS-SQL queries are parsed to ensure that they are syntactically correct. Based on the parsed trees constructed, the queries are validated against the global schema to ensure that all relations and attributes in the queries exist and are properly used. Given a global FTS-SQL fuzzy query, the fuzzy query mediator decomposes it into sub-queries to be evaluated by the fuzzy query agents. Here the local database involved in global FTS-SQL fuzzy query will be determined. Some fuzzy query optimization heuristics are introduced to reduce the processing overhead. Similar strategies have been adopted for optimizing queries for other multidatabase systems (Evrendilek, Dogac, Nural and Ozcan, 1997; Finance, Smahi and Fessy, 1995). Decomposed sub-queries disseminated to the appropriate fuzzy query agents for execution. Fuzzy query agents further translate the sub-queries to the local database queries and return the sub-fuzzy query results to the fuzzy query mediator. The fuzzy query mediator assembles the sub-fuzzy query results and computes the final fuzzy query result if there exist some sub-fuzzy query operations that could not be performed by the fuzzy query agents.

Fuzzy Query Decomposition with Optimization

FTS-SQL allows source options to be attached to their SELECT and WHERE clauses. Hence a strategy should be evolved to decompose a FTS-SQL fuzzy query to handle different combination of source options. Therefore, we have designed it to meet the following objectives:

a. Fuzzy query agents are supposed to perform most of the fuzzy query processing tasks in order to maximize the parallelism in local fuzzy query evaluation.
b. To reduce the sub-fuzzy query results that have to be transferred from the local database sites to the fuzzy query mediator and heuristic fuzzy query optimization has to be performed. Fuzzy query response time can be improved with small local fuzzy query results shipped between sites.
c. Since every FTS-SQL operations can't be performed by local database systems, the decomposition process must consider the capabilities of fuzzy query agents and also determine the portion(s) of global queries to be processed by the fuzzy query mediator itself. At present we have assumed that all fuzzy query agents support the usual select-project-join FTS-SQL queries.

WHERE clause with the source option *sameDB* allows the join of tuples from the same local database only and with the source option *anyDB* it allows the join of tuples from any local database. Based on this join definition, we derive the decomposition strategies for following two categories of FTS-SQL queries:

FTS-SQL queries with WHERE $<$ ... $>$[sameDB]

As per this strategy, we decompose a global fuzzy query into a sub-fuzzy query template and a global fuzzy query residue. Sub-fuzzy query template is the sub-fuzzy query generated based on the global schema and it has to be further translated into sub-queries on the export schemas of local fuzzy databases relevant to the global fuzzy query. The global fuzzy query residue represents the remaining global fuzzy query operations that have to be handled by the fuzzy query mediator. Since *sameDB* is the source option of the WHERE clause, all *selection* and *join* predicates on the global FTS relation(s) can be performed by the fuzzy query agents together with their local database systems. Deriving the *Sub-Fuzzy query Template* and the *Global Fuzzy query Residue* from a *Global Fuzzy query* may be given as follows:

1. The SELECT clause of Sub-Fuzzy query Template is assigned the list of attributes that appear in the SELECT clause of Global Fuzzy query, including those which appear in the *aggregate* functions.
2. The FROM clause of Sub-Fuzzy query Template is assigned the global FTS-relations that appear in the FROM clause of Global fuzzy query.
3. Move the selection and join predicates in the WHERE clause of Global Fuzzy query to the WHERE clause of Sub-Fuzzy query Template.
4. The Global Fuzzy query Residue inherits the SELECT clause of the original Global Fuzzy query. It's FROM clause is defined by the union of sub-fuzzy query results. In other words, only operations to be performed by the Global Fuzzy query Residue are Projections. The WITH clause is retained in the Global Fuzzy query Residue and performed in the last phase of the fuzzy query processing.
5. The values of α and β in the HAVING clause of the global fuzzy query are assigned to the having clause of all the sub-queries.

Figure 5.

<u>Global Query(Q_a):</u>

SELECT $T_1.Name, T_2.Dname$ *[anyDB]*

FROM   Emp T_1, Dept T_2

WHERE $T_1.Name\ EQ_\alpha\ T_2.HoD\ AND\ T_2.Fund\ EQ_\alpha\ .66/mod$ *[sameDB]*

HAVING   .8, .6

<u>Sub-Query Template:</u>

SELECT $T_1.Name, T_2.Dname$

FROM   Emp T_1, Dept T_2

WHERE $T_1.Name\ EQ_\alpha\ T_2.HoD\ AND\ T_2.Fund\ EQ_\alpha\ .66/mod$

HAVING   .8, .6

<u>Global Query Residue:</u>

SELECT $T_1.Name, T_2.Dname$ *[anyDB]*

FROM   < Union of sub-query results>

HAVING   .8, .6

Example *Consider the global fuzzy database as given in Table 5 whose component local fuzzy databases are given in Table 4. In the fuzzy query Q_a (see Figure 5), we show that the join predicate ($T_1.Name\ EQ_\alpha\ T_2.HoD$) and selection predicate ($T_2.Fund\ EQ_\alpha\ .66/mod$) have been propagated to the sub-fuzzy query template for decomposition of a global fuzzy query that has been formulated using FTS-SQL. Having performed a union of sub fuzzy query results returned by the fuzzy query agents, a final projection operation on the union result will be required as specified in the global fuzzy query residue.*

FTS-SQL queries with WHERE < ...>[anyDB]

This strategy generates one Global Fuzzy query Residue and multiple Sub-Fuzzy query Templates, one for each global relation involved in the Global Fuzzy query. In other words, a Global Fuzzy query with n relations in it's FROM clause, will be decomposed into n Sub-Fuzzy query Templates. This is necessary because join predicates in Global Fuzzy query can't be propagated to the Sub Queries. Given below are the sequential steps to derive *Sub-Fuzzy query Templates* and *Global Fuzzy query Residue* from a *Global Fuzzy query*.

1.   For each global FTS-relation R involved in the FROM clause we generate its corresponding sub-
     queries as follows:

Figure 6.

Global Query(Q_b):

SELECT T_1.Name, T_2.Dname [sameDB]

FROM   Emp T_1, Dept T_2

WHERE T_1.Name EQ_α T_2.HoD AND T_2.Fund EQ_α .66/mod [anyDB]

HAVING   .8, .6

Sub-Query Template-1(for Emp):

SELECT T_1.Name

FROM   Emp T_1

HAVING   .8,.6

Sub-Query Template-2(for Dept):

SELECT T_2.Dname, T_2.Fund, T_2.HoD

FROM   Dept T_2

WHERE T_2.Fund EQ_α .66/mod

HAVING   .8,.6

Global Query Residue:

SELECT T_1.Name, T_2.Dname[sameDB]

FROM   <union of Sub-query results for Emp> T_1,

         <union of Sub-query results for Dept> T_2

WHERE T_1.Name EQ_α T_2.HoD

HAVING   .8, .6

a. The SELECT clause of Sub-Fuzzy query Template is assigned the list of R's attributes that appears in the SELECT clause or join predicates of the Global Fuzzy query, including those which appear in the *aggregate* functions.

b. Selection and join predicates using R's attributes in the Global Fuzzy query are propagated to Sub-Fuzzy query Template.

c. The FROM clause of Sub-Fuzzy query Template is assigned R.

2. For the inter-global relation *join* predicates in the WHERE clause of Global Fuzzy query, the *projections* are retained in WHERE clause of Global Fuzzy query Residue. The clause WITH SOURCE CONTEXT is also retained, however, processed at last.

3. The values of α and β in the HAVING clause of the global fuzzy query are assigned to the having clause of all the sub-queries.

Example: *Consider here again a similar fuzzy query as in above Example but with* anyDB *option attached to WHERE clause. Thus, a new global fuzzy query Qb has been formulated which is decomposed as shown in Figure 6.*

It can be shown that the join predicate T_1.Name EQ_α T_2.HoD can't be evaluated before the two Global FTS-relations Dept and *Emp* are derived. Nevertheless, the selection predicate

$T_2.Fund \quad EQ_\alpha \quad .66 / \mod$ can still be propagated to the sub-queries for local relations corresponding to *Dept*. Having performed *unions* of sub-fuzzy query results to construct the global relations *Dept* and *Emp*, a final *join* and *projection* of the global relations will be required as specified in the Global Fuzzy query Residue.

Translation of Sub-Fuzzy Query Templates into Sub-Queries

Although the fuzzy query agents support Sub-queries on the export schemas which are compatible to the global schema, translating Sub-fuzzy query templates into Sub-queries is still necessary for the following reasons:

a. **Missing Export Fuzzy Relations:** In our FTS relational model, a FTS relation may not always have its corresponding export fuzzy relation in every export fuzzy schema. When a FTS relation in the FROM clause of a Sub-fuzzy query template cannot be found in an export fuzzy schema, no fuzzy Sub-fuzzy query will be generated for the corresponding fuzzy query agent.
b. **Missing Fuzzy Attributes:** Some attributes of FTS relation may not be found in the export fuzzy schema. If any FTS relation attribute involved in a WHERE clause of a Sub-fuzzy query template cannot be found in the export fuzzy schema defined upon a local fuzzy database, it is not required to translate the Sub-fuzzy query template for the fuzzy query agent of the local fuzzy database. However, a translated Sub-fuzzy query is still required for each fuzzy query agent, if the WHERE clause involves an explicit check for Null values.

Correctness of FTS Relational Model

Although FTS relational data model is designed for representing global fuzzy relations, it is closely related to the component export fuzzy relational databases due to existence of source attribute. It is; therefore, appropriate to characterize the correctness of FTS relational data model by showing that the FTS relational operations are consistent with the fuzzy relational operations on export fuzzy relations. Henceforth, we call these fuzzy relational operations the export fuzzy relational operations. Nevertheless, for FTS relational operations that combine fuzzy tuples from different export fuzzy relational databases, i.e. $\overset{fs}{_\pi}any$, $\overset{fs}{_\bowtie}any$, $\overset{fs}{_\cup}any$, $\overset{fs}{_\cap}any$, and $\overset{fs}{_-}any$, it is not possible to show their consistency with respect to the export fuzzy relational operations because these FTS relational operations offer fuzzy query expressiveness beyond that of the export fuzzy relational operations. Hence, we have shown the correctness only for the FTS relational operations that can be mapped into export fuzzy relational operations.

Definition: (Consistency of Global Fuzzy Relational Operations)

Let $DB_1,...,DB_n$ be n export fuzzy databases and merge() be integrating operation that integrates the export fuzzy relations into global fuzzy relations. Then the global fuzzy relational operation OP_G is consistent with the export fuzzy relational operations OP_L iff $\exists$ a one to one mapping (denoted by opMap) from OP_G to $\left\langle (OP_{L_1} \cup \{op_\phi\}),\cdots,(OP_{L_m} \cup \{op_\phi\}) \right\rangle$ such that $\forall L_{ij} \in Rel(DB_i)$, $\forall op_G \in OP_G$ (say, OP_G

is m-ary), op_ϕ is an operation that returns an empty relation for any given input export fuzzy relation

$$op_G(G_1,\cdots,G_m) = merge\left(op_{L_1}(L_{11},\cdots,L_{n1}),\cdots,op_{L_m}(L_{1m},\cdots,L_{nm})\right) \text{n}.$$

where $G_i=merge(L_{1i},\ldots,L_{ni})$(i.e. global fuzzy relation G_i is derived by combining export fuzzy relations $L_{1i},\ldots,L_{ni}$ from $DB_1,\ldots,DB_n$ respectively). We assume that for DB_k that has no export fuzzy relation for deriving G_i will have $L_{ki} = \phi$, and $opMap(op_G) = \left\langle op_{L_1},\cdots,op_{L_m}\right\rangle$. A set of one to one operation mapping function from global fuzzy relational operations to export fuzzy relational operations is shown below:

$$opMap(\overset{fs}{\sigma}_{p\alpha\wedge(s\in DB_{set}),\beta}) = \left\langle op_1,\cdots,op_n\right\rangle where \begin{cases} \overset{fs}{\sigma}_{p\alpha,\beta} & DB_i \in DB_{set} \\ op_\phi & otherwise. \end{cases}$$

$$opMap(\overset{fs}{\sigma}_{p\alpha,\beta}) = \left\langle \overset{fs}{\sigma}_{p\alpha,\beta},\ldots,\overset{fs}{\sigma}_{p\alpha,\beta}\right\rangle$$

$$opMap(\overset{fs\,sameDB}{\pi}_{A,\alpha,\beta}) = \left\langle \overset{fs}{\pi}_{A,\alpha,\beta},\ldots,\overset{fs}{\pi}_{A,\alpha,\beta}\right\rangle$$

$$opMap(\overset{fs\,sameDB}{\bowtie}_{p\alpha,\beta}) = \left\langle \overset{fs}{\bowtie}_{p\alpha,\beta},\ldots,\overset{fs}{\bowtie}_{p\alpha,\beta}\right\rangle$$

$$opMap(\overset{fs\,sameDB}{\cup}_{\alpha,\beta}) = \left\langle \overset{fs}{\cup}_{\alpha,\beta},\ldots,\overset{fs}{\cup}_{\alpha,\beta}\right\rangle$$

$$opMap(\overset{fs\,sameDB}{\cap}_{\alpha,\beta}) = \left\langle \overset{fs}{\cap}_{\alpha,\beta},\ldots,\overset{fs}{\cap}_{\alpha,\beta}\right\rangle$$

$$opMap(\overset{fs\,sameDB}{-}_{\alpha,\beta}) = \left\langle \overset{fs}{-}_{\alpha,\beta},\ldots,\overset{fs}{-}_{\alpha,\beta}\right\rangle$$

All these mapping functions shall be used to prove the consistency of the FTS relational operations with the *sameDB* option as given below:

Proofs of Consistent Global Fuzzy Operations

The following two lemmas show that global FTS selection is consistent with or without source predicates.

Lemma 1.1

$$\forall L_{1j},\cdots,L_{nj}, G_j = merge(L_{1j},\cdots,L_{nj}),$$

$$\overset{fs}{\sigma}_{p\alpha\wedge(s\in DB_{set}),\beta}) = merge(op_1 L_{1j},\cdots,op_n L_{nj)}$$

$$where \begin{cases} \overset{fs}{\sigma}_{p\alpha,\beta} & DB_i \in DB_{set} \\ op_\phi & otherwise. \end{cases}$$

Proof: $g \in^{fs}_{\sigma_{p\alpha\wedge(g.s\in DBset),\beta}} G_j \Leftrightarrow$

$g \in G_j \wedge p_\alpha(g) \wedge \mu_{Gj}(g) \geqslant \beta \wedge \exists DB_i \in DBset, g.s = DB_i \Leftrightarrow$

$\exists DB_i \in DBset, g.A \in^f_{\sigma_{p\alpha\beta}} L_{ij}$ where $A = \text{Attr}(G_j) = \text{Attr}(L_{ij})$ for $i-1,\ldots,\text{n} \Leftrightarrow$

$g \in merge(op_1 L_{1j},\ldots,op_n L_{nj}).$

$$where \; op_i \begin{cases} \overset{f}{\sigma}_{p\alpha\beta} & DB_i \in DBset \\ op_\phi & otherwise. \end{cases}$$

In the above proof, the source predicate constrains the result of global fuzzy selection to contain only tuples with DB_i as source values. This implies that the tuple attributes come from an export fuzzy relation in DB_i. Hence a global fuzzy selection operation produces result identical to that produced by first performing a selection on the export fuzzy relation from DB_i followed by making the fuzzy tuples global using the merge operation.

Lemma 1.2 : $\forall L_{1j,\dots,}L_{nj}, G = merge(L_{1j,\dots,}L_{nj}), \sigma^{fs}_{p\alpha,\beta} G_j = merge(\sigma^{fs}_{p\alpha,\beta}L_{1j}, \cdots, \sigma^{fs}_{p\alpha,\beta}L_{nj}).$

Proof:

$g \in^{fs}_{\sigma_{p\alpha,\beta}} G_j \Leftrightarrow \exists i \in \{1, \cdots, n\}, g.A \in^{fs}_{\sigma_{p\alpha,\beta}} L_{ij}$ where $A = Attr(G_j) = Attr(L_{ij}) \Leftrightarrow g \in merge(\sigma^{fs}_{p\alpha,\beta}L_{1j}, \cdots, \sigma^{fs}_{p\alpha,\beta}L_{nj}).$

Lemma 1.3 $\forall L_{1j}, \dots, L_{nj}, G_j = merge(L_{1j}, \dots, L_{nj}),$
$\sigma^{fs}_{p\alpha,\beta} G_j = merge(\sigma^{fs}_{p\alpha,\beta}L_{1j}, \dots, \sigma^{fs}_{p\alpha,\beta} L_{nj})$
Proof: $g^{fs}_{\sigma_{p\alpha,\beta}} G_j \Leftrightarrow$
$\exists i \in \{1, \dots, n\}, g.A \in^{fs}_{\sigma_{p\alpha,\beta}} L_{ij}$ where $A = Attr(G_j) = Attr(L_{ij}) \Leftrightarrow$
$g \in merge(\sigma^{fs}_{p\alpha,\beta}L_{1j}, \dots, \sigma^{fs}_{p\alpha,\beta} L_{nj}).$

A global projection operation with *sameDB* option is equivalent to projecting the required attributes from the export relations first followed by integrating the projected export relations. Hence the global FTS *project* operation is consistent as given below.

Lemma 1.4 $\forall L_{1j}, \dots, L_{nj}, G_j = merge(L_{1j}, \dots, L_{nj}),$
$\pi^{fs\,sameDB}_{A,\alpha,\beta} G_j = merge(\pi^{fs\,sameDB}_{A,\alpha,\beta}L_{1j}, \dots, \pi^{fs\,sameDB}_{A,\alpha,\beta} L_{nj})$
Proof: Let $G = (\pi^{fs\,sameDB}_{A,\alpha,\beta} G_j)$ and $L = (\pi^{fs}_{A,\alpha,\beta}L_{ij}).$
$g \in G$ and $g.s = DB_i$ for some $i \in \{1, \dots, n\} \Leftrightarrow$
$g \in \pi^{fs\,sameDB}_{A,\alpha,\beta} G_j$ and $g.s = DB_i$ for some $i \in \{1, \dots, n\} \Leftrightarrow$
$g.A \in \pi^{f}_{A,\alpha,\beta} L_{ij}$ for some $i \in \{1, \dots, n\} \Leftrightarrow$
$g = (g.A, \mu_L(g.A), DB_i) \wedge \mu_L(g.A) \geqslant \beta$ for some $i \in \{1, \dots, n\} \Leftrightarrow$
$g \in L \Leftrightarrow$
$g \in (\pi^{f}_{A,\alpha,\beta}L_{ij}) \Leftrightarrow$
$g \in merge(\pi^{f}_{A,\alpha,\beta}L_{1j}, \dots, \pi^{f}_{A,\alpha,\beta}L_{nj}).$

Using similar proof techniques, we have proved that global FTS *join, union, intersection,* and *minus* operations are also consistent with the respective fuzzy relational operations on the export fuzzy relations as given below:

Lemma 1.5 $\forall L_{1j},...,L_{nj},L_{1k},...,L_{nk}$, and $G_j = merge(L_{1j},...,L_{nj})$,
$G_k = merge(L_{1k},...,L_{nk}), G_j \overset{fs\ sameDB}{\underset{p\alpha,\beta}{\bowtie}} G_k = merge(L_{1j}\overset{fs}{\underset{p\alpha,\beta}{\bowtie}} L_{1k},...,L_{nj}\overset{fs}{\underset{p\alpha,\beta}{\bowtie}} L_{nk})$.

Proof: $g \in (G_j \overset{fs\ sameDB}{\underset{p\alpha,\beta}{\bowtie}} G_k) \wedge g.s = DB_i$ for some $i \in \{1,...,n\} \Leftrightarrow$
$((g.A_j, \mu_{Gj}(g.A_j), DB_i) \in G_j) \wedge ((g.A_k, \mu_{Gk}(g.A_k), DB_i) \in G_k) \wedge$
$\mu_{(Gj\overset{f}{\underset{p\alpha,\beta}{\bowtie}} Gk)}(g) = \min(\mu_{Gj}(g.A_j), \mu_{Gk}(g.A_k)) \geqslant \beta \wedge p_\alpha(g.A_j, g.A_k)$ for some $i \Leftrightarrow$
$(g.A_j \in L_{i,j} \wedge \mu_{L_{ij}}(g.A_j) \geqslant \beta) \wedge ((g.A_k \in L_{i,k} \wedge \mu_{L_{ik}}(g.A_k) \geqslant \beta) \wedge p_\alpha(g.A_j, g.A_k)$ for some $i \Leftrightarrow$

$((g.A_j, \mu_{Gj}(g.A_j)), (g.A_k, \mu_{L_{ik}}(g.A_k))) \in (L_{ij}\overset{f}{\underset{p\alpha,\beta}{\bowtie}} L_{ik})$ for some $i \Leftrightarrow$
$g = ((g.A_j, g.A_k), \min(\mu_{L_{ij}}(g.A_j), \mu_{L_{ik}}(g.A_k)), DB_i)$ for some $i \Leftrightarrow$
$merge(L_{1j}\overset{f}{\underset{p\alpha,\beta}{\bowtie}} L_{1k},...,L_{nj}\overset{f}{\underset{p\alpha,\beta}{\bowtie}} L_{nk})$.

Lemma 1.6 $\forall L_{1j},...,L_{nj},L_{1k},...,L_{nk}$, and $G_j = merge(L_{1j},...,L_{nj})$,
$G_k = merge(L_{1k},...,L_{nk}), G_j \overset{fs\,sameDB}{\underset{\cup\ p\alpha,\beta}{}} G_k = merge(L_{1j}\overset{fs}{\underset{\cup\ p\alpha,\beta}{}} L_{1k},...,L_{nj}\overset{fs}{\underset{\cup\ p\alpha,\beta}{}} L_{nk})$.

Proof: Let $G = (G_j \overset{fs\,sameDB}{\underset{\cup\ p\alpha,\beta}{}} G_k)$ and Let $L = (L_{ij}\overset{fs}{\underset{\cup\,\alpha,\beta}{}} L_{ik})$.
$g \in G \wedge g.s = DB_i$ for some $i \in \{1,...,n\} \Leftrightarrow$

$g \in (G_j \overset{fs\,sameDB}{\underset{\cup\ p\alpha,\beta}{}} G_k) \wedge g.s = DB_i$ for some $i \in \{1,...,n\} \Leftrightarrow$
$(\mu_{EQ}(g.A, g_{Gj}.A) \geqslant \alpha \wedge \mu_G(g.A) = \max(\mu_G(g.A), \mu_{Gj}(g_{Gj}.A)) \geqslant \beta) \vee (\mu_{EQ}(g.A, g_{Gk}.A) \geqslant$
$\alpha \wedge \mu_G(g.A) = \max(\mu_G(g.A), \mu_{Gk}(g_{Gk}.A)) \geqslant \beta) \wedge g.s = DB_i$ for some $i \in \{1,...,n\} \Leftrightarrow$
$(\mu_{EQ}(g.A, g_{L_{ij}}.A) \geqslant \alpha \wedge \mu_L(g.A) = \max(\mu_L(g.A), \mu_{L_{ij}}(g_{Lij}.A)) \geqslant \beta) \vee (\mu_{EQ}(g.A, L_{ik}.A) \geqslant$
$\alpha \wedge \mu_L(g.A) = \max(\mu_L(g.A), \mu_{L_{ik}}(g_{L_{ik}}.A)) \geqslant \beta)$ for some $i \in \{1,...,n\} \Leftrightarrow$
$g.A \in (L_{ij}\overset{f}{\underset{\cup\,\alpha,\beta}{}} L_{ik})$ for some $i \in \{1,...,n\} \Leftrightarrow$
$merge(L_{ij}\overset{f}{\underset{\cup\,\alpha,\beta}{}} L_{ik},...,L_{nj}\overset{f}{\underset{\cup\,\alpha,\beta}{}} L_{nk})$.

Lemma 1.7 $\forall L_{1j},...,L_{nj},L_{1k},...,L_{nk}$, and $G_j = merge(L_{1j},...,L_{nj})$,
$G_k = merge(L_{1k},...,L_{nk}), G_j \overset{fs\,sameDB}{\underset{\cap\,\alpha,\beta}{}} G_k = merge(L_{1j}\overset{f}{\underset{\cap\,\alpha,\beta}{}} L_{1k},...,L_{nj}\overset{f}{\underset{\cap\,\alpha,\beta}{}} L_{nk})$.

Proof: Let $G = (G_j \overset{fs\,sameDB}{\underset{\cap\,\alpha,\beta}{}} G_k)$ and Let $L = (L_{ij}\overset{f}{\underset{\cap\,\alpha,\beta}{}} L_{ik})$.
$g \in G \wedge g.s = DB_i$ for some $i \in \{1,...,n\} \Leftrightarrow$
$g \in (G_j \overset{fs\,sameDB}{\underset{\cap\,\alpha,\beta}{}} G_k) \wedge g.s = DB_i$ for some $i \in \{1,...,n\} \Leftrightarrow$
$(\mu_{EQ}(g.A, g_{Gj}.A) \geqslant \alpha \wedge \mu_G(g.A) = \max(\mu_G(g.A), \mu_{Gj}(g_{Gj}.A)) \geqslant \beta) \vee (\mu_{EQ}(g.A, g_{Gk}.A) \geqslant$
$\alpha \wedge \mu_G(g.A) = \max(\mu_G(g.A), \mu_{Gk}(g_{Gk}.A)) \geqslant \beta) \wedge g.s = DB_i$ for some $i \in \{1,...,n\} \Leftrightarrow$
$(\mu_{EQ}(g.A, g_{L_{ij}}.A) \geqslant \alpha \wedge \mu_L(g.A) = \max(\mu_L(g.A), \mu_{L_{ij}}(g_{Lij}.A)) \geqslant \beta) \vee (\mu_{EQ}(g.A, L_{ik}.A) \geqslant$
$\alpha \wedge \mu_L(g.A) = \max(\mu_L(g.A), \mu_{L_{ik}}(g_{L_{ik}}.A)) \geqslant \beta)$ for some $i \in \{1,...,n\} \Leftrightarrow$
$g.A \in (L_{ij}\overset{f}{\underset{\cap\,\alpha,\beta}{}} L_{ik})$ for some $i \in \{1,...,n\} \Leftrightarrow$
$merge(L_{ij}\overset{f}{\underset{\cap\,\alpha,\beta}{}} L_{ik},...,L_{nj}\overset{f}{\underset{\cap\,\alpha,\beta}{}} L_{nk})$.

Lemma 1.8 $\forall L_{1j}, ..., L_{nj}, L_{1k}, ..., L_{nk}$, and $G_j = merge(L_{1j}, ..., L_{nj})$,
$G_k = merge(L_{1k}, ..., L_{nk}), G_{j^-\alpha,\beta}^{fs\,sameDB}G_k = merge(L_{1j^-\alpha,\beta}^f L_{1k}, ..., L_{nj^-\alpha,\beta}^f L_{nk})$.

Proof: *Let* $G = (G_{j^-\alpha,\beta}^{fs\,sameDB}G_k)$
and Let $L = (L_{ij^-\alpha,\beta}^f L_{ik})$.
$g \in G \wedge g.s = DB_i \; for \; some \; i \in \{1, ..., n\} \Leftrightarrow$
$g \in (G_{j^-\alpha,\beta}^{fs\,sameDB}G_k) \wedge g.s = DB_i \; for \; some \; i \in \{1, ..., n\} \Leftrightarrow$
$(\mu_{EQ}(g.A, g_{Gj}.A) \geqslant \alpha \wedge \mu_G(g.A) = \max(\mu_G(g.A), \mu_{Gj}(g_{Gj}.A)) \geqslant \beta) \vee (\mu_{EQ}(g.A, g_{Gk}.A) <$
$\alpha \vee \max(\mu_G(g.A), \mu_{Gk}(g_{Gk}.A)) < \beta) \wedge g.s = DB_i \; for \; some \; i \in \{1, ..., n\} \Leftrightarrow$
$(\mu_{EQ}(g.A, g_{L_{ij}}.A) \geqslant \alpha \wedge \mu_L(g.A) = \max(\mu_L(g.A), \mu_{L_{ij}}(g_{Lij}.A)) \geqslant \beta) \wedge (\mu_{EQ}(g.A, L_{ik}.A) <$
$\alpha \vee \max(\mu_L(g.A), \mu_{L_{ik}}(g_{L_{ik}}.A)) < \beta) \; for \; some \; i \in \{1, ..., n\} \Leftrightarrow$
$g.A \in (L_{ij^-\alpha,\beta}^f L_{ik}) \; for \; some \; i \in \{1, ..., n\} \Leftrightarrow$
$merge(L_{ij^-\alpha,\beta}^f L_{ik}, ..., L_{nj^-\alpha,\beta}^f L_{nk})$.

Having proved the consistency of the above FTS relational operations, the following corollary becomes apparent.

Corollary: The set of FTS relational operations $\{ \overset{fs}{\sigma}, \overset{fs\,sameDB}{\pi}, \overset{fs}{\bowtie}sameDB, \overset{fs\,sameDB}{\cup}, \overset{fs\,sameDB}{\cap}, and \overset{fs\,sameDB}{-} \}$
is consistent with respect to the export fuzzy relational operations.

Algebraic Properties of FTS Relational Model

Given a global multidatabase fuzzy query written in FTS-SQL, a distributed fuzzy query processor derives its equivalent FTS relational expression and evaluates the FTS relational operations in the expression. As part of the fuzzy query evaluation process, the fuzzy query processor may have to transform the relational expression in order to obtain an algebraically equivalent relational expression that requires the least evaluation cost (in terms of disk and communication overheads). Such transformation of FTS queries can only be possible when the algebraic properties of FTS relational model are known. In this section, we will present a few important algebraic properties related to the *Union* operation in the FTS relational model.

Theorem: $\overset{fs\,sameDB}{\cup}_{\alpha,\beta}$ is commutative.
Proof: The definition is independent of the ordering of operands, so it can be proved.
Theorem: $\overset{fs\,sameDB}{\cup}_{\alpha,\beta}$ is associative. i.e. $Z = (R \overset{fs\,sameDB}{\cup}_{\alpha,\beta} S) \overset{fs\,sameDB}{\cup}_{\alpha,\beta} T = R \overset{fs\,sameDB}{\cup}_{\alpha,\beta} (S \overset{fs\,sameDB}{\cup}_{\alpha,\beta} T)$
Proof: Let S, R and T be FTS relations of same arity and domain of ith attribute of S,R,T is the same. In case of *sameDB* option, result must have non-'*' source attribute value. Let FTS relation $X = (R \overset{fs\,sameDB}{\cup}_{\alpha,\beta} S)$ and FTS relation $Y = S \overset{fs\,sameDB}{\cup}_{\alpha,\beta} T)$. Hence,

$(t.A, \mu_Z(t.A), t.s) \in Z \Leftrightarrow$
$(t.A, \mu_Z(t.A), t.s) \in (X \overset{fs\,sameDB}{\cup}_{\alpha,\beta} T) \Leftrightarrow$
$(\mu_{EQ}(t.A, t_X.A) \geqslant \alpha \wedge \mu_Z(t.A) = \max(\mu_Z(t.A), \mu_X(t_X.A)) \geqslant \beta \wedge (t.s = t_X.s \neq *))$

$$(\mu_{EQ}(t.A, t_T.A) \geqslant \alpha \wedge \mu_Z(t.A) = \max(\mu_Z(t.A), \mu_T(t_T.A)) \geqslant \beta \wedge (t.s = t_T.s \neq *)) \Leftrightarrow$$

$$(\mu_{EQ}(t.A, t_R.A) \geqslant \alpha \wedge \mu_Z(t.A) = \max(\mu_Z(t.A), \mu_R(t_R.A)) \geqslant \beta \wedge (t.s = t_R.s \neq *)) \vee$$

$$(\mu_{EQ}(t.A, t_S.A) \geqslant \alpha \wedge \mu_Z(t.A) = \max(\mu_Z(t.A), \mu_S(t_S.A)) \geqslant \beta \wedge (t.s = t_S.s \neq *)) \vee$$

$$(\mu_{EQ}(t.A, t_T.A) \geqslant \alpha \wedge \mu_Z(t.A) = \max(\mu_Z(t.A), \mu_T(t_T.A)) \geqslant \beta \wedge (t.s = t_T.s \neq *)) \Leftrightarrow$$

$$(\mu_{EQ}(t.A, t_R.A) \geqslant \alpha \wedge \mu_Z(t.A) = \max(\mu_Z(t.A), \mu_R(t_R.A)) \geqslant \beta \wedge (t.s = t_R.s \neq *)) \vee$$

$$(\mu_{EQ}(t.A, t_Y.A) \geqslant \alpha \wedge \mu_Z(t.A) = \max(\mu_Z(t.A), \mu_Y(t_Y.A)) \geqslant \beta \wedge (t.s = t_Y.s \neq *)) \Leftrightarrow$$

$$(t.A, \mu_Z(t.A), t.s) \in (R \overset{fs\,sameDB}{\underset{\cup_{\alpha,\beta}}{}} Y) \Leftrightarrow$$

$$(t.A, \mu_Z(t.A), t.s) \in (R \overset{fs\,sameDB}{\underset{\cup_{\alpha,\beta}}{}} (S \overset{fs\,sameDB}{\underset{\cup_{\alpha,\beta}}{}} T))$$

Theorem: $\overset{fs\,anyDB}{\cup_{\alpha,\beta}}$ is associative. i.e. $Z = (R \overset{fs\,anyDB}{\cup_{\alpha,\beta}} S) \overset{fs\,anyDB}{\cup_{\alpha,\beta}} T = R \overset{fs\,anyDB}{\cup_{\alpha,\beta}} (S \overset{fs\,anyDB}{\cup_{\alpha,\beta}} T)$

Proof: Tuples in the result of $\overset{fs\,anyDB}{\cup_{\alpha,\beta}}$ can have either non-`*' or `*' as its source value.

Case 1: Resultant tuple with its source value non-`*' (say `s'). It can be shown by using the procedure similar to that of previous proof that:

$$(t.A, \mu_Z(t.A), t.s) \in (R \overset{fs\,anyDB}{\cup_{\alpha,\beta}} S) \overset{fs\,anyDB}{\cup_{\alpha,\beta}} T \Leftrightarrow (t.A, \mu_Z(t.A), t.s) \in R \overset{fs\,anyDB}{\cup_{\alpha,\beta}} (S \overset{fs\,anyDB}{\cup_{\alpha,\beta}} T)$$

Case 2: Resultant tuple with `*' value of its source attribute.

Proof: Let S, R and T be FTS relations of same arity and domain of ith attribute of S,R,T is the same. In case of *anyDB* option, result must have non-`*' source attribute value.

Let FTS relation Let FTS relation $X = (R \overset{fs\,anyDB}{\cup_{\alpha,\beta}} S)$ and FTS relation $Y = S \overset{fs\,anyDB}{\cup_{\alpha,\beta}} T)$. Hence,

$$(t.A, \mu_Z(t.A), *) \in Z \Leftrightarrow$$

$$(t.A, \mu_Z(t.A), *) \in (X \overset{fs\,sameDB}{\underset{\cup_{\alpha,\beta}}{}} T) \Leftrightarrow$$

$$t.A \in (\overset{f}{\pi}_{A,\alpha,\beta} X \overset{f}{\underset{\cup_{\alpha,\beta}}{}} \overset{f}{\pi}_{A,\alpha,\beta} T) \wedge \mu_Z(t.A) \geqslant \beta \wedge (t.s = * \vee t_X.s \neq t_T.s)) \Leftrightarrow$$

$$t.A \in (\overset{f}{\pi}_{A,\alpha,\beta} R \overset{f}{\underset{\cup_{\alpha,\beta}}{}} \overset{f}{\pi}_{A,\alpha,\beta} S \overset{f}{\underset{\cup_{\alpha,\beta}}{}} \overset{f}{\pi}_{A,\alpha,\beta} T) \wedge \mu_Z(t.A) \geqslant \beta \wedge (t.s = * \vee t_R.s \neq t_S.s \neq t_T.s)) \Leftrightarrow$$

$$t.A \in (\overset{f}{\pi}_{A,\alpha,\beta} R \overset{f}{\underset{\cup_{\alpha,\beta}}{}} \overset{f}{\pi}_{A,\alpha,\beta} Y) \wedge \mu_Z(t.A) \geqslant \beta \wedge (t.s = * \vee t_R.s \neq t_Y.s)) \Leftrightarrow$$

$$(t.A, \mu_Z(t.A), *) \in (R \overset{fs\,sameDB}{\underset{\cup_{\alpha,\beta}}{}} Y) \Leftrightarrow$$

$$(t.A, \mu_Z(t.A), *) \in (R \overset{fs\,sameDB}{\underset{\cup_{\alpha,\beta}}{}} (S \overset{fs\,sameDB}{\underset{\cup_{\alpha,\beta}}{}} T)).$$

Although $\overset{fs\,sameDB}{\cup_{\alpha,\beta}}$ and $\overset{fs\,anyDB}{\cup_{\alpha,\beta}}$ and are associative, however, they are mutually non-associative.

Theorem: $(R \overset{fs\,sameDB}{\cup_{\alpha,\beta}} S) \overset{fs\,anyDB}{\cup_{\alpha,\beta}} T \neq R \overset{fs\,sameDB}{\cup_{\alpha,\beta}} (S \overset{fs\,anyDB}{\cup_{\alpha,\beta}} T)$

Proof: This can be proved using a counter example given in Figure 7.

Similarly properties related with other FTS relational operations can also be proved.

CONCLUSION

In real life multidatabases it is not always desirable to perform complete instance integration, as there are global users/ applications that require a global schema just to query the local databases. For them it is important to identify the source of instances in order to make decisions. Hence in this work, we have described an extended relational model in the context of fuzzy multidatabases with instance integration (level-0) performed on export fuzzy relations. While integrating instances, semantic conflicts are resolved suitably and information about the source database identity is attached with each of the resulting fuzzy tuples. A set of such fuzzy tuples having source information attached with them are called Fuzzy Tuple Source (FTS)-relation. A set of such FTS relations form a fuzzy multidatabase of type-2 under FTS relational model as per our proposal. We have proposed and implemented a full set of FTS relational algebraic operations capable of manipulating an extensive set of fuzzy relational multidatabases of type-2 that include fuzzy data values in their instances.

In this chapter we have also proposed a fuzzy query language FTS-SQL to formulate a global fuzzy query on a fuzzy relational multidatabase of type-2 under FTS relational model. *FTS relational operations* operate on FTS relations to produce a resultant FTS relation. We have also provided architecture for distributed fuzzy query processing with a strategy for fuzzy query decomposition and optimization. Sub-queries obtained as a result of fuzzy query decomposition are allowed to get processed in parallel at respective local fuzzy databases. This reduces the fuzzy query processing time effectively. We have proved the correctness of FTS relational data model by showing that the FTS relational operations are consistent with the fuzzy relational operations on export fuzzy relations of component local fuzzy relational databases. Finally, we have described some algebraic properties of the FTS relational model that may help the fuzzy query processor to transform the relational expression in order to obtain an algebraically equivalent relational expression that require the least evaluation cost in terms of disk space and communication overhead.

SCOPE FOR FUTURE WORK

The future work will explore an appropriate extension to the relational model for integrated fuzzy databases with level-1 instance integration using information on fuzzy inclusion dependencies among component fuzzy relational databases. A user-friendly fuzzy query interface can be designed and developed for FTS-SQL queries in the heterogeneous database environment.

REFERENCES

Agrawal, S., Keller, A. M., Wiederhold, G., & Saraswat, K. (1995). Flexible relation: An approach for integrating data from multiple, possibly inconsistent databases", *In: Proc, Intl. Conf. on Data Engineering*, pp 495-504.

Batini, C., Lenzerini, M., Navade, S.B. (1986). A coperative analysis of methodlogies for database schema integration. *ACM Computing Surveys*, *18*(4), 323–364.

Buckles, B. P. and Petry, E.F. (1983). Information-Theoretical Characterization of Fuzzy Relational Databases", *IEEE Transactions on Systems, Man, and Cybernetics*, Vol. SMC-13, No.1, pp 74-77. Chiang, R.H.L.,

Barron, T.M., Storey, V.C.(1994). Reverse engineering of relational databases: Extraction of an EER model from a relational database". *Data andKnowledge Engineering*, 12(2), pp 107-142.

Clements, D. Ganesh. M., Hwang, S.Y., Lim, E.-P., Mediratta, K., Srivastava, J., Stenoein, J., Myriad, H. Yang, (1994). Design and Implementation of a Federated Database Prototype", *In: Proc. ACM SID-MOD Conf.*, pp 518.

Chen P. (1976). The Entity-Relationship Model-Toward a Uni̅ed View of Data", *ACM Trans on Database Systems* 1, 1, pp 9-36.

Codd, E. F. (1970). A relational Model of Data for Large Shared Data Banks", *ACM Comm.*, 13,6, pp 377-387.

Codd, E.F. (1971). Further Normalization of the Database Relational Model", *In Database Systems, Courant Computer Science Symposia*, 6, R. Rustin, Ed. Printice Hall, Englewood Claffs, N.J., pp 65-98.

Codd, E. F. (1972). Relational Completeness of Database Sublanguages", *In R Rustin, Ed, Database Systems*, Printice-Hall, New Jersey.

Chatterjee, A., Segev, A.(1991). Data manipulation in heterogeneous databases", *SIGMOD Record*, 20(4), pp 64-68.

DeMichiel, L. G. (1989). Resolving database incompatibility: an approach to performing relational operations over mismatched domains. *IEEE Transactions on Knowledge and Data Engineering*, 1(4), 485–493. doi:10.1109/69.43423

Evrendilek, C., Dogac, A., Nural, S., & Ozcan, F. (1997). Fuzzy query optimization in multidatabase systems", *Jouranal of Distrubuted and Parallel Databases*, 5(1) pp 77-114.

Fahrner C., Vossen G.,(1995). A servey of database design transformations based on entity relationship model. *Data & Knowledge Engineering*, 15(3), 213–250.

Finance, B., Smahi, V., & Fessy, J. (1995). Fuzzy query processing in IRO-DB", In: *Proc. 4th Intl. Conf. On Deductive and Object Oriented Databases (DOOD95)*, Singapore, pp 299-318.

Galindo J., Medina J.M., Pons O., Cubero J.C. (1998). A Server for Fuzzy SQL Queries, Flexible Fuzzy query Answering Systems", eds. T. Andreasen, H. Christiansen and H.L. Larsen, *Lecture Notes in Arti̅cial Intelligence (LNAI)*, 1495, Ed. Springer, pp. 164-174.

Galindo, J., Medina, J. M., Cubero, J. C., & Garca, M. T. (2001). Relaxing the Universal Quantifier of the Division in Fuzzy Relational Databases", *International Journal of Intelligent Systems*, Vol. 16-6, pp 713-742.

Hayne, S., Ram, S. (1990). Multi-user view integration system (MUVIS): An expert system for view integration", In: *Proc. Intl. Conf. on Data Engineering*, pp 402-409.

Grant, J., Litwin, W., Roussopoulos, N., & Sellis, T. (1993). Fuzzy query languages for relational multidatabases", *The VLDB Journal*, Volume 2, Issue 2, pp 153-172.

Juan C. Lavariega, Susan D. Urban, (2002). An Object Algebra Approach to Multidatabase Fuzzy query Decomposition in Donaj. *Distributed and Parallel Databases*, *12*(Issue 1), 27–71.

Kandel, A. (1986). *Fuzzy Mathematical Techniques with Applications", Addison Wesley Publishing Co., California.*

Kaufman, A. *(1975). Inroduction to the Theory of Fuzzy Subsets", Vol-I, Academic Press.* New York: Sanfrancisco.

Kaul, M., Drosten, K., & Neuhold, E. J. (1990). Integrating heterogeneous information bases by object-oriented views", In: *Proc. Intl. Conf. on Data Engineering*, pp 2-10.

Litwin W. and Abdellatif A. (1986). Multidatabase Interoperabilty", *IEEE. The Computer Journal*, *12*(19), 10–18.

Lakshman, L. V. S., Saderi, F., & Subramanian, L. N. \Schema SQL-Alanguage for interoperability in relational multidatabase systems". In: *Proc. Intl. Conf. Very Large Databases*, (1996), pp 239-250.

Meier A. et al.(1994). Hierarchical to relational database migration", *IEEE Software*, pp 21-27.

Larson, J. A., Navade, S. B., & Elmasari, R. (1989), A theory of attribute equivalence in database with application to schema integration", *IEEE Trans. on Software Engineering*, 15(4), pp 449-463.

Liu, L., Pu, C., Lee, Y.(1996). An adoptive approach to query mediation across heterogeneous databases". In: *Proc. Intl. Conf. on Cooperative Information Systems*, pp 144-156.

Lim, E. P., Srivastava, J., & Shekhar, S. (1994), Resolving attribute incompatibility in database integration: An evidential reasoning approach". In: *Proc, Intl. Conf. on Data Engineering*, pp 154-163.

Litwin W. et al (1982). SIRIUS Systems for Distributed Data Management", In: chneider, H.J., ed., *Distributed Databases*, New Yark: North-Holland.

Lim Ee Peng. Chiang Roger H.L., Cao Yinyan (1999). Tuple source relational model: A source aware data model for multidatabase", *Data and Knowledge Engineering*, 29, pp 83-114.

Lim E.P., Srivastava J., Prabhakar S., Richardson J. (1993). Entity identification problem in database integration". In: *Proc, Intl. Conf. on Data Engineering*, 294-301.

Litwin, W., Abdellatif, A., Zeroual, A., & Nicolas, B. (1989). MSQL: A multidatabase language", *Information sciences*, 49, pp 59-101.

Lee, Jeong-Oog, Baik, Doo-Kwon (1999). SemQL: a semantic fuzzy query language for multidatabase systems",In: *Proceedings of the eighth international conference on Information and knowledge management*, United States, pp 259-266.

Ma, Z. M., Zhang, W., & Ma, W. (2000). Semantic con°icts and solutions in fuzzy multidatabase systems", *DNIS*, pp 80-90.

Prade, H., Testemale, C. (1984). Generalizing Database Relational Algebra for the Treatment of Incomplete and Uncertain Information and Vague Queries. *Information Science*, 115–143.

Rundensteiner, E. A., Hawkes, L. W., & Bandler, W. (1989). On Nearness Measures in Fuzzy Relational Data Models", *International Journal of Approximate Reasoning*, (3), 267-298. Raju, K.V.S.V.N., Majumdar, A.K. (1986). Fuzzy functional dependencies in fuzzy relations", In Proc. *Second Intl. Conf. on Data Engg.*, Los Angeles, California, pp 312-319.

Saltor, F., Castellanos, M., & Garcia-Solaco, M. (1991). Suitability of data models as canonical models for federated databases", *SIGMOD Record*, 20(4), pp 44-48.

Seth, A.P., Larson, J.A. (1990). Federated database systems for managing distributed heterogeneous and autonomous databases. *ACM Computing Surveys*, *22*(3), 183–236.

Sharma, A. K., Goswami, A., & Gupta, D. K. (2004). Fuzzy Inclusion Dependencies in Fuzzy Relational Databases", In *Proceedings of International Conference on Information Technology: Coding and Computing (ITCC 2004)*, Las Vegas, USA, IEEE Computer Society Press, USA, Volum-1, pp 507-510.

Sharma, A. K., Goswami, A., & Gupta, D. K. (2008). Fuzzy Inclusion Dependencies in Fuzzy Databases. In Galindo, J. (Ed.), *Handbook of Research on Fuzzy Information Processing in Databases* (pp. 657–683). Hershey, PA, USA: Information Science Reference.

Spaccapietra, S., Parent, C., & Dupont, Y. (1992). Model independent assertions for integration of heterogeneous schemas", *Very Large Database Journal*, l(1), pp 81-126.

Tasi, P.S.M., Chen, A.L.P. (1993), Querying uncertain data in heterogeneous databases", In: *Proc. RIDE-IMS Conf.*, pp 161-168.

Wang, Y. R., & Madnick, S. E. (1989), The inter-database instance identi‾cation problem in integrating autonomous systems", In: *Proc. Intl. Conf. on Data Engineering*, pp 46-55.

Wang, Y.R., Madnick, S.E., R. Wang, S. Madnick. (1990), A polygen model for heterogeneous database systems: The source tagging perspective", In: *Proc. Intl. Conf. on Very Large Data Bases*, pp 519-538.

Zadeh, L. A. (1965). Fuzzy Sets, Information and Control", 8, pp 338-353.

Zaniolo C. (1979). Design of relational views over network schemas", In: *Proc. ACM SIGMOD Intl. Conf. on Management of Data*, pp 179-190.

Zemankova, M., & Kandel, A. (1984). Fuzzy Relational Database-A Key to Expert Systems", *Verlag*, TÄUV Rheinland, Cologne.

Zemankova, M., Kandel, A. (1985). Implementing Imprecision in Information Systems. *Information Sciences*, *37*(3), 107–141. doi:10.1016/0020-0255(85)90008-8

Zhang, W., Laun, E., & Meng, W. (1997). A methodology of integrating fuzzy relational database in multidatabase systems", In: *Proc, Intl. Conf. on Database Systems for Advance Applications*.

Zhao, J.L., Segev, A., Chatterjee, A. (1995). A universal relation approach to federated database management", In: *Proc, Intl. Conf. on Data Engineering*, pp 261-270.

KEY TERMS AND DEFINITIONS

A Proximity Relation: A universe of discourse U is reflexive, symmetric and transitive fuzzy relation with $\mu_p(u_1, u_2) \in [1, 0]$, where $u_1, u_2 \in U$ (Kandel, 1986).

EQ: A resemblance relation, EQ of U is a fuzzy binary relation on $U \times U$, that fulfills the following properties $\forall x, y \in U$, where U is the universe of discourse. (i) Reflexive: $\mu_{EQ}(x, x) = 1$, (ii) Symmetric: $\mu_{EQ}(x, y) = \mu_{EQ}(y, x)$

FTS Relation & Fuzzy Multidatabase: In some way the merge operation is similar to an outer-union except that an additional source attribute is added before they are outer-unioned. An integrated global fuzzy relation thus obtained by the use of merge operation is given the name FTS relations. A set of such FTS relations is called Fuzzy Multidatabase where integrated fuzzy relations have fuzzy tuples with the source (DB_{id}) information.

FTS Relational Operations: These operations refer to the fundamental relational algebraic operators as defined in chapter-1 that is operative on global fuzzy as well as crisp relations.

FTS-SQL: It is an extended SQL that addresses fuzzy as well as crisp databases for fuzzy query formulations using FTS relational operators.

Fuzzy Comparison Operators: To supports queries that may contain qualifications involving imprecise and uncertain values, FTS relational model is equipped with fuzzy comparison operators. These operators (EQ, NEQ) and (GT, GOE, LT, LOE) are defined as follows:

Fuzzy Query Agents: For each local fuzzy database there is one fuzzy query agent to transform sub-queries into local queries that can be directly processed by the local fuzzy database systems and to transform back the local fuzzy query results into a format that is acceptable to the fuzzy query mediator.

Fuzzy Query Mediator: Fuzzy query processor has a fuzzy query mediator who has to take the global queries as input given by fuzzy multidatabase applications, and decompose it into multiple sub-queries and forward the same to fuzzy query agents for its evaluation. It is also responsible for the compilation of results given back by the different fuzzy query agents.

Fuzzy Relational Database of Type-1: In type-1 fuzzy relations, $dom(A_i)$ may be a classical subset or a fuzzy subset of U_i. Let the membership function of $dom(A_i)$ be denoted by μ_{A_i}, for $i=1,2,\ldots,n$. Then from the definition of Cartesian product of fuzzy sets, $dom(A_1) \times dom(A_2) \times \cdots \times dom(A_n)$ is a fuzzy subset of $U^* = U_1 \times U_2 \times \ldots \times U_n$. Hence a type-1 fuzzy relation r is also a fuzzy subset of U^* with membership function μ_r.

Fuzzy Relational Database of Type-2: A type-2 fuzzy relation r is a fuzzy subset of D, where $\mu_r : D \to [0,1]$ must satisfy the condition $\mu_r(t) \leq \max\limits_{(u_1, u_2, \cdots, u_n) \in U^*} \left[\min \left(\mu_{a_1}(u_1), \mu_{a_2}(u_2), \cdots, \mu_{a_n}(u_n) \right) \right]$ where $t = (a_1, a_2, \cdots, a_n) \in D$.

Fuzzy Value Equivalent (FVEQ): Let A and B be two fuzzy sets with their membership functions μ_A and μ_B respectively. A fuzzy value $\alpha \in A$ is said to be equivalent to some other fuzzy value $b \in B$, iff $b \in \mu_B(x)$, for some $x \in S$, where S is the set of crisp values that are returned by $\mu_A^{-1}(a)$, where μ_A^{-1} is the inverse of the membership function of fuzzy set A.

GT: Let P_1 is a proximity relation defined over U. Fuzzy relational operator GT is defined to be a fuzzy subset of $U \times U$, where μ_{GT} satisfies the following properties $\forall u_1, u_2 \in U$:

$$\mu_{GT}(u_1, u_2) = \begin{cases} 0 & if \quad u_1 \leq u_2 \\ \mu_{P_1}(u_1, u_2) & otherwise. \end{cases}$$

LT: Let P_2 is a proximity relation defined over a universe of discourse U. The fuzzy relational operator LT is defined to be a fuzzy subset of $U \times U$, where μ_{LT} satisfies the following properties $\forall u_1, u_2 \in U$:

$$\mu_{LT}(u_1, u_2) = \begin{cases} 0 & if \quad u_1 \geq u_2 \\ \mu_{P_1}(u_1, u_2) & otherwise. \end{cases}$$

NEQ, GOE, LOE: Membership functions of fuzzy relations `NOT EQUAL' (*NEQ*), `GREATER THAN OR EQUAL' (*GOE*) and `LESS THAN OR EQUAL' (*LOE*) can be defined based on that of *EQ*, *GT* and *LT* as follows:

$$\mu_{NEQ}(u_1, u_2) = [1 - \mu_{EQ}(u_1, u_2)]$$
$$\mu_{GOE}(u_1, u_2) = \max[\mu_{GT}(u_1, u_2), \mu_{EQ}(u_1, u_2)]$$
$$\mu_{LOE}(u_1, u_2) = \min[\mu_{LT}(u_1, u_2), \mu_{EQ}(u_1, u_2)]$$

α-Cut: Given a fuzzy set A defined on U and any number $\alpha \in [0,1]$, the α-cut $^{\alpha}A$, and the strong α-cut, $^{\alpha+}A$, are the crisp sets

$$^{\alpha}A = \{u \mid \mu_A(u) \geq \alpha\}$$
$$^{\alpha+}A = \{u \mid \mu_A(u) > \alpha\}$$

α-Resemblance: Given a set U with a resemblance relation EQ as previously defined. Then, $\langle U, EQ \rangle$ is called a resemblance space. An α-level set EQ_α induced by EQ is termed as an α-resemblance set. Define the relationship of two values x,y∈U that resemble each other with a degree larger than or equal to α (i.e. $\mu_{EQ}(x, y) \geq \alpha$) as α-resemblant. The following notation is proposed for the notion of two values x,y being α-resemblant: $xEQ_{\alpha y}$. A set P⊆U is called an α-preclass on $\langle U, EQ \rangle$, if $x, y \in P$, x and y are α-resemblant (i.e. $xEQ_{\alpha y}$ holds).

Section 2

Chapter 9

Pattern–Based Schema Mapping and Query Answering in Peer–to–Peer XML Data Integration System

Tadeusz Pankowski
Poznan University of Technology, Poland

ABSTRACT

This chapter addresses the problem of data integration in a P2P environment, where each peer stores schema of its local data, mappings between the schemas, and some schema constraints. The goal of the integration is to answer queries formulated against a chosen peer. The answer must consist of data stored in the queried peer as well as data of its direct and indirect partners. The chapter focuses on defining and using mappings, schema constraints, query propagation across the P2P system, and query answering in such scenario. Schemas, mappings, constraints (functional dependencies) and queries are all expressed using a unified approach based on tree-pattern formulas. The chapter discusses how functional dependencies can be exploited to increase information content of answers (by discovering missing values) and to control merging operations and propagation strategies. The chapter proposes algorithms for translating high-level specifications of mappings and queries into XQuery programs, and it shows how the discussed method has been implemented in SixP2P (or 6P2P) system.

DOI: 10.4018/978-1-60960-475-2.ch009

INTRODUCTION

The goal of data integration is to enable rapid development of new applications requiring information from multiple sources (Haas, 2007). Data integration consists in combining data from different sources into a unified format (Bernstein & Haas, 2008). There is a number of different research fields relevant to data integration. Among them we can distinguish: identification of the best data sources to use, cleansing and standardizing data coming from these sources, dealing with uncertainty and tracing data provenance, the way of querying diverse sources and optimizing queries and execution plans. Integration activities cover any form of data reuse, such as exchanging data between different application's databases, translating data for business-to-business e-commerce, and providing access to structured data and documents via a Web portal (Bernstein & Haas, 2008).

A variety of architectural approaches can be used to deal with the problem of data integration. The most popular is the *materialized integration* realized by means of *data warehouse* that consolidates data from multiple sources. Other approaches use paradigm of *virtual integration*. While warehouses materialize the integrated data, virtual data integration offers a mediated schema against which users can pose queries. The query is translated into queries on the data sources and results of those queries are merged so that it appears to have come from a single integrated database (Miller et al., 2000, Pankowski & Hunt, 2005). In a peer-to-peer (P2P) data integration the role of the mediated schema can play schema of any peer database. Then the user issues a query against an arbitrarily chosen peer and expects that the answer will include relevant data stored in all P2P connected data sources. The data sources are related by means of XML *schema mappings*. A query must be propagated to all peers in the system along semantic paths of mappings and reformulated accordingly. The partial answers must be merged and sent back to the user's peer (Madhavan & Halevy, 2003; Pankowski, 2008c; Tatarinov & Halevy, 2004).

Much work has been done on data integration systems both with a mediated (global) schema and in P2P architecture, where the schema of any peer can play the role of the mediated schema (Arenas & Libkin, 2005; Madhavan & Halevy, 2003; Melnik et al., 2005, Yu & Popa, 2004). There is also a number of systems built in P2P data integration paradigm (Koloniari & Pitoura, 2005), notably Piazza (Tatarinov et al., 2003), PeerDB (Ooi et al., 2003). In these works the focus was on overcoming syntactic heterogeneity and schema mappings were used to specify how data structured under one schema (the source schema) can be transformed into data structured under another schema (the target schema) (Fagin et al., 2004; Fuxman et al., 2006). Some attention has been paid to the question of how schema constraints influence the query propagation.

This chapter describes formal foundations and some algorithms used for XML data integration in P2P system. Schemas of XML data are described by means of a class of tree-pattern formulas, like in (Arenas & Libkin, 2005). These formulas are used to define both schema mappings and queries. In contrast to (Arenas & Libkin, 2005), except for schemas we use tree-pattern formulas also to specify constraints (functional dependencies) over schemas. Schemas, mappings, queries and constraints are specified in a uniform way as a class of tree-pattern formulas. Thanks to this, we are able to translate high-level specifications into XQuery programs. We also discuss the problem of query propagation between peers. We show how mutual relationships between schema constraints and queries can influence both propagation of queries and merging of answers. Taking into account such interrelationships may improve both, efficiency of the system and information content included in answers. We show in brief how the issues under consideration have been implemented in 6P2P system (*SixP2P, Semantic Integration of XML data in P2P environment*).

PATTERN-BASED APPROACH TO XML SCHEMAS AND INSTANCES

XML Schemas

Schemas for XML data are usually specified by means of XSDL (*XML Schema Definition Language*) (XML Schema, 2009) or DTD (*Document Type Definition*) (Martens et al., 2007). The aim of such a schema is to control well-formedness and validity of XML documents. We assume that the structure of XML documents conform to their DTDs and that attributes are represented by so called *terminal elements* labeled with *terminal labels* of *Text type* (we ignore mixed elements).

Let L be a set of labels, $Ter \subseteq L$ be a set of terminal labels, and $top \in L - Ter$ be the outermost (top) label.

Definition 1. (*DTD*) A tuple $D = (top, L, Ter, \sigma)$ is a DTD, if σ is a function assigning regular expressions over $L - \{top\}$ to non-terminal labels, and *Text* to terminal labels, i.e.

- $\sigma: L - Ter \rightarrow Reg$
- $\sigma: Ter \rightarrow \{Text\}$,

the set *Reg* of regular expressions is defined by the grammar:

$$e ::= l \mid (e) \mid e? \mid e* \mid e^+ \mid e + e \mid e\,e.$$

Example 1. In Figure 1 there are graphical representations of the following DTDs (D_a is a recursive DTD, while D_1 is non-recursive):

```
D₁ = (pubs, {pubs, pub, title, year, author, name, university}, {title, year,
name, university}, σ),
        where
σ(pubs) = pub*, σ(pub) = title year? author+, σ(author) = name university?
             σ(title) = σ(year) = σ(name) = σ(university) = Text.
Dₐ = (parts, {parts, part, pid}, {pid}, σ),
        where:
            σ(parts) = part*, σ(part) = pid part*, σ(pid) = Text.
```

In this chapter, we assume that all XML documents are valid, so we will not be interested in checking their validity against DTDs. Instead, we are interested in such a formal description of the structures of XML documents that would be convenient for defining mappings and transforming data in XML data integration processes.

Since every XML document is a finite tree, thus its structure can be specified by a *tree pattern* (Xu & Ozsoyoglu, 2005). For documents having recursive DTDs their tree patterns are restricted to finite depths. The notion of tree-patterns can be used to define *tree-pattern formulas* (Arenas & Libkin, 2005). A tree-pattern formula arises from a tree pattern by assigning variables to terminal labels (i.e. to paths starting in the root and ending with this terminal label). In Figure 1 the tree-pattern formulas, S_1 and S_a,

Figure 1. Graphical representation of DTDs (D_1 and D_a) and tree-pattern formulas (schemas) S_1 and S_a for documents conforming to those DTDs, S_a is restricted to depth of 3

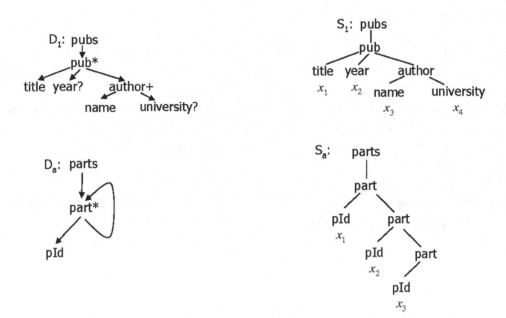

are represented in a form of trees, whose leaves are labeled with text-valued variables. We will consider two classes of tree-pattern formulas: *schemas* and *functional dependencies*.

Definition 2. (*tree pattern*) A *tree pattern* over $D = (top, L, Ter, \sigma)$ is an expression that can be defined recursively by the following grammar:

```
TP::=  /E | EE::=  l | l[E₁, ..., Eₖ] | E/E', and first(Eᵢ) ∈ σ(l), for i = 1,
..., k; and first(E') ∈ σ(last(E)),
```

- $first(l) = last(l) = l$,
- $first(l[E_1, ..., E_k]) = last(l[E_1, ..., E_k]) = l$,
- $first(E/E') = first(E)$,
- $last(E/E') = last(E')$.

Example 2. For $L = \{pubs, pub, title, year, author, name, university\}$, the following expressions are tree patterns over L:

```
TP₁ = /pubs[pub[title, year[author[name, university]]]],
TP₂ = pubs/pub[title, author]/year,
TP₃ = pub/author.

TPₐ = /parts[part[pid, part[pid part[pid]]]].
```

By *Path*(*TP*) we will denote the set of all paths defined by the tree pattern *TP*. This set is defined recursively as follows:

- $Path(/E) = \{/p \mid p \in Path(E)\}$,
- $Path(l) = \{l\}$,
- $Path(E/E') = \{p/p' \mid p \in Path(E), p' \in Path(E')\}$,
- $Path(l[E_1, ..., E_k]) = \{ l/p_i \mid p_i \in Path(E_i), i \in [1, ..., k] \}$.

Definition 3. (*schema pattern*) A tree pattern *TP* over $D = (top, L, Ter, \sigma)$ is called a *schema pattern* over *D*, if the following two conditions hold:

- *TP* is of the form $/top[E]$,
- each path in *Path*(*TP*) ends with a terminal label.

Tree pattern TP_1 and TP_a from Example 2 are tree-pattern schemas over D_1 and D_a, respectively.

Definition 4. (*arity of tree patterns*) A tree pattern *TP* over $D = (top, L, Ter, \sigma)$ is of *arity m* if there are *m* paths in *Path*(*TP*) ending with a terminal label from *Ter*. To indicate these terminal labels (possibly with more that one occurrences) and their ordering we use the notation $TP(l_1, ..., l_m)$ meaning that the occurrence of the terminal label l_1 proceeds the occurrence of l_2, and so on.

Note that a label can have many occurrences in a tree pattern (e.g. for S_a in Example 1, we have $S_a(pid, pid, pid)$).

Definition 5. (*tree-pattern formula, schema*) Let *TP* be a tree pattern of arity *m* over $D = (top, L, Ter, \sigma)$, and $(l_1, ..., l_m)$ be a list of (not necessarily distinct) terminal labels occurring in *TP* and $\mathbf{x} = (x_1, ..., x_m)$ be a tuple of distinct text-valued variables. Then the formula $TP(\mathbf{x})$ created from *TP* by replacing the *i*-th terminal label l_i with the equality $l_i = x_i$, is called a *tree-pattern formula*. If *TP* is a schema pattern, then $TP(\mathbf{x})$ will be referred to as a *schema*.

Schemas will be denoted by $S(\mathbf{x})$, or by *S* if variable names are not important or clear from the context. Note that a schema $S(\mathbf{x})$ is an XPath expression (XPath, 2006}, where the first slash, /, denotes the root of the corresponding XML document. Any variable *x* occurring in the schema has the *type* being the sequence of labels (the path) leading from the root to the leaf the variable *x* is assigned to.

Definition 6. (*variable types*) Let *S* be a schema over $\mathbf{x}$ and let an atom $l = x$ occur in *S*. Then the path *p* starting with *top* and ending with *l* is called the *type* of the variable *x*, denoted $type_S(x) = p$.

A tree pattern has the type being the type of the elements returned by its evaluation according to the XPath semantics. This type is a path determined as follows:

- $type(/E) = /type(E)$,
- $type(l) = l$,
- $type(E/E') = type(E)/ type(E')$,

- $type(E[E']) = type(E)$.

Example 3. Schemas S_1 and S_a from Figure 1 can be specified as follows:

```
S₁(x₁, x₂, x₃, x₄) := /pubs[pub[title = x₁, year = x₂, author[name = x₃, univer-
sity = x₄]]]
Sₐ(x₁, x₂, x₃)      := /part[pId = x₁, part[pId = x₂, part[pId = x₃]]]

typeₛ₁(x₁) = /pubs/pub/title,

type(S₁) = /pubstype(TP₂) = /pubs/pub/year (see Example 2).
```

Instances of XML Schemas

An XML database consists of a set of XML data. We define XML data as an unranked rooted node-labeled tree (*XML tree*) over a set L of labels, and a set $Str \cup \{\bot\}$ of strings (*Str*) and the distinguished null value $\bot$ – both strings and the null value are used as values of text (i.e. terminal) nodes. The value $\bot$ denotes that the path with this value is in fact missing in the XML tree under consideration.

Definition 7. (*XML tree*) An *XML tree* I is a tuple $(r, N^e, N^t, child, \lambda, v)$, where:

- r is a distinguished *top node*, N^e is a finite set of *element nodes*, and N^t is a finite set of *text nodes*;
- $child \subseteq (\{r\} \cup N^e) \times (N^e \cup N^t)$ – a relation introducing tree structure into the set $\{r\} \cup N^e \cup N^t$, where r is the root, each element node has at least one child (being an element or text node), text nodes are leaves;
- $\lambda: N^e \rightarrow L$ – a function labeling element nodes with *names* (labels);
- $v: N^t \rightarrow Str \cup \{\bot\}$ – a function labeling text nodes with *text values* from *Str* or with the null value $\bot$.

It will be useful to perceive an XML tree I with a schema $S(\mathbf{x})$, as a pair $(S(\mathbf{x}), \Omega)$ (called the *instance description*), where Ω is a set of *valuations* of variables in $\mathbf{x}$.

Definition 8. (*variable valuation*) Let $Str \cup \{\bot\}$ be a set of values of text nodes. Let $\mathbf{x}$ be a set of variable names. A *valuation* ω for variables in $\mathbf{x}$ is a function

$$\omega: \mathbf{x} \rightarrow Str \cup \{\bot\}$$

assigning values in $Str \cup \{\bot\}$ to variables in $\mathbf{x}$.

An XML tree I satisfies a description (S, Ω), denoted $I \leq (S, \Omega)$, if I satisfies (S, ω) for every $\omega \in \Omega$, where this satisfaction is defined as follows.

Definition 9. (*schema satisfaction*) Let S be a schema, $\mathbf{x}$ be a set of variables in S, and ω be a valuation of variables in $\mathbf{x}$. An XML tree $I = (r, N^e, N^t, child, \lambda, v)$ satisfies S by ω, denoted $I \leq (S, \omega)$, if the root r of I satisfies S by ω, denoted $(I, r) \leq (S, \omega)$, where:

Figure 2. Two XML trees as equivalent instances of S_1; J_2 is a canonical instance, whereas J_1 is not

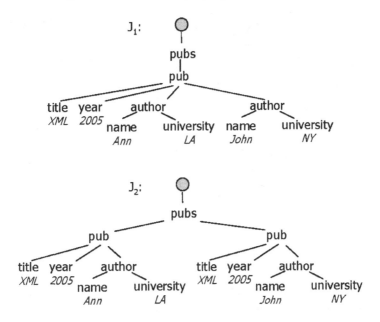

- $(I, r) \leq (/top[E], \omega)$, iff $\exists n \in N^e$ $(child(r, n) \wedge (I, n) \leq (top[E], \omega))$;
- $(I, n) \leq (l[E_1, ..., E_k], \omega)$, iff $\lambda(n) = l$ and $\exists n_1, ..., n_k \in N^e$ $(child(n, n_1) \wedge (I, n_1) \leq (E_1, \omega) \wedge ... \wedge child(n, n_k) \wedge (I, n_k) \leq (E_k, \omega))$;
- $(I, n) \leq (l/E, \omega)$, iff $\lambda(n) = l \wedge \exists n' \in N^e$ $(child(n, n') \wedge (I, n') \leq (E, \omega))$;
- $(I, n) \leq (l = x, \omega)$, iff $\lambda(n) = l$ and $\exists n' \in N^t$ $(child(n, n') \wedge v(n') = \omega(x))$.

In fact, a description (S, Ω) represents a class of instances of S with the same set of valuations Ω, since elements in instance trees can be grouped and nested in different ways.

For example, both XML trees J_1 and J_2 in Figure 2 conform to the schema S_1 from Example 1, and satisfy the description $(S_1, \{(XML, 2005, Ann, LA), (XML, 2005, John, NY)\}$, although they are organized in different ways.

By a *canonical instance* we will understand the instance with the maximal width, i.e. the instance where subtrees corresponding to valuations are pair-wise disjoint. For example, the instance J_2 in Figure 2 is a canonical instance, whereas J_1 is not since two authors are nested under one publication.

SCHEMA MAPPINGS

Further on in this chapter, we will refer to the running example depicted in Figure 3. There are three XML schema trees S_1, S_2, S_3, along with their instances I_1, I_2, and I_3, respectively. S_1 is the same as S_1 in Figure 1, and its instance I_1 is empty. The schemas and their instances are on peers P_1, P_2, and P_3, respectively.

The key issue in data integration is this of *schema mapping*. Schema mapping is a specification defining how data structured under one schema (the *source schema*) is to be transformed into data structured under another schema (the *target schema*). In the theory of relational data exchange, *source-to-*

Figure 3. XML schemas, S_1, S_2, S_3, and their instances I_1, I_2 and I_3, located in peers P_1, P_2, and P_3

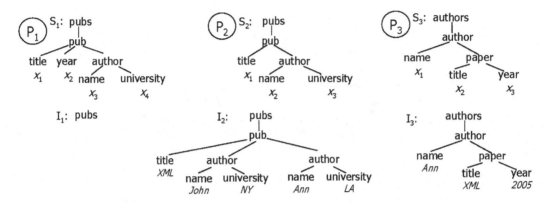

target dependencies (STDs) (Abiteboul et al., 1995) are usually used to express schema mappings (Fagin et al., 2004).

We adopt the approach proposed in (Fagin et al., 2004), but instead of relational schemas we will deal with XML schemas (Arenas & Libkin, 2005; Pankowski et al., 2007). An XML schema mapping specifies the semantic relationship between a source XML schema and a target XML schema.

Definition 10. (*schema mapping*) A mapping from a source schema $S(\mathbf{x})$ to a target schema $T(\mathbf{x'}, \mathbf{y})$, where $\mathbf{x'} \subseteq \mathbf{x}$, and $\mathbf{y} \cap \mathbf{x} = \varnothing$, is a formula of the form

$m_{ST} := \forall \mathbf{x} \, (S(\mathbf{x}) \Rightarrow \exists \mathbf{y} T(\mathbf{x'}, \mathbf{y})).$

In other words, a mapping m_{ST} states, that for any valuation of variables in $\mathbf{x}$, if this valuation satisfies a tree-pattern formula $S(\mathbf{x})$, then there is such a valuation of $\mathbf{y}$ that $T(\mathbf{x'}, \mathbf{y})$ is also satisfied.

Variable names in a mapping are used to indicate correspondences between text values of paths bound to variables. In practice, a correspondence can also involve functions that transform values of source and target variables. These functions are irrelevant to our discussion, so they will be omitted.

The result of a mapping is a canonical instance of the right-hand side schema, where each variable $y \in \mathbf{y}$ has the $\bot$ (*null*) value. The target instance can be obtained using the *chase* procedure (Abiteboul et al., 1995; Fagin et al., 2005; Pankowski, 2008d). In this work, however, we will propose an algorithm (Algorithm 1) translating the high-level specification of a mapping into an XQuery program (XQuery, 2002; Pankowski, 2008c) producing the target instance from a given source instance.

Example 4. The mapping m_{S3S1} from S_3 to S_1 (Figure 3) is specified as:

```
m_{S3S1} := ∀x_1, x_2, x_3 (S_3(x_1, x_2, x_3) ⇒ ∃x_4 S_1(x_2, x_3, x_1, x_4)) =
       = ∀x_1, x_2, x_3 (/authors[author[name = x_1, paper[title = x_2, year = x_3]]] ⇒
       ⇒ ∃x_4 /pubs[pub[title = x_2, year = x_3, author[name = x_1, university = x_4]]]).
```
Then, for $I_3 = (S_3(x_1, x_2, x_3), \{(Ann, XML, 2005)\})$,

```
m_{S3S1}(I_3) = (S_1(x_2, x_3, x_1, x_4), {(XML, 2005, Ann, ⊥)}).
```

Algorithm 1 translates a mapping into an appropriate XQuery program. By x, y, v (possibly with subscripts) we denote variables, while x, y, v are the corresponding XQuery variables.

Algorithm 1. (*translating a mapping* m_{ST} *to XQuery program*)

```
Input:              A mapping ∀x (S(x) ⇒ ∃yT(x', y)), where:
 S:= /l'[E'],  T:= /l[E],  y = (y₁, ..., yₘ).
Output: Query in XQuery over S transforming an instance of S into the corre-
sponding
  canonical instance of T.
mappingToXQuery(∀x (/l'[E'] ⇒ ∃y₁, ..., yₘ /l[E]) =
<l>{let $y₁: = "null", ..., $yₘ := "null"
for $vin doc("...")/l',
τ($v, E')
return
   ρ(E)}
</l>
```

where:

1. $\tau(v, l = x) = x$ **in if** ($v[l]$) **then** $v/l/text()$ **else** "*null*",
2. $\tau(v, l[E]) = v$ '**in if** ($v[l]$) **then** v/l **else** /, $\tau(v', E)$,
3. $\tau(v, E_1, ..., E_k) = \tau(v, E_1), ..., \tau(v, E_k)$,

and

4. $\rho(l = x) = $ <l>{x}</l>
5. $\rho(l[E]) = $ <l>$\rho(E)$</l>
6. $\rho(E_1, ..., E_k) = \rho(E_1) ... \rho(E_k)$

For the mapping from Example 4, Algorithm 1 generates the following XQuery program:

```
Query 1:
<pubs>{
  let $x4:="null"
  for $_v in doc("I3.xml")/authors,
  $_v1 in if ($_v[author]) then $_v/author else /,
    $x1 in if ($_v1[name]) then $_v1/name/text() else "null",
    $_v2 in if ($_v1[paper]) then $_v1/paper else /,
      $x2 in if ($_v2[title]) then $_v2/title/text() else "null",
      $x3 in if ($_v2[year]) then $_v2/year/text() else "null"
  return
  <pub>
    <title>{$x2}</title>
```

```
    <year>{$x3}</year>
    <author>
      <name>{$x1}</name>
      <university>{$x4}</university>
    </author>
  </pub> }
</pubs>
```

The program creates a canonical instance of S_1, i.e. elements are not grouped and all missing values are replaced with nulls ($\perp$).

SCHEMA CONSTRAINTS

Over a schema, we can define XML *functional dependencies* (XFD), which constrain dependencies between values or values and nodes in instances of the schema.

Definition 11. (*TP-XFD*) A tree-pattern formula $F(x_1, ..., x_k)$ over a schema $S(\mathbf{x})$ defines an XML functional dependency $p_1, ..., p_k \rightarrow p$ (Arenas & Libkin, 2004) if:

- $type_S(x_i) = p_i$, for $i = 1,...,k$,
- $type(S) = p$.

Such TPFs will be referred to as *tree-pattern XML functional dependencies* (TP-XFDs), p is then the *dependent path*, and $p_1, ..., p_k$ are *determining paths*.

An XFD $p_1, ..., p_k \rightarrow p$ denotes that a tuple of text values corresponding to the left-hand side uniquely determines the value of the right-hand side. It is assumed that each path p_i on the left-hand ends with a terminal label, whereas the path p on the right-hand side can end with a terminal or non-terminal label. In general, there can also be a *context* determined by a path q in which the XFD is defined, then XFD has the following form (Arenas & Libkin, 2004):

$$q; \{p_1, ..., p_k\} \rightarrow p$$

Example 5. For example, to specify that in S_1 (Figure 3) the *university* is determined by the author's *name*, we can write:

```
XFD: pubs.pub.author.name → pubs.pub.author.university, or
TP-XFD: /pubs/pub/author[name = x]/university.
```

To express that the constraint is valid in a subtree denoted by the path *pubs.pub* (the context), we write:

```
XFD: pubs.pub; pubs.pub.author.name → pubs.pub.author.university, or
TP-XFD: /pubs/pub[title = x₁]/author[name = x₂]/university.
```

In the last TP-XFD a *key* for the context subtree must be given (we assume that the context subtree is uniquely determined by the *title* of the publication) (see Buneman et al., 2003).

Note that TP-XFDs are XPath expressions, so their semantics is precisely defined. Moreover, they can be easily incorporated into XQuery-based procedures exploiting these constraints.

Definition 12. We say that a TP-XFD $F(\mathbf{x'})$ is defined over a schema $S(\mathbf{x})$, if $\mathbf{x'} \subseteq \mathbf{x}$ and $type_S(x) = type_F(x)$ for each $x \in \mathbf{x'}$.

Definition 13. (*satisfaction of TP-XFD*) An instance $I = (S(\mathbf{x}), \Omega)$ satisfies a TP-XFD $F(\mathbf{x'})$ defined over $S(\mathbf{x})$, if for any two valuation $\omega_1, \omega_2 \in \Omega$ the following implication holds

$$\omega_1(\mathbf{x'}) = \omega_2(\mathbf{x'}) \Rightarrow F(\omega_1(\mathbf{x'})) = F(\omega_2(\mathbf{x'})), \tag{1}$$

where $F(\omega_1(\mathbf{x'}))$ and $F(\omega_2(\mathbf{x'}))$ denote results of computing XPath expression $F(\mathbf{x'})$ by valuations ω_1 and ω_2, respectively.

Example 6. Over schema S_3 (Figure 3), we can specify the following TP-XFD:

$F_1(x_2):= /authors/author/paper[title = x_2]/year,$

(the title of a paper determines the year of its publication), whereas over S_2 (Figure 3) one of the following two TP-XFDs can be specified, either

$F'_2(x_1):= /pubs/pub[title = x_1],$

or

$F''_2(x_1, x_2):= /pubs/pub[title = x_1, author[name= x_2]].$

Any instance satisfying $F'_2(x_1)$ must have at most one subtree of the type */pubs/pub* for any distinct value of *title* (see J_1 in Figure 2), whereas any instance satisfying $F''_2(x_1, x_2)$ must have at most one subtree of the type */pubs/pub* for any distinct pair of values (*title, author/name*) (see J_2 in Figure 2).

Further on, we will use TP-XFDs to discover some *missing values*. Thus, we will restrict ourselves to TP-XFDs determining text values.

Definition 14. (*text-valued TP-XFDs*) We say that a TP-XFD $F(\mathbf{x'})$ over a schema $S(\mathbf{x})$ determines text values (or is *text-valued*), if there is such $x \in \mathbf{x}$, that $type_S(x) = type(F(\mathbf{x'}))$. Then this TP-XFD will be denoted by $(F(\mathbf{x'}), x)$.

Proposition 1. (*discovering missing values*) Let $(F(\mathbf{x'}), x)$ be a text-valued TP-XFD over $S(\mathbf{x})$, and $I = (S(\mathbf{x}), \Omega)$ be an instance of $S(\mathbf{x})$ satisfying $(F(\mathbf{x'}), x)$. Let $\omega_1, \omega_2 \in \Omega$ be such valuations that:

- $\omega_1(\mathbf{x'}) = \omega_2(\mathbf{x'})$,
- $\omega_1(x) = \bot, \omega_2(x) \neq \bot,$

then in force of (1) (Definition 13) we take

$$\omega_1(x):= \omega_2(x)$$

Then we say that the *missing value* of x for the valuation ω_1 *is discovered* as $\omega_2(x)$.

The following algorithm generates an XQuery program for a given schema and a set of TP-XFDs over this schema. The program discovers all possible missing values, with respect to the given set of TP-XFDs. We say that in this way the instance is being *repaired*.

Algorithm 2. (*generation of XQuery program discovering missing values*)

```
Input:    A schema S(x) = /top[E] and a set F of text-valued TP-XFDs over S(x).
Output: Program in XQuery over instances of  S(x) returning a repaired version
of the given   instance of S(x).
Method:
xfdToXQuery(/top[E]) - identical to the translation function
mappingToXQuery(∀x (/top[E] ⇒ /top[E]) in Algorithm 1, except that the rule
(4) is replaced with the rule:
4'.  ρ(l = x)  = <l>{
        if ($x = "null") thenF(x')[text() != "null"] /text()
                  else $x}
                    </l>,
          where (F(x'), x) ∈ F.
```

Example 7. Discovering missing values in an instance of S_1 (Figure 3) can be done using the XQuery program (Query2) generated for the schema S_1 where TP-XFD constraints are:

$$F_1(x_1):= /pubs/pub[title = x_1]/year,$$

and

$$F_2(x_3):=/pubs/pub/author[name = x_3]/university.$$

The corresponding XQuery program is similar to this for Query 1. However, expressions defining elements *year* and *university* attempt to discover missing values, when the current values of $x2 or $x3 are null:

```
Query 2:
<pubs>{
    for $_v in doc("I1.xml")/pubs,
    $_v1 in if ($_v[pub]) then $_v/pub else /,
      $x1 in if ($_v1[title]) then $_v1/title/text()
          else "null",
      $x2 in if ($_v1[year]) then $_v1/year/text()
```

```
        else "null",
    $_v2 in if ($_v1[author]) then $_v1/author
        else /,
    $x3 in if ($_v2[name]) then $_v2/name/text()
        else "null",
    $x4 in if ($_v2[university]) then $_v2/university/text()
        else "null"

return
<pub>
    <title>{$x1}</title>
    <year>{if ($x2="null") then
        doc("I1.xml")/pubs/pub[title=$x1]/year[text()!="null"]/text()
        else $x2}</year>
    <author>
        <name>{$x3}</name>
        <university>{if ($x4="null") then
            doc("I1.xml")/pubs/pub/author[name=$x3]/university
                [text()!="null"]/text() else $x4}</university>
    </author>
</pub> }
</pubs>
```

As the result of repairing, all nulls violating TP-XFDs are replaced with non-null values.

QUERIES AND QUERY REFORMULATION

A *query* will be understood as a mapping where its left-hand side is extended with a filter (the *query qualifier*).

Definition 15. (*query*) Let $m_{ST} := \forall \mathbf{x} \, (S(\mathbf{x}) \Rightarrow \exists \mathbf{y} T(\mathbf{x'}, \mathbf{y}))$ be a mapping from a source schema $S(\mathbf{x})$ to a target schema $T(\mathbf{x'}, \mathbf{y})$ and $\varphi(\mathbf{x})$ be a formula over $\mathbf{x}$. A *query q* from S to T with qualifier φ is a formula of the form

$$q_{ST} := \forall \mathbf{x} \, (S(\mathbf{x}) \wedge \varphi(\mathbf{x}) \Rightarrow \exists \mathbf{y} T(\mathbf{x'}, \mathbf{y})) \, .$$

Such a query will be denoted as the pair (m_{ST}, φ).

The answer to a query $q = (m_{ST}, \varphi)$ over an instance $I = (S, \Omega)$ of S, is an instance $J = (T, \Omega')$ of T. Valuations in Ω' are created from the valuations in Ω satisfying the query qualifier. Such valuations are restricted to variables occurring in both S and T and extended with null values, $\perp$, assigned to those variables in T which do not occur in S. More precisely:

Figure 4. Reformulation of a query ($m_{T(z)T(z)}$, $\varphi(z)$) into a query ($m_{S(x)T(x',y)}$, $\varphi'(x)$) using the mapping $\forall x(S(x) \Rightarrow \exists y T(x', y))$

$$
\begin{array}{c}
S(\mathbf{x}) \xrightarrow{\; S(\mathbf{x}) \Rightarrow \exists \mathbf{y}\, T(\mathbf{x'},\mathbf{y}) \;} T(\mathbf{z}) \\[4pt]
\varphi'(\mathbf{x}) \qquad \varphi(\mathbf{z}) \\[4pt]
\varphi'(\mathbf{x}) := \varphi(\mathbf{z}).rewrite(T(\mathbf{z}),T(\mathbf{x'},\mathbf{y})), \\[4pt]
\text{for each } z \in \mathbf{z}, \text{ replace: } z \rightarrow x, \text{ such that} \\[4pt]
x \in \mathbf{x'} \text{ and } type_{T(\mathbf{z})}(z) = type_{T(\mathbf{x'},\mathbf{y})}(x)
\end{array}
$$

Definition 16. (*answer to a query*) Let $q = (m_{ST}, \varphi)$ be a query from $S(\mathbf{x})$ to $T(\mathbf{x'}, \mathbf{y})$ and $I = (S, \Omega)$ be an instance of S. The answer to $q(I)$ is such the instance $J = (T, \Omega')$ that

$$\Omega' = \{\omega.restrict(\mathbf{x'}) \cup null(\mathbf{y}) \mid \omega \in \Omega \wedge \varphi(\omega(\mathbf{x})) = true\},$$

where $\omega.restrict(\mathbf{x'})$ is the restriction of the valuation ω to the variables in $\mathbf{x'}$, and $null(\mathbf{y})$ is a valuation assigning nulls to all variables in $\mathbf{y}$.

Example 8. The query $q_{12} = (m_{S1(x1,x2,x3,x4)S2(x1,x3,x4)}, x_3 = \text{``John''} \wedge x_2 = \text{``2005''})$, filters an instance of the source schema S_1 according to the qualifier and produces an instance of the schema S_2.

A query is issued by the user against an arbitrarily chosen peer schema (the target schema). The user perceives a target schema $T(\mathbf{z})$, and defines a qualifier $\varphi(\mathbf{z})$, so initially the query is from T to T, and is of the form $q = (m_{T(\mathbf{z})T(\mathbf{z})}, \varphi(\mathbf{z}))$. When the query is propagated to a source peer with the schema $S(\mathbf{x})$, it must be reformulated into a query from S to T, i.e. to $q' = (m_{S(\mathbf{x})T(\mathbf{x'},\mathbf{y})}, \varphi'(\mathbf{x}))$. The *query reformulation* concerns the left-hand side of the query, and consists in the appropriate renaming of variables.

The reformulation is performed as follows (Figure 4):

1. We want to determine the qualifier $\varphi'(\mathbf{x})$ over the source schema $S(\mathbf{x})$. To do this we use the mapping $m_{S(\mathbf{x})T(\mathbf{x'},\mathbf{y})}$.

The qualifier $\varphi'(\mathbf{x})$ is obtained as the result of the following rewriting of the qualifier $\varphi(\mathbf{z})$

$$\varphi'(\mathbf{x}) := \varphi(\mathbf{z}).rewrite(T(\mathbf{z}), T(\mathbf{x'}, \mathbf{y})),$$

The rewriting consists in appropriate replacement of variable names. A variable $z \in \mathbf{z}$ occurring in $\varphi(\mathbf{z})$ is replaced by such a variable $x \in \mathbf{x'}$ that the type of z in $T(\mathbf{z})$ is equal to the type of x in $T(\mathbf{x'}, \mathbf{y})$. If such $x \in \mathbf{x'}$ does not exist, the query is not rewritable.

Example 9. For the query

$$q_{11} = (m_{S1(x1,x2,x3,x4)S1(x1,x2,x3,x4)}, x_3 = \text{``John''}),$$

we have the following reformulation for its propagation to S_2

$$q_{21} = (m_{S2(x1,x2,x3)S1(x1,x4,x2,x3)}, x_2 = \text{``John''}),$$

since

$$type_{S1(x1,x2,x3,x4)}(x_3) = type_{S1(x1,x4,x2,x3)}(x_2) = /pubs/pub/author/name.$$

Deciding about Merging Modes for Answers and Propagation

Answers to a query propagated across the P2P systems must be collected and merged. In the merge operation we try also to discover missing values, i.e. we try to replace null values with real values everywhere where it is possible. This replacement is based on TP-XFD constraints.

It is important to decide which of the following two merging modes should be applied in the peer while partial answers are to be merged:

- **partial merge:** all partial answers are merged without taking into account the source instance stored in the peer, i.e. only partial answers are taken into account in discovering missing values;
- **full merge:** the whole source instance in the peer is merged with all received partial answers, therefore the whole peer's instance participates in discovering procedure; finally the query is evaluated on the result of the merge.

The possibility of discovering missing values during the process of merging constitutes the criterion of the selection of one of these two modes. To make the decision, relationships between TP-XFD constraints specified for the peer's schema, and the query qualifier must be analyzed.

Further on in this section, we formulate a theorem (Theorem 1) that states the sufficient condition when there is no sense in applying full merge because no missing value can be discovered (Pankowski, 2008a).

Query Execution Strategies

In this subsection we discuss how the propagation and merging strategies influence the cost of merging answers (with discovering missing values), and amount of information contained in the answer.

Let us consider some possible strategies of execution of the following query q_{11} against S_1 at peer P_1 (see Figure 3):

$$q_{11} = (m_{S1S1}, x_3 = \text{``John''}).$$

The answer to the query should contain information stored in all three sources shown in Figure 3. Thus, one of the following three strategies can be performed (Figure 5):

Strategy (a). Query q_{11} is sent to P_2 and P_3, where it is reformulated to, respectively, q_{21} (from P_2 to P_1) and q_{31} (from P_3 to P_1). The answers $q_{21}(I_2)$ and $q_{31}(I_3)$ are returned to P_1. In P_1 these partial answers are merged with the local answer $q_{11}(I_1)$ and a final answer Ans_a is obtained. This process can be written as follows:

Figure 5. Three execution strategies for query q_{11}

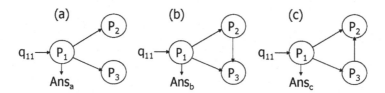

$$Ans_a = merge(\{Ans_{11}^a, Ans_{21}^a, Ans_{31}^a\}),$$

$$Ans_{11}^a = q_{11}(I_1) = \{(x_1 :\perp, x_2 :\perp, x_3 :\perp, x_4 :\perp)\},$$

$$Ans_{21}^a = q_{21}(I_2) = \{(x_1 : XML, x_3 : John, x_4 : NY)\},$$

$$Ans_{31}^a = q_{31}(I_3) = \{(x_3 :\perp, x_1 :\perp, x_2 :\perp)\},$$

$$Ans_a = \{(x_1 : XML, x_2 :\perp, x_3 : John, x_4 : NY)\}.$$

Strategy (b). It differs from strategy (a) in that P_2 after receiving the query propagates it to P_3 and waits for the answer $q_{32}(I_3)$. It is obvious that the result Ans_b is equal to Ans_a:

$$\begin{aligned} Ans_b &= merge(\{Ans_{11}^b, Ans_{21}^b, Ans_{31}^b\}) \\ &= \{(x_1 : XML, x_2 :\perp, x_3 : John, x_4 : NY)\}. \end{aligned}$$

Strategy (c). In contrast to the strategy (b), the peer P_3 propagates the query to P_2 and waits for the answer. Next, the peer P_3 decides to merge the obtained answer $q_{23}(I_2)$. with the whole its instance I_3. The decision follows from the fact that the functional dependency */authors/author/paper[title = x_1]/year* is defined over the local schema of P_2, and satisfies the necessary condition for discovering missing values of variable x_2 of the type */authors/author/paper/year* (Theorem 1). So we have:

$$Ans_c = merge(\{Ans_{11}^c, Ans_{23}^c, Ans_{31}^c\}),$$

$$Ans_{23}^c = \{(x_1 : XML, x_2 :\perp, x_3 : John)\},$$

$$\begin{aligned} Ans_{31}^c &= q_{31}(merge(\{I_3, Ans_{23}^c\}) \\ &= \{(x_1 : XML, x_2 : 2005, x_3 : John)\}, \end{aligned}$$

$$Ans_c = \{(x_1 : XML, x_2 : 2005, x_3 : John, x_4 : NY)\}.$$

While computing $merge(\{I_3, Ans_{23}^c\})$ a missing value of x_2 is discovered. Thus, the answer Ans_c provides more information than those in strategies (a) and (b).

This discussion above shows that it is useful to analyze relationships between the query and functional dependencies defined over the peer's schema. The analysis can influence the decision about the propagation and merging modes.

Sufficient Condition for Merging Modes

It is quite obvious that the full merge is more expensive than the partial one. However, during full merge more missing values can be discovered. Thus, full merge should be performed when there is a chance to discover missing values. The following Theorem 1 states the sufficient condition when there is no sense in applying full merge because no missing value can be discovered.

Theorem 1. Let $S(\mathbf{x})$ be a target schema, $F(\mathbf{z})$ be a TP-XFD over $S(\mathbf{x})$, where $type(F) = type_S(x)$ for some $x \in \mathbf{x}$. Let q be a query with qualifier $\varphi(\mathbf{y})$, $\mathbf{y} \subseteq \mathbf{x}$, and I be an instance of S and Ans be an answer to q received from a propagation. Then

$$q(merge(Ans, I)) = merge(Ans, q(I)) \qquad (2)$$

holds if one of the following two conditions holds

(a) $x \in \mathbf{y}$ (i.e. the query qualifier constraints the value of the dependent path), or
(b) $\mathbf{z} \subseteq \mathbf{y}$ (i.e. the query qualifier constraints values of all determining paths).

Proof. The equality (2) does not hold if there are valuations $\omega_1 \in \Omega_{Ans}$, $\omega_2 \in \Omega_I$, such that $\omega_1(x) = \bot$, $\omega_2(x) \neq \bot$, and $\omega_1(\mathbf{z}) = \omega_2(\mathbf{z})$ (see Proposition 1). Let us consider conditions (a) and (b):

1. *Condition (a).* Let $x \in \mathbf{y}$. Let us assume that there is $\omega_1 \in \Omega_{Ans}$, such that $\omega_1(x) = \bot$. But then $\varphi(\omega_1(\mathbf{y}))$ could not be true and this contradicts the assumption. Thus, the theorem holds.
2. *Condition (b).* Let $\mathbf{z} \subseteq \mathbf{y}$. Let us assume that there are valuations $\omega_1 \in \Omega_{Ans}$, $\omega_2 \in \Omega_I$, such that $\omega_1(x) = \bot$, $\omega_2(x) \neq \bot$, and $\omega_1(\mathbf{z}) = \omega_2(\mathbf{z})$. Then:
   ○ Let $\varphi(\omega_2(\mathbf{y})) = true$. Then ω_2 must be also in $\Omega_{q(I)}$, and $\Omega_{q(I)}$ can be used for discovering missing values instead of the whole Ω_I. Thus the equality (2) holds.
   ○ Let $\varphi(\omega_2(\mathbf{y})) \neq true$. Because ω_1 and ω_2 must coincide on $\mathbf{y}$, then also $\varphi(\omega_1(\mathbf{y})) \neq true$ and ω_1 cannot be in Ans that contradicts the assumption. Thus the equality (2) holds.

To illustrate application of the above theorem let us consider a query about *John's* data in peers P_2 and P_3 in Figure 3.

1. Let q be a query with the qualifier $\varphi_2(x_2) := x_2 = $ "*John*" in the peer P_2. There is also TP-XFD $F_2(x_2) :=$ */pubs/pub/author[name = x_2]/university* specified over $S_2(x_1, x_2, x_3)$. In force of Theorem 1 there is no chance to discover any missing value of *John's* university. Indeed, if we obtain an answer with *university* $= \bot$, then the real value is either in the local answer $q(I_2)$ or it does not occur in I_2 at all. So, in P_2 the partial merge should be performed. Performing the full merge in this case is pointless. Let q be a query with the qualifier $\varphi_3(x_1) := x_1 = $ "*John*" issued against the peer P_3. There is TP-XFD $F_3(x_2) :=$ */authors/author/paper[title = x_2]/year* specified over $S_3(x_1, x_2, x_3)$. Assumptions of

Theorem 1 are not satisfied, so there is a chance to discover missing value of *year* using the full merge. Indeed, from P_2 we obtain the answer $q(I_2) := (S_3, \{(\text{"}John\text{"}, \text{"}XML\text{"}, \perp)\})$. The local answer $q(I_3)$ is empty. But performing the full merge and using $F_3(x_2)$, we obtain:

$$q(merge((S_3, \{(\text{"}John\text{"}, \text{"}XML\text{"}, \perp)\}), (S_3, \{(\text{"}Ann\text{"}, \text{"}XML\text{"}, \text{"}2005\text{"})\}))) = = (S_3, \{(\text{"}John\text{"}, \text{"}XML\text{"}, \text{"}2005\text{"}\}).$$

Thus, the year of *John's* publication has been discovered and the using of full merge is justified.

The consequences of Theorem 1 impact also the way of query propagation. The P2P propagation (i.e. to all partners with the *P2P propagation mode*) may be rejected because of avoiding cycles. However, when the analysis of the query qualifier and TP-XFD's shows that there is a chance to discover missing values, the peer can decide to propagate the query with the *local propagation mode* (i.e. the peer expects only the local answer from a partner, without further propagation) instead of rejecting it. Such an action can take place in peer P_3 in the case (2) discussed above.

QUERY ANSWERING IN 6P2P

Overall Architecture

6P2P is built around a set of peers having a common architecture and communicating with each other by sending (*propagating*) queries and returning answers. According to the P2P technology, there is not any central control over peer's behavior and each peer is autonomous in performing operations, such as accepting queries, query answering and query propagation. The overall architecture of the system is depicted in Figure 6.

Each peer in 6P2P has its own local database consisting of two parts: *data repository* of data available to other peers, and *6P2P repository* of data necessary for performing integration processes (e.g.,

Figure 6. Overall architecture of 6P2P system

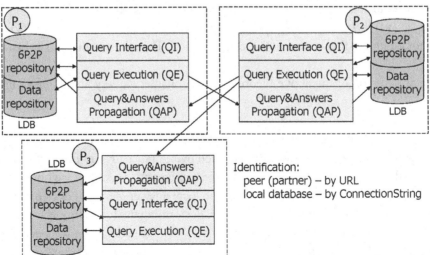

information about partners, schemas constraints, mappings, answers). Using the query interface (QI) a user formulates a query. The query execution module (QE) controls the process of query reformulation, query propagation to partners, merging of partial answers, discovering missing values, and returning partial answers (Brzykcy et al., 2008; Pankowski, 2008b; Pankowski, 2008c; Pankowski et al., 2007; Pankowski, 2008d). Communication between peers (QAP) is realized by means of Web Services technology.

6P2P Modeling Concepts

Basic notions constituting the 6P2P data model are: peers, data sources, schemas, constraints, mappings, queries, answers, and propagation.

1. A *peer*, *@P*, is identified by its URL address identifying also the Web Service representing the peer. There are two methods exported by a peer: *sendAnswer* – used by peers to send to *@P* the answer to a query received from *@P*, and *propagateQuery* – used by peers to send to *@P* a query to be answered (possibly with further propagation).

2. A *data source* is an XML document or an XML view over a centralized or distributed data. Different techniques can be used to implement such a view – it can be AXML documents (Abiteboul et al., 2002; Milo et al., 2005), a gateway to another 6P2P system or even to different data integration systems. Thus, a community of various collaborating information integration engines can be created.

3. A *schema* is used to specify structural properties of the data source and also the structure of the intermediate answers to queries. In 6P2P, schemas are defined as tree-pattern formulas discussed in previous sections.

4. *Constraints* delivers additional knowledge about data. Two kinds of constraints are taken into consideration: *tree-pattern XML functional dependencies* (TP-XFD) and XML *keys* (Arenas & Libkin, 2004; Buneman et al., 2003; Pankowski, 2008c). TP-XFD will be used to control query propagation and answer merging (especially to discover some missing data), and keys for eliminating duplicates and appropriate nesting of elements. In this chapter we restrict ourselves only to TP-XFDs.

5. *Mappings* specify how data structured under a source schema is to be transformed into data conforming to a target schema (Fagin et al., 2004; Pankowski, 2008c). Information provided by mappings is also used to query reformulation. In previous sections we presented algorithms translating high level specifications of mappings, queries and constraints into XQuery programs.

6. A *query* issued against a peer can be split up to many *query threads* – one query thread for one trace incoming to the peer (corresponding to one propagation). Partial answers to all query threads are merged to produce the answer to the query. A peer can receive many threads of the same query.

7. An *answer* is the result of query evaluation. There are *partial* and *final* answers. A partial answer is an answer delivered by a partner who the query was propagated to. All partial answers are merged and transformed to obtain the final answer. In some cases (when the peer decides about discovering missing values), a whole peer's data source may be involved into the merging process. In (Pankowski, 2008b) we discuss a method of dealing with hard inconsistent data, i.e. data that is other than null and violates TP-XFDs. The method proposed in (Pankowski, 2008b) is based on trustworthiness of data sources.

Figure 7. Structure of tables peer, constraints and partners in 6P2P database

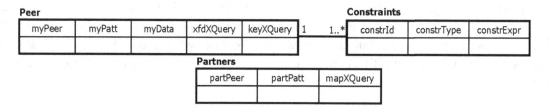

8.   A *propagation* is a relationship between a peer (the *target peer*) and another peer (the *source peer*) where the query has been sent (propagated) to. While propagating queries, the following three objectives are taken into account: (1) avoiding cycles, (2) deciding about propagation modes (*P2P* or *local*), and (3) deciding about merging modes (*full* or *partial*).

6P2P Database

A peer's database consists of five tables: *Peer, Constraints, Partners* (Figure 7), *Queries*, and *Propagations* (Figure 8).

1.   *Peer(myPeer, myPatt, myData, xfdXQuery, keyXQuery)* – has exactly one row, where: *myPeer* – the URL of the peer owning the database; *myPatt* – the schema (tree-pattern formula) of the data source; *myData* – the peer's data source, i.e. an XML document or an XML view over some data repositories. *xfdXQuery* and *keyXQuery* are XQuery programs obtained by the translation of constraints specifications, TP-XFDs and keys, respectively.
2.   *Constraints(constrId, constrType, constrExp)* – stores information about the local data constraints (in this chapter we discuss only TP-XFDs).
3.   *Partners(partPeer, partPatt, mapXQuery)* – stores information about all peer's partners (acquaintances), where: *partPeer* – the URL of the partner; *partPatt* – the right-hand side of the schema mapping to the partner (variable names reflect correspondences between paths in the source and in the target schema). *mapXQuery* is an XQuery program obtained by translation(by means of Algorithm 1) of the mapping determined by the *Peer.myPatt* (left-hand side of the mapping) and *Partners.partPatt* (right-hand side of the mapping).
4.   *Queries* and *Propagations* (Figure 8) maintain information about queries, *qryId*, and their threads, *qryThreadId*, managed in the 6P2P system. The user specifies a qualifier of the query, *myQualif*, as well as propagation (*propagMode*) and merging (*mergeMode*) modes.

Query Propagation in 6P2P

Symbolic values in tables (Figure 8) indicate relationships between tuples in tables maintained by peers *@P* and *@P'*. Algorithm 3 describes propagation of a query (more precisely, a thread of the query) stored in *@P:Queries*. The propagation mode can be either *P2P* (a query is to be propagated to all partners with *P2P* mode), or *local* (a query is to be answered in the peer's data source without propagation).

In Algorithm 3, the tuple *q*1 contains a query and its context (e.g. *q*1.*myPatt* is the schema against which *q*1.*myQualif* has been formulated). *LeadsToCycle(q1, @P')* returns *true* if the propagation causes

Figure 8. Queries and propagations tables in 6P2P. Sample data illustrates instances of tables when a query is propagated from a peer @P to a peer @P'

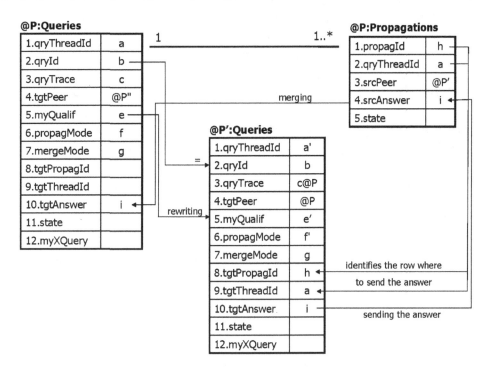

a cycle, i.e. @P' occurs in $q1.qryTrace$. $discoveryMayBeDone(q1, @P)$ is *true* if the hypothesis of Theorem 1 does not hold. $acceptedPropagation(q1, @P')\$$ is *true* if @P' accepts the propagation of $q1$ with the given parameters.

Algorithm 3. (*query propagation*)

```
Input: @P - a current peer; @P:Peer, @P:Partners, @P:Queries, @P:Propagations
- tables in the peer's @P database.
Output: New states of tables @P:Queries and @P:Propagations, if a partner peer
@P' accepts the propagation.
Method:
q:= @P:Queries; // a row describing the query thread to be propagatedifq.
propagMode = 'P2P' {
    q1                      := newpropagationParametersType;
                                // used to prepare propagations to all partners
    q1.propagId             := newpropagId;
    q1.qryThreadId          := q.qryThreadId;
    q1.qryId                := q.qryId;
    q1.qryTrace             := q.qryTrace + @P;
                                // the sequence of visited peers used to avoid cycles
    q1.myPeer               := @P; // the peer where the answer should be returned
```

```
q1.myQualif          := q.myQualif; // the query qualifier
q1.propagMode        := "P2P";
q1.mergeMode         := q.mergeMode;
q1.myPatt            := @P:Peer.myPatt; // the schema of @P
foreach $@P'in @P:Partners.partPeer {
    // attempt to propagate the query to all partners
    if LeadsToCycle(q1, @P') and not discoveryMayBeDone(q1,@P)
    then next
    if LeadsToCycle(q1, @P') then q1.propagMode := "local";
    if acceptedPropagation(q1, @P') then
        insert into @P:Propagations
        values (q1.propagId, q1.qryThreadId, @P', null, "Waiting")
    }
}
```

If the source peer *@P'* accepts the propagation *q1* then it creates the following tuple *q2* and inserts it into the *@P':Queries* table:

```
q2.qryThreadId         := newqryThreadId,
q2.qryId               := q1.qryId,
q2.qryTrace            := q1.qryTrace,
q2.tgtPeer             := q1.myPeer,
q2.myQualif            := (q1.myQualif).rewrite(q1.myPatt,@P':Partners.partPatt
wherePartners.partPeer = q1.myPeer),
q2.propagMode          := q1.propagMode,
q2.mergeMode           := q1.mergeMode,
q2.tgtPropagId         := q1.propagId,
q2.tgtThreadId         := q1.qryThreadId,
q2.tgtAnswer           := null,
q2.tgtAnswer           := "Waiting",
q2.myXQuery            := XQuery program obtained by automatic translation
of the query into XQuery.
```

CONCLUSION

The chapter discusses a method for schema mapping and query reformulation in a P2P XML data integration system. The discussed formal approach enables us to specify schemas, schema constraints, schema mappings, and queries in a uniform and precise way. Based on this approach we define some basic operations used for query reformulation and data merging, and propose algorithms for automatic generation of XQuery programs performing these operations in real. We discussed some issues concerning query propagation strategies and merging modes, when missing data is to be discovered in the P2P integration processes. The approach is implemented in 6P2P system. We presented its general architecture, and sketched the way how queries and answers were sent across the P2P environment.

ACKNOWLEDGMENT

The work was supported in part by the Polish Ministry of Science and Higher Education under Grant 3695/B/T02/2009/36.

REFERENCES

Abiteboul, S., Benjelloun, O., Manolescu, I., Milo, T., & Weber, R. (2002). Active XML: Peer-to-peer data and Web services integration. In *Proceedings of 28th International Conference on Very Large Data Bases,* (pp. 1087-1090). August 20-23, 2002, Hong Kong, China, Morgan Kaufmann.

Abiteboul, S., Hull, R., & Vianu, V. (1995). *Foundations of databases.* Reading, MA: Addison-Wesley.

Arenas, M., & Libkin, L. (2004). A normal form for XML documents. *ACM Transactions on Database Systems, 29*(1), 195–232. doi:10.1145/974750.974757

Arenas, M., & Libkin, L. (2005). XML data exchange: Consistency and query answering. In L. Chen (Ed.), *Proceedings of the 24th ACM SIGACT-SIGMOD-SIGART Symposium on Principles of Database Systems,* (pp. 13-24). June 13-15, 2005, Baltimore, Maryland, USA, ACM.

Bernstein, P. A., & Haas, L. M. (2008). Information integration in the enterprise. *Communications of the ACM, 51*(9), 72–79. doi:10.1145/1378727.1378745

Brzykcy, G., Bartoszek, J., & Pankowski, T. (2008). Schema mappings and agents' actions in P2P data integration system. *Journal of Universal Computer Science, 14*(7), 1048–1060.

Buneman, P., Davidson, S. B., Fan, W., Hara, C. S., & Tan, W. C. (2003). Reasoning about keys for XML. *Information Systems, 28*(8), 1037–1063. doi:10.1016/S0306-4379(03)00028-0

Fagin, R., Kolaitis, P. G., & Popa, L. (2005). Data exchange: Getting to the core. *ACM Transactions on Database Systems, 30*(1), 174–210. doi:10.1145/1061318.1061323

Fagin, R., Kolaitis, P. G., Popa, L., & Tan, W. C. (2004). Composing schema mappings: Second-order dependencies to the rescue. In: A. Deutsch (Ed.), *Proceedings of the 23rd ACM SIGACT-SIGMOD-SIGART Symposium on Principles of Database Systems,* (pp. 83-94). June 14-16, 2004, Paris, France, ACM.

Fuxman, A., Kolaitis, P. G., Miller, R. J., & Tan, W. C. (2006). Peer data exchange. *ACM Transactions on Database Systems, 31*(4), 1454–1498. doi:10.1145/1189769.1189778

Haas, L. M. (2007). Beauty and the beast: The theory and practice of information integration. In Schwentick, T., & Suciu, D. (Eds.), *Database theory. (LNCS 4353)* (pp. 28–43). Springer.

Koloniari, G., & Pitoura, E. (2005). Peer-to-peer management of XML data: Issues and research challenges. *SIGMOD Record, 34*(2), 6–17. doi:10.1145/1083784.1083788

Madhavan, J., & Halevy, A. Y. (2003). Composing mappings among data sources. In J. Ch., Freytag, et al. (Eds.), *VLDB 2003, Proceedings of 29th International Conference on Very Large Data Bases,* (pp. 572-583). September 9-12, 2003, Berlin, Germany. Morgan Kaufmann.

Martens, W., Neven, F., & Schwentick, T. (2007). Simple off the shelf abstractions for XML schema. *SIGMOD Record, 36*(3), 15–22. doi:10.1145/1324185.1324188

Melnik, S., Bernstein, P. A., Halevy, A. Y., & Rahm, E. (2005). Supporting executable mappings in model management. In F. Özcan (Ed.), *Proceedings of the 24th ACM SIGMOD International Conference on Management of Data,* (pp. 167-178). Baltimore, Maryland, USA, June 14-16, ACM.

Miller, R. J., Haas, L. M., & Hernandez, M. A. (2000). Schema mapping as query discovery. In: A.E. Abbadi, et al. (Eds.), *VLDB 2000, Proceedings of 26th International Conference on Very Large Data Bases,* (pp. 77-88). September 10-14, 2000, Cairo, Egypt. Morgan Kaufmann

Milo, T., Abiteboul, S., Amann, B., Benjelloun, O., & Ngoc, F. D. (2005). Exchanging intensional XML data. *ACM Transactions on Database Systems, 30*(1), 1–40. doi:10.1145/1061318.1061319

Ooi, B. C., Shu, Y., & Tan, K.-L. (2003). Relational data sharing in peer-based data management systems. *SIGMOD Record, 32*(3), 59–64. doi:10.1145/945721.945734

Pankowski, T. (2008a). Query propagation in a P2P data integration system in the presence of schema constraints. In A. Hameurlain (Ed.): *Data management in Grid and peer-to-peer systems, (LNCS 5187).* (pp. 46-57). Springer.

Pankowski, T. (2008b). Reconciling inconsistent data in probabilistic XML data integration . In Gray, W. A., Jeffery, K. G., & Shao, J. (Eds.), *Sharing data, information and knowledge, (LNCS 5071)* (pp. 75–86). Springer. doi:10.1007/978-3-540-70504-8_8

Pankowski, T. (2008c). XML data integration in SixP2P–a theoretical framework. In A. Doucet, S. Gançarski, & E. Pacitti (Eds.), *Proceedings of the 2008 International Workshop on Data Management in Peer-to-Peer Systems, DaMaP 2008,* (pp. 11-18). Nantes, France, March 25, 2008. ACM International Conference Proceeding Series.

Pankowski, T. (2008d). XML schema mappings using schema constraints and Skolem functions . In Cotta, C., Reich, S., Schaefer, R., & Ligeza, A. (Eds.), *Knowledge engineering and intelligent computations, knowledge-driven computing* (pp. 199–216). Springer.

Pankowski, T., Cybulka, J., & Meissner, A. (2007). XML schema mappings in the presence of key constraints and value dependencies. In M. Arenas & J. Hidders (Eds.), *Proceedings of the 1st Workshop on Emerging Research Opportunities for Web Data Management (EROW 2007) Collocated with the 11th International Conference on Database Theory (ICDT 2007),* (pp. 1-15). Barcelona, Spain, January 13, 2007.

Pankowski, T., & Hunt, E. (2005). Data merging in life science data integration systems . In Klopotek, M. A., Wierzchon, S. T., & Trojanowski, K. (Eds.), *Intelligent Information Systems. New trends in intelligent information processing and Web mining, advances in soft computing* (pp. 279–288). Berlin, Heidelberg: Springer. doi:10.1007/3-540-32392-9_29

Schema, X. M. L. (2009). *W3C XML schema definition language (XSD) 1.1 part 2: Datatypes*. Retrieved from www.w3.org/TR/xmlschema11-2

Tatarinov, I., & Halevy, A. Y. (2004). Efficient query reformulation in peer-data management systems. In G. Weikum, A.C. König & S. Deßloch (Eds.), *Proceedings of the ACM SIGMOD International Conference on Management of Data,* (pp. 539-550). Paris, France, June 13-18, 2004. ACM.

Tatarinov, I., & Ives, Z. G. (2003). The Piazza peer data management project. *SIGMOD Record, 32*(3), 47–52. doi:10.1145/945721.945732

XPath. (2006). *XML path language 2.0.* Retrieved from www.w3.org/TR/xpath20

XQuery. (2002). *XQuery 1.0: An XML query language.* W3C Working Draft. Retrieved from www.w3.org/TR/ xquery

Xu, W., & Ozsoyoglu, Z. M. (2005). Rewriting XPath queries using materialized views. In K. Böhm, et al. (Eds.), *Proceedigns of the 31st International Conference on Very Large Data Bases,* (pp. 121-132). Trondheim, Norway, August 30 - September 2, 2005, ACM.

Yu, C., & Popa, L. (2004). Constraint-based XML query rewriting for data integration. In G. Weikum, A.C. König, & S. Deßloch (Eds.), *Proceedings of the ACM SIGMOD International Conference on Management of Data,* (pp. 371-382). Paris, France, June 13-18, 2004. ACM.

KEY TERMS AND DEFINITIONS

Data Integration: Data integration consists in combining data from different sources into a unified format. The goal of data integration is to enable rapid development of new applications requiring information from multiple sources. In particular, in P2P integration when an answer is issued against an arbitrarily chosen peer then the answer should consist of data stored in the queried peer as well as data stored in its direct and indirect partners (acquaintances) .

Schema Mapping: Schema mapping is a specification defining how data structured under one schema (the *source schema*) is to be transformed into data structured under another schema (the *target schema*). The specification is based on source-to-target dependences involving atomic relational formulas (relating to relational data) or tree-pattern formulas (relating to XML data).

Tree Pattern: Tree pattern is an expression defining a part of an XML tree; a branch in the tree is denoted by square brackets ([ ]), a node-to-child relationship is denoted by slash (/), a node-to-descendant relationship is denoted by double slash (//), nodes are denoted by labels (*l* denotes nodes labeled with *l*) or by wildcard (*) that denotes a node labeled with any label. Depending on the set of permitted operators we have different classes of tree patterns. (In this chapter, operators // and * have not been considered). A tree pattern can be treated as a kind of a variable-free XPath query.

Tree-Pattern Formula: A tree-pattern formula is created from a tree pattern after assigning variables to some symbols representing nodes (i.e. to labels or to wildcards). Variables assigned to text and attribute nodes are text-valued variables. Otherwise, they are node-valued variables. Values of variables constrain trees matching the pattern. A TPF can be understood as a simple query defining the answer by means of the underlying tree pattern and values of variables. (In this chapter we considered only text-valued variables).

XML Functional Dependency (XFD): An XML functional dependency is a constraint saying that a path value (i.e. a node or a text value denoted by the path) is functionally determined by a set of text values of a given set of paths. On the contrary to the relational counterpart, an XFD can have a non-text valued path on its right-hand side, and XFD can be considered in an XML subtree denoted by a context path. XFDs can be specified by a class of tree-pattern formulas.

Query Reformulation: Query reformulation is a process in which a query (Q) formulated against a target schema (T) is rewritten to a form conforming to a source schema (S), using a mapping (m) from S to T. Query reformulation implements the virtual data integration as opposed to data exchange in materialized data integration. However, in both cases answer to Q must be the same, i.e. $Q(m(I_S)) = ref_m(Q)(I_S)$, where $m(I_S)$ transforms an instance of schema S into an instance of schema T, and $ref_m(Q)$ reformulates query Q into a query over schema S.

Query Propagation: Query propagation is a process of sending a query across a network of peer-to-peer connected nodes along semantic paths determined by schema mappings between schemas of peer databases. A peer receives a query from one of its partners (acquaintances), reformulates it and sends forward (propagates) to all other partners. The answer obtained from the peer's database is then merged with answers obtained from partners to whom the query was propagated. The result is next sent back to the partner who delivered the query.

Chapter 10
Deciding Query Entailment in Fuzzy OWL Lite Ontologies

Jingwei Cheng
Northeastern University, China

Z. M. Ma
Northeastern University, China

Li Yan
Northeastern University, China

ABSTRACT

Significant research efforts in the Semantic Web community are recently directed toward the representation and reasoning with fuzzy ontologies. Description logics (DLs) are the logical foundations of standard Web ontology languages. Conjunctive queries are deemed as an expressive reasoning service for DLs. This chapter focuses on fuzzy (threshold) conjunctive queries over knowledge bases encoding in fuzzy DL $\mathcal{SHIF}(\mathbf{D})$, the logic counterpart of fuzzy OWL Lite language. It shows decidability of fuzzy query entailment in this setting by providing a corresponding tableau-based algorithm. The chapter shows data complexity for answering fuzzy conjunctive queries in fuzzy $\mathcal{SHIF}(\mathbf{D})$ is in coNP, as long as only simple roles occur in the query. Regarding combined complexity, this research proves a co3NExpTime upper bound in the size of the knowledge base and the query.

INTRODUCTION

The Semantic Web is an extension of the current Web in which the Web information can be given well-defined semantics, and thus enabling better cooperation between people and computers. In order to represent and reason with structured knowledge in the Semantic Web, W3C has developed and recommended the Web Ontology Language (OWL) (Bechhofer, Van Harmelen, Hendler, Horrocks, McGuinness, Patel-Schneider, Stein, et al., 2004), which comprises three sublanguages of increasing expressive power: OWL Lite, OWL DL and OWL Full. Description logics (DLs) (Baader, Calvanese, McGuinness,

DOI: 10.4018/978-1-60960-475-2.ch010

Nardi, & Patel-Schneider, 2003), as the logical foundation of the standard Web Ontology Languages, support knowledge representation and reasoning by means of the concepts and roles. The logical counterparts of OWL Lite and OWL DL are the DLs $\mathcal{SHIF}(\mathbf{D})$ and $\mathcal{SHOIN}(\mathbf{D})$, respectively. The most prominent feature of DLs is their built-in reasoning mechanism through which implicit knowledge is discovered from explicit information stored in a DL knowledge base (KB).

In the real world, there exists a great deal of uncertainty and imprecision which is likely the rule than an exception. Thus, the problems that emerge are how to represent these non-crisp knowledge within ontologies and DLs. Based on Zadeh's fuzzy set theory (Zadeh, 1965), there have been substantial amounts of work carried out in the context of fuzzy extensions of DLs (Straccia, 2001; Stoilos, Stamou, Pan, Tzouvaras, & Horrocks, 2007), and fuzzy ontologies (Stoilos, Simou, Stamou, & Kollias, 2006) are thus established. For a comprehensive review of fuzzy ontologies and fuzzy DLs, the readers can refer to (Lukasiewicz & Straccia, 2008).

Fuzzy DL reasoners (Bobillo & Straccia, 2008; Stoilos et al., 2006) implement most of the standard fuzzy inference services (Straccia, 2001), including checking of fuzzy concept satisfiability, fuzzy concept subsumption, and ABox consistency. In addition, some fuzzy DL reasoners support different kinds of simple queries over a KB $\mathcal{K}$ for obtaining assertional knowledge, such as *retrieval*, i.e., given a fuzzy KB $\mathcal{K}$, a fuzzy concept C, and $n \in (0,1]$, to retrieve all instances o occurring in the ABox, such that $\mathcal{K}$ entails $C(o) \geq n$, written as $\mathcal{K} \vDash C(o) \geq n$. In fact, fuzzy DL reasoners deal with these queries by transforming them into standard inference tasks. For example, the retrieval problem $\mathcal{K} \vDash C(o) \geq n$ can be reduced to the (un)satisfiability problem of the KB $\mathcal{K} \cup \{C(a) < n\}$, while the latter one is a standard inference problem.

With the emergence of a good number of large-scale domain ontologies encoding in OWL languages, it is of particular importance to provide users with expressive querying service. Conjunctive queries (CQs) originated from research in relational databases, and, more recently, have also been identified as a desirable form of querying DL knowledge bases. Conjunctive queries provide an expressive query language with capabilities that go beyond standard instance retrieval. For example, consider a user query "find me hotels that are very close to the conference venue (with membership degree at lest 0.9) and offer inexpensive (with membership degree at lest 0.7) rooms", which can be formalized in as

$$Hotel(x) \geq 1 \wedge closeTo(x, venue) \geq 0.9 \wedge hasRoom(x, y) \geq 1$$

$$\wedge hasPrice(y, z) \geq 1 \wedge \neg Expensive(z) \geq 0.7 .$$

Existing DL reasoners are limited to providing basic reasoning services. There is, however, no support for queries that ask for *n*-tuples of related individuals or for the use of variables to formulate a query, just as conjunctive queries do. The reason for this lies in the fact that a fuzzy conjunctive query is not expressible as a part of a fuzzy DL knowledge base. Thus a fuzzy conjunctive query entailment problem cannot be reduced into a basic reasoning problem so as to be dealt with by existing fuzzy DL reasoners.

There is also the need for sufficient expressive power of fuzzy DLs to support reasoning in a full fuzzy extension of the OWL Web ontology language (Stoilos et al., 2006). In this study, we thus deal with fuzzy conjunctive query entailment for an expressive fuzzy DL f-$\mathcal{SHIF}(\mathbf{D})$, the logic counterpart of fuzzy OWL Lite language.

- We present a novel tableau-based algorithm for checking query entailment over $f\text{-}\mathcal{SHIF}(\mathbf{D})$ KBs. We generalize the mapping conditions from a fuzzy query into a completion forest, reducing the times required for checking mapping in different completion forests.
- We close the open problem of the complexity for answering fuzzy conjunctive queries in expressive fuzzy DLs by establishing two complexity bounds: for data complexity, we prove a coNP upper bound, as long as only simple roles occur in the query. Regarding combined complexity, we prove a co3NExpTime upper bound in the size of the knowledge base and the query.

PRELIMINARIES

Syntax and Semantics of $f\text{-}\mathcal{SHIF}(\mathbf{D})$

Fuzzy DL $f\text{-}\mathcal{SHIF}(\mathbf{D})$ allows to reason with fuzzy data types, such as *Young* and *Small*, by relying on so-called fuzzy concrete domains. We recall that $\mathcal{SHIF}(\mathbf{D})$ is the basic DL $\mathcal{ALC}$ (Baader & Nutt, 2003) extended with transitive role axioms ($\mathcal{S}$), role hierarchy ($\mathcal{H}$), inverse roles ($\mathcal{I}$), functional roles ($\mathcal{F}$) and concrete domains allowing to deal with data types such as strings and integers. In fuzzy $\mathcal{SHIF}(\mathbf{D})$, however, concrete domains are treated as fuzzy sets. More specially, a fuzzy data type theory $\mathbf{D} = (\Delta^{\mathbf{D}}, \cdot^{\mathbf{D}})$ consists of a data type domain $\Delta^{\mathbf{D}}$ and a mapping $\cdot^{\mathbf{D}}$ that assigns to each data value an element of $\Delta^{\mathbf{D}}$, to each n-ary data type predicate d an n-ary fuzzy relation over $\Delta^{\mathbf{D}}$. For example, we define *Young* : $\mathbb{N} \to [0,1]$ to be a fuzzy data type predicate over the natural numbers denoting the degree of youngness of a person's age. Then, *YoungPerson = Person $\sqcap \exists age.Young$* denotes young persons.

Let $\mathbf{A}, \mathbf{R}, \mathbf{R}_c, \mathbf{I}, \mathbf{I}_c$ and $\mathbf{M}$ be countable infinite and pairwise disjoint sets of concept names (denoted by A), abstract role names (denoted by R), concrete role names (denoted by T), abstract individual names (denoted by o), and concrete individual names (denoted by v). We assume that the set of abstract role names $\mathbf{R}$ can be divided into two disjoint subsets, $\mathbf{R}_t$ and $\mathbf{R}_n$, which stands for the subset of *transitive role names* and *non-transitive role names*, respectively. $f\text{-}\mathcal{SHIF}(\mathbf{D})$ abstract roles (or abstract roles for short) are defined as $R \to R_N \mid R^-$, where $R_N \in \mathbf{R}$, R^- is called the *inverse role* of R. A role inclusion axiom is of the form $R \sqsubseteq S$, with R, S abstract roles. A role hierarchy (also called a RBox) $\mathcal{R}$ is a finite set of role inclusion axioms.

For the sake of brevity and clarity, we use following notations: (i) we use an abbreviation $Inv(R)$ to denote inverse role of R, (ii) for a RBox $\mathcal{R}$, we define $\sqsubseteq_{\mathcal{R}}^*$ as the reflexive transitive closure of $\sqsubseteq$ over $\mathcal{R} \cup \{Inv(R) \sqsubseteq Inv(S) \mid R \sqsubseteq S \in \mathcal{R}\}$, ($iii$) for a RBox $\mathcal{R}$ and a role S, we define the set $Trans_{\mathcal{R}}$ of transitive roles as $\{S \mid$ there is a role R with $R \equiv_{\mathcal{R}}^* S$ and $R \in \mathbf{R}_t$ or $Inv(R) \in \mathbf{R}_t\}$, ($iv$) a role S is called simple w.r.t. a RBox $\mathcal{R}$ if, for each role R such that $R \sqsubseteq_{\mathcal{R}}^* S$, $R \notin Trans_{\mathcal{R}}$. The subscript $\mathcal{R}$ of $\sqsubseteq_{\mathcal{R}}^*$ and $Trans_{\mathcal{R}}$ is dropped if clear from the context.

$f\text{-}\mathcal{SHIF}(\mathbf{D})$ complex concepts (or simply concepts) are defined by concept names according to the following abstract syntax:

$$C \to \top \mid \bot \mid A \mid C_1 \sqcap C_2 \mid C_1 \sqcup C_2 \mid \neg C \mid \forall R.C \mid \exists R.C \mid \leq 1S \mid \geq 2S \mid \forall T.D \mid \exists T.D,$$

$D \to d \mid \neg d$.

For decidability reasons, roles in functional restrictions of the form $\leq 1S$ and their negation $\geq 2S$ are restricted to be simple abstract roles.

A fuzzy TBox is a finite set of fuzzy concept axioms. Fuzzy concept axiom of the form $A \equiv C$ are called *fuzzy concept definitions*, fuzzy concept axiom of the form $A \sqsubseteq C$ are called *fuzzy concept specializations*, and fuzzy concept axiom of the form $C \sqsubseteq D$ are called *general concept inclusion* (GCIs) axioms.

A fuzzy ABox consists of fuzzy assertions of the form $C(o) \vartriangleright\vartriangleleft n$ (*fuzzy concept assertions*), $R(o,o') \vartriangleright n$ (*fuzzy abstract role assertions*), $T(o,v) \vartriangleright n$ (*fuzzy data type role assertions*), or $o \neq o'$ (*inequality assertions*), where $o,o' \in \mathbf{I}$, $v \in \mathbf{I}_c$, $\vartriangleright\vartriangleleft$ stands for any type of inequality, i.e., $\vartriangleright\vartriangleleft \in \{\geq,>,\leq,<\}$. We use $\vartriangleright$ to denote $\geq$ or $>$, and $\vartriangleleft$ to denote $\leq$ or $<$. We call ABox assertions defined by $\vartriangleright$ *positive assertions*, while those defined by $\vartriangleleft$ *negative assertions*. Note that, we consider only positive fuzzy role assertions, since negative role assertions would imply the existence of role negation, which would lead to undecidability (Mailis, Stoilos, & Stamou, 2007). An f-$\mathcal{SHIF}(\mathbf{D})$ knowledge base $\mathcal{K}$ is a triple $\langle \mathcal{T}, \mathcal{R}, \mathcal{A} \rangle$ with $\mathcal{T}$ a TBox, $\mathcal{R}$ a RBox and $\mathcal{A}$ an ABox.

For a fuzzy concept D, we denote by $sub(D)$ the set that contains D and it is closed under subconcepts of D, and define $sub(\mathcal{K})$ as the set of all the sub-concepts of the concepts occurring in $\mathcal{K}$. We abuse the notion $sub(\mathbf{D})$ to denote the set of all the data type predicates occurring in a knowledge base.

The semantics of f-$\mathcal{SHIF}(\mathbf{D})$ are provided by a fuzzy interpretation which is a pair $\mathcal{I} = (\Delta^{\mathcal{I}}, \cdot^{\mathcal{I}})$. Here $\Delta^{\mathcal{I}}$ is a non-empty set of objects, called the domain of interpretation, disjoint from $\Delta^{\mathbf{D}}$, and $\cdot^{\mathcal{I}}$ is an interpretation function that coincides with $\cdot^{\mathbf{D}}$ on every data value and fuzzy data type predicate, and maps (i) different individual names into different elements in $\Delta^{\mathcal{I}}$, (ii) a concept name A into a membership function $A^{\mathcal{I}} : \Delta^{\mathcal{I}} \to [0,1]$, ($iii$) an abstract role name R into a membership function $R^{\mathcal{I}} : \Delta^{\mathcal{I}} \times \Delta^{\mathcal{I}} \to [0,1]$, ($iv$) a data type role T into a membership function $T^{\mathcal{I}} : \Delta^{\mathcal{I}} \times \Delta^{\mathbf{D}} \to [0,1]$. The semantics of f-$\mathcal{SHIF}(\mathbf{D})$ concepts and roles are depicted as follows.

$$\mathrm{T}^{\mathcal{I}}(o) = 1 \quad \perp^{\mathcal{I}}(o) = 0$$

$$(\neg C)^{\mathcal{I}}(o) = 1 - C^{\mathcal{I}}(o)$$

$$(C \sqcap D)^{\mathcal{I}}(o) = \min\{C^{\mathcal{I}}(o), D^{\mathcal{I}}(o)\}$$

$$(C \sqcup D)^{\mathcal{I}}(o) = \max\{C^{\mathcal{I}}(o), D^{\mathcal{I}}(o)\}$$

$$(\forall R.C)^{\mathcal{I}}(o) = \inf_{o' \in \Delta^{\mathcal{I}}} \{\max(1 - R^{\mathcal{I}}(o,o'), C^{\mathcal{I}}(o'))\}\}$$

$$(\exists R.C)^{\mathcal{I}}(o) = \sup_{o' \in \Delta^{\mathcal{I}}} \{\min(R^{\mathcal{I}}(o,o'), C^{\mathcal{I}}(o'))\}$$

$$(\forall T.d)^{\mathcal{I}}(o) = \inf_{v \in \Delta^{\mathbf{D}}} \{\max(1 - T^{\mathcal{I}}(o,v), d^{\mathcal{I}}(v))\}\}$$

$$(\exists T.d)^{\mathcal{I}}(o) = \sup_{v \in \Delta^{\mathbf{D}}} \{\min(T^{\mathcal{I}}(o,v), d^{\mathcal{I}}(v))\}$$

$$(\geq 2S)^{\mathcal{I}}(o) = \sup_{o_1, o_2 \in \Delta^{\mathcal{I}}} \{\min_{i=1}^{2}\{R^{\mathcal{I}}(o,o_i)\}\}$$

$$(\leq 1S)^{\mathcal{I}}(o) = \inf_{o_1, o_2 \in \Delta^{\mathcal{I}}} \{\max_{i=1}^{2}\{1 - R^{\mathcal{I}}(o,o_i)\}\}$$

$$(R^{-})^{\mathcal{I}}(o,o') = R^{\mathcal{I}}(o',o)$$

A fuzzy interpretation $\mathcal{I}$ satisfies a fuzzy concept specification $A \sqsubseteq C$, if $A^{\mathcal{I}}(o) \leq C^{\mathcal{I}}(o)$ for any $o \in \Delta^{\mathcal{I}}$, written as $\mathcal{I} \vDash A \sqsubseteq C$. Similarly, $\mathcal{I} \vDash A \equiv C$ if $A^{\mathcal{I}}(o) = C^{\mathcal{I}}(o)$ for any $o \in \Delta^{\mathcal{I}}$, and $\mathcal{I} \vDash C \sqsubseteq D$, if $C^{\mathcal{I}}(o) \leq D^{\mathcal{I}}(o)$ for any $o \in \Delta^{\mathcal{I}}$. For ABox assertions, $\mathcal{I} \vDash C(o) \rhd\lhd n$ (resp. $\mathcal{I} \vDash R(o,o') \rhd n$), iff $C^{\mathcal{I}}(o^{\mathcal{I}}) \rhd\lhd n$ (resp. $R^{\mathcal{I}}(o^{\mathcal{I}}, o'^{\mathcal{I}}) \rhd n$), and $\mathcal{I} \vDash o \approx /o'$ iff $o^{\mathcal{I}} \neq o'^{\mathcal{I}}$. If an interpretation $\mathcal{I}$ satisfies all the axioms and assertions in a KB $\mathcal{K}$, we call it a model of $\mathcal{K}$. A KB is *satisfiable* iff it has at least one model. A KB $\mathcal{K}$ *entails* (logically implies) a fuzzy assertion φ, iff all the models of $\mathcal{K}$ are also models of φ, written as $\mathcal{K} \vDash \varphi$.

Given a KB $\mathcal{K}$, we can w.l.o.g assume that

1. all concepts are in their negative normal forms (NNFs), i.e. negation occurs only in front of concept names. Through de Morgan law, the duality between existential restrictions ($\exists R.C$) and universal restrictions ($\forall R.C$), and the duality between functional restrictions ($\leq 1S$) and their negations ($\geq 2S$), each concept can be transformed into its equivalent NNF by pushing negation inwards.

2. all fuzzy concept assertions are in their positive inequality normal forms (PINFs). A negative concept assertion can be transformed into its equivalent PINF by applying fuzzy complement operation on it. For example, $C(o) < n$ is converted to $\neg C(o) > 1 - n$.

3. all fuzzy assertions are in their normalized forms (NFs). By introducing a positive, infinite small value ε, a fuzzy assertion of the form $C(o) > n$ can be normalized to $C(o) \geq n + \varepsilon$. The model equivalence of a KB $\mathcal{K}$ and its normalized form was shown to justify the assumption (Stoilos, Straccia, Stamou, & Pan, 2006).

4. there are only fuzzy GCIs in the TBox. A fuzzy concept specification $A \sqsubseteq C$ can be replaced by a fuzzy concept definition $A \equiv A' \sqcap C$ (Stoilos et al., 2007), where A' is a new concept name, which stands for the qualities that distinguish the elements of A from the other elements of C. A fuzzy concept definition axiom $A \equiv C$ can be eliminated by replacing every occurrence of A with C. The elimination is also known as *knowledge base expansion*. Note that the size of the expansion can be exponential in the size of the TBox. But if we follow the principle of "Expansion is done on demand" (Baader & Nutt, 2003), the expansion will have no impact on the algorithm complexity of deciding fuzzy query entailment.

Example 1. As a running example, we use the f-$\mathcal{SHIF}(\mathbf{D})$ KB $\mathcal{K} = \langle \mathcal{T}, \mathcal{R}, \mathcal{A} \rangle$ with $\mathcal{T} = \{C \sqsubseteq \exists R.C, \top \sqsubseteq \exists T.d\}$, $\mathcal{R} = \varnothing$, and $\mathcal{A} = \{C(o) \geq 0.8\}$.

Fuzzy Query Language

We now provide the formal definition of the syntax and semantics of the fuzzy querying language used in this paper, extending Mallis's work (Mailis et al., 2007) to allow for querying concrete domains.

Let $\mathbf{V}$ be a countable infinite set of variables and is disjoint from $\mathbf{A}$, $\mathbf{R}$, $\mathbf{R}_c$, $\mathbf{I}$, and $\mathbf{I}_c$. A *term* t is either an individual name from $\mathbf{I}$ or $\mathbf{I}_c$, or a variable name from $\mathbf{V}$. A *fuzzy query atom* is an expression of the form $\langle C(t) \geq n \rangle$, $\langle R(t,t') \geq n \rangle$, or $\langle T(t,t') \geq n \rangle$ with C a concept, R a simple abstract role, T a data type role, and t, t' terms. As with fuzzy assertions, we refer to these three different types of atoms as *fuzzy concept atoms*, *fuzzy abstract role atoms*, and *fuzzy data type role atoms*, respectively. The fuzzy abstract role atoms and the fuzzy data type role atoms are collectively referred to as *fuzzy role atoms*.

Definition 1. (Fuzzy Boolean Conjunctive Queries) A fuzzy boolean conjunctive query q is a non-empty set of fuzzy query atoms of the form $q = \{\langle at_1 \geq n_1 \rangle, \ldots, \langle at_k \geq n_k \rangle\}$. Then for every fuzzy query atom, we can say $\langle at_i \geq n_i \rangle \in q$.

We use $Vars(q)$ to denote the set of variables occurring in q, $AInds(q)$ and $CInds(q)$ to denote the sets of abstract and concrete individual names occurring in q, $Inds(q)$ to denotes the union of $AInds(q)$ and $CInds(q)$, and $Terms(q)$ for the set of terms in q, i.e. $Terms(q) = Vars(q) \cup Inds(q)$.

The semantics of a fuzzy query is given in the same way as for the related fuzzy DL by means of fuzzy interpretation consisting of an interpretation domain and a fuzzy interpretation function.

Definition 2. (Models of Fuzzy Queries) Let $\mathcal{I} = (\Delta^{\mathcal{I}}, \cdot^{\mathcal{I}})$ be a fuzzy interpretation of an $f\text{-}\mathcal{SHIF}(\mathbf{D})$ KB, q a fuzzy boolean conjunctive query, and t, t' terms in q. We say $\mathcal{I}$ is a model of q, if there exists a mapping $\pi : Terms(q) \to \Delta^{\mathcal{I}} \cup \Delta^{\mathbf{D}}$ such that $\pi(a) = a^{\mathcal{I}}$ for each $a \in Ind(q)$, $C^{\mathcal{I}}(\pi(t)) \geq n$ for each fuzzy concept atom $C(t) \geq n \in q$, $R^{\mathcal{I}}(\pi(t), \pi(t')) \geq n$ (resp. $T^{\mathcal{I}}(\pi(t), \pi(t')) \geq n$) for each fuzzy role atom $R(t,t') \geq n$ (resp. $T(t,t') \geq n$) $\in q$.

If $\mathcal{I} \models^{\pi} at$ for every atom $at \in q$, we write $\mathcal{I} \models^{\pi} q$. If there is a π, such that $\mathcal{I} \models^{\pi} q$, we say $\mathcal{I}$ satisfies q, written as $\mathcal{I} \models q$. We call such a π a *match* of q in $\mathcal{I}$. If $\mathcal{I} \models q$ for each model $\mathcal{I}$ of a KB $\mathcal{K}$, then we say $\mathcal{K}$ entails q, written as $\mathcal{K} \models q$. The *query entailment problem* is defined as follows: given a knowledge base $\mathcal{K}$ and a query q, decide whether $\mathcal{K} \models q$.

Example 2. Considering the following fuzzy boolean CQ:

$$q = \{R(x, y) \geq 0.6, R(y, z) \geq 0.8, T(y, y_c) \geq 1, C(y) \geq 0.6\}.$$

We observe that $\mathcal{K} \models q$. Given the GCI $C \sqsubseteq \exists R.C$, we have that, for each model $\mathcal{I}$ of $\mathcal{K}$, $\exists R.C^{\mathcal{I}}(o^{\mathcal{I}}) \geq C^{\mathcal{I}}(o^{\mathcal{I}}) \geq 0.8 > 0.6$ holds. By the definition of fuzzy interpretation, there exists some element b in $\Delta^{\mathcal{I}}$, such that $R(o^{\mathcal{I}}, b) \geq 0.8 > 0.6$ and $C(b) \geq 0.8 > 0.6$ holds. Similarly, there is some element c in $\Delta^{\mathcal{I}}$, such that $R^{\mathcal{I}}(b, c) \geq 0.8$ and $C^{\mathcal{I}}(c) \geq 0.8$ holds. Since $\top \sqsubseteq \exists T.d$, there is some element v in $\Delta^{\mathbf{D}}$, such that $T^{\mathcal{I}}(b,v) \geq 1 \geq 0.8$ and $d^{\mathcal{I}}(v) \geq 1$ holds. By constructing a mapping π with $\pi(x) = o^{\mathcal{I}}$, $\pi(y) = b$, $\pi(z) = c$, and $\pi(y_c) = v$, we have $\mathcal{I} \vDash q$.

RELATED WORK

The first conjunctive query algorithm (Calvanese, De Giacomo, & Lenzerini, 1998) over DLs was actually specified for the purpose of deciding conjunctive query containment for $\mathcal{DLR}_{reg}$. Recently, query entailment and answering have been extensively studied for tractable DLs, i.e., DLs that have reasoning problems of at most polynomial complexity. For example, the constructors provided by DL-Lite family (Calvanese, De Giacomo, Lembo, Lenzerini, & Rosati, 2007) are elaborately chosen such that the basic reasoning tasks are PTime-complete and query entailment is in LogSpace with respect to data complexity. Moreover, in DL-Lite family, as TBox reasoning can usually be done independently of the ABox, ABox storage can be transformed into database storage, thus knowledge base users can achieve efficient queries by means of well-established DBMS query engines. Another tractable DL comes from $\mathcal{EL}$ with PTime-complete reasoning complexity. It was shown that union of conjunctive queries (UCQs) entailment in $\mathcal{EL}$ and in its extensions with role hierarchies is NP-complete regarding the combined complexity (Rosati, 2007b). The data complexity of UCQ entailment in $\mathcal{EL}$ is PTime-complete (Rosati, 2007a). Allowing, additionally, role composition in the logic as in $\mathcal{EL}^{++}$, leads to undecidability (Krtzsch, Rudolph, & Hitzler, 2007).

Query answering algorithms for expressive DLs are being tracked with equal intensity. CARIN system (Levy & Rousset, 1998), the first framework for combining a description logic knowledge base with rules, provided a decision procedure for conjunctive query entailment in the description logic $\mathcal{ALCNR}$, where $\mathcal{R}$ stands for role conjunction. Decision procedures for more expressive DLs, i.e., the whole $\mathcal{SH}$ family, were presented (Ortiz, Calvanese, & Eiter, 2006; Ortiz, Calvanese, & Eiter, 2008), and the coNP-complete data complexity for a whole range of sublogics of $\mathcal{SHOIQ}$, as long as only simple roles in the query, was proved. The algorithms for answering CQs with transitive roles over $\mathcal{SHIQ}$ (Glimm, Lutz, Horrocks, & Sattler, 2008) and $\mathcal{SHOQ}$ (Glimm, Horrocks, & Sattler, 2007) KBs are provided and also a coNP upper bound was established.

Following current research developments in crisp DLs, there also have been efforts for answering CQs over fuzzy DL knowledge bases. In particular, a fuzzy extension of DL-Lite was proposed in (Straccia, 2006), along with an algorithm for answering conjunctive queries over fuzzy DL-Lite KBs. Since the query language for fuzzy DL-Lite has the same syntax as that of crisp DLs, the technique for efficiently computing the top-k answers of a conjunctive query was shown. In (Pan, Stamou, Stoilos, Taylor, & Thomas, 2008), a general framework of the aforementioned query language was proposed, covering all the existing query languages for fuzzy ontologies as well as some new ones that can be customized by users. The algorithms for these queries were implemented in the system ONTOSEARCH2 and evaluation showed that these can still be answered in a very efficient way. Clearly, threshold queries give users more flexibility in that users can specify different thresholds for different atoms. Maillis et al. (Mailis et al., 2007) proposed a fuzzy extension of CARIN system called fuzzy CARIN, and provided the ability of answering to union of conjunctive queries.

However, there is still no report for query answering over fuzzy DLs with data types. We tackle this issue in the next section.

QUERY ENTAILMENT ALGORITHM

As with the algorithms for basic inference services and simple query answering, our algorithm for deciding fuzzy query entailment is also based on tableau algorithms. However, the query entailment problem can not be reduced to the knowledge base satisfiability problem, since the negation of a fuzzy conjunctive query is not expressible with existing constructors provided by an f-$\mathcal{SHIF}(\mathbf{D})$ knowledge base. For this reason, tableau algorithms for reasoning over knowledge bases is not sufficient. A knowledge base $\mathcal{K}$ may have infinitely many possibly infinite models, whereas tableau algorithms construct only a subset of finite models of the knowledge base. The query entailment holds only if the query is true in all models of the knowledge base, we thus have to show that inspecting only a subset of the models, namely the *canonical* ones, suffices to decide query entailment.

Our algorithm works on a data structure called *completion forest*. A completion forest is a finite relational structure capturing a set of models of a KB $\mathcal{K}$. Roughly speaking, models of $\mathcal{K}$ are represented by an initial completion forest $\mathcal{F}_{\mathcal{K}}$. Then, by applying *expansion rules* repeatedly, new completion forests are generated. Since every model of $\mathcal{K}$ is preserved in some completion forest that results from the expansion, $\mathcal{K} \vDash q$ can be decided by considering a set $\mathbb{F}_{\mathcal{K}}$ of sufficiently expanded forests. From each such an $\mathcal{F}$, a single *canonical model* is constructed. Semantically, the finite set of these canonical models is sufficient for answering all queries q of bounded size. Furthermore, we prove that entailment in the canonical model obtained from $\mathcal{F}$ can be checked effectively via a syntactic mapping of the terms in q to the nodes in $\mathcal{F}$.

Completion Forests

Definition 3. (Completion Forest) A completion tree T for an f-$\mathcal{SHIF}(\mathbf{D})$ KB is a tree all of whose nodes are generated by expansion rules, except for the root node which might correspond to an abstract individual name in $\mathbf{I}$. A completion forest $\mathcal{F}$ for an f-$\mathcal{SHIF}(\mathbf{D})$ KB consists of a set of completion trees whose root nodes correspond to abstract individual names occurring in the ABox, an equivalent relation $\approx$ and an inequivalent relation $\not\approx$ among nodes.

The nodes in a completion forest $\mathcal{F}$, denoted Nodes($\mathcal{F}$), can be divided into abstract nodes (denoted ANodes($\mathcal{F}$)) and concrete nodes (or data type nodes, denoted CNodes($\mathcal{F}$)). Each abstract node o in a completion forest is labeled with a set $\mathcal{L}(o) = \{\langle C, \geq, n\rangle\}$, where $C \in sub(\mathcal{K})$, $n \in (0,1]$. The concrete nodes v can only serve as leaf nodes, each of which is labeled with a set $\mathcal{L}(v) = \{\langle d, \geq, n\rangle\}$, where $d \in sub(\mathbf{D})$, $n \in (0,1]$. Similarly, the edges in a completion forests can be divided into abstract edges and concrete edges. Each abstract edge $\langle o, o'\rangle$ is labeled with a set $\mathcal{L}(\langle o, o'\rangle) = \{\langle R, \geq, n\rangle\}$, where $R \in \mathbf{R}$. Each concrete edge $\langle o, v\rangle$ is labeled with a set $\mathcal{L}(\langle o, v\rangle) = \{\langle T, \geq, n\rangle\}$, where $T \in \mathbf{R}_c$.

If $\langle o, o'\rangle$ is an edge in a completion forest with $\langle R, \geq, n\rangle \in \mathcal{L}(\langle o, o'\rangle)$, then o' is called an $R_{\geq,n}$-*successor* of o and o is called an $R_{\geq,n}$-*predecessor* of o'. Ignoring the inequality and membership degree, we can also call o' an R-successor of o and o an R-predecessor of o'. *Ancestor* and *descendant* are the transitive closure of predecessor and successor, respectively. The union of the successor and predecessor relation is the *neighbor* relation. The *distance* between two nodes o, o' in a completion forest is the shortest path between them.

Starting with an f-$\mathcal{SHIF}(\mathbf{D})$ KB $\mathcal{K} = \langle \mathcal{T}, \mathcal{R}, \mathcal{A} \rangle$, the completion forest $\mathcal{F}_\mathcal{K}$ is initialized such that it contains (i) a root node o, with $\mathcal{L}(o) = \{\langle C, \geq, n \rangle \mid C(o) \geq n \in \mathcal{A}\}$, for each abstract individual name o occurring in $\mathcal{A}$, (ii) a leaf node v, with $\mathcal{L}(v) = \{\langle d, \geq, n \rangle \mid d(v) \geq n \in \mathcal{A}\}$, for each concrete individual name v occurring in $\mathcal{A}$, (iii) an abstract edge $\langle o, o' \rangle$ with $\mathcal{L}(\langle o, o' \rangle) = \{\langle R, \geq, n \rangle \mid \langle R(o, o') \geq n \rangle \in \mathcal{A}\}$, for each pair $\langle o, o' \rangle$ of individual names for which the set $\{R \mid R(o, o') \geq n \in \mathcal{A}\}$ is non-empty, and (iv) a concrete edge $\langle o, v \rangle$ with $\mathcal{L}(\langle o, v \rangle) = \{\langle T, \geq, n \rangle \mid \langle T(o, v) \geq n \rangle \in \mathcal{A}\}$. We initialize the relation $\not\approx$ as $\{\langle o, o' \rangle \mid o \neq o' \in \mathcal{A}\}$, and the relation $\approx$ to be empty.

Example 3. In our running example, $\mathcal{F}_\mathcal{K}$ contains only one node o labelled with $\mathcal{L}(o) = \{\langle C, \geq, 0.8 \rangle\}$.

Now we can formally define a new blocking condition, called k-*blocking*, for fuzzy query entailment depending on a depth parameter $k > 0$.

Definition 4. (k-tree equivalence) The k-tree of a node v in T, denoted as T_v^k, is the subtree of T rooted at v with all the descendants of v within distance k. We use $Nodes(T_v^k)$ to denote the set of nodes in T_v^k. Two nodes v and w in T are said to be k-tree equivalent in T, if T_v^k and T_w^k are isomorphic, i.e., there exists a bijection $\psi : Nodes(T_v^k) \to Nodes(T_w^k)$ such that (i) $\psi(v) = w$, (ii) for every node $o \in Nodes(T_v^k)$, $\mathcal{L}(o) = \mathcal{L}(\psi(o))$, (iii) for every edge connecting two nodes o and o' in T_v^k, $\mathcal{L}(\langle o, o' \rangle) = \mathcal{L}(\langle \psi(o), \psi(o') \rangle)$.

Definition 5. (k-witness) A node w is a k-witness of a node v, if v and w are k-tree equivalent in T, w is an ancestor of v in T and v is not in T_w^k. Furthermore, T_w^k tree-blocks T_v^k and each node o in T_w^k tree-blocks node $\psi^{-1}(o)$ in T_v^k.

Definition 6. (k-blocking) A node o is k-blocked in a completion forest $\mathcal{F}$ iff it is not a root node and it is either directly or indirectly k-blocked. Node o is directly k-blocked iff none of its ancestors is k-blocked, and o is a leaf of a tree-blocked k-tree. Node o is indirectly k-blocked iff one of its ancestors is k-blocked or it is a successor of a node o' and $\mathcal{L}(\langle o', o \rangle) = \varnothing$.

An initial completion forest is expanded according to a set of *expansion rules* that reflect the constructors in f-$\mathcal{SHIF}(\mathbf{D})$. The expansion rules, which syntactically decompose the concepts in node labels, either infer new constraints for a given node, or extend the tree according to these constraints (see Table 1). Termination is guaranteed by k-blocking. We denote by $\mathbb{F}_\mathcal{K}$ the set of all completion forests obtained this way.

For a node o, $\mathcal{L}(o)$ is said to contain a *clash*, if it contains one of the followings: (i) a pair of triples $\langle C, \geq, n \rangle$ and $\langle \neg C, \geq, m \rangle$ with $n + m > 1$, (ii) one of the triples: $\langle \bot, \geq, n \rangle$ with $n > 0$, $\langle C, \geq, n \rangle$ with $n > 1$, (iii) some triple $\langle \leq 1 S, \geq, n \rangle$, and o has two $R_{\geq, n'}$-neighbors o_1, o_2 with $n + n' > 1$ and $o_1 \approx / o_2$.

Definition 7. (k-complete and clash-free completion forest) A completion forest is called k-complete and clash-free if under k-blocking no rule can be applied to it, and none of its nodes and edges contains a clash. We denote by $\mathrm{ccf}_k(\mathbb{F}_\mathcal{K})$ the set of k-complete and class-free completion forests in $\mathbb{F}_\mathcal{K}$.

Table 1. Expansion rules

Rule	Description
$\sqcap_\geq$	if 1. $\langle C \sqcap D, \geq, n \rangle \in \mathcal{L}(x)$, x is not indirectly k-blocked, and 2. $\{\langle C, \geq, n \rangle, \langle D, \geq, n \rangle\} \not\subseteq \mathcal{L}(x)$, then $\mathcal{L}(x) \to \mathcal{L}(x) \cup \{\langle C, \geq, n \rangle, \langle D, \geq, n \rangle\}$
$\sqcup_\geq$	if 1. $\langle C \sqcup D, \geq, n \rangle \in \mathcal{L}(x)$, x is not indirectly k-blocked, and 2. $\{\langle C, \geq, n \rangle, \langle D, \geq, n \rangle\} \cap \mathcal{L}(x) = \varnothing$ then $\mathcal{L}(x) \to \mathcal{L}(x) \cup \{C'\}$, where $C' \in \{\langle C, \geq, n \rangle, \langle D, \geq, n \rangle\}$
$\exists_\geq$	if 1. $\langle \exists R.C, \geq, n \rangle$ (or $\langle \exists T.d, \geq, n \rangle$) $\in \mathcal{L}(x)$, x is not k-blocked. 2. x has no $R_{\geq,n}$-neighbor(resp. no $T_{\geq,n}$-neighbor) y s.t. $\langle C, \geq, n \rangle$ (resp. $\langle d, \geq, n \rangle$) $\in \mathcal{L}(y)$, then create a new node y with $\mathcal{L}(x,y) = \{\langle R, \geq, n \rangle\}$ and $\mathcal{L}(y) = \{\langle C, \geq, n \rangle\}$(resp. with $\mathcal{L}(x,y) = \{\langle T, \geq, n \rangle\}$ and $\mathcal{L}(y) = \{\langle d, \geq, n \rangle\}$).
$\forall_\geq$	if 1. $\langle \forall R.C, \geq, n \rangle$ (or $\langle \forall T.d, \geq, n \rangle$) $\in \mathcal{L}(x)$, x is not indirectly k-blocked. 2. x has an $R_{\geq,n'}$-neighbor y (resp. a $T_{\geq,n'}$-neighbor) with $\langle C, \geq, n \rangle$ (resp. $\langle d, \geq, n \rangle$) $\notin \mathcal{L}(y)$, where $n' = 1 - n + \varepsilon$, then $\mathcal{L}(y) \to \mathcal{L}(y) \cup \{\langle C, \geq, n \rangle\}$ (resp. $\mathcal{L}(y) \to \mathcal{L}(y) \cup \{\langle d, \geq, n \rangle\}$)
$\forall_+$	if 1. $\langle \forall R.C, \geq, n \rangle \in \mathcal{L}(x)$ with $Trans(R)$, x is not indirectly k-blocked, and 2. x has an $R_{\geq,n'}$-neighbor y with $\langle \forall R.C, \geq, n \rangle \notin \mathcal{L}(y)$, where $n' = 1 - n + \varepsilon$, then $\mathcal{L}(y) \to \mathcal{L}(yy \cup \{\langle \forall R.C, \geq, n \rangle\}$
$\forall_{+'}$	if 1. $\langle \forall S.C, \geq, n \rangle \in \mathcal{L}(x)$, x is not indirectly k-blocked, and 2. there is some R, with $Trans(R)$ and $R \sqsubseteq^* S$, 3. x has an $R_{\geq,n'}$-neighbor y with $\langle \forall R.C, \geq, n \rangle \notin \mathcal{L}(y)$, where $n' = 1 - n + \varepsilon$, then $\mathcal{L}(y) \to \mathcal{L}(yy \cup \{\langle \forall R.C, \geq, n \rangle\}$
$\geq_\geq$	if 1. $\langle \geq 2S, \geq, n \rangle \in \mathcal{L}(x)$, x is not k-blocked, 2. $\#\{x_i \in N_I \mid \langle R, \geq, n \rangle \in \mathcal{L}(x, x_i)\} < 2$, then introduce new nodes, s.t. $\#\{x_i \in N_I \mid \langle R, \geq, n \rangle \in \mathcal{L}(x, x_i)\} \geq 2$
$\leq_\geq$	if 1. $\langle \leq 1S, \geq, n \rangle \in \mathcal{L}(x)$, x is not indirectly k-blocked, 2. $\#\{x_i \in N_I \mid \langle R, \geq, 1 - n + \varepsilon \rangle \in \mathcal{L}(x, x_i)\} > 1$ and 3. there exist x_l and x_k, with no $x_i \approx /x_k$, 4. x_l is neither a root node nor an ancestor of x_k. then (i) $\mathcal{L}(x_k) \to \mathcal{L}(x_k) \cup \mathcal{L}(x_l)$ (ii) $\mathcal{L}(x, x_k) \to \mathcal{L}(x, x_k) \cup \mathcal{L}(x, x_l)$ (iii) $\mathcal{L}(x, x_l) \to \varnothing$, $\mathcal{L}(x_l) \to \varnothing$ (iv) set $x_i \approx /x_k$ for all x_i with $x_i \approx /x_l$.
··	if 1. $\langle \leq 1S, \geq, n \rangle \in \mathcal{L}(x)$, 2. $\#\{x_i \in N_I \mid \langle R, \geq, 1 - n + \varepsilon \rangle \in \mathcal{L}(x, x_i)\} > 1$ and 3. there exist x_l and x_k, both root nodes, with no $x_l \approx /x_k$, then 1. $\mathcal{L}(x_k) \to \mathcal{L}(x_k) \cup \mathcal{L}(x_l)$ 2. For all edges $\langle x_l, x' \rangle$, i. if the edge $\langle x_k, x' \rangle$ does not exist, create it with $\mathcal{L}(\langle x_k, x' \rangle) = \varnothing$, ii. $\mathcal{L}(\langle x_k, x' \rangle) \to \mathcal{L}(\langle x_k, x' \rangle) \cup \mathcal{L}(\langle x_l, x' \rangle)$. 3. For all edges $\langle x', x_l \rangle$, i. if the edge $\langle x', x_k \rangle$ does not exist, create it with $\mathcal{L}(\langle x', x_k \rangle) = \varnothing$, ii. $\mathcal{L}(\langle x', x_k \rangle) \to \mathcal{L}(\langle x', x_k \rangle) \cup \mathcal{L}(\langle x', x_l \rangle)$. 4. Set $\mathcal{L}(x_l) = \varnothing$ and remove all edges to/from x_l. 5. Set $x'' \approx /x_k$ for all x'' with $x'' \approx /x_l$ and set $x_l \approx x_k$.
$\sqsubseteq$	if 1. $C \sqsubseteq D \in \mathcal{T}$ and 2. $\{\langle \neg C, \geq, 1 - n + \varepsilon \rangle, \langle D, \geq, n \rangle\} \cap \mathcal{L}(x) = \varnothing$ for $n \in N^A \cup N^q$, then $\mathcal{L}(x) \to \mathcal{L}(x) \cup \{C'\}$ for some $C' \in \{\langle \neg C, \geq, 1 - n + \varepsilon \rangle, \langle D, \geq, n \rangle\}$.

Example 4. Figure 1 shows a 2-complete and clash-free completion forest $\mathcal{F}$ for $\mathcal{K}$, i.e., $\mathcal{F} \in \mathrm{ccf}_2(\mathbb{F}_\mathcal{K})$, where $\mathcal{L}_o = \{\langle C, \geq, 0.8 \rangle, \langle \exists R.C, \geq, 0.8 \rangle\}$, $\mathcal{L}_d = \{\langle d, \geq, 1 \rangle\}$, $\mathcal{L}_R = \{\langle R, \geq, 0.8 \rangle\}$, $\mathcal{L}_T = \{\langle T, \geq, 1 \rangle\}$. In $\mathcal{F}$, o_1 and o_4 are 2-tree equivalent, and o_1 is a 2-witness of o_4. $T^2_{o_1}$ tree-blocks $T^2_{o_4}$, and o_1 tree-blocks o_5. The node o_6 in $T^2_{o_4}$ is directly blocked by o_3 in $T^2_{o_1}$-tree, indicated by the dashed line.

Figure 1. A 2-complete and clash-free completion forest $\mathcal{F}$ of $\mathcal{K}$.

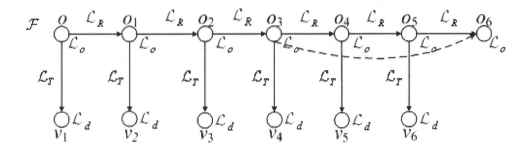

Models of Completion Forests

We now show that every model of a KB $\mathcal{K}$ is preserved in some complete and clash-free completion tree $\mathcal{F}$. If we view all the nodes (either root nodes or generated nodes) in a completion forest $\mathcal{F}$ as individual names, we can define models of $\mathcal{F}$ in terms of models of $\mathcal{K}$ over an extended vocabulary.

Definition 8. (Models of completion forests) An interpretation $\mathcal{I}$ is a model of a completion forest $\mathcal{F}$ for $\mathcal{K}$, denoted $\mathcal{I} \vDash \mathcal{F}$, if $\mathcal{I} \vDash \mathcal{K}$ and for all abstract nodes o, o' and concrete nodes v in $\mathcal{F}$ it holds that (i) $C^{\mathcal{I}}(o^{\mathcal{I}}) \geq n$ if $\langle C, \geq, n \rangle \in \mathcal{L}(o)$, (ii) $d^{\mathcal{I}}(v^{\mathcal{I}}) \geq n$ if $\langle d, \geq, n \rangle \in \mathcal{L}(v)$, (iii) $R^{\mathcal{I}}(o^{\mathcal{I}}, o'^{\mathcal{I}}) \geq n$ if there exists an abstract edge $\langle o, o' \rangle$ in $\mathcal{F}$ and $\langle R, \geq, n \rangle \in \mathcal{L}(\langle o, o' \rangle)$, (iv) $T^{\mathcal{I}}(o^{\mathcal{I}}, v^{\mathcal{I}}) \geq n$ if there exists a concrete edge $\langle o, v \rangle$ in $\mathcal{F}$ and $\langle T, \geq, n \rangle \in \mathcal{L}(\langle o, v \rangle)$, (v) $o^{\mathcal{I}} \neq o'^{\mathcal{I}}$ if $o \neq o' \in \mathcal{F}$.

We first show that the models of the initial completion forest $\mathcal{F}_{\mathcal{K}}$ and of $\mathcal{K}$ coincide.

Lemma 1. $\mathcal{I} \vDash \mathcal{F}_{\mathcal{K}}$ iff $\mathcal{I} \vDash \mathcal{K}$.

Proof. The only if direction follows from Definition 8. For the if direction, we need to show that, for all nodes v, w in $\mathcal{F}_{\mathcal{K}}$, Property (i)-(v) in Definition 8 hold. By Definition 3, each node in $\mathcal{F}_{\mathcal{K}}$ corresponds to an individual name in $\mathcal{K}$. For each abstract individual o in $\mathbf{I}$, the label of node o in $\mathcal{F}_{\mathcal{K}}$ is $\mathcal{L}(o) = \{\langle C, \geq, n \rangle \mid C(o) \geq n \in \mathcal{A}\}$. Since $\mathcal{I} \vDash \mathcal{K}$, then we have $C^{\mathcal{I}}(o^{\mathcal{I}}) \geq n$ and Property (i) thus holds. Property (ii)-(v) can be proved in a similar way with (i).

We then show that, each time an expansion rule is applied, all models are preserved in some resulting forest.

Lemma 2. Let $\mathcal{F}$ be a completion forest in $\mathbb{F}_{\mathcal{K}}$, r a rule in Table 1, $\mathbf{F}$ a set of completion forests obtained from $\mathcal{F}$ by applying r, then for each model $\mathcal{I}$ of $\mathcal{F}$, there exist an $\mathcal{F}'$ in $\mathbf{F}$ and an extension $\mathcal{I}'$ of $\mathcal{I}$, such that $\mathcal{I}' \vDash \mathcal{F}'$.

Proof. $\exists_{\geq}$-rule. Since $\langle \exists R.C, \geq, n \rangle \in \mathcal{L}(x)$ and $\mathcal{I} \vDash \mathcal{F}$, then there exists some $o \in \Delta^{\mathcal{I}}$, such that $R^{\mathcal{I}}(x^{\mathcal{I}}, o) \geq n$ and $C^{\mathcal{I}}(o) \geq n$ hold. In the completion forest $\mathcal{F}'$ obtained from $\mathcal{F}$ by applying $\exists_{\geq}$-rule, a new node y is generated such that $\langle R, \geq, n \rangle \in \mathcal{L}(\langle x, y \rangle)$ and $\langle C, \geq, n \rangle \in \mathcal{L}(y)$. By setting $y^{\mathcal{I}'} = o$, we obtain an extension $\mathcal{I}'$ of $\mathcal{I}$, and thus $\mathcal{I}' \vDash \mathcal{F}'$. The case of $\geq_\geq$-rule is analogous to the $\exists_\geq$-rule. The proofs for other rules are in similar way.

Since the set of k-complete and clash-free completion forests for $\mathcal{K}$ semantically captures $\mathcal{K}$ (modulo new individuals), we can transfer query entailment $\mathcal{K} \vDash q$ to logical consequence of q from completion forests as follows. For any completion forest $\mathcal{F}$ and any CQ q, let $\mathcal{F} \vDash q$ denote that $\mathcal{I} \vDash q$ for every model $\mathcal{I}$ of $\mathcal{F}$.

Theorem 1. Let $k \geq 0$ be arbitrary. Then $\mathcal{K} \vDash q$ iff $\mathcal{F} \vDash q$ for each $\mathcal{F} \in ccf_k(\mathbb{F}_\mathcal{K})$.

Proof. By Lemma 1 and Lemma 2, for each model $\mathcal{I}$ of $\mathcal{K}$, there exists some $\mathcal{F} \in \mathbb{F}_\mathcal{K}$ and an extension $\mathcal{I}'$ of $\mathcal{I}$, such that $\mathcal{I}' \vDash \mathcal{F}$. Assume $\mathcal{F} \notin ccf_k(\mathbb{F}_\mathcal{K})$, then there still have rules applicable to $\mathcal{F}$. We thus obtain an expansion $\mathcal{F}'$ from $\mathcal{F}$ and an extension $\mathcal{I}''$ of $\mathcal{I}'$, such that $\mathcal{I}'' \vDash \mathcal{F}'$, and so forth until no rule is applicable. Now we either obtain a complete and clash free completion forest, or encounter a clash. The former is conflict with the assumption, and the latter is conflict with the fact that $\mathcal{F}$ have models.

Checking Query Entailment Within Completion Forests

We now show that, if k is large enough, we can decide $\mathcal{F} \vDash q$ for each $\mathcal{F} \in ccf_k(\mathbb{F}_\mathcal{K})$ by syntactically mapping the query q into $\mathcal{F}$.

Definition 9. (Query mapping) A fuzzy query q can be mapped into $\mathcal{F}$, denoted $q \rightarrowtail \mathcal{F}$, if there is a mapping $\mu : Terms(q) \rightarrow Nodes(\mathcal{F})$, such that ($i$) $\mu(a) = a$, if $a \in \mathrm{Inds}(q)$, (ii) for each fuzzy concept atom $C(x) \geq n$ (resp. $d(x) \geq n$) in q, $\langle C(x), \geq, m \rangle$ (resp. $\langle d(x), \geq, m \rangle$) $\in \mathcal{L}(\mu(x))$ with $m \geq n$, (iii) for each fuzzy role atom $R(x, y) \geq n$ (resp. $T(x, y) \geq n$) in q, $\mu(y)$ is a $R_{\geq m}$-neighbor (resp. a $T_{\geq m}$-neighbor) of $\mu(x)$ with $m \geq n$.

Example 5. By setting $\mu(x) = o_1$, $\mu(y) = o_2$, $\mu(z) = o_3$, and $\mu(y_c) = v_1$, we can construct a mapping μ of q into $\mathcal{F}_1$.

In fact, for completion forests $\mathcal{F}$ of a KB $\mathcal{K}$, syntactic mapping $q \rightarrowtail \mathcal{F}$ implies semantic consequence $\mathcal{F} \vDash q$.

Lemma 3. *If* $q \rightarrowtail \mathcal{F}$, *then* $\mathcal{F} \vDash q$.

Proof. If $q \rightarrowtail \mathcal{F}$, then there is a mapping $\mu : \mathrm{Terms}(q) \rightarrow \mathrm{Nodes}(\mathcal{F})$ satisfying Definition 9. For any model $\mathcal{I} = (\Delta^{\mathcal{I}}, \cdot^{\mathcal{I}})$ of $\mathcal{F}$, it satisfies Definition 8. We construct a mapping $\pi : \mathrm{Terms}(q) \rightarrow \Delta^{\mathcal{I}}$ such that, for each term $x \in \mathrm{Terms}(q)$, $\pi(x) = (\mu(x))^{\mathcal{I}}$. It satisfies $C^{\mathcal{I}}(\pi(x)) = C^{\mathcal{I}}((\mu(x))^{\mathcal{I}}) \geq m \geq n$, for each fuzzy concept atom $C(x) \geq n \in q$. The proof for fuzzy role atoms can be shown in a similar way. Hence $\mathcal{I} \vDash q$, which by Theorem 1 implies $\mathcal{F} \vDash q$.

Lemma 3 shows the soundness of our algorithm. We prove, in next subsection, the converse (the completeness) also holds. We show that provided the completion forest $\mathcal{F}$ has been sufficiently expanded, a mapping from q to $\mathcal{F}$ can be constructed from a single canonical model.

Fuzzy Tableaux and Canonical models

The construction of the canonical model $\mathcal{I}_{\mathcal{F}}$ for $\mathcal{F}$ is divided into two steps. First, $\mathcal{F}$ is unravelled into a fuzzy tableau. Then, the canonical model is induced from the tableau. The interpretation domain $\Delta^{\mathcal{I}_{\mathcal{F}}}$ of $\mathcal{I}_{\mathcal{F}}$ consists of a set of (maybe infinite) paths. The reason lies in that a KB $\mathcal{K}$ may have infinite models, whereas the canonical model $\mathcal{I}_{\mathcal{F}}$ is constructed from $\mathcal{F}$, which is a finite representation decided by the termination of the algorithm. This requires some nodes in $\mathcal{F}$ represent several elements in $\Delta^{\mathcal{I}_{\mathcal{F}}}$. The paths is chosen to distinguish different elements represented in $\mathcal{F}$ by the same node. The definition of fuzzy tableau is based on the one in (Stoilos et al., 2006, 2007).

Definition 10. (Fuzzy tableau) Let $\mathcal{K} = \langle \mathcal{T}, \mathcal{R}, \mathcal{A} \rangle$ be a $f\text{-}\mathcal{SHIF}(\mathbf{D})$ KB, $\mathbf{R}_{\mathcal{K}}$, $\mathbf{R}_{\mathbf{D}}$ the sets of abstract and concrete roles occurring in $\mathcal{K}$, $\mathbf{I}_{A}$ the set of individual names occurring in $\mathcal{A}$, $T = \langle \mathbf{S}, \mathcal{H}, \mathcal{E}_{a}, \mathcal{E}_{c}, \mathcal{V} \rangle$ is the fuzzy tableau of $\mathcal{K}$ if (i) $\mathbf{S}$ is a nonempty set, (ii) $\mathcal{H}: \mathbf{S} \times sub(\mathcal{K}) \rightarrow [0,1]$ maps each element in $\mathbf{S}$ and each concept in $sub(\mathcal{K})$ to the membership degree the element belongs to the concept, (iii) $\mathcal{E}_{a}: \mathbf{S} \times \mathbf{S} \times \mathbf{R}_{\mathcal{K}} \rightarrow [0,1]$ maps each pair of elements in $\mathbf{S}$ and each role in $\mathbf{R}_{\mathcal{K}}$ to the membership degree the pair belongs to the role, (iv) $\mathcal{E}_{c}: \mathbf{S} \times \Delta^{\mathbf{D}} \times \mathbf{R}_{\mathbf{D}} \rightarrow [0,1]$ maps each pair of elements and concrete values and each concrete role in $\mathbf{R}_{\mathbf{D}}$ to the membership degree the pair belongs to the role, (v) $\mathcal{V}: \mathbf{I}_{A} \rightarrow \mathbf{S}$ maps each individual in $\mathbf{I}_{A}$ to a element in $\mathbf{S}$. Additionally, for each $s,t \in \mathbf{S}$, $C, D \in sub(\mathcal{K})$, $R \in \mathbf{R}_{\mathcal{K}}$, and $n \in [0,1]$, T satisfies:

1. *for each $s \in \mathbf{S}$, $\mathcal{H}(s, \bot) = 0$, $\mathcal{H}(s, \top) = 1$;*
2. *if $\mathcal{H}(s, C \sqcap D) \geq n$, then $\mathcal{H}(s, C) \geq n$ and $\mathcal{H}(s, D) \geq n$;*
3. *if $\mathcal{H}(s, C \sqcup D) \geq n$, then $\mathcal{H}(s, C) \geq n$ or $\mathcal{H}(s, D) \geq n$;*
4. *if $\mathcal{H}(s, \forall R.C) \geq n$, then for all $t \in \mathbf{S}$, $\mathcal{E}(\langle s,t \rangle, R) \leq 1 - n$ or $\mathcal{H}(t, C) \geq n$;*
5. *if $\mathcal{H}(s, \exists R.C) \geq n$, then there exists $t \in \mathbf{S}$, such that $\mathcal{E}_{a}(\langle s,t \rangle, R) \geq n$ and $\mathcal{H}(t, C) \geq n$;*
6. *if $\mathcal{H}(s, \forall R.C) \geq n$, and $\mathrm{Trans}(R)$, then $\mathcal{E}_{a}(\langle s,t \rangle, R) \leq 1 - n$ or $\mathcal{H}(t, \forall R.C) \geq n$;*
7. *if $\mathcal{H}(s, \forall S.C) \geq n$, $\mathrm{Trans}(R)$, and $R \sqsubseteq^{*} S$, then $\mathcal{E}_{a}(\langle s,t \rangle, R) \leq 1 - n$ or $\mathcal{H}(t, \forall R.C) \geq n$;*
8. *if $\mathcal{H}(s, \geq 2S) \geq n$, then $\#\{t \in \mathbf{S} \mid \mathcal{E}_{a}(\langle s,t \rangle, R) \geq n$;*
9. *if $\mathcal{H}(s, \leq 1S) \geq n$, then $\#\{t \in \mathbf{S} \mid \mathcal{E}_{a}(\langle s,t \rangle, R) \geq 1 - n + \varepsilon$;*
10. *if $\mathcal{E}_{a}(\langle s,t \rangle, R) \geq n$, and $R \sqsubseteq^{*} S$, then $\mathcal{E}_{a}(\langle s,t \rangle, S) \geq n$;*
11. *$\mathcal{E}_{a}(\langle s,t \rangle, R) \geq n$ iff $\mathcal{E}_{a}(\langle t,s \rangle, Inv(R)) \geq n$;*
12. *if $C \sqsubseteq D \in \mathcal{T}$, then for all $s \in \mathbf{S}$, $n \in N^{A} \cup N^{q}$, $\mathcal{H}(s, \neg C) \geq 1 - n + \varepsilon$ or $\mathcal{H}(s, D) \geq n$;*
13. *if $C(o) \geq n \in \mathcal{A}$, then $\mathcal{H}(\mathcal{V}(o), C) \geq n$;*
14. *if $R(o, o') \geq n \in \mathcal{A}$, then $\mathcal{E}_{a}(\langle \mathcal{V}(o), \mathcal{V}(o') \rangle, R) \geq n$;*
15. *if $o \approx /o' \in \mathcal{A}$, then $\mathcal{V}(o) \neq \mathcal{V}(o')$.*

16. *if* $\mathcal{H}(s, \forall T.d) \geq n$, then for all $t \in \Delta^{\mathbf{D}}$, $\mathcal{E}_c(\langle s, t \rangle, T) \leq 1 - n$ or $d^{\mathbf{D}}(t) \geq n$;

17. *if* $\mathcal{H}(s, \exists T.d) \geq n$, then there exists $t \in \Delta^{\mathbf{D}}$, such that $\mathcal{E}_c(\langle s, t \rangle, T) \geq n$ and $d^{\mathbf{D}}(t) \geq n$.

The process of inducing a fuzzy tableau from a completion forest $\mathcal{F}$ is as follows.

Each element in $\mathbf{S}$ corresponds to a path in $\mathcal{F}$. We can view a blocked node as a loop so as to define infinite paths. To be more precise, a path $p = [v_0 / v_{0'}, \ldots, v_n / v_{n'}]$ is a sequence of node pairs in $\mathcal{F}$. We define $Tail(p) = v_n$, and $Tail'(p) = v_{n'}$. We denote by $[p \mid v_{n+1} / v_{n+1}']$ the path $[v_0 / v_{0'}, \ldots, v_n / v_{n'}, v_{n+1} / v_{n+1}']$ and use $[p \mid v_{n+1} / v_{n+1}', v_{n+2} / v_{n+2}']$ as the abbreviation of $[[p \mid v_{n+1} / v_{n+1}'], v_{n+2} / v_{n+2}']$. The set Paths$(\mathcal{F})$ of paths in $\mathcal{F}$ is inductively defined as follows:

- if v is a root node in $\mathcal{F}$, then $[v / v'] \in$ Paths$(\mathcal{F})$;
- if $p \in$ Paths$(\mathcal{F})$, and $w \in$ Nodes$(\mathcal{F})$,
  - if w is the R-successor of $Tail(p)$ and is not k-blocked, then $[p \mid w / w] \in$ Paths$(\mathcal{F})$;
  - if there exists $w' \in$ Nodes$(\mathcal{F})$ and is the R-successor of $Tail(p)$, and is directly k-blocked by w, then $[p \mid w / w'] \in$ Paths$(\mathcal{F})$.

Definition 11. (Induced fuzzy tableau) The fuzzy tableau $T_{\mathcal{F}} = \langle \mathbf{S}, \mathcal{H}, \mathcal{E}_a, \mathcal{E}_c, \mathcal{V} \rangle$ induced by $\mathcal{F}$ is as follows.

- $\mathbf{S} = $ Paths$(\mathcal{F})$,
- $\mathcal{H}(p, C) \geq \sup\{n_i \mid \langle C, \geq, n_i \rangle \in \mathcal{L}(Tail(p))\}$,
- $\mathcal{E}_a(\langle p, [p \mid [p \mid w / w']] \rangle, R) \geq \sup\{n_i \mid \langle R, \geq, n_i \rangle \in \mathcal{L}(\langle Tail(p), w' \rangle)\}$,
  $\mathcal{E}_a(\langle [p \mid [p \mid w / w']], p \rangle, R) \geq \sup\{n_i \mid \langle Inv(R), \geq, n_i \rangle \in \mathcal{L}(\langle Tail(p), w' \rangle)\}$,
  $\mathcal{E}_a(\langle [v / v, w / w] \rangle, R) \geq \sup\{n_i \mid \langle R^*, \geq, n_i \rangle \in \mathcal{L}(\langle v, w \rangle)\}$, where v, w are root nodes, v is the R^*-neighbour of w, and R^* denotes R or $Inv(R)$,
- $\mathcal{E}_c(\langle p, [p \mid v_c / v_c] \rangle, T) \geq n$ with $\langle T, \geq, n \rangle \in \mathcal{L}(\langle Tail(p), v_c \rangle)\}$, where v_c is a concrete node,
- $\mathcal{V}(a_i) = \begin{cases} [a_i / a_i], & \text{if } a_i \text{ is a root node, and } \mathcal{L}(a_i) \neq \varnothing, \\ [a_j / a_j], & \text{if } a_i \text{ is a root node, and } \mathcal{L}(a_i) = \varnothing, \\ \quad \text{with } a_i \approx a_j \text{ and } \mathcal{L}(a_j) \neq \varnothing. \end{cases}$

From the fuzzy tableau of a fuzzy KB $\mathcal{K}$, we can obtain the canonical model of $\mathcal{K}$.

Definition 12. (Canonical model) Let $T = \langle \mathbf{S}, \mathcal{H}, \mathcal{E}_a, \mathcal{E}_c, \mathcal{V} \rangle$ be a fuzzy tableau of $\mathcal{K}$, the canonical model of T, $\mathcal{I}_T = (\Delta^{\mathcal{I}_T}, \cdot^{\mathcal{I}_T})$, is defined as follows.

- $\Delta^{\mathcal{I}_T} = \mathbf{S}$;
- for each individual name o in $\mathbf{I}_A$, $o^{\mathcal{I}_T} = \mathcal{V}(o)$;
- for each $s \in \mathbf{S}$ and each concept name A, $A^{\mathcal{I}_T}(s) = \mathcal{H}(s, A)$;

- for each $\langle s,t \rangle \in \mathbf{S} \times \mathbf{S}$, $R^{\mathcal{I}_T}(s,t) = \begin{cases} R_{\mathcal{E}}^+(s,t), & \text{if } Trans(R), \\ \max\limits_{S \sqsubseteq^* R, S \neq R}(R_{\mathcal{E}}(s,t), S^{\mathcal{I}_T}(s,t)), & \text{otherwise.} \end{cases}$ where

  $R_{\mathcal{E}}(s,t) = \mathcal{E}_a(\langle s,t \rangle, R)$, and $R_{\mathcal{E}}^+(s,t)$ is the sup-min transitive closure of $R_{\mathcal{E}}(s,t)$.

- for each $\langle s,t \rangle \in \mathbf{S} \times \Delta^{\mathbf{D}}$, $T^{\mathcal{I}_T}(s,t) = \mathcal{E}_c(s,t)$.

Lemma 4. Let T be the fuzzy tableau of an $f\text{-}\mathcal{SHIF}(\mathbf{D})$ KB $\mathcal{K} = \langle \mathcal{T}, \mathcal{R}, \mathcal{A} \rangle$, then the canonical model $\mathcal{I}_T$ of T is a model of $\mathcal{K}$.

Proof. Property 12 in Definition 10 ensures that $\mathcal{I}_T$ is a model of $\mathcal{T}$. For a detailed proof, see Proposition 3 in (Stoilos et al., 2006). Property 1-11 and 13-17 in Definition 10 ensures that $\mathcal{I}_T$ is a model of $\mathcal{A}$ and $\mathcal{R}$. For a detailed proof, see Lemma 5.2 and 6.5 in (Stoilos et al., 2007).

Example 6. By unraveling $\mathcal{F}$ in Figure 1, we obtain a model $\mathcal{I}_{\mathcal{F}}$ which has as domain the infinite set of paths from o to each o_i. Note that a path actually comprises a sequence of pairs of nodes, in order to witness the loops introduced by the blocked variables. When a node is not blocked, like o_1, the pair $o_1 \,/\, o_1$ is added to the path. Since $T_{o_1}^2$ tree-blocks $T_{o_4}^2$, each time a path reaches o_6, which is a leaf node of a blocked tree, we add $o_3 \,/\, o_6$ to the path and 'loop' back to the successors of o_3. This set of paths constitute the domain $\Delta^{\mathcal{I}_{\mathcal{F}}}$. For each concept name A, we have $A^{\mathcal{I}_{\mathcal{F}}}(p_i) \geq n$, if $\langle A, \geq, n \rangle$ occurs in the label of the last node in p_i. For each role R, $R^{\mathcal{I}_{\mathcal{F}}}(p_i, p_j) \geq n$ if the last node in p_j is an $R_{\geq,n}$-successor of p_i. If role $R \in Trans$, the extension of R is expanded according to the sup-min transitive semantics. Therefore, $C^{\mathcal{I}_{\mathcal{F}}}(p_i) \geq 0.8$ for $i \geq 0$, and $R^{\mathcal{I}_{\mathcal{F}}}(p_i, p_j) \geq 0.8$ for $0 \leq i < j$.

From a complete and clash-free completion forest $\mathcal{F}$, we can obtain a fuzzy tableau $T_{\mathcal{F}}$, through which a canonical model $\mathcal{I}_{\mathcal{F}}$ is constructed.

Lemma 5. Let $\mathcal{F} \in ccf_k(\mathbb{F}_{\mathcal{K}})$, then $\mathcal{I}_{\mathcal{F}} \vDash \mathcal{K}$, where $k \geq 1$.

Proof. It follows from Lemma 5.9 and 6.10 in (Stoilos et al., 2007) and Proposition 5 in (Stoilos et al., 2006) that the induced tableau in Definition 11 satisfies Property 1-15 in Definition 10. By Lemma 4, the canonical model $\mathcal{I}_{\mathcal{F}}$ constructed from $T_{\mathcal{F}}$ is a model of $\mathcal{K}$.

Now we illustrate how to construct a mapping of q to $\mathcal{F}$ from a mapping of q to $\mathcal{I}_{\mathcal{F}}$.

Definition 13. (Mapping graph) Let $\mathcal{F} \in ccf_k(\mathbb{F}_{\mathcal{K}})$ with $k \geq 0$, and a fuzzy query q, such that $\mathcal{I}_{\mathcal{F}} \vDash q$. π is a mapping in Definition 2, then the mapping graph $G_{\pi} = \langle V, E \rangle$ is defined as:

$V(G_{\pi}) = \{\pi(x) \in \Delta^{\mathcal{I}_{\mathcal{F}}} \cup \Delta^{\mathbf{D}} \mid x \in Terms(q)\}$,

$E(G_{\pi}) = \{\langle \pi(x), \pi(y) \rangle \in \Delta^{\mathcal{I}_{\mathcal{F}}} \times \Delta^{\mathcal{I}_{\mathcal{F}}} \mid R(x,y) \geq n \in q\} \cup$

$$\{\langle \pi(x), \pi(y) \rangle \in \Delta^{\mathcal{I}_{\mathcal{F}}} \times \Delta^{\mathbf{D}} \mid T(x, y) \geq n \in q\} .$$

$V(G_\pi)$ is divided into $Vr(G_\pi)$ and $Vn(G_\pi)$, i.e., $V(G_\pi) = Vr(G_\pi) \cup Vn(G_\pi)$ and $Vr(G_\pi) \cap Vn(G_\pi) = \varnothing$, where $Vr(G_\pi) = \{[v \mid v] \mid v$ is a root node in $\mathcal{F}\}$.

Definition 14. (Maximal q-distance) For any $x, y \in Terms(q)$, if $\pi(x), \pi(y) \in Vn(G_\pi)$, then we use $d^\pi(x, y)$ to denote the length of the shortest path between $\pi(x)$ and $\pi(y)$ in $G\pi$. If $\pi(x)$ and $\pi(y)$ are in two different connected components respectively, then $d^\pi(x, y) = -1$. We define maximal q-distance $d_q^\pi = \max_{x, y \in Terms(q)} \{d^\pi(x, y)\}$.

Example 7. Consider a mapping π such that $\pi(x) = p_6$, $\pi(y) = p_7$, $\pi(z) = p_8$, and $\pi(y_c) = v_5$. The mapping graph G_π contains the nodes p_6, p_7 and p_8, where $Vr(G_\pi) = \varnothing$, $Vn(G_\pi) = \{p_6, p_7, p_8, v_5\}$, and $E(G_\pi) = \{\langle p_6, p_7 \rangle, \langle p_7, p_8 \rangle, \langle p_7, v_5 \rangle\}$. Moreover, $d^\pi(p_6, p_7) = 1$, $d^\pi(p_7, p_8) = 1$, $d^\pi(p_6, p_8) = 2$, $d^\pi(p_6, v_5) = 2$, and $d^\pi(v_5, p_8) = 2$, thus $d_q^\pi = 2$.

We use n_q to denote the number of fuzzy role atoms in a fuzzy query q. We only consider fuzzy role atoms $R(x, y) \geq n$ with R a simple role, so $d^\pi(x, y) = 1$ and $d_q^\pi \leq n_q$. We show provided the k in the k-blocking condition is greater than or equal to n_q, it suffices to find a mapping from q to $\mathcal{F}$.

Lemma 6. Let $\mathcal{F} \in ccf_k(\mathbb{F}_{\mathcal{K}})$ with $k \geq n_Q$, and $\mathcal{I}_{\mathcal{F}}$ is the canonical model of $\mathcal{F}$. If $\mathcal{I}_{\mathcal{F}} \vDash q$, then $q \rightarrowtail \mathcal{F}$.

Proof. Since $\mathcal{I}_{\mathcal{F}} \vDash q$, then there exists a mapping $\pi : Terms(q) \rightarrow \Delta^{\mathcal{I}_F} \cup \Delta^{\mathbf{D}}$ such that $\pi(a) = a^{\mathcal{I}_F}$ for each $a \in Ind(q)$, $C^{\mathcal{I}_{\mathcal{F}}}(\pi(t)) \geq n$ for each fuzzy concept atom $C(t) \geq n \in q$, $R^{\mathcal{I}_{\mathcal{F}}}(\pi(t), \pi(t')) \geq n$ (resp. $T^{\mathcal{I}_{\mathcal{F}}}(\pi(t), \pi(t')) \geq n$) for each fuzzy role atom $R(t, t') \geq n$ (resp. $T(t, t') \geq n$) $\in q$.

We construct the mapping $\mu : Terms(q) \rightarrow Nodes(\mathcal{F})$ from the mapping π. First, we consider G, a subgraph of G_π, which is obtained by eliminating the vertices of the form $[a \mid a]$ with a a individual name and the arcs that enter or leave these vertices. G consists of a set of connected components- written as $G_1, \ldots, G_m$. We define $Blocked(G_i)$ as the set of all the vertices p such that $Tails(p) \neq Tails'(p)$. Then, for every ancestor p' of p in G_i, $Tails(p) = Tails'(p)$. We use $AfterBlocked(G_i)$ to denote the set of the descendants of the vertices in $Blocked(G_i)$.

Recalling the definition of $Nodes(\mathcal{F})$, since $\mathcal{F}$ is k-blocked, if there are two node pairs $v \mid v'$ and $w \mid w'$ in a path (also a vertex) p with $v \neq v'$ and $w \neq w'$, then the distance between these two node pairs must greater than k. A path p always begins with $v \mid v$, if it contains a node pair $w \mid w'$ with $w \neq w'$, then the distance between $v \mid v$ and $w \mid w'$ must greater than k.

We prove two properties of G_i as follows.

(1) If $\pi(x) \in AfterBlocked(G_i)$, then $Tail(\pi(x)) = Tail'(\pi(x))$. If $\pi(x) \in AfterBlocked(G_i)$, then there exists some $y \in Vars(q)$, such that $\pi(y) \in Blocked(G_i)$, i.e., $Tail(\pi(y)) \neq Tail'(\pi(y))$, and $\pi(x)$ is a descendant of $\pi(y)$. $\pi(x)$ is of the form $[p \mid v_0 / v_0', \dots, v_m / v_m']$, where $Tail(p) \neq Tail'(p)$. Assume that $v_m \neq v_m'$, then the length of the path $\pi(x)$ is larger than k, which contradicts with the fact that $d^\pi(x, y) \leq d_q^\pi \leq n_q \leq k$.

(2) If $\pi(x) \in V(G_i)$ for some G_i with $afterblocked(G_i) \neq \varnothing$ and $\pi(x) \notin afterblocked(G_i)$, then $Tail'(\pi(x))$ is tree-blocked by $\psi(Tail'(\pi(x)))$. If $afterblocked(G_i) \neq \varnothing$, then there exists some $y \in Vars(q)$, such that $\pi(y) \in Nodes(G_i)$ has some proper sub-path p such that $Tail(p) = Tail'(p)$. Since $\pi(x)$ and $\pi(y)$ are in the same G_i, then either $\pi(x)$ is an ancestor of $\pi(y)$ or there is some $z \in Terms(q)$ such that $\pi(z)$ is a common ancestor of $\pi(x)$ and $\pi(y)$ in $Nodes(G_i)$. In the first case, if $Tail'(\pi(x))$ was not tree-blocked, we would have that $d^\pi(x, y) > n \geq n_q$, which is a contradiction. In the second case, if $Tail'(\pi(x))$ was not tree-blocked, then $Tail'(\pi(z))$ would not be tree-blocked either, and thus we also derive a contradiction since $d^\pi(z, y) > n \geq n_q$.

We thus can construct the mapping $\mu : Terms(q) \to Nodes(\mathcal{F})$ as follows.

- For each $a \in Inds(q)$, $\mu(a) = Tail(\pi(a)) = a$;
- For each $x \in Vars(q)$ with $\pi(x) \in afterblocked(G_i)$, $\mu(x) = Tail(\pi(x))$;
  - If $afterblocked(G_i) = \varnothing$, then $\mu(x) = Tail(\pi(x))$,
  - If $afterblocked(G_i) \neq \varnothing$, then $\mu(x) = \begin{cases} Tail'(\pi(x)) & if \ \pi(x) \in afterblocked(G_i), \\ \psi(Tail'(\pi(x))) & otherwise. \end{cases}$

We now prove that μ satisfies Property 1-3 in Definition 9.

Property 1 follows from the construction of μ;

Property 2: For each fuzzy concept atom $C(x) \geq n \in q$, since $\mathcal{I}_\mathcal{F} \vDash q$, $\mathcal{H}(\pi(x), C) \geq n$ holds. It follows that $\langle C, \geq, n \rangle \in \mathcal{L}(Tail'(\pi(x)))$ or $\langle C, \geq, n \rangle \in \mathcal{L}(\psi(Tail'(\pi(x))))$, then we have $\langle C, \geq, n \rangle \in \mathcal{L}(\mu(x))$.

Property 3: For each fuzzy role atom $R(x, y) \geq n \in q$, $\mathcal{E}(\langle \pi(x), \pi(y) \rangle, R) \geq n$ holds. Then, either (1) $Tail'(\pi(y))$ is a $R_{\geq,n}$-successor of $Tail'(\pi(x))$, or (2) $Tail'(\pi(x))$ is a $Inv(R)_{\geq,n}$-successor of $Tail'(\pi(y))$.

case (1): For each connected component G_i, if $AfterBlocked(G_i) = \varnothing$, then for each term x such that $\pi(x) \in G_i$, $Tail(\pi(x) = Tail'(\pi(x)$. If $Tail'(\pi(y))$ is a $R_{\geq,n}$-successor of $Tail'(\pi(x))$, then $\mu(y) = Tail'(\pi(y))$ is a $R_{\geq,n}$-successor of $\mu(x) = Tail'(\pi(x))$.

If $AfterBlocked(G_i) \neq \varnothing$, we make case study as follows.

(a) If $\pi(x), \pi(y) \in AfterBlocked(G_i)$, then $\mu(x) = Tail'(\pi(x))$ and $\mu(y) = Tail'(\pi(y))$. If $Tail'(\pi(y))$ is a $R_{\geq,n}$-successor of $Tail(\pi(x))$, then $\mu(y) = Tail'(\pi(y))$ is a $R_{\geq,n}$-successor of $\mu(x) = Tail'(\pi(x)) = Tail(\pi(x))$.

(b) If $\pi(x), \pi(y) \notin AfterBlocked(G_i)$, then $Tail'(\pi(x)) = Tail(\pi(x))$. Otherwise, there will be $\pi(y) \in AfterBlocked(G_i)$. By Property (2), $Tail'(\pi(x))$ is tree-blocked by $\psi(Tail'(\pi(x)))$,

$Tail'(\pi(y))$ is tree-blocked by $\psi(Tail'(\pi(y)))$. If $Tail'(\pi(y))$ is a $R_{\geq,n}$-successor of $Tail(\pi(x))$, then $\mu(y) = \psi(Tail'(\pi(y)))$ is a $R_{\geq,n}$-successor of $\mu(x) = \psi(Tail'(\pi(x)))$.

(c) If $\pi(x) \notin AfterBlocked(G_i)$ and $\pi(y) \in AfterBlocked(G_i)$, then $Tail(\pi(x)) \neq Tail'(\pi(x))$ and $Tail(\pi(x)) = \psi(Tail'(\pi(x)))$. If $Tail'(\pi(y))$ is a $R_{\geq,n}$-successor of $Tail(\pi(x))$, then $\mu(y) = Tail'(\pi(y))$ is a $R_{\geq,n}$-successor of $\mu(x) = \psi(Tail'(\pi(x)))$.

The proof for case (2) is in a similar way with case (1).

Since μ has the Property 1-3, $q \rightarrowtail \mathcal{F}$ holds.

Example 8. Since $Vr(G_\pi) = \varnothing$ and G_π is connected, the only connected component of G_π is itself. We have $Blocked(G_\pi) = \{p_6\}$, and $AfterBlocked(G_\pi) = \{p_7, p_8, v_5\}$. We obtain the mapping μ_1 from π by setting $\mu_1(x) = \psi(Tail'(p_6)) = o_3$, $\mu_1(y) = Tail'(p_7) = o_4$, $\mu_1(z) = Tail'(p_8) = o_5$, and $\mu_1(y_c) = v_5$. By Definition 9, $q_1 \rightarrowtail \mathcal{F}_1$.

Theorem 2. Let $k \geq n_q$. Then $\mathcal{K} \models q$ iff for each $\mathcal{F} \in \mathrm{ccf}_k(\mathbb{F}_\mathcal{K})$, it holds that $q \rightarrowtail \mathcal{F}$.

Proof. The if direction is easy. By Lemma 3, for each $\mathcal{F} \in \mathrm{ccf}_k(\mathbb{F}_\mathcal{K})$, $\mathcal{F} \models q$. Then, by Theorem 1, $\mathcal{K} \models q$. For the converse side, by Theorem 1, $\mathcal{F} \models q$ for each $\mathcal{F} \in \mathrm{ccf}_k(\mathbb{F}_\mathcal{K})$. By Lemma 6, $q \rightarrowtail \mathcal{F}$.

We can, from the only if direction of Theorem 2, establish our key result, which reduce query entailment $\mathcal{K} \models q$ to finding a mapping of q into every $\mathcal{F}$ in $\mathrm{ccf}_k(\mathbb{F}_\mathcal{K})$.

TERMINATION AND COMPLEXITY

For the standard reasoning tasks, e.g., knowledge base consistency, the combined complexity is measured in the size of the input knowledge base. For query entailment, the size of the query is additionally taken into account. The size of a knowledge base $\mathcal{K}$ or a query q is simply the number of symbols needed to write it over the alphabet of constructors, concept, role, individual, and variable names that occur in $\mathcal{K}$ or q, where numbers are encoded in binary. As for data complexity, we consider the ABox as the only input for the algorithm, i.e., the size of the TBox, the role hierarchy, and the query is fixed. When the size of the TBox, role hierarchy, and query is small compared to the size of the ABox, the data complexity of a reasoning problem is a more useful performance estimate since it tells us how the algorithm behaves when the number of assertions in the ABox increases.

Let $\mathcal{K} = \langle \mathcal{T}, \mathcal{R}, \mathcal{A} \rangle$ a $f\text{-}\mathcal{SHIF}(\mathbf{D})$ KB and q a fuzzy conjunctive query, we denote by $\| \mathcal{K}, q \|$ the string length of encoding $\mathcal{K}$ and q, $|\mathcal{A}|$ the sum of the numbers of fuzzy assertions and inequality assertions, $|\mathcal{R}|$ the number of role inclusion axioms, $|\mathcal{T}|$ the number of fuzzy GCIs, $\mathbf{c}$ the $sub(\mathcal{K}) \cup sub(C_q)$, where C_q is the set of concepts occurring in q, $\mathbf{r}$ the cardinality of $\mathbf{R}_\mathcal{K}$, $\mathbf{d} = |N^A| + |N^q|$. Note that, when the size of q, TBox $\mathcal{T}$, and RBox $\mathcal{R}$ is fixed, $\mathbf{c}$, $\mathbf{d}$, and $\mathbf{r}$ is linear in the size of $\| \mathcal{K}, q \|$, and is constant in $\mathcal{A}$.

Lemma 7. In a completion forest of $\mathcal{K}$, the maximal number of non-isomorphic k-trees is $T_k = 2^{p(\mathbf{c},\mathbf{d},\mathbf{r})^{k+1}}$, where $p(\mathbf{c},\mathbf{d},\mathbf{r})$ is some polynomial w.r.t. $\mathbf{c}, \mathbf{d}$, and $\mathbf{r}$.

Proof. Since $\mathcal{L}(x) \subseteq (sub(\mathcal{K}) \cup sub(C_q)) \times \{\geq\} \times (N^A \cup N^q)$, there are at most $2^{\mathbf{c}}\mathbf{d}$ node labels in a k-complete clash free completion forest $\mathcal{F}$ of $\mathcal{K}$. Each successor of such a node v may be a root node of a $(k-1)$-tree. If a node label of a k-tree contains some tripes of the form $\langle \exists R.C, \geq, n \rangle$ or $\langle \geq 2S, \geq, n \rangle$, the $\exists_{\geq}$-rule or $\geq_{\geq}$-rule is triggered and new nodes are added. The generating rules can be applied to each node at most $\mathbf{c}$ times. Each time it is applied, it generates at most two R-successors (if the label of the node contains $\langle \geq 2S, \geq, n \rangle$) for each role R. This gives a bound of $2\mathbf{c}$ R-successors for each role, and a bound of 2 $\mathbf{cr}$ successors for each node. Since $\mathcal{L}(\langle x, y \rangle) \subseteq \mathbf{R}_{\mathcal{K}} \times \{\geq\} \times (N^A \cup N^q)$, there are at most $2^{\mathbf{r}}\mathbf{d}$ different edge labels, and thus can link a node to one of its successor in $2^{\mathbf{r}}\mathbf{d}$ ways. Hence, there can be at most $2^{\mathbf{r}}\mathbf{d}$ combinations from a single node in a completion forest to its successors. Thus, the upper bound of the number of non-isomorphic k-trees is $T_k = 2^{\mathbf{c}}\mathbf{d}(2^{\mathbf{r}}\mathbf{d}T_{k-1})^{2\mathbf{cr}}$. Let $y = 2\mathbf{cr}$, $x = \mathbf{c} + \mathbf{r}y$, then

$$T_k = 2^x \mathbf{d}^{1+y}(T_{k-1})^y = 2^x \mathbf{d}^{1+y}(2^x \mathbf{d}^{1+y}(T_{k-2})^y)^y = \ldots$$
$$= (2^x \mathbf{d}^{1+y})^{1+y+\ldots+y^{k-1}}(T_0)^{y^k} \leq (2^x \mathbf{d}^{1+y}T_0)^{y^k}.$$

Since $T_0 = 2^{\mathbf{c}}\mathbf{d}$, we have for $y \geq 2$ (It also holds for $y = 1$) that

$$T_k \leq (2^{\mathbf{c}+2\mathbf{cr}^2}\mathbf{d}^{1+2\mathbf{cr}}2^{\mathbf{c}})^{(2\mathbf{cr})^k} \leq (2^{2\mathbf{c}+2\mathbf{cr}^2+(1+2\mathbf{cr})\mathbf{d}})^{(2\mathbf{cr})^k}$$
$$\leq (2^{2\mathbf{c}^2+4\mathbf{c}^2\mathbf{r}^3+4\mathbf{c}^2\mathbf{r}^2\mathbf{d}})^{k+1} = 2^{p(\mathbf{c},\mathbf{d},\mathbf{r})^{k+1}}$$

where $p(\mathbf{c},\mathbf{d},\mathbf{r}) = 2\mathbf{c}^2 + 4\mathbf{c}^2\mathbf{r}^3 + 4\mathbf{c}^2\mathbf{r}^2\mathbf{d}$.

Lemma 8. The upper bound of the number of nodes in $\mathcal{F}$ is $O(\mathbf{I}_{\mathcal{K}}((\mathbf{cr})^{d+1}))$, where $d = (T_k + 1)k$.

Proof. By Lemma 7, there are at most T_k non-isomorphic k-trees. If there exists a path from v' to v with its length greater than $(T_k + 1)k$, then v would appear after a sequence of $T_k + 1$ non-overlapping k-trees, and one of them would have been blocked so that v would not be generated. The number of nodes in a k-tree is bounded by $(\mathbf{cr})^{d+1}$. The number of nodes in a $\mathcal{F}$ is bounded by $|\mathbf{I}_{\mathcal{K}}|(2\mathbf{cr})^{d+1}$.

Corollary 1. If k is linear in the size of $\| \mathcal{K}, q \|$, then the number of nodes in $\mathcal{F}$ is at most triple exponential in the size of $\| \mathcal{K}, q \|$; if the size of q, TBox $\mathcal{T}$, and RBox $\mathcal{R}$ is fixed, and k is a constant, then the number of nodes in $\mathcal{F}$ is polynomial in the size of $\mathcal{A}$.

Theorem 3. (Termination) The expansion of $\mathbb{F}_{\mathcal{K}}$ into a complete and clash free completion forest $\mathcal{F} \in \text{ccf}_k(\mathbb{F}_{\mathcal{K}})$ terminates in triple exponential time w.r.t. $\| \mathcal{K}, q \|$, and in polynomial time w.r.t. $|\mathcal{A}|$ if the size of q, TBox $\mathcal{T}$, and RBox $\mathcal{R}$ is fixed, and k is a constant.

Proof. By Lemma 8, the number of nodes in $\mathcal{F}$ is at most $|\mathbf{I}_\mathcal{K}|(2\mathbf{cr})^{d+1}$, written as M. We now make a case study of the numbers of the application of rules for expanding $\mathcal{F}_\mathcal{K}$ into $\mathcal{F}$. For each node, the $\sqcap$-rule and the $\sqcup$-rule may be used at most $O(\mathbf{c})$ times, and the $\exists_\geq$, $\forall_\geq$, $\forall_+$, $\forall_{+'}$ and $\geq_\geq$-rules may be used at most $O(cr)$ times. The number of the application of these rules is at most $O(Mcr)$ times. The number of the application of $\leq_{r_\geq}$-rule is at most $O(|\mathbf{I}_\mathcal{K}|)$ times. For each node, The number of the application of $\sqsubseteq$-rule is at most $O(\mathbf{d}|\mathcal{T}|)$ times, and is at most $O(M\mathbf{d}|\mathcal{T}|)$ times for M nodes. To sum up, the total number for the application of rules is at most $O(Mcr + M\mathbf{d}|\mathcal{T}|)$ times.

Theorem 4. Let $\mathcal{K}$ be a $f\text{-}\mathcal{SHIF}(\mathbf{D})$ KB and q a fuzzy conjunctive query in which all the roles are simple, deciding whether $\mathcal{K} \vDash q$ is in co3NexpTime w.r.t. combined complexity, and is in coNP w.r.t. data complexity.

Proof. If $\mathcal{K} \nvDash q$, there must exists a $\mathcal{F} \in \mathrm{ccf}\ \mathbb{F}_\mathcal{K}$, such that $q \rightarrowtail \mathcal{F}$ does not hold. Due to the existence of the nondeterministic rules, and by Theorem 3, the construction of $\mathcal{F}$ can be done in nondeterministic tripe exponential time in the size of $\|\mathcal{K},q\|$. By Corollary 1, the number of the nodes in $\mathcal{F}$ is at most triple exponential in the size of $\|\mathcal{K},q\|$. For a fuzzy CQ q with k variables, checking $\mathcal{F}$ for a mapping takes M^k times, which is tripe exponential in the size of $\|\mathcal{K},q\|$. Hence, deciding $\mathcal{K} \nvDash q$ is in 3NexpTime, and deciding $\mathcal{K} \models q$ is in co3NexpTime. Similarly, the data complexity deciding $\mathcal{K} \models q$ is in coNP.

CONCLUSION

Fuzzy Description Logics-based knowledge bases are envisioned to be useful in the Semantic Web. Existing fuzzy DL reasoners either are not capable of answering complex queries (mainly conjunctive queries), or only apply to DLs with less expressivity. We thus present an algorithm for answering expressive fuzzy conjunctive queries over the relative expressive DL, namely fuzzy $\mathcal{SHIF}(\mathbf{D})$. The algorithm we suggest here can easily be adapted to existing (and future) DL implementations. Future direction concern applying the proposed technique to more expressive fuzzy query language, e.g. in (Pan et al., 2008).

REFERENCES

Baader, F., Calvanese, D., McGuinness, D. L., Nardi, D., & Patel-Schneider, P. F. (Eds.). (2003). *The description logic handbook: Theory, implementation, and applications*. Cambridge University Press.

Baader, F., & Nutt, W. (2003). *Basic description logics* (pp. 43–95).

Bechhofer, S., Van Harmelen, F., Hendler, J., Horrocks, I., McGuinness, D., Patel-Schneider, P., et al. (2004). *OWL Web ontology language reference*. W3C recommendation.

Bobillo, F., & Straccia, U. (2008). fuzzydl: An expressive fuzzy description logic reasoner. *Proceedings of the 2008 IEEE International Conference on Fuzzy Systems*, (pp. 923–930).

Calvanese, D., De Giacomo, G., Lembo, D., Lenzerini, M., & Rosati, R. (2007). Tractable reasoning and efficient query answering in description logics: The dl-lite family. *Journal of Automated Reasoning, 39*(3), 385–429. doi:10.1007/s10817-007-9078-x

Calvanese, D., De Giacomo, G., & Lenzerini, M. (1998). On the decidability of query containment under constraints. *Proceedings of the 17th ACM SIGACT SIGMOD SIGART Symposium on Principles of Database Systems* (PODS'98), (pp. 149–158).

Glimm, B., Horrocks, I., & Sattler, U. (2007). Conjunctive query entailment for shoq. *Proceedings of the 2007 International Workshop on Description Logic* (DL 2007). CEUR Electronic Workshop Proceedings.

Glimm, B., Lutz, C., Horrocks, I., & Sattler, U. (2008). Conjunctive query answering for the description logic shiq. [JAIR]. *Journal of Artificial Intelligence Research, 31*, 157–204.

Krtzsch, M., Rudolph, S., & Hitzler, P. (2007). Conjunctive queries for a tractable fragment of owl 1.1. *Proceedings of the 6th International Semantic Web Conference* (ISWC 2007), 310–323.

Levy, A. Y., & Rousset, M.-C. (1998). Combining horn rules and description logics in carin. *Artificial Intelligence, 104*(1-2), 165–209. doi:10.1016/S0004-3702(98)00048-4

Lukasiewicz, T., & Straccia, U. (2008). Managing uncertainty and vagueness in description logics for the semantic Web. *Journal of Web Semantics, 6*(4), 291–308. doi:10.1016/j.websem.2008.04.001

Mailis, T. P., Stoilos, G., & Stamou, G. B. (2007). Expressive reasoning with horn rules and fuzzy description logics. *Proceedings of 2nd International Conference on Web Reasoning and Rule Systems* (RR'08).

Ortiz, M., Calvanese, D., & Eiter, T. (2006). Data complexity of answering unions of conjunctive queries in shiq. *Proceedings of the 2006 International Workshop on Description Logic.* CEUR Electronic Workshop Proceedings.

Ortiz, M., Calvanese, D., & Eiter, T. (2008). Data complexity of query answering in expressive description logics via tableaux. *Journal of Automated Reasoning, 41*(1), 61–98. doi:10.1007/s10817-008-9102-9

Pan, J. Z., Stamou, G. B., Stoilos, G., Taylor, S., & Thomas, E. (2008). Scalable querying services over fuzzy ontologies. *Proceedings of the 17th International World Wide Web Conference* (WWW2008), (pp. 575–584).

Rosati, R. (2007a). The limits of querying ontologies. *Proceedings of the 11th International Conference on Database Theory* (ICDT 2007), (pp. 164–178).

Rosati, R. (2007b). On conjunctive query answering in EL. *Proceedings of the 2007 International Workshop on Description Logic* (DL 2007). CEUR Electronic Workshop Proceedings.

Stoilos, G., Simou, N., Stamou, G. B., & Kollias, S. D. (2006). Uncertainty and the semantic Web. *IEEE Intelligent Systems, 21*(5), 84–87. doi:10.1109/MIS.2006.105

Stoilos, G., Stamou, G. B., Pan, J. Z., Tzouvaras, V., & Horrocks, I. (2007). Reasoning with very expressive fuzzy description logics. [JAIR]. *Journal of Artificial Intelligence Research, 30*, 273–320.

Stoilos, G., Straccia, U., Stamou, G. B., & Pan, J. Z. (2006). General concept inclusions in fuzzy description logics. *Proceedings of the 17th European Conference on Artificial Intelligence* (ECAI 2006), (pp. 457–461).

Straccia, U. (2001). Reasoning within fuzzy description logics. [JAIR]. *Journal of Artificial Intelligence Research, 14*, 137–166.

Straccia, U. (2006). Answering vague queries in fuzzy dl-lite. *Proceedings of the 11th International Conference on Information Processing and Management of Uncertainty in Knowledge-Based Systems* (IPMU-06), (pp. 2238–2245).

Zadeh, L. A. (1965). Fuzzy sets. *Information and Control, 8*(3), 338–353. doi:10.1016/S0019-9958(65)90241-X

KEY TERMS AND DEFINITIONS

Semantic Web: is a term coined by World Wide Web Consortium (W3C) director Sir Tim Berners-Lee. It describes methods and technologies to allow machines to understand the meaning - or "semantics" - of information on the World Wide Web.

Ontology: a formal, explicit specification of a shared conceptualisation.

Description Logics: a family of formal knowledge representation languages.

Conjunctive Queries: are simply the fragment of first-order logic given by the set of formulae that can be constructed from atomic formulae using conjunction and existential quantification, but not using disjunction, negation, or universal quantification.

Knowledge Base: is a special kind of database for knowledge management, providing the means for the computerized collection, organization, and retrieval of knowledge.

Tableau: is a decision procedure for sentential and related logics, and a proof procedure for formulas of first-order logic. The tableau method can also determine the satisfiability of finite sets of formulas of various logics. It is the most popular proof procedure for modal logics. The method of semantic tableaux was invented by the Dutch logician Evert Willem Beth.

Completion Forests: are finite relational structures that represent sets of models of a knowledge base.

Chapter 11
Relational Techniques for Storing and Querying RDF Data:
An Overview

Sherif Sakr
University of New South Wales, Australia

Ghazi Al-Naymat
University of New South Wales, Australia

ABSTRACT

The Resource Description Framework (RDF) is a flexible model for representing information about resources in the Web. With the increasing amount of RDF data which is becoming available, efficient and scalable management of RDF data has become a fundamental challenge to achieve the Semantic Web vision. The RDF model has attracted attentions in the database community and many researchers have proposed different solutions to store and query RDF data efficiently. This chapter focuses on using relational query processors to store and query RDF data. It gives an overview of the different approaches and classifies them according to their storage and query evaluation strategies.

INTRODUCTION

The *Semantic Web* term is coined by W3C founder Tim Berners-Lee in a Scientific American article describing the future of the Web (Berners-Lee et al., 2001). The main purpose of the Semantic Web vision is to provide a common framework for data-sharing across applications, enterprises, and communities. By giving data semantic meaning (through metadata), this framework allows machines to consume, understand, and reason about the structure and purpose of the data. The core of the Semantic Web is built on the Resource Description Framework (RDF) data model (Manola & Miller, 2004).

The RDF model is designed to have a simple data model, with a formal semantics and provable inference, with an extensible URI-based vocabulary that allows anyone to make statements about any

DOI: 10.4018/978-1-60960-475-2.ch011

resource. Hence, in the RDF model, the universe is modeled as set of resources where a resource is defined as anything that can have a universal resource identifier (URI). RDF describes a particular resource using a set of RDF statements of the form (subject, predicate, object) triples, also known as (subject, property, value). The *subject* is the resource, the *predicate* is the characteristic being described, and the *object* is the value for that characteristic.

Efficient and scalable management of RDF data is a fundamental challenge at the core of the Semantic Web. Several research efforts have been proposed to address these challenges (Abadi et al., 2009; Alexaki et al., 2001; Broekstra et al., 2002; Harth & Decker, 2005; Ma et al., 2004; Weiss et al., 2008). Relational database management systems (RDBMSs) have repeatedly shown that they are very efficient, scalable and successful in hosting types of data which have formerly not been anticipated to be stored inside relational databases such complex objects (TÆurker & Gertz, 2001), spatio-temporal data (Botea et al., 2008) and XML data (Grust et al., 2004). RDMBSs derive much of their performance from sophisticated optimizer components which makes use of physical properties that are specific to the relational model such as: sortedness, proper join ordering and powerful indexing mechanisms.

This chapter focuses on using relational query processors to store and query RDF data. We give an overview of the different approaches and classifies them according to their storage and indexing strategy. The rest of the chapter is organized as follows. Section (RDF-SPARQL Preliminaries) introduces preliminaries of RDF data model and the W3C standard RDF query language, SPARQL. It also introduces the main alternative relational approaches for storing and querying RDF. Sections (Vertical (Triple) Stores, Property Table Stores, and Horizontal Stores) provide the details of the different techniques in each of the alternative relational approaches. Section (Experimental Evaluation) presents an experimental comparison between representatives of the different approaches. Finally, Section (Concluding Remarks) concludes the chapter and provides some suggestions for possible future research directions on the subject.

RDF-SPARQL PRELIMINARIES

The Resource Description Framework (RDF) is a W3C recommendation that has rapidly gained popularity a means of expressing and exchanging semantic metadata, i.e., data that specifies semantic information about data. RDF was originally designed for the representation and processing of metadata about remote information sources and defines a model for describing relationships among resources in terms of uniquely identified attributes and values. The basic building block in RDF is a simple tuple model, (subject, predicate, object), to express different types of knowledge in the form of fact statements. The interpretation of each statement is that subject S has property P with value O, where S and P are resource URIs and O is either a URI or a literal value. Thus, any object from one triple can play the role of a subject in another triple which amounts to chaining two labeled edges in a graph-based structure. Thus, RDF allows a form of reification in which any RDF statement itself can be the subject or object of a triple. One of the clear advantage of the RDF data model is its schema-free structure in comparison to the entity-relationship model where the entities, their attributes and relationships to other entities are strictly defined. RDF is not a syntax (i.e. data format). There exist various RDF syntaxes (e.g. Notation 3 (N3) language, Turtle, XML) and depending on the application space one syntax may be more appropriate than another. In RDF, the schema may evolve over the time which fits well with the modern notion of data management, dataspaces, and its *pay-as-you-go* philosophy (Jeffery et al., 2008). Figure 1 illustrates a sample RDF graph.

Figure 1. Sample RDF graph

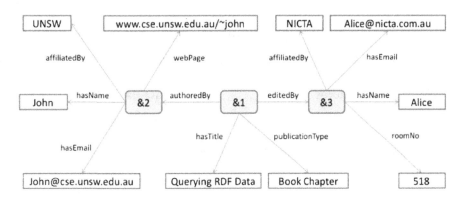

Figure 2. Sample SPARQL query

```
SELECT   ?Z
WHERE    ?X  hasTitle "Querying RDF Data"
         ?X  publicationType "Book Chapter"
         ?X  authoredBy ?Y
         ?y  webPage ?Z
```

The SPARQL query language is the official W3C standard for querying and extracting information from RDF graphs (Prud'hommeaux & Seaborne, 2008). RDF is a directed labeled graph data format and, thus, SPARQL is essentially a graph-matching query language. It represents the counterpart to *select-project-join* queries in the relational model. It is based on a powerful graph matching facility, allows binding variables to components in the input RDF graph and supports conjunctions and disjunctions of triple patterns. In addition, operators akin to relational joins, unions, left outer joins, selections, and projections can be combined to build more expressive queries. A basic SPARQL query has the form:

```
select ?variable1 ?variable2...
 where { pattern1. pattern2.... }
```

Figure 3 illustrates a general classification for RDF tripe stores based on their storage models Ma et al. (2008). In principle, RDF stores can be divided into two major categories: *native* stores and *database-based* stores. Native stores are directly built on the file system, whereas database based repositories use relational or object relational databases as the backend store. Representative native stores include OWLIM (Kiryakov et al., 2005), HStar (Ma et al., 2008), AllegroGraph (*AllegroGraph RDFStore*, 2009) and YARs (Harth & Decker, 2005). Representative of ontology-dependent stores include DLDB (Pan & Heflin, 2003; Pan et al., 2008) and Sesame (Broekstra et al., 2002). The main focus of this chapter is to give an overview of the *generic relational* approaches for processing RDF data.

In general, relational database management systems (RDBMSs) have repeatedly shown that they are very efficient, scalable and successful in hosting types of data which have formerly not been anticipated to be stored inside relational databases. In addition, RDBMSs have shown its ability to handle

Figure 3. Classification of RDF triple stores

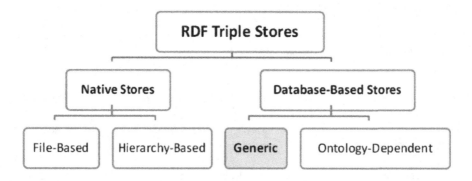

Figure 4. Relational representation of triple RDF stores

Subject	Predicate	Object
Id1	publicationType	Book Chapter
Id1	hasTitle	Querying RDF Data
Id1	authoredBy	Id2
Id2	hasName	John
Id2	affiliatedBy	UNSW
Id2	hasEmail	John@cse.unsw.edu.au
Id2	webPage	www.cse.unsw.edu.au/~john
Id1	editedBy	Id3
Id3	hasName	Alice
Id3	affiliatedBy	NICTA
Id3	hasEmail	Alice@nicta.com.au
Id3	roomNo	518

```
Select T3.Object
From Triples as T1, Triples as T2,
        Triples as T3, Triples as T4
Where
T1.Predicate="publicationType" and
T1.Object="Book Chapter"
and T2.predicate="hasTitle"
and T2.Object="Querying RDF Data"
and T3.Predicate="webPage"
and T1.subject=T2.subject
and T4.subject=T1.subject
and T4.Predicate="authoredBy"
and T4.Object = T3.Subject
```

vast amounts of data very efficiently using its powerful indexing mechanisms. In principle, RDMBSs derive much of their performance from sophisticated optimizer components which makes use of physical properties that are specific to the relational model such as: sortedness, proper join ordering and powerful indexing mechanisms. In fact, a main advantage of the relational-based approach of processing RDF data is that it can makes use of a large and robust body of work on query planning and optimization available in the infrastructure of relation query engines to implement efficient and scalable SPARQL query processors. For example, Cyganiak (2005) presented an approach for compiling SPARQL queries into standard relational algebraic plans. The relational RDF stores can be mainly classified to the following categories:

1. **Vertical (triple) table stores**: where each RDF triple is stored directly in a three-column table (subject, predicate, object).
2. **Property (n-ary) table stores**: where multiple RDF properties are modeled as n-ary table columns for the same subject.
3. **Horizontal (binary) table stores**: where RDF triples are modeled as one horizontal table or into a set of vertically partitioned binary tables (one table for each RDF property).

Figure 5. Relational representation of property tables RDF stores

Publication

ID	publicationType	hasTitle	authoredBy	editedBy
Id1	Book Chapter	Querying RDF Data	Id2	id3

Person

ID	hasName	affiliatedBy	hasEmail	webPage	roomNo
Id2	John	UNSW	John@cse.unsw.edu.au	www.cse.unsw.edu.au/~john	
Id3	Alice	NICTA	Alice@nicta.com.au		518

```
Select  Person.webPage
From Person, Publication
Where Publication.publicationType = "Book Chapter"
and  Publication.hasTitle = "Querying RDF Data"
and  Publication.authoredBy = Person.ID
```

Figure 6. Relational representation of binary tables RDF stores

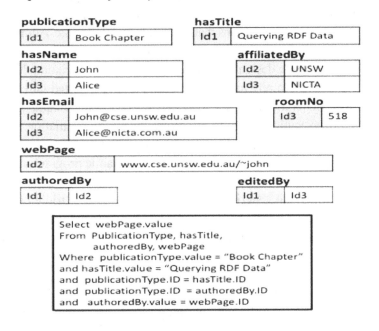

```
Select  webPage.value
From  PublicationType, hasTitle,
        authoredBy, webPage
Where  publicationType.value = "Book Chapter"
and hasTitle.value = "Querying RDF Data"
and  publicationType.ID = hasTitle.ID
and  publicationType.ID  = authoredBy.ID
and  authoredBy.value = webPage.ID
```

Figures 4, 5 and 6 illustrate examples of the three alternative relational representation of the sample RDF graph (Figure 1) and their associated SQL queries for evaluating the sample SPARQL query (Figure 2).

VERTICAL (TRIPLE) STORES

A naive way to store a set of RDF statements is using a relational database with a single table including columns for subject, property, and object. While simple, this schema quickly hits scalability limitations.

Therefore, several approaches have been proposed to deal with this limitation by using extensive set of indexes or by using selectivity estimation information to optimize the join ordering.

Harris & Gibbins (2003) have described the 3store RDF storage system. The storage system of 3Store is based on a central triple table which holds the hashes for the subject, predicate, object and graph identifier. The graph identifier equal to zero if the triple resides in the anonymous background graph. A symbols table is used to allow reverse lookups from the hash to the hashed value, for example, to return results. Furthermore it allows SQL operations to be performed on pre-computed values in the data types of the columns without the use of casts. For evaluating SPARQL queries, the triples table is joined once for each triple in the graph pattern where variables are bound to their values when they encounter the slot in which the variable appears. Subsequent occurrences of variables in the graph pattern are used to constrain any appropriate joins with their initial binding. To produce the intermediate results table, the hashes of any SPARQL variables required to be returned in the results set are projected and the hashes from the intermediate results table are joined to the symbols table to provide the textual representation of the results.

Neumann & Weikum (2008) have presented the RDF-3X (RDF Triple eXpress) RDF query engine which tries to overcome the criticism that triples stores incurs too many expensive self-joins by creating the exhaustive set of indexes and relying on fast processing of merge joins. The physical design of RDF-3x is workload-independent and eliminates the need for physical-design tuning by building indexes over all 6 permutations of the three dimensions that constitute an RDF triple. Additionally, indexes over count-aggregated variants for all three two-dimensional and all three one-dimensional projections. The query processor follows RISC-style design philosophy (Chaudhuri & Weikum, 2000) by using the full set of indexes on the triple tables to rely mostly on merge joins over sorted index lists. The query optimizer relies upon its cost model in finding the lowest-cost execution plan and mostly focuses on join order and the generation of execution plans. In principle, selectivity estimation has a huge impact on plan generation. While this is a standard problem in database systems, the schema-free nature of RDF data makes the problem more challenging. RDF-3X employs dynamic programming for plan enumeration, with a cost model based on RDF-specific statistical synopses. It relies on two kinds of statistics: 1) specialized histograms which are generic and can handle any kind of triple patterns and joins. The disadvantage of histograms is that it assumes independence between predicates. 2) frequent join paths in the data which give more accurate estimation. During query optimization, the query optimizer uses the join-path selectivity information when available and otherwise assume independence and use the histograms information. Neumann & Weikum (2009) have extended the work further by introducing a runtime technique for accelerating query executions. It uses a light-weight, RDF-specific technique for sideways information passing across different joins and index scans within the query execution plans. They have also enhanced the selectivity estimator of the query optimizer by using very fast index lookups on specifically designed aggregation indexes, rather than relying on the usual kinds of coarse-grained histograms. This provides much more accurate estimates at compile-time, at a fairly small cost that is easily amortized by providing better directives for the join-order optimization.

Weiss et al. (2008) have presented the Hexastore RDF storage scheme with main focuses on scalability and generality in its data storage, processing and representation. Hexastore is based on the idea of indexing the RDF data in a multiple indexing scheme (Harth & Decker, 2005). It does not discriminate against any RDF element and treats subjects, properties and objects equally. Each RDF element type have its special index structures built around it. Moreover, every possible ordering of the importance or precedence of the three elements in an indexing scheme is materialized. Each index structure in a Hexastore centers around one RDF element and defines a prioritization between the other two elements. Two vectors are associated with each RDF element (e.g., subject), one for each of the other two RDF elements (e.g., property and object). In addition, lists of the third RDF element are appended to the elements in these vectors. In total, six distinct indices are used for indexing the RDF data. These indices materialize all possible orders of precedence of the three RDF elements. A clear disadvantage of this approach is that Hexastore features a worst-case fivefold storage increase in comparison to a conventional triples table.

PROPERTY TABLE STORES

Due to the proliferations of self-joins involved with the triple-store, the property table approach was proposed. The main idea of this approach is to create separate *n-ary* tables (property tables) for subjects that tend to have common properties together in a single table. Hence, designing the schema of the property tables depends on the availability of either explicit or implicit information about the characteristics of the objects in the RDF dataset.

Jena is a an open-source toolkit for Semantic Web programmers (McBride, 2002). It implements persistence for RDF graphs using an SQL database through a JDBC connection. The schema of the first version of Jena, Jena1, consisted of a statement table, a literals table and a resources table. The statement table *(Subject, Predicate, ObjectURI, ObjectLiteral)* contained all statements and referenced the resources and literals tables for subjects, predicates and objects. To distinguish literal objects from resource URIs, two columns were used. The literals table contained all literal values and the resources table contained all resource URIs in the graph. However, every query operation required multiple joins between the statement table and the literals table or the resources table.

To address this problem, the Jena2 schema trades-off space for time. It uses a denormalized schema in which resource URIs and simple literal values are stored directly in the statement table. In order to distinguish database references from literals and URIs, column values are encoded with a prefix that indicates which the kind of value. A separate literals table is only used to store literal values whose length exceeds a threshold, such as blobs. Similarly, a separate resources table is used to store long URIs. By storing values directly in the statement table it is possible to perform many queries without a join. However, a denormalized schema uses more database space because the same value (literal or URI) is stored repeatedly. The increase in database space consumption is addressed by using string compression schemes. Both Jena1 and Jena2 permit multiple graphs to be stored in a single database instance. In Jena1, all graphs were stored in a single statement. However, Jena2 supports the use of multiple statement tables in a single database so that applications can flexibly map graphs to different tables. In this way, graphs that are often accessed together may be stored together while graphs that are never accessed together may be stored separately.

In principle, applications typically have access patterns in which certain subjects and/or properties are accessed together. For example, a graph of data about persons might have many occurrences of objects with properties name, address, phone, and gender that are referenced together. Jena2 uses property table as a general facility for clustering properties that are commonly accessed together. A property table is a separate table that stores the subject-value pairs related by a particular property. A property table stores all instances of the property in the graph where that property does not appear in any other table used for the graph. In Jena1, each query is evaluated with a single SQL select query over the statement table. In Jena2, queries have to be generalized because there can be multiple statement tables for a graph.

Using the knowledge of the frequent access patterns to construct the property-tables and influence the underlying database storage structures can provide a performance benefit and reduce the number of join operations during the query evaluation process.

Chong et al. (2005) have introduced an Oracle-based SQL table function *RDFMATCH* to query RDF data. The results of RDFMATCH table function can be further processed by SQLs rich querying capabilities and seamlessly combined with queries on traditional relational data. The core implementation of RDFMATCH query translates to a self-join query on Triple-based RDF table store. The resulting query is executed efficiently by making use of B-tree indexes as well as creating materialized join views for specialized subject-property. Subject-Property Matrix materialized join views is used To minimize the query processing overheads that are inherent in the canonical triples-based representation of RDF. The materialized join views are incrementally maintained based on user demand and query workloads. A special module is provided to analyze table of RDF triples and estimate the size of various materialized views, based on which a user can define a subset of materialized views. For a group of subjects, the system defines a set of single-valued properties that occur together. These can be direct properties of these subjects or nested properties. A property p1 is a direct property of subject x_1 if there is a triple (x_1,p_1,x_2). A property pm is a nested property of subject x_1 if there is a set of triples such as, $(x_1,p_1,x_2),...,$ (x_m,p_m,x_{m+1}), where m> 1. For example, if there is a set of triples, (John, address, addr1), (addr1, zip, 03062), then zip is a nested property of *John*.

Levandoski & Mokbel (2009) have presented another property table approach for storing RDF data without any assumption about the query workload statistics. The main goals of this approach are: (1) reducing the number of join operations which are required during the RDF query evaluation process by storing related RDF properties together (2) reducing the need to process extra data by tuning null storage to fall below a given threshold. The approach provides a *tailored* schema for each RDF data set which represents a balance between property tables and binary tables and is based on two main parameters: 1) *Support threshold* which represents a value to measure the strength of correlation between properties in the RDF data. 2) The *null threshold* which represents the percentage of null storage tolerated for each table in the schema. The approach involves two phases: *clustering* and *partitioning*. The clustering phase scans the RDF data to automatically discover groups of related properties (i.e., properties that always exist together for a large number of subjects). Based on the support threshold, each set of n properties which are grouped together in the same cluster are good candidates to constitute a single n-ary table and the properties which are not grouped in any cluster are good candidates for storage in binary tables. The partitioning phase goes over the formed clusters and balances the tradeoff between storing as many RDF properties in clusters as possible while keeping null storage to a minimum based on the null threshold. One of the main concerns of the partitioning phase is twofold: is to ensure the non-overlapping between the clusters and that each property exists in a single cluster and reduces the number of table accesses and unions necessary in query processing.

Matono et al. (2005) have proposed a path-based relational RDF database. The main focus of this approach is to improve the performance for path queries by extracting all reachable path expressions for each resource, and store them. Thus, there is no need to perform join operations unlike the flat tripe stores or the property tables approach. In this approach, the RDF graph is divided into subgraphs and then each subgraph is stored by applicable techniques into distinct relational tables. More precisely, all classes and properties are extracted from RDF schema data, and all resources are also extracted from RDF data. Each extracted item is assigned an identifier and a path expression and stored in corresponding relational table.

HORIZONTAL STORES

Abadi et al. (2009) have presented *SW-Store* a new DBMS which is storing RDF data using a fully decomposed storage model (DSM) (Copeland & Khoshafian, 1985). In this approach, the triples table is rewritten into *n* two-column tables where *n* is the number of unique properties in the data. In each of these tables, the first column contains the subjects that define that property and the second column contains the object values for those subjects while the subjects that do not define a particular property are simply omitted from the table for that property. Each table is sorted by subject, so that particular subjects can be located quickly, and that fast merge joins can be used to reconstruct information about multiple properties for subsets of subjects. For a multivalued attribute, each distinct value is listed in a successive row in the table for that property. One advantage of this approach is that while property tables need to be carefully constructed so that they are wide enough but not too wide to independently answer queries, the algorithm for creating tables in the vertically partitioned approach is straightforward and need not change over time. Moreover, in the property-class schema approach, queries that do not restrict on class tend to have many union clauses while in the vertically partitioned approach, all data for a particular property is located in the same table and thus union clauses in queries are less common. The implementation of SW-Store relies on a column-oriented DBMS, C-store (Stonebraker et al., 2005), to store tables as collections of columns rather than as collections of rows. In standard row-oriented databases (e.g., Oracle, DB2, SQLServer, Postgres, etc.) entire tuples are stored consecutively. The problem with this is that if only a few attributes are accessed per query, entire rows need to be read into memory from disk before the projection can occur. By storing data in columns rather than rows projection occurs for freeonly those columns relevant to a query need to be read.

Beckmann et al. (2006); Chu et al. (2007) have argued that storing a sparse data set (like RDF) in multiple tables can cause problems. They suggested storing a sparse data set in a single table while the complexities of sparse data management can be handled inside an RDBMS with the addition of an interpreted storage format. The proposed format starts with a header which contains fields such as relation-id, tuple-id, and a tuple length. When a tuple has a value for an attribute, the attribute identifier, a length field (if the type is of variable length), and the value appear in the tuple. The attribute identifier is the id of the attribute in the system catalog while the attributes that appear in the system catalog but not in the tuple are null for that tuple. Since the interpreted format stores nothing for null attributes, sparse data sets in a horizontal schema can in general be stored much more compactly in the format. While the interpreted format has storage benefits for sparse data, retrieving the values from attributes in tuples is more complex. In fact, the format is called interpreted because the storage system must discover the attributes and values of a tuple at tuple-access time, rather than using precompiled position information from a catalog, as the positional format allows. To tackle this problem, a new operator (called EXTRACT operator) is introduced to the query plans to precede any reference to attributes stored in the interpreted format and returns the offsets to the referenced interpreted attribute values which is then used to retrieve the values. Value extraction from an interpreted record is a potentially expensive operation that is dependent on the number attributes stored in a row, or the length of the tuple. Moreover, if a query evaluation plan fetches each attribute individually and uses an EXTRACT call per attribute, the record will be scanned for each attribute and will be very slow. Thus, a batch EXTRACT technique is used to allow one scan of the present values and saves time. Table 1 provides a summary of the relational techniques for processing RDF queries in terms of their representative approaches and their specific query optimization techniques.

Table 1. Summary of relational techniques for processing RDF queries

Query Engine	Class	Optimization Technique(s)
3store (Harris & Gibbins, 2003)	Vertical Store	Hash tables
RDF-3X (Neumann & Weikum, 2008)	Vertical Store	Exhaustive indexing of all permutations of (S,P,O) Merge joins, Cost-based query optimization
Hexastore (Weiss et al., 2008)	Vertical Store	Materialization of all orders of the 3 RDF elements
RDFMATCH (Chong et al., 2005)	Property Tables	Materialized join views based on user demand and query workloads
(Levandoski & Mokbel, 2009)	Property Tables	Automated inference independent of query workloads
(Matono et al., 2005)	Property Tables	Path-based storage of RDF data
SW-Store (Abadi et al., 2009)	Horizontal Stores	Column-oriented storage of RDF data

EXPERIMENTAL EVALUATION

In this section, we present an experimental evaluation for the different approaches which are relying on the relational infrastructure to provide scalable engines to store and query RDF data (MahmoudiNasab & Sakr, 2010).

SP²Bench Performance Benchmark

Schmidt et al. (2009) have presented the **SP**ARQL **P**erformance **Bench**mark (SP²Bench) which is based on the DBLP scenario (*DBLP XML Records*, 2009). The DBLP database presents an extensive bibliographic information about the field of Computer Science and, particularly, databases. The benchmark is accompanied with a data generator which supports the creation of arbitrarily large DBLP-like models in RDF format. This data generator mirrors the vital key characteristics and distributions of the original DBLP dataset. The logical RDF schema for the DBLP dataset consists of *Authors* and *Editors* entities which are representation types of *Persons*. A superclass *Document* which is decomposed into several sub-classes: *Proceedings, Inproceedings, Journal, Article, Book, PhDThesis, MasterThesis, Incollection, WWW resources*. The RDF graph representation of these entities reflects their instantiation and the different types of relationship between them.

In addition, the benchmark provides 17 queries defined using the SPARQL query language on top of the structure of the DBLP dataset in a way to cover the most important SPARQL constructs and operator constellations. The defined queries vary in their complexity and result size. Table 2 lists the SP²Bench Benchmark Queries. For more details about the benchmark specification, data generation algorithm and SPARQL definition of the benchmark queries, we refer the reader to (Schmidt et al., 2009).

Experimental Settings

Our experimental evaluation of the alternative relational RDF storage techniques are conducted using the IBM DB2 DBMS running on a PC with 3.2 GHZ Intel Xeon processors, 4 GB of main memory storage and 250 GB of SCSI secondary storage. We used the SP2Bench data generator to produce four different testing datasets with number of triples equal to: 500K, 1M, 2M and 4M Triples. In our evaluation, we consider the following four alternative relational storage schemes:

Table 2. SP²bench benchmark queries

Q1	Return the year of publication of "Journal 1 (1940)"
Q2	Extract all proceedings with properties: creatore, booktitle, issued, part of, seeAlso, title, pages, homepage, and optionally abstract, including their values
Q3abc	Select all articles with property (a) pages (b) month (c) isbn
Q4	Select all distinct pairs of article author names for authors that have published in the same journal
Q5	Return the names of all persons that occur as author o at least one proceeding and at least one article
Q6	Return, for each year, the set of all publications authored by persons that have not published in years before
Q7	Return the titles of all papers that have been cited at least once, but not by any paper that has not been cited itself
Q8	Compute authors that have published with Paul Erdos or with an author that has published with Paul Erdos
Q9	Return incoming and outgoing properties of persons
Q10	Return publications and venues in which "Paul Erdos" is involved either as author or as editor.
Q11	Return top 10 electronic edition URLs starting from the 51th publication, in lexicographical order.
Q12abc	(a) Return yes if a person is an author of at least one proceeding and article. (b) return yes if an author has published with "Paul Erdos" or with an author that has published with "Paul Erdos" (c) Return yes if person "John Q. Public" exists.

1. **Triple Stores (TS)**: where a single relational table is used to store the whole set of RDF triples (subject, predicate, object). We follow the RDF-3X and build indexes over all 6 permutations of the three fields of each RDF triple.
2. **Binary Table Stores (BS)**: for each unique predicate in the RDF data, we create a binary table (ID, Value) and two indexes over the permutations of the two fields are built.
3. **Traditional Relational Stores (RS)**: In this scheme, we use the Entity Relationship Model of the DBLP dataset and follow the traditional way of designing normalized relational schema where we build a separate table for each entity (with its associated descriptive attributes) and use foreign keys to represent the relationships between the different objects. We build specific partitioned B-tree indexes Graefe (2003) for each table based on the referenced attributes in the benchmark queries.
4. **Property Table Stores (PS)**: where we use the schema of RS and decompose each entity with number of attributes ≥ 4 into two subject-property tables. The decomposition is done blindly and based on the order of the attributes without considering the benchmark queries (workload independent).

Performance Metrics

We measure and compare the performance of the alternative relational RDF storage techniques using the following metrics:

1. **Loading Time**: represents the period of time for shredding the RDF dataset into the relational tables of the storage scheme.
2. **Storage Cost**: depicts the size of the storage disk space which is consumed by the relational storage schemes for storing the RDF dataset.
3. **Query Performance**: represents the execution times for the different SQL-translation of the SPARQL queries of SP²Bench over the alternative relational storage schemes.

All reported numbers of the query performance metric are the average of five executions with the highest and the lowest values removed. The rational behind this is that the first reading of each query is always expensively inconsistent with the other readings. This is because the relational database uses buffer pools as a caching mechanism. The initial period when the database spends its time loading pages into the buffer pools is known as the warm up period. During this period the response time of the database declines with respect to the normal response time. For all metrics: the lower the metric value, the better the approach.

Experimental Results

Table 3 summarizes the loading times for shredding the different datasets into the alternative relational representations. The *RS* scheme is the fastest due to the less required number of insert tuple operations. Similarly, the *TS* requires less loading time than *BS* since the number of inserted tuples and updated tables are smaller for each triple.

Table 4 summarizes the storage cost for the alternative relational representations. The *RS* scheme represents the cheapest approach because of the normalized design and the absence of any data redundancy. Due to the limited percentage of the sparsity in the DBLP dataset, the *PS* does not introduce any additional cost in the storage space except a little overhead due to the redundancy of the object identification attributes in the decomposed property tables. The *BS* scheme represents the most expensive approach due to the redundancy of the *ID* attributes for each binary table. It should be also noted that the storage cost of *TS* and *BS* are affected by the additional sizes of their associated indexes.

Table 5 summarizes the query performance for the SP²Bench benchmark queries over the alternative relational representations using the different sizes of the dataset. Remarks about the results of this experiment are given as follows:

1. There is no clear winner between the triple store (*TS*) and the binary table (*BS*) encoding schemes. Triple store (*TS*) with its simple storage and the huge number of tuples in the encoding relation is still very competitive to the binary tables encoding scheme because of the full set of B-tree physical indexes over the permutations of the three encoding fields (subject, predicate, object).

2. The query performance of the (*BS*) encoding scheme is affected badly by the increase of the number of the predicates in the input query. It is also affected by the *subject-object* or *object-object* type of joins where no index information is available for utilization. Such problem could be solved by building materialized views over the columns of the most frequently referenced pairs of attributes.

Table 3. A comparison between the alternative relational RDF storage techniques in terms of their loading times

Dataset	Loading Time (in seconds)			
	Triple Stores	**Binary Tables**	**Traditional Relational**	**Property Tables**
500K	282	306	212	252
1M	577	586	402	521
2M	1242	1393	931	1176
$M	2881	2936	1845	2406

3. Although their generality, there is still a clear gap between the query performance of the (*TS*) and (*BS*) encoding schemes in comparison with the tailored relational encoding scheme (*RS*) of the RDF data. However, designing a tailored relational schema requires a detailed information about the structure of the represented objects in the RDF dataset. Such information is not always available and designing a tailored relational schema limits the schema-free advantage of the RDF data because any new object with a variant schema will require applying a change in the schema of the underlying relational structure. Hence, we believe that there is still required efforts to improve the performance of these generic relational RDF storages and reduce the query performance gap with the tailored relational encoding schemes.

4. The property tables encoding schemes (*PS*) are trying to fill the gap between the generic encoding schemes (*TS* and *BS*) and the tailored encoding schemes (*RS*). The results of our experiments show that the (*PS*) encoding scheme can achieve a comparable query performance to the (*RS*) encoding scheme. However, designing the schema of the property tables requires either explicit or implicit

Table 4. A comparison between the alternative relational RDF storage techniques in terms of their storage cost

Dataset	Storage Cost (in KB)			
	Triple Stores	Binary Tables	Traditional Relational	Property Tables
500K	24721	32120	8175	10225
1M	48142	64214	17820	21200
2M	96251	128634	36125	43450
4M	192842	257412	73500	86200

Table 5. A comparison between the alternative relational RDF storage techniques in terms of their query performance (in milliseconds)

	1M				2M				4M			
	TS	BS	RS	PS	TS	BS	RS	PS	TS	BS	RS	PS
Q1	1031	1292	606	701	1982	2208	1008	1262	3651	3807	1988	2108
Q2	1672	1511	776	1109	2982	3012	1606	1987	5402	5601	2308	3783
Q3a	982	1106	61	116	1683	1873	102	198	3022	3342	191	354
Q3b	754	883	46	76	1343	1408	87	132	2063	2203	176	218
Q3c	1106	1224	97	118	1918	2109	209	275	3602	3874	448	684
Q4	21402	21292	11876	14116	38951	37642	20192	25019	66354	64119	39964	48116
Q5	1452	1292	798	932	2754	2598	1504	1786	5011	4806	3116	35612
Q6	2042	1998	1889	2109	3981	3966	3786	4407	7011	6986	6685	8209
Q7	592	30445	412	773	1102	58556	776	1546	2004	116432	1393	2665
Q8	9013	8651	1683	1918	15932	13006	3409	3902	27611	24412	8012	8609
Q9	2502	15311	654	887	4894	26113	1309	1461	9311	37511	2204	2671
Q10	383	596	284	387	714	1117	554	708	1306	2013	1109	1507
Q11	762	514	306	398	1209	961	614	765	2111	1704	1079	1461

information about the characteristics of the objects in the RDF dataset. Such explicit information cannot be always available and the process of inferring such implicit information introduces an additional cost of a pre-processing phase. Such challenges call for new techniques for flexible designs for the property tables encoding schemes.

CONCLUDING REMARKS

RDF is a main foundation for processing semantic information stored on the Web. It is the data model behind the Semantic Web vision whose goal is to enable integration and sharing of data across different applications and organizations. The naive way to store a set of RDF statements is using a relational database with a single table including columns for subject, property, and object. While simple, this schema quickly hits scalability limitations. Therefore, several approaches have been proposed to deal with this limitation by using extensive set of indexes or by using selectivity estimation information to optimize the join ordering (Neumann & Weikum, 2008; Weiss et al., 2008).

Another approach to reduce the self-join problem is to create separate tables (property tables) for subjects that tend to have common properties defined (Chong et al., 2005; Levandoski & Mokbel, 2009). Since Semantic Web data is often semi-structured, storing this data in a row-store can result in very sparse tables as more subjects or properties are added. Hence, this normalization technique is typically limited to resources that contain a similar set of properties and many small tables are usually created. The problem is that this may result in union and join clauses in queries since information about a particular subject may be located in many different property tables. This may complicate the plan generator and query optimizer and can degrade performance.

Abadi et al. (2009) has explored the trade-off between triple-based stores and binary tables-based stores of RDF data. The main advantages of binary tables are:

1. **Improved bandwidth utilization**: In a column store, only those attributes that are accessed by a query need to be read off disk. In a row-store, surrounding attributes also need to be read since an attribute is generally smaller than the smallest granularity in which data can be accessed.
2. **Improved data compression**: Storing data from the same attribute domain together increases locality and thus data compression ratio. Hence, bandwidth requirements are further reduced when transferring compressed data.

On the other side, binary tables have the following main disadvantages:

1. **Increased cost of inserts**: Column-stores perform poorly for insert queries since multiple distinct locations on disk have to be updated for each inserted tuple (one for each attribute).
2. **Increased tuple reconstruction costs**: In order for column-stores to offer a standards-compliant relational database interface (e.g., ODBC, JDBC, etc.), they must at some point in a query plan stitch values from multiple columns together into a row-store style tuple to be output from the database.

Abadi et al. (2009) reported that the performance of binary tables is superior to clustered property table while Sidirourgos et al. (2008) reported that even in column-store database, the performance of binary tables is not always better than clustered property table and depends on the characteristics of the data set. Moreover, the experiments of Abadi et al. (2009) reported that storing RDF data in column-store database is better than that of row-store database while Sidirourgos et al. (2008) experiments have shown that the gain of performance in column-store database depends on the number of predicates in a data set. Our experimental evaluation in addition to other independent benchmarking projects (Bizer & Schultz, 2008; Schmidt et al., 2008, 2009) have shown that no approach is dominant for all queries and none of these approaches can compete with a purely relational model. Therefore, it is clear that there is still room for optimization in the proposed generic relational RDF storage schemes and thus new techniques for storing and querying RDF data are still required to bring forward the Semantic Web vision.

REFERENCES

Abadi, D. J., Marcus, A., Madden, S., & Hollenbach, K. (2009). SW-Store: A vertically partitioned DBMS for Semantic Web data management. *The VLDB Journal, 18*(2), 385–406. doi:10.1007/s00778-008-0125-y

Alexaki, S., Christophides, V., Karvounarakis, G., Plexousakis, D., & Tolle, K. (2001). The ICS-FORTH RDFSuite: Managing voluminous RDF description bases. In *Proceedings of the 2nd International Workshop on the Semantic Web (semWeb)*.

AllegroGraph RDFStore. (2009). *Allegrograph*. Retrieved from http://www.franz.com/agraph/allegrograph/

Beckmann, J. L., Halverson, A., Krishnamurthy, R., & Naughton, J. F. (2006). Extending RDBMSs to support sparse datasets using an interpreted attribute storage format. In *Proceedings of the 22nd International Conference on Data Engineering,* (p. 58).

Berners-Lee, T., Hendler, J. & Lassila, O. (2001). The Semantic Web: A new form of Web content that is meaningful to computers will unleash a revolution of new possibilities. *Scientific American.*

Bizer, C., & Schultz, A. (2008). Benchmarking the performance of storage systems that expose SPARQL endpoints. In *Proceedings of the 4th International Workshop on Scalable Semantic Web Knowledge Base Systems.*

Botea, V., Mallett, D., Nascimento, M. A., & Sander, J. (2008). PIST: An efficient and practical indexing technique for historical spatio-temporal point data. *GeoInformatica, 12*(2), 143–168. doi:10.1007/s10707-007-0030-3

Broekstra, J., Kampman, A., & van Harmelen, F. (2002). Sesame: A generic architecture for storing and querying RDF and RDF schema. In *Proceedings of the First International Semantic Web Conference,* (p. 54-68).

Chaudhuri, S., & Weikum, G. (2000). Rethinking database system architecture: Towards a self-tuning RISC-style database system. In *Proceedings of 26th International Conference on Very Large Data Bases,* (p. 1-10).

Chong, E. I., Das, S., Eadon, G., & Srinivasan, J. (2005). An efficient SQL-based RDF querying scheme. In *Proceedings of the 31st International Conference on Very Large Data Bases,* (pp. 1216-1227).

Chu, E., Beckmann, J. L., & Naughton, J. F. (2007). The case for a wide-table approach to manage sparse relational data sets. In *Proceedings of the ACM SIGMOD International Conference on Management of Data,* (pp. 821-832).

Copeland, G. P., & Khoshafian, S. (1985). A decomposition storage model. In *Proceedings of the ACM SIGMOD International Conference on Management of Data,* (pp. 268-279).

Cyganiak, R. (2005). *A relational algebra for SPARQL.* (Tech. Rep. No. HPL-2005-170). HP Labs.

DBLP XML Records. (2009). *Home page information.* Retrieved from http://dblp.uni-trier.de/xml/

Graefe, G. (2003). Sorting and indexing with partitioned B-trees. In *Proceedings of the 1st International Conference on Data Systems Research.*

Grust, T., Sakr, S., & Teubner, J. (2004). XQuery on SQL hosts. In *Proceedings of the Thirtieth International Conference on Very Large Data Bases,* (pp. 252-263).

Harris, S., & Gibbins, N. (2003). 3store: Efficient bulk RDF storage. In *Proceedings of the First International Workshop on Practical and Scalable Semantic Systems.*

Harth, A., & Decker, S. (2005). Optimized index structures for querying RDF from the Web. In *Proceedings of the Third Latin American Web Congress,* (pp. 71-80).

Jeffery, S. R., Franklin, M. J., & Halevy, A. Y. (2008). Pay-as-you-go user feedback for dataspace systems. In *Proceedings of the ACM SIGMOD International Conference on Management of Data,* (pp. 847-860).

Kiryakov, A., Ognyanov, D., & Manov, D. (2005). Owlim-a pragmatic semantic repository for owl. In *Proceedings of the Web Information Systems Engineering Workshops,* (pp. 182-192).

Levandoski, J. J., & Mokbel, M. F. (2009). RDF data-centric storage. In *Proceedings of the IEEE International Conference on Web Services.*

Ma, L., Su, Z., Pan, Y., Zhang, L., & Liu, T. (2004). RStar: An RDF storage and query system for enterprise resource management. In *Proceedings of the ACM International Conference on Information and Knowledge Management,* (pp. 484-491).

Ma, L., Wang, C., Lu, J., Cao, F., Pan, Y., & Yu, Y. (2008). Effective and efficient Semantic Web data management over DB2. In *Proceedings of the ACM SIGMOD International Conference on Management of Data,* (pp. 1183-1194).

Mahmoudi Nasab, H., & Sakr, S. (2010). An experimental evaluation of relational RDF sorage and querying techniques. In *Proceedings of the 2nd International Workshop on Benchmarking of XML and Semantic Web Applications.*

Manola, F., & Miller, E. (2004). *RDF primer.* W3C recommendation. Retrieved from http://www.w3.org/TR/REC-rdf-syntax/

Matono, A., Amagasa, T., Yoshikawa, M., & Uemura, S. (2005). A path-based relational RDF database. In *Proceedings of the 16th Australasian Database Conference,* (pp. 95-103).

McBride, B. (2002). Jena: A Semantic Web toolkit. *IEEE Internet Computing, 6*(6), 55–59. doi:10.1109/MIC.2002.1067737

Neumann, T., & Weikum, G. (2008). RDF-3X: A RISC-style engine for RDF. [PVLDB]. *Proceedings of the VLDB Endownment, 1*(1), 647–659.

Neumann, T., & Weikum, G. (2009). Scalable join processing on very large RDF graphs. In *Proceedings of the ACM SIGMOD International Conference on Management of Data,* (pp. 627-640).

Pan, Z., & Heflin, J. (2003). DLDB: Extending relational databases to support Semantic Web queries. In *Proceedings of the First International Workshop on Practical and Scalable Semantic Systems.*

Pan, Z., Zhang, X., & Heflin, J. (2008). DLDB2: A scalable multi-perspective Semantic Web repository. In *Proceedings of the IEEE/WIC /ACM International Conference on Web Intelligence,* (pp. 489-495).

Prud'hommeaux, E., & Seaborne, A. (2008). *SPARQL query language for RDF.* W3C recommendation. Retrieved from http://www.w3.org/TR/rdf-sparql-query/

Schmidt, M., & Hornung, T. K®uchlin, N., Lausen, G. & Pinkel, C. (2008). An experimental comparison of RDF data management approaches in a SPARQL benchmark scenario. In *Proceedings of the 7th International Semantic Web Conference,* (pp. 82-97).

Schmidt, M., Hornung, T., Lausen, G., & Pinkel, C. (2009). SP2Bench: A SPARQL performance benchmark. In *Proceedings of the 25th International Conference on Data Engineering,* (pp. 222-233).

Sidirourgos, L., Goncalves, R., Kersten, M. L., Nes, N., & Manegold, S. (2008). Column-store support for RDF data management: Not all swans are white. [PVLDB]. *Proceedings of the VLDB Endownment, 1*(2), 1553–1563.

Stonebraker, M., Abadi, D. J., Batkin, A., Chen, X., Cherniack, M., Ferreira, M., et al. (2005). C-Store: A column-oriented DBMS. In *Proceedings of the 31st International Conference on Very Large Data Bases,* (pp. 553-564).

Türker, C. & Gertz, M. (2001). Semantic integrity support in SQL: 1999 and commercial object-relational database management systems. *The VLDB Journal, 10*(4), 241–269. doi:10.1007/s007780100050

Weiss, C., Karras, P., & Bernstein, A. (2008). Hexastore: Sextuple indexing for Semantic Web data management. [PVLDB]. *Proceedings of the VLDB Endownment, 1*(1), 1008–1019.

Section 3

Chapter 12

Making Query Coding in SQL Easier by Implementing the SQL Divide Keyword:
An Experimental Query Rewriter in Java

Eric Draken
University of Calgary, Canada

Shang Gao
University of Calgary, Canada

Reda Alhajj
University of Calgary, Canada & Global University, Beirut, Lebanon

ABSTRACT

Relational Algebra (RA) and structured query language (SQL) are supposed to have a bijective relationship by having the same expressive power. That is, each operation in SQL can be mapped to one RA equivalent and vice versa. Actually, this is an essential fact because in commercial database management systems, every SQL query is translated into equivalent RA expression, which is optimized and executed to produce the required output. However, RA has an explicit relational division symbol (÷), whereas SQL does not have a corresponding explicit division keyword. Division is implemented using a combination of four core operations, namely cross product, difference, selection, and projection. In fact, to implement relational division in SQL requires convoluted queries with multiple nested select statements and set operations. Explicit division in relational algebra is possible when the divisor is static; however, a dynamic divisor forces the coding of the query to follow the explicit expression using the four core operators. On the other hand, SQL does not provide any flexibility for expressing division when the divisor is static. Thus, the work described in this chapter is intended to provide SQL expression equivalent to

DOI: 10.4018/978-1-60960-475-2.ch012

explicit relational algebra division (with static divisor). In other words, the goal is to implement a SQL query rewriter in Java which takes as input a divide grammar and rewrites it to an efficient query using current SQL keywords. The developed approach could be adapted as front-end or wrapper to existing SQL query system. Users will be able to express explicit division in SQL which will be translated into an equivalent expression that involves only the standard SQL keywords and structure. This will turn SQL into more attractive for specifying queries involving explicit division.

INTRODUCTION

Since its development as the standard query language for relational databases, the Structured Query Language (SQL) has witnessed a number of developments and extensions. Different research groups have worked on different aspects of SQL (Brantner et al., 2007; Chong et al., 2005; Harris & Shadbolt, 2005; Hung et al., 2005; Karvounarakis et al., 2002; Pan & Hein, 2003; Prudhommeaux, 2005). We realized the gap between relational algebra and SQL as far as the division operation is concerned. While the relational algebra has an operator for explicit division, SQL does not provide any keyword for explicit division. Hence from the user perspective the translation between SQL and the relational algebra is not one to one. A user who is able to express explicit division in relational algebra does not find the same flexibility with SQL. The work described in this paper is intended to cover this gap.

Given two tables S and T such that the schema of S is subset from the schema of T; a common type of database query requires finding all tuples of a table or view that are related to each and every one of the tuples of a second table or group, and is called *Relational Division*. For instance, it is very common to code queries for finding employees working on all projects; students who have completed a certain set of courses, etc. Such kind of queries require a division operator which is normally expressed internally as equivalent to a combination of four core relational algebra operators, namely, selection, projection, difference and cross-product.

The research community realized the importance of the division process and hence defined a stand-alone operator for explicitly expressing division as in the above two examples. However, the explicit division operator is not applicable when the divisor is dynamic. For instance, queries such as finding students who completed all first year courses in their departments, finding persons who ate at every restaurant in their neighborhood, etc, are not doable using explicit division; these queries qualify as requiring implicit division because the divisor changes for different instances of the dividend. Implicit division could be coded by explicitly using the four core operators, though expressing implicit division is not an easy task. Having no *divide* keyword for expressing explicit division in SQL, as many as six query types in different SQL dialects have been identified using nested *select, exists, not exists, except, contains and count* keywords (Elmasri & Navathe, 2006; McCann, 2003). We argue that it is necessary to provide for explicit division in SQL.

The division operator is firstly instantiated from the perspective of relational algebra (Dadashzadeh, 1989) and further extended to relational databases in terms of flexible implementation (Bosc et al., 1997). Further discussions shift the focus to advanced computation, such as Fuzzy systems (Galindo et al., 2001; Bosc & Pivert, 2006)

Once integrated into SQL, the explicit division will allow users to express their queries easier and hence one of the main targets of SQL (ease of use by end users) will be satisfied better. Realizing this gap, the goal of this work is twofold: to devise a minimal division grammar that when encountered will be rewritten to two contemporary SQL division queries; and to implement such a query rewriter in Java, execute both rewritten queries on a sample database, and compare their returned sets for consistency. It is not intended to expand the existing SQL syntax or the already accepted SQL standard; rather we have developed a wrapper that could be integrated on the top of the existing SQL. This way, the end users will be able to express explicit division using DIVIDE as if it is one of the agreed upon keywords for SQL. Then, the developed rewriter translates the SQL query with DIVIDE into an equivalent SQL query where the division is expressed using the traditional way in SQL and hence our approach does not affect the underlying query system.

The rest of this paper is organized as follows. Next section describes the division operator, followed by the discussion of proposed explicit division in SQL. We then cover the division grammar parser, and report the results of the testing process. A special divide-by-zero case is discussed before our conclusion of findings.

RELATIONAL DEVISION

Relational division is one of the eight basic operations in Codd's relational algebra (Darwen & Date, 1992). Though it can be coded using four of the five core relational algebra operators, it has been defined as standalone operator to make the coding of queries involving explicit division easier. The concept is that a divisor relation is used to partition a dividend relation and produce a quotient or results table. The quotient table is made up of those values of one group of columns (or a single column) for which a second group of columns (or column) had all of the values in the divisor.

Division in Relational Algebra

Let $R_1(A \cup B)$ and $R_2(B)$ be relation schemas, where $A = \{a_1,..,a_j\}$ and $B = \{b_1,..,b_s\}$ are non-empty, disjoint sets of ordered attributes. Let $r_1(R_1)$ and $r_2(R_2)$ be relations on these schemas with $r_1 \div r_2 = r_3$, where by definition the schema of r_3 is $R_3(A)$. Table r_1 is the *dividend*, r_2 is the *divisor*, and r_3 is the *quotient* of the relational division operation. Healy's division (Date, 1995) is defined as follows:

$$r_1 \div r_2 = \pi_A(r_1) - \pi_A((\pi_A(r_1) \times r_2) - r_1) = r_3$$

A visual example of relational division is given below. This query could be interpreted as follows. For A in R_1 (schema of R_1 minus schema of R_2) find every value which is related with all values in R_2.

Relational Division in SQL

The highly-regarded database textbook by Elmasri and Navathe describes the division operation using the SQL formulation of D0 (see below) (Elmasri & Navathe, 2006). The use of the NOT EXISTS predicates is for speed because most SQL parsers in DBMSs will look up a value in an index rather than scan the whole table (Harris & Shadbolt, 2005). This query for relational division was made popular by Chris Date in his textbooks (Codd, 1972).

```
D0: SELECT DISTINCT x.A
       FROM T1 AS x
       WHERE NOT EXISTS
           (SELECT *
              FROM T2 AS y
            WHERE NOT EXISTS
                    (SELECT *
                       FROM T1 AS z
                  WHERE (z.A=x.A) AND (z.B=y.B)));
```

D1 is an alternate formulation which is simpler to implement (Brantner et al., 2007). It uses membership test, *group-by*, counting, and *having* SQL constructs, yet computationally it is much faster (less table scanning) and closer semantically to the division in relational algebra.

```
D1: SELECT A
       FROM T1
       WHERE B IN
           (SELECT B
              FROM T2)
           GROUP BY A
           HAVING COUNT(*) =
                 (SELECT COUNT (*)
                    FROM T2);
```

PROPOSED SQL DIVIDE GRAMMARS

In this study, two SQL relational division grammars are proposed and each is examined to determine the minimum number of keywords needed to implement.

First SQL Divide Grammar

The first form of the proposed divide grammar is

```
G1: (table1) DIVIDE (table2)

G1a: (SELECT i..j,r..s,t..v FROM table1 WHERE …) DIVIDE
     (SELECT r..s FROM table2 WHERE …)
```

This divide grammar is a departure from that posited by Rantzau (Harris & Shadbolt, 2005) because this paper assumes a complete SQL query may be contained within each of the dividend and divisor clauses. This is possible as long as the projection of the final dividend relation contains an ordered set of attributes which is a superset of the projection of the final divisor relation's attributes.

Table 1. Symbol representations

T1	**table1**
T2	**table2**
A	SELECT **i..s** FROM T1
B	SELECT **r..s** FROM T2
W1	SELECT A FROM T1 WHERE **(..)**
W2	SELECT B FROM T2 WHERE **(..)**

The following symbols denote their corresponding query entity in bold. These will be used in the rewrite templates in the next sections.

Count Method Rewrite

The above query G1a can be rewritten to a template using the partition-and-count method such as the following (Brantner et al., 2007; Hung et al., 2005). Note that quantities in square brackets require evaluation beforehand.

```
R0: SELECT [A-B]
     FROM [T1]
     WHERE [W1]
     AND [A∩B] IN
          (SELECT [B]
             FROM [T2]
             WHERE [W2])
     GROUP BY [A-B]
     HAVING COUNT (*) =
          (SELECT COUNT(*)
             FROM [T2]
             WHERE [W2]);
```

By replacing the entities in square brackets with their appropriate values, a single divide grammar can be rewritten in a straightforward manner.

Not Exists/Not Exists Method Rewrite

This is the original so-called classic division (originally from Matos (Brantner, 2007) which borrows from Date (Codd, 1972)) which has been transformed into a rewrite template. Prefix letters must be fixed to each of the *select* attributes.

```
R1: SELECT DISTINCT x.[A-B]
     FROM [T1] AS x
     WHERE NOT EXISTS
```

```
(SELECT [A∩B]
  FROM [T2] AS y
WHERE NOT EXISTS
      (SELECT [A∩B]
        FROM [T1] AS z
      WHERE (z.[A-B]=x.[A-B]) AND (z.[A∩B]=y.[A∩B])));
```

However, it was discovered early on in this research project that R1 suffers from two important flaws: if T1 or T2 or both consist of more than one table, this template fails; the second is that the where-clauses of T1 and T2 collide with the template's where-not-exists clauses. That is why R2 is used instead.

```
R2: SELECT DISTINCT x.[A-B]
    FROM (SELECT [A-B]
                    FROM [T1]
                    WHERE [W1]) AS x
    WHERE NOT EXISTS
        (SELECT *
        FROM (SELECT [A∩B]
              FROM [T2]
              WHERE [W2]) AS y
        WHERE NOT EXISTS
            (SELECT *
            FROM (SELECT [A∩B]
                  FROM [T1]
                  WHERE [W1]) AS z
            WHERE (z.[A-B]=x.[A-B]) AND (z.[A∩B]=y.[A∩B])));
```

In R2, both the dividend and the divisor are each encased within a *from* statement which uses an alias to maintain the x-y-z relationship. Complete SQL statements may be retained in the dividend and divisor clauses. This is a highly impractical solution to the query rewrite problem because now there are six *select* statements. However, the classic rewrite is not intended as a solution to this project, rather it serves as the comparison query against R0.

Divide-On Grammar

Consider a scenario where the dividend is known and the divisor is not entirely known. Such a divisor might be a stored query, a view, or a table where SELECT * is used but division is not desired across all of its attributes. Even more common might be that the SELECT * is desired, but the attributes are not in a compatible order with those of the dividend. A way to refine or limit which attributes to divide on is desired.

The second form of the proposed divide grammar is

```
G2: (table1) DIVIDE (table2) ON {attributes}

G2a: (SELECT i..j,r..s,t..v
     FROM table1
     WHERE ...)
DIVIDE
     (SELECT *
     FROM table2
     WHERE ...) ON {r..s}
```

Virtually all conceivable forms of G2 can be written as G1. That is, the *on* keyword is not needed, but is included as a convenience. In fact, when implemented in Java, if the *on* keyword is present, the B attributes will simply be replaced with them. This is different from Rantzau's proposed grammar (Harris & Shadbolt, 2005) in which this *on* keyword is necessary.

DIVIDE GRAMMAR PARSER

In designing a custom SQL parser, several considerations are made. One of them is being able to handle nested divide grammars. Another consideration is if the divide query can be part of another query, perhaps as a *join* or *union*. As long as each select-from-where clause in the whole query is correct, then both of these issues can be addressed simultaneously with the algorithm included in Section 4.1.

Iterative Parsing Algorithm

This is an overview of how nested divide queries may be identified and rewritten:

1. Are brackets matched?
2. Is a **DIVIDE grammar** present?
3. Find **DIVIDE** token
4. Find the correctly nested brackets before **DIVIDE**
5. Find the correctly nested brackets after **DIVIDE**
6. Find the ON attributes, if any
7. If **DIVIDE grammar** found in dividend, repeat steps 3-9 on it
8. If **DIVIDE grammar** found in divisor, repeat steps 3-9 on it
9. Rewrite sub-query in-place

Parse and Rewrite Example

Below is simple example of a query rewrite using the count method from the authors JUnit tests. A more complicated example is presented in Section 4.3. The steps of the above algorithm are applied in sequence as follows.

```
Example 1. A basic rewrite example

Input query:
(SELECT a, b
 FROM T1)
DIVIDE
(SELECT b
 FROM T2)
Rewritten query:
SELECT a
FROM T1
WHERE b IN
     (SELECT b
       FROM T2)
GROUP BY a
HAVING COUNT(a) = (SELECT COUNT(b)
                                  FROM T2)
```

- **Step 1:** Are the brackets matched? Yes - This step checks that the number of left brackets equals the number of right brackets.
- **Step 2:** Is the *divide* keyword present? Yes – If missing, no rewrite is performed. A trivial regular expression checks for this keyword in any case.
- **Step 3:** Locate the position in the query where the first *divide* keyword occurs. Actually, the *divide* keyword and its immediate surrounding brackets must be matched. This is to prevent a rogue table with the word *divide* in it from damaging the rewrite.

```
(SELECT a, b
   FROM T1)
DIVIDE
(SELECT b
   FROM T2)
```

- **Step 4:** Scan leftward until the number of left brackets matches the number of right brackets from the beginning of the *divide* keyword.

```
(SELECT a, b
   FROM T1)
DIVIDE
(SELECT b
   FROM T2)
```

- **Step 5:** Scan rightward until the number of right brackets matches the number of left brackets from the end of the *divide* keyword.

```
(SELECT a, b
   FROM T1)
DIVIDE
(SELECT b
   FROM T2)
```

- **Step 6:** Find the ON keyword and attributes, if any. None found.
- **Steps 7 and 8:** Is another *divide* keyword present in either the dividend or divisor? None found.
- **Step 9:** Rewrite the query. A general SQL parser called Zql (Karvounarakis et al., 2002) is used to extract from the dividend and divisor the *select* attributes, the *from* tables, and any *where* qualifiers. The final rewritten query is in Example 1. An analogous process exists for the R2 template rewrite.

A More Complex Rewrite Example

```
Input query:
((SELECT a, b, c
   FROM T1, T2
  WHERE T1.a = T2.a AND T1.b > 0)
Divide
(SELECT b, c
 FROM T3, T4
 WHERE T3.d = T4.d)
ON {b})
DIVIDE
((SELECT a, d
   FROM T1, T2
   WHERE T1.a = T2.a AND T1.b < 0)
Divide
(SELECT d, c
  FROM T3, T4
  WHERE T3.d = T4.d)
  ON {d})
  ON {a}
*The divide keywords are highlighted for ease of reading.
First found divide query:
(SELECT a, b, c
 FROM T1, T2
WHERE T1.a = T2.a AND T1.b > 0)
Divide
(SELECT b, c
 FROM T3, T4
WHERE T3.d = T4.d) ON {b}
Dividend:   SELECT a, b, c
```

```
                FROM T1, T2
    WHERE T1.a = T2.a AND T1.b > 0
Divisor:       SELECT b, c
    FROM T3, T4
    WHERE T3.d = T4.d
On:                b
Replacing
(SELECT a, b, c
 FROM T1, T2
WHERE T1.a = T2.a AND T1.b > 0)
Divide
(SELECT b, c
 FROM T3, T4
 WHERE T3.d = T4.d) ON {b}
with
SELECT a, c
 FROM T1, T2
 WHERE ((T1.a = T2.a) AND (T1.b > 0)) AND b IN
       (SELECT b, c
  FROM T3, T4
 WHERE (T3.d = T4.d))
 GROUP BY a, c
 HAVING COUNT(*) =
       (SELECT COUNT(*)
  FROM T3, T4
 WHERE (T3.d = T4.d)).
The original query now looks like:
SELECT a, c
 FROM T1, T2
 WHERE ((T1.a = T2.a) AND (T1.b > 0)) AND b IN
       (SELECT b, c
FROM T3, T4
WHERE (T3.d = T4.d))
 GROUP BY a, c
 HAVING COUNT(*) =
       (SELECT COUNT(*)
  FROM T3, T4
 WHERE (T3.d = T4.d)))
DIVIDE
((SELECT a, d
    FROM T1, T2
  WHERE T1.a = T2.a AND T1.b < 0)
Divide
(SELECT d, c
```

```
 FROM T3, T4
  WHERE T3.d = T4.d) ON {d}) ON {a}
A divide grammar was found in the dividend:
(SELECT a, c
 FROM T1, T2
 WHERE ((T1.a = T2.a) AND (T1.b > 0)) AND b IN
      (SELECT b, c
FROM T3, T4
WHERE (T3.d = T4.d))
 GROUP BY a, c
 HAVING COUNT(*) =
      (SELECT COUNT(*)
                    FROM T3, T4
  WHERE (T3.d = T4.d)))
DIVIDE
((SELECT a, d
   FROM T1, T2
  WHERE T1.a = T2.a AND T1.b < 0)
Divide
(SELECT d, c
 FROM T3, T4
WHERE T3.d = T4.d) ON {d}) ON {a}
Dividend:    SELECT a, c
 FROM T1, T2
 WHERE ((T1.a = T2.a) AND (T1.b > 0)) AND b IN
      (SELECT b, c
FROM T3, T4
WHERE (T3.d = T4.d))
 GROUP BY a, c
 HAVING COUNT(*) =
      (SELECT COUNT(*)
FROM T3, T4
WHERE (T3.d = T4.d))
Divisor:     (SELECT a, d
   FROM T1, T2
  WHERE T1.a = T2.a AND T1.b < 0)
Divide
(SELECT d, c
 FROM T3, T4
WHERE T3.d = T4.d) ON {d}
On:          a
Another divide grammar was found in the divisor:
 (SELECT a, d
  FROM T1, T2
```

```
    WHERE T1.a = T2.a AND T1.b < 0)
Divide
(SELECT d, c
 FROM T3, T4
WHERE T3.d = T4.d) ON {d}
Dividend:     SELECT a, d
    FROM T1, T2
    WHERE T1.a = T2.a AND T1.b < 0
Divisor:      SELECT d, c
    FROM T3, T4
WHERE T3.d = T4.d
On:               d
Replacing
(SELECT a, d
 FROM T1, T2
 WHERE T1.a = T2.a AND T1.b < 0)
Divide
(SELECT d, c
 FROM T3, T4
WHERE T3.d = T4.d) ON {d}
with
 SELECT a
 FROM T1, T2
 WHERE ((T1.a = T2.a) AND (T1.b < 0)) AND d IN
     (SELECT d, c
FROM T3, T4
WHERE (T3.d = T4.d))
 GROUP BY a
 HAVING COUNT(a) =
     (SELECT COUNT(*)
FROM T3, T4
WHERE (T3.d = T4.d)).
```

The original query now looks like:

```
(SELECT a, c
 FROM T1, T2
 WHERE ((T1.a = T2.a) AND (T1.b > 0)) AND b IN
     (SELECT b, c
FROM T3, T4
WHERE (T3.d = T4.d))
 GROUP BY a, c
 HAVING COUNT(*) =
     (SELECT COUNT(*)
FROM T3, T4
WHERE (T3.d = T4.d)))
```

```
DIVIDE
(SELECT a
 FROM T1, T2
 WHERE ((T1.a = T2.a) AND (T1.b < 0)) AND d IN
       (SELECT d, c
FROM T3, T4
WHERE (T3.d = T4.d))
 GROUP BY a
 HAVING COUNT(a) =
       (SELECT COUNT(*)
FROM T3, T4
WHERE (T3.d = T4.d))) ON {a}
```

The final rewrite would then proceed exactly as before for the last divide keyword.

Limitations

The logic of the rewrite algorithm is sound. The experimental parser and rewriter, however, have some limitations. Notably, the target database's metadata is not polled to make sure tables exist, attributes exist, and attributes are on domains that make sense. As this is a pure character string rewriter, it is not expected to do this. These have been left out because the DBMS, of course, will check the final rewritten query for correctness so that these limitations are relegated to the DBMS. Actually, this is not a limitation even if it is seen because our target is to turn into easy task the coding of queries that involve explicit division. The target is assumed achieved one a query explicit division is translated into an equivalent SQL query. Then it is the duty of the SQL parser within the DBMS to check the syntax of the query for correctness.

The Zql parser used in this experiment cannot properly parse complicated *select* statements. A new light-weight general SQL parser is needed for exhaustive query handling.

Also, extracting aggregate functions, *having* and *group by* clauses inside the dividend or divisor were not included in this experiment so they would not interfere with the count method template. This limited nested query rewriting abilities.

EXPERIMENTS

A suite of JUnit tests were created to test varying complexities of divide queries. For each division query, a count-method rewrite and a not-exists/not-exists method rewrite were performed. As long as the dividend and divisor each were valid with *select* attributes that could be extracted with Zql, the rewrites succeeded.

The implemented front end has been integrated into a complete system that communicates with MySQL. The integrated system takes any SQL statement, rewrite the query if it contains explicit division (expressed using DIVIDE), and then executes the query to return the results. All the translated queries were successful run. Finally, the verbatim translation process has been tested by coding queries that does not refer to existing tables/attributes. The queries were correctly translated by the front end into

Figure 1. Visual example of relational division

R1	A	B			R2	A			R3	B
	4	3	÷			4	=			3
	4	1				8				1
	4	7								7
	8	3								
	8	1								
	8	7								

corresponding SQL queries that involve same tables/attributes. However the MySQL parser reported them as erroneous queries because they refer to non-existing tables/attributes.

Software Used

Zql: A Java SQL Parser

An established SQL lexical parser is needed to check and validate ordinary SQL queries and to explode clauses such as *select*, *from* and *where*. Zql (Karvounarakis et al., 2002) is appropriately-suited for this as it is light-weight and easy to use. Unfortunately it is deprecated and unmaintained by its authors.

MySQL with XAMPP

XAMPP is an Apache distribution (Leinders & den Bussche, 2005) which contains MySQL – a popular DBMS which is free, widespread and easy to install.

Performance

Consistently, the count method division returned results more than an order of magnitude faster that the not-exists/except division method while returning the same results set[1]. Leinders and den Bussche show an interesting theoretical result about the divide operation (http://www.gibello.com/code/zql/). Algorithms implementing the divide operation based on sorting and counting, as in R0, can achieve a time complexity of $O(n \log n)$. In contrast, they show that any expression of the divide operator in the relational algebra with union, difference, projection, selection, and equi-joins must produce intermediate results of quadratic size. The resources and time needed to rewrite a character string as outlined in this paper are negligible.

The implementation is tested on Windows XP Professional (3.39GHz, 1GB of RAM). We randomonly sample DIVIDE queries from a pool of different cases. The performance chart is shown in Figure 1, where data labels are average time(ms) per query, we observe that the parsing and rewrite execute efficently on avarage, including large sampled data set.

Figure 2. Performance chart

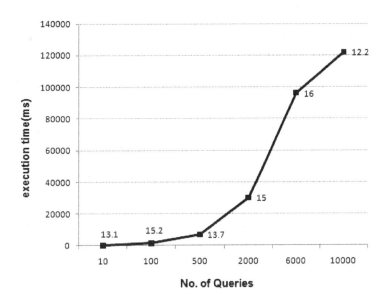

DIVISION BY ZERO

An interesting question arises when the divisor table is empty: what should the result be? Using the count method rewrite, the empty set is returned. Using the not-exists/except method rewrite, on the other hand, enumerates all the rows from the dividend table. It makes the most sense to return an empty set in the authors' opinion because just as algebraic division by zero produces a nonsense result, so does returning all the rows of the dividend table.

CONCLUSION

As a proof-of-concept, this project succeeded. Divide grammars outlined in this paper can be rewritten into more than one contemporary SQL division methods. Therefore, it is possible to add the *divide* keyword to the standard SQL language. It should be up to each vendor how they would like to implement a division algorithm but they should agree that the division grammar proposed in this paper is very straightforward. It has been successfully integrated into MySQL and the testing has been very encouraging. Currently we are trying to develop a nice user interface for the integrated system.

REFERENCES

Bosc, P., Dubois, D., Pivert, O., & Prade, H. (1997). Flexible queries in relational databases-the example of the division operator. *Theoretical Computer Science*, *171*(1/2), 281–302. doi:10.1016/S0304-3975(96)00132-6

Bosc, P., & Pivert, O. (2006). About approximate inclusion and its axiomatization. *Fuzzy Sets and Systems, 157*, 1438–1454. doi:10.1016/j.fss.2005.11.011

Brantner, M., May, N., & Moerkotte, G. (2007). Unnesting scalar SQL queries in the presence of disjunction. In *Proceedings of IEEE ICDE.*

Chong, E. I., Das, S., Eadon, G., & Srinivasan, J. (2005). An efficient SQL-based RDF querying scheme. In *Proceedings of VLDB.*

Codd, E. (1972). Relational completeness of database sub-languages. In R. Rustin, (Ed.), *Courant Computer Science Symposium 6: Database Systems*, (pp. 65-98). Prentice-Hall.

Dadashzadeh, M. (1989). An improved division operator for relational algebra. *Information Systems, 14*(5), 431–437. doi:10.1016/0306-4379(89)90007-0

Darwen, H., & Date, C. (1992). Into the great divide. In Date, C., & Darwen, H. (Eds.), *Relational database: Writings 1989-1991* (pp. 155–168). Reading, MA: Addison-Wesley.

Date, C. (1995). *An introduction to database systems* (6th ed.).

Elmasri, R., & Navathe, S. R. (2006). *Fundamentals of database systems* (5th ed.). Addison Wesley.

Galindo, J., Medina, J. M., & Aranda-Garridoa, M. C. (2001)... *Fuzzy Sets and Systems, 121*(3), 471–490. doi:10.1016/S0165-0114(99)00156-6

Gibello, P. (2010). *Zql: A Java SQL parser*. Retrieved June 2010, from http://www.gibello.com/code/zql/

Harris, S., & Shadbolt, N. (2005). SPARQL query processing with conventional relational database systems. In *Proceedings of SSWS.*

Hung, E., Deng, Y., & Subrahmanian, V. S. (2005). RDF aggregate queries and views. In *Proceedings of IEEE ICDE.*

Karvounarakis, G., Alexaki, S., Christophides, V., Plexousakis, D., & Scholl, M. (2002). RQL: A declarative query language for RDF. In *Proceedings of WWW.*

Leinders, D., & den Bussche, J. V. (2005). On the complexity of division and set joins in the relational algebra. In *Proceedings of ACM PODS*, Baltimore, MD USA.

Maier, D. (1983). *The theory of relational databases*. Computer Science Press.

Matos, V. M., & Grasser, R. (2002). A simpler (and better) SQL approach to relational division. *Journal of Information Systems Education, 13*(2).

McCann, L. (2003). On making relational division comprehensible. In *Proceedings of ASEE/IEEE Frontiers in Education Conference.*

Pan, Z., & Hein, J. (2003). DLDB: Extending relational databases to support SemanticWeb queries. In *Proceedings of PSSS.*

Prudhommeaux, E. (2005). Notes on adding SPARQL to MySQL. Retrieved from http://www.w3.org/2005/05/22-SPARQL-MySQL/

Rantzau, R., & Mangold, C. (2006). Laws for rewriting queries containing division operators. In the *Proceedings of IEEE ICDE*.

XAMPP. (2010). An apache distribution containing MySQL. Retrieved June 2010, from http://www.apachefriends.org/en/xampp.html

KEY TERMS AND DEFINITIONS

Relational Algebra (RA): an offshoot of first-order logic (and of algebra of sets), deals with a set of finitary relations which is closed under certain operators. These operators operate on one or more relations to yield a relation.

Structured Query Language (SQL): a database computer language designed for managing data in relational database management systems (RDBMS), and originally based upon relational algebra.

MySQL: a relational database management system (RDBMS) that runs as a server providing multi-user access to a number of databases.

Divide Operator: Relational division is one of the eight basic operations in relational algebra. Though it can be coded using four of the five core relational algebra operators, it has been defined as standalone operator to make the coding of queries involving explicit division easier. The concept is that a divisor relation is used to partition a dividend relation and produce a quotient or results table. The quotient table is made up of those values of one group of columns (or a single column) for which a second group of columns (or column) had all of the values in the divisor.

Zql: An established SQL lexical parser to check and validate ordinary SQL queries and to explode clauses such as *select*, *from* and *where*.

XAMPP: an Apache distribution which contains MySQL – a popular DBMS which is free, widespread and easy to install.

Grammar: a set of rules or standards that specifiy the query language.

ENDNOTE

[1] The result differed only when division by an empty set occurred.

Chapter 13
Querying Graph Databases:
An Overview

Sherif Sakr
University of New South Wales, Australia

Ghazi Al-Naymat
University of New South Wales, Australia

ABSTRACT

Recently, there has been a lot of interest in the application of graphs in different domains. Graphs have been widely used for data modeling in different application domains such as: chemical compounds, protein networks, social networks, and Semantic Web. Given a query graph, the task of retrieving related graphs as a result of the query from a large graph database is a key issue in any graph-based application. This has raised a crucial need for efficient graph indexing and querying techniques. This chapter provides an overview of different techniques for indexing and querying graph databases. An overview of several proposals of graph query language is also given. Finally, the chapter provides a set of guidelines for future research directions.

INTRODUCTION

The field of graph databases and graph query processing has received a lot of attention due to the constantly increasing usage of graph data structure for representing data in different domains such as: chemical compounds (Klinger & Austin, 2005), multimedia databases (Lee et al., 2005), social networks (Cai et al., 2005), protein networks (Huan et al., 2004) and semantic web (Manola & Miller, 2004). To effectively understand and utilize any collection of graphs, a graph database that efficiently supports elementary querying mechanisms is crucially required. Hence, determining graph database members which constitute the answer set of a graph query q from a large graph database is a key performance issue

DOI: 10.4018/978-1-60960-475-2.ch013

in all graph-based applications. A primary challenge in computing the answers of graph queries is that pair-wise comparisons of graphs are usually really hard problems. For example, subgraph isomorphism is known to be NP-complete (Garey & Johnson, 1979). A naive approach to compute the answer set of a graph query q is to perform a sequential scan on the graph database and to check whether each graph database member satisfies the conditions of q or not. However, the graph database can be very large which makes the sequential scan over the database impracticable. Thus, finding an efficient search technique is immensely important due to the combined costs of pair-wise comparisons and the increasing size of modern graph databases. It is apparent that the success of any graph database application is directly dependent on the efficiency of the graph indexing and query processing mechanisms. Recently, there are many techniques that have been proposed to tackle these problems. This chapter gives an overview of different techniques of indexing and querying graph databases and classifies them according to their target graph query types and their indexing strategy.

The rest of the chapter is organized as follows. The Preliminary section introduces preliminaries of graph databases and graph query processing. In Section (Subgraph Query Processing), a classification of the approaches of subgraph query processing problem and their index structures is given while the section (Supergraph Query Processing) focuses on the approaches for resolving the supergraph query processing problem. Section (Graph Similarity Queries) discusses the approach of approximate graph matching queries. Section (Graph Query Languages) gives an overview of several proposals of graph query languages. Finally, Section (Discussion and Conclusions) concludes the chapter and provides some suggestions for possible future research directions on the subject.

PRELIMINARIES

In this section, we introduce the basic terminologies used in this chapter and give the formal definition of graph querying problems.

Graph Data Structure

Graphs are vey powerful modeling tool. They are used to model complicated structures and schemaless data. In graph data structures, *vertices* and edges represent the *entities* and the relationships between them respectively. The attributes associated with these entities and relationships are called labels. A graph database D is defined as a collection of member graphs $D = \{g_1, g_2, ..., g_n\}$ where each member graph database member g_i is denoted as $(V, E, L_v, L_e, F_v, F_e)$ where V is the set of vertices; $E \subseteq V * V$ is the set of edges joining two distinct vertices; L_v is the set of vertex labels; L_e is the set of edge labels; F_v is a function $V \rightarrow L_v$ that assigns labels to vertices and F_e is a function $E \rightarrow L_e$ that assigns labels to edges. In general, graph data structures can be classified according to the direction of their edges into two main classes:

- *Directed-labeled graphs*: such as XML, RDF and traffic networks.
- *Undirected-labeled graphs*: such as social networks and chemical compounds.

In principle, there are two main types of graph databases. The first type consists of few numbers of very large graphs such as the Web graph and social networks (*non-transactional graph databases*). The second type consists of a large set of small graphs such as chemical compounds and biological pathways (*transactional graph databases*). The main focus of this chapter is on giving an overview of the efficient indexing and querying mechanisms on the second type of graph databases.

Graph Queries

In principle, queries in transactional graph databases can be broadly classified into the following main categories:

1. **Subgraph queries:** this category searches for a specific pattern in the graph database. The pattern can be either a small graph or a graph where some parts of it are uncertain, e.g., vertices with wildcard labels. Therefore, given a graph database $D = \{g_1, g_2, ..., g_n\}$ and a subgraph query q, the query answer set $A = \{g_i | q \subseteq g_i, g_i \in D\}$. A graph q is described as a subgraph of another graph database member gi if the set of vertices and edges of q form subset of the vertices and edges of g_i. To be more formal, let us assume that we have two graphs $g_1(V_1, E_1, L_{v1}, L_{e1}, F_{v1}, F_{e1})$ and $g_2(V_1, E_2, L_{v2}, L_{e2}, F_{v2}, F_{e2})$, g_1 is defined as subgraph of g_2, if and only if:

   ○ For every distinct vertex $x \in V_1$ with a label $v_1 \in L_{v1}$, there is a distinct vertex $y \in V_2$ with a label $v_1 \in L_{v2}$.

   ○ For every distinct edge edge $ab \in E_1$ with a label $e_1 \in L_{e1}$, there is a distinct edge $ab \in E_2$ with a label $e_1 \in L_{e2}$.

   Figure 1(a) illustrates the subgraph search problem. Figure 2(a) shows an example of a graph database. Figure 2(b) illustrates examples of graph queries (q_1 and q_2). Let us assume that these queries are subgraph queries. If we evaluate these queries over the sample graph database (Figure 2(a)) then the answer set of q_1 will consist of the graph database members g_1 and g_2 while the answer set of q_2 will be empty. The more general type of the subgraph search problem is the *subgraph isomorphism* search problem, which is defined as follows. Let $g_1 = (V_1, E_1, L_{v1}, L_{e1}, F_{v1}, F_{e1})$ and $g_1 = (V_2, E_2, L_{v2}, L_{e2}, F_{v2}, F_{e2})$ be two graphs, g_1 is defined as a graph isomorphism to g_2, if and only if there exists at least one bijective function $f: V_1 \rightarrow V_2$ such that: 1) for any edge $uv \in E_1$, there is an edge $f(u)f(v) \in E_2$. 2) $F_{v1}(u) = F_{v2}(f(u))$ and $F_{v1}(v) = F_{v2}(f(v))$. 3) $F_{e1}(uv) = F_{e2}(f(u)f(v))$.

2. **Supergraph queries:** searches for the graph database members of which their whole structures are *contained* in the input query. Therefore, given a graph database $D = \{g_1, g_2, ..., g_n\}$ and a supergraph query q, the query answer set $A = \{g_i | q \supseteq g_i, g_i \in D\}$. Figure 1(b) illustrates the subgraph search problem. Let us assume that the graph queries of Figure 2(b) are supergraph queries.

   If we evaluate these queries over the sample graph database (Figure 2(a)) then the answer set of q_1 will be empty while the answer set of q_2 will contain the graph database member g_3.

3. **Similarity (Approximate Matching) queries:** this category finds graphs which are *similar*, but not necessarily isomorphic to a given query graph. Given a graph database $D = \{g_1, g_2, ..., g_n\}$ and a query graph q, similarity search is to discover all graphs that are approximately similar to the graph query q. A key question in graph similarity queries is how to measure the similarity between a target graph member of the database and the query graph. In fact, it is difficult to give a precise definition of graph similarity. Different approaches have proposed different similarity metrics for graph data structures (Bunke & Shearer, 1998; Fern•andez & Valiente, 2001; Raymond et al., 2002). Discussing these different similarity metrics is out of the scope of this chapter. We refer the interested reader to a detailed survey in (Gao et al., 2009).

Figure 1. Graph database querying

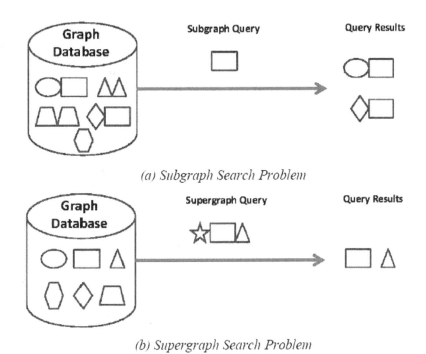

(a) Subgraph Search Problem

(b) Supergraph Search Problem

SUBGRAPH QUERY PROCESSING

There are many graph indexing techniques that have been recently proposed to deal with the problem of subgraph query processing (Sakr, 2009; Yan et al., 2004; Zhang et al., 2007; Zhao et al., 2007). Subgraph query processing techniques can be divided into the following two approaches:

- **Non Mining-Based Graph Indexing Techniques:** The techniques of this approach focus on indexing the whole constructs of the graph database instead of indexing only some selected features (Giugno & Shasha, 2002; He & Singh, 2006; Jiang et al., 2007; Sakr, 2009; Williams et al., 2007). The main criticisms of these approaches are that: 1) they can be less effective in their pruning power; 2) they may need to conduct expensive structure comparisons in the filtering process and thus degrades the filtering efficiency. Therefore, these techniques need to employ efficient filtering and pruning mechanisms to overcome these limitations. However, The techniques of this approach have a clear advantage in that they can handle the graph updates with less cost as they do not rely on the effectiveness of the selected features and they do not need to rebuild their whole indexes.
- **Mining-Based Graph Indexing Techniques:** The techniques of this approach apply graph-mining methods (Kuramochi & Karypis, 2001, 2004; Wang et al., 2004; Washio & Motoda, 2003; Yan & Han, 2002, 2003) to extract some features (sub-structures) from the graph database members (Cheng et al., 2007; Yan et al., 2004; Zhang et al., 2007; Zhao et al., 2007). An inverted index is created for each feature. Answering a subgraph query q is achieved through two steps:

Figure 2. An example graph database and graph queries

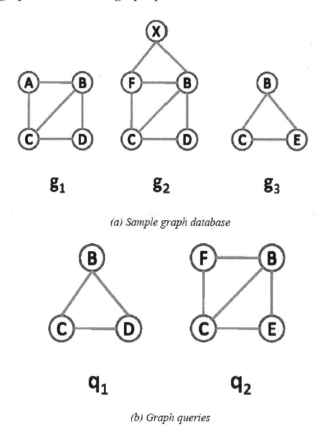

(a) Sample graph database

(b) Graph queries

1. Identifying the set of features of the subgraph query.
2. Using the inverted index to retrieve all graphs that contain the same features of q.

The rationale behind this type of query processing techniques is that if some features of graph q do not exist in a data graph G, then G cannot contain q as its subgraph (inclusion logic). Formally, Clearly, the effectiveness of these filtering methods depends on the quality of mining techniques to effectively identify the set of *features*. Therefore, important decisions need to be made about: the indexing feature, the number and the size of indexing features. These decisions crucially affect the cost of the mining process and the pruning power of the indexing mechanism. A main limitation of these approaches is that the quality of the selected features may degrade over time after lots of insertions and deletions. In this case, the set of features in the whole updated graph database need to be re-identified and the index needs to be re-build from scratch. It should be noted that, achieving these tasks is quite time consuming.

Non Mining-Based Graph Indexing Techniques

GraphGrep

The *GraphGrep* (Giugno & Shasha, 2002) index structure uses enumerated paths as index features to filter unmatched graphs. For each graph database member, it enumerates all paths up to a certain maximum

Figure 3. Sample graph decomposition

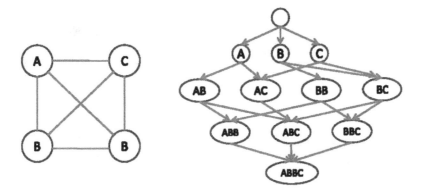

length and records the number of occurrences of each path. Hence, in this index table, each row stands for a path and each column stands for a graph. Each entry in the table is the number of occurrences of the path in the graph. In the query processing, the path indexes is used to find a set of candidate graphs which contains paths in the query structure and to check if the counts of such paths are beyond the threshold specified in the query. In the verification step, each candidate graph is examined by subgraph isomorphism to obtain the final results. The main strength of this approach is that the indexing process of paths with limited lengths is usually fast. However, the size of the indexed paths could drastically increase with the size of graph database. In addition, the filtering power of paths data structure is limited. Therefore, the verification cost can be very high due to the large size of the candidate set.

GDIndex

Williams et al. (2007) have presented an approach for graph database indexing using a structured graph decomposition named GDIndex. In this approach, all connected and induced subgraphs of a given graph are enumerated. Therefore, a graph of size n is decomposed into at most 2^n subgraphs when each of the vertices has a unique label. However, due to isomorphism between enumerated graphs, a complete graph with multiple occurrences of the same label may decompose into fewer subgraphs. If all labels are identical, a complete graph of size n is decomposed into just $n + 1$ subgraphs. A directed acyclic graph (DAG) is constructed to model the decomposed graphs and the contained relationships between them. In this DAG, there is always one node that represents the whole graph G, and one node that represents the null graph. The children of a node P are all graphs Q where there is a directed link in the DAG between P and Q. Moreover, the descendants of a node P are all nodes that are reachable from P in the DAG. Figure 3 depicts a sample of graph decomposition using the GDIndex approach.

A hash table is used to index the subgraphs enumerated during the decomposition process. The hash key of each subgraph is determined from the string value given by the canonical code of the subgraph. This canonical code is computed from its adjacency matrix. In this way, all isomorphic graphs produce the same hash key. Since all entries in the hash table are in canonical form, only one entry is made for each unique canonical code. This hash table enables the search function to quickly locate any node in the decomposition DAG, which is isomorphic to a query graph, if it exists. Therefore, in the query-processing step, the hash key of the graph query q is computed from the query's canonical code. This

Figure 4. Sample graph representation using GString basic structures

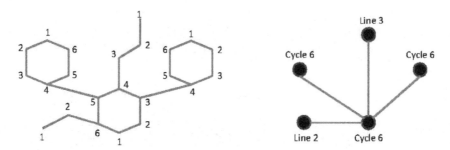

computed hash value of the graph query is then used to identify and verify the set of queries that matches the canonical codes of the graph query. A clear advantage of the GDIndex approach is that no candidate verification is required. However, the index is designed for databases that consist of relatively smaller graphs and do not have a large number of distinct graphs.

GString

The *GString* approach (Jiang et al., 2007) considers the semantics of the graph structures in the database. It focuses on modeling graph objects in the context of organic chemistry using basic structures (*Line*, *Star* and *Cycle*) that have semantic meaning and use them as indexing features. *Line* structure denotes a structure consisting of a series of vertices connected end to end, *Cycle* structure denotes a structure consisting of a series of vertices that form a close loop and *Star* structure denotes a structure where a core vertex directly connects to several vertexes. For a graph g, GString first extracts all Cycle structures, then it extracts all Star structures, and finally, it identifies the remaining structures as Line structures. Figure 4 represents a sample graph representation using the GString basic structures. GString represents both graphs and queries on graphs as string sequences and transforms the subgraph search problem to the subsequence string-matching domain.

A suffix tree-based index structure for the string representations is then created to support an efficient string matching process. Given a basic structure, its GString has three components: *type*, *size*, and a set of annotations (*edits*). For Line or Cycle, the size is the number of vertices in the structure. For Star, the size indicates the fanout of the central vertex. For a query graph q, GString derives its summary string representation which is then matched against the suffix-tree of the graph database. An element of a summary string matches a node in the suffix-tree if their types match, sizes are equal or the size in the query is no more than the size in the node and the counts of corresponding types of edits in the query are no larger than those in the node. A key disadvantage of the GString approach is that converting subgraph search queries into a string matching problem could be an inefficient approach especially if the size of the graph database or the subgraph query is large. Additionally, GString focuses on decomposing chemical compounds into basic structures that have semantic meaning in the context of organic chemistry and it is not trivial to extend this approach in other domain of applications.

Figure 5. Sample GraphREL encoding of graph databases

graphID	vertexID	vLabel
1	1	A
1	2	A
1	3	D
1	4	A
1	5	C
1	6	B
2	1	A
2	2	C
2	3	D
2	4	C
2	5	B

Vertices Table

graphID	sVertex	dVertex	eLabel
1	1	2	n
1	1	3	m
1	2	3	n
1	4	3	x
1	5	4	x
1	6	5	y
1	5	2	z
1	1	6	m
2	1	2	e
2	2	3	m
2	4	3	m
2	4	2	n
2	5	4	x
2	1	5	f

Edges Table

GraphREL

Sakr (2009) has presented a purely relational framework for processing graph queries named GraphREL. In this approach, the graph data set is encoded using an intuitive Vertex-Edge relational mapping scheme ((Figure 5) and the graph query is translated into a sequence of SQL evaluation steps over the defined storage scheme. An obvious problem in the relational-based evaluation approach of graph queries is the huge cost which may result from the large number of join operations which are required to be performed between the encoding relations. Several relational query optimization techniques have been exploited to speed up the search efficiency in the context of graph queries. The main optimization technique of GraphREL is based on the observation that the size of the intermediate results dramatically affects the overall evaluation performance of SQL scripts (Teubner et al., 2008). Therefore, GraphREL keeps statistical information about the less frequently existing nodes and edges in the graph database in the form of simple Markov Tables.

For a graph query q, the maintained statistical information is used to identify the highest pruning point on its structure (nodes or edges with very low frequency) to firstly filter out, as many as possible, of the false positives graphs that are guaranteed to not exist in the final results first before passing the candidate result set to an optional verification process. This statistical information is also used to influence the decision of relational query optimizers by selectivity annotations of the translated query predicates to make the right decision regarding the selection of most efficient join order and the cheapest execution plan (Bruno et al., 2009).

Based on the fact that the number of distinct vertices and edges labels are usually far less than the number of vertices and edges in graph databases, GraphREL utilizes the powerful partitioned B-trees indexing mechanism of the relational databases to reduce the access costs of the secondary storage to a minimum. GraphREL applies an optional verification process only if more than one vertex of the set of query vertices has the same label. For large graph queries, GraphREL applies a decomposition mechanism to divide the large and complex SQL translation query into a sequence of intermediate queries (using temporary tables) before evaluating the final results. This decomposition mechanism reuses the statistical summary information an effective selectivity-aware decomposition process and reduces the size of the intermediate result of each step.

Mining-Based Graph Indexing Techniques

Graph-Based Mining

The *GIndex* technique (Yan et al., 2004) is the first work that used pattern-mining techniques to index graph databases. It makes use of frequent subgraphs as the basic indexing unit. The main observation of this approach is that graph-based index can significantly improve query performance over a path-based one due to the high pruning power of graph data structures. However, the limitation of using subgraphs as the indexing unit is that the number of graph structures is usually much larger than the number of paths in a graph database. To deal with this problem, GIndex considers only frequent subgraphs. Therefore, in order to avoid the exponential growth of the number of frequent subgraphs, the support threshold is progressively increased when the subgraphs grow large. Any subgraph is considered as being frequent if its support is greater than a minimum support threshold. GIndex uses low support for small subgraphs and high support for large subgraphs. Given a query graph q, if q is a frequent subgraph, the exact set of query answers containing q can be retrieved directly without performing any candidate verification since q is indexed. Otherwise, q probably has a frequent subgraph f whose support maybe close to the support threshold. A candidate answer set of query q is then retrieved and verified. If the query graph q is infrequent that means this subgraph is only contained in a small number of graphs in the database. Therefore, the number of subgraph isomorphism tests is going to be small. Among similar fragments with the same support, GIndex only index the smallest common fragment since more query graphs may contain the smallest fragment. Therefore, the subgraph indexes can be more compact and more effective.

Cheng et al. (2007) have extended the ideas of GIndex (Yan et al., 2004) by using nested inverted-index in a new graph index structure named *FG-Index*. In this index structure, a memory-resident inverted-index is built using the set of frequent subgraphs. A disk-resident inverted-index is built on the closure of the frequent graphs. If the closure is too large, a local set of closure frequent subgraphs can be computed from the set of frequent graphs and a further nested inverted-index can be constructed. The main advantage of this approach is that it can answer an important subset of queries (frequent graph queries) directly without verification.

Tree-Based Mining

Zhang et al. (2007) have presented an approach for using frequent subtrees as the indexing unit for graph structures named *TreePI*. The main idea of this approach is based on two main observations: 1) Tree data structures are more complex patterns than paths and trees can preserve almost equivalent amount of structural information as arbitrary subgraph patterns. 2) The frequent subtree mining process is relatively easier than general frequent subgraph mining process. Therefore, the TreePI starts by mining the frequent tree on the graph database and then selecting a set of frequent trees as index patterns. In the query processing, for a query graph q, the frequent subtrees in q are identified and then and then matched with the set of indexing features to obtain a candidate set. In the verification phase, the advantage of the location information partially stored with the feature trees is utilized for devising an efficient subgraph isomorphism tests. As the canonical form of any tree can be calculated in polynomial time, the indexing and searching operations can be effectively improved. Moreover, operations on trees, such as isomorphism and normalization are asymptotically simpler than graphs, which are usually NP-complete (Fortin, 1996).

Zhao et al. (2007) have extended the ideas of TreePi (Zhang et al., 2007) to achieve better pruning ability by adding a small number of discriminative graphs (Δ) to the frequent tree-features in the index structure. They propose a new graph indexing mechanism, named (Tree+Δ), which first selects frequent tree-features as the basis of a graph index, and then on-demand selects a small number of discriminative graph-features that can prune graphs more effectively than the selected tree-features, without conducting costly graph mining beforehand.

SUPERGRAPH QUERY PROCESSING

The *supergraph* query-processing problem is important in practice. However, it has not been extensively considered in the research literature. Only two approaches have been presented to deal with this problem. Chen et al. (2007) have presented an approach named *cIndex* as the first work on supergraph query processing. The indexing unit of this approach is the subgraphs which extracted from graph databases based on their rarely occurrence in historical query graphs. Sometimes, the extracted subgraphs are very similar to each other. Therefore, cIndex tries to find a set of contrast subgraphs that collectively perform well. It uses a redundancy-aware selection mechanism to sort out the most significant and distinctive contrast subgraphs. The distinctive subgraph is stored in a hierarchical fashion using bottom-up and top-down proposed approaches. During query processing, cIndex reduces the number of subgraph isomorphism testing by using the filtering and verification methodology. An advantage of the cIndex approach is that the size of the feature index is small. On the other hand, the query logs may frequently change over time so that the feature index maybe outdated quite often and need to be recomputed to stay effective.

Zhang et al. (2009) have investigated the supergraph query-processing problem from another angle. They proposed an approach for compact organization of graph database members named *GPTree*. In this approach, all of the graph database members are stored into one graph where the common subgraphs are stored only once. An algorithm for extracting the key features from graph databases is used to construct the feature indexes on graph database members. Based on the containment relationship between the support sets of the extracted features, a mathematical approach is used to determine the ordering of the feature set which can reduce the number of subgraph isomorphism tests during query processing.

GRAPH SIMILARITY QUERIES

The problem of similarity (approximate) subgraph queries has been addressed by different research efforts in the literature. Given a query graph and a database of graphs, these approaches try to find subgraphs in the database that are *similar* to the query. Therefore, these approaches can allow for node mismatches, node gaps (Gap node is a node in the query that cannot be mapped to any node in the target graph), as well as graph structural differences. Approximate graph matching techniques are used in some cases when the graph databases are noisy or incomplete. In these cases, using approximate graph matching query-processing techniques can be more useful and effective than exact matching. In this section, we give an overview of the main approaches which address this problem.

Grafil

Yan et al. (2005) have proposed a feature-based structural filtering algorithm, named *Grafil* (*Gra*ph Similarity *Fil*tering) to perform substructure similarity search in graph databases. Grafil models each query graph as a set of features and transforms the edge deletions into the feature misses in the query graph. With an upper bound on the maximum allowed feature misses, Grafil can filter many graphs directly without performing pair-wise similarity computation. It uses two data structures: *feature-graph matrix* and *edge-feature matrix*.

The feature-graph matrix is used to compute the difference in the number of features between a query graph and graphs in the database. In this matrix, each column corresponds to a target graph in the graph database, each row corresponds to a feature being indexed and each entry records the number of the embeddings of a specific feature in a target graph. The edge-feature matrix is used to compute a bound on the maximum allowed feature misses based on a query relaxation ratio. In this matrix, each row represents an edge while each column represents an embedding of a feature. Grafil uses a multi-filter composition strategy, where each filter uses a distinct and complimentary subset of the features. The filters are constructed by a hierarchical, one-dimensional clustering algorithm that groups features with similar selectivity into a feature set.

During the query processing, the feature-graph matrix is used to calculate the difference in the number of features between each graph database member g_i and the query q. If the difference is greater than a user-defined parameter d_{max} then it is discarded while the remaining graphs constitute a candidate answer set. The substructure similarity is then calculated for each candidate to prune the false positives candidates. A loop of query relaxation steps can be applied if the user needs more matches than those returned from the current value of d_{max}.

Closure Tree

He & Singh (2006) have proposed a tree-based index structure named *CTree* (*Closure-T*ree). CTree index is very similar to the R-tree indexing mechanism (Guttman, 1984) but extended to support graph-matching queries. In this index structure, each node in the tree contains discriminative information about its descendants in order to facilitate effective pruning. The closure of a set of vertices is defined as a generalized vertex whose attribute is the union of the attribute values of the vertices. Similarly, the closure of a set of edges is defined as a generalized edge whose attribute is the union of the attribute values of the edges. The closure of two graphs g_1 and g_2 under a mapping *M* is defined as a generalized graph *(V, E)* where *V* is the set of vertex closures of the corresponding vertices and *E* is the set of edge closures of the corresponding edges (Figure 6). Hence, a graph closure has the same characteristics of a graph. However, the only difference is that the graph database member has singleton labels on vertices and edges while the graph closure can have multiple labels.

In a closure tree, each node is a graph closure of its children where the children of an internal node are nodes and the children of a leaf node are database graphs. A subgraph query is processed in two phases. The first phase traverses the CTree and the nodes are pruned based on a *pseudo subgraph isomorphism*. A candidate answer set is returned. The second phase verifies each candidate answer for exact subgraph isomorphism and returns the answers. In addition to pruning based on pseudo subgraph isomorphism, a lightweight histogram-based pruning is also employed. The histogram of a graph is a vector that counts the number of each distinct attribute of the vertices and edges. For similarity queries,

Figure 6. Graph closure

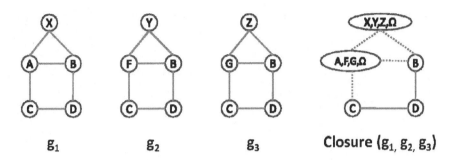

CTree defines graph similarity based on edit distance, and computes it using heuristic graph mapping methods. It conceptually approximates subgraph isomorphism by sub-isomorphism using adjacent subgraphs then it approximates sub-isomorphism by using adjacent subtrees.

SAGA

Tian et al. (2007) have presented an approach of approximate graph query matching named *SAGA* (substructure index-based approximate graph alignment). SAGA measures graph similarity by a distance value such that graphs that are more similar have a smaller distance. The distance model contains three components:

1. The *StructDist* component measures the structural differences for the matching node pairs in the two graphs.
2. The *NodeMismatches* component is the penalty associated with matching two nodes with different labels.
3. The *NodeGaps* component is used to measure the penalty for the gap nodes in the query graph.

SAGA index is built on small substructures of graphs in the database (*Fragment Index*). Each fragment is a set of k nodes from the graphs in the database where K is a user-defined parameter. The index does not enumerate all possible k-node sets. It uses another user-defined parameter $dist_{max}$ to avoid indexing any pair of nodes in a fragment if its distance measure is greater than $dist_{max}$. The fragments in SAGA do not always correspond to connected subgraphs. The reason behind this is to allow node gaps in the matching process. To efficiently evaluate the subgraph distance between a query graph and a database graph, an additional index called *DistanceIndex* is also maintained. This index is used to look up the pre-computed distance between any pair of nodes in a graph. The graph matching process goes through the following three steps:

1. The query is broken into small fragments and the Fragment Index is probed to find database fragments that are similar to the query fragments.
2. The hits from the index probes are combined to produce larger candidate matches. A hit-compatible graph is built for each matching graph. Each node in the hit-compatible graph corresponds to a pair of matching query and database fragments. An edge is drawn between two nodes in the hit-compatible

Table 1. Summary of the graph indexing and querying techniques

Indexing Technique	Supported Query Types	Indexing Unit	Indexing Mechanism
CIndex (Chen et al., 2007)	Supergraph queries	Subgraph structure	Rarely occurring features
Closure-Tree (He & Singh, 2006)	Subgraph and similarity	Closure Tree	Enumeration of graph closures
FG-Index (Cheng et al., 2007	Subgraph queries	Subgraph structure	Frequent features
GDIndex (Williams et al., 2007)	Subgraph queries	Decomposed subgraph	Full enumeration
GIndex (Yan et al., 2004)	Similarity queries	Subgraph structure	Frequent features
GPTree (Zhang et al., 2009)	Supergraph queries	Subgraph structure	Full enumeration
Grafil (Yan et al., 2005)	Similarity queries	Any	Full enumeration
GraphGrep (Guigno & Shasha, 2002)	Subgraph queries	Path structure	Full enumeration
GraphREL (Sakr, 2009)	Subgraph queries	Nodes and Edges	Full enumeration
GString (Jiang et al., 2007)	Subgraph queries	Subgraph structure	Full enumeration
SAGA (Tian et al., 2007)	Similarity queries	Subgraph structure	Full enumeration
TreeDelta (Zhao et al., 2007)	Subgraph queries	Tree structure	Frequent features
TreePi (Zhang et al., 2007)	Subgraph queries	Tree structure	Frequent features

graph if and only if two query fragments share zero or more nodes, and the corresponding database fragments in the hit-compatible graph also share the same corresponding nodes. An edge between two nodes tells us that the corresponding two hits can be merged to form a larger match which is then a candidate match.

3. Each candidate is examined to produce the query results. For each candidate, the percentage of the gap nodes is checked. If it exceeds a user-defined threshold P_g, then the candidate match is ignored otherwise, the *DistanceIndex* is probed to calculate the real subgraph matching distance. If two matches have the same matching distance and one is a submatch of the other, only the supermatch is considered.

Table 1 provides a comparison between the different graph indexing techniques in terms of their supported query types, indexing unit and indexing strategy.

GRAPH QUERY LANGUAGES

With the prevalence of graph data in a variety of application domains, there is an increasing need for a suitable language to query and manipulate graph data structure (Angles & Guti•errez, 2008). In this section, we give an overview of representative proposals for graph query languages in the literature.

In (Leser, 2005) Leser has proposed a special-purpose graph query language for biological networks called *PQL* (Pathway Query Language). PQL is a declarative language whose syntax is similar to SQL. The language targets retrieving specific parts of large, complex networks. It is based on a simple graph data model with extensions reflecting properties of biological objects. PQL queries match arbitrary subgraphs in the database based on node properties and paths between nodes. The general syntax of PQL is as follows:

```
SELECT subgraph-specification FROM node-variables
WHERE node-condition-set
```

During query evaluation node variables are bound to nodes of the database graph such that all node-conditions in the WHERE clause evaluate to TRUE. The query result is constructed from these variable bindings according to the subgraph-specification of the SELECT clause. Query evaluation considers each node variable in the FROM clause. For each of these variables, all possible assignments of the variable to nodes of the graph are determined for which the conditions of the WHERE clause mentioning only this variable evaluates to TRUE. Node variables are equally assigned to molecules and interactions. Once all possible bindings are computed for each node variable, the Cartesian product of these sets is computed. From this set, all instances are removed for which the entire WHERE clause evaluates to FALSE and all distinct assignments from the remaining elements of the Cartesian product are combined to form the match graph. In general, SQL query operates on tables and produces a table (a set of rows), in the same manner as a PQL query operates on a graph and produces a graph (a set of nodes) and not a set of graphs. In the result of the SQL query the rows from the Cartesian product are preserved, columns might be removed, added, or changed in their value. In PQL, the concrete combinations of bindings of different node variables that together fulfill the WHERE clause are not preserved in the match graph of a PQL query. The match graph simply consists of all bindings present in the filtered Cartesian product into a flat, duplicate-free list of nodes.

In (He & Singh, 2008) He and Singh have proposed a general graph query and manipulation languages called GraphQL. In this language, graphs are considered as the basic unit of information and each query manipulates one or more collections of graphs. It also targets graph databases that supports arbitrary attributes on nodes, edges, and graphs. The core of GraphQL is its data model and its graph algebra. In the GraphQL data model, a graph pattern is represented as a graph structure and a predicate on attributes of the graph. Each node, edge, or graph can have arbitrary attributes. A tuple with a list of name and value pairs is used to denote these attributes. In GraphQL algebra, graphs are the basic unit of information. Each operator takes one or more collections of graphs as input and generates a collection of graphs as output. For example, the selection operator takes a collection of graphs as input and produces a collection of graphs that match the graph pattern as an output. A graph pattern can match a specific graph database member many times. Therefore, an exhaustive option is used to specify whether it should return one or all possible matches. A Cartesian product operator takes two collections of graphs *C* and *D* and produces a collection of graphs as output where each output graph is composed of a graph from *C* and another from *D*. The join operator is defined as a Cartesian product operator followed by a selection operator. The composition operator generates new graphs by combining information from matched graphs based on graph templates that specify the output structure of the graphs.

Consens & Mendelzon (1990) have proposed a graphical query language for graph databases called GraphLog. Graphlog queries ask for patterns that must be present or absent in the database graph. In GraphLog, the query graph can define a set of new edges that are added to the graph whenever the search pattern is found. Awad has followed a similar approach in (Awad, 2007) where he presented a visual query language for business process definitions called BPMN-Q. BPMN-Q allows expressing structural queries and specifies proceedings of determining whether a given process model graph is structurally similar to a query graph. BPMN-Q relies on the notations of BPMN languages as its concrete syntax and provides a set of new visual constructs that can be seen as abstractions over the existing modeling constructs. For example a Path construct connecting two nodes in a query represents an abstraction over

Table 2. Summary graph query languages

Query Language	Target Domain	Query Units	Query Style
BPMN-Q (Awad, 2007)	Business Process Models	Subgraphs	Graphical
GOOD (Gyssens et al., 1994)	General	nodes/edges	Declarative (OQL-Like)
GOQL (Sheng et al., 1999)	General	nodes/edges	Declarative (OQL-Like)
GraphLog (Consens & Mendelzon, 1990)	General	nodes/edges	Graphical
GraphQL (He & Singh, 2008)	General	Subgraphs	Declarative (XQuery-Like)
PQL (Leser, 2005)	Biological networks	Subgraphs	Declarative (SQL-Like)
SPARQL (Prud'hommeaux & Seaborne, 2008)	Semantic Web	Subgraphs	Declarative (SQL-Like)

whatever nodes could be in between in the matching process model while Negative Path used to express that two nodes must have no connection between them.

There are some other proposal for graph query languages that have been proposed in the literature such as: GOQL (Sheng et al., 1999), GOOD (Gyssens et al., 1994) and SPARQL (Prud'hommeaux & Seaborne, 2008). For example, GOQL and GOOD are designed based on an extension of OQL (Object-Oriented Query Language) and rely on an object-oriented graph data model. SPARQL query language is a W3C recommendation for querying RDF graph data. It describes a directed labeled graph by a set of triples, each of which describes a (attribute, value) pair or an interconnection between two nodes. The SPARQL query language works primarily through a primitive triple pattern matching techniques with simple constraints on query nodes and edges.

Table 2 provides a comparison between the graph query languages in terms of their target domain, query unit and query style.

DISCUSSION AND CONCLUSION

In this chapter, we give an overview of the problem of graph indexing and querying techniques. The problem is motivated by the continued emergence and increase of massive and complex structural data. Due to the very expensive cost of pair-wise comparison of graph data structures, recently proposed graph query processing techniques rely on a strategy which consists of two steps: *filtering* and *verification*. For a given graph database D and a graph query q, the main objective of the filtering and verification methodology is to avoid comparing the query graph q with each graph database member g_i that belongs to D to check whether gi satisfies the conditions of q or not. Therefore, most of the proposed graph indexing strategies shift the high online graph query processing cost to the off-line index construction phase. Index construction is thus, always computationally expensive because it requires the use of high quality indexing features with great pruning power from the graph database. However, the number of indexing features should be as small as possible to keep the whole index structure compact so that it is possible to be held in the main memory for efficient access and retrieval. Hence, a high quality graph indexing mechanism should be time-efficient in index construction and indexing features should be compact and powerful for pruning purposes. Moreover, candidate verification can be still very expensive as the size of the candidate answer set is *at least* equal to that of the exact answer set in the optimal case but it is usually larger. Hence, reducing the size of the candidate answer set by removing as much as possible of the false positive graphs is the main criteria to evaluate the effectiveness of any filtering technique.

There is a clear imbalance between the number of developed techniques for processing supergraph queries and the other types of graph queries. The reason behind this is that the supergraph query type can be considered to be relatively new. Therefore, there are many technical aspects which still remain unexplored.

A clear gap in the research efforts in the domain of graph database is the absence of a *standard* graph query language which plays the same role as that SQL for the relational data model or XPath and XQuery for the XML hierarchical model. Although there are a number of query languages that have been proposed in the literature (Consens & Mendelzon, 1990; Gyssens et al., 1994; Sheng et al., 1999), none of them has been universally accepted as they are designed to deal with different representations of the graph data model. A *standard* definition of a general purpose graph query language with more powerful and flexible constructs is essentially required. A concrete algebra behind this expected query language is also quite important.

The proposed graph query processing techniques concentrate on the retrieval speed of their indexing structures in addition to their compact size. Further management of these indexes is rarely taken into account. Although efficient query processing is an important objective, efficient update maintenance is also an important concern. In the case of dynamic graph databases, it is quite important that indexing techniques avoid the costly recomputation of the whole index and provide more efficient mechanisms to update the underneath index structures with minimum effort. Therefore, efficient mechanisms to handle dynamic graph databases are necessary.

Finally, query processing usually involves a cost-based optimization phase in which query optimizers rely on cost models to attempt on choosing an optimal query plan from amongst several alternatives. A key issue of any cost model is the cardinality estimation of the intermediate and final query results. Although there is an initial effort has been proposed by Stocker et al. (2008) for estimating the selectivity estimation of basic graph patterns, there is still a clear need for summarization and estimation frameworks for graph databases. These frameworks need to provide accurate selectivity estimations of more complex graph patterns which can be utilized in accelerating the processing of different types of graph queries.

REFERENCES

Angles, R., & Gutierrez, C. (2008). Survey of graph database models. *ACM Computing Surveys, 40*(1), 1–39. doi:10.1145/1322432.1322433

Awad, A. (2007). BPMN-Q: A language to query business processes. In *Proceedings of the 2nd International Workshop on Enterprise Modelling and Information Systems Architectures,* (pp. 115-128).

Bruno, N., Chaudhuri, S., & Ramamurthy, R. (2009). Power hints for query optimization. In *Proceedings of the 25th International Conference on Data Engineering,* (pp. 469-480).

Bunke, H., & Shearer, K. (1998). A graph distance metric based on the maximal common subgraph. *Pattern Recognition Letters, 19*(3-4), 255–259. doi:10.1016/S0167-8655(97)00179-7

Cai, D., Shao, Z., He, X., Yan, X., & Han, J. (2005). Community mining from multi-relational networks. In *Proceedings of the 9th European Conference on Principles and Practice of Knowledge Discovery in Databases,* (pp. 445-452).

Chen, C., Yan, X., Yu, P. S., Han, J., Zhang, D.-Q., & Gu, X. (2007). Towards graph containment search and indexing. In *Proceedings of the 33rd International Conference on Very Large Data Bases,* (pp. 926-937).

Cheng, J., Ke, Y., Ng, W., & Lu, A. (2007). FG-Index: Towards verification-free query processing on graph databases. In *Proceedings of the ACM SIGMOD International Conference on Management of Data,* (pp. 857-872).

Consens, M. P., & Mendelzon, A. O. (1990). GraphLog: A visual formalism for real life recursion. In *Proceedings of the Ninth ACM SIGACT-SIGMOD-SIGART Symposium on Principles of Database Systems,* (pp. 404-416).

Fern•andez, M.-L. & Valiente, G. (2001). A graph distance metric combining maximum common subgraph and minimum common supergraph. *Pattern Recognition Letters, 22*(6/7), 753-758.

Fortin, S. (1996). *The graph isomorphism problem. (Technical Report)*. Department of Computing Science, University of Alberta.

Gao, X., Xiao, B., Tao, D. & Li, X. (2009). A survey of graph edit distance. *Pattern Analysis & Applications*.

Garey, M. R., & Johnson, D. S. (1979). *Computers and intractability: A guide to the theory of NP-completeness*. W.H. Freeman.

Giugno, R., & Shasha, D. (2002). GraphGrep: A fast and universal method for querying graphs. In *IEEE International Conference in Pattern Recognition,* (pp. 112-115).

Guttman, A. (1984). R-Trees: A dynamic index structure for spatial searching. In *Proceedings of the ACM SIGMOD International Conference on Management of Data,* (pp. 47-57).

Gyssens, M., Paredaens, J., den Bussche, J. V., & Gucht, D. V. (1994). A graph-oriented object database model. [TKDE]. *IEEE Transactions on Knowledge and Data Engineering, 6*(4), 572–586. doi:10.1109/69.298174

He, H., & Singh, A. K. (2006). Closure-Tree: An index structure for graph queries. In *Proceedings of the 22nd International Conference on Data Engineering,* (pp. 38-52).

He, H., & Singh, A. K. (2008). Graphs-at-a-time: Query language and access methods for graph databases. In *Proceedings of the ACM SIGMOD International Conference on Management of Data,* (pp. 405-418).

Huan, J., Wang, W., Bandyopadhyay, D., Snoeyink, J., Prins, J., & Tropsha, A. (2004). Mining protein family specific residue packing patterns from protein structure graphs. In *Proceedings of the Eighth Annual International Conference on Computational Molecular Biology,* (pp. 308-315).

Jiang, H., Wang, H., Yu, P. S., & Zhou, S. (2007). GString: A novel approach for efficient search in graph databases. In *Proceedings of the 23rd International conference on Data Engineering,* (pp. 566-575).

Klinger, S., & Austin, J. (2005). Chemical similarity searching using a neural graph matcher. In *Proceedings of the 13th European Symposium on Artificial Neural Networks,* (p. 479-484).

Kuramochi, M., & Karypis, G. (2001). Frequent subgraph discovery. In *Proceedings of the IEEE International Conference on Data Mining,* (pp. 313-320).

Kuramochi, M., & Karypis, G. (2004). GREW-a scalable frequent subgraph discovery algorithm. In *Proceedings of the IEEE International Conference on Data Mining,* (pp. 439-442).

Lee, J., Oh, J.-H., & Hwang, S. (2005). STRG-index: Spatio-temporal region graph indexing for large video databases. In *Proceedings of the ACM SIGMOD International Conference on Management of Data,* (pp. 718-729).

Leser, U. (2005). A query language for biological networks. In *Proceedings of the Fourth European Conference on Computational Biology/Sixth Meeting of the Spanish Bioinformatics Network,* (p. 39).

Manola, F., & Miller, E. (2004). *RDF primer: World Wide Web consortium proposed recommendation.* Retrieved from http://www.w3.org/TR/rdf-primer/

Prud'hommeaux, E., & Seaborne, A. (2008). *SPARQL query language for RDF.* World Wide Web consortium proposed recommendation. Retrieved from http://www.w3.org/TR/rdf-sparql-query/

Raymond, J. W., Gardiner, E. J., & Willett, P. (2002). RASCAL: Calculation of graph similarity using maximum common edge subgraphs. *The Computer Journal, 45*(6), 631–644. doi:10.1093/comjnl/45.6.631

Sakr, S. (2009). GraphREL: A decomposition-based and selectivity-aware relational framework for processing sub-graph queries. In *Proceedings of the 14th International Conference on Database Systems for Advanced Applications,* (pp. 123-137).

Sheng, L., Ozsoyoglu, Z. M., & Ozsoyoglu, G. (1999). A graph query language and its query processing. In *Proceedings of the 15th International Conference on Data Engineering,* (pp. 572-581).

Stocker, M., Seaborne, A., Bernstein, A., Kiefer, C., & Reynolds, D. (2008). SPARQL basic graph pattern optimization using selectivity estimation. In *Proceedings of the 17th International Conference on World Wide Web,* (pp. 595-604).

Teubner, J., Grust, T., Maneth, S., & Sakr, S. (2008). Dependable cardinality forecasts for XQuery. [PVLDB]. *Proceedings of the VLDB Endowment, 1*(1), 463–477.

Tian, Y., McEachin, R. C., Santos, C., States, D. J., & Patel, J. M. (2007). SAGA: A subgraph matching tool for biological graphs. *Bioinformatics (Oxford, England), 23*(2), 232–239. doi:10.1093/bioinformatics/btl571

Wang, C., Wang, W., Pei, J., Zhu, Y., & Shi, B. (2004). Scalable mining of large disk-based graph databases. In *Proceedings of the Tenth ACM SIGKDD International Conference on Knowledge Discovery and Data Mining,* (pp. 316-325).

Washio, T., & Motoda, H. (2003). State of the art of graph-based data mining. *SIGKDD Explorations, 5*(1), 59–68. doi:10.1145/959242.959249

Williams, D. W., Huan, J., & Wang, W. (2007). Graph database indexing using structured graph decomposition. In *Proceedings of the 23rd International Conference on Data Engineering,* (pp. 976-985).

Yan, X., & Han, J. (2002). gSpan: Graph-based substructure pattern mining. In *Proceedings of the IEEE International Conference on Data Mining,* (pp. 721-724).

Yan, X., & Han, J. (2003). CloseGraph: Mining closed frequent graph patterns. In *Proceedings of the 9th ACM SIGKDD International Conference on Knowledge Discovery and Data Mining,* (pp. 286-295).

Yan, X., Yu, P. S., & Han, J. (2004). Graph indexing: A frequent structure-based approach. In *Proceedings of the ACM SIGMOD International Conference on Management of Data,* (pp. 335-346).

Yan, X., Yu, P. S., & Han, J. (2005). Substructure similarity search in graph databases. In *Proceedings of the ACM SIGMOD International Conference on Management of Data,* (pp. 766-777).

Zhang, S., Hu, M., & Yang, J. (2007). TreePi: A novel graph indexing method. In *Proceedings of the 23rd International Conference on Data Engineering,* (pp. 966-975).

Zhang, S., Li, J., Gao, H., & Zou, Z. (2009). A novel approach for efficient supergraph query processing on graph databases. In *Proceedings of the 12th International Conference on Extending Database Technology,* (pp. 204-215).

Zhao, P., Yu, J. X., & Yu, P. S. (2007). Graph indexing: Tree + delta >= Graph. In *Proceedings of the 33rd International Conference on Very Large Data Bases,* (pp. 938-949).

Chapter 14
Querying Multimedia Data by Similarity in Relational DBMS

Maria Camila Nardini Barioni
Federal University of ABC, Brazil

Daniel dos Santos Kaster
University of Londrina, Brazil

Humberto Luiz Razente
Federal University of ABC, Brazil

Agma Juci Machado Traina
University of São Paulo at São Carlos, Brazil

Caetano Traina Júnior
University of São Paulo at São Carlos, Brazil

ABSTRACT

Multimedia objects – such as images, audio, and video – do not present the total ordering relationship, so the relational operators ('<', '≤', '≥', '>') are not suitable to compare them. Therefore, similarity queries are the most useful, and often the only types of queries adequate to search multimedia objects stored in a database. Unfortunately, the ubiquitous query language SQL – the most widely employed language in Database Management Systems (DBMS) – does not provide effective support for similarity queries. This chapter presents an already validated strategy that adds similarity queries to SQL, supporting a powerful set of similarity operators. The chapter also describes techniques to store and retrieve multimedia objects in an efficient way and shows existing DBMS alternatives to execute similarity queries over multimedia data.

DOI: 10.4018/978-1-60960-475-2.ch014

INTRODUCTION

With the increasing availability and capacity of recording equipments, managing the huge amount of multimedia data generated has been more and more challenging. Without a proper retrieval mechanism, such data is usually forgotten on a storage device and most of them are never touched again.

As the information embedded into multimedia data is intrinsically complex and rich, the retrieval approaches for such data usually rely on its contents. However, Multimedia Objects (MO) are seldom compared directly, because their binary representation is of little help to understand their content. Rather, a set of predefined features is extracted from the MO, which is thereafter used in place of the original object to perform the retrieval. For example, in Content-Based Image Retrieval (CBIR), images are preprocessed by specific feature extraction algorithms to retrieve their color or texture histograms, polygonal contours of the pictured objects, etc. The features are employed to define a mathematical signature that represents the content of the image regarding specific criteria. The features are employed in the search process.

Although many progress have been achieved in the recent years to handle multimedia content, the development of large-scale applications has been facing problems because existing Database Management Systems (DBMS) lack support for such data. The operators usually employed to compare numbers and small-texts in traditional DBMS are not useful to compare MO. Moreover, MO demand specific indexing structures and other advanced resources, for example, maintaining the query context during a user interaction with a multimedia database.

The most promising approach to overcome these issues is to add support for similarity-based data management inside the DBMS. Similarity can be defined through a function that compares pairs of MO and returns a value stating how similar (close) they are. As it is shown later in this chapter, employing similarity as the basis of the retrieval process allows writing very elaborated queries using a reduced set of operators and developing a consistent and efficient query execution mechanism.

Although a number of works has been reported in the literature describing the basic algorithms to execute similarity retrieval operations on multimedia and other complex object datasets (Roussopoulos et al., 1995, Hjaltason and Samet, 2003, Bohm et al., 2001), there are few works on how to integrate similarity queries into the DBMS core. Some DBMS provide proprietary modules to handle multimedia data and perform a limited set of similarity queries (IBM Corp., 2003, Oracle Corp., 2005, Informix Corp., 1999). However, such approaches are generalist and do not allow including domain-specific resources, which prevent many applications from using them. Moreover, it is worth to note that it is important considering the support of similarity queries in SQL as native predicates to allow representing queries that mix traditional and similarity-based predicates and to execute them efficiently in a Relational DBMS (RDBMS) (Barioni et al., 2008).

This chapter presents the key foundations toward supporting similarity queries as a native resource in RDBMS, addressing the fundamental aspects related to the representation of similarity queries in SQL. It also describes case studies showing how it is possible to perform similarity queries within existing DBMS (Barioni et al., 2006, Kaster et al., 2009).

In the following sections, we describe related work and fundamental concepts, including the general strategy usually adopted to represent and to compare MO, the kinds of similarity queries that can be employed to query multimedia data and some adequate indexing methods. We also discuss issues regarding the support of similarity queries in relational DBMS, presenting the current alternatives and also an already validated approach to seamlessly integrate similarity queries in SQL. There is also a description of case studies for the enhancement of existing DBMS with appropriate techniques to store multimedia data and algorithms to efficiently execute similarity queries over them. Finally, we conclude the chapter and give future research directions on multimedia retrieval support in DBMS.

QUERYING BY SIMILARITY

The Query Representation Problem

One of the reasons why the DBMS are widely adopted is related to its capacity to support the storage and retrieval of large data volumes, enforcing concurrent and safety data access among several applications. They are also characterized by supporting efficient languages that allow both, the definition of data structures (Data Definition Language – DDL) and the specification of queries and data updates (Data Manipulation Language - DML), in such a way that the user has to worry in state what data is wanted but not how to obtain them.

The Structured Query Language (SQL), the *de facto* standard language of DBMS, provides a plentiful set of operators to represent queries involving "simple" data, such as numbers and short texts. However, the modalities of querying operations based on multimedia content bring many more possibilities than those feasible for simple data. If on the one hand searching over sets of numeric attributes usually allows employing total order relationships or well-defined mathematical functions over them, on the other hand searching over sets of multimedia data can involve non-trivial abstractions inferred from their content.

For example, the following queries are relevant for multimedia applications:

- **Q1**: return the images that have a mass of abnormal size in a radiological imaging exam;
- **Q2**: return the images that show a sunset over the sea;
- **Q3**: return the videos that contain parts of other copyrighted videos;
- **Q4**: return the videos of children playing with pets;
- **Q5**: return the songs that have a given drum solo.

Each of these queries requires a particular processing over the data content to be answered. The point is: how to represent the query to be answered by a general-purpose retrieval system? By general-purpose we mean a system that provides sets of primitives that can be reused and specialized by distinct applications, and that share a common group of retrieval requirements. In the following subsections two approaches to answer these problems are discussed.

The Content-Based Operators Approach

The strategy that aims at defining a specific function or operator to every abstraction identified on the data content we call as the *Content-based Operators approach*. For example, to represent the query Q1, this approach requires having a function that identifies a specific pattern in the images (a mass) and another that calculates the area. In a similar way, Q2 demands functions to identify the desired elements (sun and sea) in the scene and operators based on the spatial relationship among them (e.g. north, south, east and west).

Although this approach is suitable to specific applications, the amount of operators needed to represent queries can be excessively high. The operators employed to identify objects should be specialized to each application domain to acquire higher semantics, yielding a variety of functions to represent each (class of) object(s). Moreover, although there are works aimed at retrieving images by spatial similarity between segmented regions, such as (Huang et al., 2008, Yeh and Chang, 2008), queries are usually represented using a sketch or an example of the desired spatial relationships, because representing the association among various objects can be very difficult.

The representation of more complex classes of queries is even harder using content-based operators. Queries Q3, Q4 and Q5 would require defining respectively: what determines a video to be copyrighted, what is the visual pattern that represents the act of playing, and what a drum solo is. It is easy to notice that this approach would lead to an explosion on the amount of operators to meet every situation and the variety of relationships among complex elements and among their components.

The Similarity Operators Approach

We define the *Similarity Operators approach* as the one that provides a few similarity-based operators to be employed in a wide range of situations. These operators have the goal of computing the similarity regarding a predefined pattern between the stored data and the (set of) element(s) provided in the query, verifying when this similarity satisfies a given criteria.

The support for the Similarity Operators approach is twofold: providing an example of the desired pattern is generally more feasible than trying to describe it; and providing a restricted set of operators is sufficient to represent queries over complex data, because the peculiarity of each domain is carried by its definition of similarity.

The first supporting idea is derived from the query-by-example strategy that has been employed in databases for long time. Most of the existing content-based multimedia retrieval tools use this method. The second idea aims at simplifying the overall query answering process to allow developing a consistent retrieval environment. This simplification can be done without losing the generality of the approach because the definition of similarity is *problem-dependent*. For instance, a good similarity measure to answer Q2 would focus on the color distribution pattern of the images. This measure would probably produce poor results if applied to Q1, because what identifies a mass in a radiograph is usually the difference between the mass and its surrounding texture tissue, which is not adequately captured by a standard color-based evaluation, thus requiring a texture extractor. The domain knowledge of each problem class is embedded into the similarity evaluation process, which must be specialized according to the requirements of each case. This allows stating specialized query conditions to a broad range of domains employing few query operators.

The reader may ask whether we are not just transferring the aforementioned problem of the explosion on the amount of operators for multimedia data querying to the explosion of similarity measures. In part this observation is correct. Nevertheless, maintaining a reduced set of similarity operators allows developing a common framework with well-defined query optimization alternatives and with basic primitives and structures that can be applied to a variety of situations. Providing such common framework is not feasible using the Content-based Operators approach.

Therefore, this chapter adopts the Similarity Operators approach for representing queries. The next section discusses similarity evaluation regarding multimedia data.

Similarity Evaluation

Similarity evaluation requires a sequence of computational tasks that results in a value quantifying how close two multimedia objects are. In the philosophical and the psychological literature, the notion of *similarity space* states that the mind embodies a representational hyperspace. In this space, dimensions represent ways in which objects can be distinguished, points represent possible objects and distances between points are inversely proportional to the perceived similarity between those objects (Gauker, 2007).

When dealing with multimedia data, the driving rules of the similarity space that correspond to the human perception is fairly unknown yet. Different users can have different perceptions of a same image or movie depending on their intent and background. Moreover, usually the similarity between two pairs of objects does not always follow the same measurement, the perceived distances may vary according to the user intent in the moment.

The similarity evaluation process is usually quite complex and specialized, thus a great deal of approaches is encountered in the literature. We will organize the building blocks of this process around an abstraction of the similarity space concept. It is assumed that a multimedia data can be modeled through a set of features summarizing its content, which is usually called the data's feature vector, although the features do not need to compose a vector space (e.g. complex objects of a same dataset can have feature vectors of varying sizes). The features along with the distance functions constitute a *descriptor*, which determines the similarity value (Torres et al., 2009). If we interpret each pair *<feature vector-distance function>* as a similarity space instance, the whole set of possible instances forms our abstraction of the human similarity space, in which the instances are switched according to the user perception at each instant.

Therefore, at the base level, it is only necessary to have the feature vector and the distance function to compute the similarity. Although having a manner to compute the similarity suffices to answer similarity queries (see 'Similarity Queries' section), we will discuss herein the internals of similarity evaluation.

In some domains, to choose the right combination is not a problem. For instance, geoprocessing applications usually treat similarity as the distance among objects in the Earth's surface (e.g. return the restaurants that are at most 1 mile from me, return the closest hospital to a given kindergarten). In this case, the (spatial) features of the elements are well-defined (their geographical coordinates) and the function used to compute the proximity is mainly restricted to the Euclidean distance or a shortest path algorithm if the routes are modeled as a graph. On the other hand, for multimedia data it is mandatory to identify which pair *<feature vector-distance function>* forms the space that closely represents the user interpretation in each situation. Assessing the best combination between them improves the query precision (Bugatti et al., 2008).

The challenge is to identify the similarity space instance that best fits the user expectation. This "ideal" instance is usually called the semantic (similarity) space (He et al., 2002). There are many fields and techniques employed to pursue this challenge, as shown in Figure 1. This illustration is not intended to be exhaustive, but to include the most usual concepts regarding similarity. We highlight in this figure that several concepts directly affect the components of a similarity space instance, such as feature extraction, selection and transformation and feature/partial distance weighting. Every modification promoted by any of these elements produces a new alternative instance. On a higher level are the techniques, algorithms and external information that are employed to define how each of these elements will be addressed to accomplish the user needs. In this level are: data processing algorithms, knowledge discovery techniques, relevance feedback, machine learning and others.

Figure 1. The basis of a similarity space instance – a feature vector and a distance function – and the fields and techniques employed to drive its semantics

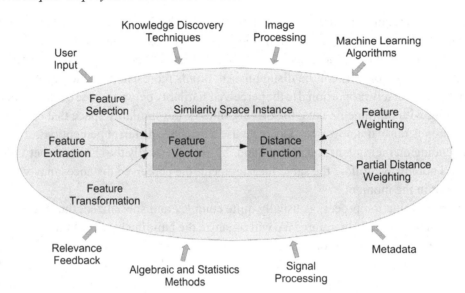

A Look on the Feature Vector Component

Features describing multimedia data can be classified in three abstraction levels, according to the kinds of queries that could be answered (Eakins and Graham, 1999).

- **Level 1.** Comprises retrieval by primitive features directly obtained from the multimedia object, without referring to external knowledge. Examples of such features for still images are general patterns regarding color, texture, shape or location of elements in the scene. Features describing videos include these elements plus motion patterns.
- **Level 2.** Comprises retrieval by derived attributes, identified through some degree of logical inference about the data content. Features capable of identify elements (e.g. a person or an object) and/or simple movements (e.g. an airplane taking off) are included in this level.
- **Level 3.** Comprises retrieval by abstract features, involving a significant amount of high-level reasoning. Features in this level can represent more elaborated actions, such as dancing pictures or videos of children playing with pets.

The abstraction levels present increasing complexity and a tendency to narrow the domain. The lack of coincidence between the low-level features automatically extracted from the multimedia data (Level 1) and the high-level human interpretation (based on features of levels 2 and 3) is known in the literature as the *semantic gap* (Smeulders et al., 2000). Many research efforts have been directed to extract higher-semantic features in order to bridge the gap.

Feature extraction is the first step on which the multimedia data is processed generating a feature vector. The algorithms that identify the features that aim at inferring the data content are called feature extractors. There are many feature extractors for multimedia data proposed in the literature. Images are usually represented through their color, texture and shape patterns extracted either globally in the image or locally in regions identified by segmentation methods. Examples of color feature extractors are the normalized histograms (Long et al., 2003) and the descriptors being considered for inclusion on the MPEG-7 standard (Manjunath et al., 2001), which also include texture descriptors. Regarding texture, it can be cited the Haralick's descriptors (Haralick, 1979), features obtained using the wavelet transform (Santini and Gupta, 2001) and the Gabor filters (Jain and Farrokhnia, 1991). Shape extractors include the contour-based Fourier descriptors (Zahn and Roskies, 1972), the Curvature Scale Space (CSS) descriptors (Mokhtarian and Mackworth, 1986) and the region-based Zernike moments (Khotanzad and Hong, 1990).

With respect to videos, their representation is much more complex due to their intrinsic temporal information. However, they borrow the techniques developed for content-based image retrieval because digital videos are essentially sequences of frames, which are still images. As sequential frames have slight differences, the extraction algorithms are usually based on shots, which are sets of contiguous frames that show an action. Therefore, shot boundary detection is a fundamental process applied in video content and there are many approaches developed to address it (Lienhart, 2001). After having detected the shots, usually a key frame is selected to represent it, which is submitted to image feature extractors. Other features available in videos include the sound track, texts appearing in the scenes, subtitle data that can be extracted and closed captions.

Feature extractors for audio also segment the files in frames. Frames whose sound energy is below a predefined threshold are considered as silence and ignored. From the non-silence frames, features are extracted regarding time, frequency and coefficient domains. Examples of audio extractors are the Mel-Frequency Cepstral Coefficients (MFCC), features based on the Short Time Fourier Transform (STFT) (Tzanetakis and Cook, 2002) and approaches based on audio fingerprintings (Baluja and Covell, 2008).

Other concepts that directly affect the feature vector component are feature selection and feature transformation. Both aims at reducing the dimensionality of the feature vector, simplifying the representation through the elimination of redundant information and also requires fewer memory and time resources. Feature selection consists in obtaining a subset of the feature vector that includes the most relevant features to discriminate the objects. Feature selection is based on statistics and machine learning algorithms (refer to (Guyon and Elisseeff, 2003) to an overview). Feature transformation create new features by combining and transforming the original features. The most widely adopted transformation methods are the Principal Component Analysis (PCA) and the Linear Discriminant Analysis (LDA) (Blanken et al., 2007). Many works use feature transformation to allow indexing multimedia datasets, which usually are high-dimensional, in index structures tailored to low-dimensional data, such as the R-tree.

The Role of the Distance Function Component

Distance functions measure the dissimilarity between two objects, assigning smaller values for more similar objects, being zero the distance between two identical objects. There are a variety of distance functions in the literature (Wilson and Martinez, 1997). When the space is also multidimensional, that is, all of the elements are composed of equal sized arrays, the most used distance function are the Minkowski distances L_p, which are defined by the equation $\delta(x, y) = \sqrt[p]{\sum_{i=1}^{n} |x_i - y_i|^p}$, where n is the dimension of the embedded vector space and p is an integer. When p is 1, 2 and ∞, we have respectively the distances L_1 (Manhattan), L_2 (Euclidean) and L_∞ (Chebychev).

Distance functions that are able to define *metric spaces* are particularly interesting, because metric spaces allow handling multi-dimensional feature datasets as well as feature datasets for whom the concept of dimensions do not apply (as for example shapes defined by polygons with distinct number of vertices). Formally, a metric space is a pair $\langle \mathbb{S}, \delta \rangle$, where $\mathbb{S}$ is the set of all objects complying with the properties of the domain and δ is a distance function that complies with the following three properties: **symmetry**: $\delta(s_1, s_2) = \delta(s_2, s_1)$; **non-negativity**: $0 < \delta(s_1, s_2) < \infty$ if $s_1 \neq s_2$ and $\delta(s_1, s_1) = 0$; and **triangular inequality**: $\delta(s_1, s_2) \leq \delta(s_1, s_3) + \delta(s_3, s_2)$, $\forall s_1, s_2, s_3 \in \mathbb{S}$. A function that satisfies these properties is called a *metric*. The Minkowski distances with $p \geq 1$ are metrics, therefore vector spaces ruled by any of such functions are special cases of metric spaces. Another important property of metric spaces is that they allow developing fast indexing structures (see 'Indexing Methods for Multimedia' section). Other examples of metrics are the Canberra distance (Kokare et al., 2003) and the Weak Attribute Interaction Distance (WAID), which allows users to define the influence between features according to their perception (Felipe et al., 2009).

Distance functions can be affected by weighting techniques, producing distinct similarity space instances and tuning the evaluation. These techniques can be classified in: feature weighting and partial distance weighting. Feature weighting has the goal of establishing the ideal balance among the relevance of each feature for the similarity that best satisfies the user needs. The trivial strategy for weighting features is based on exhaustive experimental evaluation. Nonetheless, there is an increasing number of approaches dynamically guided by information provided in the query formulation and/or in relevance feedback cycles (Liu et al., 2007, Wan and Liu, 2006, Lee and Street, 2002). Partial distance weighting is employed when an object is represented by many feature vectors and the similarity evaluation between two objects first computes the (partial) distance between each feature vector, usually employing distinct distance functions, and then uses another function to aggregate these values to calculate the final distance. The automatic partial distance weighting methods can be classified into supervised (e.g. (Bustos et al., 2004)) and unsupervised (e.g. (Bueno et al., 2009)).

Now that we already know how to represent and compare the similarity of multimedia objects, it is time to learn how to query these data. There are several types of similarity queries that can be employed to query multimedia data. These types of queries are discussed in the next section.

Similarity Queries

Let us remember a few fundamental concepts of the relational model to provide a proper definition of similarity queries following the database theory. It is worth to stress that every traditional concept of the relational model remains valid when retrieving multimedia objects by the similarity of their contents.

Suppose R is a relation with n attributes described by a relational schema $\mathfrak{R} = (S_1, \ldots, S_n)$, composed of a set of m tuples t_i, such that $R = \{t_1, \ldots, t_m\}$. Each attribute S_j, $1 \leq j \leq n$, indicates a role for domain $\mathbb{S}_j$, that is $S_j \subset \mathbb{S}_j$. Therefore, when $\mathbb{S}_j$ is the multimedia domain from a metric space, each attribute S_j stores multimedia values. Each tuple of the relation stores one value for each attribute S_j, where each value s_i, $1 \leq i \leq m$, assigned to S_j is an element taken from domain $\mathbb{S}_j$ and the dataset S_j is composed of the set of elements s_i that are assigned to the attribute S_j in at least one tuple of the stored relation. Notice that more than one attribute S_j, S_k from $\mathfrak{R}$ can share the same domain, that is, it is possible to have $\mathbb{S}_j = \mathbb{S}_k$. Regarding the multimedia domain from a metric space, the elements must be compared by similarity, using a distance function δ defined over the respective domain. Elements can be compared using the properties of the domain, regardless of the attributes that store the elements. Therefore, every pair

Table 1. Table of symbols

Symbol	Definition
$\langle \mathbb{S}, \delta \rangle$	A metric space
R	A database relation
$\mathfrak{R}$	Squema of relation R
$\mathbb{S}_j, \mathbb{S}_k$	Metric data domains
S_j, S_k	Attribute of a relation, $S_j \subset \mathbb{S}_j$, $S_k \subset \mathbb{S}_k$
$\delta()$	Distance function or dissimilarity function
d_g	Similarity aggregation function
ξ	Query radius
k	Maximum number of elements to be returned in a query
g	Grip factor
Q	Set of query centers
s_q	Query center, $s_q \in Q$

of elements from one attribute and from distinct attributes sharing the same domain can be compared. The symbols employed in this chapter are summarized on Table 1.

There are several types of similarity queries that can be employed to compare multimedia data. A similarity query is expressed using a similarity predicate. There are basically two families of similarity predicates: those limiting the answer based on a given similarity threshold ξ, and those limiting the answer based on the number *k* of elements that should be retrieved. Moreover, the operators involved in similarity queries can be either unary or binary.

Similarity Selections

Similarity selections are performed by unary operators that compare the elements of S_j with one or more reference elements $s_q \in \mathbb{S}_j$ given as part of the predicate. A similarity selection over an attribute S_j of the relation R can be represented as $(\hat{\sigma}_{<selection-predicate>} R)$ where the selection predicate has the form $\langle S_j \, \theta \, Q \rangle$ and θ denotes a similarity operator. This predicate expresses a similarity comparison between the set of values $S_j \subset \mathbb{S}_j$ of an attribute S_j and a set of constant values $Q \subset \mathbb{S}_j$, called the reference or query centers set, taken from the domain $\mathbb{S}_j$ and given as part of the query predicate. The answer of a similarity selection is the subset of tuples t_i from R whose values s_i from attribute S_j meet the selection predicate. It is important to note that similarity selections exhibit properties distinct from those of the traditional selections (for example, they do not possess the commutative property, see (Ferreira, 2009), so we use the $(\hat{\sigma})$ symbol instead of the traditional σ.

When Q is an unitary set, the similarity selection correspond to the traditional range and k-nearest-neighbor queries. These two types of similarity selections can be represented in the following manner:

- **Range selection (Rq):** given a maximum query distance ξ, the query $\hat{\sigma}_{(S_j \; R_q[\delta(),\xi] \; \{s_q\})} R$ retrieves every tuple t_i from R whose value s_i from attribute S_j satisfies $\delta(s_i, s_q) \leq \xi$. Considering R to be a set of images, an example is: "Select the images that are similar to the image P by up to 5 units", represented as $\hat{\sigma}_{(image \; R_q[\delta(),5] \; \{P\})} Images$;

- **k-Nearest Neighbor selection (kNN):** given an integer value $k \geq 1$, the query $\hat{\sigma}_{(S_j \; kNN[\delta(),k] \; \{s_q\})} R$ retrieves the k tuples t_i from R whose values s_i from attribute S_j have the smallest distance from the query element s_q, according to the distance function δ. An example is: "Select the 3 images most similar to the image P", represented as $\hat{\sigma}_{(image \; kNN_q[\delta(),3] \; \{P\})} Images$.

Figures 2 (a) and (b) illustrate the range and k-nearest neighbor selections in a 2-dimensional Euclidean space.

When the query centers set Q has more than one object, the similarity selection correspond to aggregate similarity queries. In order to perform the comparison, these queries require the definition of a similarity aggregation function d_g, which evaluates the aggregate similarity of each element $s_i \in S_j$ regarding its similarity measured by the metric δ to every element $s_q \in Q$. The aggregate range and the aggregate k-nearest neighbor selections can be represented as follows (Razente et al., 2008b):

- **Aggregate Range selection (ARq):** given a maximum aggregate query distance ξ, a similarity aggregation function d_g and a set of query centers Q, the query ARq retrieves every tuple t_i from R whose value s_i from attribute S_j satisfies $d_g(s_i, Q) \leq \xi$. An aggregate range selection can be expressed as $\hat{\sigma}_{(S_j \; AR_q[d_g(),\xi] \; Q)} R$. An example is: "Select the images that are similar to the set of images composed by the images P, M and N by up to 5 units", represented as $\hat{\sigma}_{(S_j \; AR_q[d_g(),5] \; \{P,M,N\})} Images$;

- **Aggregate k-Nearest Neighbor selection ($kANNq$):** given an integer value $k \geq 1$, the query $kANNq$ retrieves the k tuples t_i from R whose values s_i from attribute S_j minimize the similarity aggregation function d_g regarding the query centers Q. An aggregate k-nearest neighbor selection can be expressed as $\hat{\sigma}_{(S_j \; kANN_q[d_g(),k] \; Q)} R$. An example is: "Select the 3 images most similar to the set of images composed by the images P, M and N", represented as $\hat{\sigma}_{(S_j \; kANN_q[d_g(),3] \; \{P,M,N\})} Images$.

The predicate of aggregate similarity selections uses the value of the similarity aggregation function to rank the elements in S_j with respect to Q. There are several ways to define the similarity aggregation function d_g. Herein, we consider the class of functions analyzed in (Razente et al., 2008b) and generated by:

$$d_g(Q, s_i) = \sqrt[g]{\sum_{s_q \in Q} \delta(s_q, s_i)^g} \tag{1}$$

Figure 2. Examples of similarity queries considering the Euclidean distance. (a) Range selection. (b) k-Nearest-Neighbor selection considering k=4. (c) Aggregate Range selection. (d) k-Aggregate Nearest Neighbor selection considering k=1 and g=2. (e) Range join. (f) k-Nearest Neighbors join considering k=2. (g) k-Closest Neighbors join considering k=3

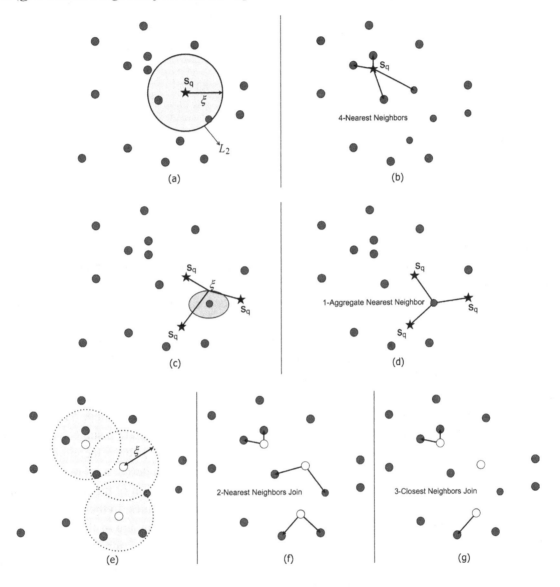

where δ is a distance function over $\mathbb{S}_j$, Q is the set of query centers, s_i is a dataset element, and the power $g \in \mathbb{R}^*$ is a non-zero real value that we call the *grip factor* of the similarity aggregation function. Considering Equation 1, the aggregate range and the aggregate k-nearest neighbor queries applied over a unitary set Q correspond to the traditional range and k-NN queries respectively.

It is important to note that, different values for the grip factor g can provide interesting different interpretations. For example, $g = 1$ defines the minimization of the sum of the distances, $g = 2$ defines the minimization of the mean square distance (see Figures 2(c) and (d)), and $g = \infty$ defines the minimization

Figure 3. Illustration of the effect of the grip factor g in an Euclidean 2-dimensional space, considering |Q| = 3

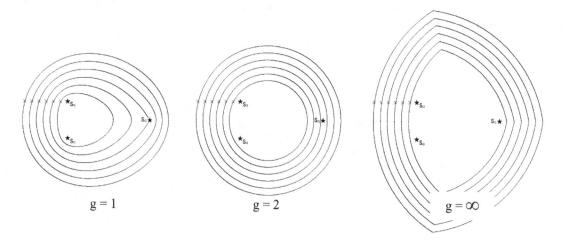

of the maximum distance. Figure 3 helps on getting the intuition of the meaning of these grip factors presenting the effect of g in a 2-dimensional Euclidean space and considering Q composed of the three query centers shown. Each curve represents the geometric place where Equation 1 has the same value. Therefore, each curve is an isoline representing a different covering radius, thus defining both range and k-limited queries.

There are several applications that can benefit from the use of queries that employ this type of similarity predicates. For instance, multimedia data (such as images, audio or video) require extracting features that are used in place of the data element when performing the comparisons in a similarity query. The features are usually the result of mathematical algorithms, resulting in low level features. Considering an image domain, the features are usually based on color, texture and shape. However, there exists a semantic gap between the low level features and the human interpretation subjectivity. To deal with the semantic gap, relevance feedback techniques have been developed. In these techniques, positive and/or negative examples are informed by the user to allow the system to derive a more precise representation of the user intent (Zhou and Huang, 2003). The new representation of the user intent can be achieved by query point movement or by multiple point movement techniques. In these techniques, the system learns from the search results provided by the user and takes advantage of this information to adapt ranking functions. One way to tell to the system what is the user's intention is specifying, in the same query, other elements besides the query center, which are positive or negative examples of the intend answer. This representation is based on multiple query centers.

Similarity Joins

Binary operators correspond to similarity joins. A similarity join over an attribute S_j in relation R_1 and an attribute S_k in relation R_2 can be represented as ($R_1 \overset{<join-predicate>}{\otimes} R_2$), where the join predicate is of the form $\langle S_j \, \theta \, S_k \rangle$ and θ denotes a similarity operator. This predicate expresses a similarity comparison between the set of values $S_j \subset \mathbb{S}_j$ of an attribute S_j from the relation R_1 and a set of values $S_k \subset \mathbb{S}_k$ of an attribute S_k from the relation R_2, taken from the domains of attributes S_j and S_k (that is, $\mathbb{S}_j = \mathbb{S}_k$) and given as part of the query predicate. The answer of a similarity join is composed of the concatenation of tuples from R_1 and R_2 whose values s_i from attribute S_j and s_m from attribute S_k meet the join predicate. There are basically three types of similarity joins, as follows.

- **Range join** – $\otimes$: given a maximum query distance ξ, the query $R_1 \overset{S_j\, R_q[\delta(),\xi]\, S_k}{\otimes} R_2$ retrieves the pairs of tuples $< t_i,\, t_m >$ from R_1 and R_2 whose values s_i from attribute S_j and s_m from attribute S_k satisfies $\delta(s_i, s_m) \leq \xi$. An example is: "Select the European landscapes that differ from American landscapes by at most 5 units", represented as

  $$EuropeanLandscapes \overset{europeanimage\; R_q[\delta(),5]\; americanimage}{\otimes} AmericanLandscapes,$$

  considering that both American and European landscapes are elements from the images domain.

- **k-Closest Neighbors join** – $\otimes$: given an integer value $k \geq 1$, the query $R_1 \overset{S_j\, kCN_q[\delta(),k]\, S_k}{\otimes} R_2$ retrieves the k closest pairs of tuples $< t_i,\, t_m >$ from R_1 and R_2, according to the distance function δ. An example is: "Select the 20 most similar pairs of European and American landscapes", represented as

  $$EuropeanLandscapes \overset{europeanimage\; kCN_q[\delta(),20]\; americanimage}{\otimes} AmericanLandscapes;$$

- **k-Nearest Neighbors join** – $\otimes$: given an integer value $k \geq 1$, the query $R_1 \overset{S_j\, kNN_q[\delta(),k]\, S_k}{\otimes} R_2$ retrieves pairs of tuples $< t_i,\, t_m >$ from R_1 and R_2, such that there are k pairs for each value s_i from attribute S_j together with its nearest values s_m from attribute S_k, according to the distance function δ. An example is: "Select the 10 European landscapes that are the most similar to each American landscape", represented as

  $$EuropeanLandscapes \overset{europeanimage\; kNN_q[\delta(),10]\; americanimage}{\otimes} AmericanLandscapes.$$

  The k-Nearest neighbor join is not commutative.

Figures 2 (e), (f) and (g) present an illustration of the three types of similarity joins described previously. In these figures, the white circles represent elements of the attribute S_j and the gray circles represent elements of the attribute S_k.

Every similarity operator allows a number of variations, such as retrieving the most dissimilar elements instead of the most similar, and taking into account occurrences of ties in k-limited predicates. Predicates can also be limited by both k and ξ, so the most restrictive condition is the one that applies.

Indexing Methods for Multimedia

From a system's perspective, not only the semantics must be fulfilled but also performance and usability aspects are fundamental to the acceptance of an application, which are also gaps to be bridged (Deserno et al., 2009]. Despite the fact that the queries described in the 'Similarity Queries' section can be answered running a sequential search in the database, this is not the most appropriate strategy to be used in large databases, once the computational cost involved can be very high. Therefore, another important issue to consider to query multimedia data is related to using indexing methods specially tailored to efficiently answer similarity queries.

Indexing methods, such as B-tree and its variations, and hashing structures (a description of these methods can be found in (Garcia-Molina et al., 2002)) are normally provided by DBMS. However, although these indexing methods are enough to attend the needs of traditional application users, they are not suitable for systems that require similarity searches, which usually deal with data that present high dimensionality and do not present the total ordering property. In order to answer similarity queries in generic metric spaces the most suitable indexing structures are the Metric Access Methods (MAM).

A MAM is a distance-based indexing method that employs only metrics (such as those described in the 'The Role of the Distance Function Component' section) to organize the objects in the database. There are several works presenting MAM proposals in the literature. Among the first proposed, there were the ones called BK-trees (Burkhard-Keller-trees). The main idea of these structures consists in choosing an arbitrary central object and applying a distance function to split the remaining objects into several subsets. In this way, the indexing structure is built recursively, executing this procedure for each non empty subset. A good overview about these and other indexing structures widely mentioned in the literature, such as the VP-tree (Vantage Point tree) (Yianilos, 1993), the MVP-tree (Multi-Vantage Point tree) (Bozkaya and Ozsoyoglu, 1997), the GNAT (Geometric Near-neighbor Access Tree) (Brin, 1995), the M-tree (Ciaccia et al., 1997) and Slim-tree (Traina-Jr et al., 2002), can be found in (Hjaltason and Samet, 2003).

Many of the methods mentioned above were developed to improve single-center similarity search operations (such as k-nearest neighbor and range queries), using the triangle inequality property to prune branches of the trees. Considering the k-NN queries, for example, there are several approaches proposed to improve its performance, such as: branch-and-bound (Roussopoulos et al., 1995, Ciaccia et al., 1997, Hjaltason and Samet, 2003), incremental (Hjaltason and Samet, 1995, Hjaltason and Samet, 1999) and multi-step algorithms (Korn et al., 1996, Seidl and Kriegel, 1998). Other approaches are to estimate a final limiting range for the query and to perform a sequence of "start small and grow" steps (Tasan and Ozsoyoglu, 2004). All of these works refer to algorithms dealing with just one query center.

Regarding the case of multiple query centers, the proposals found in the literature are more recent. The aggregate range query was first proposed in (Wu et al., 2000) and was used as a relevance feedback mechanism for content-based image retrieval in a system named Falcon. Considering the aggregate k-nearest neighbor queries, the first approach appeared in 2005 with the work presented in (Papadias et al., 2005), which deals only with spatial data. The first strategies proposed considering the case of metric space appeared more recently with the works presented in (Razente et al., 2008b, Razente et al., 2008a).

Moreover, there are also works considering the improvement of similarity join algorithms. The first strategies were designed primarily for data in a vector space (Brinkhoff et al., 1993), but others were developed considering data lying in metric spaces (Dohnal et al., 2003a, Dohnal et al., 2003b, Jacox and Samet, 2008). The use of this type of query for improving data mining processes has also been explored in works such as (Bohm and Krebs, 2002, Bohm and Krebs, 2004).

SUPPORTING SIMILARITY QUERIES IN RELATIONAL DBMS

There are several systems developed to query multimedia data by content, including similarity searching. Many of them are prototypes aimed at testing techniques, without concerns about performance issues.

Others were built on top of a DBMS, but with retrieval mechanisms detached from its query processor. Nevertheless, this approach prevents using several optimization alternatives when executing complex queries, especially when search conditions also contain operators over simple data, which are efficiently handled by DBMS.

In order to add support for similarity queries in a RDBMS it is necessary: (i) to create a representation for multimedia data, (ii) to define how the similarity evaluation is carried out, (iii) to state how a query involving similarity operations is written and (iv) to provide mechanisms to execute the queries efficiently. The last requisite have been fulfilled by several works reporting basic algorithms to execute similarity retrieval operations on data sets of multimedia objects (as described in the 'Indexing Methods for Multimedia' section). The first two requisites have also been extensively addressed in the literature, as it was discussed in the 'Similarity Evaluation' section. The third requirement is directly related to the most widely employed language in DBMS, the SQL. Although a few works focused on languages to represent similarity queries (Carey and Kossmann, 1997, Carey and Kossmann, 1998, Melton and Eisenberg, 2001, Gao et al., 2004), none of them is able to provide a production-strength support seamlessly integrated with the other features of the language.

This section presents existing DBMS solutions aimed at similarity retrieval and their limitations, and introduces an extension to SQL that allows managing similarity data inside a DBMS in a consistent way.

Current DBMS Solutions for Similarity Searching

The ISO/IEC SQL/MM (Melton and Eisenberg, 2001) is the piece of the SQL standard devoted to multimedia data. It defines data types and operators to manage multimedia information, such as multidimensional data, images and large texts. Concerning similarity, the Still Image part of SQL/MM defines an abstract data type that encapsulates a binary image and its metadata, a set of basic image processing functions and data types aimed at executing similarity queries over the image contents. However, it addresses too superficially the internals of the image representation and the query representation and processing.

A few DBMS vendors released modules to query multimedia data by content. The precursors were the Audio, Image and Video (AIV) Extenders of the IBM DB2 database (IBM Corp., 2003), which were based on QBIC (the first commercial strength system for multimedia retrieval) (Flickner et al., 1995). Other examples are the Informix Excalibur Image Data Blade (Informix Corp., 1999) and the Oracle interMedia (Oracle Corp., 2005) (now called Oracle Multimedia). They provide proprietary data types with feature extractors and similarity functions that are used in SQL statements.

As an example, consider a relation to store photographs of landscapes defined as: (see Algorithm 1)

Algorithm 1.

```
CREATE TABLE Landscapes (
 Id INTEGER,
 Place CHAR(20),
 Picture IMAGETYPE,
 Photographer CHAR(30),...);
```

The Landscapes relation includes attributes of traditional data types (e.g. Id, Place and Photographer) and one attribute of a multimedia data type: Picture. As Picture stores images and each vendor use a proprietary data type to this intend, in the example we employ the fictitious type IMAGETYPE to represent them. After having the table created and the data loaded, the features representing the image are extracted and stored, so they can be later employed in content-based queries. These tasks require several instructions to be accomplished in all the aforementioned modules and are omitted in the example. Thereafter, suppose a user wants to retrieve the images which differ at most 1.5 similarity units from a query example (example.jpg), regarding color and texture features. Such range query can be written as follows, respectively using the DB2 QbScoreFromStr (a) or the Oracle ORDImageSignature.evaluate-Score (b)[1] similarity functions: (see Algorithm 2)

Although these modules allow querying images by similarity, they have some drawbacks. The first one is that their source code are not available to make improvements and to include domain-specific knowledge. The built-in functions provided are of general purpose and usually yield poor results when applied over specific domains, precluding many applications from using these modules. Other major shortcoming is that the data definition and manipulation instructions are very verbose and sometimes error-prone, requiring to write sentences to perform intermediary steps which should be transparent to the user.

To circumvent those drawbacks, it would be interesting to provide architectures allowing the development of multimedia systems capable of adapting themselves to the particular needs of each application domain. Moreover, to address the latter drawback, it would be interesting to develop a simple language with a syntax close to the widely adopted standard SQL. The next subsection presents a seamless way to extend SQL to include similarity-related handling constructions.

A SQL Extension for Similarity Data Management

In order to meet the requirement of introducing similarity queries into SQL, there are several issues that must be addressed. The first one is how to represent similarity queries over multimedia domains – such as images and video. It can be done defining the domains where the similarity will be measured as new data types. In this chapter we restrict the examples to images, defining a new SQL data type called

Algorithm 2.

```
(a) SELECT * FROM Landscapes
      WHERE QbScoreFromStr (
        Picture,
        'QbTextureFeatureClass file=<example.jpg> weight=1.0
        and QbColorFeatureClass file=<example.jpg> weight=2.0'
      ) <= 1.5
(b) SELECT * FROM Landscapes
      WHERE ORDImageSignature.evaluateScore(
        Picture_Features,
        ORDImageSignature.generateSignature('example.jpg'),
        'color="2.0" texture="1.0"'
      ) <= 1.5
```

STILLIMAGE and all the needed requirements to process it. However, other complex domains, such as video and audio, can be manipulated following the same approach. Other important issues are related to the need of incorporating constructions in the SQL that allow:

- In the Data Definition Language (DDL):
  ○ To define similarity measures that specify the distance function to be employed and the structure that represents the data to be compared by similarity. Each data domain demands structures and similarity functions tailored to the inherent features of the underlying data;
  ○ To specify multimedia data types when defining a table;
  ○ To associate multimedia domain attributes with the available similarity measures;
  ○ To define indexes for multimedia domain attributes.
- In the Data Manipulation Language (DML):
  ○ To insert and/or update the data in a multimedia database;
  ○ To allow specifying similarity queries in an integrated manner with the other resources of the SQL, including operations such as selection and join.

In the following subsections, we describe a strategy that addresses all these issues, extending the syntax of DDL and DML commands. The definition of these extensions requires both, the description of the new constructors (i.e., the language syntax) and their meaning (i.e., the language semantics). In order to specify the syntax of the SQL extension we employ the BNF (Backus-Naur Form), a widely adopted notation for the specification of program languages. For the meaning specification of the new constructors, we use suggestive examples and informal descriptions.

Extending DDL Commands

Each image is stored as the value of an attribute of the STILLIMAGE data type. Thus, recalling the Landscapes example table of the previous section, the Picture attribute should be of type STILLIMAGE.

As pointed previously, a key functionality of a DBMS enriched with similarity data management is how to allow the similarity evaluation to be domain-specific. Since there is no concept resembling the definition of comparison operators in SQL, it is needed to create new commands to do so. Metrics should be stored in the database catalog, thus their manipulation commands should follow the DDL command style. Hence, three new commands were defined to handle similarity comparisons: the CREATE METRIC, the ALTER METRIC and the DROP METRIC commands. Note that they are the only new commands needed to support similarity queries, as the other modifications are just extensions on existing commands. These commands rely on feature extractors to define the feature vectors used in the similarity measures. Feature extractors, on the other hand, do not require new SQL constructions, as they can be defined as stored procedures that receive a multimedia object and return the features.

Only the CREATE METRIC is described here as the other constructions are alike to it. The syntax of this command is as follows: (see Algorithm 3)

As it can be seen, the CREATE METRIC syntax defines an instance of a similarity space, including the distance function and the feature vector components. The feature vector is stated as a linear combination of existing feature extractors, allowing the DBMS to take into account various feature types in the similarity evaluation. As an illustration, suppose two extractors are available: the HistogramEXT, which returns an array of integers representing the color histogram of one image; and the LargestOb-

Algorithm 3.

```
CREATE METRIC <metric_name>
  USING <distance_function> FOR <complex_data_type>
  (<extractor_name> (
     <parameter_name> AS <parameter_alias> [weight],...)
    [, <extractor_name> (
     <parameter_name> AS <parameter_alias> [weight],...),
   ...]
);
```

jectEXT, which returns the features Area (in number of pixels) and the center pixel XYCenter of the largest continuous area of the same color in the image. If one wants to define a metric that evaluates the similarity of two images, considering their histogram and the position of the largest continuous area (but not its area), with the histogram weighting twice the center, the following command can be used: (see Algorithm 4)where the Area parameter of the LargestObjectEXT was not provided, indicating that this feature should not be treated by the extractor.

Once a metric was created, it can be associated with one or several image attributes defined in any relation. The METRICs are associated with complex attributes as constraints following any of the two usual ways to define constraints in the table definition commands: column constraint or table constraint. In the example following, the metric Histo&Center is associated to the Picture attribute of the table Landscape: (see Algorithm 5)

When defining a METRIC constraint using a column constraint syntax, it is only necessary to provide the USING <metric_name> clause in the attribute definition.

Note that we do no intend that comparing two landscapes using the Histo&Center metric guarantee obtaining the most similar images by human standards – a much better comparison metric should be developed – it is used here only as an example of the proposed syntax. With regard to multimedia

Algorithm 4.

```
CREATE METRIC Histo&Center USING LP1
  FOR STILLIMAGE (
    HistogramEXT (Histogram AS Histo 2),
    LargestObjectEXT (XYCenter AS XYLargestObj)
);
```

Algorithm 5.

```
ALTER TABLE Landscapes ADD METRIC (Picture) USING (Histo&Center);
```

retrieval, it is expected that users gradually enhance the similarity evaluation algorithms, adding new feature extractors, distance functions and experimenting with several combinations. In this sense, a single multimedia attribute can be employed in queries considering different metrics. Therefore, the presented SQL extension allows associating several metrics with the same complex attribute, and allows the user to choose one of them to be employed in each query formulation. When more than one metric is associated with the same attribute, the DEFAULT keyword must follow the name to be used as the default one, i.e., the metric that should be employed if none is explicitly provided in a query.

Other SQL extended command is the CREATE INDEX. As the indexes that apply to multimedia searching by similarity depends on the employed metric (see 'Indexing Methods for Multimedia' section), this information must be provided in order to be possible to create them. This requirement is accomplished in the SQL extension adding the USING <metric_name> clause to the CREATE INDEX syntax. Note that this command implicitly adds a corresponding METRIC constraint to the referred attribute. Regarding our example, considering that a metric called Texture was defined for the STILLIMAGE type, the following command creates an index to execute queries using this metric over the Picture attribute and sets Texture as its default metric: (see Algorithm 6)

Extending DML Commands

The syntax of the DML commands (SELECT, UPDATE and DELETE) needs new constructions to allow expressing similarity predicates. In this chapter we only describe the new constructions of the SELECT command, as the other commands are equivalent. The syntax of the INSERT command does not need changes (although its implementation does).

The new constructions required in the SELECT command occur in the FROM and the WHERE clauses. The new construction in the WHERE clause allows expressing every similarity predicate described in the 'Similarity Queries' section, that is, similarity selection, and similarity join queries. The simplest expression in a non-similarity selection predicate compares an attribute with a constant value, in the format *attr θ value*, or it compares an attribute with another compatible attribute, in the format *attr$_1$ θ attr$_2$*. To express a similarity predicate, the attributes must be of complex data types (e.g. a multimedia data type), the constant *value* must be an element in the corresponding domain, and the operator θ must be a similarity operator using a metric defined over the attributes. The syntax to express similarity selection predicates is: (see Algorithm 7)

Following this syntax, the reserved word NEAR corresponds to the θ operator, and value is employed to state similarity selections, which can be obtained considering two approaches. The first is expressing a constant as a path in the file system where the image is stored. For example, to select the five landscapes with pictures more similar to a given example stored in the example.jpg file, the following command can be used: (see Algorithm 8)

Algorithm 6.

```
CREATE INDEX TextureIndex ON Landscapes (Picture)
  USING Texture DEFAULT;
```

Algorithm 7.

```
<complex_attr> NEAR [ANY] {<value>|<complex_attr2>}
  [STOP AFTER <k>] [RANGE <ξ>]
```

Algorithm 8.

```
SELECT * FROM Landscapes
WHERE     Picture NEAR 'example.jpg' STOP AFTER 5;
```

The second approach obtains the value from the database. Then, in order to answer the same query regarding a landscape stored in the database, the following command can be used. (see Algorithm 9)

It is worth to note that the inner SELECT of the previous command can return more than one tuple when a non key attribute is used in the WHERE clause. In this case, the result of the inner SELECT can potentially return a set with several query centers for the similarity predicate. Therefore, the command turns into an aggregate similarity query and a grip factor must be selected according to Equation 1 presented in the 'Similarity Queries' section. To specify which grip factor must be used, one of the following keywords can be inserted after the keyword NEAR: SUM to ask for $g = 1$, ALL to ask for $g = 2$ and MAX to ask for $g = \infty$. For example, to retrieve the three pictures whose landscapes looks more similar to those of Paris, regarding a grip factor of 2, the following command can be issued: (see Algorithm 10)

Algorithm 9.

```
SELECT * FROM Landscapes
 WHERE Picture NEAR
  (SELECT Picture
    FROM Landscapes WHERE Id = 123) STOP AFTER 5;
```

Algorithm 10.

```
SELECT * FROM Landscapes
  WHERE Picture NEAR ALL
    (SELECT Picture
       FROM Landscapes
      WHERE place = 'Paris') STOP AFTER 3;
```

The construction to express a similarity join compares a complex attribute from the left table R to a compatible attribute from the right table S, in the format $R.attr_1$ NEAR $S.attr_2$ <...>. The similarity join syntaxes are expressed as regular joins, either in the FROM or in the WHERE clauses. Two complex attributes are compatible if they are associated with the same metric (consequently, they are of the same type). The construction $R.attr_1$ NEAR $S.attr_2$ RANGE ξ expresses a range join, the construction $R.attr_1$ NEAR $S.attr_2$ STOP AFTER k expresses a nearest join, and the construction $R.attr_1$ NEAR ANY $S.attr_2$ STOP AFTER k expresses a closest join. For example, the following command retrieves the 5 landscapes pairs whose pictures look more similar to each other: (see Algorithm 11)

Variations on the basic command can be expressed with modifiers in the command. If one wants to retrieve the most dissimilar elements instead of the most similar, the keyword NEAR is replaced by the keyword FAR. If more than one metric was defined, the default one is used, unless the clause BY <metric name> is declared. Concerning the running example, to select up to fifty landscapes that are among the most similar pictures to a given query image considering the Histo&Center metric and the fifty most similar pictures to another query image regarding the Texture metric, the following command can be stated: (see Algorithm 12)

Queries with predicates limited to k neighbors (either selections or joins) can take into account the occurrence of ties. The default behavior of a k-limited query is retrieving k elements without ties, as it is the behaviour of most of the works reported in the literature. However, the SQL extension allows specifying WITH TIE LIST following the STOP AFTER specification, to ask for every element tied at the same distance of the k-th nearest neighbor to the query element.

Both STOP AFTER and RANGE can be specified in the same query. In this case, the answer is limited by having at most k elements and elements not farther (or nearer) than a distance ξ from the query center. For example, the command (see Algorithm 13) retrieves from the 5 images most similar to the query image that are not farther than 0.03 units from the query image. On the other hand, if neither STOP AFTER nor RANGE is specified, then RANGE 0 (zero) is assumed.

Algorithm 11.

```
SELECT * FROM Landscapes L1, Landscapes L2
  WHERE L1.Picture NEAR L2.Picture STOP AFTER 5;
```

Algorithm 12.

```
SELECT * FROM Landscapes WHERE
  Picture NEAR 'example1.jpg' By Histo&Center STOP AFTER 50 AND
  Picture NEAR 'example2.jpg' By Texture STOP AFTER 50;
```

Algorithm 13.

```
SELECT * FROM Landscapes
  WHERE Picture NEAR 'example.jpg' STOP AFTER 5 RANGE 0.03;
```

PERFORMING SIMILARITY QUERIES USING DBMS

Besides including new constructions in the SQL language to represent similarity queries, it is also needed to deal with adequate techniques to store multimedia data and algorithms to execute similarity queries over them. This section describes two case studies that developed experimental systems to tackle such requirements on existing DBMS.

Both of them are open source software and can be enhanced with domain-specific feature extractors and distance functions. The first one ('A Blade for Similarity Query Processing' section) is implemented as a intermediate layer over the DBMS interface that recognizes the SQL extension for similarity described in the 'A SQL Extension for Similarity Data Management' section. It is conceived as a layer to be DBMS-independent, since it introduces new logic to the query processor. It allows managing similarity data integrated with simple data in a plain and transparent way and executes the similarity operations using efficient algorithms. The second system ('A DBMS Module for Similarity Searching' section) is implemented as a module attached to the DBMS core. It is tightly coupled to the DBMS query processor and also executes similarity operations efficiently. However, as it does not interpret the extended commands, it relies on the verbose standard SQL syntax and is limited to the built-in query rewrite rules.

A Blade for Similarity Query Processing

This section presents an academic open source engine, called SIREN (SImilarity Retrieval ENgine) (Barioni et al., 2006), which was developed intending both to validate the extension of the SQL presented in the previous section and to explore the issues related with supporting similarity queries from inside SQL in a native form, which is important to allow optimizing the full set of search operations involved in each query posed.

SIREN acts like a blade between a conventional DBMS and the application programs intercepting every SQL command sent from the application. If it has no similarity construction nor a reference to complex objects, it sends the unchanged command to the underlying DBMS and relays the answer from the DBMS to the application program. Therefore, when only conventional commands are posed by the application, SIREN is transparent. When the SQL command has similarity-related constructions or references to complex data, the command is re-written, the similarity-related operations are executed internally, and the underlying DBMS is used only to execute the conventional data operations.

Multimedia data types are stored as Binary Large Objects (BLOB data types) as well as their extracted features. Feature extraction is usually costly, but it must be executed for each object once, when the object is stored in the database. As the user does not provide places in the relations to store the extracted attributes, the system provides their storage and association to the multimedia objects in a transparent way to the user.

To store a complex object along with its extracted feature vectors, SIREN changes the definition of user defined tables that have the complex attributes as follows. Each complex attribute (e.g. a STILLIMAGE column) is changed to a reference to a system-controlled table that has as its attributes both the object's binary data and the attributes that store all features gotten by every extractor used in each metric associated with the attribute. A new table is created for each complex attribute. Whenever a new image is stored in the database, SIREN intercepts the INSERT command, stores the non-image attributes in the user table and the images in the corresponding system tables. Thereafter, SIREN calls the feature extractors and stores their outputs in the corresponding system tables. Whenever the user asks for data from its tables, SIREN joins the system tables and the user tables, removing the feature attributes, thus the user never sees the table split nor the features. This is the same approach for the treatment of BLOB data in DBMS, which are stored apart from the original table into system-controlled areas and only references to them are stored in the table.

When the user poses queries involving similarity predicates, SIREN uses the extracted features to execute the similarity operators. The current version of SIREN has three types of feature extractors regarding the STILLIMAGE data type: a texture extractor (TEXTUREEXT), a shape extractor based on Zernike Moments (ZERNIKEEXT) and a color extractor based on the normalized color histogram (HISTOGRAMEXT). For sound objects storing music, there are the a sound-texture extractor (SOUND-TEXTUREEXT), which extracts the Mel-Frequency Cepstral Coefficients (MFCC) and features based on the Short Time Fourier Transform (STFT). The 'A Look on the Feature Vector Component' section presented references of these extractors.

The similarity operators implemented consist of the similarity selections for single query centers, the similarity selections for multiple query centers and the similarity joins, as presented in the 'Similarity Queries' section. The traditional single center similarity selections, that is, the similarity range query and the *k*-nearest-neighbor query operators, are available in several MAM presented in the literature. However, regarding the multiple center similarity selections, there are operators available only for the Slim-tree MAM. Therefore, the Slim-tree MAM (Traina-Jr et al., 2002) is employed to index the multimedia attributes. The Slim-tree is implemented in a C++ access method library, which is called from the SIREN Indexer subsystem to execute the similarity-related operations. Unfortunately, there is no procedure already published to execute similarity joins in this MAM. Therefore, in SIREN they are always executed using sequential scan implementations.

Following, it is used the previous example to illustrate how SIREN executes a query asking for the five closest landscapes from a given picture. (see Algorithm 14)

This command is analyzed and rewritten by SIREN following the steps shown in Figure 4. Initially, the application program submits the SQL command. The command interpreter analyzes the original command and detects that it contains a similarity predicate refering to a query image that is not stored in the DBMS (Step 1). The interpreter also identifies the type of similarity operation that needs to be executed (a *kNN* query in the case), the multimedia attribute involved (Picture) and the parameters of the predicate (the query center sq = 'example.jpg', the number of neighbors *k*=5 and the metric that is the attribute's default). Thereafter, it queries the SIREN data dictionary (Step 2). The data dictionary is searched to obtain information regarding the complex attribute Picture: the attribute's default metric (Texture in the example), the feature extractors that are employed by the metric (the TextureEXT extractor), the distance function to be used (), and the index structure *Ix* to be employed (Step 3). The query image s_q is submitted to the required feature extractors (Step 4) and the extracted feature vector V is

Algorithm 14.

```
SELECT * FROM Landscapes
  WHERE Picture NEAR 'example.jpg'
  STOP AFTER 5;
```

Figure 4. An example of the command execution process in SIREN

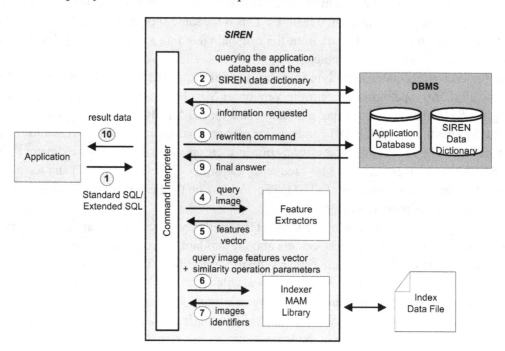

Algorithm 15.

```
SELECT Id, Place, Photographer, IPV$Landscapes_Picture.Image AS Picture
  FROM Landscapes JOIN IPV$Landscapes_Picture
    ON Landscapes.Picture = IPV$Landscapes_Picture.Image_id
  WHERE Picture IN (6969, 6968, 6975, 8769, 9721);
```

returned (Step 5). The interpreter sends to the indexer the following parameters: the feature vector V, the similarity operation (kNN) and its respective parameters (s_q, k), and the index structure Ix (Step 6). The indexer returns the set of images identifiers S_{oid} that answers the command (Step 7). The command interpreter uses the identifiers S_{oid} to rewrite the original command submitted by the application program and resubmits it to the underlaying DBMS (Step 8). The command rewritten by SIREN for the current example is presented below: (see Algorithm 15)where (6969, 6968, 6975, 8769, 9721) are examples of identifiers returned and IPV$Landscapes_Picture is the SIREN controlled table that stores the real image and the feature vectors.

Finally, the DBMS answers the query, obtaining the images and the traditional attributes requested (Step 9) and the result data is returned to the application program. It is worth noting that if a query image stored in the DBMS was specified in the original command submitted by the application program, it would not be sent to the features extractors. In this case, Steps 4 and 5 are replaced by a query to the DBMS in order to retrieve the feature vector of the stored image, which is much more efficient.

Algorithm 16.

```
SELECT * FROM Landscapes
WHERE Place = 'Paris' AND
 Figure NEAR 'example.jpg' RANGE 0.03 AND
 Figure NEAR 'example.jpg' STOP AFTER 5;
```

Figure 5. The FMI-SiR$_O$ architecture

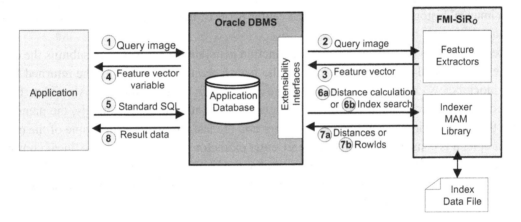

SIREN allows executing simple queries, as well as any combination of operations among themselves and among traditional selections and joins, providing a powerful way to execute similarity queries in multimedia databases. For instance, the following query mixes two similarity-based select conditions and one regular condition: (see Algorithm 16)

As SIREN intercepts the SQL commands, it can detect that the two similarity conditions considers the same query center and thus they can be executed in only one pass using the kAndRange algorithm (Traina-Jr et al., 2006). On the other hand, it will always execute first the similarity operations and then the regular conditions, even if the selectivity of the regular condition is higher. In addition to the example provided herein, there are others considering real datasets and several query statements in (Barioni et al., 2006, Barioni et al., 2008).

A DBMS Module for Similarity Searching

FMI-SiR (user-defined Features, Metrics and Indexes for Similarity Retrieval) (Kaster et al., 2009) is an open-source module that can be attached to a commercial DBMS to provide mechanisms to answer similarity queries efficiently. This section presents its implementation over the Oracle Database called the FMI-SiR$_O$. Applications employing multimedia data can take advantage of FMI-SiR$_O$, defining its own domain specific feature extractors and/or distance functions, whereas retaining the ability of using all the powerful resources of the Oracle DBMS in an integrated way.

FMI-SiR$_O$ is attached to Oracle Database using its extensibility interfaces, as shown in Figure 5. It includes feature extractors embedded into C++ external functions and it relies on the same access method library used in SIREN to provide the distance functions and the MAMs. As FMI-SiR$_O$ follows the Oracle Extensibility Framework, it is integrated to the query processor and its operations are all under the DBMS transactional control, except the index updates, whose concurrency control is responsibility of the indexing library.

Multimedia data and their feature vectors are stored in BLOB columns in FMI-SiR$_O$. However, unlike SIREN the attributes that store the feature vectors must be explicitly defined and handled by users. As a consequence, if there are various feature vectors representing complementary characteristics of the same data, they will be stored in a set of attributes to be employed in queries either individually or combined in multiple ways. With regard to the chapter's running example, the attributes Picture_Histo&Center and Picture_Texture must be added to the Landscapes table by the user to store respectively the images' histogram together with the center pixel of the largest continuous area and the images' texture features.

Feature extraction is performed through the function generateSignature, which submits the complex data to the respective algorithms and populates the feature vector attribute with the returned features. The SQL block below creates the image feature vectors used in the example: (see Algorithm 17)

The second and third parameters of function generateSignature are, respectively, the names of the attributes that hold the image and the feature vector and the last parameter is the name of the extractor. In this example, it is considered that the Histo&Center extractor internally codes the linear combination of the Histogram and LargestObject extractors cited in the 'A SQL Extension for Similarity Data Management' section. Note that the attributes storing the feature vectors are IN/OUT parameters. Hence, it is necessary to select the data using an exclusive lock, expressed in the example by the FOR UPDATE clause.

In FMI-SiR$_O$, the association between the feature vector and the distance function to form the desired similarity space does not need to be previously stated, as it is done in query time. This syntax allows high flexibility, although it is prone to misuse. In FMI-SiR$_O$, there are several distance functions, such as the Manhattan_distance, Euclidean_distance and Canberra_distance. However, new distance functions can be included according to application requirements. These functions can be employed to formulate similarity queries executed using sequential scans. For example, the following two instructions execute respectively a range query and a 5-NN query. (see Algorithm 18)where Example is a variable containing the BLOB feature vector of the query center, 0.03 is the maximum query distance for the range query and 5 is the number of neighbors for the k-NN query. Using standard SQL requires numbering the rows according to the ordering criterion (the distance in similarity queries), which is used to filter the k neighbors. This is done through SQL-99 *window functions* as showed in the example.

Algorithm 17.

```
SELECT Picture, Picture_Histo&Center, Picture_Texture
  INTO Pic, Pic_Histo&Center, Pic_Texture
  FROM Landscapes FOR UPDATE;
generateSignature(Pic, Pic_Histo&Center, 'Histo&Center');
generateSignaturePic, Pic_Texture, 'Texture');
```

Algorithm 18.

```
SELECT * FROM Landscapes
  WHERE Manhattan_distance(Picture_Histo&Center, Example) <= 0.03;
SELECT * FROM (
  SELECT Id, Place, Photographer, ROW_NUMBER() OVER (
    ORDER BY Manhattan_distance(Picture_Histo&Center, Example) AS rn
  FROM Landscapes
) WHERE rn <= 5;
```

Algorithm 19.

```
CREATE OPERATOR Manhattan_dist BINDING (BLOB, BLOB)
  RETURN FLOAT USING Manhattan_distance;
```

The execution of queries in FMI-SiR$_O$ is illustrated in Figure 5. Before posing a query it is necessary to load the feature vector of the query center into a database variable. If the feature vector is already stored in the database, it is queried and stored in the variable. Otherwise, the application calls the generateSignature function, providing the query image (Step 1). The DBMS submits the image to the FMI-SiR$_O$'s feature extractor, which generates the feature vector that is in turn stored in the variable (steps 2 to 4). Thereafter, the query is submitted to the DBMS (Step 5), which forwards the distance calculation to the FMI-SiR$_O$'s access method library (Step 6a), obtaining the distances (Step 7a). Based on the distances, the DBMS executes the query and returns the result data to the application (Step 8).

FMI-SiR$_O$ also provides new metric index structures to speed up similarity queries. They are built on the associated access method library and are accessible by the query processor through *SQL operators*, which are defined in the Oracle DBMS as links between user-defined functions and index types. FMI-SiR$_O$ defines operators to enable the indexed execution of both range and *k*-NN queries. For instance, the following instruction creates an operator for range queries employing the Manhattan distance: (see Algorithm 19)

To create a new index type it is necessary to have a data type implementing the methods required by the Oracle Extensible Indexing Interface. Such data types in FMI-SiR$_O$ have the following header: (see Algorithm 20)where each of these methods maps to an external C++ function that executes the respective action on the index using access method library. The new index types associate the operators and the implementation types, as exemplified below: (see Algorithm 21)

The FMI-SiR$_O$ indexes are managed in the same way as the built-in ones. To execute indexed similarity queries, the user must create an index for the feature vector and write the queries using the operators associated to the respective index type. For example, the following instructions create an index and executes the same aforementioned queries, but now using the index: (see Algorithm 22)

The value provided in the PARAMETERS clause of the index creation instruction is the index page size. Note that indexed k-NN queries in FMI-SiR$_O$ do not require explicitly ordering the rows according to their distances to the query center, because the k-NN condition is tested during the index search. The

Algorithm 20.

```
CREATE OR REPLACE TYPE index_im_type AS OBJECT (
  scanctx RAW(4),
  STATIC FUNCTION ODCIIndexCreate(),
  STATIC FUNCTION ODCIIndexDrop(),
  STATIC FUNCTION ODCIIndexInsert(),
  STATIC FUNCTION ODCIIndexDelete(),
  STATIC FUNCTION ODCIIndexUpdate(),
  STATIC FUNCTION ODCIIndexStart(),
  MEMBER FUNCTION ODCIIndexFetch(),
  MEMBER FUNCTION ODCIIndexClose());
```

Algorithm 21.

```
CREATE INDEXTYPE Slim_Manhattan FOR
  Manhattan_dist(BLOB, BLOB), Manhattan_kNN(BLOB, BLOB)
  USING index_im_type;
```

Algorithm 22.

```
CREATE INDEX new_index ON Landscapes(Picture_Histo&Center)
  INDEX TYPE IS Slim_Manhattan PARAMETERS ('8192');
SELECT * FROM Landscapes
  WHERE Manhattan_dist(Picture_Histo&Center, Example) <= 0.03;
SELECT * FROM Landscapes
  WHERE Manhattan_kNN(Picture_Histo&Center, Example) <= 5;
```

execution of indexed queries is alike to the execution of sequential ones, except that the DBMS query processor requests an index scan to FMI-SiR$_O$ (Step 6b of Figure 5), which returns the physical row identifiers (RowIds) satisfying the predicate (Step 7b of Figure 5). To retrieve the most dissimilar elements instead of the most similar, the comparison operator <= should be reversed (e.g. Manhattan_dist(...) > 1.5 returns the elements out of this range from the query center).

Similarity joins and aggregated selections can also be represented in FMI-SiR$_O$. To be employed in join operations, the distance function parameters are the joining attributes of the involved tables. For instance, the following query is a similarity range join: (see Algorithm 23)

Aggregated selections employ functions that accept multiple query centers as parameters and compute the aggregated similarity. Such queries are written in the same way as the regular similarity selections, but using the aggregated similarity functions in place of the distance functions.

Complex queries interleaving similarity and regular selection predicates also can be posed in FMI-SiR$_O$. The command that states a query equivalent as the last example of the previous section is the following. (see Algorithm 24)

Algorithm 23.

```
SELECT * FROM Landscapes L1, Landscapes L2
  WHERE Manhattan_dist(L1.Picture_Texture, L2.Picture_Texture) <= 0.03
```

Algorithm 24.

```
SELECT * FROM Landscapes
  WHERE Place = 'Paris' AND
        Manhattan_dist(Figure_Texture, Example) <= 0.03 AND
        Manhattan_knn(Figure_Texture, Example) <= 5;
```

FMI-SiR$_O$ allows the query processor to choose the best execution strategy regarding all query conditions. Therefore, the most selective condition can be used to filter the results or intersections can be employed between the individual index results before accessing the data blocks. However, optimizer cannot detect special similarity constructions, as a Range and a k-NN query with the same query center. This happens because only the built-in rewriting rules of the query processor are evaluated. To overcome this issue, it would be necessary to modify the DBMS query processor. Another alternative would be to combine the two approaches described in this section: a blade that intercepts SQL instructions and rewrite them in the best query plan using the standard DBMS resources as well as those provided by a module for similarity searching. However, this is a solution that only can be implemented changing the code of the underlying DBMS, and thus only can be implemented in a way specific for a given product.

CONCLUSION

Most of the systems available to query multimedia data by similarity were developed considering a specific data domain and presenting a closed architecture. This approach does not allow applications to extend the access over traditional data in order to also deal with other data types, such as images and audio. This can be a big issue, for example, for the extension of typical applications of a medical information system, such as the electronic patient record system, in a way that they could also support image retrieval by similarity to support decision making.

Commercial products, such as Oracle InterMedia and IBM DB2 AIV Extenders, support the management of several types of multimedia data through user-defined functions and types. Although this approach can use the existing highly optimized algorithms for each specific similarity operation, it does not allow optimizations among the operators nor their integration with the other operators used in a query.

Therefore, it is fundamental that DBMS support the management of multimedia data by similarity through native predicates in SQL, built into an architecture that is capable to be easily adjusted to the particular needs of each application domain. This chapter contributes to support similarity queries as a built-in resource in relational DBMS, addressing the fundamental aspects related to the representation of similarity queries in SQL. Having this goal in mind, the solutions for similarity query representation and execution presented herein have several interesting characteristics.

First, the SQL extension presented enables representing similarity queries as just one more type of predicate, leading to the integration of similarity as operations in relational algebra. This characteristic enables extending the optimizers of the relational DBMS to treat and optimize similarity queries as well.

Second, the presented retrieval engines shows how to benefit from improvements on data retrieval techniques aimed at similarity, such as techniques involved in the similarity evaluation and index structures that support similarity operators.

Third, the presented solutions can act as a hub for the development of algorithms to perform broadly employed similarity operations regarding data analysis. For example, data mining processes often require performing similarity operations, and having them integrated in the database server, possibly optimized by a MAM, can be feasible in the future.

FUTURE RESEARCH DIRECTIONS

There is a diversity of application areas for similarity retrieval systems, including: medicine, education, entertainment and others, each of which usually presenting different requirements. We observed that important requirements for several applications, such as getting a timely answer for a similarity query, have been widely explored in many works. However, many other topics regarding representation, indexing and searching of multimedia data are still open issues to be explored.

With concern to the retrieval quality, approaches that aims at improving the semantics of multimedia queries are highly desired. Current techniques yet require much improvement to satisfy the requirements of specialized applications. The chapter presented several methods that represent a starting point to do this, such as the multiple center queries, which are a straightforward way to support relevance feedback requirements.

Regarding the retrieval efficiency, existing structures and algorithms suffer from the *dimensionality curse* and the search space deserves to be mapped into simpler and more relevant subspaces. Moreover, algorithms for executing similarity operations are worth improving, such as those for aggregate similarity and similarity joins.

Currently, another issue to be tackled is the lack of flexibility of the available system architectures to query multimedia data by similarity. As the techniques for inferring the content of complex data and the process of similarity evaluation evolve, each system for multimedia retrieval tends more and more to rely on particularized solutions. This panorama can lead to interoperability problems as well as to redundant development efforts. Therefore, it is necessary to conceive software architectures to manage multimedia data in such a way that base functionalities and structures can be encapsulated in a manner equivalent to those that have made DBMS so successful in the past 40 years.

REFERENCES

Baluja, S., & Covell, M. (2008). Waveprint: Efficient wavelet-based audio fingerprinting. *Pattern Recognition, 41*(11), 3467–3480. doi:10.1016/j.patcog.2008.05.006

Barioni, M. C. N., Razente, H., Traina, A. J. M., & Traina-Jr, C. (2006). Siren: A similarity retrieval engine for complex data. In International Conference on Very Large Databases (VLDB), (pp.1155–1158). Seoul, Korea.

Barioni, M. C. N., Razente, H., Traina, A. J. M., & Traina-Jr, C. (2008). Seamlessly integrating similarity queries in sql. *Software, Practice & Experience*, *39*, 355–384. doi:10.1002/spe.898

Blanken, H. M., de Vries, A. P., Blok, H. E., & Feng, L. (Eds.). (2007). *Multimedia retrieval (Data-centric systems and applications)*. Springer.

Bohm, C., & Krebs, F. (2002). High performance data mining using the nearest neighbor join. In International Conference on Data Mining (ICDM), (pp. 43–50). Maebashi City, Japan.

Bohm, C., & Krebs, F. (2004). The k-nearest neighbour join: Turbo charging the KDD process. *Knowledge and Information Systems*, *6*(6), 728–749. doi:10.1007/s10115-003-0122-9

Bohm, C., Stefan, B., & Keim, D. A. (2001). Searching in high-dimensional spaces: Index structures for improving the performance of multimedia databases. *ACM Computing Surveys*, *33*(3), 322–373. doi:10.1145/502807.502809

Bozkaya, T., & Ozsoyoglu, M. (1997). *Distance-based indexing for high-dimensional metric spaces*. In ACM International Conference on Management of Data (SIGMOD), (pp. 357–368). Tucson: ACM Press.

Brin, S. (1995). *Near neighbor search in large metric spaces*. In International Conference on Very Large Databases (VLDB), (pp. 574–584). Zurich, Switzerland. Morgan Kaufman.

Brinkhoff, T., Kriegel, H.-P., & Seeger, B. (1993). Efficient processing of spatial joins using r-trees. In ACM International Conference on Management of Data (SIGMOD), (pp. 237–246). New York: ACM.

Bueno, R., Kaster, D. S., Paterlini, A. A., Traina, A. J. M., & Traina-Jr, C. (2009). *Unsupervised scaling of multi-descriptor similarity functions for medical image datasets*. In IEEE International Symposium on Computer-Based Medical Systems (CBMS), (pp. 1–8). Albuquerque, NM: IEEE.

Bugatti, P. H., Traina, A. J. M., & Traina-Jr, C. (2008). *Assessing the best integration between distance-function and image-feature to answer similarity queries*. In ACM Symposium on Applied Computing (SAC), (pp. 1225–1230). Fortaleza, CE, Brazil. ACM.

Bustos, B., Keim, D., Saupe, D., Schreck, T., & Vranic, D. (2004). *Automatic selection and combination of descriptors for effective 3D similarity search*. In IEEE International Symposium on Multimedia Software Engineering, (pp. 514–521). Miami: IEEE.

Carey, M. J., & Kossmann, D. (1997). *On saying enough already! in SQL*. In ACM International Conference on Management of Data (SIGMOD), (pp. 219–230).

Carey, M. J., & Kossmann, D. (1998). *Reducing the braking distance of an SQL query engine*. In International Conference on Very Large Databases (VLDB), (pp. 158–169). New York.

Ciaccia, P., Patella, M., & Zezula, P. (1997). *M-tree: An efficient access method for similarity search in metric spaces*. In International Conference on Very Large Databases (VLDB), (pp. 426–435). Athens, Greece. Morgan Kaufmann.

IBM Corp. (2003). *Image, audio, and video extenders administration and programming guide*. DB2 universal database version 8.

Deserno, T. M., Antani, S., & Long, R. (2009). Ontology of gaps in content-based image retrieval. *Journal of Digital Imaging, 2*(22), 1–14.

Dohnal, V., Gennaro, C., Savino, P., & Zezula, P. (2003a). *Similarity join in metric spaces*. In European Conference on Information Retrieval Research(ECIR), (pp 452–467). Pisa, Italy.

Dohnal, V., Gennaro, C., & Zezula, P. (2003b). Similarity join in metric spaces using ed-index. In 14th International Conference on Database and Expert Systems Applications (DEXA), (pp. 484–493). Prague, Czech Republic.

Eakins, J., & Graham, M. (1999). *Content-based image retrieval*. (Technical Report 39), University of Northumbria at Newcastle.

Felipe, J. C., Traina-Jr, C., & Traina, A. J. M. (2009). A new family of distance functions for perceptual similarity retrieval of medical images. *Journal of Digital Imaging, 22*(2), 183–201. doi:10.1007/s10278-007-9084-x

Ferreira, M. R. P., Traina, A. J. M., Dias, I., Chbeir, R., & Traina-Jr, C. (2009). *Identifying algebraic properties to support optimization of unary similarity queries*. 3rd Alberto Mendelzon International Workshop on Foundations of Data Management, Arequipa, Peru, (pp. 1–10).

Flickner, M., Sawhney, H. S., Ashley, J., Huang, Q., Dom, B., & Gorkani, M. (1995). Query by image and video content: The QBIC system. *IEEE Computer, 28*(9), 23–32.

Gao, L., Wang, M., Sean Wang, X., & Padmanabhan, S. (2004). *Uexpressing and optimizing similarity-based queries in SQLs*. (Technical Report CS-04-06), University of Vermont. Retrieved from http://www.cs.uvm.edu /csdb/ techreport.shtml

Garcia-Molina, H., Ullman, J. D., & Widom, J. (2002). *Database systems: The complete book*. Upper Saddle River, NJ: Prentice Hall.

Gauker, C. (2007). A critique of the similarity space theory of concepts. *Mind & Language, 22*(4), 317–345. doi:10.1111/j.1468-0017.2007.00311.x

Guyon, I., & Elisseeff, A. (2003). An introduction to variable and feature selection. *Journal of Machine Learning Research, 3*, 1157–1182. doi:10.1162/153244303322753616

Haralick, R. M. (1979). Statistical and structural approaches to texture. *IEEE, 67*, 786–804.

He, X., Ma, W.-Y., King, O., Li, M., & Zhang, H. (2002). *Learning and inferring a semantic space from user's relevance feedback for image retrieval*. In ACM International Conference on Multimedia (MULTIMEDIA), (pp. 343–346). New York: ACM.

Hjaltason, G. R., & Samet, H. (1995). *Ranking in spatial databases*. In International Symposium on Advances in Spatial Databases (SSD), (pp. 83–95). Portland, Maine.

Hjaltason, G. R., & Samet, H. (1999). Distance browsing in spatial databases. *ACM Transactions on Database Systems, 24*(2), 265–318. doi:10.1145/320248.320255

Hjaltason, G. R., & Samet, H. (2003). Index-driven similarity search in metric spaces. *ACM Transactions on Database Systems, 28*(4), 517–580. doi:10.1145/958942.958948

Huang, P.-W., Hsu, L., Su, Y.-W., & Lin, P.-L. (2008). Spatial inference and similarity retrieval of an intelligent image database system based on object's spanning representation. *Journal of Visual Languages and Computing, 19*(6), 637–651. doi:10.1016/j.jvlc.2007.09.001

Informix Corp. (1999). *Excalibur image DataBlade module user's guide*. Informix Press.

Jacox, E. H., & Samet, H. (2008). Metric space similarity joins. *ACM Transactions on Database Systems, 33*(2), 1–38. doi:10.1145/1366102.1366104

Jain, A. K., & Farrokhnia, F. (1991). Unsupervised texture segmentation using gabor filters. *Pattern Recognition, 24*(12), 1167–1186. doi:10.1016/0031-3203(91)90143-S

Kaster, D. S., Bugatti, P. H., Traina, A. J. M., & Traina-Jr, C. (2009). Incorporating metric access methods for similarity searching on Oracle database. In Brazilian Symposium on Databases (SBBD), (pp. 196–210). Fortaleza, Brazil.

Khotanzad, A., & Hong, Y. H. (1990). Invariant image recognition by zernike moments. *IEEE Transactions on Pattern Analysis and Machine Intelligence, 12*(5), 489–497. doi:10.1109/34.55109

Kokare, M., Chatterji, B., & Biswas, P. (2003). *Comparison of similarity metrics for texture image retrieval*. In Conference on Convergent Technologies for Asia-Pacific Region, (pp. 571–575).

Korn, F., Sidiropoulos, N., Faloutsos, C., Siegel, E., & Protopapas, Z. (1996). *Fast nearest neighbor search in medical image databases*. In International Conference on Very Large Databases (VLDB), pp(. 215–226). San Francisco.

Lee, K.-M., & Street, W. N. (2002). Incremental feature weight learning and its application to a shape-based query system. *Pattern Recognition Letters, 23*(7), 865–874. doi:10.1016/S0167-8655(01)00161-1

Lienhart, R. (2001). Reliable transition detection in videos: A survey and practitioner's guide. *International Journal of Image and Graphics, 1*, 469–486. doi:10.1142/S021946780100027X

Liu, Y., Zhang, D., Lu, G., & Ma, W.-Y. (2007). A survey of content-based image retrieval with high-level semantics. *Pattern Recognition Letters, 40*, 262–282.

Long, F., Zhang, H., & Feng, D. D. (2003). *Fundamentals of content-based image retrieval (Multimedia information retrieval and management-technological fundamentals and applications)*. Springer.

Manjunath, B. S., Ohm, J.-R., Vasudevan, V. V., & Yamada, A. (2001). Color and texture descriptors. *IEEE Transactions on Circuits and Systems for Video Technology, 11*(6), 703–715. doi:10.1109/76.927424

Melton, J., & Eisenberg, A. (2001). SQL multimedia and application packages (SQL/MM). *SIGMOD Record, 30*(4), 97–102. doi:10.1145/604264.604280

Mokhtarian, F., & Mackworth, A. (1986). Scale-based description and recognition of planar curves and two-dimensional objects. *IEEE Transactions on Pattern Analysis and Machine Intelligence, 8*(1), 34–43. doi:10.1109/TPAMI.1986.4767750

Oracle Corp. (2005). *Oracle interMedia user's guide, (10.2)*. Oracle.

Papadias, D., Tao, Y., Mouratidis, K., & Hui, C. K. (2005). Aggregate nearest neighbor queries in spatial databases. *ACM Transactions on Database Systems, 30*(2), 529–576. doi:10.1145/1071610.1071616

Razente, H., Barioni, M. C. N., Traina, A. J. M., & Traina-Jr, C. (2008a). Aggregate similarity queries in relevance feedback methods for content-based image retrieval. In ACM Symposium on Applied Computing (SAC), (pp. 869–874). Fortaleza, Brazil.

Razente, H., Barioni, M. C. N., Traina, A. J. M., & Traina-Jr, C. (2008b). *A novel optimization approach to efficiently process aggregate similarity queries in metric access methods*. In ACM International Conference on Information and Knowledge Management, (pp. 193–202). Napa, CA.

Roussopoulos, N., Kelley, S., & Vincent, F. (1995). *Nearest neighbor queries*. In ACM International Conference on Management of Data (SIGMOD), (pp. 71–79).

Santini, S., & Gupta, A. (2001). *A wavelet data model for image databases*. In IEEE International Conference on Multimedia and Expo (ICME), Tokyo, Japan. IEEE Computer Society.

Seidl, T., & Kriegel, H.-P. (1998). *Optimal multi-step k-nearest neighbor search*. In ACM International Conference on Management of Data (SIGMOD), (pp. 154–165). Seattle, Washington.

Smeulders, A. W. M., Worring, M., Santini, S., Gupta, A., & Jain, R. (2000). Content-based image retrieval at the end of the early years. [TPAMI]. *IEEE Transactions on Pattern Analysis and Machine Intelligence, 22*(12), 1349–1380. doi:10.1109/34.895972

Tasan, M., & Ozsoyoglu, Z. M. (2004). *Improvements in distance-based indexing*. In International Conference on Scientific and Statistical Database Management (SSDBM), (p. 161). Washington, DC: IEEE Computer Society.

Torres, R. S., Falcão, A. X., Gonçalves, M. A., Papa, J. P., Zhang, P., & Fan, W. (2009). A genetic programming framework for content-based image retrieval. *Pattern Recognition, 42*(2), 283–292. doi:10.1016/j.patcog.2008.04.010

Traina-Jr, C., Traina, A. J. M., Faloutsos, C., & Seeger, B. (2002). Fast indexing and visualization of metric datasets using slim-trees. [TKDE]. *IEEE Transactions on Knowledge and Data Engineering, 14*(2), 244–260. doi:10.1109/69.991715

Traina-Jr, C., Traina, A. J. M., Vieira, M. R., Arantes, A. S., & Faloutsos, C. (2006). *Efficient processing of complex similarity queries in RDBMS through query rewriting*. In International Conference on Information and Knowledge Management (CIKM), (pp.4–13). Arlington, VA.

Tzanetakis, G., & Cook, P. R. (2002). Musical genre classification of audio signals. *IEEE Transactions on Speech and Audio Processing, 10*(5), 293–302. doi:10.1109/TSA.2002.800560

Wan, C., & Liu, M. (2006). Content-based audio retrieval with relevance feedback. *Pattern Recognition Letters, 27*(2), 85–92. doi:10.1016/j.patrec.2005.07.005

Wilson, D. R., & Martinez, T. R. (1997). Improved heterogeneous distance functions. *Journal of Artificial Intelligence Research, 6*, 1–34.

Wu, L., Faloutsos, C., Sycara, K., & Payne, T. R. (2000). *Falcon: Feedback adaptive loop for content-based retrieval*. In International Conference on Very Large Databases (VLDB), (pp. 297–306). Cairo, Egypt.

Yeh, W.-H., & Chang, Y.-I. (2008). An efficient iconic indexing strategy for image rotation and reflection in image databases. [JSS]. *Journal of Systems and Software, 81*(7), 1184–1195. doi:10.1016/j.jss.2007.08.019

Yianilos, P. N. (1993). *Data structures and algorithms for nearest neighbor search in general metric spaces*. In ACM/SIGACT-SIAM Symposium on Discrete Algorithms (SODA), (pp. 311–321). Austin, TX, EUA. Society for Industrial and Applied Mathematics.

Zahn, C. T., & Roskies, R. Z. (1972). Fourier descriptors for plane closed curves. *IEEE Transactions on Computers, 21*(3), 269–281. doi:10.1109/TC.1972.5008949

Zhou, X. S., & Huang, T. S. (2003). Relevance feedback in image retrieval: A comprehensive review. *Multimedia Systems, 8*(6), 536–544. doi:10.1007/s00530-002-0070-3

ADDITIONAL READING

Antani, S., Kasturi, R., & Jain, R. (2002). A survey on the use of pattern recognition methods for abstraction, indexing and retrieval of images and video. *Pattern Recognition, 35*(4), 945–965. doi:10.1016/S0031-3203(01)00086-3

Bohm, C., Stefan, B., & Keim, D. A. (2001). Searching in high-dimensional spaces: Index structures for improving the performance of multimedia databases. *ACM Computing Surveys, 33*(3), 322–373. doi:10.1145/502807.502809

Cano, P. (2009). *Content-Based Audio Search: From Audio Fingerprinting To Semantic Audio Retrieval*. VDM Verlag.

Chávez, E., Navarro, G., Baeza-Yates, R., & Marroquín, J. L. (2001). Searching in Metric Spaces. *ACM Computing Surveys, 33*(3), 273–321. doi:10.1145/502807.502808

Datta, R., Joshi, D., Li, J., & Wang, J. Z. (2008). Image retrieval: Ideas, influences, and trends of the new age. *ACM Computing Surveys, 40*(2), 1–60. doi:10.1145/1348246.1348248

Deb, S. (2003). Multimedia Systems and Content-Based Image Retrieval. Information Science Publishing. 2003

Deserno, T. M., Antani, S., & Long, R. (2009). Ontology of Gaps in Content-Based Image Retrieval. *Journal of Digital Imaging, 22*(2), 202–215. doi:10.1007/s10278-007-9092-x

Doulamis, N., & Doulamis, A. (2006). Evaluation of relevance feedback schemes in content-based in retrieval systems. *Signal Processing Image Communication, 21*(4), 334–357. doi:10.1016/j.image.2005.11.006

Geetha, P., & Narayanan, V. (2008). A Survey of Content-Based Video Retrieval. *Journal of Computer Science, 4*(6), 474–486. doi:10.3844/jcssp.2008.474.486

Gibbon, D. C., & Liu, Z. (2008). *Introduction to Video Search Engines* (1st ed.). Springer.

Groff, J. R., & Weinberg, P. N. (2002). *SQL: The Complete Reference* (2nd ed.). McGraw-Hill, Osborne Media.

Kosch, H. (2003). *Multimedia Database Management Systems: Indexing, Access, and MPEG-7*. Boca Raton, FL, USA: CRC Press, Inc.

Lew, M. S., Sebe, N., Djeraba, C., & Jain, R. (2006). Content-based multimedia information retrieval: State of the art and challenges. [TOMCCAP]. *ACM Transactions on Multimedia Computing, Communications, and Applications*, *2*(1), 1–19. doi:10.1145/1126004.1126005

Melton, J. (2001). *SQL:1999 - Understanding Relational Language Components. The Morgan Kaufmann Series in Data Management Systems* (1st ed.). Morgan Kaufmann.

Mostefaoui, A. (2006). A modular and adaptive framework for large scale video indexing and content-based retrieval: the SIRSALE system. *Software, Practice & Experience*, *36*(8), 871–890. doi:10.1002/spe.722

Muller, H. (2008). Medical multimedia retrieval 2.0. *IMIA Yearbook of Medical Informatics*, *2008*, 55–63.

Samet, H. (2006). *Foundations of Multidimensional and Metric Data Structures*. San Francisco, CA: Morgan Kaufmann.

Vasconcelos, N. (2008). From Pixels to Semantic Spaces: Advances in Content-Based Image Retrieval. *IEEE Computer*, *40*(7), 20–26.

Vaswani, V. (2004). The Future of SQL. In *MySQL: The Complete Reference*. McGraw-Hill/Osborne.

Zezula, P., Amato, G., Dohnal, V., & Batko, M. (2006). Similarity Search: The Metric Space Approach (Series Advances in Database Systems, vol. 32), Springer.

Zhang, Z., & Zhang, R. (2008). Multimedia Data Mining: A Systematic Introduction to Concepts and Theory. Chapman & Hall/CRC Data Mining and Knowledge Discovery Series. Chapman & Hall; 1 edition.

Zhou, S. X., & Huang, T. S. (2003). Relevance feedback in image retrieval: A comprehensive review. *Multimedia Systems*, *8*(6), 536–544. doi:10.1007/s00530-002-0070-3

KEY TERMS AND DEFINITIONS

Content-Based Image Retrieval: consists of the retrieval of images based on the dissimilarity of features extracted from the images.

Similarity Evaluation: an operation that consists of a sequence of computational tasks in order to obtain a value quantifying how close (or far) two multimedia objects are.

Similarity Queries: are those queries where the search criteria is computed based on the similarity among multimedia objects

Feature Extraction Algorithms: mathematical routines that generate numerical vectors that represent an image

Query-By-Example: a query where the user gives an example of what he wants to retrieve

Semantic Gap: the gap between what the user wants and the results based on features extracted automatically from multimedia data

ENDNOTE

[1] In Oracle, feature vectors are stored explicitly in other attributes of the table containing the image. Thus, the Oracle example considers that the table *Landscapes* also has another attribute holding the features (*Picture_Features*).

Compilation of References

Abadi, D. J., Marcus, A., Madden, S., & Hollenbach, K. (2009). SW-Store: A vertically partitioned DBMS for Semantic Web data management. *The VLDB Journal*, *18*(2), 385–406. doi:10.1007/s00778-008-0125-y

Abiteboul, S., & Kanellakis, P. C. (1998). Object identity as a query language primitive. [JACM]. *Journal of the ACM, 45*(5), 798–842. doi:10.1145/290179.290182

Abiteboul, S., Hull, R., & Vianu, V. (1995). *Foundations of databases*. Reading, MA: Addison-Wesley.

Abiteboul, S., Benjelloun, O., Manolescu, I., Milo, T., & Weber, R. (2002). Active XML: Peer-to-peer data and Web services integration. In *Proceedings of 28th International Conference on Very Large Data Bases*, (pp. 1087-1090). August 20-23, 2002, Hong Kong, China, Morgan Kaufmann.

Agrawal, S., Chaudhuri, S., Das, G., & Gionis, A. (2003). Automated ranking of database query results. *ACM Transactions on Database Systems, 28*(2), 140–174.

Agrawal, R., Gupta, A., & Sarawagi, S. (1997). *Modeling multidimensional databases*. In 13th International Conference on Data Engineering (ICDE'97), (pp. 232–243).

Agrawal, R., Rantzau, R., & Terzi, E. (2006). Context-sensitive ranking. *Proceedings of the ACM SIGMOD International Conference on Management of Data*, (pp. 383-394).

Ahlberg, C., & Shneiderman, B. (1994). *Visual information seeking: tight coupling of dynamic query filters with starfield displays* (pp. 313–317). Proceedings on Human Factors in Computing Systems.

Alexaki, S., Christophides, V., Karvounarakis, G., Plexousakis, D., & Tolle, K. (2001). The ICS-FORTH RDF Suite: Managing voluminous RDF description bases. In *Proceedings of the 2nd International Workshop on the Semantic Web (semWeb)*.

AllegroGraph RDF Store. (2009). *Allegrograph*. Retrieved from http://www.franz.com/agraph/allegrograph/

Allen, J. F. (1983). Maintaining knowledge about temporal intervals. *Communications of the ACM*, 832–843. doi:10.1145/182.358434

Angles, R., & Gutierrez, C. (2008). Survey of graph database models. *ACM Computing Surveys, 40*(1), 1–39. doi:10.1145/1322432.1322433

Arenas, M., & Libkin, L. (2004). A normal form for XML documents. *ACM Transactions on Database Systems, 29*(1), 195–232. doi:10.1145/974750.974757

Arenas, M., & Libkin, L. (2005). XML data exchange: Consistency and query answering. In L. Chen (Ed.), *Proceedings of the 24th ACM SIGACT-SIGMOD-SIGART Symposium on Principles of Database Systems*, (pp. 13-24). June 13-15, 2005, Baltimore, Maryland, USA, ACM.

Awad, A. (2007). BPMN-Q: A language to query business processes. In *Proceedings of the 2nd International Workshop on Enterprise Modelling and Information Systems Architectures*, (pp. 115-128).

Baader, F., Calvanese, D., McGuinness, D. L., Nardi, D., & Patel-Schneider, P. F. (Eds.). (2003). *The description logic handbook: Theory, implementation, and applications*. Cambridge University Press.

Baader, F., & Nutt, W. (2003). *Basic description logics* (pp. 43–95).

Balke, W., & Güntzer, U. (2004). Multi-objective query processing for database systems. In *Proceedings of the International Conference on Very Large Databases* (VLDB), (pp. 936-947).

Balke, W., Güntzer, U., & Zheng, J. (2004). Efficient distributed skylining for Web Information Systems. In *Proceedings of International Conference on Extending Database Technology* (EDBT), (pp. 256-273).

Baluja, S., & Covell, M. (2008). Waveprint: Efficient wavelet-based audio fingerprinting. *Pattern Recognition*, *41*(11), 3467–3480. doi:10.1016/j.patcog.2008.05.006

Bancilhon, F. (1996). Object databases. [CSUR]. *ACM Computing Surveys*, *28*(1), 137–140. doi:10.1145/234313.234373

Barioni, M. C. N., Razente, H., Traina, A. J. M., & Traina-Jr, C. (2008). Seamlessly integrating similarity queries in sql. *Software, Practice & Experience*, *39*, 355–384. doi:10.1002/spe.898

Barioni, M. C. N., Razente, H., Traina, A. J. M., & Traina-Jr, C. (2006). Siren: A similarity retrieval engine for complex data. In International Conference on Very Large Databases (VLDB), (pp.1155–1158). Seoul, Korea.

Bechhofer, S., Van Harmelen, F., Hendler, J., Horrocks, I., McGuinness, D., Patel-Schneider, P., et al. (2004). *OWL Web ontology language reference*. W3C recommendation.

Beckmann, J. L., Halverson, A., Krishnamurthy, R., & Naughton, J. F. (2006). Extending RDBMSs to support sparse datasets using an interpreted attribute storage format. In *Proceedings of the 22nd International Conference on Data Engineering*, (p. 58).

Bentley, J., Kung, H.T., Schkolnick, M. & Thompson, C.D. (1978). On the average number of maxima in a set of vectors and applications. *Journal of ACM* (JACM).

Berners-Lee, T., Hendler, J. & Lassila, O. (2001). The Semantic Web: A new form of Web content that is meaningful to computers will unleash a revolution of new possibilities. *Scientific American*.

Bernstein, P. A., & Haas, L. M. (2008). Information integration in the enterprise. *Communications of the ACM*, *51*(9), 72–79. doi:10.1145/1378727.1378745

Bizer, C., & Schultz, A. (2008). Benchmarking the performance of storage systems that expose SPARQL endpoints. In *Proceedings of the 4th International Workshop on Scalable Semantic Web Knowledge Base Systems*.

Blanken, H. M., de Vries, A. P., Blok, H. E., & Feng, L. (Eds.). (2007). *Multimedia retrieval (Data-centric systems and applications)*. Springer.

Bobillo, F., & Straccia, U. (2008). fuzzydl: An expressive fuzzy description logic reasoner. *Proceedings of the 2008 IEEE International Conference on Fuzzy Systems*, (pp. 923–930).

Bohm, C., & Krebs, F. (2004). The k-nearest neighbour join: Turbo charging the KDD process. *Knowledge and Information Systems*, *6*(6), 728–749. doi:10.1007/s10115-003-0122-9

Bohm, C., Stefan, B., & Keim, D. A. (2001). Searching in high-dimensional spaces: Index structures for improving the performance of multimedia databases. *ACM Computing Surveys*, *33*(3), 322–373. doi:10.1145/502807.502809

Bohm, C., & Krebs, F. (2002). High performance data mining using the nearest neighbor join. In International Conference on Data Mining (ICDM), (pp. 43–50). Maebashi City, Japan.

Bookstein, A. (1980). Fuzzy requests: An approach to weighted Boolean searches. *Journal of the American Society for Information Science American Society for Information Science*, *31*, 240–247. doi:10.1002/asi.4630310403

Bordogna, G., & Pasi, G. (1995). Linguistic aggregation operators of selection criteria in fuzzy information retrieval. *International Journal of Intelligent Systems*, *10*(2), 233–248. doi:10.1002/int.4550100205

Bordogna, G., Carrara, P., & Pasi, G. (1991). Query term weights as constraints in fuzzy information retrieval. *Information Processing & Management*, *27*(1), 15–26. doi:10.1016/0306-4573(91)90028-K

Bordogna, G., & Pasi, G. (2007). A flexible approach to evaluating soft conditions with unequal preferences in fuzzy databases. *International Journal of Intelligent Systems*, *22*(7), 665–689. doi:10.1002/int.20223

Bordogna, G., & Psaila, G. (2008). Customizable flexible querying classic relational databases. In Galindo, J. (Ed.), *Handbook of research on fuzzy information processing in databases* (pp. 191–217). Hershey, PA: Information Science Reference.

Bordogna, G., Carrara, P., Pagani, M., Pepe, M., & Rampini, A. (2009). Extending INSPIRE metadata to imperfect temporal descriptions, In the *Proceedings of the Global Spatial Data Infrastructures Conference (GSDI11), June 15-19 2009, Rotterdam (NL)*, CD Proceedings, Ref 235.

Börzsönyi, S., Kossmann, D., & Stocker, K. (2001). The skyline operator. In *Proceedings of the 17th International Conference on Data Engineering*, (pp. 421- 430). Washington, DC, USA. IEEE Computer Society.

Bosc, P., Kraft, D., & Petry, F. E. (2005). Fuzzy sets in database and Information Systems: Status and opportunities. *Fuzzy Sets and Systems*, *153*(3), 418–426. doi:10.1016/j.fss.2005.05.039

Bosc, P., Lietard, L., & Pivert, O. (2003). Sugeno fuzzy integral as a basis for the interpretation of flexible queries involving monotonic aggregates. *Information Processing & Management*, *39*(2), 287–306. doi:10.1016/S0306-4573(02)00053-5

Bosc, P., & Pivert, O. (1995). SQLf: A relational database language for fuzzy querying. *IEEE Transactions on Fuzzy Systems*, *3*, 1–17. doi:10.1109/91.366566

Bosc, P., Dubois, D., Pivert, O., & Prade, H. (1997). Flexible queries in relational databases-the example of the division operator. *Theoretical Computer Science*, *171*(1/2), 281–302. doi:10.1016/S0304-3975(96)00132-6

Bosc, P., & Pivert, O. (2006). About approximate inclusion and its axiomatization. *Fuzzy Sets and Systems*, *157*, 1438–1454. doi:10.1016/j.fss.2005.11.011

Bosc, P. (1999). Fuzzy databases. In Bezdek, J. (Ed.), *Fuzzy sets in approximate reasoning and Information Systems* (pp. 403–468). Boston: Kluwer Academic Publishers.

Bosc, P., & Pivert, O. (1993). An approach for a hierarchical aggregation of fuzzy predicates. In *Proceedings of the 2nd IEEE International Conference on Fuzzy Systems (FUZZ-IEEE'93)*, (pp. 1231—1236). San Francisco, USA.

Bosc, P., & Pivert, O. (2000). On the specification of representation-based conditions in a context of incomplete databases. In the *Proceedings of Database and Expert Systems Applications, 10th International Conference (DEXA '99), August 30 - September 3, 1999, Florence (It)*, (pp. 594-603).

Bosc, P., & Pivert, O. (2000). SQLf query functionality on top of a regular relational RDBMS. *Knowledge Management in Fuzzy Databases*, 171-190. Heidelberg: Physica-Verlag.

Bosc, P., Pivert, O., & Lietard, L. (2001). Aggregate operators in database flexible querying. In *Proceedings of the IEEE International Conference on Fuzzy Systems (FUZZ-IEEE 2001)*, (pp. 1231-1234), Melbourne, Australia.

Botea, V., Mallett, D., Nascimento, M. A., & Sander, J. (2008). PIST: An efficient and practical indexing technique for historical spatio-temporal point data. *GeoInformatica*, *12*(2), 143–168. doi:10.1007/s10707-007-0030-3

Boulos, J., Dalvi, N., & Mandhani, B. Mathur, S., Re, C. & Suciu, D. (2005). *MystiQ: A system for finding more answers by using probabilities*. System Demo in 2005 ACM SIGMOD International Conference on Management of Data. Retrieved October 18, 2009, from http://www.cs.washington.edu/homes/suciu/demo.pdf

Bozkaya, T., & Ozsoyoglu, M. (1997). *Distance-based indexing for high-dimensional metric spaces*. In ACM International Conference on Management of Data (SIGMOD), (pp. 357–368). Tucson: ACM Press.

Brantner, M., May, N., & Moerkotte, G. (2007). Unnesting scalar SQL queries in the presence of disjunction. In *Proceedings of IEEE ICDE*.

Breiman, L., Friedman, J., Stone, C. J., & Olshen, R. (1984). *Classification and regression trees*. Boca Raton, FL: CRC Press.

Brin, S. (1995). *Near neighbor search in large metric spaces*. In International Conference on Very Large Databases (VLDB), (pp. 574–584). Zurich, Switzerland. Morgan Kaufman.

Brinkhoff, T., Kriegel, H.-P., & Seeger, B. (1993). Efficient processing of spatial joins using r-trees. In ACM International Conference on Management of Data (SIGMOD), (pp. 237–246). New York: ACM.

Broekstra, J., Kampman, A., & van Harmelen, F. (2002). Sesame: A generic architecture for storing and querying RDF and RDF schema. In *Proceedings of the First International Semantic Web Conference,* (p. 54-68).

Bruno, N., Chaudhuri, S., & Ramamurthy, R. (2009). Power hints for query optimization. In *Proceedings of the 25th International Conference on Data Engineering,* (pp. 469-480).

Bruno, N., Gravano, L., & Marian, A. (2002). Evaluating top-k queries over Web-accessible databases. *Proceedings of the 18th International Conference on Data Engineering,* (pp. 369-380).

Brzykcy, G., Bartoszek, J., & Pankowski, T. (2008). Schema mappings and agents' actions in P2P data integration system. *Journal of Universal Computer Science, 14*(7), 1048–1060.

Buckles, B. P., Petry, F. E., & Sachar, H. S. (1989). A domain calculus for fuzzy relational databases. *Fuzzy Sets and Systems, 29,* 327–340. doi:10.1016/0165-0114(89)90044-4

Bueno, R., Kaster, D. S., Paterlini, A. A., Traina, A. J. M., & Traina-Jr, C. (2009). *Unsupervised scaling of multi-descriptor similarity functions for medical image datasets.* In IEEE International Symposium on Computer-Based Medical Systems (CBMS), (pp. 1–8). Albuquerque, NM: IEEE.

Bugatti, P. H., Traina, A. J. M., & Traina-Jr, C. (2008). *Assessing the best integration between distance-function and image-feature to answer similarity queries.* In ACM Symposium on Applied Computing (SAC), (pp. 1225–1230). Fortaleza, CE, Brazil. ACM.

Buneman, P., Davidson, S. B., Fan, W., Hara, C. S., & Tan, W. C. (2003). Reasoning about keys for XML. *Information Systems, 28*(8), 1037–1063. doi:10.1016/S0306-4379(03)00028-0

Bunke, H., & Shearer, K. (1998). A graph distance metric based on the maximal common subgraph. *Pattern Recognition Letters, 19*(3-4), 255–259. doi:10.1016/S0167-8655(97)00179-7

Bustos, B., Keim, D., Saupe, D., Schreck, T., & Vranic, D. (2004). *Automatic selection and combination of descriptors for effective 3D similarity search.* In IEEE International Symposium on Multimedia Software Engineering, (pp. 514–521). Miami: IEEE.

Cai, D., Shao, Z., He, X., Yan, X., & Han, J. (2005). Community mining from multi-relational networks. In *Proceedings of the 9th European Conference on Principles and Practice of Knowledge Discovery in Databases,* (pp. 445-452).

Calvanese, D., De Giacomo, G., Lembo, D., Lenzerini, M., & Rosati, R. (2007). Tractable reasoning and efficient query answering in description logics: The dl-lite family. *Journal of Automated Reasoning, 39*(3), 385–429. doi:10.1007/s10817-007-9078-x

Calvanese, D., De Giacomo, G., & Lenzerini, M. (1998). On the decidability of query containment under constraints. *Proceedings of the 17th ACM SIGACT SIGMOD SIGART Symposium on Principles of Database Systems (PODS'98),* (pp. 149–158).

Card, S., MacKinlay, J., & Shneiderman, B. (1999). *Readings in information visualization: using vision to think.* Morgan Kaufmann.

Carey, M. J., & Kossmann, D. (1997). *On saying enough already! in SQL.* In ACM International Conference on Management of Data (SIGMOD), (pp. 219–230).

Carey, M. J., & Kossmann, D. (1998). *Reducing the braking distance of an SQL query engine.* In International Conference on Very Large Databases (VLDB), (pp. 158–169). New York.

Cater, S. C., & Kraft, D. H. (1989). A generalization and clarification of the Waller-Kraft wish-list. *Information Processing & Management, 25,* 15–25. doi:10.1016/0306-4573(89)90088-5

Chakrabarti, K., Chaudhuri, S., & Hwang, S. (2004). Automatic categorization of query results. *Proceedings of the ACM SIGMOD International Conference on Management of Data,* (pp. 755–766).

Chambers, C., Ungar, D., Chang, B., & Hölzle, U. (1991). Parents are shared parts of objects: Inheritance and encapsulation in self. *Lisp and Symbolic Computation, 4*(3), 207–222. doi:10.1007/BF01806106

Chaudhuri, S., & Weikum, G. (2000). Rethinking database system architecture: Towards a self-tuning RISC-style database system. In *Proceedings of 26th International Conference on Very Large Data Bases*, (p. 1-10).

Chaudhuri, S., Das, G., Hristidis, V., & Weikum, G. (2004). Probabilistic ranking of database query results. *Proceedings of the 30th International Conference on Very Large Data Base*, (pp. 888–899).

Chen, C., Yan, X., Yu, P. S., Han, J., Zhang, D.-Q., & Gu, X. (2007). Towards graph containment search and indexing. In *Proceedings of the 33rd International Conference on Very Large Data Bases*, (pp. 926-937).

Chen, Z. Y., & Li, T. (2007). Addressing diverse user preferences in SQL-Query-Result navigation. *Proceedings of the ACM SIGMOD International Conference on Management of Data*, (pp. 641-652).

Cheng, J., Ke, Y., Ng, W., & Lu, A. (2007). FG-Index: Towards verification-free query processing on graph databases. In *Proceedings of the ACM SIGMOD International Conference on Management of Data*, (pp. 857-872).

Chong, E. I., Das, S., Eadon, G., & Srinivasan, J. (2005). An efficient SQL-based RDF querying scheme. In *Proceedings of the 31st International Conference on Very Large Data Bases*, (pp. 1216-1227).

Chrobak, M., Keynon, C., & Young, N. (2005). The reverse greedy algorithm for the metric k-median problem. *Information Processing Letters*, *97*, 68–72. doi:10.1016/j.ipl.2005.09.009

Chu, E., Beckmann, J. L., & Naughton, J. F. (2007). The case for a wide-table approach to manage sparse relational data sets. In *Proceedings of the ACM SIGMOD International Conference on Management of Data*, (pp. 821-832).

Ciaccia, P., Patella, M., & Zezula, P. (1997). *M-tree: An efficient access method for similarity search in metric spaces*. In International Conference on Very Large Databases (VLDB), (pp. 426–435). Athens, Greece. Morgan Kaufmann.

Codd, E. F. (1979). Extending the database relational model to capture more meaning. [TODS]. *ACM Transactions on Database Systems*, *4*(4), 397–434. doi:10.1145/320107.320109

Connolly, T., & Begg, C. (2005). *Database systems-a practical approach to design, implementation, and management*. United Kingdom: Pearson Education Limited.

Consens, M. P., & Mendelzon, A. O. (1990). GraphLog: A visual formalism for real life recursion. In *Proceedings of the Ninth ACM SIGACT-SIGMOD-SIGART Symposium on Principles of Database Systems*, (pp. 404-416).

Copeland, G. P., & Khoshafian, S. (1985). A decomposition storage model. In *Proceedings of the ACM SIGMOD International Conference on Management of Data*, (pp. 268-279).

Cross Drafting Teams, I. N. S. P. I. R. E. (2007). *INSPIRE technical architecture overview, INSPIRE cross drafting teams report*. Retrieved on February 17, 2009, from http://inspire.jrc.ec.europa.eu/reports.cfm

Cyganiak, R. (2005). *A relational algebra for SPARQL*. (Tech. Rep. No. HPL-2005-170). HP Labs.

Dadashzadeh, M. (1989). An improved division operator for relational algebra. *Information Systems*, *14*(5), 431–437. doi:10.1016/0306-4379(89)90007-0

Darwen, H., & Date, C. (1992). Into the great divide. In Date, C., & Darwen, H. (Eds.), *Relational database: Writings 1989-1991* (pp. 155–168). Reading, MA: Addison-Wesley.

Das, G., Hristidis, V., Kapoor, N., & Sudarshan, S. (2006). Ordering the attributes of query results. *Proceedings of the ACM SIGMOD International Conference on Management of Data*, (pp. 395-406).

DBLP XML Records. (2009). *Home page information*. Retrieved from http://dblp.uni-trier.de/xml/

De Caluwe, R., Devis, F., Maesfranckx, P., De Trè, G., & Van der Cruyssen, B. (1999). Semantics and modelling of flexible time indication. In Zadeh, L. A., & Kacprzyk, J. (Eds.), *Computing with words in Information/Intelligent Systems* (pp. 229–256). Physica Verlag.

De Caluwe, R., & De Tré, G. G., Van der Cruyssen, B., Devos, F. & Maesfranckx, P. (2000). Time management in fuzzy and uncertain object-oriented databases. In O. Pons, A. Vila & J. Kacprzyk (Eds.), *Knowledge management in fuzzy databases*. (pp. 67-88). Heidelberg: Physica-Verlag.

De Kunder, M. (2010). *The size of the World Wide Web.* Retrieved from http://www.worldwidewebsize.com

De Tré, G., De Caluwe, R., Tourné, K., & Matthé, T. (2003). Theoretical considerations ensuing from experiments with flexible querying. In T. Bilgiç, B. De Baets & O. Kaynak (Eds.), *Proceedings of the IFSA 2003 World Congress,* (pp. 388—391). (LNCS 2715). Springer.

De Tré, G., Verstraete, J., Hallez, A., Matthé, T., & De Caluwe, R. (2006). The handling of select-project-join operations in a relational framework supported by possibilistic logic. In *Proceedings of the 11th International Conference on Information Processing and Management of Uncertainty in Knowledge-based Systems (IPMU),* (pp. 2181—2188). Paris, France.

De Tré, G., Zadrożny, S., Matthe, T., Kacprzyk, J., & Bronselaer, A. (2009). *Dealing with positive and negative query criteria in fuzzy database querying.* (LNCS 5822), (pp. 593-604).

Dekkers, M. (2008). *Temporal metadata for discovery-a review of current practice.* M. Craglia (Ed.), (EUR 23209 EN, JRC Scientific and Technical Report).

DeMichiel, L. G. (1989). Resolving database incompatibility: an approach to performing relational operations over mismatched domains. *IEEE Transactions on Knowledge and Data Engineering, 1*(4), 485–493. doi:10.1109/69.43423

Deng, L., Cai, Y., Wang, C., & Jiang, Y. (2009). Fuzzy temporal logic on fuzzy temporal constraint metworks. In the *Proceedings of the Sixth International Conference on Fuzzy Systems and Knowledge Discovery, 6,* (pp. 272-276).

Deserno, T. M., Antani, S., & Long, R. (2009). Ontology of gaps in content-based image retrieval. *Journal of Digital Imaging, 2*(22), 1–14.

Dhillon, I. S., Mallela, S., & Kumar, R. (2002). Enhanced word clustering for hierarchical text classification. *Proceedings of the 8th ACM SIGKDD International Conference,* (pp. 191–200).

Directive, I. N. S. P. I. R. E. 2007/2/EC of the European Parliament and of the Council of 14. (2007). *INSPIRE.* Retrieved on February 17, 2009, from www.ecgis.org/inspire/directive/l_10820070425en00010014.pdf

Dittrich, K. R. (1986). Object-oriented database systems: The notions and the issues. In *Proceedings of the International Workshop on Object-Oriented Database Systems,* (pp. 2–4).

Dubois, D., & Prade, H. (1997). Using fuzzy sets in flexible querying: Why and how? In Andreasen, T., Christiansen, H., & Larsen, H. L. (Eds.), *Flexible query answering systems.* Dordrecht: Kluwer Academic Publishers.

Dubois, D., & Prade, P. (2008). Handling bipolar queries in fuzzy information processing. In Galindo, J. (Ed.), *Handbook of research on fuzzy information processing in databases* (pp. 97–114). New York: Information Science Reference.

Dubois, D., & Prade, H. (2002). *Bipolarity in flexible querying.* (LNAI 2522), (pp. 174-182).

Eakins, J., & Graham, M. (1999). *Content-based image retrieval.* (Technical Report 39), University of Northumbria at Newcastle.

Eliassen, F., & Karlsen, R. (1991). Interoperability and object identity. *SIGMOD Record, 20*(4), 25–29. doi:10.1145/141356.141362

Elmasri, R., & Navathe, S. R. (2006). *Fundamentals of database systems* (5th ed.). Addison Wesley.

European Commission. (2007). *Draft implementing rules for metadata* (v. 3). INSPIRE Metadata Report. Retrieved on February 17, 2009, from http://inspire.jrc.ec.europa.eu/reports.cfm

European Commission. (2009). *INSPIRE metadata implementing rules: Technical guidelines based on EN ISO 19115 and EN ISO 19119.* INSPIRE Metadata Report. Retrieved on February 18, 2009, from http://inspire.jrc.ec.europa.eu/reports.cfm

Fagin, R. (2002). Combining fuzzy information: An overview. *SIGMOD Record, 31*(2), 109–118. doi:10.1145/565117.565143

Fagin, R., Kolaitis, P. G., & Popa, L. (2005). Data exchange: Getting to the core. *ACM Transactions on Database Systems, 30*(1), 174–210. doi:10.1145/1061318.1061323

Fagin, R., Kolaitis, P. G., Popa, L., & Tan, W. C. (2004). Composing schema mappings: Second-order dependencies to the rescue. In: A. Deutsch (Ed.), *Proceedings of the 23rd ACM SIGACT-SIGMOD-SIGART Symposium on Principles of Database Systems,* (pp. 83-94). June 14-16, 2004, Paris, France, ACM.

Felipe, J. C., Traina-Jr, C., & Traina, A. J. M. (2009). A new family of distance functions for perceptual similarity retrieval of medical images. *Journal of Digital Imaging, 22*(2), 183–201. doi:10.1007/s10278-007-9084-x

Ferreira, M. R. P., Traina, A. J. M., Dias, I., Chbeir, R., & Traina-Jr, C. (2009). *Identifying algebraic properties to support optimization of unary similarity queries.* 3rd Alberto Mendelzon International Workshop on Foundations of Data Management, Arequipa, Peru, (pp. 1–10).

Finkelstein, L., Gabrilovich, E., Matias, Y., Rivlin, E., Solan, Z., Wolfman, G., et al. (2001). Placing search in context: The concept revisited. *Proceedings of the 9th International World Wide Web Conference,* (pp. 406–414).

Flickner, M., Sawhney, H. S., Ashley, J., Huang, Q., Dom, B., & Gorkani, M. (1995). Query by image and video content: The QBIC system. *IEEE Computer, 28*(9), 23–32.

Fortin, S. (1996). *The graph isomorphism problem. (Technical Report).* Department of Computing Science, University of Alberta.

Fuxman, A., Kolaitis, P. G., Miller, R. J., & Tan, W. C. (2006). Peer data exchange. *ACM Transactions on Database Systems, 31*(4), 1454–1498. doi:10.1145/1189769.1189778

Galindo, J., Urrutia, A., & Piattini, M. (2006). *Fuzzy databases: Modeling, design and implementation.* Hershey, PA: Idea Group Publishing.

Galindo, J. (2005). New characteristics in FSQL, a fuzzy SQL for fuzzy databases. *WSEAS Transactions on Information Science and Applications, 2*(2), 161–169.

Galindo, J., Medina, J. M., Pons, O., & Cubero, J. C. (1998). A server for Fuzzy SQL queries. In T. Andreasen, H. Christiansen & H.L. Larsen (Eds.), *Proceedings of the Third International Conference on Flexible Query Answering Systems,* (pp. 164-174). (LNAI 1495). London: Springer-Verlag.

Gao, L., Wang, M., Sean Wang, X., & Padmanabhan, S. (2004). *Uexpressing and optimizing similarity-based queries in SQLs.* (Technical Report CS-04-06), University of Vermont. Retrieved from http:// www.cs.uvm.edu / csdb/ techreport.shtml

Gao, X., Xiao, B., Tao, D. & Li, X. (2009). A survey of graph edit distance. *Pattern Analysis & Applications.*

Garcia-Molina, H., Ullman, J. D., & Widom, J. (2002). *Database systems: The complete book.* Upper Saddle River, NJ: Prentice Hall.

Garey, M. R., & Johnson, D. S. (1979). *Computers and intractability: A guide to the theory of NP-completeness.* W.H. Freeman.

Gauker, C. (2007). A critique of the similarity space theory of concepts. *Mind & Language, 22*(4), 317–345. doi:10.1111/j.1468-0017.2007.00311.x

Geerts, F., Mannila, H., & Terzim, E. (2004). Relational link-based ranking. *Proceedings of the 30th International Conference on Very Large Data Base,* (pp. 552-563).

Gibello, P. (2010). *Zql: A Java SQL parser.* Retrieved June 2010, from http://www.gibello.com/code/zql/

Giugno, R., & Shasha, D. (2002). GraphGrep: A fast and universal method for querying graphs. In *IEEE International Conference in Pattern Recognition,* (pp. 112-115).

Glimm, B., Lutz, C., Horrocks, I., & Sattler, U. (2008). Conjunctive query answering for the description logic shiq. [JAIR]. *Journal of Artificial Intelligence Research, 31,* 157–204.

Glimm, B., Horrocks, I., & Sattler, U. (2007). Conjunctive query entailment for shoq. *Proceedings of the 2007 International Workshop on Description Logic* (DL 2007). CEUR Electronic Workshop Proceedings.

Godfrey, P., Shipley, R., & Gryz, J. (2005). Maximal vector computation in large data sets. In VLDB '05: *Proceedings of the 31st International Conference on Very Large Data Bases* (VLDB), (pp. 229-240).

Goncalves, M., & Tineo, L. (2008). SQLfi y sus aplicaciones. [Medellín, Colombia]. *Avances en Sistemas e Informática, 5*(2), 33–40.

Goncalves, M., & Vidal, M.-E. (2009). Reaching the top of the Skyline: An efficient indexed algorithm for Top-k Skyline queries. In *Proceedings of International Conference on Database and Expert Systems Applications* (DEXA), (pp. 471-485).

Grabisch, M., Greco, S., & Pirlot, M. (2008). Bipolar and bivariate models in multicriteria decision analysis: Descriptive and constructive approaches. *International Journal of Intelligent Systems, 23,* 930–969. doi:10.1002/int.20301

Graefe, G. (2003). Sorting and indexing with partitioned B-trees. In *Proceedings of the 1st International Conference on Data Systems Research.*

Grust, T., Sakr, S., & Teubner, J. (2004). XQuery on SQL hosts. In *Proceedings of the Thirtieth International Conference on Very Large Data Bases,* (pp. 252-263).

Guttman, A. (1984). R-Trees: A dynamic index structure for spatial searching. In *Proceedings of the ACM SIGMOD International Conference on Management of Data,* (pp. 47-57).

Guyon, I., & Elisseeff, A. (2003). An introduction to variable and feature selection. *Journal of Machine Learning Research, 3,* 1157–1182. doi:10.1162/153244303322753616

Gyssens, M., Paredaens, J., den Bussche, J. V., & Gucht, D. V. (1994). A graph-oriented object database model. [TKDE]. *IEEE Transactions on Knowledge and Data Engineering, 6*(4), 572–586. doi:10.1109/69.298174

Gyssens, M., & Lakshmanan, L. V. S. (1997). A foundation for multi-dimensional databases. In *Proceedings of the 23rd International Conference on Very Large Data Bases (VLDB'97),* (pp. 106–115).

Haas, L. M. (2007). Beauty and the beast: The theory and practice of information integration. In Schwentick, T., & Suciu, D. (Eds.), *Database theory. (LNCS 4353)* (pp. 28–43). Springer.

Haralick, R. M. (1979). Statistical and structural approaches to texture. *IEEE, 67,* 786–804.

Harris, S., & Gibbins, N. (2003). 3store: Efficient bulk RDF storage. In *Proceedings of the First International Workshop on Practical and Scalable Semantic Systems.*

Harris, S., & Shadbolt, N. (2005). SPARQL query processing with conventional relational database systems. In *Proceedings of SSWS.*

Harth, A., & Decker, S. (2005). Optimized index structures for querying RDF from the Web. In *Proceedings of the Third Latin American Web Congress,* (pp. 71-80).

He, H., & Singh, A. K. (2006). Closure-Tree: An index structure for graph queries. In *Proceedings of the 22nd International Conference on Data Engineering,* (pp. 38-52).

He, H., & Singh, A. K. (2008). Graphs-at-a-time: Query language and access methods for graph databases. In *Proceedings of the ACM SIGMOD International Conference on Management of Data,* (pp. 405-418).

He, X., Ma, W.-Y., King, O., Li, M., & Zhang, H. (2002). *Learning and inferring a semantic space from user's relevance feedback for image retrieval.* In ACM International Conference on Multimedia (MULTIMEDIA), (pp. 343–346). New York: ACM.

Hjaltason, G. R., & Samet, H. (1999). Distance browsing in spatial databases. *ACM Transactions on Database Systems, 24*(2), 265–318. doi:10.1145/320248.320255

Hjaltason, G. R., & Samet, H. (2003). Index-driven similarity search in metric spaces. *ACM Transactions on Database Systems, 28*(4), 517–580. doi:10.1145/958942.958948

Hjaltason, G. R., & Samet, H. (1995). *Ranking in spatial databases.* In International Symposium on Advances in Spatial Databases (SSD), (pp. 83–95). Portland, Maine.

Huan, J., Wang, W., Bandyopadhyay, D., Snoeyink, J., Prins, J., & Tropsha, A. (2004). Mining protein family specific residue packing patterns from protein structure graphs. In *Proceedings of the Eighth Annual International Conference on Computational Molecular Biology,* (pp. 308-315).

Huang, P.-W., Hsu, L., Su, Y.-W., & Lin, P.-L. (2008). Spatial inference and similarity retrieval of an intelligent image database system based on object's spanning representation. *Journal of Visual Languages and Computing, 19*(6), 637–651. doi:10.1016/j.jvlc.2007.09.001

Hull, R., & King, R. (1987). Semantic database modeling: Survey, applications, and research issues. [CSUR]. *ACM Computing Surveys, 19*(3), 201–260. doi:10.1145/45072.45073

Hung, E., Deng, Y., & Subrahmanian, V. S. (2005). RDF aggregate queries and views. In *Proceedings of IEEE ICDE*.

IBM Corp. (2003). *Image, audio, and video extenders administration and programming guide*. DB2 universal database version 8.

Informix Corp. (1999). *Excalibur image DataBlade module user's guide*. Informix Press.

ISO8601. (2004). *Data elements and interchange formats–information interchange- Representation of dates and times*. (Ref: ISO 8601).

Jacox, E. H., & Samet, H. (2008). Metric space similarity joins. *ACM Transactions on Database Systems, 33*(2), 1–38. doi:10.1145/1366102.1366104

Jain, A. K., & Farrokhnia, F. (1991). Unsupervised texture segmentation using gabor filters. *Pattern Recognition, 24*(12), 1167–1186. doi:10.1016/0031-3203(91)90143-S

Jeffery, S. R., Franklin, M. J., & Halevy, A. Y. (2008). Pay-as-you-go user feedback for dataspace systems. In *Proceedings of the ACM SIGMOD International Conference on Management of Data*, (pp. 847-860).

Jiang, H., Wang, H., Yu, P. S., & Zhou, S. (2007). GString: A novel approach for efficient search in graph databases. In *Proceedings of the 23rd International conference on Data Engineering*, (pp. 566-575).

Joachims, T. (1998). Text categorization with support vector machines: Learning with many relevant features. *Proceedings of the European Conference on Machine Learning*, (pp. 137–142).

Joachims, T. (2002). Optimizing search engines using clickthrough data. *Proceedings of the ACM Conference on Knowledge Discovery and Data Mining*, (pp. 133–142).

Kacprzyk, J., & Yager, R. R. (2001). Linguistic summaries of data using fuzzy logic. *International Journal of General Systems, 30*, 133–154. doi:10.1080/03081070108960702

Kacprzyk, J., Yager, R. R., & Zadrożny, S. (2000). A fuzzy logic based approach to linguistic summaries of databases. *International Journal of Applied Mathematics and Computer Science, 10*, 813–834.

Kacprzyk, J., & Zadrożny, S. (2005). Linguistic database summaries and their protoforms: Towards natural language based knowledge discovery tools. *Information Sciences, 173*, 281–304. doi:10.1016/j.ins.2005.03.002

Kacprzyk, J., & Zadrożny, S. (2009). Protoforms of linguistic database summaries as a human consistent tool for using natural language in data mining. *International Journal of Software Science and Computational Intelligence, 1*(1), 100–111.

Kacprzyk, J., Zadrożny, S., & Ziółkowski, A. (1989). FQUERY III+: A human-consistent database querying system based on fuzzy logic with linguistic quantifiers. *Information Systems, 14*, 443–453. doi:10.1016/0306-4379(89)90012-4

Kacprzyk, J., & Ziółkowski, A. (1986). Database queries with fuzzy linguistic quantifiers. *IEEE Transactions on Systems, Man, and Cybernetics, 16*, 474–479. doi:10.1109/TSMC.1986.4308982

Kacprzyk, J., & Zadrożny, S. (1995). FQUERY for Access: Fuzzy querying for windows-based DBMS. In Bosc, P., & Kacprzyk, J. (Eds.), *Fuzziness in database management systems* (pp. 415–433). Heidelberg, Germany: Physica-Verlag.

Kacprzyk, J., & Zadrozny, S. (2010). Computing with words and systemic functional linguistics: Linguistic data summaries and natural language generation. In Huynh, V.-N., Nakamori, Y., Lawry, J., & Inuiguchi, M. (Eds.), *Integrated uncertainty management and applications* (pp. 23–36). Heidelberg: Springer-Verlag. doi:10.1007/978-3-642-11960-6_3

Kacprzyk, J., & Zadrożny, S. (1997). Implementation of OWA operators in fuzzy querying for Microsoft Access. In Yager, R. R., & Kacprzyk, J. (Eds.), *The ordered weighted averaging operators: Theory and applications* (pp. 293–306). Boston: Kluwer Academic Publishers.

Kandel, A. (1986). *Fuzzy Mathematical Techniques with Applications", Addison Wesley Publishing Co., California. Kaufman, A. (1975). Inroduction to the Theory of Fuzzy Subsets", Vol-I, Academic Press*. New York: Sanfrancisco.

Karvounarakis, G., Alexaki, S., Christophides, V., Plexousakis, D., & Scholl, M. (2002). RQL: A declarative query language for RDF. In *Proceedings of WWW*.

Kaster, D. S., Bugatti, P. H., Traina, A. J. M., & Traina-Jr, C. (2009). Incorporating metric access methods for similarity searching on Oracle database. In Brazilian Symposium on Databases (SBBD), (pp. 196–210). Fortaleza, Brazil.

Kaul, M., Drosten, K., & Neuhold, E. J. (1990). Integrating heterogeneous information bases by object-oriented views", In: *Proc. Intl. Conf. on Data Engineering*, pp 2-10. Litwin W. and Abdellatif A. (1986). Multidatabase Interoperabilty", *IEEE. The Computer Journal, 12*(19), 10–18.

Kent, W. (1991). A rigorous model of object references, identity and existence. *Journal of Object-Oriented Programming, 4*(3), 28–38.

Khoshafian, S. N., & Copeland, G. P. (1986). Object identity. *Proceedings of OOPSLA '86, ACM SIGPLAN Notices, 21*(11), 406–416.

Khotanzad, A., & Hong, Y. H. (1990). Invariant image recognition by zernike moments. *IEEE Transactions on Pattern Analysis and Machine Intelligence, 12*(5), 489–497. doi:10.1109/34.55109

Kießling, W. (2002). Foundations of preferences in database systems. *Proceedings of the 28th International Conference on Very Large Data Bases*, (pp. 311-322).

Kiryakov, A., Ognyanov, D., & Manov, D. (2005). Owlim-a pragmatic semantic repository for owl. In *Proceedings of the Web Information Systems Engineering Workshops*, (pp. 182-192).

Klement, E. P., Mesiar, R., & Pap, E. (Eds.). (2000). *Triangular norms*. Dordrecht, Boston, London: Kluwer Academic Publishers.

Klinger, S., & Austin, J. (2005). Chemical similarity searching using a neural graph matcher. In *Proceedings of the 13th European Symposium on Artificial Neural Networks*, (p. 479-484).

Koch, C. (2009). MayBMS: A database management system for uncertain and probabilistic data. In Aggarwal, C. (Ed.), *Managing and mining uncertain data* (pp. 149–184). Springer. doi:10.1007/978-0-387-09690-2_6

Kokare, M., Chatterji, B., & Biswas, P. (2003). *Comparison of similarity metrics for texture image retrieval*. In Conference on Convergent Technologies for Asia-Pacific Region, (pp. 571–575).

Koller, D., & Sahami, M. (1997). Hierarchically classifying documents using very few words. *Proceedings of the 14th International Conference on Machine Learning*, (pp. 170–178).

Koloniari, G., & Pitoura, E. (2005). Peer-to-peer management of XML data: Issues and research challenges. *SIGMOD Record, 34*(2), 6–17. doi:10.1145/1083784.1083788

Korn, F., Sidiropoulos, N., Faloutsos, C., Siegel, E., & Protopapas, Z. (1996). *Fast nearest neighbor search in medical image databases*. In International Conference on Very Large Databases (VLDB), pp(. 215–226). San Francisco.

Kossmann, D., Ramsak, F., & Rost, S. (2002). Shooting stars in the sky: An online algorithm for skyline queries. In *Proceedings of the 28th International Conference on Very Large Data Bases* (VLDB), (pp. 275-286).

Koutrika, G., & Ioannidis, Y. (2004). Personalization of queries in database systems. *Proceedings of the 20th International Conference on Database Engineering*, (pp. 597-608).

Krtzsch, M., Rudolph, S., & Hitzler, P. (2007). Conjunctive queries for a tractable fragment of owl 1.1. *Proceedings of the 6th International Semantic Web Conference* (ISWC 2007), 310–323.

Kuramochi, M., & Karypis, G. (2001). Frequent subgraph discovery. In *Proceedings of the IEEE International Conference on Data Mining*, (pp. 313-320).

Kuramochi, M., & Karypis, G. (2004). GREW-a scalable frequent subgraph discovery algorithm. In *Proceedings of the IEEE International Conference on Data Mining*, (pp. 439-442).

Lacroix, M., & Lavency, P. (1987). Preferences: Putting more knowledge into queries. In *Proceedings of the 13 International Conference on Very Large Databases*, (pp. 217-225). Brighton, UK.

Laurent, A. (2003). Querying fuzzy multidimensional databases: Unary operators and their properties. *International Journal of Uncertainty. Fuzziness and Knowledge-Based Systems, 11*, 31–46. doi:10.1142/S0218488503002259

Lee, K.-M., & Street, W. N. (2002). Incremental feature weight learning and its application to a shape-based query system. *Pattern Recognition Letters*, *23*(7), 865–874. doi:10.1016/S0167-8655(01)00161-1

Lee, J., Oh, J.-H., & Hwang, S. (2005). STRG-index: Spatio-temporal region graph indexing for large video databases. In *Proceedings of the ACM SIGMOD International Conference on Management of Data*, (pp. 718-729).

Leinders, D., & den Bussche, J. V. (2005). On the complexity of division and set joins in the relational algebra. In *Proceedings of ACM PODS*, Baltimore, MD USA.

Leser, U. (2005). A query language for biological networks. In *Proceedings of the Fourth European Conference on Computational Biology/Sixth Meeting of the Spanish Bioinformatics Network*, (p. 39).

Levandoski, J. J., & Mokbel, M. F. (2009). RDF data-centric storage. In *Proceedings of the IEEE International Conference on Web Services*.

Levy, A. Y., & Rousset, M.-C. (1998). Combining horn rules and description logics in carin. *Artificial Intelligence*, *104*(1-2), 165–209. doi:10.1016/S0004-3702(98)00048-4

Ley, M. (2010). *The dblp computer science bibliography*. Retrieved from http://www.informatik.uni-trier.de/~ley/db

Li, C., & Wang, X. S. (1996). A data model for supporting on-line analytical processing. In *Proceedings of the Conference on Information and Knowledge Management*, Baltimore, MD, (pp. 81–88).

Li, C., Chen-chuan, K., Ihab, C., Ilyas, F., & Song, S. (2005). RankSQL: Query algebra and optimization for relational top-k queries. *In Proceedings of the 2005 ACM SIGMOD International Conference on Management of Data*, (pp. 131-142). ACM Press.

Lieberman, H. (1986). Using prototypical objects to implement shared behavior in object-oriented systems. In *Proceedings of OOPSLA '86, ACM SIGPLAN Notices*, *21*(11), 214–223.

Lienhart, R. (2001). Reliable transition detection in videos: A survey and practitioner's guide. *International Journal of Image and Graphics*, *1*, 469–486. doi:10.1142/S021946780100027X

Lin, X., Yuan, Y., Zhang, Q., & Zhang, Y. (2007). Selecting Stars: The k Most Represen-tative Skyline Operator. In Proceedings of International Conference on Database Theory (ICDE), pp. 86-95.

Liu, Y., Zhang, D., Lu, G., & Ma, W.-Y. (2007). A survey of content-based image retrieval with high-level semantics. *Pattern Recognition Letters*, *40*, 262–282.

Liu, F., Yu, C., & Meng, W. (2002). Personalized Web search by mapping user queries to categories. *Proceedings of the ACM International Conference on Information and Knowledge Management*, (pp. 558-565).

Long, F., Zhang, H., & Feng, D. D. (2003). *Fundamentals of content-based image retrieval (Multimedia information retrieval and management-technological fundamentals and applications)*. Springer.

López, Y., & Tineo, L. (2006). About the performance of SQLf evaluation mechanisms. *CLEI Electronic Journal*, *9*(2), 8. Retrieved October 10, 2009, from http://www.clei.cl/cleiej/papers/v9i2p8.pdf

Lukasiewicz, T., & Straccia, U. (2008). Managing uncertainty and vagueness in description logics for the semantic Web. *Journal of Web Semantics*, *6*(4), 291–308. doi:10.1016/j.websem.2008.04.001

Ma, L., Su, Z., Pan, Y., Zhang, L., & Liu, T. (2004). RStar: An RDF storage and query system for enterprise resource management. In *Proceedings of the ACM International Conference on Information and Knowledge Management*, (pp. 484-491).

Ma, L., Wang, C., Lu, J., Cao, F., Pan, Y., & Yu, Y. (2008). Effective and efficient Semantic Web data management over DB2. In *Proceedings of the ACM SIGMOD International Conference on Management of Data*, (pp. 1183-1194).

Madhavan, J., & Halevy, A. Y. (2003). Composing mappings among data sources. In J. Ch., Freytag, et al. (Eds.), *VLDB 2003, Proceedings of 29th International Conference on Very Large Data Bases*, (pp. 572-583). September 9-12, 2003, Berlin, Germany. Morgan Kaufmann.

Mahmoudi Nasab, H., & Sakr, S. (2010). An experimental evaluation of relational RDF sorage and querying techniques. In *Proceedings of the 2nd International Workshop on Benchmarking of XML and Semantic Web Applications*.

Maier, D. (1983). *The theory of relational databases.* Computer Science Press.

Mailis, T. P., Stoilos, G., & Stamou, G. B. (2007). Expressive reasoning with horn rules and fuzzy description logics. *Proceedings of 2nd International Conference on Web Reasoning and Rule Systems* (RR'08).

Maiocchi, R., Pernici, B., & Barbic, F. (1992). Automatic deduction of temporal indications. *ACM Transactions on Database Systems, 17*(4), 647–668. doi:10.1145/146931.146934

Manjunath, B. S., Ohm, J.-R., Vasudevan, V. V., & Yamada, A. (2001). Color and texture descriptors. *IEEE Transactions on Circuits and Systems for Video Technology, 11*(6), 703–715. doi:10.1109/76.927424

Manola, F., & Miller, E. (2004). *RDF primer.* W3C recommendation. Retrieved from http://www.w3.org/TR/REC-rdf-syntax/

Martens, W., Neven, F., & Schwentick, T. (2007). Simple off the shelf abstractions for XML schema. *SIGMOD Record, 36*(3), 15–22. doi:10.1145/1324185.1324188

Matono, A., Amagasa, T., Yoshikawa, M., & Uemura, S. (2005). A path-based relational RDF database. In *Proceedings of the 16th Australasian Database Conference,* (pp. 95-103).

Matos, V. M., & Grasser, R. (2002). A simpler (and better) SQL approach to relational division. *Journal of Information Systems Education, 13*(2).

Matthé, T., & De Tré, G. (2009). Bipolar query satisfaction using satisfaction and dissatisfaction degrees: Bipolar satisfaction degrees. In S.Y. Shin & S. Ossowski (Eds.), *Proceedings of the SAC Conference,* (pp. 1699-1703). ACM.

McBride, B. (2002). Jena: A Semantic Web toolkit. *IEEE Internet Computing, 6*(6), 55–59. doi:10.1109/MIC.2002.1067737

McCann, L. (2003). On making relational division comprehensible. In *Proceedings of ASEE/IEEE Frontiers in Education Conference.*

Melnik, S., Bernstein, P. A., Halevy, A. Y., & Rahm, E. (2005). Supporting executable mappings in model management. In F. Özcan (Ed.), *Proceedings of the 24th ACM SIGMOD International Conference on Management of Data,* (pp. 167-178). Baltimore, Maryland, USA, June 14-16, ACM.

Melton, J., & Eisenberg, A. (2001). SQL multimedia and application packages (SQL/MM). *SIGMOD Record, 30*(4), 97–102. doi:10.1145/604264.604280

Meng, X. F., & Ma, Z. M. (2008). A context-sensitive approach for Web database query results ranking. *Proceedings of IEEE/WIC/ACM International Conference on Web Intelligence and Intelligent Agent Technology,* (pp. 836-839).

Miller, R. J., Haas, L. M., & Hernandez, M. A. (2000). Schema mapping as query discovery. In: A.E. Abbadi, et al. (Eds.), *VLDB 2000, Proceedings of 26th International Conference on Very Large Data Bases,* (pp. 77-88). September 10-14, 2000, Cairo, Egypt. Morgan Kaufmann

Milo, T., Abiteboul, S., Amann, B., Benjelloun, O., & Ngoc, F. D. (2005). Exchanging intensional XML data. *ACM Transactions on Database Systems, 30*(1), 1–40. doi:10.1145/1061318.1061319

Mokhtarian, F., & Mackworth, A. (1986). Scale-based description and recognition of planar curves and two-dimensional objects. *IEEE Transactions on Pattern Analysis and Machine Intelligence, 8*(1), 34–43. doi:10.1109/TPAMI.1986.4767750

Morin, E. (1999). *Seven complex lessons in education for the future.* United Nations Educational, Scientific and Cultural Organization. Retrieved October 18, 2009, from http://www.unesco.org/education/tlsf/TLSF/theme_a/mod03/img/sevenlessons.pdf

Neumann, T., & Weikum, G. (2008). RDF-3X: A RISC-style engine for RDF. [PVLDB]. *Proceedings of the VLDB Endowment, 1*(1), 647–659.

Neumann, T., & Weikum, G. (2009). Scalable join processing on very large RDF graphs. In *Proceedings of the ACM SIGMOD International Conference on Management of Data,* (pp. 627-640).

Ooi, B. C., Shu, Y., & Tan, K.-L. (2003). Relational data sharing in peer-based data management systems. *SIGMOD Record, 32*(3), 59–64. doi:10.1145/945721.945734

Ortiz, M., Calvanese, D., & Eiter, T. (2008). Data complexity of query answering in expressive description logics via tableaux. *Journal of Automated Reasoning, 41*(1), 61–98. doi:10.1007/s10817-008-9102-9

Ortiz, M., Calvanese, D., & Eiter, T. (2006). Data complexity of answering unions of conjunctive queries in shiq. *Proceedings of the 2006 International Workshop on Description Logic.* CEUR Electronic Workshop Proceedings.

Pan, J. Z., Stamou, G. B., Stoilos, G., Taylor, S., & Thomas, E. (2008). Scalable querying services over fuzzy ontologies. *Proceedings of the 17th International World Wide Web Conference* (WWW2008), (pp. 575–584).

Pan, Z., & Heflin, J. (2003). DLDB: Extending relational databases to support Semantic Web queries. In *Proceedings of the First International Workshop on Practical and Scalable Semantic Systems.*

Pan, Z., & Hein, J. (2003). DLDB: Extending relational databases to support Semantic Web queries. In *Proceedings of PSSS.*

Pan, Z., Zhang, X., & Heflin, J. (2008). DLDB2: A scalable multi-perspective Semantic Web repository. In *Proceedings of the IEEE/WIC/ACM International Conference on Web Intelligence,* (pp. 489-495).

Pankowski, T., & Hunt, E. (2005). Data merging in life science data integration systems. In Klopotek, M. A., Wierzchon, S. T., & Trojanowski, K. (Eds.), *Intelligent Information Systems. New trends in intelligent information processing and Web mining, advances in soft computing* (pp. 279–288). Berlin, Heidelberg: Springer. doi:10.1007/3-540-32392-9_29

Pankowski, T., Cybulka, J., & Meissner, A. (2007). XML schema mappings in the presence of key constraints and value dependencies. In M. Arenas & J. Hidders (Eds.), *Proceedings of the 1st Workshop on Emerging Research Opportunities for Web Data Management (EROW 2007) Collocated with the 11th International Conference on Database Theory (ICDT 2007),* (pp. 1-15). Barcelona, Spain, January 13, 2007.

Papadias, D., Tao, Y., Mouratidis, K., & Hui, C. K. (2005). Aggregate nearest neighbor queries in spatial databases. *ACM Transactions on Database Systems, 30*(2), 529–576. doi:10.1145/1071610.1071616

Papadias, D., Tao, Y., Fu, G., & Seeger, B. (2003). An optimal and progressive algorithm for skyline queries. In SIGMOD '03: *Proceedings of the 2003 ACM SIGMOD International Conference on Management of Data,* (pp. 467-478). New York: ACM Press.

Peckham, J., & Maryanski, F. (1988). Semantic data models. [CSUR]. *ACM Computing Surveys, 20*(3), 153–189. doi:10.1145/62061.62062

Pedersen, T. B., & Jensen, C. S. (2001). Multidimensional database technology. *IEEE Computers, 34*(12), 40–46.

Pei, J., Yuan, Y., Lin, X., Jin, W., Ester, M., & Wang, Q. L. W. (2006). Towards multidimensional subspace skyline analysis. *ACM Transactions on Database Systems, 31*(4), 1335–1381. doi:10.1145/1189769.1189774

Prud'hommeaux, E., & Seaborne, A. (2008). *SPARQL query language for RDF.* W3C recommendation. Retrieved from http://www.w3.org/TR/rdf-sparql-query/

Prudhommeaux, E. (2005). Notes on adding SPARQL to MySQL. Retrieved from http://www.w3.org/2005/05/22-SPARQL-MySQL/

Quinlan, J. R. (1986). Induction of decision trees. *Machine Learning, 1*(1), 81–106. doi:10.1007/BF00116251

Quinlan, J. R. (1993). *C4.5: Programs for machine learning.* San Francisco: Morgan Kaufmann Publishers Inc.

Rantzau, R., & Mangold, C. (2006). Laws for rewriting queries containing division operators. In the *Proceedings of IEEE ICDE.*

Raymond, J. W., Gardiner, E. J., & Willett, P. (2002). RASCAL: Calculation of graph similarity using maximum common edge subgraphs. *The Computer Journal, 45*(6), 631–644. doi:10.1093/comjnl/45.6.631

Raymond, D. (1996). *Partial order databases.* Unpublished doctoral thesis, University of Waterloo, Canada

Rosado, A., Ribeiro, R., Zadrożny, S., & Kacprzyk, J. (2006). Flexible query languages for relational databases: An overview. In Bordogna, G., & Psaila, G. (Eds.), *Flexible databases supporting imprecision and uncertainty* (pp. 3–53). Berlin, Heidelberg: Springer Verlag. doi:10.1007/3-540-33289-8_1

Roussopoulos, N., Kelley, S., & Vincent, F. (1995). *Nearest neighbor queries*. In ACM International Conference on Management of Data (SIGMOD), (pp. 71–79).

Roussos, Y., Stavrakas, Y., & Pavlaki, V. (2005). Towards a context-aware relational model. *Proceedings of the International Workshop on Context Representation and Reasoning, Paris*, (pp. 101-106).

Rui, Y., Huang, T. S., & Merhotra, S. (1997). Content-based image retrieval with relevance feedback in MARS. *Proceedings of the IEEE International Conference on Image Processing*, (pp. 815-818).

Sakr, S. (2009). GraphREL: A decomposition-based and selectivity-aware relational framework for processing sub-graph queries. In *Proceedings of the 14th International Conference on Database Systems for Advanced Applications*, (pp. 123-137).

Salton, G. (1989). *Automatic text processing: The transformation, analysis and retrieval of information by computer*. Addison Wesley.

Santini, S., & Gupta, A. (2001). *A wavelet data model for image databases*. In IEEE International Conference on Multimedia and Expo (ICME), Tokyo, Japan. IEEE Computer Society.

Savinov, A. (2008). Concepts and concept-oriented programming. *Journal of Object Technology*, 7(3), 91–106. doi:10.5381/jot.2008.7.3.a2

Schema, X. M. L. (2009). *W3C XML schema definition language (XSD) 1.1 part 2: Datatypes*. Retrieved from www.w3.org/TR/xmlschema11-2

Schmidt, M., Hornung, T., Lausen, G., & Pinkel, C. (2009). SP2Bench: A SPARQL performance benchmark. In *Proceedings of the 25th International Conference on Data Engineering*, (pp. 222-233).

Seidl, T., & Kriegel, H.-P. (1998). *Optimal multi-step k-nearest neighbor search*. In ACM International Conference on Management of Data (SIGMOD), (pp. 154–165). Seattle, Washington.

Sharma, A. K., Goswami, A., & Gupta, D. K. (2008). Fuzzy Inclusion Dependencies in Fuzzy Databases. In Galindo, J. (Ed.), *Handbook of Research on Fuzzy Information Processing in Databases* (pp. 657–683). Hershey, PA, USA: Information Science Reference.

Sharma, A. K., Goswami, A., & Gupta, D. K. (2004). Fuzzy Inclusion Dependencies in Fuzzy Relational Databases", In *Proceedings of International Conference on Information Technology: Coding and Computing (ITCC 2004)*, Las Vegas, USA, IEEE Computer Society Press, USA, Volum-1, pp 507-510.

Shen, X., Tan, B., & Zhai, C. (2005). Context-sensitive information retrieval using implicit feedback. *Proceedings of the 28th Annual International ACM SIGIR Conference on Research and Development in Information Retrieval*, (pp. 43–50).

Sheng, L., Ozsoyoglu, Z. M., & Ozsoyoglu, G. (1999). A graph query language and its query processing. In *Proceedings of the 15th International Conference on Data Engineering*, (pp. 572-581).

Shipman, D. W. (1981). The functional data model and the data language DAPLEX. [TODS]. *ACM Transactions on Database Systems*, 6(1), 140–173. doi:10.1145/319540.319561

Sibley, E. H., & Kerschberg, L. (1977). Data architecture and data model considerations. In *Proceedings of the AFIPS Joint Computer Conferences*, (pp. 85-96).

Sidirourgos, L., Goncalves, R., Kersten, M. L., Nes, N., & Manegold, S. (2008). Column-store support for RDF data management: Not all swans are white. [PVLDB]. *Proceedings of the VLDB Endownment*, 1(2), 1553–1563.

Smeulders, A. W. M., Worring, M., Santini, S., Gupta, A., & Jain, R. (2000). Content-based image retrieval at the end of the early years. [TPAMI]. *IEEE Transactions on Pattern Analysis and Machine Intelligence*, 22(12), 1349–1380. doi:10.1109/34.895972

Smith, J. M., & Smith, D. C. P. (1977). Database abstractions: Aggregation and generalization. [TODS]. *ACM Transactions on Database Systems, 2*(2), 105–133. doi:10.1145/320544.320546

Stein, L. A. (1987). Delegation is inheritance. In *Proceedings of OOPSLA'87, ACM SIGPLAN Notices, 22*(12), 138–146.

Stocker, M., Seaborne, A., Bernstein, A., Kiefer, C., & Reynolds, D. (2008). SPARQL basic graph pattern optimization using selectivity estimation. In *Proceedings of the 17th International Conference on World Wide Web,* (pp. 595-604).

Stoilos, G., Simou, N., Stamou, G. B., & Kollias, S. D. (2006). Uncertainty and the semantic Web. *IEEE Intelligent Systems, 21*(5), 84–87. doi:10.1109/MIS.2006.105

Stoilos, G., Stamou, G. B., Pan, J. Z., Tzouvaras, V., & Horrocks, I. (2007). Reasoning with very expressive fuzzy description logics. [JAIR]. *Journal of Artificial Intelligence Research, 30*, 273–320.

Stoilos, G., Straccia, U., Stamou, G. B., & Pan, J. Z. (2006). General concept inclusions in fuzzy description logics. *Proceedings of the 17th European Conference on Artificial Intelligence* (ECAI 2006), (pp. 457–461).

Stonebraker, M., Abadi, D. J., Batkin, A., Chen, X., Cherniack, M., Ferreira, M., et al. (2005). C-Store: A column-oriented DBMS. In *Proceedings of the 31st International Conference on Very Large Data Bases,* (pp. 553-564).

Straccia, U. (2001). Reasoning within fuzzy description logics. [JAIR]. *Journal of Artificial Intelligence Research, 14*, 137–166.

Straccia, U. (2006). Answering vague queries in fuzzy dl-lite. *Proceedings of the 11th International Conference on Information Processing and Management of Uncertainty in Knowledge-Based Systems* (IPMU-06), (pp. 2238–2245).

Sugiyama, K., Hatano, K., & Yoshikawa, M. (2004). Adaptive Web search based on user profile constructed without any effort from users. *Proceedings of the 13th International World Wide Web Conference,* (pp. 975-990).

TÆurker, C. & Gertz, M. (2001). Semantic integrity support in SQL: 1999 and commercial object-relational database management systems. *The VLDB Journal, 10*(4), 241–269. doi:10.1007/s007780100050

Tahani, V. (1977). A conceptual framework for fuzzy query processing: A step toward very intelligent database systems. *Information Processing & Management, 13*, 289–303. doi:10.1016/0306-4573(77)90018-8

Takahashi, Y. (1995). A fuzzy query language for relational databases. In Bosc, P., & Kacprzyk, J. (Eds.), *Fuzziness in database management systems* (pp. 365–384). Heidelberg, Germany: Physica-Verlag.

Tan, K., Eng, P., & Ooi, B. (2001). Efficicient progressive skyline computation. In *Proceedings of the 28th International Conference on Very Large Data Bases* (VLDB), (pp. 301-310).

Tasan, M., & Ozsoyoglu, Z. M. (2004). *Improvements in distance-based indexing.* In International Conference on Scientific and Statistical Database Management (SSDBM), (p. 161). Washington, DC: IEEE Computer Society.

Tatarinov, I., & Ives, Z. G. (2003). The Piazza peer data management project. *SIGMOD Record, 32*(3), 47–52. doi:10.1145/945721.945732

Tatarinov, I., & Halevy, A. Y. (2004). Efficient query reformulation in peer-data management systems. In G. Weikum, A.C. König & S. Deßloch (Eds.), *Proceedings of the ACM SIGMOD International Conference on Management of Data,* (pp. 539-550). Paris, France, June 13-18, 2004. ACM.

Teubner, J., Grust, T., Maneth, S., & Sakr, S. (2008). Dependable cardinality forecasts for XQuery. [PVLDB]. *Proceedings of the VLDB Endowment, 1*(1), 463–477.

Tian, Y., McEachin, R. C., Santos, C., States, D. J., & Patel, J. M. (2007). SAGA: A subgraph matching tool for biological graphs. *Bioinformatics (Oxford, England), 23*(2), 232–239. doi:10.1093/bioinformatics/btl571

Timarán, R. (2001). Arquitecturas de integración del proceso de descubrimiento de conocimiento con sistemas de gestión de bases de datos: Un estado del arte. [Universidad del Valle, Colombia.]. *Ingeniería y Competitividad, 3*(2), 44–51.

Tineo, L. (2006) *A contribution to database flexible querying: Fuzzy quantified queries evaluation.* Unpublished doctoral dissertation, Universidad Simón Bolívar, Caracas, Venezuela.

Torres, R. S., Falcão, A. X., Gonçalves, M. A., Papa, J. P., Zhang, P., & Fan, W. (2009). A genetic programming framework for content-based image retrieval. *Pattern Recognition, 42*(2), 283–292. doi:10.1016/j.patcog.2008.04.010

Traina-Jr, C., Traina, A. J. M., Faloutsos, C., & Seeger, B. (2002). Fast indexing and visualization of metric datasets using slim-trees. [TKDE]. *IEEE Transactions on Knowledge and Data Engineering, 14*(2), 244–260. doi:10.1109/69.991715

Traina-Jr, C., Traina, A. J. M., Vieira, M. R., Arantes, A. S., & Faloutsos, C. (2006). *Efficient processing of complex similarity queries in RDBMS through query rewriting.* In International Conference on Information and Knowledge Management (CIKM), (pp.4–13). Arlington, VA.

Tsichritzis, D. C., & Lochovsky, F. H. (1976). Hierarchical data-base management: A survey. [CSUR]. *ACM Computing Surveys, 8*(1), 105–123. doi:10.1145/356662.356667

Tsotras, V. J., & Kumar, A. (1996). Temporal database bibliography update. *SIGMOD Record, 25*(1), 41–51.

Tweedie, L., Spence, R., Williams, D., & Bhogal, R. S. (1994). The attribute explorer. *Proceedings of the International Conference on Human Factors in Computing Systems,* (pp. 435–436).

Tzanetakis, G., & Cook, P. R. (2002). Musical genre classification of audio signals. *IEEE Transactions on Speech and Audio Processing, 10*(5), 293–302. doi:10.1109/TSA.2002.800560

Umano, M., & Fukami, S. (1994). Fuzzy relational algebra for possibility-distribution-fuzzy relational model of fuzzy data. *Journal of Intelligent Information Systems, 3*, 7–27. doi:10.1007/BF01014018

Vila, L. (1994). A survey on temporal reasoning in artificial intelligence. *AI Communications, 7*(1), 4–28.

Vila, M. A., Cubero, J.-C., Medina, J.-M., & Pons, O. (1997). Using OWA operator in flexible query processing. In Yager, R. R., & Kacprzyk, J. (Eds.), *The ordered weighted averaging operators: Theory and applications* (pp. 258–274). Boston: Kluwer Academic Publishers.

Vila, L., & Godo, L. (1995). Query answering in fuzzy temporal constraint networks. In the *Proceedings of FUZZ-IEEE/IFES'95,* Yokohama, Japan. IEEE Press.

Vlachou, A., & Vazirgiannis, M. (2007). Link-based ranking of skyline result sets. In *Proceedings of the 3rd Multidisciplinary Workshop on Advances in Preference Handling* (M-Pref).

W3C Semantic Web discussion list. (2010). *Kit releases 14 billion triples to the linked open data cloud.* Retrieved from http://permalink.gmane.org/gmane.org.w3c.semantic-web/12889

Wan, C., & Liu, M. (2006). Content-based audio retrieval with relevance feedback. *Pattern Recognition Letters, 27*(2), 85–92. doi:10.1016/j.patrec.2005.07.005

Wang, X. S., Bettini, C., Brodsky, A., & Jajodia, S. (1997). Logical design for temporal databases with multiple granularities. *ACM Transactions on Database Systems, 22*(2), 115–170. doi:10.1145/249978.249979

Wang, C., Wang, W., Pei, J., Zhu, Y., & Shi, B. (2004). Scalable mining of large disk-based graph databases. In *Proceedings of the Tenth ACM SIGKDD International Conference on Knowledge Discovery and Data Mining,* (pp. 316-325).

Washio, T., & Motoda, H. (2003). State of the art of graph-based data mining. *SIGKDD Explorations, 5*(1), 59–68. doi:10.1145/959242.959249

Weiss, C., Karras, P., & Bernstein, A. (2008). Hexastore: Sextuple indexing for Semantic Web data management. [PVLDB]. *Proceedings of the VLDB Endowment, 1*(1), 1008–1019.

Widom, J. (2009). Trio: A system for integrated management of data, uncertainty, and lineage. In Aggarwal, C. (Ed.), *Managing and mining uncertain data* (pp. 113–148). Springer. doi:10.1007/978-0-387-09690-2_5

Wieringa, R., & de Jonge, W. (1995). Object identifiers, keys, and surrogates-object identifiers revisited. *Theory and Practice of Object Systems, 1*(2), 101–114.

Williams, D. W., Huan, J., & Wang, W. (2007). Graph database indexing using structured graph decomposition. In *Proceedings of the 23rd International Conference on Data Engineering,* (pp. 976-985).

Wilson, D. R., & Martinez, T. R. (1997). Improved heterogeneous distance functions. *Journal of Artificial Intelligence Research, 6,* 1–34.

Wu, L., Faloutsos, C., Sycara, K., & Payne, T. (2000). FALCON: Feedback adaptive loop for content-based retrieval. *Proceedings of the 26th International Conference on Very Large Data Bases,* (pp. 297-306).

Wu, L., Faloutsos, C., Sycara, K., & Payne, T. R. (2000). *Falcon: Feedback adaptive loop for content-based retrieval.* In International Conference on Very Large Databases (VLDB), (pp. 297–306). Cairo, Egypt.

XAMPP. (2010). An apache distribution containing MySQL. Retrieved June 2010, from http://www.apache-friends.org/en/xampp.html

XPath. (2006). *XML path language 2.0.* Retrieved from www.w3.org/TR/xpath20

XQuery. (2002). *XQuery 1.0: An XML query language.* W3C Working Draft. Retrieved from www.w3.org/TR/xquery

Xu, W., & Ozsoyoglu, Z. M. (2005). Rewriting XPath queries using materialized views. In K. Böhm, et al. (Eds.), *Proceedigns of the 31st International Conference on Very Large Data Bases,* (pp. 121-132). Trondheim, Norway, August 30 - September 2, 2005, ACM.

Yager, R. R. (1982). A new approach to the summarization of data. *Information Sciences, 28,* 69–86. doi:10.1016/0020-0255(82)90033-0

Yager, R. R. (1988). On ordered weighted averaging aggregation operators in multi-criteria decision making. *IEEE Transactions on Systems, Man, and Cybernetics, 18,* 183–190. doi:10.1109/21.87068

Yager, R. R., & Kacprzyk, J. (1997). *The ordered weighted averaging operators: Theory and applications.* Boston: Kluwer.

Yan, X., & Han, J. (2002). gSpan: Graph-based substructure pattern mining. In *Proceedings of the IEEE International Conference on Data Mining,* (pp. 721-724).

Yan, X., & Han, J. (2003). CloseGraph: Mining closed frequent graph patterns. In *Proceedings of the 9th ACM SIGKDD International Conference on Knowledge Discovery and Data Mining,* (pp. 286-295).

Yan, X., Yu, P. S., & Han, J. (2004). Graph indexing: A frequent structure-based approach. In *Proceedings of the ACM SIGMOD International Conference on Management of Data,* (pp. 335-346).

Yan, X., Yu, P. S., & Han, J. (2005). Substructure similarity search in graph databases. In *Proceedings of the ACM SIGMOD International Conference on Management of Data,* (pp. 766-777).

Yeh, W.-H., & Chang, Y.-I. (2008). An efficient iconic indexing strategy for image rotation and reflection in image databases. [JSS]. *Journal of Systems and Software, 81*(7), 1184–1195. doi:10.1016/j.jss.2007.08.019

Yianilos, P. N. (1993). *Data structures and algorithms for nearest neighbor search in general metric spaces.* In ACM/SIGACT-SIAM Symposium on Discrete Algorithms (SODA), (pp. 311–321). Austin, TX, EUA. Society for Industrial and Applied Mathematics.

Yu, C., & Popa, L. (2004). Constraint-based XML query rewriting for data integration. In G. Weikum, A. C. König, & S. Deßloch (Eds.), *Proceedings of the ACM SIGMOD International Conference on Management of Data,* (pp. 371-382). Paris, France, June 13-18, 2004. ACM.

Yuan, Y., Lin, X., Liu, Q., Wang, W., Yu, J. X., & Zhang, Q. (2005). Efficient computation of the skyline cube. In VLDB '05: *Proceedings of the 31st International Conference on Very Large Data Bases* (VLDB), (pp. 241-252). VLDB Endowment.

Zadeh, L. A. (1965). Fuzzy sets. *Information and Control, 8*(3), 338–353. doi:10.1016/S0019-9958(65)90241-X

Zadeh, L. A. (1983). A computational approach to fuzzy quantifiers in natural languages. *Computers & Mathematics with Applications (Oxford, England), 9,* 149–184. doi:10.1016/0898-1221(83)90013-5

Zadeh, L. A. (1978). Fuzzy sets as a basis for a theory of possibility. *Fuzzy Sets and Systems, 1,* 3–28. doi:10.1016/0165-0114(78)90029-5

Zadeh, L. (1994). Soft computing and fuzzy logic. *IEEE Software, 11*(6), 48–56. doi:10.1109/52.329401

Zadeh, L. A. (1965). Fuzzy sets. *Information and Control, 8*(3), 338–353. doi:10.1016/S0019-9958(65)90241-X

Zadeh, L. A. (2006). From search engines to question answering systems-the problems of world knowledge relevance deduction and precisiation. In Sanchez, E. (Ed.), *Fuzzy logic and the Semantic Web* (pp. 163–210). Amsterdam: Elsevier.

Zadrożny, S., & Kacprzyk, J. (2007). *Bipolar queries using various interpretations of logical connectives* (pp. 181–190).

Zadrożny, S., De Tré, G., De Caluwe, R., & Kacprzyk, J. (2008). An overview of fuzzy approaches to flexible database querying. In Galindo, J. (Ed.), *Handbook of research on fuzzy information processing in databases* (pp. 34–54). Hershey, PA/ New York: Idea Group, Inc.

Zadrożny, S. (2005). Bipolar queries revisited. In V. Torra, Y. Narukawa & S. Miyamoto (Eds.), *Modelling decisions for artificial intelligence (MDAI 2005),* (pp. 387-398). (LNAI 3558). Berlin, Heidelberg: Springer-Verlag.

Zadrożny, S., & Kacprzyk, J. (1996) Multi-valued fields and values in fuzzy querying via FQUERY for Access. In *Proceedings of FUZZ-IEEE.96 - Fifth International Conference on Fuzzy Systems New Orleans, USA,* (pp. 1351-1357).

Zadrożny, S., & Kacprzyk, J. (2002). Fuzzy querying of relational databases: A fuzzy logic view. In *Proceedings of the EUROFUSE Workshop on Information Systems,* (pp. 153-158). Varenna, Italy.

Zadrożny, S., & Kacprzyk, J. (2006). Bipolar queries and queries with preferences. In *Proceedings of the 17th International Conference on Database and Expert Systems Applications (DEXA'06)*, Krakow, Poland, (pp. 415-419). IEEE Computer Society.

Zahn, C. T., & Roskies, R. Z. (1972). Fourier descriptors for plane closed curves. *IEEE Transactions on Computers, 21*(3), 269–281. doi:10.1109/TC.1972.5008949

Zemankova, M., & Kacprzyk, J. (1993). The roles of fuzzy logic and management of uncertainty in building intelligent Information Systems. *Journal of Intelligent Information Systems, 2,* 311–317. doi:10.1007/BF00961658

Zemankova-Leech, M., & Kandel, A. (1984). *Fuzzy relational databases-a key to expert systems.* Cologne, Germany: Verlag TÜV Rheinland.

Zeng, H. J., He, Q. C., Chen, Z., Ma, W. Y., & Ma, J. (2004). Learning to cluster Web search results. *Proceedings of the 19th Annual International ACM SIGIR Conference on Research and Development in Information Retrieval,* (pp. 210–217).

Zhang, S., Hu, M., & Yang, J. (2007). TreePi: A novel graph indexing method. In *Proceedings of the 23rd International Conference on Data Engineering,* (pp. 966-975).

Zhang, S., Li, J., Gao, H., & Zou, Z. (2009). A novel approach for efficient supergraph query processing on graph databases. In *Proceedings of the 12th International Conference on Extending Database Technology,* (pp. 204-215).

Zhao, P., Yu, J. X., & Yu, P. S. (2007). Graph indexing: Tree + delta >= Graph. In *Proceedings of the 33rd International Conference on Very Large Data Bases,* (pp. 938-949).

Zhou, X. S., & Huang, T. S. (2003). Relevance feedback in image retrieval: A comprehensive review. *Multimedia Systems, 8*(6), 536–544. doi:10.1007/s00530-002-0070-3

About the Contributors

Li Yan received her Ph.D. degree from Northeastern University, China. She is currently an Associate Professor of the School of Software at Northeastern University, China. Her research interests include database modeling, XML data management, as well as imprecise and uncertain data processing. She has published papers in several journals such as Data and Knowledge Engineering, Information and Software Technology, International Journal of Intelligent Systems and some conferences such as WWW and CIKM.

Zongmin Ma (Z. M. Ma) received the Ph. D. degree from the City University of Hong Kong and is currently a Full Professor in College of Information Science and Engineering at Northeastern University, China. His current research interests include intelligent database systems, knowledge representation and reasoning, the Semantic Web and XML, knowledge-bases systems, and semantic image retrieval. He has published over 100 papers in international journals, conferences and books in these areas since 1999. He also authored and edited several scholarly books published by Springer-Verlag and IGI Global, respectively. He has served as member of the international program committees for several international conferences and also spent some time as a reviewer of several journals. Dr. Ma is a senior member of the IEEE.

* * *

Ana Aguilera received her PhD in Computer Systems from University of Rennes I, France, in 2008 with a PhD thesis award très honorable, her MSc in Computer Science from Universidad Simón Bolívar in 1998 and her Engineer in Computer Systems from UCLA in 1994 with great praise. She is Associate Professor and staff member of University of Carabobo (since 1997). She has received the distinction: Orden José Felix Ribas in third class 1993, member of program to research promotion PPI (1998-2000), and Outstanding Teacher of UC (1997). She is coordinator of Research Group in Databases (since 2004). In the area of Fuzzy Databases and Medical Computer Science, she has more than twenty articles in indexed journal and international arbitrated conferences and more than ten advisories of works conducing to academic titles. She is the responsible of the project "Creation and Application of Fuzzy Databases Management Systems" supported by FONACIT (since 2009).

Reda Alhajj received his B.Sc. degree in Computer Engineering in 1988 from Middle East Technical University, Ankara, Turkey. After he completed his BSc with distinction from METU, he was offered a full scholarship to join the graduate program in Computer Engineering and Information Sciences at

Bilkent University in Ankara, where he received his M.Sc. and Ph.D. degrees in 1990 and 1993, respectively. Currently, he is Professor in the Department of Computer Science at the University of Calgary, Alberta, Canada. He has published over 275 papers in refereed international journals and conferences. He served on the program committee of several international conferences including IEEE ICDE, IEEE ICDM, IEEE IAT, SIAM DM; program chair of IEEE IRI 2008, OSIWM 2008, SONAM 2009, IEEE IRI 2009. He is editor in chief of International Journal of Social Networks Analysis and Mining, associate editor of IEEE SMC- Part C and he is member of the editorial board of the Journal of Information Assurance and Security; he has been guest editor for a number of special issues and edited a number of conference proceedings. He recently received the Grad Studies Outstanding Achievement in Supervision Award. Dr. Alhajj's primary work and research interests are in the areas of biocomputing and biodata analysis, data mining, multiagent systems, schema integration and re-engineering, social networks, and XML. He currently leads a research group of 10 PhD and 8 MSc candidates.

Ghazi Al-Naymat received his PhD degree in May 2009 from the School of Information Technologies at The University of Sydney, Australia. He is a Postdoctoral Fellow at the School of Computer Science and Engineering at The University of New South Wales, Australia. His research focuses on developing novel data mining techniques for different applications and datasets such as: graph, spatial, spatio-temporal, and time series databases. The Australian Research Council and (ARC) and The University of new South Wales are supporting Dr. Al-Naymat's current research. He has published a number of papers in excellent international journals and conferences.

Maria Camila N. Barioni received the B.Sc. degree in Computer Science from the Federal University of Uberlandia, Brazil, in 2000, and the M.Sc. and the Ph.D. in Computer Science in 2002 and 2006 at University of Sao Paulo at Sao Carlos, Brazil. She is currently an assistant professor with the Mathematics, Computing and Cognition Center of the Federal University of ABC and the undergraduate students officer for the Computer Science course. Her research interests include multimedia databases, multimedia data mining, indexing methods for multidimensional data and information visualization.

Mounir Bechchi studied Computer Science at the ENSIAS engineering school (Rabat – Morocco). Then, he worked as a research engineer at the INRIA-Rocquencourt until December 2005. He did his Ph.D. in Computer Science under the supervision of Prof. N. Mouaddib at the University of Nantes from January 2006 to September 2009. The subject of his study was "Clustering-based Approximate Answering of Query Result in Large and Distributed Databases." He currently works as a database administrator in Bimedia, La Roche sur Yon, France. His areas of expertise include database design, administration, performance tuning and optimization, database recovery, and data warehousing architecture.

Gloria Bordogna is a senior researcher of the National Research Council (CNR) and contract professor at the Faculty of Engineering of Bergamo University, where she teaches IR and GIS. She graduated in Physics at the University of Milano. Her research interests concern soft computing techniques in the area of information retrieval, flexible query languages and Geographic Information Systems. She was involved in several European projects such as Ecourt, PENG, and IDE-Univers, edited three volumes and a special issue of JASIST in her research area, and participated in the program committee of several conferences such as FUZZ-IEEE, ACM SIGIR, ECIR, FQAS, CIKM, IEEE-ACM WI/IAT, WWW.

Francesco Bucci received the "Laurea Specialistica" in Computer Science Engineering from Bergamo University in 2007, and worked at the Italian National Research Council within the IDE-Univers project during 2008, for which he developed the discovery service of IREA CNR SDI.

José Tomás Cadenas is a PhD Student in Computer Science and Information Technology, Granada University, Spain (2009-present). He received his MSc on Industrial Engineering from Carabobo University, Valencia, Venezuela, in 2010, his MSc on Computer Science from Simón Bolívar University, Caracas, Venezuela, in 2008 and his Computer Engineering from Simón Bolívar University, Caracas, Venezuela, in 1985. He is an Assistant Professor (April 2008 – present) at Computer and I.T. Department of Simón Bolívar University, Caracas, Venezuela, and was an Academic Assistant (April 2006 - April 2008) at Computer and I.T. Department of Simón Bolívar University, Caracas, Venezuela. He spent 1999 thru 2006 in other higher education institutes in Venezuela (IUETLV- La Victoria and CULTCA- Los Teques) in informatic departments, where he taught Database, Software Engineering and programming (grade and postgrades). He was co-responsible on the project "Creating and Applying Fuzzy Database Management Systems" support by FONACIT (January 2009 - December 2009) and was an Associate Investigator (February 2008 – december 2008). Also he has experience for 20 years in different companies (public and privates) in Venezuela. His interest areas include database systems, software engineering and Information and Communication Technologies in Education.

Paola Carrara is graduated in Physics at the University of Milan, Italy. She has been a researcher of the National Research Council (CNR) of Italy since 1986. Her scientific activity regards designing and managing Information Systems. Her main interests are in (Fuzzy) Information Retrieval, spatio-temporal archives of images, architectures, technologies and standards for geographic information on the Internet, in particular Spatial Data Infrastructures and the Sensor Web initiative. She was responsible for the Italian branch of the project IDE-Univers which created the first European Spatial Data Infrastructure in the research field. With Gloria Bordogna, she promoted and organized the special session Management of Uncertain information in the "Digital Earth" at IPMU 2010.

Jingwei Cheng received his BSc from Jilin University in 1995. He is currently a PhD candidate in the College of Information Science and Engineering at Northeastern University under the supervision of Prof. Z. M. Ma. He has published in conference proceedings of DEXA, WI/IAT, ASWC and Fuzz-IEEE. His current research interests include description logics, RDF, SPARQL, and Semantic Web.

Guy De Tré is Professor at the Faculty of Engineering of Ghent University and leading the Database, Document and Content Management research group. His research interests include the handling of imperfect information, (fuzzy) database modeling, flexible querying, information retrieval and content based retrieval of multimedia. His publications comprise three books (one as author and two as co-editor), 17 chapters in various books, and 30 papers in international journals. He was guest editor of special issues in Fuzzy Sets and Systems, International Journal of Intelligent Systems, and Control and Cybernetics and is reviewer of several journals and conferences in the areas of databases and fuzzy information processing. He co-coordinates SCDMIR, the Eusflat Working Group on Soft Computing in Database Management and Information Retrieval.

Eric Draken is an undergraduate student in the Department of Computer Science at the University of Calgary with a focus on relational database development and software design. He is active in designing and optimizing Web applications where any given Web page may assemble data from multiple resources asynchronously using XML-based protocols.

Shang Gao received his BSc in Computer Science from the University of Waterloo in 2006, and MSc in Computer Science from the University of Calgary in 2009. He is currently a PhD candidate in the Department of Computer Science at the University of Calgary under the supervision of Prof. Reda Alhajj. He received a number of prestigious awards and scholarships including iCore graduation studies scholarship, Department of Computer Science research award and University of Calgary Queen Elizabeth II Scholarship. He published over 10 papers in fully refereed conferences and journals. His research interests cover data mining, financial data analysis, social networks, bioinformatics, and XML.

Marlene Goncalves Da Silva received her Bachelor on Computer Science in 1998 from Central of Venezuela University, and her Master on Computer Science in 2002 and PhD on Computer Science in 2009 from the University Simón Bolívar, Caracas Venezuela. She is an Associate Professor of the Computer Science department at the University Simón Bolívar, and Visitor Scholar at Youngstown State University (2009-2010). She has reported her research on DEXA and OTM. Her current research interests are Preference based queries. Her home page is http://www.ldc.usb.ve/~mgoncalves

A. Goswami obtained his Ph.D. degree from Jadavpur University, Kolkata, India and joined the IIT as a regular faculty member in 1992. He has published several papers at national & international level, and guided many M.Tech. & Ph.D. Thesis. His research areas are: theoretical computer science and operation research. He is a Member, Editorial Board of the Journals: (i) International Journal of Fuzzy Systems and Rough Systems (ii) International Journal of Mathematics in Operational Research (IJMOR). At present he is holding the post of Chairman, HMC (Hall Management Centre) of the institute as an additional responsibility.

D. K. Gupta obtained his Ph.D. degree from IIT Kharagpur, India and joined the institute as a regular faculty member in 1985. He has published several papers at the national and international level, and guided many M.Tech. and PhD thesis. His research areas are: computer science, constraint satisfaction problems and numerical & interval analysis. He is a member of The National Academic of Sciences and Life member of ISTAM. He is Co-Principal-Investigators of projects (i) FIST Program Department of Mathematics (ii) Multi objective and Multi level Decision making model with an application to environment and Regional planning, that are sponsored by DST, New Delhi.

Janusz Kacprzyk is Professor at the Systems Research Institute, Polish Academy of Sciences, and Honorary Professor at Yli Normal University, Shanxi, China. He is an Academician (Member of the Polish Academy of Sciences). His research interests include soft computing, fuzzy logic, decisions, database querying, and information retrieval. His publication record is: 5 books, 30 volumes, 300 papers. He is Fellow of IEEE and IFSA. He received The 2005 IEEE CIS Fuzzy Pioneer Award, and The Sixth Kaufmann Prize and Gold Medal for pioneering works on uncertainty. He is Editor in chief of three Springer's book series, is on editorial boards of ca. 25 journals, and a member of the IPC at ca. 200 conferences.

Daniel S. Kaster received the B.Sc. degree in Computer Science from the University of Londrina, Brazil, in 1998 and the M.Sc. degree in Computer Science from the University of Campinas, Brazil, in 2001. He is currently a Lecturer with the Computer Science Department of the University of Londrina, Brazil, and a Ph.D. candidate in Computer Science from the University of S?o Paulo at S?o Carlos, Brazil. His research interests include searching complex data and multimedia databases.

Xiangfu Meng received his Ph.D. degree from Northeastern University, China. He is currently a Lecturer of the College of Electronic and Information Engineering at Liaoning Technical University, China. His research interests include Web database flexible query, query results ranking and categorization, XML data management, and the Semantic Web. He teaches computer networks, database systems, and software architecture.

Noureddine Mouaddib received his Ph. D. degree and Habilitation in Computer Science from the University Poincaré (Nancy I) in 1989 and 1995, respectively. Since 1996, he is a full Professor at Polytechnic School of University of Nantes in France. He is the founder and President of the International University of Rabat (www.uir.ma). He was the founder and the head of the Atlas-GRIM team of LINA Laboratory, pursuing research in databases, particularly in summarization of large databases, flexible querying, and fuzzy databases. He has authored and co-authored over 100 technical papers in international conferences and journals. He was member of several program committees and executive chair of international conferences.

Tadeusz Pankowski, Ph.D., D.Sc., is a professor of computer science at Poznan University of Technology, Poland. His research interests are in foundations of database models, data languages, and information integration from heterogeneous databases (relational and XML). His research concerning semantic data integration in peer-to-peer systems has been supported by Polish Ministry of Science and Higher Education. He is the author or coauthor of two recognized books: "Foundations of Databases", and "Security of Data in Information Systems" (both in Polish). He teaches courses on database systems, data mining, information integration and software engineering. He serves as a member of program committees of numerous international conferences, such as XSym in conjunction with VLDB, IEEE ICIIC. He is a member of the ACM, IEEE and PTI (Polish Society of Computer Science).

Monica Pepe received the master degree in Geology in 1993 and the PhD in Physical Geography from the University of Pavia, Italy. She has been with the National Research Council (CNR) of Italy since 1994. Her research activity regards the use of remote sensing for environmental studies and for pattern recognition tasks. She has worked on automatic interpretation methods of multisource data for thematic and environmental mapping, on the basis of the combined use of remote sensing image analysis and domain knowledge representation. In the last few years she has been interested in Spatial Data Infrastructures (SDI) and OpenGIS Web Services (OWS) issues in order to make geographic information derived from her research activity retrievable, accessible, and exploitable in an interoperable framework, with particular focus on the INSPIRE Directive.

Guillaume Raschia studied CS at the Polytech'Nantes engineering school. He graduated (Engineer and Master) in 1998. He did his Ph.D. under the supervision of Prof. N. Mouaddib at the University of Nantes from 1999 to 2001. He studied the database summarization paradigm with fuzzy set theoretic background. He had a lecturer position in 2002 and obtained an assistant professor position in September 2003 in the CS department of Polytech'Nantes. Since then, he is affiliated to the LINA labs and he is a member of the INRIA-Atlas research group as well. Guillaume Raschia's main research topics are database indexing and data reduction techniques, flexible querying, and approximate answering systems.

Anna Rampini has worked at the Italian National Research Council since 1984. Her research interests are in image processing, pattern recognition, remote sensing images interpretation, and GIS. Her main research activities regard the definition and development of knowledge-based systems for the automatic interpretation of remote sensing images aimed to produce thematic maps on the basis of the combined use of remote sensing data analysis and domain knowledge representation, and support experts in the evaluation and prevention of environmental risks. She has been involved in several national and international projects and coordinated the European Projects FIREMEN Project (Fire Risk Evaluation in Mediterranean Environment) and AWARE (A tool for monitoring and forecasting Available WAter REsource in mountain environment).

Humberto L. Razente received the B.Sc. degree in Computer Science from the Federal University of Mato Grosso, Brazil, in 2000, and the M.Sc. and the Ph.D. in Computer Science in 2004 and 2009 at University of Sao Paulo at Sao Carlos, Brazil. He is currently an assistant professor with the Mathematics, Computing and Cognition Center of the Federal University of ABC. His research interests include access methods for complex data, similarity searching, multimedia databases and information visualization.

Sherif Sakr received his PhD degree in computer science from Konstanz University, Germany in 2007. He received his BSc and MSc degree in computer science from the Faculty of Computers and Information, Cairo University, Egypt, in 2000 and 2003 respectively. He is a senior research associate/lecturer in the Service Oriented Computing (SOC) research group at School of Computer Science and Engineering (CSE), University of New South Wales (UNSW), Australia. Prior to taking up the current position, he worked as a postdoctoral research fellow at National ICT Australia (NICTA). His research interest is data and information management in general, particularly in areas of indexing techniques, query processing and optimization techniques, graph data management, social networks, and data management in cloud computing. His work has been published in international journals and conferences such as: Proceedings of the VLDB endowment (PVLDB), Journal of Database Management (JDM), International Journal of Web Information Systems (IJWIS), Journal of Computer Systems and Science (JCSS), VLDB, SIGMOD, WWW, DASFAA, and DEXA. One of his papers has awarded the Outstanding Paper Excellence Award 2009 of Emerald Literati Network.

Alexandr Savinov received his PhD from the Technical University of Moldova in 1993 and his MS degree from the Moscow Institute of Physics and Technology (MIPT) in 1989. He is currently a researcher at SAP Research Center Dresden, Germany. His primary research interests include data modeling, programming and knowledge management methodologies with applications to database systems, Grid and cloud computing, distributed systems, peer-to-peer technologies, Semantic Web, and other areas. He is an author of two novel methodologies in computer science: concept-oriented model (COM) and concept-oriented programming (COP). Previous research interests include fuzzy expert systems and data mining. In particular, he developed a novel matrix-based approach to fuzzy knowledge representation and inference implemented in the expert system shell EDIP. In data mining, he proposed an original algorithm for mining dependence rules and developed a data mining system with component architecture, SPIN!

Awadhesh Kumar Sharma obtained his M.Tech. & Ph.D. degrees from IIT Kharagpur, India and joined the college as a regular faculty member in January 1988. He has been bearing the responsibility of Head the Department in addition to teaching at UG & PG level. He is FIE, FIETE, MISTE, MCSI, MIAENG, and Expert-DOEACC, Government of India. He has published several research papers at national and international level. His research area is database systems. He is a member of Editorial Board & Review Committees of some International Journals & Conferences.

Leonid Tineo received his PhD in Computing from Universidad Simón Bolívar (USB), Venezuela, in 2006. Tineo received his MSc in Computer Science from USB in 1992 and his Eng. in Computing from USB in 1990. He is Titular Professor (since 2007), Staff Member of USB (since 1991), Level I Accredited Researcher of Venezuelan Researcher Promotion Program (since 2003), Outstanding Professor CONABA (2002), and Outstanding Educational Work USB (1999). He was the Coordinator of USB Database Research Group (2002-2008). He has exerted the post of Information and Integration Coordinator of the Research and Development Deanship at USB (2002-2007). In Fuzzy Databases area, he has more than twenty articles in extenso in arbitrated Proceedings, more than fifteen published brief notes, eight papers in indexed journals, two book chapters, and more than fifteen advisories of works conducing to academic titles. Tine is responsible for the project "Creation and Application of Fuzzy Databases Management Systems" supported by Venezuelan National Foundation for Sciences, Innovation and Technology FONACIT, Grant G-2005000278 (2006-2008).

Agma J. M. Traina received the B.Sc. the M.Sc. degrees in Computer Science from the University of S?o Paulo, Brazil, in 1983, 1987 and the and Ph.D. in Computational Physics in 1991. She is currently a full Professor with the Computer Science Department of the University of Sao Paulo at Sao Carlos, Brazil and the graduate students officer for the Computer Science program. Her research interests include image databases, image mining, indexing methods for multidimensional data, information visualization and image processing for medical applications. She has supervised more than 20 graduate students.

Caetano Traina Jr. received the B.Sc. degree in Electrical Engineering, the M.Sc. in Computer Science and the Ph.D. in Computational Physics from the University of São Paulo, Brazil, in 1978, 1982 and 1987, respectively. He is currently a full professor with the Computer Science Department of the University of São Paulo at São Carlos, Brazil. His research interests include indexing and access methods for complex data, data mining, similarity searching, query rewriting, and multimedia databases. He has supervised more than 30 graduate students

María-Esther Vidal received her Bachelor on Computer Engineering in 1987, Master on Computer Science in 1991 and PhD on Computer Science in 2000 from the University Simón Bolívar, Caracas Venezuela. She is a Full Professor of the Computer Science department at the University Simón Bolívar and has been Assistant Researcher at the Institute of Advanced Computer Studies in the University of Maryland (UMIACS) (1995-1999), and Visitor Professor at UMIACS (2000-2009) and in Universidad Politecnica de Catalunya (2003). She has reported her research in AAAI, IJCAI, SIGMOD, CoopIs, WIDM, WebDB, ICDE, DILS, DEXA, ALPWS, ACM SAC, CAISE, OTM, EDBT, SIGMOD RECORDS and TPLP Journal. Her current research interests are query rewriting and optimization in emerging infrastructures. Prof. Vidal is member of SIGMOD. Her home page is http://www.ldc.usb.ve/~mvidal.

Sławomir Zadrożny is Associate Professor (Ph.D. 1994, D.Sc. 2006) at the Systems Research Institute, Polish Academy of Sciences. His current scientific interests include applications of fuzzy logic in database management systems, information retrieval, decision support, and data analysis. He is the author and co-author of approximately 150 journal and conference papers. He has been involved in the design and implementation of several prototype software packages. He is also a teacher at the Warsaw School of Information Technology in Warsaw, Poland and at the Technical University of Radom, Poland.

Index

Symbols

ε-Range Query 36

A

abstract roles 249, 250
agglomerative single-link approach 46
Algorithmic Solution 11
ARES system 34, 35
automated ranking 29, 37, 42, 58
AWARE project 145

B

Basic Distributed Skyline (BDS) 107
Basic Multi-Objective Retrieval (BMOR) 107
Berners-Lee, Tim 269, 283
bipolar queries 118, 120, 128, 130, 131, 134, 135
Block-Nested-Loops (BNL) 107
Bottom-Up Skycube algorithm (BUS) 108, 109, 112, 113, 115
Branch-and-Bound Skyline (BBS) 107
brushing histogram 4, 5

C

C4.5-Categorization 2, 3, 20, 21, 22
C4.5 decision tree constructing algorithm 4
cartesian product, symmetric 35
categorization approach 1, 5, 20, 24
categorization case 3
Categorization Cost Experiment 20
category tree 1, 2, 3, 4, 5, 6, 7, 8, 13, 14, 15, 17, 21, 22, 24, 27
Category Tree Construction 8
Chakrabarti et al's System 45

Chaudhuri's system 40, 41
cIndex indexing structure 313
cluster-based retrieval 44
Cluster Hypothesis 59
clustering 4, 5, 7, 8, 10, 11, 12, 14, 22, 23, 24, 25
clustering approach 4
clustering-based techniques 29, 58, 59
clustering of query results 29, 48, 77
Clustering Problem 10
cluster queries 4, 11
CoBase 31, 32, 33
completion forests 249, 254, 255, 256, 257, 258, 259, 260, 264, 265
Complexity Analysis 19
concept assertions (ABox) 248, 250, 251, 253, 254, 264
concept axioms (TBox) 250, 251, 253, 264, 265
concept-oriented model (COM) 85, 86, 87, 89, 90, 92, 93, 94, 96, 97, 98, 99, 101
concept-oriented programming (COP) 86
concept-oriented query language (COQL) 85, 86, 89, 91, 92, 95, 98, 99
conjunctive queries (CQs) 247, 248, 253, 267, 268
content-based image retrieval (CBIR) 324, 357, 358
content-based operators approach 325, 326

D

Data Asphyxiation 29
database 323, 324, 330, 331, 335, 336, 337, 339, 342, 344, 348, 349, 354, 355
database integration 186, 187, 188, 189, 216

Database Integration Process 189

database management systems (DBMS) 289, 299, 300, 303, 323, 324, 325, 335, 336, 337, 339, 340, 344, 345, 346, 347, 348, 349, 350, 351, 352

database migration 189, 216

database query processing models 30

databases 270, 271, 273, 274, 275, 276, 277, 280, 282, 283, 284, 285

Database systems 28, 30, 49, 59

Data Clustering 8

data clusters 3, 12, 20, 27

data definition language (DDL) 325, 339

data integration 221, 222, 223, 227, 239, 242, 243, 244, 245, 246

data integration, materialized 222

data integration, virtual 222

data manipulation language (DML) 325, 339, 341

data manipulation operations 188

data modeling 85, 86, 87, 89, 90, 91, 92, 96, 97, 98, 99, 101

data provenance 222

Data Smog 29

dataspaces 270

data strings 249

DATA TUPLES 8

data warehouse 189

data warehouses 222

DB Clustering Techniques 45

DBXplorer 56

decision support systems 28, 59

decomposed storage model (DSM) 277

description logics (DL) 247, 248, 249, 252, 253, 266, 267

dimension 86, 87, 88, 92, 93, 94, 95, 96, 97, 98, 99, 101

direct acyclic graph (DAG) 97

Divide and Conquer (DC) 108, 115

divide keyword 288, 294, 295, 299, 301

dividend relation 289, 290, 303

divide operator 303

divide query 293, 295

DIVIDE system 289, 290, 293, 294, 295, 296, 297, 299, 300

division 287, 288, 289, 290, 291, 292, 299, 300, 301, 302, 303

divisor relation 289, 290, 303

DL knowledge base (KB) 248, 251, 252, 254, 255, 257, 258, 259, 260, 261, 264, 266

document type definition (DTD) 223

domain-specific identities 85, 86, 96, 98

domain-specific structure 89, 90

Duality principle 86

dynamic query slider 4

E

edges 305, 306, 311, 314, 317, 318

efficient implementation of Top-k Skyline (EI-TKS) 108

Efficient Top-k Query Processing 42

e-merchant 30

EmpDB 31, 32, 34, 52, 53, 54

empty-answer problem 30, 31

European Spatial Data Infrastructure (ESDI) 141

Executor 164, 170, 178

Exploitation activity 143

Exploration activity 143

exploration model 5, 7

exploratory data retrieval 28, 59, 61, 76

Explore-Select algorithm (ESA) 61, 66, 67, 69, 70, 71, 73, 74

Explore-Select-Rearrange Algorithm (ESRA) 29, 30, 61, 70, 71, 72, 73, 74, 76, 77

extensible markup language (XML) 221, 222, 223, 225, 226, 227, 228, 230, 238, 239, 240, 242, 243, 244, 245, 246, 270, 278, 284

extension operator 87, 88

EXTRACT operator 277

F

feature extraction algorithms 358

feature weighting 330

feature weighting technique 330

Feedback-Based Systems 42

flexible fuzzy queries 119, 121, 129

flexible fuzzy querying 118, 119, 124, 132

flexible querying 118, 119, 124, 128, 132, 134, 135

flexible querying languages 118

flexible query processing 50

flexible relations 188

functional dependencies 221, 222, 224, 230, 237, 239

functional roles 249

fuzziness 190

fuzzy comparison operators 51, 53

fuzzy concept assertions 250, 251

fuzzy concept axioms 250

fuzzy concrete domains 249

fuzzy conjunctive queries 247, 249, 266

fuzzy database framework 142, 155, 157

fuzzy database identifiers (DBids) 196, 197

fuzzy database instances 191

fuzzy databases 122, 136, 140, 141, 158, 187, 192, 197, 198, 205, 206, 208, 214

fuzzy data types 249

fuzzy data values 185, 190, 214

fuzzy extension 122, 124

fuzzy logic 118, 120, 121, 122, 123, 127, 128, 130, 134, 136, 138, 167, 184, , , 247, 248, 249, 250, 251, 252, 253, 254, 255, 258, 259, 260, 261, 262, 263, 264, 266, 267, 268, 288, 302

fuzzy modifiers 51

fuzzy multidatabases 185, 200, 214

fuzzy multidatabase system 190

fuzzy ontologies 247, 248, 253, 267

fuzzy OWL Lite 247, 248

Fuzzy Plan Tree 177, 180, 184

fuzzy probabilistic relational data model 190

fuzzy quantifiers 51, 53

fuzzy queries 50, 118, 119, 120, 121, 128, 129, 132, 134, 137, 162, 163, 164, 166, 168, 169, 170, 172, 173, 175, 178, 179, 180, 181, 182, 184,

fuzzy query 185, 199, 200, 201, 202, 203, 204, 205, 206, 207, 208, 212, 214, 216, 218

FuzzyQUERY (FQUERY) 124, 125, 126, 127, 131, 132, 133, 134, 136, 138

fuzzy querying 118, 119, 120, 124, 132, 133, 134, 135, 136, 138

fuzzy querying systems 124

Fuzzy Query Language (FQL) 122

fuzzy query processor 160

Fuzzy Query Tree 168, 169, 170, 171, 172, 175, 177, 178, 179, 184

fuzzy relation 190, 194, 195, 196, 201, 208, 209, 210, 218, 219

fuzzy relational databases 185, 187, 190, 192, 195, 208, 214

fuzzy relational data model 187, 192

fuzzy relations 190, 191, 193, 194, 195, 201, 208, 209, 210, 211, 214, 215, 218, 219

fuzzy set framework 141

fuzzy sets 50, 51, 66, 67, 119, 121, 124, 126, 127, 128, 131, 149, 152, 156, 162, 164, 165, 166, 167, 169, 172, 173, 178, 184, 185, 190, 200, 218, 219

fuzzy set theory 50, 51, 119, 248, 249

fuzzy systems 288

fuzzy temporal indications 148

fuzzy terms 50, 51, 53, 162, 164, 166, 168, 170, 174, 177, 179

fuzzy tuple source (FTS) 185, 191, 192, 193, 194, 196, 197, 198, 199, 200, 201, 202, 203, 204, 205, 206, 207, 208, 209, 210, 212, 213, 214, 218

fuzzy tuple source structured query language (FTS-SQL) 185, 199, 200, 201, 202, 203, 204, 205, 206, 212, 214, 218

fuzzy values 51, 52, 53, 148

G

GDIndex index structure 309, 310, 316

generated trees 5, 20

geodata 140, 141, 142, 143, 144, 145, 148, 157, 159

Geodata Discovery 143

geoprocessing applications 327

GIndex index structure 312, 316

global data model 186, 187, 188

Godfrey's System 33

GPTree index structure 313, 316

grammar 290, 292, 303

graph databases 304, 305, 306, 311, 312, 313, 314, 317, 319, 320, 321, 322

graph data structure 304, 305, 316

GraphGrep index structure 308, 316, 320

graph indexing techniques 304, 305, 307, 313, 316, 318, 319, 322

graph indexing techniques, mining-based 307, 308, 312
graph query languages 304, 316, 319, 321
graph query processing 304, 305, 318, 319
GraphREL index structure 311, 316, 321
graphs 304, 305, 306, 308, 309, 310, 311, 312, 313, 314, 315, 317, 319, 320, 321
graphs, directed-labeled 305
graphs, undirected-labeled 305
greedy algorithm 4, 25
Greedy catagorization 2, 11, 20, 21, 22, 23
Greedy-Refine 11, 23
Greedy-Refine algorithm 23
GString index structure 310, 320, 321

H

Healy's division 289
Hexastore RDF storage scheme 274, 278, 285,
Hierarchical address spaces 86
hierarchical data model (HDM) 96
high-dimensional Skyline spaces 102, 114
HITS algorithm 39

I

IDE-Univers 145
imperfect temporal metadata 140, 141, 142, 156
Imperfect Time Indications 149, 150
Inclusion principle 86, 87
index scan 164, 168, 169, 171, 178
Infoglut 29
Information Fatigue Syndrome 29
information overload 1, 2, 3, 29, 37, 59, 80, 82
Information Pollution 29
Information Retrieval (IR) 38, 44, 45, 81
Information Technology 141
INSPIRE 140, 141, 142, 143, 144, 145, 146, 151, 157, 158
instance integration process 189
integers 249
interactive approach 132, 136
inverse roles 249
inverted indexes 307, 308
IQE approach 34, 35, 36

J

Java programming language 287, 288, 289, 293, 300, 302
Jena1 schema 275
Jena2 schema 275
join query 293
JUnit tests 293, 299

K

keywords 287, 288, 293, 294, 295, 299, 301
k-median problem 10, 25
k-Nearest Neighbor Query 36
Koutrika et al's approach 49

L

Linear Elimination Sort for Skyline (LESS) 107
link-based ranking methods 38, 39
local database 187, 189, 191, 202, 203, 204, 205
local fuzzy databases 187, 192, 197, 205, 206, 214

M

many-answers problem 30, 37, 42, 61, 67
mappings 221, 222, 223, 228, 239, 242, 243, 244, 246
maXimal Generalizations that Fail (XGFs) 31, 32, 33
mediated schemas 222
metadata 140, 141, 142, 143, 144, 145, 146, 147, 148, 149, 150, 151, 152, 153, 155, 156, 157, 158, 159, 269, 270, 299
Minimal Generalizations that Succeed (MGSs) 31, 32, 33
multidatabase system (MDBS) 188, 189, 190, 199, 204, 215, 216, 217
Multidimensional Analysis 95
multidimensional index structures 36
Multidimensionality 86
multidimensional models 97
multimedia objects, audio 323, 329, 334, 339, 351, 352, 354, 356

multimedia objects, images 323, 324, 325, 326, 327, 328, 329, 332, 334, 335, 336, 337, 338, 339, 340, 341, 343, 344, 345, 346, 348, 349, 351, 353, 354, 355, 356, 357, 358, 359

multimedia objects (MO) 323, 324

multimedia objects, video 323, 326, 327, 329, 334, 338, 339, 354, 357, 358

MySQL database management system 299, 300, 301, 302, 303

N

nearest neighbor (NN) algorithm 36, 107

Normalized Skyline Frequency value (NSF) 112, 113

O

Online Analytical Processing (OLAP) model 98, 120

ontologies 247, 248, 253, 267

optimizer module 168, 169, 177

Order principle 86

P

parser 164, 289, 293, 295, 299, 300, 302, 303

partial distance weighting 330

partial distance weighting technique 327, 330

partially ordered set 87, 88, 97, 98

partition point 14

pattern-mining 312

PeerDB system 222

peers 221, 222, 234, 235, 236, 237, 238, 239, 240, 241, 242, 243, 244, 245, 246

peer to peer (P2P) environments 221, 222, 235, 238, 240, 241, 242, 243, 244, 245

physical fuzzy relational operators 160

Piazza system 222, 245

PIR system 40, 41

Planner Module 177

Planner-Optimizer 164

platform-specific references 86

platform-specific structure 89

possibility theory 118

primitive value 87, 89

probabilistic-based approaches 38

probabilistic model 38

problem-dependent 326

progressive algorithm 107, 116

property-class schema 277

proportional linguistic quantifiers 127

protoform 132, 133, 134

Q

qualitative approach 50

query-by-example 359

Query Clustering 9

query clusters 3, 11, 12, 21

query entailment 247, 248, 249, 251, 252, 253, 254, 255, 258, 264, 267

query graphs 304, 306, 309, 310, 312, 313, 314, 315, 317, 318

query history 1, 3, 4, 5, 6, 7, 8, 9, 10, 11, 12, 13, 19, 20, 22, 23

query model 37

query personalization 4

query propagation 221, 222, 238, 239, 241, 243, 244, 246

Query Prune 9

query pruning algorithm 9

query reformulation 246

Query Relaxation 31

query results 28, 29, 30, 37, 38, 39, 41, 42, 44, 45, 46, 47, 58, 59, 68, 69, 70, 73, 76, 77, 78

query tree 164, 168, 170, 177

R

RDF, horizontal tables stores for 270, 272, 278

RDF, property tables stores for 270, 279

RDF triple stores 271, 272, 273, 274, 275, 276, 282, 283

RDF, vertical tables stores for 270, 272, 273, 274, 278

reflexive 35

relational algebra (RA) 121, 122, 137, 139, 287, 288, 289, 290, 300, 302, 303

relational algebra tree 184,

relational calculus 121, 122, 139

relational database 120, 135, 139

relational database management systems (RD-BMS) 160, 161, 162, 163, 164, 166, 167, 168, 172, 180, 182, 183, 270, 271, 272, 277, 283, 303

relational databases 248

relational division 288, 289, 303

relational fuzzy data model 191

relational model 185, 188, 192, 194, 200, 208, 212, 214, 216, 218

relational multimedia databases 5

relational query processors 269, 270

relation schema 120

relevance 29, 37, 38, 39, 40, 42, 44, 47, 54, 56, 58, 59, 60, 80

resource description framework (RDF) 269, 270, 271, 272, 273, 274, 275, 276, 277, 278, 279, 280, 281, 282, 283, 284, 285

resources 270, 275, 276, 284

result tuples 5

retrieved tuples 37

rewrite algorithm 299

rewriter 288, 289, 299

role hierarchy (RBox) 249, 250, 264, 265

role names, non-transitive 249

role names, transitive 249

R*-tree 36

R-Tree 36

S

SAINTETIQ model 29, 61, 62, 63, 64, 65, 66, 67, 69, 72, 73, 76, 81

SAINTETIQ System 61

scalability 29, 59, 60

schema constraints 221, 222, 242, 244

Schema Integration Process 189

schema mapping 227, 244, 245

schema patterns 225

schemas 221, 222, 223, 224, 225, 227, 228, 237, 239, 245, 246

SEAVEii system 31

SEAVE system 31, 32

selection predicates 331, 341

semantic gap 328, 334, 359

semantic metadata 270

Semantics 87

Semantic Search 102

semantic space 327

Semantic Web 102, 115, 247, 266, 267, 268, 269, 270, 275, 282, 283, 284, 285,

sequential permutation 11

sequential scan 164, 168, 171, 178

SHIF(D) algorithm 247, 248, 249, 250, 251, 254, 255, 259, 261, 264, 266

similarity evaluation 326, 327, 358

similarity operators approach 326

similarity predicates 331, 334, 341, 342, 345

similarity queries 323, 324, 325, 327, 330, 331, 332, 333, 335, 336, 337, 338, 339, 341, 342, 344, 345, 346, 347, 348, 349, 351, 352, 353, 354, 356, 358

Similarity Search 34

similarity selections 331

similarity space 327, 328, 330, 339, 340, 354

simple query language (SQL) 323, 324, 325, 337, 338, 339, 341, 343, 344, 345, 347, 348, 349, 351, 352, 353, 355, 358

SixP2P system 221, 222, 244

Skycube 104, 106, 108, 117

Skycube computation 104, 108

skyline frequency metric (SFM) 105, 108, 109, 110, 111, 112

Skyline system 102, 103, 104, 105, 106, 107, 108, 109, 110, 111, 112, 113, 114, 115, 116, 117, 162

Sort-Filter-Skyline (SFS) 107

SPARQL query language 270, 271, 272, 273, 274, 278, 279, 283, 285

Spatial Data Infrastructures (SDI) 140, 141, 142, 143, 144, 145, 151, 157

SQL-based query 30

SQLf system 163, 164, 166, 167, 168, 170, 171, 172, 173, 180, 181, 182, 183, 184,

SQL query language 5

SS-Tree 36

stores, database-based 271

stores, native 271

strict inclusion relation 87

structured data repositories 28

structured query language (SQL) 273, 275, 276, 279, 280, 283, 285, , 287, 288, 289, 290, 292, 293, 295, 299, 300, 301, 302, 303

sub-elements 87, 91
subgraph isomorphism 305, 306, 309, 312, 313, 314, 315
subgraph query processing 305, 307
super-elements 87, 91
supergraph queries 306, 316, 319
supergraph query processing 305, 313, 322
systemic functional linguistics (SFL) 133, 134

T

tableaus 247, 249, 254, 259, 260, 261, 268
Tahani's Approach 52
Target Entry List (tlist) 178
TechnoStress 29, 82
terminal elements 223
terminal labels 223, 225
text categorization methods 4
text type 223
texture extractor 326, 345
Threshold Algorithm (TA) 43, 44
TKSI algorithm 102, 108, 109, 110, 111, 112, 113, 115
Top-Down Skycube algorithm (TDS) 108
top-k queries 37, 43
Top-k Skyline approach 102, 104, 108
Top-k Skyline problem 102, 104
top-k subset 29, 37, 58
traditional database management systems 118
transitive 35
transitive role axioms 249
trapezoidal fuzzy membership functions 64
tree-pattern formulas 221, 222, 223, 224, 225, 228, 230, 239, 240, 245, 246
tree patterns 223, 224, 225, 245
tree patterns, finite 223
TreePI index structure 312, 313, 316, 322
tuples 1, 2, 3, 4, 5, 6, 7, 8, 12, 13, 14, 15, 16, 17, 18, 19, 20, 21, 22, 24, 27, 87, 97, 120, 129, 130, 131

type constraint 88

U

uniform resource identifier (URI) 269, 270, 275
union query 293, 300
United Nations Conference on Environment and Development 141
user assistance 132

V

VAGUE approach 34, 35, 83
Vector space model 38
vertices 305, 306, 309, 310, 311, 314

W

Web database queries 1
Web ontology language (OWL) 247, 248, 266
World Wide Web Consortium (W3C) 269, 270, 271, 284, 285

X

XAMPP Apache distribution 300, 303
XML functional dependency (XFD) 230, 231, 232, 235, 237, 238, 239, 245, 246
XML schema mappings 222, 244
XQuery programs 221, 222, 239, 240, 242
X-Tree 36

Z

Zadeh, Lotfi 119, 120, 123, 124, 127, 128, 132, 133, 134, 137, 248, 268
Zql lexical parser 295, 299, 300, 302, 303